16th Edition

# Technology in Action

## Introductory

Alan Evans • Kendall Martin • Mary Anne Poatsy

330 Hudson Street, NY NY 10013

**Vice President, Career & IT Skills:** Andrew Gilfillan
**Executive Portfolio Manager:** Jenifer Niles
**Managing Producer:** Laura Burgess
**Development Editor:** Shannon LeMay-Finn
**Director of Product Marketing:** Brad Parkins
**Director of Field Marketing:** Jonathan Cottrell
**Field Marketing Manager:** Bob Nisbet
**Product Marketing Manager:** Heather Taylor
**Operations Specialist:** Maura Garcia
**Senior Product Model Manager:** Eric Hakanson
**Lead, Production and Digital Studio:** Heather Darby
**Course Producer:** Amanda Losonsky

**Digital Content Producer:** Tanika Henderson
**Senior Art Director:** Mary Siener
**Cover Design:** Pearson CSC
**Cover Image Credits:** keving3/Alamy Stock Photo
**Full-Service Project Management:** Susan Hannahs
**Composition:** Pearson CSC
**Printer/Binder:** LSC Communications
**Cover Printer:** Phoenix Color
**Text Font:** 10/12 Helvetica Neue LT W1G Roman

Credits and acknowledgments borrowed from other sources and reproduced, with permission, in this textbook appear on the appropriate page within text.

Microsoft and/or its respective suppliers make no representations about the suitability of the information contained in the documents and related graphics published as part of the services for any purpose. All such documents and related graphics, are provided "as is" without warranty of any kind. Microsoft and/or its respective suppliers hereby disclaim all warranties and conditions with regard to this information, including all warranties and conditions of merchantability, whether express, implied or statutory, fitness for a particular purpose, title and non-infringement. In no event shall Microsoft and/or its respective suppliers be liable for any special, indirect or consequential damages or any damages whatsoever resulting from loss of use, data or profits, whether in an action of contract, negligence or other tortious action, arising out of or in connection with the use or performance of information available from the services.

The documents and related graphics contained herein could include technical inaccuracies or typographical errors. Changes are periodically added to the information herein. Microsoft and/or its respective suppliers may make improvements and/or changes in the product(s) and/or the program(s) described herein at any time. Partial screen shots may be viewed in full within the software version specified.

Microsoft©, Windows©, and Microsoft Office© are registered trademarks of the Microsoft Corporation in the U.S.A. and other countries.

### Library of Congress Cataloging-in-Publication Data

Names: Evans, Alan (Alan D.), author. | Martin, Kendall (Kendall E.), author. | Poatsy, Mary Anne, author.
Title: Technology in action : introductory / Alan Evans, Kendall Martin, Mary Anne Poatsy.
Description: 16th edition. | NY, NY : Pearson, 2019.
Identifiers: LCCN 2018057008| ISBN 9780135480144 | ISBN 0135480140
Subjects: LCSH: Microcomputers. | Computer science. | Computer networks. | Information technology.
Classification: LCC QA76.5 .E9195 2019 | DDC 004—dc23
LC record available at https://lccn.loc.gov/2018057008

3 2019

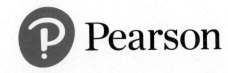 Pearson

ISBN 10: 0-13-548014-0

ISBN 13: 978-0-13-548014-4

# Contents at a Glance

# Contents

# Chapter 2

## Looking at Computers: Understanding the Parts ................................................. 36

# Chapter 3

## Using the Internet: Making the Most of the Web's Resources .............. 80

## Chapter 4

# Application Software: Programs That Let You Work and Play ..................... 120

## Chapter 5

## System Software: The Operating System, Utility Programs, and File Management ................................................................ 158

# Chapter 6

# Understanding and Assessing Hardware: Evaluating Your System ................... 198

# Chapter 7

# Chapter 8

## Managing Your Digital Lifestyle: Challenges and Ethics ............................ 272

## Chapter 9

## Securing Your System: Protecting Your Digital Data and Devices ...... 322

## Appendix A

## Appendix B

# Learn Technology by Using
## *Technology in Action* 16e

The best-selling *Technology in Action* continues to deliver an engaging approach to teaching the topics and skills students need to be digitally literate. Using practical content, hands-on projects, and interactive simulation activities students are engaged in learning.

Today's students are more tech savvy than ever—they know how to use their smartphones, YouTube, Snapchat, and Instagram—and that's how they want to learn. *Technology in Action* is written knowing that many students are digital natives, so the instruction and practice offer students a consistent and engaging experience from chapter to chapter. They don't just read about technology, they engage with it in familiar ways.

For the 16th edition, students will engage with their peers at the beginning of each chapter of the etext by taking a Web-based survey and then analyzing the results with *What Do You Think?* questions. From there students continue to engage with the content by watching videos, working through interactive Helpdesk activities, Sound Byte lessons, IT simulations, and a variety of hands-on projects. Using these resources and the practical content, students learn the concepts and skills they need to be digitally literate in today's workplace. And, if they are using MyLab IT, they can earn the *Digital Competency* badge to demonstrate their skills to potential employers.

## Hallmarks

- Engaging **question-and-answer writing style** that approaches topics as students do.

- **Ethics coverage** throughout, including in end-of-chapter activities, Point/Counterpoint ethical debate content found in relevant chapters, and a Sound Byte lesson on how to discuss and debate ethical issues.

- **Hands-on learning** with projects throughout each chapter:

  - **Try This** projects allow students to practice and demonstrate their proficiency with important topics. Each project is accompanied by a how-to video.

  - **Solve This** projects put the concepts students are learning into action through real-world problem solving using Microsoft Office programs. Grader project versions of most of these projects are in MyLab IT.

  - **Make This** projects provide activities where students build programs that run on their mobile devices. Twelve of the chapters have activities that build fully functional mobile apps, compatible with either Android or iOS. Each project includes instructions and a how-to video.

- **Interactive activities** engage students in active learning and *demonstration* of understanding:

  - **Helpdesk** interactive activities provide a review of chapter objectives by having students play the role of a helpdesk staffer assisting customers via a live chat using a decision-based simulation with a quiz.

  - **Sound Byte** audio lessons provide coverage of additional topics related to the chapter, including a brief quiz.

  - **IT Simulations** provide an in-depth chapter scenario that students work through in an active learning environment and complete with a brief quiz to

demonstrate understanding. Newly redesigned for a more engaging and easier-to-use learning experience that helps students actively demonstrate understanding. Now includes a "presentation mode" so instructors can walk through the simulation in class or with students.

- **Review and Quizzes**

  - **Check Your Understanding Quizzes** provide a self-check covering objectives in each part of the chapter so that students can see how well they are learning the content.

  - The **Chapter Quiz** provides a way for students to test that they have learned the material from the entire chapter.

  - New **"Chew on This"** critical thinking questions require that students demonstrate their understanding through written answers that are manually graded.

  - **Testbank Exams** provide customizable prebuilt, autograded, objective-based questions covering the chapter objectives.

- **Videos**

  - **Chapter Overview Videos** provide an objective-based review of what students should have learned.

  - **Try This** and **Make This** project videos

- **Helpful Resources**

  - **PowerPoint and Audio Presentations** can be used in class for lecture or assigned to students, particularly online students, for instruction and review.

  - **Instructor Chapter Guides** provide teaching tips; homework and assessment suggestions; a brief overviews of each chapter's *Try This*, *Make This*, and *Solve This* exercises; as well as select Sound Byte talking points and ethics debate starters.

# What's New?

- **What Do You Think?** discussion topics begin each chapter with surveys that students complete. They then respond to follow-up questions related to the topic at the end of the chapter to encourage critical thinking.
- **Chew on This** critical thinking questions at the end of each chapter part, encourage students to think critically about the impact of technology on society.
- **Technology in the News** (formerly *TechBytes Weekly*) lets you keep your class current with weekly technology news. This currency widget is included in the etext or Revel versions of *Technology in Action* to provide new and updated content, discussion points, and activities every week.
- **Chapter 8** has been expanded to discuss the challenges students face in managing an active digital lifestyle such as the Dark Web, keeping data private, and using cryptocurrency.
- **Images and quizzes** have been updated throughout.
- A new **Try This project in Chapter 1**—*What Does Facebook Know About You?*—lets students explore the detailed information collected about them by the social media platform.

## Summary of Chapter Updates

All chapter Learning Outcomes and Learning Objectives have been revised as needed and throughout the text, figures and photos have been updated with new images, current topics, and state-of-the art technology coverage.

### Chapter 1

A new *Try This* exercise leading students through the steps to examine the data stored about them by social media platforms has been added.

The section on technology and careers has been updated with current trends and an emphasis on the impact of artificial intelligence.

### Chapter 5

Discussions on additional mobile operating systems like watchOS and tvOS have been added.

Coverage of the latest smarthome devices and open-source solutions has been added.

### Chapter 7

The *Bits&Bytes: Net Neutrality* has been updated.

The *Bits&Bytes: Is Dial-Up Still an Option?* has been updated.

The *Bits&Bytes: 5G Is Coming—Is It Worth the Wait?* has been deleted and content has been added to the text.

*Ethics in IT: Ethical Challenges of the Internet of Things* has moved to Chapter 8.

A new *Bits&Bytes: Power Your Devices Wirelessly* has been added.

Revisions to setting up a Windows home network have been made to remove concept of homegroups.

The *Bits&Bytes: The Rise of Wearable Technology* has moved to Chapter 8.

A new *Ethics in IT: Privacy Challenges of Delivering Free Wi-Fi* has been added.

### Chapter 8

*Ethics in IT: Ethical Challenges of the Internet of Things* has been relocated from Chapter 7.

A new objective, "Discuss the challenges in managing an active digital lifestyle," has been added to the chapter.

A new *Dig Deeper, Deep Web versus Dark Web: Are There Places You Shouldn't Go?*, has been added to the chapter.

*Bits&Bytes: The Rise of Wearable Technology* has been relocated from Chapter 7.

### Chapter 9

A Bits&Bytes addressing the role of social media and computer security in maintaining democratic elections has been added.

Extended treatment of password managers and biometric options for access control has been added.

# The Program

To maximize student results, we recommend using *Technology in Action* with **MyLab IT**, the teaching and learning platform that empowers you to reach every student. By combining trusted author content with digital tools and a flexible platform, MyLab IT personalizes the learning experience and will help your students learn and retain key course concepts while developing skills that future employers seek.

With MyLab IT for *Technology in Action*, students have access to all of the instruction, practice, review, and assessment resources in one place. There are two ways you can set up your course:

1. You can choose to use the new *sequential learning modules* that allow you to create activities in the order you want students to complete them, providing a consistent, measurable learning experience from chapter to chapter.

2. You can take a second approach for an interactive learning experience, where students use the interactive etext to read and learn actively with Helpdesk activities, Sound Bytes, IT Simulations, *What's New in Technology* currency updates, *What do You Think?* surveys and critical thinking questions, hands-on projects, videos, accessible PowerPoint presentations, and more. You assign the etext chapter, students engage in learning and practice, and go back to their assignments to take the chapter quizzes.

# Solving Teaching and Learning Challenges

*Technology in Action*, 16e provides a hands-on approach to learning computer concepts in which students learn a little and then apply what they are learning in a project or simulation or watch a video to dive deeper. Within the etext, students are engaged through interactive surveys, *What's New in Technology* currency updates, videos, IT Simulations, interactives, fun study tools, and quiz questions with immediate feedback. And with the new *What do you think?* surveys at the beginning of each chapter, the follow-up question at the end of the chapter related to the survey results, as well as new *Chew on This* critical thinking questions at the end of each chapter part, students are encouraged to think critically about the impact of technology on society.

The optimal way to experience *Technology in Action* is with MyLab IT. All of the instruction, practice, review, and assessment resources are in one place, allowing you to arrange your course from an instructional perspective that gives students a consistent, measurable learning experience from chapter to chapter.

# Developing Employability Skills

Digital literacy is a top skill required in today's job market! Developing these skills involves conceptual as well as hands-on learning. With *Technology in Action*, students get both—they learn the fundamentals of computers and have opportunities to apply what they are learning in real-world projects and simulations. Using MyLab IT and *Technology in Action*, students can learn, practice, and demonstrate their digital literacy.

- **High-Demand Office Skills** are evaluated in the auto-graded *Solve This* projects in each chapter.

- **Essential Digital Literacy Skills** are taught and practiced throughout the book *in Try This*, *Solve This*, and *Make This* projects.

| | Employability Skills Matrix (ESM) | | | | | | | |
|---|---|---|---|---|---|---|---|---|
| | Ethics Projects | Try This Projects | Solve This Projects | Make This Projects | What do you think? | Interactives: Helpdesks, Sound Bytes, IT Sims | Team Time Projects | Badge |
| Critical Thinking | x | | x | x | x | | X | |
| Communication | x | | | | x | x | X | |
| Collaboration | x | | | | x | x | X | |
| Knowledge Application and Analysis | x | X | x | x | x | x | X | |
| Social Responsibility | x | X | | | x | | | |

# Applied Learning Opportunities Throughout

Using MyLab IT with *Technology in Action* provides students with a variety of ways to get instruction, practice, review, and assessment.

### Technology in the News

Formerly *TechBytes Weekly*, these weekly currency updates deliver the latest technology news stories to you to use in your classroom. The update is live in the etext chapter, so no matter where you are in the content, you'll have this weekly update to use for in-class discussion or as a reading assignment.

### *Try This* Projects

These projects have students apply what they are learning in a practical project that uses skills they'll need in the workforce and everyday life. Each project includes a video to guide students through the project.

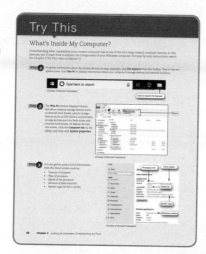

### *Make This* Projects

These hands-on activities lead students to explore mobile app development in either an Android or iOS environment.

### Helpdesk Activities

The Helpdesk training content, created specifically for *Technology in Action*, enables students to take on the role of a helpdesk staffer fielding questions posed by computer users so that students demonstrate their understanding in an active learning environment. Each Helpdesk ends with a quiz, ensuring students have grasped the content.

### *Solve This* Projects

These exercises integrate and reinforce chapter concepts with Microsoft Office skills.

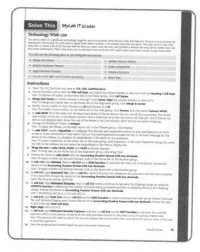

### Sound Bytes

Sound Bytes expand student mastery of complex topics through engaging lessons with a brief quiz to check understanding.

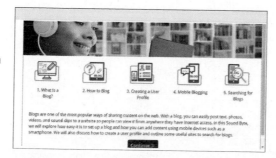

### IT Simulations

These detailed interactive scenarios cover a core chapter topic in a hands-on environment where students can apply what they have learned and demonstrate understanding through active engagement.

# Instructor Teaching Resources

This program comes with the following teaching resources.

| Supplements available to instructors at www.pearsonhighered.com/techinaction | Features of the Supplement |
|---|---|
| Accessible PowerPoint Presentation | PowerPoints meet accessibility standards for students with disabilities. Features include, but are not limited to:<br>• Keyboard and Screen Reader Access<br>• Alternative Text for Images<br>• High Color Contrast between Background and Foreground Colors |
| End-of-Chapter Answer Key, Check Your Understanding Answer Key, Chapter Quiz Answer Key | Answers to all end-of-chapter questions. |
| Image Library | Every image in the book. |
| Instructor Chapter Guide | • Content Instruction<br>• Student Preparation and Review<br>• Active Learning Options<br>• Chapter Assessment<br>• End-of-Chapter Exercises<br>• Currency Topics<br>• Soft Skills and Team Work<br>• Instructor Resources |
| *Make This* Projects | Activities where students build programs that run on their mobile devices. Each project includes instructions and a how-to video. |
| Objectives Mapping | Outline of the objectives in every chapter. |
| *Solve This* Projects | Real-world problem solving using Microsoft Office programs. Grader versions of most of these projects are in MyLab IT. |
| Syllabus Template | Sample syllabus for help in setting up your course. |
| Test Bank (Textbook, Helpdesk, Sound Bytes) | Over 1,000 multiple-choice, true/false, short-answer, and matching questions with these annotations:<br>• Difficulty level (1 for straight recall, 2 for some analysis, 3 for complex analysis)<br>• Objective, which provides location in the text<br>Provided for:<br>• Textbook<br>• Helpdesk<br>• Sound Byte |
| Computerized TestGen | TestGen allows instructors to:<br>• Customize, save, and generate classroom tests<br>• Edit, add, or delete questions from the Test Item files<br>• Analyze test results<br>• Organize a database of tests and student results |
| Transition Guide | Detailed explanation of changes between the previous and current edition. |
| Web Projects | Discussion questions and additional projects that can be done on the Internet. |

## Our 16th Edition—A Letter from the Authors

### Why We Wrote This Book

The pace of technological change is ever increasing. In education, we have seen this impact us more than ever recently—the Maker movement, the Internet of Things, MOOCs, touch-screen mobile delivery, and Hangouts are now fixed parts of our environment.

Even the most agile of learners and educators need support in keeping up with this pace of change. Our students have easier access to more information than any generation before them. We recognize the need for them to be able to think critically and investigate the data they see. In this edition, we introduce the use of chapter-opening features called *What do you think?* that allow students to critically think about a chapter topic. Students then follow up at the end of the chapter by answering additional related critical thinking questions in a *What do you think now?* feature.

We have also responded by integrating material to help students develop skills for web application and mobile programming. We see the incredible value of these skills and their popularity with students and have included *Make This* exercises for each chapter. These exercises gently bring the concepts behind mobile app development to life. In addition, there is a *Solve This* exercise in each chapter that reinforces chapter content while also applying Microsoft Office skills. These projects help to promote students' critical-thinking and problem-solving skills, which employers value highly.

The Helpdesk and Sound Byte training modules and IT Simulations continue to provide students with an active learning environment in which they can reinforce their learning of chapter objectives. In this edition, we have put the spotlight on critical thinking. We've integrated real-time surveys on important technology topics to foster classroom discussion and analytical skills. We have also included additional material on key challenges of a digital lifestyle, such as using digital currency, avoiding the Dark Web, and protecting privacy.

We also continue to emphasize the many aspects of ethics in technology debates. Some of the Helpdesks and IT Simulations support instruction on how to conduct thoughtful and respectful discussion on complex ethical issues.

Our combined 70 years of teaching computer concepts have coincided with sweeping innovations in computing technology that have affected every facet of society. From iPads to Web 2.0, computers are more than ever a fixture of our daily lives—and the lives of our students. But although today's students have a much greater comfort level with their digital environment than previous generations, their knowledge of the machines they use every day is still limited.

Part of the student-centered focus of our book has to do with making the material truly engaging to students. From the beginning, we have written *Technology in Action* to focus on what matters most to today's student. Instead of a history lesson on the microchip, we focus on tasks students can accomplish with their computing devices and skills they can apply immediately in the workplace, in the classroom, and at home.

We strive to keep the text as current as publishing timelines allow, and we are constantly looking for the next technology trend or gadget. We have augmented the etext with weekly *What's New in Technology* automatic updates. These updates will be in each chapter, so regardless of where you are in the text, you'll have current topics to talk about in class related to the latest breaking developments.

We also continue to include a number of multimedia components to enrich the classroom and student learning experience. The result is a learning system that sparks student interest by focusing on the material they want to learn (such as how to integrate devices into a home network) while teaching the material they need to learn (such as how networks work). The sequence of topics is carefully set up to mirror the typical student learning experience.

As they read this text, your students will progress through stages and learning outcomes of increasing difficulty:

- Thinking about how technology offers them the power to change their society and their world and examining why it's important to be computer fluent
- Understanding the basic components of computing devices
- Connecting to and exploring the Internet
- Exploring application software
- Learning about the operating system and personalizing their computer
- Evaluating and upgrading computing devices
- Understanding home networking options
- Creating digital assets and understanding how to legally distribute them
- Keeping computing devices safe from hackers

We strive to structure the book in a way that makes navigation easy and reinforces key concepts. We continue to design the text around learning outcomes and objectives, making them a prominent part of the chapter structure. Students will see the learning outcomes and objectives in the chapter opener, throughout the text itself, as well as in the summary so they understand just what they are expected to learn.

We also continue to structure the book in a progressive manner, intentionally introducing on a basic level in the earlier chapters concepts that students traditionally have trouble with and then later expanding on those concepts in more detail when students have become more comfortable with them. Thus, the focus of the early chapters is on practical uses for the computer, with real-world examples to help the students place computing in a familiar context. For example, we introduce basic hardware components in Chapter 2, and then we go into increasingly greater detail on some hardware components in Chapter 6.

In addition to extensive review, practice, and assessment content, each chapter contains several problem-solving, hands-on activities that can be carried out in the classroom or as homework:

- The *Try This* exercises lead students to explore a particular computing feature related to the chapter.
- The *Make This* exercises are hands-on activities that lead students to explore mobile app development in both the Android and iOS environments.
- The *Solve This* exercises integrate and reinforce chapter concepts with Microsoft Office skills.

Throughout the years we have also developed a comprehensive multimedia program to reinforce the material taught in the text and to support both classroom lectures and distance learning:

- New chapter-opening features called *What do you think?* allow students to critically think about a chapter topic. Students then follow up at the end of the chapter by answering additional related critical thinking questions in a *What do you think now?* feature.
- New *Chew on This* critical-thinking questions require that students demonstrate their understanding through written answers that are manually graded.
- The Helpdesk training content, created specifically for *Technology in Action*, enables students to take on the role of a helpdesk staffer fielding questions posed by computer users so that students can demonstrate their understanding in an active learning environment.
- Sound Bytes expand student mastery of complex topics through engaging lessons with a brief quiz to check understanding.
- IT Simulations are detailed, interactive scenarios covering the core chapter topic. As students work through the simulation, they apply what they have learned and demonstrate understanding in an active learning environment.
- The *What's New in Technology* (formerly *TechBytes Weekly*) is a weekly currency update that delivers the latest technology news stories to you for use in your classroom. In addition, the currency items have discussion points or activities included. The update is live in the etext chapters, so no matter where you are in the content, you'll have this weekly update to use for an in-class discussion or reading assignment.

# About the Authors

## Alan Evans, MS, CPA
aevans@mc3.edu

Alan is currently a faculty member at Moore College of Art and Design and Montgomery County Community College, teaching a variety of computer science and business courses. He holds a BS in accounting from Rider University and an MS in Information Systems from Drexel University, and he is a certified public accountant. After a successful career in business, Alan finally realized that his true calling is education. He has been teaching at the college level since 2000. He enjoys attending technical conferences and exploring new methods of engaging students.

## Kendall Martin, PhD
kmartin@mc3.edu

Kendall is a full professor of Computer Science at Montgomery County Community College with teaching experience at both the undergraduate and graduate levels at a number of institutions, including Villanova University, DeSales University, Ursinus College, and Arcadia University. Her education includes a BS in electrical engineering from the University of Rochester and an MS and a PhD in engineering from the University of Pennsylvania. Kendall has industrial experience in research and development environments (AT&T Bell Laboratories) as well as experience with several start-up technology firms.

## Mary Anne Poatsy, MBA
mpoatsy@mc3.edu

Mary Anne is a senior faculty member at Montgomery County Community College, teaching various computer application and concepts courses in face-to-face and online environments. She enjoys speaking at various professional conferences about innovative classroom strategies. Mary Anne holds a BA in psychology and education from Mount Holyoke College and an MBA in finance from Northwestern University's Kellogg Graduate School of Management. She has been in teaching since 1997, ranging from elementary and secondary education to Montgomery County Community College, Gwynedd-Mercy College, Muhlenberg College, and Bucks County Community College, as well as training in the professional environment. Before teaching, Mary Anne was a vice president at Shearson Lehman Hutton in the Municipal Bond Investment Banking Department.

# Acknowledgments

For my wife, Patricia, whose patience, understanding, and support continue to make this work possible, especially when I stay up past midnight writing! And to my parents, Jackie and Dean, who taught me the best way to achieve your goals is to constantly strive to improve yourself through education.

**—Alan Evans**

For all the teachers, mentors, and gurus who have popped in and out of my life.

**—Kendall Martin**

For my husband, Ted, who unselfishly continues to take on more than his fair share to support me throughout this process, and for my children, Laura, Carolyn, and Teddy, whose encouragement and love have been inspiring.

**—Mary Anne Poatsy**

First, we would like to thank our students. We constantly learn from them while teaching, and they are a continual source of inspiration and new ideas.

We could not have written this book without the loving support of our families. Our spouses and children made sacrifices (mostly in time not spent with us) to permit us to make this dream into a reality.

Although working with the entire team at Pearson has been a truly enjoyable experience, a few individuals deserve special mention. The constant support and encouragement we receive from Jenifer Niles, Executive Portfolio Product Manager, and Andrew Gilfillan, VP, Editorial Director, continually make this book grow and change. Our heartfelt thanks go to Shannon LeMay-Finn, our Developmental Editor. Her creativity, drive, and management skills helped make this book a reality. We also would like to extend our appreciation to Pearson Content Producers, particularly Laura Burgess, and the vendor teams, who work tirelessly to ensure that our book is published on time and looks fabulous. The timelines are always short, the art is complex, and there are many people with whom they have to coordinate tasks. But they make it look easy! We'd like to extend our thanks to the media and MyLab IT team—Eric Hakanson, Becca Golden, Amanda Losonsky, and Heather Darby—for all of their hard work and dedication.

There are many people whom we do not meet at Pearson and elsewhere who make significant contributions by designing the book, illustrating, composing the pages, producing the media, and securing permissions. We thank them all.

And finally, we would like to thank the reviewers and the many others who contribute their time, ideas, and talents to this project. We appreciate their time and energy, as their comments help us turn out a better product each edition. A special thanks goes to Rick Wolff, a wonderfully talented infographic designer who helped by creating the infographics for this text.

**Chapter**

# The Impact of Technology in a Changing World

 For a chapter overview, watch the **Chapter Overview videos**.

**PART 1**

## Technology in Society

| **Learning Outcome 1.1** | You will be able to discuss the impact of the tools of modern technology on national and global issues. |

### Technology in a Global Society   4

**Objective 1.1**   *Describe various technological tools being used to impact national and global issues.*

**Objective 1.2**   *Describe various global social issues that are being affected by technology.*

### Technology Connects Us with Others   6

**Objective 1.3**   *Describe how technology is changing how and why we connect and collaborate with others.*

**Objective 1.4**   *Summarize how technology has impacted the way we choose and consume products and services.*

**Helpdesk:** Technology Impacts

### The Importance of Computer Literacy   8

**Objective 1.5**   *Characterize computer literacy and explain why it is important to be computer literate.*

**Sound Byte:** Virtual Computer Tour

**PART 2**

## Emerging Technologies and Ethical Computing

| **Learning Outcome 1.2** | You will be able to describe emerging technologies, such as artificial intelligence, and how technology creates new ethical debates. |

### Artificial Intelligence   13

**Objective 1.6**   *Describe artificial intelligence systems and explain their main goals.*

**Helpdesk:** The Impact of Artificial Intelligence

### Working with Artificial Intelligence and Other Information Technologies   17

**Objective 1.7**   *Describe how artificial intelligence and other emerging technologies are important in many careers.*

### Ethical Computing   22

**Objective 1.8**   *Define ethics and describe various ethical systems.*

**Objective 1.9**   *Describe influences on the development of your personal ethics.*

**Objective 1.10**   *Present examples of how technology creates ethical challenges.*

**Sound Byte:** How to Debate Ethical Issues

 All media accompanying this chapter can be found here.

 **Make This** A Virtual Assistant on **page 12**

*(John Lund/Getty Images; Carlos Castilla/Shutterstock; Winui/Shuttertock; Ivan Trifonenko/123RF; Sergey Nivens/Shutterstock; Stuart Miles/Fotolia)*

2

Journalism
Robotics
Education
Psychology
Medicine
Literature
Theater
Biology
Economics

# What do you think?

Having a **background in technology and computer science** enables you to be a powerful contributor in many career fields. More universities are realizing this and **creating a new department, CS + X**. What is CS + X? The CS stands for Computer Science, while the **X stands for a second area of study** that blends with computer technology. For example, the X might be Music, with the combined degree including study of the perception of music and use of digital techniques to enhance our experiences. Or the X might be Archaeology, with the curriculum including courses on the computer simulation of human behavior and creating virtual reality models. Universities that are creating CS + X departments argue that **combining computer science with other skills produces students who are better journalists, artists, scientists, and so on**. The possibilities for collaboration between your passions and technology are endless.

 Which field would you be most curious about combining with CS?
- Literature
- Statistics
- Business
- Nursing
- Criminal Justice
- Anthropology
- Art
- Other

*See the end of the chapter for a follow-up question.*

3

# Technology in Society

**Learning Outcome 1.1    You will be able to discuss the impact of the tools of modern technology on national and global issues.**

Ask yourself: Why are you in this class? Maybe it's a requirement for your degree, or maybe you want to improve your computer skills. But let's step back and look at the bigger picture.

Technology is a tool that enables us all to make an impact beyond our own lives. We've all seen movies that dangle the dream in front of us of being the girl or guy who saves the world—and gets to drive a nice car while doing it!

Technology can be your ticket to doing just that by influencing and participating in projects that will change the world.

# Technology in a Global Society

Recent national and global issues are showing that technology is accelerating change around the world and galvanizing groups of people in new ways. Let's look at a few examples.

## Impact of Tools of Modern Technology

**Objective 1.1**    *Describe various technological tools being used to impact national and global issues.*

### Social Media Tools

Social media platforms like Twitter, Facebook, and Instagram enable people to connect and exchange ideas. These platforms also bring together people facing similar problems to fight for social change. For example, the Twitter hashtag #MeToo began as a way of supporting women facing sexual harassment and assault but evolved to galvanize an international movement. A simple hashtag brought to light an important social issue and was a key means for revealing how widespread the problem was.

How we conduct informed discussion in the age of social media is still developing, however. Bot accounts, automated programs retweeting news stories and quotes, have been used to create discord around controversial topics in many countries—enflaming the gun control debate in the United States or fanning prejudice into violence in Sri Lanka. For these and other reasons, knowing how to use and critically evaluate social media is an important skill needed by all (see Figure 1.1).

### Crisis-Mapping Tool

Another example of the interaction of technology and society is the software tool Ushahidi. Following a disputed election in Kenya, violence broke out all over the country. Nairobi lawyer Ory Okolloh tried to get word of the violence out to the world through her blog, but she couldn't keep up with the volume of reports. However, two programmers saw her request for help and in a few days created Ushahidi. It is a crisis-mapping tool that collects information from

**Figure 1.1** Social media has changed how we access, distribute, and evaluate information. *(Rudmer Zwerver/Shutterstock)*

**Figure 1.2** Ushahidi crisis-mapping software has been used to identify areas of violence against women in India. *(Pixhall/Alamy Stock Photo)*

e-mails, text messages, blog posts, and tweets and then maps them, instantly making the information publicly available. The developers then made Ushahidi a free platform anyone in the world can use (see Figure 1.2). It has since been used in several international disasters. In what other ways may technology help us face times of crisis?

## Global Issues

**Objective 1.2** *Describe various global social issues that are being affected by technology.*

Let's look at the different global social issues that are being affected by technology.

### Health Care

Infectious diseases account for about one-fifth of all deaths worldwide. Researchers say the odds of a flu pandemic occurring in the next century are nearly 100%. Could technology help us develop and deliver vaccines to save lives? Using scientific visualization tools, scientists are developing antibodies for flu viruses and even HIV, viruses that are difficult to target because they continually change shape. Computationally intense modeling software is helping researchers increase the pace of vaccine production.

As we learn more about the terrible consequences of concussion injuries, technology is playing a part in providing a solution. Researchers now know that even without an actual concussion, athletes can sustain serious damage from repeated impacts of their brain against the skull. Computer programs have collected sensor data from impacts on the field, which scientists have analyzed and used to create a new kind of helmet. College programs and the NFL now use enhanced helmets, designed to better distribute the impact of collisions.

### The Environment

What if every cell phone in the world had built-in atmospheric sensors? Then millions of points of data measuring air and water quality from around the world could be acquired. The data could be tagged with geographical information, alerting scientists to new trends in our environment. Ideas like these are being explored by researchers around the world.

Smart Internet-connected water sprinklers are another technology that is already saving water in California and other dry areas of the country. The sprinkler system checks the weather forecast so it won't use water when rain is coming the next day. The system is showing a 30% reduction in water usage.

**Figure 1.3** The Next Einstein Initiative (NEI) is rallying the support of the world to identify and encourage mathematical genius.
*(Alistair Cotton/123RF)*

### The Digital Divide

There is a serious gap in the levels of Internet access and the availability of technical tools in different regions of the world. The term for this difference in access to technology is the digital divide. One danger of a digital divide is that it prevents us from using all the minds on the planet to solve global problems. But this challenge created by technology is also being answered by it.

The Next Einstein Initiative (NEI) is a plan to focus resources on the talented mathematical minds of Africa (see Figure 1.3). Cambridge professor Neil Turok founded the African Institute of Mathematical Sciences (AIMS) to bring together the brightest young minds across Africa with the best lecturers in the world. By capturing the enthusiasm of the world with presentations distributed through TED (*ted.com*) and Google's Project $10^{100}$, there is now a push to create additional AIMS centers across Africa.

Table 1.1 shows additional examples of people putting technology into action to impact the world. How will you join them?

**Table 1.1  Technology in Action: Taking on Global Problems**

| Person/ Organization | Global Problem | Technology Used | Action | Find Out More . . . |
|---|---|---|---|---|
| Start Network | Corruption | Blockchain, a digitized public ledger for recording a series of transactions | Blockchain technology can help track humanitarian aid funds as they flow from donors to recipients. | Start Network: *startnetwork.org* |
| SolaRoad/ Netherlands | The need for a renewable, nonpolluting energy resource | Solar cells | Solar cells are integrated into the asphalt roadway. They collect solar energy and distribute electricity all day. | Netherlands SolaRoad: *solaroad.nl* |
| United Nations World Food Programme (WFP) | Issues of hunger for 1 in 7 of the world's population | GIS (geographical information systems) and mobile devices | The WFP can analyze the location and need for food, positioning it where it will help the most. | World Food Programme: *wfp.org* |
| Gates Foundation | The threat of global pandemic disease, like Ebola, or weaponized biological warfare | Mobile apps, data analytics, and enhanced global communications | Worldwide organizations like the Gates Foundation are taking steps to build better networks to detect outbreaks and deliver vaccines. | Gates Foundation: *gatesfoundation.org* |

# Technology Connects Us with Others

Technology is also allowing us to redefine fundamental parts of our social makeup—how we think, how we connect with each other, and how we purchase and consume products.

## Technology Impacts How and Why We Connect and Collaborate

**Objective 1.3**  *Describe how technology is changing how and why we connect and collaborate with others.*

### Collaborating for the Benefit of Others

With the arrival of many web applications that allow individuals to become "creators" of the web, a new kind of Internet has come into being. Nicknamed Web 2.0, the web now allows users to easily contribute content and connect with each other. Web 2.0 has fostered a dramatic shift across the world, from simply consuming to having the ability to volunteer and collaborate on projects. The term cognitive surplus was coined to reflect the combination of leisure time and the tools to be creative. The availability of media tools and the easy connectivity of Web 2.0, along with generosity and a need to share, also enable projects like Ushahidi to emerge.

## Connecting Through Business

One of the most profound ways we can connect with each other is to support other people's dreams. Kickstarter helps us connect in this way by allowing people to post their ideas and to ask for direct funding. Donors are given rewards for different levels of pledges, such as a signed edition of a book or a special color of a product. This means of generating capital to start a business is known as crowdfunding, asking for small donations from a large number of people. Successful Kickstarter projects have included ice chests with integrated blenders, DNA analysis machines that could inexpensively diagnose disease, and many entertainment projects. Over $3.0 billion of funding for businesses has been raised using Kickstarter. Business ideas are not the only projects benefiting from crowdfunding. Sites like GoFundMe allow people to crowdfund to raise money for things such as medical bills or tuition.

## Technology Impacts How We Consume

**Objective 1.4** *Summarize how technology has impacted the way we choose and consume products and services.*

Technology is also changing how we decide what we'll purchase and how we actually buy goods and services.

(Pearson Education)

### Marketing

Marketing strategies are counting on the fact that most people have a cell phone with a camera and Internet access. Quick response (QR) codes like the one shown here let any piece of text host a direct link to online information and video content.

Marketers also have to be aware of the phenomenon of crowdsourcing—checking in with the voice of the crowd. Forward-thinking companies are using this input to improve their products and services. AT&T, for example, has an app called Mark the Spot that lets customers report locations of dropped calls to help the company improve its coverage.

## Access Versus Ownership

Even the idea of ownership is evolving. Items like cars and bikes can become "subscriptions" instead of purchases. Services like Uber and Lyft let you use your car to provide rides for others while Zipcar allows you to use a shared car whenever you need it. Bicycles can be shared in most cities with programs like New York City's Citi Bike. It has already seen riders take over 50 million trips. These new sharing options have revolutionized the transportation industry (see Figure 1.4).

Such collaborative consumption implies that we are joining together as a group to use a specific product more efficiently. There are increasing opportunities to share the services a product provides instead of owning it outright. Mounting environmental concerns and global financial pressures are other forces pushing us toward collaborative consumption (see Figure 1.5).

**Figure 1.4** With smartphones and constant networking, sharing services like CitiBike, Zipcar, Uber, and Lyft have revolutionized transportation options. *(MShieldsPhotos/Alamy Stock Photo; Metamorworks/Shutterstock; Mr.Whiskey/Shutterstock; Piotr Swat/Shutterstock)*

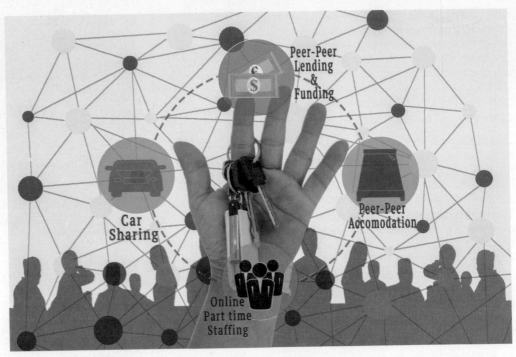

**Figure 1.5** Collaborative consumption means that we use networking to share a resource (for example, a car or home) so many people can use the same object. *(Montri Nipitvittaya/Shutterstock)*

# The Importance of Computer Literacy

Everywhere you go, you see ads for computers and other devices. Do you know what all the words in the ad mean? What is a GPU? How fast do you need your computer to be, and how much memory should it have? If you're computer literate, you'll be a more informed consumer when it comes time to buy computers, peripherals, and technology services. Understanding computer terminology and keeping current with technology will help you better determine which computers and devices you need.

## Computer Literacy

**Objective 1.5**   *Characterize computer literacy and explain why it is important to be computer literate.*

Let's look at a few examples of what it means to be a savvy computer user and consumer.

**Computer literacy.** When you are computer literate (see Table 1.2), you understand the capabilities and limitations of computers and you know how to use them safely and efficiently. The topics listed in Table 1.2 and more are covered in detail in the remaining chapters.

**Avoiding hackers and viruses.** Hackers and viruses can threaten a computer's security. Being aware of how they operate and knowing the damage they can cause can help you avoid falling prey to them.

**Protecting your privacy.** If your identity is stolen, your credit rating can be quickly ruined. Do you know how to protect yourself from identity theft when you're online?

**Understanding the real risks.** Being computer literate means being able to separate real privacy and security risks from things you don't have to worry about. Do you know whether cookies pose a privacy risk when you're on the Internet? Do you know how to configure a firewall for your needs?

**Using the web wisely.** People who are computer literate know how to find reliable, accurate information effectively. They also know how to use the web to work well with others. Are you effective in how you use the web?

**Avoiding online annoyances.** How can you avoid spam—unsolicited electronic junk mail? Do you know what adware and spyware are? Do you know the difference between viruses, worms,

 **MyLab IT**

**Technology Impacts**

In this Helpdesk, you'll play the role of a helpdesk staffer fielding questions about ways in which technology affects society.

 **MyLab IT**

**Virtual Computer Tour**

In this Sound Byte, you'll take a video tour of the inside of a desktop system unit; locate the power supply, CPU, and memory; and learn more about what's inside a computer.

## Table 1.2  What Does It Mean to Be Computer Literate?

| | | |
|---|---|---|
| You can **avoid falling prey to hackers and viruses** because you are aware of how they operate. | You know how to **protect yourself from identity theft.** | You can **separate the real privacy and security risks from things you don't have to worry about.** |

| | | |
|---|---|---|
| You know how to find information and **use the web effectively**. | You can **avoid being overwhelmed by spam, adware, and spyware**. | You can how to **diagnose and fix problems** with your hardware and software. |

*(Peter Dazeley/The Image Bank/Getty Images; Yuri_Arcurs/E+/Getty Images; Zakai/DigitalVision Vectors/Getty Images; Justin Lewis/Stone/Getty Images; Argus/Fotolia; Ivanastar/E+/Getty Images)*

and Trojan horses? What software—the instructions that tell the computer what to do—should you install on your computer to avoid online annoyances?

**Being able to maintain, upgrade, and troubleshoot your computer.** Learning how to care for and maintain your computer and knowing how to diagnose and fix certain problems can save you time and money. Do you know how to upgrade your computer if you want more memory? Do you know which software and computer settings can keep your computer in top shape?

**Keeping up to date.** Finally, becoming computer literate means knowing about new technologies and how to integrate them into your life. Can you connect your TV to your wireless network? What is a media server, and do you need one? Can a USB type C connection carry HDMI video signals? Being able to stay up to date with technology is an important skill.

This book will help you become computer literate. In Chapter 3, you'll find out how to get the most from the web while staying free from the spam and clutter Internet surfing can leave behind on your computer. Chapter 6 shows you how to determine whether your hardware is limiting your computer's performance and how to upgrade or shop for a new device. Chapter 9 covers how to keep your computer and your digital life secure. You'll be able to save money, time, and frustration by understanding the basics of how computer systems operate.

---

### Before moving on to Part 2:

1. 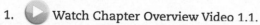 Watch Chapter Overview Video 1.1.
2. Then take the Check Your Understanding quiz.

# Check Your Understanding // Review & Practice

For a quick review to see what you've learned so far, answer the following questions.

## multiple choice

1. Automated bot accounts use social media
   a. responsibly.
   b. to help humans who are busy.
   c. to manipulate opinion by posting news stories and quotes massive numbers of times.
   d. in some countries but they are illegal in the U.S.

2. The digital divide occurred because
   a. the United States has the fastest Internet access.
   b. not everyone has equal access to the Internet.
   c. crowdfunding is increasing.
   d. everyone now has a smartphone.

3. Cognitive surplus means that we now find many people with
   a. more money than free time.
   b. limited access to the Internet.
   c. mobile devices.
   d. excess time and free tools for collaboration.

4. Crowdfunding helps startup businesses by
   a. selling stock more easily.
   b. using QR codes to advertise and market products.
   c. gathering financial contributions from supporters.
   d. replacing Web 2.0 technology.

5. Collaborative consumption is when people get together to
   a. find the best prices on products.
   b. increase the use of a single product by sharing access to it.
   c. fight diseases of the respiratory tract.
   d. exchange reviews on services and goods they have purchased.

### chew on this

Our thoughts are influenced by the information fed to our mind all day long. Web 2.0 has created numerous channels for people to offer their own work for free—open source software and free music, text, and artwork, to name a few. How has this affected your thinking, what you create, and what value you put on creative work?

(mdorottya/123RF)

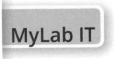

Go to **MyLab IT** to take an autograded version of the *Check Your Understanding* review and to find all media resources for the chapter.

> **For the IT Simulation for this chapter, see MyLab IT.**

# Try This

## What Does Facebook Know about You?

Social media sites like Facebook and Twitter do not charge you a fee. They make a profit by selling information about your behavior to marketers. By watching what groups you join and what posts you read, their algorithms make conclusions about what kind of person you are. In this exercise we'll show you how to check what information these sites have deduced about who you are. For more step-by-step instructions, watch the Chapter 1 Try This video on MyLab IT.

### What You Need

A Facebook account

A Twitter account

*(rvlsoft/Shutterstock; Solomon7/Shutterstock)*

**Step 1** **From the Facebook website, download your Facebook data.** On the top line of your Facebook page, click the dropdown arrow on the far right and select **Settings**. Next, select **Your Facebook Information** and click **Download Your Information**. Click the **Create File** button. Facebook will e-mail you when the file is ready.

*(Used with Permission from Kendall Martin)*

**Step 2** **From the Twitter website, download the information Twitter has created on you.** Click on your Twitter avatar and select **Settings and privacy**. From the list on the left, select **Your Twitter data**. Scroll to the bottom and under **Download your Twitter data**, and click the **Request data** button. It will be e-mailed to you when the report is ready.

> **Demographics > Stay-at-home moms**
> **Demographics > Trailing baby boomers**
> **Demographics > Trendy moms**
> **Demographics > Veteran in household**
> **Demographics > Wife**
> **Demographics > Working-class families**
> **Demographics > Working-class moms**
> **Demographics > Young adult age 18-25**
> **Dining > Likely to dine at Chili's Grill & Bar**
> **Dining > Likely to dine at Chipotle Mexican Grill**
> **Dining > Likely to dine at Panera Bread Company**

**Step 3** **Examine what these algorithms have decided about you.** Check the list of interests and what items they think you will likely buy. How accurately have they guessed your household income, your politics, and your finances?

## TOOL: IFTTT.com (If This Then That)

### A Virtual Assistant

If This Then That (*IFTTT.com*) is an Internet-based tool that helps you get things done automatically. By using "recipes" within this web-based tool, you can automate tasks you do during the day, such as:

- automatically silencing your phone when you go into class,
- automatically texting your manager when you're on your way to work, or
- notifying you when the president signs a new law.

In this exercise, you'll explore using IFTTT to create recipes like these.

Make the Internet work for you by knowing this one programming statement: IF THIS, THEN THAT.

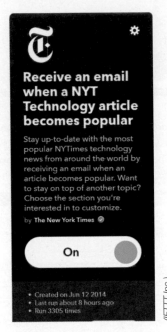

(IFTTT Inc.)

**For the instructions for this exercise, go to MyLab IT.**

# Emerging Technologies and Ethical Computing

**Learning Outcome 1.2** You will be able to describe emerging technologies, such as artificial intelligence, and how technology creates new ethical debates.

Can computing devices really think? Are virtual assistants like Alexa intelligent, or do they just mimic thinking? Rapid developments in the field of artificial intelligence have forced us to consider many new ethical debates. It's important to learn about new advancements in technology, such as artificial intelligence, as well as to understand the ethical dilemmas technology presents.

 ## Artificial Intelligence

Artificial intelligence focuses on creating computer systems that have an ability to perform tasks associated with human intelligence. Let's explore in detail what artificial intelligence is and how it impacts you.

### Artificial Intelligence Basics

**Objective 1.6** *Describe artificial intelligence systems and explain their main goals.*

**What exactly is intelligence?** Intelligence is the ability to acquire and apply knowledge and skills. Sociologists point to characteristics that make human beings intelligent, such as learning from experiences, reasoning, problem solving, perception, and using language. Animals can exhibit complex behavior, such as birds flying south for the winter, but this is attributed to instinct rather than intelligence. Some animals can even solve problems, such as sea otters that use rocks to crack open shellfish so they can consume them. But what separates us from other animals is the ability to combine behaviors as opposed to demonstrating one specific rote behavior (such as flying south for the winter).

**What is artificial intelligence?** Artificial intelligence (AI) is a branch of computer science that focuses on creating computer systems able to perform tasks that are usually associated with human intelligence. By this definition, any computer-controlled device that accomplishes something thought of as "intelligent" by humans is considered AI.

**Do computers "think" like human beings?** In the 1950s, the goal was to create a machine that could think like a human. Early examples included expert systems that mimicked doctors in diagnosing illnesses. But this goal has shifted somewhat toward creating machines that generate intelligent output but that do not necessarily mimic the human thought process.

Consider visiting the library. You could tell a human librarian your interests and the librarian could ask you some questions and then recommend books you might like. The Amazon recommendation engine fulfills the same purpose. However, the Amazon recommendation engine doesn't mimic a human librarian's thought process but instead analyzes vast amounts of data about you and other shoppers to make its recommendations. It provides intelligent results, but it does not arrive at those results the same way a human would.

**Helpdesk** MyLab IT

**The Impact of Artificial Intelligence**

In this Helpdesk, you'll play the role of a helpdesk staffer, fielding questions about artificial intelligence.

**What are the main areas of research for AI?** AI's central goals can be grouped into a number of categories (see Table 1.3):

- Natural language processing (NLP): NLP works to develop AI systems that understand written and spoken words and can interact with humans using language.
- Perception: AI systems have senses just as we do. AI systems use sonar, accelerometers, infrared, magnetic, and other electronic sensors to gather data. Being able to combine all the data from sensors and then construct information from it is a difficult challenge.
- Knowledge representation: Knowledge representation involves encoding information about the world into formats that the AI system can understand. Humans possess a vast collection of general knowledge based on their experiences in the world. AI systems need to build knowledge bases to solve problems. Developing a knowledge base and using it efficiently are active areas of research and have been demonstrated effectively by IBM's artificial intelligence computer Watson.
- Planning: AI systems need to set goals and then achieve them. An AI system might need to plan how to move a blue block out of the way to reach a red one or how to rotate a block as it moves to fit through a narrow opening.
- Problem solving: Humans tend to make intuitive judgments when solving a problem rather than perform a step-by-step analysis. AI programming combines a rules-based approach, along with trying to make judgments with incomplete information.
- Learning: Like humans, AI algorithms adapt and learn through experience. Supervised learning is used when the system can be trained with a huge number of examples. Unsupervised learning is when a system can look at data and build rules on its own to decide what it is seeing.

---

**Table 1.3   Main Areas of AI Research**

**Natural Language Processing**

Understanding
Written and spoken words

**Perception**

Using sensors to gather data

**Knowledge Representation**

Storing and accessing
information about the world

**Planning**

Goal must be set
and achieved

**Problem Solving**

Using even incomplete information
to achieve solution

**Learning**

Improve through
experience

A project like a self-driving (autonomous) car requires research in many of these areas. The car must have computer vision—the ability to interpret visual information the way humans do. The AI system needs to be able to tell the difference between trees and pedestrians, but it also needs to know many things about trees and people. Is the tree going to run into the path of the car? The car must scan the scene with sensors, recognize objects, and consult a knowledge base to create and execute a plan.

**What has enabled us to deploy effective AI systems?** Many information technology developments have contributed to the functional AI systems that we have today.

### Artificial Neural Networks

Expert systems, computer programs that mimic the experience of human experts such as doctors or lawyers, were among the first attempts at producing AI. Rules-based systems, software that asks questions and responds based on preprogrammed algorithms, were the first expert systems designed. These systems asked questions ("Do you have a fever?") and initiated other questions or actions based on the answers ("How long have you had a fever?") and worked adequately for some settings. But just a list of rules is not sophisticated enough to handle difficult tasks.

Artificial neural networks (ANNs) are designed based on the structure of the human brain (see Figure 1.6), which is a network of loosely connected neurons. When signals are received by a neuron, it fires an electrical impulse and the signal travels to all the neurons connected to it. In ANNs, digital signals take the place of biological signals. Many modern ANNs feature different layers of neurons that allow many degrees of complexity. ANNs have allowed researchers to tackle complex problems such as speech recognition.

### Machine Learning

Machine learning (ML) is a type of AI that doesn't need to be specifically programmed. Instead, it analyzes patterns in data, then uses the patterns to draw conclusions and adjust the actions of the AI system accordingly. By learning, the AI system can adapt itself and become constantly better at its task. You have interacted with these kinds of systems if you use Alexa, the Amazon voice recognition device. Alexa gathers input from human speech and uses this information to become better at understanding language over time.

Deep learning (DL) is a subset of the ML field that describes systems capable of learning from mistakes, just as humans do. DL algorithms can learn from data that is not labeled as "correct" or "incorrect." The algorithm adapts to improve its final result without being presented with a huge, labeled set of training data. This is known as unsupervised learning.

Having a basic understanding about AI systems is necessary to becoming a digitally literate citizen. In the next section, we'll explore various workplace systems that use AI.

**Figure 1.6** Human neurons can either send a signal or block one. Artificial neurons mimic this behavior digitally. *(LuckyStep48/Alamy Stock Photo)*

# Ethics in IT

## Ethics in Computing

Should there be rules for conduct in a virtual world? If so, what should they be? What does plagiarism mean in a world where people can easily copy, paste, and upload content of all kinds? Should workplaces be allowed to monitor their employees' computing activities without their knowledge? Should websites be allowed to capture data related to what visitors do on their sites and analyze and sell that data? Should programmers be responsible if their software malfunctions and leads to personal injury or financial loss? Should Internet access be provided for free by communities to their citizens who cannot afford it? How should artificial intelligence be designed to behave ethically? These are the sorts of ethical questions and challenges that technology poses—questions that did not even exist just a few years ago.

As the reach of technology continues to spread, these are questions that more and more societies must face and develop their own answers to. Because different societies have different ideas of what it means to behave ethically, there will be many solutions to ethical questions. How we navigate cultural responses to ethical challenges becomes more important as the pace of technology quickens. How should U.S. companies respond to censorship of their websites in countries such as China? A state in the United States can declare that online gambling is illegal, but what does that mean when its citizens have access to foreign websites hosting gambling (see Figure 1.7)?

Answering challenging ethical questions related to technology is part of being a digitally literate citizen. This text will help you understand technology and the ethical issues it poses. Taking the time to think deeply about the connection between technology and ethics is one step in being a more knowledgeable and thoughtful global citizen.

**Figure 1.7** How do we enforce ethical standards in our global, Internet-enabled environment? (*lucadp/123RF*)

# Working with Artificial Intelligence and Other Information Technologies

Information technology (IT) is a field of study focused on the management and processing of information. IT careers include working with computers, telecommunications, and software deployment. Career opportunities in IT are on the rise, but no matter what career you choose, the workplace demands new skill levels in technology from employees. Understanding how AI systems and other technologies can be utilized in the workplace is an important skill for everyone.

## Technology and Your Career

**Objective 1.7**  *Describe how artificial intelligence and other emerging technologies are important in many careers.*

One of the benefits of being digitally literate is that you will most likely be able to perform your job more effectively. Your understanding of key concepts in technology can "future-proof" you, letting you easily and quickly react to the next round of new technologies.

Let's look at a whole range of industries and examine how current and emerging technologies are a part of getting work done.

### Retail

The amount of data generated each second of the day is staggering (see Figure 1.8). AI systems deployed in the retail sector are responsible for managing huge amounts of data and performing

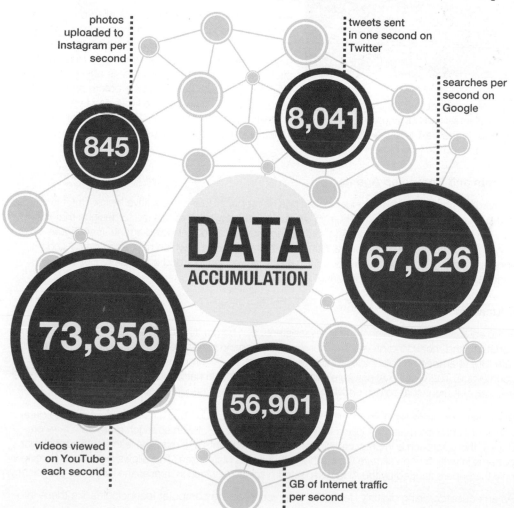

photos uploaded to Instagram per second

tweets sent in one second on Twitter

searches per second on Google

**845**

**8,041**

**67,026**

**DATA ACCUMULATION**

**73,856**

**56,901**

videos viewed on YouTube each second

GB of Internet traffic per second

**Figure 1.8** Enormous amounts of data are produced every second. Data mining is performed by sophisticated AI systems such as recommendation engines.

data mining analysis for managers. For example, retailers often study the data gathered from register terminals to determine which products are selling on a given day and in a specific location. In addition to using inventory control systems, which help managers figure out how much merchandise they need to order to replace stock, managers can use mined data to determine that if they want a certain product to sell well, they must lower its price. Such data mining thus allows retailers to respond to consumer buying patterns.

Recommendation engines are AI systems that help people discover things they may like but are unlikely to discover on their own. The secret behind recommendation engines is crunching massive amounts of data effectively. Without the ability to collect massive amounts of data and use data mining to understand it, recommendation engines wouldn't exist. Presenting effective recommendations and learning to make better recommendations are essential to Amazon's success. About 35% of Amazon's sales come from customers using the recommendation list.

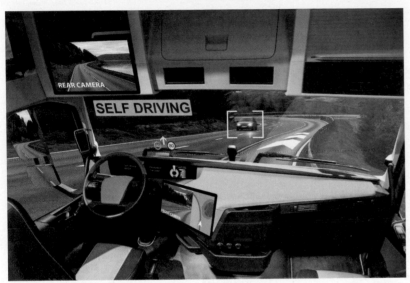

**Figure 1.9** Autonomous (self-driving) trucks are poised to revolutionize the transportation industry. *(Scharfsinn/Shutterstock)*

### Banking

Credit card processors and banks use AI systems to analyze huge volumes of transaction data to spot fraud. Banks use software to assess the risk of extending credit to customers by analyzing spending patterns, credit scores, and debt repayment. The same software also helps determine what interest rates and terms to offer on loans. Researchers at MIT determined that using AI to evaluate credit risk could help reduce an institution's loan losses by 25%.

### Transportation

Autopilots run by AI have been installed on commercial airliners for decades. Although they can't yet replace human pilots, it is estimated that the average commercial flight only requires seven to ten minutes of pilot-directed flight, most of which is during takeoff and landing. It may still be some time before airliners can fly themselves but autonomous (self-driving) cars are here now. Services like Uber and Lyft are already testing fleets of self-driving vehicles, though a fatality that occurred in 2018 has put Uber's program in limbo. In the next few years trucking companies will face major changes if self-driving trucks become common (see Figure 1.9).

### Robots and Embodied Agents

Many robots are deployed in industrial settings doing hazardous or repetitive tasks. But it is difficult to design robots that can match human dexterity and mobility. This has led to designs that mimic how humans walk and grasp objects, producing robots called embodied agents (see Figure 1.10) that look and act like human beings. Still, there are many jobs in which human empathy and understanding are highly valued, such as in medicine, education, and counseling. But we will continue to see more robots appearing in our everyday lives.

**Figure 1.10** *Embodied agents* are robots that mimic humans in appearance. *(Dmytro Zinkevych/ Shutterstock)*

### Education

In the education field, intelligent personal assistants can be created to assist students with designing, updating, and monitoring progress in individualized learning plans. Pearson has entered a partnership with IBM to embed artificial intelligence similar to the Watson computer directly into Pearson courseware. The Watson AI software will chat with students in natural language throughout a chapter and ask questions that zero in on what that particular student needs to review.

Plagiarism checkers, like Turnitin, initially relied on brute force comparisons of student work to databases of published material, looking for exact text matches. But with so much more data now produced, this approach is impractical. Modern plagiarism agents use machine learning to spot similar patterns in writing and estimate the likelihood that it was plagiarized. This allows instructors to review only the papers flagged by the AI for suspected plagiarism, which increases the instructor's efficiency.

As an educator, being digitally literate will help you integrate computer technologies like these into your classroom.

Alan Turing was an early pioneer in computer design and cryptography who inspired many designers of the first digital computers. He proposed a simple test to distinguish between a human and a computer system. The Turing test (see Figure 1.11) places a person in a room, asking written questions of two other "people." But one person is a live human being, while the other is a computer. If the questioner can't tell which one of the respondents is a computer, then Turing felt the computer had reached "intelligence." The computer is permitted to be deceptive; however, the human is required to help the questioner reach the correct conclusion.

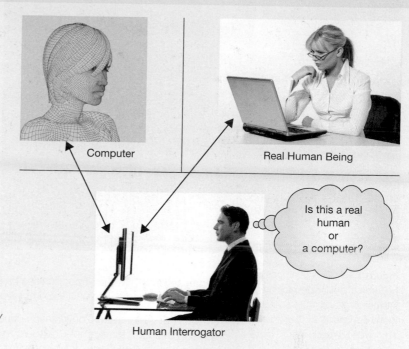

Computer

Real Human Being

Is this a real human or a computer?

Human Interrogator

**Figure 1.11** Basic Components of a Turing Test *(Design36/Shutterstock, Fotek/123RF, Ostill/123RF)*

## Law Enforcement

Today, AI systems are being used in police cars and crime labs to solve an increasing number of crimes. For example, facial reconstruction systems like the one shown in Figure 1.12 can turn a skull into a finished digital image of a face, allowing investigators to proceed far more quickly with identification than before.

Using AI-powered software, proprietary law enforcement databases can be analyzed for similarities between crimes in an attempt to detect patterns that may reveal serial crimes. In fact, a law enforcement specialty called computer forensics is growing in importance in order to fight modern crime. Computer forensics analyzes computer systems with specific techniques to gather potential legal evidence. For example, Steven Zirko was convicted of two Chicago-area murders based on computer forensics work. Computer forensics examiners trained by the FBI scoured Zirko's computer and located searches for terms like *hire a hitman*. In many cases, files, videos, and conversations conducted using a computer can be recovered by forensics specialists and can be used as evidence of criminal activity.

**Figure 1.12** Tissue-rendering programs add layers of muscle, fat, and skin to create faces that can be used to identify victims. *(Pixologicstudio/Science Photo Library/Glow Images)*

## Medicine

A career in medicine will connect you to new ways of using technology to better people's lives. Websites like Modernizing Medicine (*modmed.com*) use AI software to search through data on millions of patient visits and treatments provided by thousands of physicians. The website can help doctors quickly diagnose conditions with which they're not familiar and research alternative means of treatment for illnesses to reduce costs and side-effects for patients.

AI is also being integrated directly into patient information systems. Dashboards on the physician's computer screen can make recommendations about treatments to specific patients after the AI has analyzed their genetic traits and compared them to millions of other patients through records. The AI can recommend drugs for treatment as well as remind physicians about tests they may need to perform.

The design and construction of prosthetic devices is another area of medicine impacted by modern technology. MIT's Biomechatronics lab has developed software that uses an array of pressure sensors to gauge the softness or stiffness of a patient's remaining tissue to create a better fit for a prosthetic to the limb. Meanwhile, 3D printing is allowing more inexpensive designs for prosthetic arms and legs, and more stylish artificial limbs as well (see Figure 1.13).

**Figure 1.13** 3D printing has become a tool for developing more inexpensive, and more stylish, prosthetic devices. *(Cem Ozdel/Anadolu Agency/Getty Images)*

### Psychology

Fear of speaking in public is common, but for people with autism spectrum disorders, making proper eye contact and reacting to social cues is so difficult that it can severely limit their opportunities for relationships and jobs. Researchers at the MIT Media Lab have developed a system to help improve interpersonal skills for people who have autism.

MACH (My Automated Conversation coacH) is a computer system that generates an on-screen person that can, for example, conduct a job interview or appear ready for a first date. The computerized person (see Figure 1.14) nods and smiles in response to the user's speech and movement. This is an example of affective computing, developing systems that can recognize and simulate human emotions. MACH users can practice as many times as they wish in a safe environment. They receive an analysis that shows how well they modulated their voices, maintained eye contact, smiled, and how often they lapsed into "umms" and "uhhhs."

**Figure 1.14** My Automated Conversation coacH (MACH) generates an on-screen interviewer you can practice with over and over. *(Cultura Limited/SuperStock)*

What is *augmented reality*? And how is it different from *virtual reality*?

Augmented reality (AR) is the addition of digital information directly into our reality, either to add more detail or at times to remove unwanted visual effects. How does this happen?

AR combines our normal sense of the world around us with an additional layer of digital information. The extra information can be displayed on a separate device, such as in augmented reality apps for smartphones. Displays in stores can augment your image with the clothing you're interested in, creating a virtual fitting room (see Figure 1.15). The Microsoft HoloLens even lets you manipulate holographic images as part of your reality (see Figure 1.16).

Researcher Stephen Mann of the University of Toronto is working with wearable computers that use "point of eye" (PoE) cameras as AR devices. A PoE camera is designed so that the camera is positioned directly in front of the eye itself. The ultimate PoE camera would be one that is implanted within the eye or eye socket. Mann's research group is exploring this as a way to assist partially sighted or blind people.

Instead of adding information to the reality you perceive, virtual reality (VR) replaces it with a different world. Virtual reality creates an artificial environment that is immersive and interactive. VR environments can be as simple as a pair of goggles or as elaborate as entire "caves" that you walk into (see Figure 1.17). VR is also coming to the consumer gaming market with the introduction of VR goggles, like Sony's Project Morpheus and the Rift by Oculus (see Figure 1.18). These goggles have high pixel count displays that wrap your full field of view.

So reality may be a bit less absolute than it once seemed. Whether it is being augmented with additional information or replaced by new virtual realms, technology is expanding our sense of what is real.

**Figure 1.15** This high-tech fitting room uses augmented reality technology to allow shoppers to try on clothes virtually. *(Yoshikauz Tsuno/Staff/AFP/Getty Images)*

**Figure 1.17** Virtual reality "caves" replace our ordinary reality with a new, immersive environment. *(Idaho National Laboratory/US Department of Energy/Science Photo Library)*

**Figure 1.16** The Microsoft HoloLens augments your reality by adding holographic images you can manipulate. *(Andrija Markovic/123RF)*

**Figure 1.18** VR goggles like these wrap around your full field of view, creating a totally immersive environment. *(Philippe Plailly/Science Photo Library)*

# Ethical Computing

As noted earlier, technology has brought about a new set of ethical challenges. And because technology often moves faster than rules can be formulated to govern it, how technology is used is often left up to the individual and the guidance of his or her personal ethics. Ethical considerations are complex, and reasonable people can have different, yet valid, views. In this section, we define ethics and then examine a set of ethical systems. Next, we discuss personal ethics and how technology affects our personal ethics. Finally, we ask you to consider what your personal ethics are and how you make ethical choices.

## Defining Ethics

**Objective 1.8**  *Define ethics and examine various ethical systems.*

Ethics is the study of the general nature of morals and of the specific moral choices individuals make. Morals involve conforming to established or accepted ideas of right and wrong (as generally dictated by society) and are usually viewed as being black or white. Ethical issues often involve subtle distinctions, such as the difference between fairness and equity. Ethical principles are the guidelines you use to make decisions each day, decisions about what you will say, do, and think.

There are many systems of ethical conduct (see Table 1.4). *Relativism* states that there is no universal truth and that moral principles are dictated by the culture and customs of each society. *Divine command theory* follows the principle that God is all knowing and that moral standards are perfectly stated by God's laws, such as the Ten Commandments. *Utilitarianism* judges actions to be right or wrong solely by their consequences. Actions that generate greater happiness are deemed to be better than those actions that lead to less happiness. *Virtue ethics* teaches that we each have an internal moral compass and should try to be a person who spontaneously follows that guide. Finally, the duty-based ethical system, or *deontology,* suggests we should all follow common moral codes and apply those to all humanity.

### Systems of Ethics

What is the difference between laws and ethics? Laws are formal, written standards designed to apply to everyone. It's impossible to pass laws that cover every human behavior, though. Therefore, ethics provide a general set of unwritten guidelines for people to follow. Unethical behavior isn't necessarily illegal, however. Consider the death penalty. In many U.S. states, putting convicted criminals to death for certain crimes is legal. However, many people consider it unethical to execute a human being for any reason.

Not all illegal behavior is unethical, either. Civil disobedience, which is intentionally refusing to obey certain laws, is used as a form of protest to effect change. Gandhi's nonviolent resistance to the British rule of India, which led to India's establishment as an independent country, and Martin Luther King's protests and use of sit-ins in the civil rights movement are both examples of civil disobedience. What does civil disobedience look like in our hyper-connected age of social media and the Internet?

Note that there is also a difference between unethical behavior and amoral behavior. Unethical behavior is not conforming to a set of approved standards of behavior—cheating on an exam, for example. Amoral behavior occurs when a person has no sense of right and wrong and no interest in the moral consequences of his or her actions, such as when a murderer shows no remorse for his or her crime.

There is no universal agreement on which system of ethics is the best. Most societies use a blend of different systems. Regardless of the ethical system of the society in which you live, all ethical decisions are greatly influenced by personal ethics.

 **MyLab IT**

**How to Debate Ethical Issues**

This Sound Byte will help you consider important aspects of debating difficult issues arising from the ethical use of technology.

## Table 1.4  Systems of Ethics

| Ethical System | Basic Tenets | Examples |
| --- | --- | --- |
| **Relativism**  | • There is no universal moral truth.<br>• Moral principles are dictated by cultural tastes and customs. | Topless bathing is prevalent in Europe but generally banned on public beaches in the United States. |
| **Divine Command Theory**  | • God is all-knowing and sets moral standards.<br>• Conforming to God's law is right; breaking it is wrong. | The Ten Commandments of Christian religions<br>The Five Pillars of Islam |
| **Utilitarianism**  | • Actions are judged solely by consequences.<br>• Actions that generate greater happiness are judged to be better than actions that lead to unhappiness.<br>• Individual happiness is not important. Consider the greater good. | Using weapons of mass destruction ends a war sooner and therefore saves lives otherwise destroyed by conventional fighting. |
| **Virtue Ethics**  | • Morals are internal.<br>• Strive to be a person who behaves well spontaneously | A supervisor views the person who volunteered to clean up a park as a better person than the workers who are there because of court-ordered community service. |
| **Deontology (Duty-Based)** | • Focus on adherence to moral duties and rights.<br>• Morals should apply to everyone equally. | Human rights (like freedom of religion) should be respected for all people because human rights should be applied universally. |

(Solomin Andrey/Fotolia; Olga Galushko/Fotolia; Kentoh/Fotolia; Alexmillos/Fotolia; Scanrail/Fotolia)

## Personal Ethics

**Objective 1.9**  *Describe influences on the development of your personal ethics.*

Each day as you choose your words and actions, you're following a set of personal ethics—a set of formal or informal ethical principles you use to make decisions. Some people have a clear, well-defined set of principles they follow. Others' ethics are inconsistent or are applied differently in different situations.

A person's ethics develop in many ways. Naturally, your family plays a major role in establishing the values you cherish in your own life, and these might include a cultural bias toward certain

**Figure 1.19** Many different forces shape your personal ethics. *(lmtmphoto/Fotolia; Lisa F. Young/Shutterstock; Jovannig/Fotolia; Michael jung/Fotolia)*

ethical positions (see Figure 1.19). Your religious affiliation is another major influence on your ethics because most religions have established codes of ethical conduct. How these sets of ethics interact with the values of the larger culture is often challenging. Issues such as abortion, the death penalty, and war often create conflict between personal ethical systems and the larger society's established legal–ethical system.

As you mature, your life experiences also affect your personal ethics. Does the behavior you see around you make sense within the ethical principles that your family, your church, or your teachers taught you? Has your experience led you to abandon some ethical rules and adopt others? Have you modified how and when you apply these laws of conduct depending on what's at stake?

## Determining Your Personal Ethics

When you have a clear idea of what values are important to you, it may be easier to handle situations in your life that demand ethical action. You can follow these steps to help yourself define a list of personal values:

1. **Describe yourself.** Write down words that describe who you are, based on how others view you. Would a friend describe you as honest, helpful, or kind? These keywords will give you a hint as to the values and behaviors that are important to you.

2. **List the key principles you believe in.** Make a list of the key principles that influence your decisions. For example, would you be comfortable working in a lab that used animals for medical research? How important is it to you that you never tell a lie? List the key ideas you believe to be important in conducting your life. Do you always behave this way, or are there situations in which your answers might change?

3. **Identify external influences.** Where did your key principles come from—your parents? Your friends? Spiritual advisors? Television and movies? You may want to question some of your beliefs once you actually identify where they came from.

4. **Consider why.** After writing down your beliefs, think about why you believe them. Have you accepted them without investigation? Do they stand up in the context of your real-world experiences?

5. **Prepare a statement of values.** Distill what you have written into a short statement. Having a well-defined statement of the values you hold most important in your own life will make it easier for you to make ethical decisions in times of challenge.

# Ethics and Technology

**Objective 1.10** *Present examples of how technology creates ethical challenges.*

You'll encounter many ethical challenges relating to information technology. Your personal ethics—combined with the general ethical environment of society and ethical guidelines your company provides if your decision is related to the workplace—will help to guide your decisions.

## Intellectual Property

One obvious area of ethical challenge in technology is intellectual property rights. Intellectual property is work that is the result of someone's creativity and knowledge (such as music, writing, and software) that is protected by copyright law and documented by copyrights, patents, and trademarks. Anti-piracy efforts by various organizations and governments aim to protect intellectual property rights—an issue that has been an ongoing and important one in the technology industry.

With increased use of electronic media, challenges to enforcing copyright laws have increased. Countries such as China and the Philippines are known for their high rates of pirated software use. Businesses and individuals that use such illegal software potentially gain an advantage in the international marketplace. Companies like Microsoft have taken several measures to combat illegal piracy but still haven't managed to effectively reduce the amount of pirated software in certain countries.

Piracy challenges have also placed significant pressures on existing business models for creative arts industries such as film and music. Time will tell whether copyright laws will need to be revised to adapt to the predominant digital culture, whether regulatory agencies will need to improve the methods of controlling piracy, or whether the industries themselves will need to change their business models.

## Privacy

Technology is also posing new ethical issues related to privacy. Intelligent personal agents (like Alexa) are constantly listening to you and combing through your data (such as your e-mails and texts) to help determine your needs. Many people are concerned about the loss of privacy from such agents.

Social media sites such as Facebook and Twitter are designed to share information with others, which can be great for sharing graduation photos with family. But employers now routinely check social media sites to gather information on prospective employees. If you have privacy settings that allow them to see enough to infer your race, religion, or sexual orientation, they will have information they are not legally allowed to ask you directly. Facebook and Twitter also generate information about you based on your behavior on their sites. What is your household income? What is your political affiliation? Sophisticated algorithms make predictions about these matters from the choices you make using their sites. For example, what groups do you join? What links do you follow? The Try This exercise in this chapter will guide you in finding out exactly what information these companies have generated to describe you. The control and privacy of information will continue to be a fine balancing act for the foreseeable future.

## Social Justice

Technological processing power has led to new issues that impact social justice. Consider predictive policing—gathering data from different sources, analyzing it, and then using the results to prevent future crime. Data sources may include crime maps, traffic camera data, surveillance footage, and social media network analysis. But at what point does the possibility of a crime warrant intervention? Is predictive policing just another way to justify racial profiling? Table 1.5 lists different views on the issue of predictive policing. Where do your views fall?

Another social justice issue affected by technology is related to military and government secrets. There are military secrets and communication related to ongoing negotiations with foreign governments that the public does not have a right to see. Historically, tight controls have been in place over access to such information. With Web 2.0 tools, the entire model for the distribution of information has shifted, and now everyone can create and publish content on the Internet. This has altered the meaning of privacy in fundamental ways. WikiLeaks (*wikileaks.org*) makes private

## Table 1.5  Point/Counterpoint: Social Justice

| Issue: Predictive Policing | Ethical Question: Should police agencies act on data trends that seem to predict crime? |
|---|---|
|  **Point** | • This is just a use of modern technology to enhance law enforcement.<br>• Data trends that show areas of high criminal activity allow the police to use their resources more effectively.<br>• If law enforcement steps in before a crime has been committed, it helps both the potential victim and the potential criminal. |
|  **Counterpoint** | • This is a high-tech form of racial and socioeconomic profiling and acts to reinforce existing stereotypes.<br>• This decreases our privacy and encourages constant government surveillance of our activities.<br>• It is impossible to create predictive algorithms in a way that is not harmful to law-abiding people living in highcrime areas. |

and secret documents available for viewing on its site. These might be the script of a movie still in production or reports delivered by a whistleblower documenting abuses in the military. Does society have a right to see secret documents? And do we all have a responsibility to use technology to help achieve social justice? Where do the boundaries of those rights and responsibilities lie?

### Liability

3D printing is revolutionizing the way items are manufactured, causing a range of issues involving intellectual property rights and liability. In traditional manufacturing, it is relatively easy to enforce safety laws. Consider the manufacture of bicycle helmets. Traditional manufacturers are held accountable for delivering safely designed products free from defects in workmanship. Products are subjected to safety testing prior to being sold to the public and must conform to legal safety guidelines. If you buy a helmet and are injured while riding your bike because of a defect in the design of or materials used in the helmet, you can sue the manufacturer for damages. Manufacturers protect their designs (intellectual property) by obtaining patents.

3D printers produce objects from design plans generated with various types of software. Anyone who is reasonably proficient with design software can generate a design for an object to be printed. However, a person could also use a 3D scanner to scan an existing object (say a helmet designed and sold by a traditional manufacturer) and use design software to create his or her own plan for how to print it. If the object is patented, this would be a violation of the law. But it certainly makes it easier to steal someone's intellectual property.

Design plans for objects are often shared online. Even if the same design is used, the product quality can be vastly different depending on the type of 3D printer used and the type of plastic selected for printing.

Consider the ethics of printing a helmet from a file you downloaded from a public website. You give it to a friend as a gift. While riding her bicycle, your friend is injured because the design of the helmet was flawed and the materials you used to make it were substandard. Who is responsible for the injuries? You? The manufacturer of the printer? The owner of the printer? The manufacturer of the raw materials used to make the helmet? The creator of the flawed design plans? The person who decided to use an untested product (i.e., your friend)? What if the design you used was created from a patented product? Table 1.6 lists different views on the issue of 3D printing regulation. Where do your views fall?

### Censorship

Various countries have different answers to the question of what information their people should be allowed to see. For instance, India blocked over 800 pornographic sites recently, sparking a huge debate about free speech and personal freedom. The ban was partially lifted in a few days with only sites deemed to be promoting child pornography still blocked. Blocking child pornography is obviously a laudable goal, but other countries block many different types of websites. For example, the Chinese government has demanded that search engine providers like Google self-censor their search engines, restricting search results for sensitive information such as the details of the

**Table 1.6   Point/Counterpoint: Liability**

| Issue: 3D Printing Regulation | Ethical Question: Should 3D printing be regulated? |
|---|---|
|  | • The general public expects to buy products that are free from design and material defects. If governments do not regulate 3D printing materials and designs, the public is placed in unnecessary peril.<br>• Because designs of existing products are easy to produce, there is an increased chance of intellectual property theft.<br>• Users of 3D printers need to understand the risks, responsibilities, and liabilities of producing products on demand for their use and for resale. |
|  | • Heavily regulating 3D printing will stifle creativity and ingenuity in the design and production of new products.<br>• Manufacturers can seek legal remedies for violation of design patents under existing laws.<br>• Consumers should be aware of the principle of "caveat emptor" (let the buyer beware) when using untested or unproven products. People should use untested products cautiously. |

Tiananmen Square protests and of human rights groups. Table 1.7 lists different views on the issue of Internet censorship. What do you think?

## Social Activism

Hacktivism (derived from *hack* and *activism*) involves using computers and computer networks in a subversive way to promote an agenda usually related to causes such as free speech, human rights, or freedom of information. Essentially, it is using computer hacking to effect some sort of social change. An example of early hacktivism is "Worms Against Nuclear Killers (WANK)," a computer worm that anti-nuclear activists in Australia unleashed into the networks of NASA in 1989 to protest the launch of a shuttle that carried radioactive plutonium. As computer security has grown more sophisticated, attacks today are usually carried out by groups of hackers (such as the group Anonymous) or groups of computer scientists funded by nation states for the specific purpose of hacking.

Hacktivism often takes the form of denial-of-service attacks in which websites are bombarded with requests for information until they are overwhelmed and legitimate users can't access the site. At other times, hacktivism takes the form of cyberterrorism, where the objective is to embarrass or harass a company by penetrating its computer networks and stealing (and often publishing) sensitive information. Certain countries are rumored to maintain groups of computer scientists whose main goal is to spy on other countries by hacking into their computer networks. Table 1.8 lists different views on the issue of hacktivism. What do you think?

**Table 1.7   Point/Counterpoint: Censorship**

| Issue: Censoring the Internet | Ethical Question: Should an American company agree to restrict freedom of information to do business with a more restrictive country? |
|---|---|
|  | • It is not the place of a company to try to change laws of foreign countries. Reform must come from within.<br>• Working in China does not mean a company supports all of China's policies.<br>• U.S. companies can ethically stay in China if they make an effort to improve human rights there. U.S. companies operating in China should agree on guidelines that respect human rights. |
|  | • Policies will never change unless there are financial and political incentives to do so. The departure of U.S. companies helps pressure foreign governments to reform.<br>• If companies withdraw from China, the viability of many other resellers in China are threatened.<br>• Countries cannot expect to compete in the global marketplace while refusing to have a global exchange of ideas. |

## Table 1.8 Point/Counterpoint: Social Activism

**Issue: Hacktivism**

**Ethical Question: Is hacktivism a helpful form of civil disobedience?**

Point

- Society as a whole benefits when injustices are exposed.
- Civil disobedience is an inalienable right upon which the United States was founded.
- Methods of civil disobedience need to keep pace with modern technology in order to have the greatest impact possible.

Counterpoint

- Computer technology provides many opportunities for reaching a wide audience with a message without resorting to illegal activities such as hacking.
- Personal data of individuals needs to be protected as a basic right of privacy.
- Hacking into computer systems for alleged acts of civil disobedience are often hard to distinguish from acts of cyberterrorism.

### Automated Robotic Machinery

Automobiles now contain sophisticated AI systems to exercise control over the vehicle and respond faster than humans can. For example, using a wide set of sensors, accident-avoidance systems can apply the brakes and even change lanes to help drivers avoid accidents. In the coming years, these systems may exercise even more control of your vehicle, such as the self-driving cars that are under development by Google and major auto manufacturers.

But who controls the ethical constraints by which automated robotic machinery like this operates? Consider a selection between a set of bad choices: You suddenly find that you either have to brake, knowing you will still hit the school bus ahead of you, swerve into oncoming traffic, or swerve to the other side into a tree. Which choice would you make? Which choice would you want your automated car to make? Should owners have a choice of overriding the programming in their vehicles and adjusting the ethical parameters of their robotic systems? What should manufacturers do until laws are passed regarding robo-ethics? Table 1.9 lists different views on the issue of robotic machinery ethics. Where do your views fall?

Ethical discussions are important in many fields but especially with technology. The pace of change is forcing us to consider implications for our families and countries as well as for our personal ideas of justice and proper conduct. Being able to analyze and then discuss your ethical positions with others are important skills to develop.

## Table 1.9 Point/Counterpoint: Automated Robotic Machinery

**Issue: Ethics of Robotic Machinery**

**Ethical Question: Should owners be able to set the ethical rules of behavior for their own robots?**

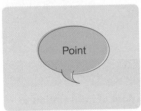
Point

- As long as choices over robotic ethics don't violate laws, individual owners should be able to choose ethical rules of behavior.
- Individuals should have the right to set ethical parameters for their robots because they may wish to be even more selfless than society dictates.
- Individuals make ethical decisions in times of crisis. Robotic systems should be an extension of the individual's ethical values.

Counterpoint

- If all robots do not contain ethical constraints that prevent harm to human beings, human lives may be lost.
- Allowing individuals to adjust the ethics of robotic devices exposes society to risks from careless, thoughtless, or psychotic individuals.
- Every robot must have ethical programming that allows them to make decisions regarding the best possible outcomes in life-and-death situations.

### Before moving on to the Chapter Review:

1.  Watch Chapter Overview Video 1.2.
2. Then take the Check Your Understanding quiz.

# Check Your Understanding // Review & Practice

For a quick review to see what you've learned so far, answer the following questions.

## multiple choice

1. _____ is a branch of computer science that focuses on creating computer systems or computer-controlled machines that have an ability to perform tasks usually associated with human intelligence.

   a. Computer literacy

   b. Artificial intelligence

   c. Natural language

   d. Information technology

2. AI systems that help people discover things they may like but may not discover on their own are known as

   a. crowdsourcing systems.

   b. Turing testers.

   c. recommendation engines.

   d. intelligent personal assistants.

3. A working definition of *ethics* is

   a. impossible because it means different things to different people.

   b. the laws of a given society.

   c. the study of the general nature of morals and of the specific moral choices individuals make.

   d. the rules of conduct presented in Christian religions.

4. The set of formal or informal ethical principles you use to make decisions is your

   a. mindset.

   b. instinct.

   c. personal ethics.

   d. personality.

5. The analysis of a computer system to gather potential legal evidence is

   a. affective computing.

   b. data mining.

   c. hacktivism.

   d. computer forensics.

**chew on this**

This part of the chapter lists many ways in which becoming computer literate is beneficial. Think about what your life will be like once you're started in your career. How would an understanding of computer hardware, software, and artificial intelligence help you in working from home, working with groups in other countries, and contributing your talents?

**MyLab IT**    Go to **MyLab IT** to take an autograded version of the *Check Your Understanding* review and to find all media resources for the chapter.

**For the IT Simulation for this chapter, see MyLab IT.**

# 1 Chapter Review

## Summary

**Learning Outcome 1.1** **You will be able to discuss the impact of the tools of modern technology on national and global issues.**

### Technology in a Global Society

**Objective 1.1** *Describe various technological tools being used to impact national and global issues.*

- Technology can be the means by which you find your voice in the world and impact others in meaningful ways.
- Social media is impacting elections and other issues worldwide.
- Crisis-mapping tools are an example of technology helping in different kinds of global conflicts and disasters.

**Objective 1.2** *Describe various global social issues that are being affected by technology.*

- Global health care issues, like the spread of disease, require international cooperation and technological solutions.
- Environmental issues are global in nature and will require technology to address.
- The digital divide, an uneven distribution of access to computer technology, will make it difficult for us to solve global problems.

### Technology Connects Us with Others

**Objective 1.3** *Describe how technology is changing how and why we connect and collaborate with others.*

- Web 2.0 is a set of features and functionality that allows Internet users to contribute content easily and to be easily connected to each other.
- Cognitive surplus is the combination of leisure time and access to tools to work on problems and be creative.
- New collaborative tools available on the Internet allow us to work together on projects with much larger groups.

- Crowdfunding is a method of people connecting through the Internet to fund projects by donation.

**Objective 1.4** *Summarize how technology has impacted the way we choose and consume products and services.*

- Marketing is changing .because most consumers now shop with Internet access on their phones and can therefore check competing prices and online reviews.
- The idea of ownership is changing because technology is allowing subscription services for products like cars and bikes to be available for sharing. Such collaborative consumption means that we are joining together as a group to use specific products more efficiently.

### The Importance of Computer Literacy

**Objective 1.5** *Characterize computer literacy and explain why it is important to be computer literate.*

- If you're computer literate, you understand the capabilities and limitations of computers and know how to use them wisely.
- By understanding how a computer is constructed and how its various parts function, you'll be able to get the most out of your computer.
- You'll be able to avoid hackers, viruses, and Internet headaches; protect your privacy; and separate the real risks of privacy and security from things you don't have to worry about.
- You'll also be better able to maintain, upgrade, and troubleshoot your computer; make good purchasing decisions; and incorporate the latest technologies into your existing equipment.
- Being computer literate also enables you to understand the many ethical, legal, and societal implications of technology today.

# Part 2

## Emerging Technologies and Ethical Computing

**Learning Outcome 1.2** **You will be able to describe emerging technologies, such as artificial intelligence, and how technology creates new ethical debates.**

 ## Artificial Intelligence

**Objective 1.6** *Describe artificial intelligence systems and explain their main goals.*

- Artificial intelligence (AI) focuses on creating computer systems that have an ability to perform tasks associated with human intelligence.
- Machines using AI do not necessarily mimic the human thought process.
- Current AI research is focused in the following areas: natural language processing, perception, knowledge representation, planning, problem solving, and learning (both supervised and unsupervised).
- A Turing test can be used to determine whether a system is a computer AI or a human being.

 ## Working with Artificial Intelligence and Other Information Technologies

**Objective 1.7** *Describe how artificial intelligence and other emerging technologies are important in many careers.*

- Artificial intelligence impacts the full range of careers, from retail and psychology to robotics and medicine.
- Understanding how to use software, how to use and maintain computer hardware, and how to take advantage of Internet resources will help you be a more

productive and valuable employee, no matter which profession you choose.

 ## Ethical Computing

**Objective 1.8** *Define ethics and describe various ethical systems.*

- Ethics is the study of moral choices.
- There are several different ethical systems. There is no universal agreement on which system is best.
- Unethical behavior is not necessarily unlawful behavior.
- Amoral behavior is when a person has no sense of right and wrong.

**Objective 1.9** *Describe influences on the development of your personal ethics.*

- Personal ethics are a set of formal or informal ethical principles you use to make decisions in your life.
- Your personal ethics develop from a number of sources: your family values, your religion, the values of the larger culture, and your life experiences.

**Objective 1.10** *Present examples of how technology creates ethical challenges.*

- Technology is posing new ethical challenges with regard to intellectual property, privacy, social justice, liability, censorship, social activism, and automated robotic machinery, among others concerns.

 Be sure to check out **MyLab IT** for additional materials to help you review and learn. And don't forget to watch the Chapter Overview videos. ▶

# Key Terms

# Chapter Quiz // Assessment

For a quick review to see what you've learned, answer the following questions. Submit the quiz as requested by your instructor. If you are using **MyLab IT**, the quiz is also available there.

## multiple choice

1. The crisis-mapping tool Ushahidi
   a. prevents two-way dialog between people.
   b. is only available in the United States.
   c. shows that a free software product can have great value.
   d. relies on people using their desktop computing power to help others.

2. Sophisticated modeling software is helping international researchers
   a. create more intricate screenplays and movie scripts.
   b. analyze computer systems to gather potential legal evidence.
   c. market new types of products to a wider audience.
   d. increase the pace of research in finding and producing vaccines.

3. Which of the following would **not** impact the digital divide?
   a. A decline in the price of internet access
   b. Less sharing of the work we produce
   c. Expansion of free wifi connectivity in major cities
   d. Legislation allowing communications companies to charge per website for access

4. Crowdfunding sites include
   a. Citi Bike and Zipcar.
   b. Bing and Google.
   c. Kickstarter and GoFundMe.
   d. Amazon and Kiva.

5. Bike-sharing programs like Citi Bike are an example of
   a. principled psychology.
   b. crowdfunding.
   c. crowdsourcing.
   d. a subscription-style business model made possible by technology.

6. Being computer literate includes being able to
   a. avoid spam, adware, and spyware.
   b. use the web effectively.
   c. diagnose and fix hardware and software problems.
   d. all of the above.

7. All of the following are current focuses of AI research EXCEPT
   a. natural language processing.
   b. perception.
   c. cognitive surplus.
   d. knowledge representation.

8. Which of the following statements is FALSE?
   a. Unethical behavior is always illegal.
   b. Ethical decisions are usually influenced by personal ethics.
   c. Individuals who have no sense of right or wrong exhibit amoral behavior.
   d. Life experience affects an individual's personal ethics.

9. Which of the following actions would NOT help to identify your personal ethics?
   a. Describe yourself.
   b. Conduct a genetic study of your extended family.
   c. Identify the influences of your work environment.
   d. Prepare a list of values that are most important to you.

10. Intellectual property
    a. is the result of someone's creative work and design.
    b. can be protected legally by the patent system.
    c. can include works of music, film, or engineering design.
    d. all of the above.

## true/false

_____ 1. Intellectual property can be legally protected even though it is not a physical object.

_____ 2. The move toward access instead of ownership is a sign of cognitive surplus.

_____ 3. Artificial intelligence systems think exactly like human beings do.

_____ 4. Web-based databases cannot be used to help investigators solve criminal cases.

_____ 5. Hacktivism is different from cyberterrorism.

## What do you think now?

1. Examine your answer to the What Do You Think question from the beginning of the chapter. Describe how the topics of this chapter have influenced you. Have they pushed you to change your answer? Reinforced your thinking? Why?

2. Using the Reilly Top 10 list (*reillytop10.com*), investigate three areas where technology is producing conflict for society. What kind of CS + X combination majors would produce people who are well equipped to solve these challenges?

# Team Time

## A Culture of Sharing

### problem

As more and more peer-to-peer music-sharing services appeared, like BitTorrent and LimeWire, many felt a culture of theft was developing. Some argued there was a mindset that property rights for intellectual works need not be respected and that people should be able to download, for free, any music, movies, or other digital content they wanted.

But there is another view of the phenomenon. Some are suggesting that the amount of constant access to other people—through texting, e-mail, blogging, and the easy exchange of digital content—has created a culture of trust and sharing.

This Team Time will explore both sides of this debate as it affects three different parts of our lives—finance, travel, and consumerism.

### task

Each of three groups will select a different area to examine—finance, travel, or consumerism. The groups will find evidence to support or refute the idea that a culture of sharing is developing. The finance group will want to explore projects like Kickstarter (*kickstarter.com*) and Kiva (*kiva.org*). The travel group should examine what is happening with Airbnb (*airbnb.com*) to start their research. The team investigating consumerism will want to look at goods-exchange programs like Freecycle (*freecycle.org*).

### process

1. Divide the class into three teams.
2. Discuss the different views of a "culture of sharing." With the other members of your team, use the Internet to research up-and-coming technologies and projects that would support your position. People use social media tools to connect into groups to exchange ideas. Does that promote trust? Does easy access to digital content promote theft, or has the value of content changed? Are there other forces like the economy and the environmental state of the world that play a role in promoting a culture of sharing? What evidence can you find to support your ideas?
3. Present your group's findings to the class for debate and discussion.
4. Write a strategy paper that summarizes your position and outlines your predictions for the future. Will the pace of technology promote a change in the future from the position you are describing?

### conclusion

The future of technology is unknown, but we do know that it will impact the way our society progresses. To be part of the developments that technology will bring will take good planning and attention, no matter what area of the culture you're examining. Begin now—learn how to stay on top of technology.

# Ethics Project

## Can Data Predict Your Grade?

### background

As you move through your academic career, you leave an enormous swath of data: which courses you chose to register for; which ones you looked at but didn't pick; and how you did on each homework assignment, test, and project. Could this massive amount of data be analyzed to predict your grade in a course? Could the data suggest which courses you should take next? Should those predictions be public to your instructor, to you, and to financial aid officers?

### research topics to consider

- Course Signals
- Degree Compass, Austin Peay State University

### process

1. Divide the class into teams. Each team will select a web-based tool that allows access to information.
2. Team members should each think of a situation where a person would benefit from the type of results data mining can bring to a campus and a situation where it might be undesirable.
3. Team members should select the most powerful and best-constructed arguments and develop a summary conclusion.
4. Team members should present their findings to the class or submit a PowerPoint presentation for review by the rest of the class, along with the summary conclusion they developed.

### conclusion

As technology becomes ever more prevalent and integrated into our lives, we will increasingly face ethical dilemmas. Being able to understand and evaluate both sides of the argument, while responding in a personally or socially ethical manner, will be an important skill.

## How Technology Is Used on the World Stage and in Your Personal Life

In this activity, you'll use Microsoft Word to reflect on how technology is affecting the world as well as you, personally and professionally. Reflect on the content in Chapter 1 as you work through this exercise.

You will use the following skills as you complete this activity:

- Open and Modify a Document Template
- Apply Styles and Advanced Font Formats
- Use Format Painter

- Insert Text
- Apply Themes
- Create a Header and Footer

## Instructions

1. Open TIA_Ch1_Start.docx. Save the document as **TIA_Ch1_LastFirst.docx**, using your own Last and First names.
2. Double-click the **Title placeholder** and type **Technology**, then double-click the **Heading 1 placeholder** and type **Introduction**. Press Enter, then type the following: **Political and global issues are showing that technology is accelerating change around the world and galvanizing groups of people in new ways. Technology allows us to refine how we connect with each other, and it also impacts our daily personal and professional experiences.** Press **Enter**.
3. Type **How Technology Impacts Society**, press **Enter**, and then type a few sentences that describe how technology is impacting global events such as political revolutions, health care, the environment, and the digital divide. In addition, address how businesses are using social media. Press **Enter**.
4. Type **How Technology Impacts Me Personally and Professionally**, press **Enter**, and then type a few sentences that describe how technology is impacting your personal life. You should address the importance of being computer literate. You should also address the kinds of technology being used in the industry of your current or desired career.
5. Click anywhere in the heading *Introduction*, then using **Format Painter**, apply the **Heading 1** format to the paragraph headers: *How Technology Impacts Society* and *How Technology Impacts Me Personally and Professionally*.
   Hint: Format Painter is in the Clipboard group on the Home tab.
6. Change the Document Theme style to the **Slice Theme**.
   Hint: Document Themes are found on the Design tab, in the Document Formatting group.
7. Select the title *Technology*, then format the font as **Small caps**. **Center align** the title.
   Hint: Click the dialog box launcher in the Font group on the Home tab to access the Small caps font effect.
8. Apply the **Whisp header style** to the document. Click to add Today's date in the Date header and delete the Document title header. Add a **File Path** to the document footer. Select the footer text and change the font size to **8**. Close the Header and Footer.
   Hint: Headers are found on the Insert tab in the Header & Footer group. File Path is found in Document Info in the Insert group on the Header & Footer Tools Design tab.
9. Save the document and submit based on your instructor's directions.

**Chapter**

**2**

# Looking at Computers: Understanding the Parts

 For a chapter overview, watch the **Chapter Overview Videos**.

**MyLab IT** All media accompanying this chapter can be found here.

**Make This** A Mobile App on **page 59**

(Bennymarty/123RF; Petr Malyshev/Fotolia; Destinacigdem/123RF; Karyna Navrotska/123RF; Ruslan Danyliuk/123RF; ale-kup/Shutterstock; Sebastian Kaulitzki/Shutterstock)

# What do you think?

Computer technology is making great strides toward **enabling individuals to overcome injuries and disabilities**. Implants that can restore sight are now being researched. Exo-skeletons, like the one shown here, are restoring the ability to walk. Cochlear implants can restore hearing. People with technology implanted in or attached to their bodies are referred to as *augmented humans*. It is anticipated that augmented technologies may some day improve to the point where **someone who uses such technology might have superior abilities** to someone who doesn't use it. Perhaps in the future, we won't need a regular Olympics and a Special Olympics. But **is it fair to let augmented humans compete against non-augmented humans**? Augmented technologies are anticipated to be expensive. Does this mean only the rich will be able to "improve" their abilities with augments?

> **?**
>
> Should augmented humans be allowed to compete in the Olympics and professional sports alongside non-augmented athletes?
>
> - Augmented humans should only be allowed to compete against other augmented humans.
> - Only augmented humans who have used technology to correct a deficiency should be allowed to compete with non-augmented humans.
> - Any human being (augmented or not) should be allowed to compete.

*See the end of the chapter for a follow-up question.*    (Anton Gvozdikov/Alamy Stock Photo)

# Understanding Digital Components

**Learning Outcome 2.1    You will be able to describe the devices that make up a computer system.**

After reading Chapter 1, you can see why becoming computer literate is important. But where do you start? You've no doubt gleaned some knowledge about computers just from being a member of society. However, even if you've used a computer before, do you really understand how it works, what all its parts are, and what those parts do?

# Understanding Your Computer

Let's start our look at computers by discussing what a computer does and how its functions make it such a useful machine.

## Computers Are Data Processing Devices

**Objective 2.1**    *Describe the four main functions of a computer system and how they interact with data and information.*

**What exactly does a computer do?** Strictly defined, a computer is a data processing device that performs four major functions:

1. **Input:** It gathers data or allows users to enter data.
2. **Process:** It manipulates, calculates, or organizes that data into information.
3. **Output:** It displays data and information in a form suitable for the user.
4. **Storage:** It saves data and information for later use.

 For information about the history of computers, see the History of Computers video.

**What's the difference between data and information?** In casual conversations, people often use the terms *data* and *information* interchangeably. However, for computers, the distinction between data and information is an important one. In computer terms, data is a representation of a fact, a figure, or an idea. Data can be a number, a word, a picture, or even a recording of sound. For example, the number 7135553297 and the names Zoe and Richardson are pieces of data. Alone, these pieces of data probably mean little to you. Information is data that has been organized or presented in a meaningful fashion. When your computer provides you with a contact listing that indicates that Zoe Richardson can be reached at (713) 555-3297, the data becomes useful—that is, it becomes information.

**How do computers interact with data and information?** Computers are excellent at processing (manipulating, calculating, or organizing) data into information. When you first arrived on campus, you probably were directed to a place where you could get an ID card. You most likely provided a clerk with personal data that was entered into a computer. The clerk then took your picture with a digital camera (collecting more data). All of the data was then processed so that it could be printed on your ID card (see Figure 2.1). This organized output of data on your ID card is useful information.

Input data → Processing data into information → Output information

**Figure 2.1** Computers process data into information. *(Mocker_bat/Fotolia)*

# Binary: The Language of Computers

**Objective 2.2** *Define bits and bytes, and describe how they are measured, used, and processed.*

**How do computers process data into information?** Unlike humans, computers work exclusively with numbers (not words). To process data into information, computers need to work in a language they understand. This language, called binary language, consists of just two digits: 0 and 1. Everything a computer does, such as processing data, printing a file, or editing a photo, is broken down into a series of 0s and 1s. Each 0 and 1 is a binary digit, or bit for short. Eight binary digits (or bits) combine to create one byte. In computers, each letter of the alphabet, each number, and each special character (such as @) consists of a unique combination of eight bits, or a string of eight 0s and 1s. So, for example, in binary language, the letter *K* is represented as 01001011. This is eight bits or one byte.

**How does a computer keep track of bits and bytes?** Computers understand only two states of existence: on and off. Inside a computer, these two states are defined using the numbers 1 and 0. Electrical switches are the devices inside the computer that are flipped between the two states of 1 and 0, signifying on and off. In fact, a computer system can be viewed as an enormous collection of on/off switches. These on/off switches are combined in different ways to perform addition and subtraction and to move data around the system.

You use various forms of switches every day. A water faucet is either on, allowing water to flow, or off. As shown in Figure 2.2, shutting off the faucet could represent the value 0, whereas turning it on could represent the value 1.

**What types of switches does a computer use?** Early computers used transistors. Transistors are electrical switches built out of layers of a special type of material called a semiconductor. A semiconductor is any material that can be controlled either to conduct electricity or to act as an insulator (to prohibit electricity from passing through). Silicon, which is found in sand, is the semiconductor material used to make transistors.

By itself, silicon doesn't conduct electricity particularly well, but if specific chemicals are added in a controlled way to the silicon, it behaves like an on/off switch. The silicon allows electric current to flow when a certain voltage is applied; otherwise, it prevents electric current from flowing.

Advances in technology began to require more transistors than circuit boards could handle. Something was needed to pack more transistor capacity into a smaller space. Thus, integrated circuits were developed.

**What are integrated circuits?** Integrated circuits (or chips) are tiny regions of semiconductor material that support a huge number of transistors (see Figure 2.3). Most integrated circuits are no more than a quarter inch in size yet can hold billions of transistors. This advancement has enabled computer designers to create small yet powerful microprocessors, which are the chips that contain a central processing unit (CPU, or processor). The CPU can be considered the "brains" of the computer, since this is where the processing of data into information takes place. Today, more than 2 billion transistors can be manufactured in a space as tiny as your little fingernail!

**What else can bits and bytes be used for?** Bits and bytes are not only used as the language that tells the computer what to do. They are also used to represent the quantity of data and information that the computer inputs and outputs. Word files, digital pictures, and software are represented inside computing devices as a series of bits and bytes. These files and applications can be quite large, containing billions of bytes.

To make it easier to measure the size of such files, we need units of measure larger than a byte. Kilobytes, megabytes, and gigabytes are therefore simply larger amounts of bytes. As shown in Figure 2.4, a kilobyte (KB) is approximately 1,000 bytes, a megabyte (MB) is about 1 million bytes, and a gigabyte (GB) is around 1 billion bytes. Today, personal computers can store terabytes (TB) (around 1 trillion bytes) of data, and many business computers can store up to a petabyte (PB) (1,000 terabytes) of data. The Google search engine processes more than 1 PB of user-generated data per hour!

**Figure 2.2** Water faucets can be used to illustrate binary switches.

**Figure 2.3** An integrated circuit is packaged in a small case but holds billions of transistors. *(Krasyuk/Fotolia)*

**Figure 2.4   How Much Is a Byte?**

**1 Byte (B)**
= a single letter
= a single wood block
1-inch cube

**1 tweet  = 280 Bytes**
= a shoebox of blocks
(Source: Twitter)

**1 small Instagram picture**
≈ **50 Kilobytes (Kb)**
≈ 50,000 bytes
≈ a typical car's cabin filled with blocks

3 minute MP3 song
≈ **5 Megabytes (Mb)**
≈ 5,000,000 bytes
≈ a standard shipping container full of blocks

1 movie,
1080p HD, compressed
≈ **5 Gigabytes (Gb)**
≈ 5,000,000,000 bytes
≈ 32.75 Olympic swimming pools full of blocks

Twitter's typical daily volume of
500,000,000 tweets × 280 bytes
≈ **140 Gigabytes (Gb)**
≈ 140,000,000,000 bytes
≈ half-fill the Vehicle Assembly Building at the Kennedy Space Center
(Sources: Twitter, NASA)

Wikipedia
≈ **10 Terabytes (Tb)**
≈ 10,000,000,000,000 bytes
≈ a layer covering Rhode Island 2.5 times
(June 2015, all pages with edit history, uncompressed. Source: Wikipedia)

Facebook's server capacity
≈ **100 Petabytes (Pb)**
≈ 100,000,000,000,000,000 bytes
≈ coating North America 2.8 times
(Media only. February 2012. Source: Facebook)

**How does a computer process bits and bytes?** A computer uses hardware and software to process data into information that lets you complete tasks such as writing a letter or playing a game. Hardware is any part of the computer you can physically touch. Software is the set of computer programs that enables the hardware to perform different tasks. Application software is what you use to help you carry out tasks such as writing a research paper. System software enables your computer's hardware devices and application software to work together. The most common type of system software is the operating system (OS)—the program that controls how your computer functions. Most likely, your computer's operating system is a version of Microsoft Windows or Apple's macOS.

# Types of Computers

**Objective 2.3** *List common types of computers, and discuss their main features.*

**What types of computers are popular for personal use?** There are two basic designs of computers: portable and stationary. For portable computers, three main categories exist: cell phones, tablets, and laptops.

## Cell Phones

**Are cell phones really computers?** All cell phones have the same components as any computer: a processor (central processing unit, or CPU), memory, and input and output devices, as shown in Figure 2.5. Cell phones also require their own operating system (OS) software and have their own application software. So, in effect, all cell phones are indeed computers.

**What makes a cell phone a smartphone?** Smartphones use a CPU and an interface so powerful that they can take on many of the same tasks as much more expensive computers: videoconferencing, recording and editing high-definition (HD) video, and broadcasting live-streaming video. Most providers, like AT&T or Verizon, label a smartphone as one that has sufficient power so that you can use Internet features easily. You often must purchase a data plan with a smartphone. Smartphones like the iPhone and tablets like the iPad illustrate the true power of digital convergence—they incorporate a range of features that used to be available only in separate, dedicated devices (see Figure 2.6):

- Internet access
- Personal information management (PIM) features
- Voice recording features
- The ability to play and organize music files
- GPS services
- Digital image and video capture
- Computing power to run programs like word processors and video-editing software
- Control of other devices in your "smart home"

**Isn't every phone a smartphone now?** Although many cell phones on the market are considered smartphones, less powerful cell phones are still available. Called feature phones, these inexpensive phones have modest processors, simpler interfaces, and often no touch screen. As more features are integrated into every cell phone product, though, it becomes difficult to distinguish a smartphone from a feature phone. We'll use the term *cell phone* to refer to all cellular phones and *smartphone* to refer to the more powerful type of cell phone that can run more complex applications.

### Understanding Bits and Bytes

In this Active Helpdesk, you'll play the role of a helpdesk staffer, fielding questions about the difference between data and information, what bits and bytes are, and how bytes are measured.

Music player

Digital camera

GPS

Remote control

**Figure 2.6** A single device like a tablet can play the role of many separate devices, illustrating the concept of digital convergence. *(Rostislav Sedlacek/Fotolia; Science Photo Library/Shutterstock; OnBlast/Shutterstock; Andrey Popov/Shutterstock; Amakar/Fotolia)*

**Figure 2.5** Inside your cell phone, you'll find a CPU; a memory chip; input devices such as a microphone and a touch screen; and output devices such as a display screen. *(iFixit)*

## Tablets

A tablet computer, such as the Apple iPad or Amazon Fire, is a portable computer integrated into a multitouch-sensitive screen. Tablet computers use an on-screen keyboard, but you can also connect external keyboards to tablets.

**How do tablets compare with smartphones?** Tablets are very light, portable devices, although not as light as smartphones. The top-selling tablets include the Apple iPad and the Samsung Galaxy, but there are more than 75 tablets on the market. One difference between tablets and smartphones is that you can't make cellular phone calls from most tablets. In addition, whereas smartphones usually have displays that are less than 5 inches, tablets come with screen sizes between 7 and 10 inches. However, manufacturers are beginning to make even larger phones, offering a phablet model of phone, with screen sizes of over 6 inches.

In most other regards, smartphones and tablets are similar. They have the following features:

- Similar operating systems: Common operating systems, such as iOS, Android, or Windows, operate on smartphones and tablets.
- Similar processors: The processing power of smartphones and tablets is often the same.
- Touch-screen interfaces: Smartphones and tablets are both equipped with touch-screen interfaces.
- Long battery life: Most tablets and smartphones run at least 10 hours on a single charge.
- Similar software applications: Most apps available for one device are available in a compatible version for the other type of device.
- Similar Internet connectivity: Both can offer cellular and wireless access to the Internet.
- Bluetooth: Most smartphones and tablets on the market today are Bluetooth-enabled, meaning they include a small Bluetooth chip that allows them to transfer data wirelessly to any other Bluetooth-enabled device. Bluetooth is a wireless transmission standard that lets you connect devices such as smartphones, tablets, and laptops to devices such as keyboards and headsets. Bluetooth technology uses radio waves to transmit data signals over distances up to approximately 1,200 feet for Bluetooth 5 devices.

**Can tablets function as a communication device?** Although tablets are currently not able to make cell phone calls, they can easily place audio or video phone calls if connected to a Wi-Fi network. An application like Skype that makes Internet phone calls is required for that. There are also apps available that allow tablets to handle texting. WhatsApp, for example, supports free national and international texting from a range of devices, including tablets.

### Laptops and Their Variants

A laptop (or notebook) computer is a portable computer that has a keyboard, monitor, and other devices integrated into a single compact case. This was the first type of portable computer, but as our demand for lighter and more portable computers accelerated, tablets and smartphones were developed. There are several variations of laptops, including 2-in-1 PCs, ultrabooks, and Chromebooks.

**What is a 2-in-1 PC?** A 2-in-1 PC is a laptop computer that can convert into a tablet-like device (see Figure 2.7). In laptop mode, there is a physical keyboard, while in tablet mode you use an on-screen keyboard. On some models, such as Microsoft Surface devices, the touch screen is detachable from the keyboard so it can be carried and used as an independent tablet. On others, such as the Lenovo Yoga, there is a hinge so that the keyboard can be folded behind the screen.

**Figure 2.7** The Microsoft Surface is an example of a 2-in-1 device: a touchscreen tablet and a detachable keyboard merged into one unit. *(Oleksiy Maksymenko/image-BROKER/Alamy Stock Photo)*

**Why would I want a 2-in-1 instead of a tablet?** Although more expensive than a tablet, 2-in-1s have a more powerful CPU so they can function as a laptop. Also, whereas a tablet runs a mobile OS, like Android or iOS, a 2-in-1 uses a full traditional OS, like Windows, and can therefore run the same software applications as a laptop. In addition, a 2-in-1 has a physical keyboard when you need it. Many people find a 2-in-1 can replace the need to carry both a tablet and a laptop.

**How are ultrabooks different from laptops?** Ultrabooks are a category of full-featured computers that focus on offering a very thin, lightweight computing solution. Examples include the Apple MacBook Air and the Asus ZenBook. Ultrabooks don't offer optical drives, so they facilitate a very thin profile. Some do not even offer traditional USB ports, instead using the more compact USB-C connector so that they are only about 13 mm at the thickest point. Most ultrabooks offer SSD drives and so have very fast response times on startup and restoring from a low power state. They weigh in at less than 3 pounds even though they feature the same operating systems and CPUs as heavier, larger laptops. They also include full-size keyboards and 13- to 15-inch screens.

**What is a Chromebook?** A Chromebook is a special type of laptop that uses the Google Chrome OS and is designed to be connected to the Internet always. Documents and apps are stored primarily in the cloud as opposed to locally. Because the Chrome OS places less demand on computing hardware than a conventional operating system (such as Windows or macOS), it can run the Chrome browser much more efficiently. If you do most of your work within a browser and need a lightweight, inexpensive computer, a Chromebook might be what you are seeking. However, remember that to use a Chromebook most effectively, you should have an active Internet connection.

### Choosing a Portable Device

**With all these choices, how do I know which device is best for me?** Use these guidelines to determine what device best fits your personal needs:

- **Power:** How much computational power do you need?
- **Screen size and resolution:** These cannot be changed later, so make sure the quality and size of screen will fit your needs for the years you'll keep the device.
- **Style of keyboard:** Do you want a touch-based interface? Is a physical keyboard important, or is an on-screen keyboard sufficient? Does the feel of the keyboard work for you?
- **Battery life:** Some devices can operate for 15 hours continuously, others less than 5. Investigate whether the battery can be upgraded and how much weight that would add.
- **Weight:** Does an additional 2 pounds matter? (Lighter devices usually cost more.) Remember to include the weight of any charging device you would need to carry when you travel as you consider the tradeoff in price for a lighter device.
- **Number of devices:** Is this your only computing device? As technology prices fall, you may be able to have more than one device. You might find an affordable solution that includes both a very mobile device and a second more powerful one.

Figure 2.8 summarizes the various mobile device categories.

**Laptop**
- 5 to 8 lbs
- Traditional OS

**Ultrabook**
- Less than 3 lbs
- Traditional OS

**2-in-1**
- 1 to 3 lbs
- Traditional OS

**Tablet**
- Less than 2 lbs
- Mobile OS

**Smartphone**
- 0.25 lbs
- Mobile OS

**Figure 2.8** A full spectrum of mobile devices is available. *(Sean Gallup/Getty Images; Josep Lago/AFP/Getty Images; Ethan Miller/Getty Images; Chris Tzou/Bloomberg/Getty Images; Peter Dazeley/Photographer's Choice/Getty Images)*

**Figure 2.9** (a) A desktop computer has a system unit that holds the main components. (b) An all-in-one computer does not need a separate system unit. *(Maxim Kazmin/123RF; Best pixels/Shutterstock)*

### Stationary Computers

**What are the main stationary computers available to consumers?** A desktop computer is intended for use at a single location, so it's stationary (see Figure 2.9a). Most desktop computers consist of a separate case or tower (called the system unit) that houses the main components of the computer and to which peripheral devices are attached. A peripheral device is a component, such as a monitor or keyboard that connects to the computer.

An all-in-one computer, such as the Apple iMac, eliminates the need for a separate tower because these computers house the computer's processor and memory in the monitor (see Figure 2.9b). Many all-in-one models also incorporate touch-screen technology.

**What are the advantages of a desktop computer?** Desktop computers are easier to upgrade than laptops or other portable computers (which often cannot be upgraded at all). Upgrades to components such as video cards are often important for gamers and graphic artists. Also, large screens are beneficial in many working environments (such as graphic design) and if a computer doesn't need portability you can use a larger monitor without a problem. Finally, miniaturization of components is usually costly. Therefore, you can often get more computing power for your dollar when you buy a desktop computer.

**Are there any other types of computers?** Although you may never come into direct contact with the following types of computers, they are still very important and do a lot of work behind the scenes of daily life:

- A mainframe is a large, expensive computer that supports many users simultaneously. Mainframes are often used in businesses that manage large amounts of data, such as insurance companies, where many people are working at the same time on similar operations, such as claims processing. Mainframes excel at executing many computer programs at the same time.

- A supercomputer is a specially designed computer that can perform complex calculations extremely rapidly. Supercomputers are used when complex models requiring intensive mathematical calculations are needed (such as weather forecasting). Supercomputers are designed to execute a few programs as quickly as possible, whereas mainframes are designed to handle many programs running at the same time but at a slower pace.

- An embedded computer is a specially designed computer chip that resides in another device, such as your car, a drone, or the electronic thermostat in your home. Embedded computers are self-contained computer devices that have their own programming and that typically don't receive input from you or interact with other systems.

Each part of your computer has a specific purpose that coordinates with one of the functions of the computer—input, processing, output, or storage (see Figure 2.10). Additional devices, such as Wi-Fi

Input

Processing

Storage

Output

**Figure 2.10** Each part of the computer serves a special function.

adapters and routers, help a computer communicate with the Internet and other computers to facilitate the sharing of documents and other resources. Let's begin our exploration of hardware by looking at your computer's input devices.

#  Input Devices

An input device lets you enter data (text, images, and sounds) and instructions (user responses and commands) into your computer. Let's look at some of the most popular input devices used today.

## Physical Keyboards and Touch Screens

**Objective 2.4**  *Identify the main types of keyboards and touch screens.*

**What is the most common way to input data and commands?** A keyboard is an input device you use to enter typed data and commands. However, as discussed earlier, computing devices such as smartphones, tablets, and many laptops now respond to touch. Touch screens are display screens that respond to commands initiated by touching them with your finger or a stylus—a device that looks like a pen and that you use to tap commands or draw on a screen. Touch-screen devices use a virtual keyboard that displays on screen when text input is required (see Figure 2.12). These keyboards show basic keyboard configurations but allow you to switch to other special keys. Virtual keyboards can also support dozens of languages and different character sets.

**Are all keyboards the same?** Whether virtual or physical, the most common keyboard layout is a standard QWERTY keyboard. This keyboard layout gets its name from the first six letters in the top-left row of alphabetic keys and is the standard English-language keyboard layout. The QWERTY layout was originally designed for typewriters and was meant to slow down typists and prevent typewriter keys from jamming. Although the QWERTY layout is considered inefficient because it slows typing speeds, efforts to change to more efficient layouts, such as that of the Dvorak keyboard (see Figure 2.13), have not been met with much public interest.

**Figure 2.12** Touch screen devices use virtual keyboards that appear on screen when needed. (*Lourens Smak/Alamy Stock Photo*)

**Figure 2.13** The Dvorak keyboard is an alternative keyboard layout that puts the most commonly used letters in the English language on "home keys"—the keys in the middle row of the keyboard. The Dvorak keyboard's design reduces the distance your fingers travel for most keystrokes, increasing typing speed. You can customize the layout of your keyboard using the Windows operating system. *(Courtesy of Microsoft Corporation)*

**How can I use my keyboard most efficiently?** All keyboards have the standard set of alphabetic and numeric keys that you regularly use when typing. As shown in Figure 2.14, many keyboards for laptop and desktop computers have additional keys that perform special functions. Knowing how to use the special keys shown in Figure 2.14 will help you improve your efficiency.

**What alternatives are there to a virtual keyboard?** Virtual keyboards are not always convenient when a great deal of typing is required. Most computing devices can accept physical keyboards as an add-on accessory. Wired keyboards plug into a data port on the computing device. Wireless keyboards send data to the computer using a form of wireless technology that uses radio frequency (RF). A radio transmitter in the keyboard sends out signals that are received either by a receiving device plugged into a port on the device or by a Bluetooth receiving device located in the

**Figure 2.14** Keyboards have a variety of keys that help you work more efficiently. (Note that on Macs, Function keys are slightly different, the Control function is the Apple key or Command key, and the Alt function is the Option key.)

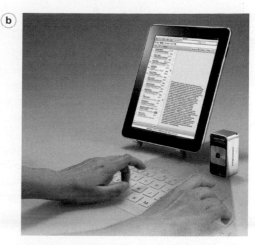

**Figure 2.15** (a) Cases with integrated physical keyboards make tablets more typing friendly. (b) Laser-projection keyboard devices project the image of a QWERTY keyboard on any surface. Sensors detect typing motions, and data is transmitted to your device via Bluetooth technology. *(guteksk7/Shutterstock; Splash News/Hammacher Schlemmer/Newscom)*

computing device. Often, Bluetooth keyboards for tablets are integrated with a case to protect your tablet (see Figure 2.15a).

Flexible keyboards are a terrific alternative if you want a full-sized keyboard for your laptop or tablet. You can roll one up, fit it in your backpack, and plug it into a USB port when you need it. Another compact keyboard alternative is a laser-projection keyboard (see Figure 2.15b), which is about the size of a matchbox. They project an image of a keyboard onto any flat surface, and sensors detect the motion of your fingers as you "type." Data is transmitted to the device via Bluetooth. These keyboards work with the latest smartphones and tablets.

## Mice and Other Pointing Devices

**Objective 2.5** *Describe the main types of mice and pointing devices.*

**What input is a mouse responsible for?** A mouse is the most common pointing device used to enter user responses and commands. One of the mouse's most important functions is to position the cursor. The cursor is an onscreen icon (often shown by a vertical bar or an arrow) that helps the user keep track of exactly what is active on the display screen. For instance, in word processing software, the cursor allows you to see exactly where the next character will be typed in a sentence based on its position. To move the cursor to another point on a touch screen you just tap the screen with your finger. Or to select an item on the screen, you just tap it with your finger. But laptops and desktop computers that are not touch enabled need other types of devices (like mice) for positioning the cursor and selecting icons (by clicking the mouse).

**What kinds of mice are there?** The most common mouse type is the optical mouse. An optical mouse uses an internal sensor or laser to detect the mouse's movement. The sensor sends signals to the computer, telling it where to move the pointer on the screen. Optical mice don't require a mouse pad, though you can use one to enhance the movement of the mouse on an uneven surface or to protect your work surface from being scratched.

Most mice have two or three buttons (mice for Macs sometimes have only one button) that let you execute commands and open shortcut menus. Many customizable mice have additional programmable buttons and wheels that let you quickly maneuver through web pages or games (see Figure 2.16). These mice are also customizable to fit any size hand and grip style by allowing for length and width adjustments. Aside from gamers, many people use customizable mice to reduce susceptibility to repetitive strain injuries or if they suffer from physical limitations that prevent them from using standard mice.

**How do wireless mice connect to a computing device?** Wireless mice usually connect the same way that wireless keyboards do—either through an integrated Bluetooth chip or a Bluetooth receiver that plugs into a USB port.

**Why would I want to use a mouse with a touch-screen device?** If you're using a physical keyboard with your touch-screen device, it's often easier to perform actions with a mouse rather than reaching to touch the screen. In addition, there are new kinds of mice,

**Figure 2.16** The R.A.I. Pro$^X$ Precision Gaming Mouse offers the ultimate in customizability for serious gamers or users with special needs. *(Mad Catz, Inc.)*

Touch-screen technology was developed in 1971 and used primarily with ATMs and fast-food order displays. The technology for monitors and other displays was made popular by the iPod Touch in 2007 and is now in smartphones, tablets, laptops, and desktop monitors. But how do touch-screen monitors know where you're touching? How do they know what you want them to do?

The basic idea behind touch screens is straightforward—when you place your finger or stylus on a screen, it changes the physical state of the screen and registers your touch. The location of your touch is then translated into a command. Three basic systems are used to recognize a person's touch: *resistive, capacitive,* and *surface acoustic wave.* These systems require the basic components of a touch-responsive glass panel, controller, and software driver, combined with a display and computer processor.

The *resistive system* maps the exact location of the pressure point created when a user touches the screen. The *capacitive system* (see Figure 2.17) uses the change in the electric charge on the glass panel of the monitor, which is created by the user's touch, to generate a location. The third technology, *surface acoustic wave system,* uses two transducers (electrical devices that convert energy from one form to another) that are placed along the x and y axes of the monitor's glass plate. Reflectors, which are also placed on the glass, are used to reflect an electric signal sent from the sending transducer to the receiving transducer. The receiving transducer determines whether the signal has been disturbed by a touch event and locates the touch instantly. With all three systems, the display's software driver then translates the touch into something the operating system can understand, like how a mouse driver translates a mouse's movements into a click or drag.

Because the resistive system uses pressure to register a touch, it doesn't matter if the touch is created by a finger or another device. On the other hand, a capacitive system must have conductive input, so generally a finger is required. The surface acoustic wave system allows touches by any object.

The iPhone introduced another complexity to the touch-screen system—a multitouch user interface. In addition to just pressing the screen in one location, multitouch technology can process multiple simultaneous touches on the screen. For example, pinching or spreading out your thumb and finger together makes the display zoom out and in, respectively. The features of each touch, such as size, shape, and location, are also determined.

A touch-sensitive screen, like the one used with the iPhone and iPad and with many other smartphones and tablets, arranges the capacitors in a coordinate system so the circuitry can sense changes at each point along the grid (see Figure 2.18). Consequently, every point on the grid generates its own signal when touched and can do so even as another signal is being generated simultaneously. The signals are then relayed to the device's processor. This allows the device to determine the location and movement of simultaneous touches in multiple locations.

After detecting the position and type of touch occurring on the display, the device's processor combines this information with the information it has about the application in use and what was being done in the application when the touch occurred. The processor relays that information to the program in use, and the command is executed. All this happens seemingly instantaneously.

**Figure 2.17** Some basic touch screens use a capacitive system to detect touches and translate them into meaningful commands that are understood by the computer's operating system.

**Figure 2.18** Multitouch screens use a coordinate-based grid to arrange the capacitors so the circuitry can detect and respond to multiple touches occurring at the same time.

called *touch mice*, which are designed with touch-screen computers in mind. Unlike traditional mice, there are no specifically defined buttons. The top surface of a touch mouse is the button. You tap one, two, or three fingers to perform touch-screen tasks such as scrolling, switching through open apps, and zooming. Touch mice also allow you to perform traditional mouse tasks, such as moving the cursor when you move the mouse.

**What pointing devices do laptops use?** Most laptops have an integrated pointing device, such as a touch pad (or trackpad)—a small, touch-sensitive area at the base of the keyboard. Mac laptops include multitouch trackpads, which don't have buttons but are controlled by various one-, two-, three-, and four-finger actions. For example, scrolling is controlled by brushing two fingers along the trackpad in any direction. Most touch pads are sensitive to taps, interpreting them as mouse clicks. Some laptops also have buttons under or near the pad to record mouse clicks.

**What input devices are used with games?** Game controllers such as joysticks, game pads, and steering wheels are also considered input devices because they send data to computing devices. Game controllers, which are like the devices used on gaming consoles such as the Xbox One, are also available for use with computers. They have buttons and miniature pointing devices that provide input to the computer.

## Image, Sound, and Sensor Input

**Objective 2.6** *Explain how images, sounds, and sensor data are input into computing devices.*

**What are popular input devices for images?** Digital cameras, camcorders, and mobile device cameras capture pictures and video and are considered input devices. Stand-alone devices can connect to your computer with a cable, transmit data wirelessly, or transfer data automatically through the Internet.

Flatbed scanners also input images. They work similarly to a photocopy machine; however, instead of generating the image on paper, they create a digital image, which you can then print, save, or e-mail. Flatbed scanners are often used in conjunction with optical character recognition (OCR) software, which digitizes and saves text in digital form. Many businesses and libraries use OCR software to reduce volumes of reports and books to manageable digital files.

The digital cameras in cell phones are also often used to scan information. For example, many health and fitness apps, like MyFitnessPal, capture data by using the cell phone's camera to scan UPC codes on food products. The devices used at supermarkets and retail stores to scan the UPC codes on your purchases are also a type of scanner that inputs information into another computer: the point-of-sale terminal (cash register).

A webcam is a front-facing camera that attaches to a desktop computer or is built into a computing device. Although webcams can capture still images, they're used mostly for capturing and transmitting live video. Videoconferencing apps let a person using a device equipped with a webcam and a microphone transmit video and audio across the Internet. Video apps such as Skype and Google Hangouts make it easy to videoconference with multiple people (see Figure 2.19).

**How do my computing devices benefit from accepting sound input?** Inputting sound to your computer requires using a microphone (or mic)—a device that lets you capture sound

**Figure 2.19** Video conferencing relies on two input devices: a webcam and a microphone. *(Andriy Popov/123RF)*

Microphone icon

**Figure 2.20** Just tap the microphone icon and ask Microsoft's intelligent personal assistant Cortana a question. She communicates using natural language processing techniques. *(Courtesy of Microsoft Corporation)*

waves (such as your voice) and transfer them to digital format on your computer. Laptops, tablets, and smartphones come with built-in microphones. In addition to letting others hear you in a videoconference, equipping your device to accept sound input enables you to conduct audio conferences, chat with people over the Internet, record podcasts, and even control computing devices with your voice.

**How can I use my voice to control my computing device?** Voice recognition software allows you to control your devices by speaking into a microphone instead of using a keyboard or mouse. Apps like Dragon Naturally Speaking are available as stand-alone apps, but voice recognition features are built into the Windows and macOS operating systems as well.

Popular extensions of voice recognition software are intelligent personal assistants such as Apple's Siri, Google Assistant, and Microsoft's Cortana (see Figure 2.20). These so-called software agents respond to voice commands and then use your input, access to the Internet, and location-aware services to perform various tasks, such as finding the closest pizza parlor to your present location.

**What types of add-on microphones are available?** For specialized situations, built-in microphones don't always provide the best performance. You may want to consider adding other types of microphones, such as those shown in Table 2.1, to your system for the best results.

### Table 2.1 Types of Microphones

| Microphone Type | Attributes | Best Used For |
|---|---|---|
| **Close Talk**  | • Attached to a headset (allows for listening) <br> • Leaves hands free | • Videoconferencing <br> • Phone calls <br> • Speech recognition software |
| **Omnidirectional**  | • Picks up sounds equally well from all directions | • Conference calls in meeting rooms |
| **Unidirectional**  | • Picks up sounds from only one direction | • Recordings with one voice (podcasts) |
| **Clip-on (Lavalier)**  | • Clips to clothing <br> • Available as wireless | • Presentations requiring freedom of movement <br> • Leaves hands free for writing on white boards |

*(Fotolia; Sumnersgraphicsinc/Fotolia; Feliks Gurevich/Shutterstock; Joseph Branston/PC Format Magazine/Getty Images)*

**What other types of input devices are found in computers?** Smartphones and tablets are now arrayed with a variety of sensors. Broadly speaking, a sensor is any device that detects or measures something. Sensors feed data into the device and are used by the hardware or apps that rely on the input provided. The following sensors can be found in almost all smartphones and many tablets today (although your particular device may not contain every one):

- *Magnetometer:* detects magnetic fields. Compass and metal detecting apps use this sensor.
- *Proximity sensor:* used in phones to determine when the phone is placed next to your ear so the phone knows to shut off the display while you are talking.
- *Light sensor:* measures ambient light brightness so the device can adjust the brightness of the display.
- *Accelerometer:* measures acceleration that the device is experiencing. It also helps determine the orientation of the device along three axes (see Figure 2.21), which allows the device to determine if it is in landscape or portrait orientation.
- *Gyroscope:* provides orientation information but with greater precision than the accelerometer.
- *Barometer:* measures atmospheric pressure to determine how high the device is above sea level. This improves GPS accuracy and also enables counting floors more accurately when step climbing.
- *Thermometer:* measures ambient temperature either inside or outside the device. This is mainly used to monitor overheating of delicate electronic components inside the device.
- *Pedometer:* used to record the number of steps taken while having the device in your possession.
- *Fingerprint sensor:* used to record and read fingerprint data to secure the device.
- *Heart rate monitor:* measures pulse rate by detecting pulsating blood vessels inside your finger.

Want to access the sensors in your smartphone? Try our Make This activity in the middle of the chapter to learn how to build your own apps that can gather information from the sensors in your smartphone.

**Figure 2.21** The accelerometer is a sensor in your devices that reports the acceleration in any direction. *(Chih Hsien Hang/123RF)*

# Output Devices

An output device lets you send processed data out of your computer in the form of text, pictures (graphics), sounds (audio), or video. Let's look at some popular output devices.

## Image and Audio Output

**Objective 2.7** *Describe options for outputting images and audio from computing devices.*

Computing devices need options for outputting data so you can transfer it to other locations. Sometimes you need only soft copies of data, such as a graph displayed on your screen. Other times you need a hard copy, such as a printed page. Let's explore the most common output device: the display screen.

### Image Output

**What are the different types of display screens?** A display screen (sometimes referred to as a monitor on desktops and laptops) displays text, graphics, and videos. The most common type of monitor for laptop and desktop computers is a liquid crystal display (LCD). An LCD monitor, also called a *flat-panel monitor*, is light and energy efficient. Some newer monitors use light-emitting diode (LED) technology, which is more energy efficient and may have better color accuracy and thinner panels than LCD monitors.

Organic light-emitting diode (OLED) displays use organic compounds that produce light when exposed to an electric current. Unlike LCDs and LEDs, OLEDs do not require a backlight to function and therefore draw less power and have a much thinner display, sometimes as thin as 3 mm. They are also brighter and more environmentally friendly than LCDs. Because of their lower power needs, OLED displays run longer on a single battery charge than do LEDs, which is why OLED technology is probably the technology used in your smartphone, tablet, and digital camera.

Companies like LG are now working on transparent and flexible OLED display screens (see Figure 2.22). These screens allow you to see what is behind the screen while still being able to

**Figure 2.22** Because they don't need a backlight, OLED displays can be made transparent and flexible. *(Yonhap/EPA/Newscom)*

**Figure 2.23** A magnification of a single pixel in an LCD monitor.

display information on the screen. These types of screens present interesting possibilities for augmentative reality. As described in Chapter 1, *augmented reality (AR)* is a view of a real-world environment whose elements are augmented (or supplemented) by some type of computer-generated sensory input such as video, graphics, or GPS data. For instance, if you had a transparent screen on your smartphone and held it up to view street signs that were in English, you could possibly have your phone display the signs in another language. Currently, applications like this exist (such as Pokémon Go) but require the use of a camera as well as your screen. But transparent screens will eliminate the need for the camera.

**How do display screens work?** Display screens are grids made up of millions of tiny dots, called pixels. When these pixels are illuminated by the light waves generated by a fluorescent panel at the back of your screen, they create the images you see on the screen or monitor. Each pixel on 4K and 8K resolution TVs and monitors is made up of four yellow, red, blue, and green subpixels. Some newer TVs further split the subpixels into upper and lower, which can brighten and darken independently. LCD monitors are made of two or more sheets of material filled with a liquid crystal solution (see Figure 2.23). A fluorescent panel at the back of the LCD monitor generates light waves. When electric current passes through the liquid crystal solution, the crystals move around and either block the fluorescent light or let the light shine through. This blocking or passing of light by the crystals causes images to form on the screen. The various combinations of yellow, red, blue, and green make up the components of color we see on our monitors.

**What factors affect the quality of a display screen?** Some portable devices don't provide a choice of screens. The current iPhone has whatever screen Apple chooses to use. But when choosing a laptop or a monitor for a desktop, you have options to compare.

The most important factors to consider are aspect ratio and resolution. The aspect ratio is the width-to-height proportion of a monitor. Traditionally, aspect ratios have been 4:3, but newer monitors are available with an aspect ratio of 16:9 to accommodate HD video. The screen resolution, or the clearness or sharpness of the image, reflects the number of pixels on the screen. An LCD monitor may have a native (or maximum) resolution of 1600 × 1200, meaning it contains 1600 vertical columns with 1200 pixels in each column. The higher the resolution, the sharper and clearer the image, but generally, the resolution of an LCD monitor is dictated by the screen size and aspect ratio. Although you can change the resolution of an LCD monitor beyond its native resolution, the images may become distorted. Generally, you should buy a monitor with the highest resolution available for the screen size (measured in inches).

**Is a bigger screen size always better?** The bigger the screen, the more you can display, and depending on what you want to display, size may matter. In general, the larger the screen, the larger the number of pixels it can display. For example, a 27-inch monitor can display 2560 × 1440 pixels, whereas a 21.5-inch monitor may only be able to display 1680 × 1050 pixels. However, new monitors have at least the 1920 × 1080 resolution (based on the HDTV resolution) required to display Blu-ray movies.

Larger screens can also allow you to view multiple documents or web pages at the same time. However, buying two smaller monitors might be cheaper than buying one large monitor. For either option—a big screen or two separate screens—check that your computer has the video hardware needed to support the display devices.

**What device provides the highest resolution?** 8K monitors and TVs are now on the market and feature a whopping 7680 × 4320 resolution. The most cost-effective high-resolution devices are probably still Ultra HD (otherwise known as 4K) monitors and TVs. Ultra HD has a resolution of 3840 × 2160, which is four times the pixels of the original HD devices. However, to take advantage of high-resolution devices, your media provider needs to stream your content at these higher resolutions. So make sure to

**Figure 2.24** Interactive white boards are now common output/input devices found in classrooms and conference rooms. *(Monkey Business Images/Shutterstock)*

check with your provider before running out and buying the newest high-resolution device the next time you need one.

**How do I show output to a large group of people?** You can always connect your computing device to an HDTV if you have one large enough to be seen by the entire group. Another option is a projector, which lets you project images from your device onto a wall or screen. Small and lightweight portable projectors are ideal for businesspeople who make presentations at client locations. Entertainment projectors include stereo speakers and multimedia connectors, making them a good option for use in the home to display TV programs, movies, or video games.

In classrooms and conference rooms, projectors are often combined with another output device, the interactive white board (see Figure 2.24). A projector projects the computer's display onto the interactive white board's surface. The touch sensitive board doubles as an input device and allows users to control and provide input to the computer using a pen, finger, or stylus. Notes and annotations can be captured and saved from the white board to the attached computer.

### Audio Output

**What are the output devices for sound?** All portable computing devices include integrated speakers, the output devices for sound. These speakers are sufficient for playing audio clips you find on the web and usually for letting you make videoconference or phone calls over the Internet. However, if you plan to digitally edit audio files or are particular about how your music sounds, you may want a more sophisticated speaker system, such as one that includes subwoofers (special speakers that produce only low bass sounds) and surround-sound speakers. A surround-sound system is a set of speakers and audio processing equipment that envelops the listener in a 360-degree field of sound. Wireless speaker systems are widely available, enabling you to connect portable devices to quality speakers easily.

Headphones or earbuds connect wirelessly or plug into the same jack on your computing device to which external speakers connect. Studies of users of portable devices have shown that hearing might be damaged by excessive volume, especially when using earbuds because they fit into the ear canals, so limit the volume when you use these devices.

## Printers

**Objective 2.8** *Describe various types of printers, and explain when you would use them.*

**What are the different types of printers?** Another common output device is the printer, which creates hard copies (copies you can touch) of text and graphics. There are two primary categories of printers common in the home and office: inkjet and laser.

**What are the advantages of inkjet printers?** Inkjet printers (see Figure 2.26) are popular because they're affordable and produce high-quality printouts quickly and quietly. Inkjet

**Figure 2.26** Inkjet printers are popular among home users, especially since high-end inkjet printers can print high-quality photographic images. *(Tankist276/Shutterstock)*

## Figure 2.27 How Laser Printers Work

Laser printer

laser beam

laser

rotating hexagonal mirror

lenses

path of laser beam

1. Residual toner removed from drum by scraping or by passing under a discharging and erasing lamp.

2. Uniform high-voltage negative charge applied to drum.

negative charger

photoreceptor drum

fuser roller

3. Laser beam selectively discharges the images areas onto the rotaing drum, reversing the strong negative charge to a weak positve charge.

toner hopper

toner roller

paper tray

blank paper

negatively charged toner particles

ABCDEFG HIJKLMN

printed side of paper

positive charger

4. Negatively charged toner particles adhere to only the areas given a positve charge by the laser.

5. Paper receives a strong positive charge.

6. Negatively charged toner particles on the drum are transferred to the paper.

7. Toner particles are fused or melted onto the paper.

*(Universal Images Group North America LLC/Alamy Stock Photo)*

printers work by spraying tiny drops of ink onto paper and are great for printing black-and-white text as well as color images. In fact, when loaded with the right paper, higher-end inkjet printers can print images that look like professional-quality photos. One thing to consider when buying an inkjet printer is the type and cost of the ink cartridges the printer needs. Some printers use two cartridges: black and color. Others use four or more cartridges: typically, cyan, magenta, yellow, and black. The four-color printing process many inkjets use is known as CMYK (cyan, magenta, yellow, and key, which is usually represented by black).

**Why would I want a laser printer?** A laser printer uses laser beams and static electricity to deliver toner (similar to ink) onto the correct areas of the page (see Figure 2.27). Heat is used to fuse the toner to the page, making the image permanent. Laser printers are often used because they print faster than inkjet printers and produce higher-quality printouts. Black-and-white and color laser printers are both affordable for home use. If you print a high volume of pages, consider a laser printer. When you include the price of ink or toner in the overall cost, color laser printers can be more economical than inkjets.

**What's the best way to print from portable devices such as tablets and smartphones?** Wireless printers are great for printing from portable devices. Wireless printers are also a good option for home networks, as they let several people print to the same printer from different devices and any location in the home. There are two types of wireless printers: Wi-Fi and Bluetooth. Both Wi-Fi and Bluetooth printers have a range of up to approximately 300 feet. Wi-Fi, however, sends data more quickly than Bluetooth.

If you're using a device running Apple's iOS (such as an iPhone), AirPrint makes printing easy. AirPrint is a feature of iOS that facilitates printing to AirPrint-compatible wireless printers, and many printers produced today are AirPrint compatible. For non-Apple devices, newer wireless printers come with their own app that enables printing from portable devices. After installing the app on your device, you can send print jobs to the wireless printer.

**Figure 2.28** Cloud-ready printers only need an Internet connection and then can be accessed from any mobile device.

Another option is Google Cloud Print, a service that lets you configure your printers so you can access them from mobile devices. Google Cloud Print uses cloud-ready printers (see Figure 2.28) that are available from manufacturers such as HP, Kodak, and Epson. These printers connect directly to the Internet and register themselves with Google Cloud Print. Once a printer is registered with Cloud Print, printing jobs can be sent to it from mobile devices (such as tablets and smartphones) using the Internet. Conventional printers that you already own can also be registered with Cloud Print, although they require connection to the Internet through a computer.

**Are there any other types of specialty printers?** Although you'll probably use laser or inkjet printers most often, you might encounter other types of printers (shown in Figure 2.29):

- An all-in-one printer combines the functions of a printer, scanner, copier, and fax into one machine. Popular for their space-saving convenience, all-in-one printers may use either inkjet or laser technology.

- A large format printer generates oversize images such as banners, posters, and infographics that require more sophisticated color detail. Some of these printers use up to 12 different inks to achieve high-quality color images.

- A 3D printer is used to print three-dimensional objects. For example, parts can be built on the spot when needed using a 3D printer. 3D printers build such objects one layer at a time from the bottom up. They begin by spreading a layer of powder on a platform. Then, depending on the technology, the printer uses nozzles to spray tiny drops of glue at specific places to solidify the powder, or the powder is solidified through a melting process. The printer repeats this process until the object is built. This technology is now used for the manufacturing of a variety of consumer goods, from toys to clothing.

(a)

(b)

(c)

**Figure 2.29** Specialty printers: (a) all-in-one printer, (b) large format printer, (c) 3D printer. *(Interior Design/Shutterstock; Koktaro/Shutterstock; Stockbroker/MBI/Alamy Stock Photo)*

3D printing is now being used in the medical community. For example, hearing aids are currently being produced using 3D printers, which allow manufacturers to offer not only a custom fit but individual skin color matching as well (to make the devices less visible). And researchers at Wake Forest Institute for Regenerative Medicine have developed a method of using similar printing technologies to build heart, bone, and blood vessel tissues in the lab. They have also developed a way to "print" restorative cells directly into a soldier's wound at the site where the injury occurred, thus significantly improving the soldier's chances of survival. So next time you visit the doctor, 3D printing might be just the cure you need!

**How do I choose the best printer?** If you're planning to print color photos and graphics, an inkjet printer or a color laser printer is a must, even though the cost per page will be higher. If you'll be printing mostly text–based documents or will be sharing your printer with others, a laser printer is best because of its speed and overall economy for volume printing. It's also important to determine whether you want just a printer or a device that prints and scans, copies, or faxes. In addition, you should decide whether you need to print from mobile devices.

Once you've narrowed down the type of printer you want, you can use the criteria listed in Table 2.2 to help you determine the best model to meet your needs.

**Table 2.2  Major Printer Attributes**

| Attribute | Considerations |
|---|---|
| Speed  | • Print speed is measured in *pages per minute* (PPM).<br>• Black-and-white documents print faster than color documents.<br>• Laser printers often print faster than inkjets. |
| Resolution  | • Resolution refers to a printer's image clarity.<br>• Resolution is measured in *dots per inch* (dpi).<br>• Higher dpi = greater level of detail and clarity.<br>• Recommended dpi:<br>   • Black-and-white text: 300<br>   • General purpose images: 1200<br>   • Photos: 4800 |
| Color Output  | • Printers with separate cartridges for each color produce the best quality output.<br>• Inkjet and laser color printers generally have four cartridges (black, cyan, magenta, and yellow).<br>• Higher-quality printers have six cartridges (the four above plus light cyan and light magenta).<br>• With separate cartridges, you only need to replace the empty one. |
| Cost of Consumables  | • Consumables are printer cartridges and paper.<br>• Printer cartridges can exceed the cost of some printers.<br>• Consumer magazines such as *Consumer Reports* can help you research costs. |

*(Freshidea/Fotolia; Michael Nivelet/Fotolia; Thomas Amby/Fotolia; Tomislav Forgo/Fotolia)*

**Before moving on to Part 2:**

1.  Watch Chapter Overview Video 2.1.
2. Then take the Check Your Understanding quiz.

# Check Your Understanding // Review & Practice

For a quick review to see what you've learned so far, answer the following questions.

## multiple choice

1. Which of the following is not one of the four major functions of a computer?

   a. indexing

   b. processing

   c. storage

   d. output

2. Which of the following statements is FALSE?

   a. Not all cell phones are smartphones.

   b. Smartphones generally have less computing power than desktop computers.

   c. Smartphones do not contain a CPU.

   d. Smartphones are considered a type of computer.

3. Which of the following can be both an input device and an output device?

   a. display screen

   b. keyboard

   c. mouse

   d. laser printer

4. The width-to-height proportion of a monitor is known as what?

   a. viewing density

   b. viewing plane

   c. aspect ratio

   d. screen resolution

5. What type of printer works by spraying ink onto the paper?

   a. inkjet

   b. laser

   c. 3D

   d. resolution

**chew on this**

Embedded computers keep turning up in new places. They can be found in cars, household appliances, smoke detectors, and thermostats, too. Embedded computers enable us to interact with even more of these "smart" devices every day. What common objects do you think might benefit from an embedded computer? What capabilities can you envision?

**MyLab IT**  Go to **MyLab IT** to take an autograded version of the *Check Your Understanding* review and to find all media resources for the chapter.

**For the IT Simulation for this chapter, see MyLab IT.**

# Try This

## What's Inside My Computer?

Understanding what capabilities your current computer has is one of the first steps toward computer literacy. In this exercise, you'll learn how to explore the components of your Windows computer. For step-by-step instructions, watch the Chapter 2 Try This video on MyLab IT.

**Step 1** To gather information about the storage devices on your computer, click **File Explorer** from the Taskbar. Then in the navigation pane, click **This PC** to display information about your computer's storage devices and network locations.

*(Courtesy of Microsoft Corporation)*

Click to launch File Explorer

**Step 2** The **This PC** window displays information about internal storage devices (such as internal hard drives), optical storage devices (such as DVD drives), and portable storage devices (such as flash drives and external hard drives). To display the System screen, click the **Computer tab** on the ribbon, and then click **System properties**.

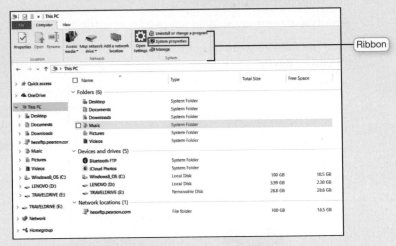

Ribbon

*(Courtesy of Microsoft Corporation)*

**Step 3** You can gather quite a bit of information from the About screen, such as:

- Version of Windows
- Type of processor
- Speed of the processor
- Amount of RAM installed
- System type (32-bit or 64-bit)

Processor info

Clock speed

RAM info

System type

Windows version

*(Courtesy of Microsoft Corporation)*

## A Mobile App

Want to build your own Android app from scratch? You can, with a simple tool called **App Inventor**. To get started, have ready:

- A computer connected to a Wi-Fi network
- The Chrome browser
- A Google account
- The MIT AI2 Companion app (available in the Google Play Store)
- [optional] An Android device connected to the same Wi-Fi network

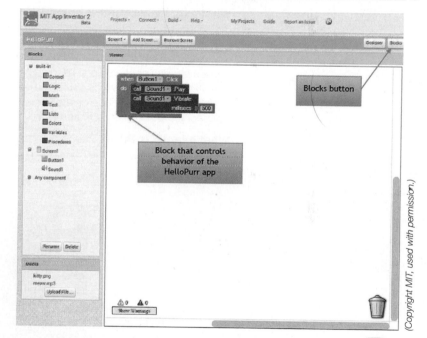

In this exercise, you'll explore the **App Inventor** tool and begin working with your first simple app. As you'll see, making your device work for you is as easy as drag and drop with **App Inventor**.

App Inventor is a programming platform used to create apps for Android devices. Using App Inventor, you can easily drag and drop components to design your app's interface and its behavior.

*(Copyright MIT, used with permission.)*

To create iOS apps, go to *Thunkable.com*, a programming platform based on App Inventor.
**For the detailed instructions for this exercise, go to MyLab IT.**

# Processing, Storage, and Connectivity

> **Learning Outcome 2.2** **You will be able to describe how computers process and store data and how devices connect to a computer system.**

So far, we have explored the components of your computer that you use to input and output data. But where does the processing take place, and where is the data stored? And how does your computer connect with peripherals and other computers?

## Processing and Memory on the Motherboard

The main processing functions of your computer take place in the CPU and memory, both of which reside on your computer's motherboard. In the following sections, we'll explore the components of the motherboard and how memory helps your computer process data.

### The Motherboard and Memory

**Objective 2.9** *Describe the functions of the motherboard and RAM.*

**What exactly is a motherboard?** The motherboard is the main circuit board that contains the central electronic components of the computing device, including the computer's processor (CPU), its memory, and the many circuit boards that help the computer function. On a desktop, the motherboard (see Figure 2.30) is located inside the system unit, the metal or plastic case that also houses the power source and all the storage devices (such as the hard drive). In a laptop, tablet, or phone, the system unit is combined with the monitor and the keyboard into a single package. Portable device motherboards are smaller, flatter, and lack expansion slots (see the image of the cell phone motherboard in Figure 2.5).

**What exactly is RAM?** Random access memory (RAM) is the place in a computer where the programs and data that the computer is currently using are stored. RAM is much faster to read

**Figure 2.30** A motherboard for a desktop computer contains the socket for the computer's processor (CPU), slots for memory (RAM) modules, ports, and slots for expansion cards. *(GIGA-BYTE Technology Co., Ltd.)*

from and write to than the hard drive and other forms of storage. The processor can request the RAM's contents, which can be located, opened, and delivered to the CPU for processing in a few nanoseconds (billionths of a second). If you look at a desktop motherboard, you'll see RAM as a series of small cards (called memory cards or memory modules) plugged into slots on the motherboard.

Because the entire contents of RAM are erased when you turn off the device, RAM is a temporary or volatile storage location. To save data permanently, you need to save it to your hard drive or to another permanent storage location, such as a flash drive or cloud storage.

**Does the motherboard contain any other kinds of memory besides RAM?** In addition to RAM, the motherboard contains a form of memory called read-only memory (ROM). ROM holds all the instructions the device needs to start up when it's powered on. Unlike data stored in RAM, which is volatile storage, the instructions stored in ROM are permanent, making ROM a nonvolatile storage location, which means the data isn't erased when the power is turned off.

**What other functionality is contained on the motherboard?** The motherboard on desktop computers also includes slots for expansion cards (or adapter cards), which are circuit boards that provide additional functionality. Typical expansion cards found in the system unit are sound and video cards. A sound card provides a connection for the speakers and microphone, whereas a video card provides a connection for the monitor. High-end gaming desktops use expansion cards to provide video and sound capabilities, making it easy for owners to upgrade to the latest video cards on the market. Laptops, tablets, and phones have video and sound capabilities integrated into their motherboards.

Other parts of the motherboard provide a means for network and Internet connections. A **network interface card (NIC)**, which enables your computer to connect with other computers or to a cable modem to facilitate a high-speed Internet connection, is often integrated into the motherboard. Wireless network interface modules provide connectivity to Wi-Fi networks. And connectivity ports such as USB and Thunderbolt ports (discussed later in this chapter) are also integrated into the motherboard.

On cell phone motherboards you'll also find a GPS (global positioning system) receiver, which is used to receive radio waves from satellites that help you pinpoint your location. The GPS receivers were initially installed in cell phones to allow the 911 emergency call operators to pinpoint the location of cell phones for people needing assistance. However, now many location-dependent apps, like Google Maps and Pokémon Go, also make use of the GPS information.

**How does GPS work?** Built and operated by the U.S. Department of Defense, the **global positioning system (GPS)** is a network of 24 satellites (plus 3 working spares) that constantly orbit Earth. GPS receivers use an antenna to pick up the signals from these satellites and use special software to transform those signals into latitude and longitude. Using the information obtained from the satellites, GPS receivers determine geographical location anywhere on the planet to within 3 feet. The exact accuracy depends on such things as atmospheric conditions and interference from obstacles like mountains or buildings.

## Processing

**Objective 2.10** *Explain the main functions of the CPU.*

**What is the CPU?** As noted earlier, the *central processing unit* (*CPU* or *processor*) is sometimes referred to as the "brains" of the computer because it controls all the functions performed by the computer's other components and processes all the commands issued to it by software instructions.

**How is processor speed measured?** Processor speed is measured in units of hertz (Hz). Hertz is a measurement of machine cycles per second. A **machine cycle** is the process of the CPU getting the data or instructions from RAM and decoding the instructions into something the computer can understand. Once the CPU has decoded the instructions, it executes them and stores the result back in system memory. Current systems run at speeds measured in gigahertz (GHz) or billions of machine cycles per second. Therefore, a 3.8 GHz processor performs work at a rate of 3.8 billion machine cycles per second. It's important to realize, however, that CPU processor speed alone doesn't determine the performance of the CPU.

Sound Byte MyLab IT

**Smartphones Are Really Smart**

In this Sound Byte, you'll learn how to use a smartphone as a powerful tool to communicate, calculate, and organize your workload.

SINGLE-CORE    DUAL-CORE

CPU            CPU

⬇ Program 1    ⬇ Program 2

**Figure 2.31** With multi-core processors, CPUs can work in parallel, processing two or more separate programs at the same time instead of switching back and forth between them.

**What else determines processor performance?** Although speed is an important consideration when determining processor performance, CPU performance is also affected by other factors. One factor is the number of cores, or processing paths, a processor has. Initially, processors could handle only one instruction at a time. Now, processors are designed so that they can have two, four, or even ten different paths, allowing them to process more than one instruction at a time (see Figure 2.31). Applications such as virus protection software and the operating system, which are always running behind the scenes, can have their own processor paths, freeing up the other paths to run other applications such as a web browser, Word, or iTunes more efficiently.

**How can I tell what processor is best for me?** The "best" processor will depend on your particular needs and is not always the processor with the highest processor speed and the greatest number of cores. Intel, one of the leading manufacturers of computer processor chips, provides a website (*ark.intel.com*) that assists in comparing the performance of different models of CPUs.

# Storing Data and Information

Because RAM is volatile storage, it can't be used to store information indefinitely. To save your data and information permanently, you need to save it to a nonvolatile storage device, such as a hard drive, cloud storage location, or flash drive.

## Storage Options on Computing Devices

**Objective 2.11**   *Describe the various means of storing data and information with computing devices.*

### Local Storage Devices

**Are there different kinds of hard drives?** The hard drive is your desktop's or laptop's primary device for permanent storage of software and documents. The hard drive is a nonvolatile storage device.

An internal hard drive resides within the desktop or laptop system unit and usually holds all permanently stored programs and data. Today's internal hard drives (see Figure 2.32) have capacities of as much as 8 TB or more. External hard drives offer similar storage capacities but reside outside the system unit and connect to the computer via a port.

The most common type of hard drive—the hard disk drive—has moveable parts—spinning platters and a moving arm with a read/write head—that can fail and lead to disk failure. However, the solid-state drive (SSD) is now a popular option for ultrabooks and laptop storage. SSDs have no moving parts, so they're more efficient, run with no noise, emit little heat, and require little power. In addition, they're less likely to fail after being bumped or dropped. Replacing a conventional hard drive in an older laptop with an SSD can often significantly improve the computer's performance.

**Figure 2.32** Internal hard drives (shown here open . . . normally they are sealed) are a desktop and laptop computer's primary nonvolatile storage. *(Mbongo/Fotolia)*

Permanent storage devices are located in your desktop or laptop computer in a space called a drive bay. There are two kinds of drive bays:

1. *Internal drive bays* cannot be seen or accessed from outside the system unit. Generally, internal drive bays are reserved for internal hard drives.

2. *External drive bays* can be seen and accessed from outside the system unit. External drive bays house DVD and Blu-ray drives, for example. On desktop computers, sometimes there are empty external drive bays that can be used to install additional drives. These extra spaces are covered by a faceplate on the front panel. Laptop computers generally do not give you the ability to add additional drives. Such expansion is done by attaching an external drive to the computer through a USB port.

## Portable Storage Options

### How can I take my files with me?
For large portable storage needs, there are portable external hard drives that are small enough to fit into your pocket and that have storage capacities of 4 TB (or more). These devices are lightweight and enclosed in a protective case. They attach to your computer via a USB port (see Figure 2.33).

A flash drive (sometimes referred to as a jump drive, USB drive, or thumb drive) uses solid-state flash memory, storing information on an internal memory chip. When you plug a flash drive into your computer's USB port, it appears in the operating system as another disk drive. You can write data to it or read data from it as you would a hard drive. Because a flash drive contains no moving parts, it's quite durable. It's also tiny enough to fit in your pocket. Despite their size, flash drives can have significant storage capacity—currently as much as 1 TB or more.

Another convenient means of portable storage is a flash memory card, such as an SD card. Like the flash drive, memory cards use solid-state flash memory. Most desktops and laptops include slots for flash memory cards. Flash memory cards let you transfer digital data between your computer and devices such as digital cameras, smartphones, tablets, video cameras, and printers. Table 2.3 compares the storage capacities of hard drives and flash drives.

### How does my cell phone store data?
Today's cell phones use various combinations of memory chips to store data. They do not contain hard drives.

### Can I increase the storage capacity of my smartphone?
Many smartphones let you add additional memory through micro SD flash cards (see Figure 2.34). Micro SD cards are easy to install inside a phone, and some models have external slots for an SD card. Not all smartphones allow memory upgrades in this way, however. For example, iPhones don't allow you to add memory.

**Figure 2.33** Smaller, portable external hard drives enable you to take a significant amount of data and programs on the road with you. *(Inga Nielsen/Shutterstock)*

**Figure 2.34** Micro SD flash cards add memory to some phones. *(Digitalr/123RF)*

| Table 2.3 | Hard Drive and Flash Drive Storage Capacity | |
| --- | --- | --- |
| **Drive Type** | **Image** | **Typical Capacity** |
| Solid-state drive (SSD) | | 1 TB or more |
| External portable hard drive | | 4 TB or more |
| Mechanical internal hard drive | | 8 TB or more |
| Flash drive | | 1 TB or more |
| Flash memory card | | 128 GB or more |

*(Oleksiy Mark/Shutterstock; Ruslan Ivantsov/Shutterstock; D. Hurst/Alamy Stock Photo; Cphoto/Fotolia; Gene Blevins/Zuma Press/Alamy Stock Photo)*

# Ethics in IT

## What Is Ethical Computing?

You've probably heard news stories about people using computers to unleash viruses or commit identity theft. You may also have read about students who were prosecuted for illegally sharing copyrighted material, such as songs and videos. These are both examples of *unethical* behavior while using a computer. However, what constitutes *ethical* behavior while using a computer?

As we discussed in Chapter 1, *ethics* is a system of moral principles, rules, and accepted standards of conduct (see Figure 2.35). So, what are the accepted standards of conduct when using computers? The Computer Ethics Institute has developed the Ten Commandments of Computer Ethics, widely cited as a benchmark for companies developing computer usage and compliance policies for employees. These guidelines are applicable for schools and students as well. The following ethical computing guidelines are based on the Computer Ethics Institute's work:

**Figure 2.35** Striving to behave ethically isn't just for "real life" interactions. It applies when using computing devices too. *(Rawpixel.com/Fotolia)*

### Ethical Computing Guidelines

1. Avoid causing harm to others when using computers.
2. Do not interfere with other people's efforts at accomplishing work with computers.
3. Resist the temptation to snoop in other people's computer files.
4. Do not use computers to commit theft.
5. Agree not to use computers to promote lies.
6. Do not use software (or make illegal copies for others) without paying the creator for it.
7. Avoid using other people's computer resources without appropriate authorization or proper compensation.
8. Do not claim other people's intellectual output as your own.
9. Consider the social consequences of the products of your computer labor.
10. Only use computers in ways that show consideration and respect for others.

The United States has enacted laws that support some of these guidelines, such as Guideline 6, the breaking of which would violate copyright laws, and Guideline 4, which is enforceable under numerous federal and state larceny laws. Other guidelines, however, require more subtle interpretation as to what behavior is unethical because there are no laws designed to enforce them.

Consider Guideline 7, which covers unauthorized use of resources. The school you attend probably provides computer resources for you to use for coursework. But if your school gives you access to computers and the Internet, is it ethical for you to use those resources to run an online business on the weekends? Although it might not be technically illegal, you're tying up computer resources that other students could use for their intended purpose: learning and completing coursework. (This behavior also violates Guidelines 2 and 10.)

Throughout the chapters in this book, we touch on various ethical situations. You will likely encounter many topics related to these guidelines. So keep them in mind as you study, and think about how they relate to the actions you take as you use computers in your life.

### Cloud Storage

**How can I easily access my files from different devices?** You may use multiple devices, such as a smartphone, laptop, and a tablet, at different times. Invariably, you'll need access to a file that is stored on a device other than the one you're using. If your devices are connected to the Internet, cloud storage provides a convenient option.

Cloud storage refers to using a service that keeps your files on the Internet (in the "cloud") rather than storing your files solely on a device. Using a cloud storage service requires that you install software or an app on your device. Popular cloud storage options include Google Drive, Microsoft's OneDrive, and Dropbox. For example, after installing the Dropbox software on your devices, any files you save in the Dropbox folder are accessible by all your other devices via the Internet. You can also share folders in Dropbox with other Dropbox users, making it ideal for group collaboration.

Most cloud storage providers give users an option of some amount of free storage, but the amount of space varies. All cloud storage providers offer additional storage space for a fee.

"Going green" is a goal for many modern businesses. Green computing (or green IT) is a movement to encourage environmentally sustainable computing. The main goal is to reduce the overall carbon footprint of a company through the strategic use of computing resources and environmentally friendly computing devices. A business's *carbon footprint* is the total amount of greenhouse gases produced directly and indirectly to support the activities of the business. Carbon footprints are expressed in equivalent tons of carbon dioxide ($CO_2$). $CO_2$ is the main greenhouse gas contributing to global warming. Reduction of greenhouse gas emissions is critical to sustaining a healthy environment.

The main goals of green computing are as follows:

1. Reducing the use of hazardous processes or materials in the production of computing equipment

2. Promoting the use of recyclable or biodegradable materials to facilitate safe disposal of products
3. Buying products that use energy efficiently
4. Using technology to reduce employee travel
5. Reducing the use of energy and consumption of materials through shared computing resources

Sharing computing resources can make a vast difference in the consumption of resources and electricity. This is one of the reasons cloud storage is becoming so popular. Rather than having 20 individual companies, each maintaining a large group of computers to hold data, savings can be achieved by having one company maintain computer resources that are able to serve the 20 other companies. However, it's not only up to businesses to practice green computing. Table 2.4 lists a few ways you can participate:

## Table 2.4    Green Computing Problems and Solutions

| Issue | Electricity | Commuting | Use Technology Longer |
|---|---|---|---|
| | | | |
| **Problems** | • Electricity is often generated using fossil fuels, which produce greenhouse gas emissions.<br>• Devices are not energy efficient. | • Cars generate greenhouse gases.<br>• Many people commute to work alone. | • Items are replaced before their useful life is over.<br>• Old items are discarded instead of continuing to be used.<br>• Technology is not disposed of or recycled properly. |
| **Solutions** | • Buy energy-efficient computing equipment with high Energy Star ratings.<br>• Turn off computing devices when not in use.<br>• Use appropriate power management settings to use less power when operating devices. | • Use technology to telecommute to your job.<br>• Use public transportation to commute, which uses energy more efficiently than cars.<br>• Use a green vehicle (bicycle, electric car) for your commute. | • Upgrade your technology only when absolutely necessary.<br>• Donate your old technology to someone who will continue to use it (friends, family, charitable organization).<br>• Dispose of electronic devices only at approved e-waste recycling facilities. |

(Kovalto1/Fotolia; MinDof/Fotolia; Marek/Fotolia)

# Connecting Peripherals to the Computer

Throughout this chapter, we have discussed peripheral devices that input, store, and output data and information. We will now look at how these types of devices are connected to computers so they can exchange data.

## Computer Ports

**Objective 2.12** *Describe common types of ports used today.*

**What is the fastest data transfer port available on today's computing devices?** A port is a place through which a peripheral device attaches to the computer so that data can be exchanged between it and the operating system. Although peripherals may connect to devices wirelessly, ports are still often used for connections. Thunderbolt is the newest input/output technology on the market. Thunderbolt ports (see Figure 2.36) are very useful for laptops and ultrabooks because one Thunderbolt port can allow you to connect up to six different peripherals to your computer. Thunderbolt 3 ports can achieve blazingly fast transfer speeds of up to 40 Gb/s. Apple was the first computer manufacturer to integrate the ports into their hardware, although other manufacturers are following suit.

**What is the most common port on digital devices?** A universal serial bus (USB) port is the port type most commonly used to connect input and output devices to the computer. This is mainly because of the ready availability of USB-compatible peripherals. USB ports can connect a wide variety of peripherals to computing devices, including keyboards, printers, mice, smartphones, external hard drives, flash drives, and digital cameras. The current USB 3.1 standard provides transfer speeds of 10 Gbps and charges devices faster than previous USB ports. USB ports come in a variety of standard and proprietary configurations (see Figure 2.37), plus the new Type-C connector (and port), which is supplanting older connector types as USB 3.1 continues to roll out (see Figure 2.38).

**Which ports help me connect with other computers and the Internet?** A connectivity port can give you access to networks and the Internet. To find a connectivity port, look for a port that resembles a standard phone jack but is slightly larger. This port is called an Ethernet port. Ethernet ports transfer data at speeds up to 10,000 Mbps. You can use an Ethernet port to connect your computer to either a cable modem or a wired network.

**How do I connect monitors and multimedia devices?** Other ports on the back and sides of the computer include audio and video ports. Audio ports are where you connect headphones, microphones, and speakers to the computer. Whether you're attaching a monitor to a desktop computer or adding a second, larger display to a laptop computer, you'll use a video port.

**Figure 2.36** Thunderbolt ports are slim and speedy, making them popular on today's ultrabooks and laptops. *(David Paul Morris/Bloomberg/ Getty Images)*

▶ Helpdesk    MyLab IT

**Exploring Storage Devices and Ports**

In this Helpdesk, you'll play the role of a helpdesk staffer, fielding questions about the computer's main storage devices and how to connect various peripheral devices to the computer.

**Figure 2.37** USB connectors come in a wide variety of styles. *(TaraPatta/Shutterstock)*

**Figure 2.38** Some computers now feature the new USB-C port that supports data transfer, video output, and charging all in a single port. *(Epa european pressphoto agency b.v/EPA/Alamy Stock Photo)*

**Figure 2.39** (a) HDMI is the industry standard digital connector type for HD monitors, TVs, and home theater equipment. (b) Cables with the appropriate connectors are available to facilitate connection of your mobile devices to your HDTV for enhanced viewing. *(Feng Yu/Shutterstock; Used with permission from Tether Tools.)*

HDMI ports are now the most common video port on computing devices. A high-definition multimedia interface (HDMI) port is a compact audio–video interface that allows both HD video and uncompressed digital audio to be carried on one cable. Because HDMI can transmit uncompressed audio and video, there's no need to convert the signal, which could ultimately reduce the quality of the sound or picture. All currently available monitors, Blu-ray players, TVs, and game consoles have at least one HDMI port (see Figure 2.39a).

If your computing device is equipped with an HDMI port, you can also choose to connect your computer directly to an HDTV using an HDMI cable. The most common HDMI connector types are shown in Figure 2.39b. Full-size (or type A) connectors are found on most TVs and laptops. Tablets and phones are more likely to have a mini (type C) or micro (type D) HDMI port.

# Power Management and Ergonomics

Conserving energy and setting up workspaces so they are comfortable are goals of many businesses. However, these are also goals to strive for at your home. In this section, we'll explore optimizing the power consumption of computing devices as well as the proper workspace setup to minimize injuries.

## Power Controls and Power Management

**Objective 2.13** *Describe how to manage power consumption on computing devices.*

**Which components of a computing device drain the battery fastest?** The number one culprit is the display. The backlights of LCD (and even OLED) displays draw a lot of power. You may love that new HD display in your phone, but your battery doesn't love it!

Wi-Fi and Bluetooth adapters also draw a lot of power because they're continuously scanning for compatible devices. In addition, any peripheral plugged into a port on your computer is most likely drawing power from the computer to function.

Certain apps are big culprits of battery drain also. Many apps continuously sync with the cloud and push alerts to you. So even though you may not be looking at an app (a *foreground* use) it is still drawing power (*background* use). Fortunately, you can determine which apps draw the most power:

- For Android devices, click Settings > Device > Battery or Settings > Power > Battery Use and you'll see a list of apps and how much battery power they're consuming.
- For iOS devices, click Settings > Battery and wait for the battery usage list to populate. Click the clock icon to display information on foreground and background power use.
- For Windows, launch Settings from the Notifications area, select System, select Battery, then click the *See which apps are affecting your battery life* link.

**Figure 2.40** The Power icon on the Windows Start menu presents several power options. *(Courtesy of Microsoft Corporation)*

> For a warm boot, choose Restart. To power down the computer completely, choose Shut down. To put your computer into a lower power mode, select Sleep.

**Figure 2.41** In Windows, you can set the options to your particular tastes to conserve power. *(Courtesy of Microsoft Corporation)*

> To access Power & sleep Settings, from the Notifications area, select **Settings**, then **System**, then select **Power & sleep**.

Consider uninstalling apps that draw a lot of background power if you rarely use them. For apps you do use frequently, consider disabling or turning off sync and alert features in the app when your battery level is low.

**How does my computer battery get its charge?** The power supply comes in the form of a brick with a cord that plugs into your portable device to charge the battery. The power supply transforms the wall voltage to the voltages required by the battery or the computer chips (if you are operating your device on a/c power). Desktop computers have their power supply housed within the system unit.

**What is the best way to turn my computer off?** In Windows and macOS, you can turn your computer completely off by displaying the power options and choosing the Shut down option (see Figure 2.40). If your computer's operating system is unresponsive, holding the power button down will force a shutdown to occur.

**Can I "rest" my computer without turning it off completely?** With many devices, an effective method of power conservation is Sleep. When your computer enters Sleep mode, all of the documents, applications, and data you were using remain in RAM (memory), where they're quickly accessible when you wake your computer.

In Sleep mode, the computer enters a state of greatly reduced power consumption, which saves energy and prolongs battery life. To put your computer into Sleep mode in Windows, display the Start menu, select Power, then select the Sleep option. To wake up your computer, press a key or the physical power button. In a few seconds, the computer will resume with the same programs running and documents displayed as when you put it to sleep.

**What's the Restart option for?** Windows and macOS power options both provide a restart option. Restarting the system while it's powered on is called a warm boot. You might need to perform a warm boot if the operating system or other software application stops responding, if you've received operating system updates, or if you've installed new apps. It takes less time to perform a warm boot than to power down completely and then restart all your hardware. Powering on your computer from a completely turned off state is called a cold boot.

**Should I turn off my computer every time I'm finished using it?** Some people argue that turning your computer on and off throughout the day subjects its components to stress because the heating and cooling process forces the components to expand and contract repeatedly. Other people say it's more environmentally friendly and less expensive to shut down your computer when you're not using it.

All modern operating systems include power-management settings that allow the most power-hungry components of the system (the hard drive and monitor) to shut down after a short idle period. The power-management options of Windows (see Figure 2.41), Android, iOS, and macOS provide you with flexibility to conserve power and battery life. Therefore, it's rarely necessary to shut your devices completely off, even when they're charging.

If you don't ever want to completely turn off your Windows laptop computer, you can change what happens when you press the power button or close the lid. By accessing the Power Options System Settings window (see Figure 2.42), you can decide if you want your computer to Sleep, Hibernate, or Shut down when you press the power button. The Hibernate option is similar to Sleep except that your data is stored on your hard drive instead of in RAM and your computer is powered off. This uses much less battery power than Sleep and is a good choice if you won't be using your laptop for a long time and won't have the opportunity to charge it.

**Define power buttons and turn on password protection**

Choose the power settings that you want for your computer. The changes you make to the settings on this page apply to all of your power plans.

🛡 Change settings that are currently unavailable

Power and sleep buttons and lid settings

|  |  | 🔋 On battery | 🔌 Plugged in |
|---|---|---|---|
| ⏻ | When I press the power button: | Sleep ⌄ | Sleep ⌄ |
| ◎ | When I press the sleep button: | Sleep ⌄ | Sleep ⌄ |
| 💻 | When I close the lid: | Sleep ⌄ | Sleep ⌄ |

| Do nothing |
| Sleep |
| Hibernate |
| Shut down |

Shutdown settings

☑ Turn on fast startup (recommended)
This helps start your PC faster after shutdown. Restart isn't affected. <u>Learn More</u>

☑ Sleep
Show in Power menu.

**Figure 2.42** You can determine what happens when you click the power button on your computer or close the lid through the Power Options System Settings screen. *(Courtesy of Microsoft Corporation)*

> *To access Power Options System Settings, from the Notifications area, select* **Settings, System, Power & sleep,** *Additional power settings, and then select* **Choose what closing the lid does.**

However, Sleep is still a good option if you just won't be using your computer for a short time. You may want to set your computer so it sleeps when you close the lid but hibernates when you press the power button, giving you quick access to either option.

## Setting It All Up: Ergonomics

**Objective 2.14** *Define ergonomics, and discuss the ideal physical setup for using computing devices.*

**What is ergonomics?** Ergonomics is the science that deals with the design and location of machines and furniture so that the people using them aren't subjected to an uncomfortable or unsafe experience. In terms of computing, ergonomics refers to how you set up your computer and other equipment to minimize your risk of injury or discomfort.

---

## Bits&Bytes    Sleep Better and Avoid Eyestrain: Use Less Blue Light

Under normal conditions, your computing device screens emit a lot of blue light. Your eyes mistake this light for that of the sun. This disrupts your biological clock and makes your brain think it needs to stay awake. To lessen this problem, most operating systems now include a setting that allows your screen to use less blue light, replacing it with warmer, softer colors (see Figure 2.43). This reduces eyestrain and helps you fall asleep faster. So check out Night Light (Windows), Night Shift (iOS), and Night Mode (Android) and fall asleep faster.

**Figure 2.43** Blue light keeps you awake, but you can set your OS to use less blue light. *(Vadym Malyshevskyi/123RF)*

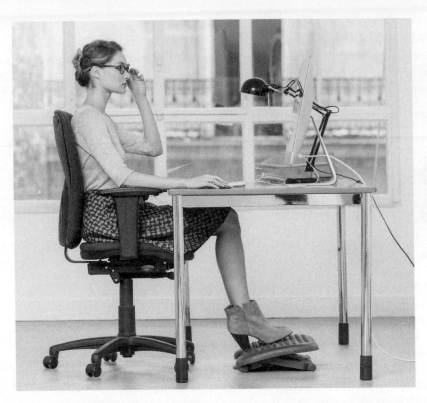

**Figure 2.44** Using proper equipment that is adjusted correctly helps prevent repetitive strain injuries while working at a computer. *(Phanie/Alamy Stock Photo)*

**Figure 2.45** To reduce the risk of repetitive strain injuries, ergonomic keyboards have curved keyboards and wrist rests to help you maintain the proper hand position while typing. *(Dgmphoto/Fotolia)*

**Why is ergonomics important?** Studies suggest that teenagers, on average, spend 7.5 hours per day using computing devices. The repetitive nature of long-term computing activities can place stress on joints, tendons, and muscles, causing repetitive stress injuries such as carpal tunnel syndrome and tendonitis. These injuries can take months or years to develop to a point where they become painful, but if you take precautionary measures now, you may prevent years of pain later.

**How can I avoid injuries when I'm working at my computer?** As Figure 2.44 illustrates, it's important to arrange your computer, chair, body, and keyboard in ways that will help you avoid injury, discomfort, and eyestrain. The following additional guidelines can help keep you comfortable and productive:

- **Position your monitor correctly.** Studies suggest it's best to place your monitor at least 25 inches from your eyes. Experts recommend that you position your monitor either at eye level or at an angle 15–20 degrees below your line of sight. If you have a laptop, this means placing the laptop on a stand (or stack of books) to achieve the correct height.
- **Purchase an adjustable chair.** Adjust the height of your chair (or use a footrest) so that your feet touch the floor. The back support needs to be adjustable so that it supports your lumbar (lower back) region. If your chair doesn't adjust, place a pillow behind your back to provide support.
- **Assume a proper position while typing.** Improperly positioned keyboards are one of the leading causes of repetitive stress injuries. Your wrists should be flat (not bent) with respect to the keyboard, and your forearms should be parallel to the floor. Additionally, your wrists should not be resting on the keyboard while typing. When using a laptop on a stand, attach an external keyboard to achieve the proper typing position. You can adjust the height of your chair or install a height-adjustable keyboard tray to ensure a proper position. Specially designed ergonomic keyboards such as the one shown in Figure 2.45 can also help you achieve the proper wrist position.
- **Take breaks.** Remaining in the same position for long periods increases stress on your body. Shift your position in your chair and stretch your hands and fingers periodically. Likewise, staring at the screen for long periods can lead to eyestrain and dry eyes, so rest your eyes periodically by taking them off the screen and focusing them on an object at least 8 feet away.
- **Ensure the lighting is adequate.** Ensuring that you have proper lighting in your work area minimizes eyestrain. Eliminate sources of direct glare (light shining directly into your eyes) or

reflected glare (light shining off the computer screen) and ensure there is enough light to read comfortably. If you still can't eliminate glare from your screen, you can buy an antiglare screen to place over your monitor.

**Is ergonomics important when using mobile devices?** Working with mobile computing devices presents interesting challenges when it comes to injury prevention. For example, many users work with laptops resting on their laps, placing the monitor outside the optimal line of sight and thereby increasing neck strain. Table 2.5 provides guidelines on preventing injuries when computing on the go.

**What devices are available for people with disabilities?** Assistive (or adaptive) technologies are products, devices, equipment, or software that are used to maintain, increase, or improve the functional capabilities of individuals with disabilities. For visually impaired users and individuals who can't type with their hand, voice recognition is a common option. For those users whose visual limitations are less severe, keyboards with larger keys are available.

People with motor control issues may have difficulty with pointing devices. To aid such users, special trackballs are available that can be manipulated with one finger and can be attached to almost any surface, including a wheelchair. When arm motion is severely restrained, head-mounted pointing devices can be used. Generally, these involve a camera mounted on the computer monitor and a device attached to the head (often installed in a hat). When the user moves his or her head, the camera detects the movement and moves the cursor. In this case, mouse clicks are controlled by a switch that can be manipulated by the user's hands or feet or even by using an instrument that fits into the mouth and senses the user blowing into it.

**Table 2.5   Preventing Injuries While on the Go**

| | Smartphone Repetitive Strain Injuries | Portable Media Player Hearing Damage | Small-Screen Vision Issues | Lap Injuries | Tablet Repetitive Strain Injuries |
|---|---|---|---|---|---|
| | | | | | |
| **Malady** | Repetitive strain injuries (such as de Quervain's disease) from constant typing of instant messages | Hearing loss from high-decibel sound levels in earbuds | Blurriness and dryness caused by squinting to view tiny screens on mobile devices | Burns on legs from heat generated by laptop | Pain caused by using tablets for prolonged periods in uncomfortable positions |
| **Preventative measures** | Restrict length and frequency of messages, take breaks, and perform other motions with your thumbs and fingers during breaks to relieve tension. | Turn down volume (you should be able to hear external noises, such as people talking), use software that limits sound levels (not to exceed 60 decibels), and use external, over-ear style headphones instead of earbuds. | Blink frequently or use eye drops to maintain moisture in eyes, after 10 minutes take a break and focus on something at least 8 feet away for 5 minutes, use adequate amount of light, and increase the size of fonts. | Place a book, magazine, or laptop cooling pad between your legs and laptop. | Restrict the length of time you work at a tablet, especially typing or gaming. Use the same ergonomic position you would use for a laptop when using a tablet. |

**Before moving on to the Chapter Review:**

1. ▶ Watch Chapter Overview Video 2.2.
2. Then take the Check Your Understanding quiz.

# Check Your Understanding // Review & Practice

For a quick review to see what you've learned so far, answer the following questions.

## multiple choice

1. Which of the following is NOT found on a motherboard?
   a. RAM
   b. hard drive
   c. ROM
   d. CPU

2. Which of these is considered the "brains" of the computer?
   a. CPU
   b. ROM
   c. RAM
   d. USB

3. Which of these has moving parts which makes them more prone to malfunction?
   a. thumb drive
   b. SSD
   c. conventional hard disk drive
   d. a flash memory card

4. Which of the following is a port?
   a. HDMI
   b. RAM
   c. ROM
   d. CPU

5. Which power control option leads to a cold boot?
   a. Sleep
   b. Restart
   c. Log off
   d. Shut down

**chew on this**

The display screen of the future may be paper-thin, flexible, and transparent. Companies like Samsung and LG are already working on it. What uses can you envision for this new technology? What advantages and disadvantages do you foresee? Do you have any suggestions for manufacturers to help make this successful?

 **MyLab IT**  Go to **MyLab IT** to take an autograded version of the *Check Your Understanding* review and to find all media resources for the chapter.

> **For the IT Simulation for this chapter, see MyLab IT.**

# 2 Chapter Review

## Summary

**Learning Outcome 2.1** **You will be able to describe the devices that make up a computer system.**

 **Understanding Your Computer**

**Objective 2.1** *Describe the four main functions of a computer system and how they interact with data and information.*

- The computer's four major functions are: (1) input: gather data or allow users to enter data; (2) process: manipulate, calculate, or organize that data; (3) output: display data and information in a form suitable for the user; and (4) storage: save data and information for later use.
- Data is a representation of a fact or idea. The number 3 and the words *televisions* and *Sony* are pieces of data.
- Information is data that has been organized or presented in a meaningful fashion. An inventory list that indicates that 3 Sony televisions are in stock is processed information. It allows a retail clerk to answer a customer query about the availability of merchandise. Information is more powerful than raw data.

**Objective 2.2** *Define bits and bytes, and describe how they are measured, used, and processed.*

- To process data into information, computers need to work in a language they understand. This language, called *binary language*, consists of two numbers: 0 and 1. Each 0 and each 1 is a binary digit or bit. Eight bits comprise one byte.
- In computers, each letter of the alphabet, each number, and each special character consists of a unique combination of eight bits (one byte)—a string of eight 0s and 1s.
- For describing large amounts of storage capacity, the terms *megabyte* (approximately 1 million bytes), *gigabyte* (approximately 1 billion bytes), *terabyte* (approximately 1 trillion bytes), and *petabyte* (1,000 terabytes) are used.

**Objective 2.3** *List common types of computers, and discuss their main features.*

- A tablet computer is a portable computer integrated into a flat multitouch-sensitive screen.
- A laptop or notebook computer is a portable computer that has a keyboard, monitor, and other devices integrated into a single compact case.
- A 2-in-1 PC is a laptop computer that can convert into a tablet-like device.
- An ultrabook is a lightweight laptop computer featuring low-power processors and solid-state drives.
- Chromebook computers use the Google Chrome OS. Documents and apps are stored primarily in the cloud.
- Desktop computers consist of a separate case (called the system unit) that houses the main components of the computer plus peripheral devices.

 **Input Devices**

**Objective 2.4** *Identify the main types of keyboards and touch screens.*

- You use physical or virtual keyboards to enter typed data and commands. Most keyboards use the QWERTY layout.
- Touch screens are display screens that respond to commands initiated by a touch with a finger or a stylus.
- Wireless keyboards mainly use Bluetooth connectivity and provide alternatives to virtual keyboards on portable computing devices.

**Objective 2.5** *Describe the main types of mice and pointing devices.*

- Mice are used to enter user responses and commands.
- Optical mice use a laser to detect mouse movement.
- Some mice can be adjusted to provide better ergonomics for users.
- Laptops have integrated pointing devices called touch pads (trackpads).

**Objective 2.6** *Explain how images, sounds, and sensor data are input into computing devices.*

- Images are input into the computer with flatbed scanners, digital cameras, camcorders, and mobile device cameras.
- Live video is captured with webcams and digital video recorders.
- Microphones capture sounds. There are many different types of microphones, including desktop, headset, and clip-on models.
- Smartphones and tablets have a variety of sensors that detect or measure a variety of inputs (such as acceleration that the device is experiencing).

 **Output Devices**

**Objective 2.7** *Describe options for outputting images and audio from computing devices.*

- Monitors display soft copies of text, graphics, and video.
- Liquid crystal display (LCD) and light-emitting diode (LED) screens are the most common types of computer monitors.

- OLED displays use organic compounds to produce light and don't require a backlight, which saves energy.
- Aspect ratio and screen resolution are key aspects to consider when choosing a monitor.
- Speakers, headphones, and earbuds are the output devices for sound.
- More sophisticated systems include subwoofers and surround sound.

**Objective 2.8** *Describe various types of printers, and explain when you would use them.*

- Printers create hard copies of text and graphics.
- There are two primary categories of printers: inkjet and laser. Laser printers usually print faster and deliver higher-quality output than inkjet printers. However, inkjet printers can be more economical for casual printing needs.
- Specialty printers are also available, such as all-in-one printers, large format printers, and 3D printers.
- When choosing a printer, you should be aware of factors such as speed, resolution, color output, and cost of consumables.

---

# Part 2
## Processing, Storage, and Connectivity

**Learning Outcome 2.2** **You will be able to describe how computers process and store data and how devices connect to a computer system.**

 **Processing and Memory on the Motherboard**

**Objective 2.9** *Describe the functions of the motherboard and RAM.*

- The motherboard, the main circuit board of the system, contains a computer's CPU, which coordinates the functions of all other devices on the computer.
- The motherboard also houses slots for expansion cards, which have specific functions that augment the computer's basic functions. Typical expansion cards are sound and video cards. In portable devices, sound and video are usually integrated directly into the motherboard.
- RAM, the computer's volatile memory, is also located on the motherboard. RAM is where data and instructions are held while the computer is running.

**Objective 2.10** *Explain the main functions of the CPU.*

- The CPU controls all the functions performed by the computer's other components. The CPU also processes all commands issued to it by software instructions.

- The performance of a CPU is mainly affected by the speed of the processor (measured in GHz) and the number of processing cores.

 **Storing Data and Information**

**Objective 2.11** *Describe the various means of storing data and information with computing devices.*

- The internal hard drive is your computer's primary device for permanent storage of software and files. The hard drive is a nonvolatile storage device, meaning it holds the data and instructions your computer needs permanently, even after the computer is turned off.
- SSD drives have no moving parts so they are more energy efficient and less susceptible to damage.
- External hard drives are essentially internal hard drives that have been made portable by enclosing them in a protective case and making them small and lightweight.
- Cloud storage refers to nonvolatile storage locations that are maintained on the Internet (in the "cloud"). Examples are OneDrive, Google Drive, and Dropbox.

- Storing your data in the cloud allows you to access it from almost any computing device that is connected to the Internet.
- Flash drives are another portable means of storing data. Flash drives plug into USB ports.
- Flash memory cards let you transfer digital data between your computer and devices such as digital cameras, smartphones, video cameras, and printers.

 **Connecting Peripherals to the Computer**

**Objective 2.12** *Describe common types of ports used today.*

- The fastest type of port used to connect devices to a computer is the Thunderbolt port.
- The most common type of port used to connect devices to a computer is the USB port.
- Connectivity ports, such as Ethernet ports, give you access to networks and the Internet.
- HDMI ports are the most common multimedia port. They are used to connect monitors, TVs, and gaming consoles to computing devices and handle both audio and video data.
- Audio ports are used to connect headphones, microphones, and speakers to computing devices.

 **Power Management and Ergonomics**

**Objective 2.13** *Describe how to manage power consumption on computing devices.*

- Turning off your computer when you won't be using it for long periods of time saves energy. In Windows, you can turn your computer off by accessing the Power option on the Start menu, then selecting Shut down.
- If you are not using your computer for short periods of time, selecting the Sleep option will help your computer save energy but allows it to be quickly "awakened" for use.

**Objective 2.14** *Define ergonomics, and discuss the ideal physical setup for using computing devices.*

- Ergonomics refers to how you arrange your computer and equipment to minimize your risk of injury or discomfort.
- Achieving proper ergonomics includes positioning your monitor correctly, buying an adjustable chair, assuming a proper position while typing, making sure the lighting is adequate, and not looking at the screen for long periods. Other good practices include taking frequent breaks and using specially designed equipment such as ergonomic keyboards.
- Ergonomics is also important to consider when using mobile devices.

**MyLab IT**   Be sure to check out **MyLab IT** for additional materials to help you review and learn. And don't forget to watch the Chapter Overview Videos.

# Key Terms

# Chapter Quiz // Assessment

For a quick review to see what you've learned, answer the following questions. Submit the quiz as requested by your instructor. If you are using **MyLab IT**, the quiz is also available there.

## multiple choice

1. Which of the following functions of a computer is mostly responsible for turning data into information?
   a. output
   b. storage
   c. input
   d. processing

2. In a computer, each _____ can represent either a 0 or a 1.
   a. byte
   b. bit
   c. integrated circuit
   d. megabyte

3. A(n) _____ is a laptop computer that can convert into a tablet-like device.
   a. 2-in-1 PC
   b. Chromebook
   c. ultrabook
   d. all-in-one PC

4. Touch-screen devices usually feature _____ keyboards.
   a. physical
   b. laser-projection
   c. virtual
   d. optical

5. Which of the following is a sensor found in certain smartphones?
   a. RAM
   b. accelerometer
   c. HDMI
   d. hygrometer

6. Ergonomics is an important consideration
   a. for all computing devices.
   b. only for laptop computers.
   c. only for laptop and desktop computers, but never for mobile devices.
   d. only for desktop computers.

7. The most common output device for hard output is a
   a. printer.
   b. scanner.
   c. speaker.
   d. display screen.

8. _____ printers work by spraying tiny drops of ink onto paper.
   a. Inkjet
   b. Cloud-ready
   c. Laser
   d. Large format

9. The most common computer port is the _____ port.
   a. USB
   b. expansion
   c. Thunderbolt
   d. Wi-Fi

10. Which component of a computing device drains the battery the fastest?
    a. hard drive
    b. display screen
    c. Wi-Fi adapter
    d. Bluetooth adapter

## true/false

_____ 1. Data and information are interchangeable terms.

_____ 2. RAM is non-volatile storage.

_____ 3. SSD drives are superior to conventional disk drives because they have no moving parts.

_____ 4. A touch pad is a pointing device usually found in tablets.

_____ 5. The "brain" of the computer is the CPU.

### What do you think now?

MIT is one of many educational institutions leading the way in researching devices for augmenting humans. Explore the Biomechatronics Group website at *biomech.media.mit.edu* and familiarize yourself with their current projects. Consider other avenues of research that you think have merit to explore. Explain what human augmentations you feel would provide the most benefits to humankind and provide rationale for your opinions.

# Team Time

## Portable Computing Options

### problem

You've joined a small business that's beginning to evaluate its technology setup. Because of the addition of several new sales representatives, customer service reps, and other administrative employees, the company needs to reconsider the various computing devices that they need. Salespeople are out in the field, as are the customer service technicians. You've been asked to evaluate options for portable computing devices.

### task

Split your class into teams of three and assign the following tasks:
- Member A explores the benefits and downfalls of smartphones.
- Member B explores the benefits and downfalls of tablets.
- Member C explores the benefits and downfalls of ultrabooks.

## process

1. Think about what the portable computing needs are for the company and what information and resources you'll need to tackle this project.
2. Research and then discuss the components of each method you're recommending. Are any of these options better suited for the particular needs of certain types of employees (sales representatives versus administrative staff)? Consider the types of battery life needed and the appropriate screen size for common tasks. How significant a factor is device weight?
3. Consider the different types of employees in the company. Would a combination of devices be better than a single solution? If so, what kinds of employees would use which type of device?
4. As a team, write a summary position paper. Support your recommendation for the company. Each team member should include why his or her portable device will or will not be part of the solution.

## conclusion

There are advantages and disadvantages to any portable computing device. Being aware of the pros and cons and knowing which device is best for a particular scenario or employee will help you to become a better consumer as well as a better computer user.

# Ethics Project

## Green Computing

Ethical conduct is a stream of decisions you make all day long. In this exercise, you'll research and then role-play a complicated ethical situation. The role you play may or may not match your own personal beliefs, but your research and use of logic will enable you to represent whichever view is assigned. An arbitrator will watch and comment on both sides of the arguments, and together, the team will agree on an ethical solution.

## background

Green computing—conducting computing needs with the least possible amount of power and impact on the environment—is on everyone's minds. Although it's hard to argue with an environmentally conscious agenda, the pinch to our pocketbooks and the loss of some comforts sometimes make green computing difficult. Businesses, including colleges, need to consider a variety of issues and concerns before jumping into a complete green overhaul.

## research areas to consider

- End-of-life management: e-waste and recycling
- Energy-efficient devices
- Renewable resources used in computer manufacturing
- Costs of green computing
- Government funding and incentives

## process

1. Divide the class into teams.
2. Research the areas cited above and devise a scenario in which your college is considering modifying its current technology setup to a greener information technology (IT) strategy.
3. Team members should take on the role of a character—for example, environmentalist, college IT administrator, or arbitrator from the scenario you devise. Each team member should write a summary that provides background information for their character and that details their character's behaviors to set the stage for the role-playing event. Then, team members should create an outline to use during the role-playing event that outlines what will occur.
4. Team members should arrange a mutually convenient time to meet, using a virtual meeting tool or by meeting in person.
5. Team members should present their case to the class or submit a PowerPoint presentation for review by the rest of the class, along with the summary and resolution they developed.

## conclusion

As technology becomes ever more prevalent and integrated into our lives, more and more ethical dilemmas will present themselves. Being able to understand and evaluate different sides of the argument, while responding in a personally or socially ethical manner, will be an important skill.

## Solve This — MyLab IT Grader

## Technology Wish List

You are in need of a significant technology upgrade, and your parents have told you they will help you finance your purchases by loaning you the money. You will need to repay them with a modest 2.5% interest rate over two years. The only catch is that they want you to create a list of all the new devices that you need, note the cost, and provide a website for each device where they can find more information. Then, they want you to calculate how much you will need to give them each month to pay them back.

You will use the following skills as you complete this activity:

- Merge and Center
- Modify Workbook Themes
- Apply Number Formats
- Use the SUM, PMT, and COUNTA Functions
- Modify Column Widths
- Insert a Hyperlink
- Create a Formula
- Wrap Text

## Instructions

1. Open *TIA_Ch2_Start.docs* and save as **TIA_Ch2_LastFirst.docx**.
2. Format the title in cell A1 with the **Title Cell Style**, and format the column headers in cells A3:F3 with the **Heading 3 Cell Style**.
   Hint: To format cell styles, on the Home tab, in the Styles group, click **Cell Styles**.
3. **Merge and Center** A1 across columns A through F, and **Center align** the column headers in cells A3:F3.
   Hint: To Merge and Center text, on the Home tab, in the Alignment group, click **Merge & Center**.
4. Modify column widths so that Column A is **25** and Column D is **45**.
   Hint: To modify column widths, on the Home tab, in the Cells group, click **Format**, and then select **Column Width**.
5. In **cells B4:E9**, fill in the table with the Brand and Model of the six devices that you would like to purchase. The device type is filled out for you. In the *Reason* column, write a brief note as to why this device will help you. (You'll format the text so it all displays later.) Enter the cost of the device in the Cost column. Don't include tax and/or shipping.
6. Change the Workbook Theme to **Integral**.
   Hint: To apply the Theme, on the Page Layout tab, in the Themes group, click Themes.
7. In **cells F4:F9**, create a **Hyperlink** to a webpage that features each respective product so your grandparents can have access to more information if they need it. Ensure that each hyperlink includes the URL to the exact webpage for the device in the Address, but displays the Make/Model of the device in the worksheet.
   Hint: To insert a hyperlink, on the Insert tab, in the Links group, click Hyperlink. In the Insert Hyperlink dialog box, enter the URL in the Address box and enter the Make/Model in the Text to display box.
8. **Wrap the text** in **cells C4:C9, D4:D9**, and **F4:F9** so all text displays.
   Hint: To wrap text, on the Home tab, in the Alignment group, click Wrap Text.
9. Format the values in **cells E4:E9** with the **Accounting Number format with two decimals**.
   Hint: To apply number and decimal formats, look on the Home tab, in the Number group.
10. In **cell A10**, type **Subtotal**, then in **cell E10** use a **SUM function** to calculate the total cost of all devices. Format the results in the **Accounting Number format with two decimals**.
    Hint: To apply number and decimal formats, look on the Home tab, in the Number group.
11. In **cell A11**, type **Estimated Tax**, then in **cell E11** create a formula that references the subtotal in cell E10 and multiplies it by a tax of 6%. Format the results in the **Accounting Number format with two decimals**.
    Hint: The formula will be =E10*0.06
12. In **cell A12**, type **Estimated Shipping**, then in **cell E12** create a formula to calculate the shipping charge by using the **COUNTA function** to determine the number of devices being purchased and then multiplying that by a $10 shipping charge. Format the results in **Accounting Number Format with two decimals**.
    Hint: The formula will be =COUNTA(B4:B9)*10.
13. In **cell A13**, type **Total Cost**, then in **cell E13** use the **SUM function** to create a formula that adds up the *Subtotal, Estimated Tax*, and *Estimated Shipping* costs. Format the results in **Accounting Number Format with two decimals**. Format the cells A13:E13 with the **Total Cell Style**.
14. **Right align** cells A10:A13.
15. In **cell D14**, type **Estimated Monthly Payment**, and then in **cell E14** use the **PMT function** to calculate the monthly payment owed to your parents to pay back the total purchase amount in two years at a 2.5% annual interest rate.
    Hint: The formula will need to adjust the annual interest rate to a monthly rate, and adjust the annual term of the loan to monthly payments.
16. Save the workbook and submit based on your instructor's directions.

# 3 Using the Internet: Making the Most of the Web's Resources

 For a chapter overview, watch the **Chapter Overview Videos**.

**MyLab IT**   All media accompanying this chapter can be found here.

**Make This**  A Web-Capable App on **page 98**

*(Smatch/Shutterstock; Marish/Shutterstock; Happy Art/Shutterstock; Robiul ctg/Shutterstock; Dinosoft Labs/Shutterstock; Panther Media GmbH/Alamy Stock Photo)*

# What do you think?

Ever seen a headline on your social media feed or in sponsored content on a website that's too tempting to ignore? You know it's probably not legit, but you click anyway. Such **sensationalized headlines are called** *clickbait*, and they're designed to tempt you to click on them. Why? Because clicking generates ad revenue. Though the term *fake news* may be reasonably new, clickbait is not. For years, people have created intentionally sensationalized headlines and photos that **bait users to click through to read what ends up being a pointless story** (hence the term clickbait). Similarly, sensationalized stories (referred to as fake news) are posted on the social web in the hopes of going viral. **Viral stories increase website traffic and that in turn generates income.** Given that sites such as Facebook and Twitter can reach billions, clickbait and fake news have become **social media plagues.** Recently, Facebook has taken strides to curtail the distribution of fake news by providing additional fact-checking information about potential fake news stories and has also cut back on the ability for clickbait sites to use Facebook advertising services. Google has also insti-tuted a policy disallowing fake news sites from using AdSense. These policy changes may help to limit fake news and clickbait, but **are we also responsible for the proliferation of this content?** If we didn't click, they wouldn't post. Where do you stand on clickbait?

Have you been enticed to click on a false story?

- Yes, I was tricked, but read the story anyway.
- Yes, I was tricked and was mad it wasted my time.
- No, I can recognize a trick headline and know not to click on it.

*See the end of the chapter for a follow-up question.*  (Prostock-studio/Shutterstock)  81

# Collaborating and Working on the Web

**Learning Outcome 3.1**  **You will be able to explain how the Internet works and how it is used for collaboration, communication, commerce, and entertainment purposes.**

You most likely know at least a bit about how to use the web's resources to communicate and collaborate with others and how business is conducted over the web. In this section, we'll explore these and related topics. But first, let's start with a brief overview of the Internet.

# The Internet and How It Works

It's hard to imagine life without the Internet. The Internet is actually a network of networks that connects billions of computer users globally, but its beginnings were much more modest.

## The Origin of the Internet

**Objective 3.1**  *Describe how the Internet got its start.*

**Why was the Internet created?** The concept of the Internet—the largest computer network in the world—was developed in the late 1950s while the United States was in the midst of the Cold War with the Soviet Union (see Figure 3.1). At that time, the U.S. Department of Defense needed a computer network that wouldn't be disrupted easily in the event of an attack.

**ASCII Code - Character to Binary**

| | | | |
|---|---|---|---|
| 0 0011 0000 | I 0100 1001 | b 0110 0010 | v 0111 0110 |
| 1 0011 0001 | J 0100 1010 | c 0110 0011 | w 0111 0111 |
| 2 0011 0010 | K 0100 1011 | d 0110 0100 | x 0111 1000 |
| 3 0011 0011 | L 0100 1100 | e 0110 0101 | y 0111 1001 |
| 4 0011 0100 | M 0100 1101 | f 0110 0110 | z 0111 1010 |
| | | g 0110 0110 | |

**1958** — The **Advanced Research Projects Agency (ARPA)** is established for the U.S. Department of Defense. This agency creates the ARPANET—the beginnings of the Internet.

**1963** — **ASCII code** is developed as the standard for computers from different manufacturers to exchange data.

**1969** — Researchers at UCLA **send the first message via a networked computer system** to researchers at Stanford University.

**1964** — A **new network scheme** is developed with multiple paths so if one communication path was destroyed (from a potential Soviet Union attack), the rest of the network would still be able to communicate.

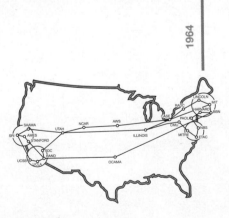

**Figure 3.1** How the Internet Began

At the same time, researchers for the Department of Defense were trying to get different computers to work with each other using a common communications method that all computers could use. The Internet was created to respond to these two concerns: establishing a secure form of communications and creating a means by which *all* computers could communicate.

**Who invented the Internet?** The modern Internet evolved from an early U.S. government-funded "internetworking" project called the Advanced Research Projects Agency Network (ARPANET). ARPANET began as a four-node network involving UCLA, Stanford Research Institute, the University of California at Santa Barbara, and the University of Utah in Salt Lake City. The first real communication occurred in 1969 between the computer at Stanford and the computer at UCLA. Although the system crashed after the third letter of "Login" was transmitted, it was the beginning of a revolution. Many people participated in the creation of the ARPANET, but two men, Vinton Cerf and Robert Kahn, are generally acknowledged as the "fathers of the Internet." These men earned this honor because in the 1970s, they were primarily responsible for developing the communications protocols (standards) still in use on the Internet today.

**So are the web and the Internet the same thing?** Because the World Wide Web (WWW or the web) is what we use the most, we sometimes think of the Internet and the web as being interchangeable. However, the web is only a subset of the Internet, dedicated to broadcasting HTML pages; it is the means by which we access information over the Internet. The web is based on the Hypertext Transfer Protocol (HTTP), which is why you see an http:// at the beginning of web addresses. What distinguishes the web from the rest of the Internet is its use of the following:

- Common communications protocols that enable computers to talk to each other and display information in compatible formats
- Special links that enable users to navigate from one place to another on the web

**Who created the web?** The web began in 1991. It was based on a protocol developed by Tim Berners-Lee, a physicist at the European Organization for Nuclear Research (CERN), who wanted a method for linking his research documents so that other researchers could access them. In conjunction with Robert Cailliau, Berners-Lee developed the basic architecture of the web and created

**1973**
**Vincent Cerf and Robert Kahn** develop a set of communication rules— the **TCP/IP protocol**— that allow different types of computers to communicate.

127.0.0.1

http://www.

**1991**
**Tim Berners-Lee** developed and made public **HTTP protocol and the World Wide Web**. WWW is a subset of the Internet that is connected via hypertext (text containing hyperlinks to other documents and media).

**1972**
**Ray Tomlinson** writes a program to send **e-mail** over the ARPANET and develops the "user@host" convention.

**1978**
By 1978, there were 111 Internet domains on ARPANET.

**1997**
By 1997, there were over 1 million Internet domains on ARPANET.

**Internet Domains (1989–1997)**

*# Domains* (y-axis: 0, 200,000, 400,000, 600,000, 800,000, 1,000,000, 1,200,000, 1,400,000, 1,600,000)

x-axis: Jul-89, Dec-89, May-90, Oct-90, Mar-91, Aug-91, Jan-92, Jun-92, Nov-92, Apr-93, Sep-93, Feb-94, Jul-94, Dec-94, May-95, Oct-95, Mar-96, Aug-96, Jan-97, Jun-97 the first web browser, software that lets you display and interact with text and other media on the web. The original browser could handle only text. Then, in 1993, the Mosaic browser, which could display graphics as well as text, was released. The once-popular Netscape Navigator browser evolved from Mosaic and heralded the beginning of the web's monumental growth.

## How the Internet Works

**Objective 3.2** *Explain how data travels on the Internet.*

**How does the Internet work?** All computers and other devices such as tablets and smartphones that are connected to the Internet create a network of networks. These Internet-connected devices communicate with each other in turns, just as we do when we ask a question or reply with an answer. Thus, a computer (or other device) connected to the Internet acts in one of two ways: Either it's a client, a computer that asks for data, or it's a server, a computer that receives the request and returns the data to the client. Because the Internet uses clients and servers, it's referred to as a client/server network.

When a client computer puts out a request for information from the server computer, the request travels along transmission lines. These transmission lines are similar to our highway system of roads, with some roads having different speed limits. The transmission lines with the fastest speeds are referred to as Internet backbones.

**How do computers talk to each other?** Suppose you want to order something from Amazon. Figure 3.2 illustrates what happens when you type *www.amazon.com* into your web browser and when Amazon's home page displays on your computer monitor. As you can see, the data request from your computer (the client computer) is sent via Internet communication pathways to a server computer. The server computer (in this case, Amazon's server) processes the request and returns the requested data to your client computer via Internet communication pathways. The data reply most likely takes a different route than did the data request. The web browser on your client computer interprets the data and displays it on its monitor.

**How does the data get sent to the correct computer?** Each time you connect to the Internet, your computer is assigned a unique identification number. This number, called an Internet Protocol (IP) address, is a set of four groups of numbers separated by periods, such as 123.45.245.91, and is commonly referred to as a dotted quad or dotted decimal. IP addresses are the means by which computers connected to the Internet identify each other. Similarly, each website is assigned a unique IP address. However, because the numbers that make up IP addresses

**STEP 4**: The server returns the requested data to your computer using the fastest pathway, which may be different from the one the request took.

**STEP 3**: Your data flows along the backbone and on to smaller pathways until it reaches its destination, which is the server computer for Amazon's website.

**STEP 5**: The web browser interprets the data and displays it on your monitor.

**STEP 2**: The request is sent to the server via a system of data pathways, similar to a roadway system.

**STEP 1**: You enter www.amazon.com in your web browser. Your computer is the client requesting information from Amazon.com's website.

Amazon.com's server

Client

**Figure 3.2** How the Internet's Client/Server Model Works *(Phonlamai Photo/Shutterstock; Cigdem/Shutterstock)*

are difficult for people to remember, websites are given text versions of their IP addresses. So, Amazon's website has an IP address of 72.21.211.176 and a name of *www.amazon.com*. When you enter *www.amazon.com* into your browser, your computer (with its unique IP address) looks for Amazon's IP address (72.21.211.176). Data is exchanged between Amazon's server computer and your computer using these unique IP addresses.

 # Collaborating and Communicating on the Web

Collaborating, or working together to achieve a common goal, is often done in the classroom, in business, and even at home. The advancement in web technologies has facilitated the collaboration process in many ways, especially enabling participants to collaborate from distant locations. In this section, we'll explore some popular means of collaborating on the web.

## Collaborating with Web Technologies

**Objective 3.3** *Evaluate the tools and technologies used to collaborate on the web.*

**How do we collaborate on the web?** Over time, our use of the web has evolved from passively browsing web pages that were created for us, to actively creating our own web content and sharing and collaborating on it with others. This collaborative, user-created web, sometimes classified as the *social web*, is possible due to Web 2.0 technologies. Web 2.0 technologies enable us to collaborate with others on documents through web applications such as Google Drive, to collaborate on projects with tools such as Slack and Basecamp, to rate and recommend products or services with Yelp, to make business connections on social networks such as LinkedIn, and to share a video on YouTube or a favorite image on Pinterest. These means of Web 2.0 communication are collectively called social media and include social networking, project collaboration and file sharing tools, blogs, podcasts, webcasts, and media sharing.

### Social Networking

**Is there more to social networking than Facebook, Snapchat, and Twitter?** Social networking refers to using the web to communicate and share information among your friends and others. Professional, business-oriented online networks such as LinkedIn are helpful for members seeking clients, business opportunities, jobs, or job candidates. Like a true business network, these sites can help you meet other professionals through connections with people you already know. In addition, businesses use social networking for marketing and communicating directly with their customers. For example, companies may post special deals and offers on their Facebook page or solicit responses from LinkedIn followers that may help with product development or future marketing campaigns. Table 3.1 lists social networking sites.

**What are some dos and don'ts of social networking?** When social networking sites first became popular, there was concern over privacy issues, especially for school-aged children who put personal information on their pages without considering the possibility of that information being misused by a stalker or identity thief. Until recently, users believed that improved privacy policies of most social media sites offered enough protection. But privacy violations, such as the Facebook/Cambridge Analytica scandal, are a reminder that personal vigilance and oversite is always necessary. Users must be cautious about the type of content they post on these sites. Consider these precautions as you use social networking sites:

- Keep your personal information personal. The year you were born, your physical address, and the routines of your life (sports games, practices, work schedules) should not be broadcast to the general public.
- Know who your friends are and know who can see the information you post. Review your privacy settings periodically, as sites change and update their privacy practices frequently.
- Do not post information you might use to set up security questions such as your pet's name.
- Use caution when posting images and know what images others are posting of you. Although privacy settings may offer some comfort, some images may be available for viewing through search engines and may not require site registration to be seen. Online images may become public property and subject to reproduction, and you might not want some—or any—of those images to be distributed.

## Table 3.1  Types of Social Networking Sites

| Social Communication | Media Sharing | Business Networking and Collaboration | Information Sharing |
|---|---|---|---|
|  |  |  |  |
| • Facebook<br>• Tumblr<br>• Twitter<br>• Snapchat<br>• Viber<br>• WhatsApp | • Bandcamp<br>• Flickr<br>• Instagram<br>• Periscope<br>• Pinterest<br>• Spotify<br>• YouTube | • Kickstarter<br>• LinkedIn<br>• Slack<br>• StartupNation | • Digg<br>• Reddit<br>• SlideShare<br>• StumbleUpon |

| Social Commerce and Payment | Social Travel | Health and Fitness |
|---|---|---|
|  |  |  |
| • GoFundMe<br>• Groupon<br>• LivingSocial<br>• PayPal<br>• SquareCash<br>• Venmo | • Airbnb<br>• TripAdvisor<br>• Uber<br>• Waze | • Fitocracy<br>• Happier<br>• MapMyFitness<br>• MyFitnessPal |

*(Rvector/Shutterstock; Best4u/Shutterstock; Aha-Soft/Shutterstock; Blan-k/Shutterstock; ValentinT/Shutterstock; Kristinasavkov/Shutterstock; Sarahdesign/Shutterstock)*

Many employers and colleges use social networks as a means of gaining information about potential applicants before granting an interview or extending admission or a job offer. In fact, people have been fired from their jobs and expelled from schools for using social media, such as Facebook, Twitter, and blogs, in a questionable way. Generally, questionable content on social media includes negative discussion about the poster's job, employer, or colleagues, or inappropriate content about the poster. The responsibility for your content rests with you. Even though you may have strong privacy settings, you can't control what those who you allow to see your content do with it. Therefore, treat all information posted on the web as public, and avoid posting damaging words and pictures. Bottom line: Make sure your profile, images, and site content project an image that positively and accurately represents you.

### Project Collaboration and File Sharing Tools

**What tools are used when collaborating on a project?** Rather than needing to pass documents back and forth via e-mail and possibly losing track of which version is the most recent, file sharing tools are very useful. Web-based document products such as Google Docs and Microsoft Office Online have features to promote online collaboration. These products offer wiki-like capabilities that allow users to add, remove, or edit a document's content in real time. A wiki is a document created collaboratively by multiple users, resulting in an emergent "common" output rather than multiple outputs of individual writers. Wikis allow all who have access to the wiki page to post their ideas and modify the content of the current version of a single document. Wikis provide the extra benefit of users being able to access, review, and even revert to past versions at any time.

**What other web tools are used to help with project collaborations?** In addition to using wikis and wiki-like documents, videoconferencing, screen sharing, and project management tools are used to facilitate collaboration. Full-featured business enterprise solutions are available, but for smaller collaborative projects, such as those you might encounter in a group project for school, you have a variety of web-based options to choose from, many of which are free. Project management tools incorporate tasks and calendars so a project can stay on schedule. Trello, for example, is a free project management tool that organizes projects onto boards and specific tasks onto cards. Cards can contain checklists, images, labels, discussion notes, and the like. All cards are searchable, shareable, and can have reminders. Slack is another popular project management tool that incorporates text messaging, file sharing, and other collaborative features.

When working with a group whose members are not in the same location, screen sharing or videoconferencing software can be helpful. Products such as Join.me and Screenleap offer free screen-sharing solutions, and Skype and Google Hangouts are handy solutions for videoconferencing.

### Blogs

**What is a blog?** A blog (short for weblog) is a personal log or journal posted on the web. Anyone can create a blog, and there are millions of blogs available to read, follow, and comment on. Blogs are generally written by a single author and are arranged as a listing of entries on a single page, with the most recent blog entry appearing at the top of the list. In addition, blogs are public, and readers can post comments on a blog, often creating an engaging, interactive experience. Blogs have searchable and organized content, making them user friendly. They're accessible from anywhere using a web browser. While blogs tend to be delivered on individual websites, some mobile apps have integrated blogs, such as the one affiliated with MyFitnessPal that gives weight loss tips and healthy recipes. Many corporations, such as Walmart and Best Buy, have blogs written by employees. BlogCatalog is a blog directory that can help you find blogs that fit your interests.

**Why do people write blogs?** Many people use blogs as a means to express themselves and share their story, experiences, or ideas. Some bloggers focus on a particular niche or demographic, at times becoming "influencers" of products or services because of their perceived knowledge and expertise. Some other blogs focus on a particular topic, such as Engadget, which discusses technogadgets. Bloggers are often attracted to this medium because of the community a blog creates through the comments and interaction of its readers. Additionally, some bloggers begin in hopes of making money by using tools such as Google's AdSense and Amazon's Associates programs. Although not every blog is guaranteed to generate large sums, bloggers with strong followings can earn a good income over time.

**Are all blogs text-based?** The traditional form of a blog is primarily text-based but may also include images and audio. A video log (vlog or video blog) is a blog that uses video as the primary content (although it can also contain text, images, and audio). Vlogs are a popular means of personal expression, and many can be found by searching YouTube.

**How do I create a blog?** Many websites provide the tools you need to create your own blog. Two sites that offer free blog hosting are Blogger and WordPress. Such tools also let you add features like pictures or subpages to your blog. You can also choose to host your blog yourself so that the URL reflects your name or the name of your business. If you choose this option, you'll need your own website and a URL so people can access it.

**Are there any problems with blogs?** The popularity of blogs has brought about spam blogs (splogs), which are artificially created blog sites filled with fake articles or stolen text (a tactic known as blog scraping). Splogs, which contain links to other sites associated with the splog's creator, have the intention of either increasing traffic to, or increasing search engine rankings for, these usually disreputable or useless websites. Although not really harmful, splogs are another unwanted form of content that continues to flourish on the web.

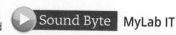 **Sound Byte**    MyLab IT

**Blogging**

In this Sound Byte, you'll see why blogs are one of today's most popular publishing mediums. You'll also learn how to create and publish your own blog.

**Figure 3.3** Many online news and radio sites offer podcasts of their programs. *(Dwd-Media/Alamy Stock Photo)*

**Are Twitter and Tumblr considered blogs?** Twitter and Tumblr are examples of microblogs, where users post short text with frequent updates. With Twitter, the posts are limited to 280 characters. Twitter and Tumblr also allow users to post multimedia and other content. Posts can be public or restricted to a certain audience.

### Podcasts

**How can I distribute audio or video files over the Internet to a wide audience?** A podcast is a series of audio or video files that are distributed over the Internet (see Figure 3.3). There are podcasts for radio shows, audiobooks, magazines, and even educational programs, which you can download to your device. Although many podcasts are news related, others offer entertaining and educational content. For example, you can access lessons on yoga, foreign language classes, or do-it-yourself tips. What makes podcasts different from other audio files found on the web is that podcasts deliver their content using Really Simple Syndication (RSS). RSS is a format that sends the latest content of the podcast series automatically to an aggregator such as Overcast or Apple Podcast. An aggregator locates all the RSS series to which you've subscribed and automatically downloads only the new content to your device. If you have several favorite websites or podcasts, rather than checking each site for updated content, aggregators collect all the site updates in one place. These updates or changes to the content are then delivered automatically if you subscribe to the podcast, instead of requiring you to search for the latest content and download it manually.

**Where can I find podcasts?** Most online news and radio sites offer podcasts of their programs. Many schools supply students with course content updates through podcasts, and instructors sometimes create podcasts of their lectures. Table 3.2 lists some websites where you can find podcasts.

**Can I create my own podcast?** It's simple to create a podcast. To record the audio content, all you need is a computer with a microphone, and if you want to make a video podcast, you also need a webcam or video camera. Although high-end equipment will produce more sophisticated output, you certainly can use whatever equipment you might own. You may also need additional software to edit the audio and video content, depending on how professional you wish the podcast to be. After you've recorded and edited the podcast content, you need to export it to MP3 format. The free program Audacity (*audacity.sourceforge.net*) lets you both edit audio files and export them to MP3 format. All that's left for you is to create an RSS feed (tricky, but doable) and then upload the content to a site that hosts podcasts, such as iTunes, PodSearch, or Stitcher.

### Webcasts

**What is a webcast?** A webcast is the (usually live) broadcast of audio or video content over the Internet. Unlike podcasts, which are prerecorded and made available for download, most webcasts are distributed in "real time," meaning they're live or one-time events. Some webcasts are archived so they can be viewed later. Unlike podcasts, webcasts are not updated automatically.

| Table 3.2  Podcast Directories and Aggregators |
|---|
| **Overcast (overcast.fm)** |
| • Podcast player for Apple mobile devices. |
| **PodSearch (podsearch.com)** |
| • Broad collection of podcasts |
| **Stitcher (stitcher.com)** |
| • Customize podcast playlists |
| **YouTube (youtube.com)** |
| • Good source for video blogs (vlogs) |

Webcasts use continuous audio and video feeds, which let you view and download large audio and video files. Webcasts can include noninteractive content, such as a simultaneous broadcast of a radio or television program, but some webcasts invite interactive responses from the audience. For example, ConcertWindow enables musicians to broadcast live to their fans, and ORLive provides surgical webcasts that demonstrate the latest surgical innovations and techniques. Webcasts also are used in the corporate world to broadcast annual meetings and in the educational arena to transmit seminars.

### Media Sharing Platforms

**Where can I share music, pictures, and videos on the web?** Social media sharing sites such as Instagram, YouTube, Flickr, and SoundCloud enable anyone to create and share multimedia. Instagram is primarily a mobile app that allows users to take photos on their device, add a caption, and then upload them. YouTube enables users to upload videos offering a variety of content. Some YouTube videos are shared or viewed by so many that they go "viral." Instagram was created to store and share photos online. Instagram enables users to tag not only their images but also others' images, thus providing a strong search capability to quickly locate images with similar tags. SoundCloud is both a distribution platform and a music streaming service. Fledgling musicians can upload original music to share, and music enthusiasts can track and follow new and favorite artists.

## Communicating over the Web

**Objective 3.4** *Summarize the technologies used to communicate over the web.*

**Why do I still need e-mail?** Despite the popularity of social media, e-mail (short for *electronic mail*)—a written message sent or received over the Internet—still remains the most widely used form of communication on the Internet. E-mail is the primary method of electronic communication worldwide because it's fast and convenient. And because it's asynchronous, users do not need to be communicating at the same time. They can send and respond to messages at their own convenience. E-mail is also convenient for exchanging files via attachments.

**How private is e-mail?** Although e-mail is a more private exchange of information than public social networking sites, e-mails are not really private. Consider the following:

- Because e-mails can be printed or forwarded to others, you never know who may read your e-mail.
- Most e-mail content is not encrypted, so you should never use e-mail to send personal or sensitive information, such as bank account or Social Security numbers. Doing so could lead to your identity being stolen.
- Employers have the right to access to e-mail sent from the workplace, so use caution when putting negative or controversial content in e-mail from your workplace.
- Even after you've deleted a message, it doesn't really vanish. Many Internet service providers and companies archive e-mail, which can be accessed or subpoenaed in the event of a lawsuit or investigation.

**What are some tips on e-mail etiquette?** When you write a casual e-mail to friends, you obviously don't need to follow any specific e-mail guidelines. But when you send e-mail for professional reasons, you should use proper e-mail etiquette. The following are a few guidelines (see Figure 3.4):

- Be concise and to the point.
- Use the spell-checker and proofread your e-mail before sending it.
- Avoid using abbreviations such as u, r, LOL, and BTW.
- Include a meaningful subject line to help recipients prioritize and organize e-mails.
- Add a signature line that includes your contact information.
- Include only those people on the e-mail who truly need to receive it.

Following such guidelines maintains professionalism, increases efficiency, and might even help protect a company from lawsuits.

**Are there different types of e-mail systems?** There are two different types of e-mail systems:

1. Web-based e-mail, such as Yahoo! Mail or Gmail, is managed with your web browser and allows you to access your e-mail with an Internet connection.
2. A desktop client requires a program, such as Microsoft Outlook, to be installed on your computer. When you open the program, your e-mail is downloaded to your computer.

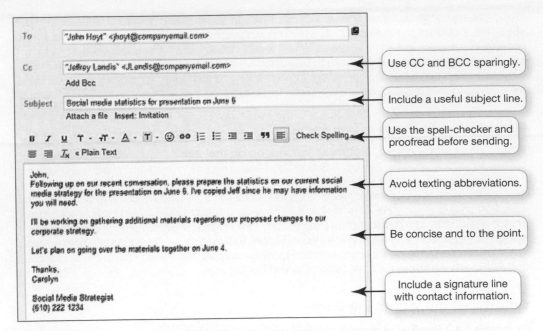

To: "John Hoyt" <jhoyt@companyemail.com>

Cc: "Jeffrey Landis" <JLandis@companyemail.com>
Add Bcc

Use CC and BCC sparingly.

Subject: Social media statistics for presentation on June 6
Attach a file   Insert: Invitation

Include a useful subject line.

B  I  U  T ▾  ᵀT ▾  A ▾  T ▾  ☺  ∞  ≔  ⋮≡  ⫤  ⫧  "  ≣   Check Spelling

Use the spell-checker and proofread before sending.

≣  ≣  𝐼ₓ  « Plain Text

John,
Following up on our recent conversation, please prepare the statistics on our current social media strategy for the presentation on June 6. I've copied Jeff since he may have information you will need.

Avoid texting abbreviations.

I'll be working on gathering additional materials regarding our proposed changes to our corporate strategy.

Be concise and to the point.

Let's plan on going over the materials together on June 4.

Thanks,
Carolyn

Social Media Strategist
(610) 222 1234

Include a signature line with contact information.

**Figure 3.4** Using simple guidelines of e-mail etiquette can promote a professional image and make your message more effective. *(Courtesy of Google, Inc.)*

The primary difference between the two is access. Web-based e-mail allows you to access e-mail from any Internet-connected device. With a desktop client, you view your e-mail on the computer on which the desktop client software has been installed. With web-based e-mail, you cannot send or receive e-mail unless you are online. Desktop clients often have integrated functionalities such as calendar, meetings, and task management, though some web-based e-mail clients are beginning to offer some of these functionalities as well. You can set up either e-mail system to display e-mail from other web-based or desktop client accounts. So, if you have separate work, school, and personal e-mail accounts, and use both desktop and web-based e-mail systems, you can limit the need to have multiple accounts and systems open at the same time.

**What is texting?** Texting (also known as text messaging) is a popular means of sending short electronic messages between two or more mobile devices. Texting uses Short Message Service (SMS) for text-based messages and Multimedia Message Service (MMS) to send images or videos. Texting uses the same cellular network you use to send voice-calls from your mobile device. Think of texting as a written voice-call. Snapchat is a popular messaging app that uses MMS so users can send brief videos or images. An aspect of Snapchat that differentiates it from text messaging is that once a message is opened, the video or image is available to be viewed for only a brief amount of time and is generally not able to be saved.

**Who uses instant messaging?** Instant messaging (IM) is a way of communicating in real time over the Internet and only requires an Internet connection. IM does not use cellular data. With greater access to WiFi, IM remains a popular means of communication and is great to use when access to your cellular network is unavailable or limited, such as when traveling abroad. Some IM programs let you conduct video chats with one or more persons using a webcam. Some of the more popular IM apps include Facebook Messenger, Google Hangouts, Viber, and WhatsApp. IM services are proprietary, meaning you can IM or chat only with those who share the same IM service. For example, you cannot use Facebook Messenger to send a message to a Google Hangouts user or vise-versa.

IM is also an important means of quick and efficient communication in the business world. In fact, some IM services, such as Cisco Jabber and Oracle Beehive, have been developed primarily for business use. IM is also great for business communications because you can monitor who is allowed to contact you, and people can communicate with you only if they know your exact e-mail or IM address.

**Can I make phone calls over the Internet?** Using apps such as Skype, FaceTime, or Google Hangouts, users can communicate using audio (voice) and video. These services use VoIP (Voice over Internet Protocol), a fully digital phone service that allows calls to be transmitted over the Internet rather than over traditional phone lines or cellular networks (see Figure 3.5).

Traditional telephone communications use analog voice data and telephone connections. In contrast, VoIP uses technology similar to that used in e-mail to transmit your voice data digitally over the

Internet. VoIP calls can be placed from anywhere you have Internet access. Major ISPs, like Comcast and Verizon, provide VoIP phone services as an option you can package with your Internet or cable plan. Sometimes these services require stand-alone VoIP phones, sometimes called IP phones.

**What are the advantages and disadvantages of VoIP?** For people who make many long-distance phone calls, the advantage of VoIP is that it is free or low cost. Portability is another advantage: As long as you are connected to the Internet, you can sign on to your VoIP service and make your call.

Some people regard sound quality and reliability issues as VoIP's primary disadvantages. Additionally, when using VoIP at home, you lose service if power is interrupted. Another issue with VoIP is security risks. Having a hacker break in to a VoIP system to make unauthorized calls is a serious but avoidable problem. Encryption services that convert data into a form not easily understood by unauthorized people are being deployed to help protect calls made over the Internet.

Table 3.3 lists the popular methods of online collaboration and communication that we've discussed.

**Figure 3.5** VoIP technology lets your computing device behave like a phone or video phone. (*David Malan/The Image Bank/Getty Images*)

## Table 3.3 Methods of Online Collaboration and Communication

| Social Networking | Project Collaboration and File Sharing | Blogs | Podcasts | Webcasts |
|---|---|---|---|---|
|  |  |  |  |  |
| • Web 2.0 technology<br>• Lets you build an online network of friends<br>• Lets you share media content | • Web-based document products such as Google Docs<br>• Screen sharing<br>• Project management<br>• Videoconferencing<br>• Wikis | • Written by a single author<br>• Chronologic entries<br>• Searchable content<br>• May include images, audio, and video | • Audio/video files delivered via RSS<br>• New RSS content collected with aggregator<br>• Can download and view content on portable media player | • Most often live, streamed broadcasts |

| Media Sharing | E-Mail | Instant Messaging | Texting | VoIP |
|---|---|---|---|---|
|  |  |  |  |  |
| • Platforms to host and share images, videos, and music<br>• Some have more social networking aspects than others | • Most common form of online communication<br>• Asynchronous (not having to be done at the same time) | • Real-time communication<br>• Requires Internet connection<br>• Used with individuals or groups<br>• Capable of doing video/audio chats | • Needs cellular network<br>• Uses Short Messaging Service (SMS) for text messages<br>• Uses Multimedia Message Service (MMS) for video and audio messages | • Voice communication via Internet<br>• Free or low-cost calls<br>• Some reliability issues |

*(Creative Stall/Shutterstock; Creative Stall/Shutterstock; VectorsMarket/Shutterstock; Icon99/Shutterstock; RedlineVector/Shutterstock; Marnikus/Shutterstock; Vlad Kochelaevskiy/Shutterstock; Jemastock/Shutterstock; Sky vectors/Shutterstock; Yuriy Vlasenko/Shutterstock)*

# Conducting Business on the Web

You can buy nearly anything on the web, including big-ticket items such as homes and cars. Now, with mobile apps, there is even greater ability to conduct business from virtually any location, at any time. In this section, we'll take a look at e-commerce and mobile commerce.

## Conducting Business Online

**Objective 3.5** *Describe how business is conducted using the Internet.*

**What are the different types of e-commerce?** E-commerce—short for electronic commerce—is the process of conducting business online. Typically, e-commerce is identified by whom the business is being conducted between:

1. Business-to-consumer (B2C) transactions take place between businesses and consumers. Such transactions include those between customers and completely online businesses, such as Amazon, and those between customers and stores that have both an online and a physical presence, such as Target. Businesses with an online and physical presence are referred to as click-and-brick businesses. Some click-and-bricks allow online purchases and in-store pickups and returns.

2. Business-to-business (B2B) transactions occur when businesses buy and sell goods and services to other businesses. An example is Omaha Paper Company, which distributes paper products to other companies.

3. Consumer-to-consumer (C2C) transactions occur when consumers sell to each other through sites such as eBay, Craigslist, and Etsy.

Social commerce is a subset of e-commerce that uses social networks to assist in marketing and purchasing products. Consumers are voicing their opinions on Facebook and other social media sites about products and services by providing ratings and reviews, and studies show that such peer recommendations have a major influence on buying behavior. When you see your friend on Facebook recommend a product or service, you're more likely to click through to that retailer and check out the product.

Other peer-influenced e-commerce trends include group-buying and individual customization. Groupon and LivingSocial are two popular deal-of-the-day group purchase services that offer discounted deals. CafePress and Zazzle sell T-shirts and other items that are customized with your own graphic designs.

E-commerce encompasses more than just online shopping opportunities from your desktop or laptop computers. Mobile commerce (or m-commerce) is conducting commercial transactions through a smartphone, tablet, or other mobile device. Apple Pay, Venmo, and other digital payment systems are becoming quite popular, as is making payments using proprietary mobile apps such as at Starbucks. Many businesses push coupons and offers through their mobile apps to customers using location-based services when the customer is nearby. Some fast-food places and restaurants such as Panera and Dominos enable you to place an order via their mobile app for in-store pick-up or delivery. Mobile commerce also includes services that enable users to check their bank and credit card account balances, deposit checks, pay bills online, and manage investment portfolios. Tickets and boarding passes can also be sent to smartphones, adding another level of convenience.

## E-Commerce Safeguards

**Objective 3.6** *Summarize precautions you should take when doing business online.*

**Just how safe are online transactions?** When you buy something online, you may use a credit card; therefore, money is exchanged directly between your credit card company and the online merchant's bank. Because online shopping eliminates a salesclerk or other human intermediary from the transaction, it can actually be safer than traditional retail shopping.

**What precautions should I take when shopping online?** In addition to using some basic common computing sense such as having a firewall and up-to-date antivirus software on your computer, and using strong passwords for all your online accounts, there are several

Have you ever done any of the following?

- Posted pictures on Instagram that your friends accessed from their iPhone
- Used Dropbox or OneDrive to store your files
- Used Google Docs or Microsoft Office Online to collaborate on a project
- Used IDrive to back up your data

By doing any of these activities, you have participated in cloud computing. So what exactly is cloud computing?

**Cloud computing** refers to storing data, files, and applications on the web and being able to access and manipulate these files and applications from any Internet-connected device. Being able to work from the cloud eliminates the need to have everything stored on your own computer's drives and lets you access your pictures, music, files, and programs from any device as long as you have access to the Internet. In addition, cloud computing makes it easier to collaborate and communicate with others and can cut down on administrative tasks for organizations maintaining large amounts of computer hardware and software.

There are two sides to cloud computing (see Figure 3.6):

1. The *front end* is the side we see as users. It involves a web browser like Google Chrome, Microsoft Edge, or Mozilla Firefox.
2. The *back end* consists of various data centers and server farms that house the files and programs you access "on the cloud." These data centers and server farms are warehouses full of computers and servers, and they are being created all over the world, providing us with "cloud storage." The computers in the data centers or server farms are designed to work together, adjusting to the varying degrees of demand placed on them at any time.

Google is one of the first true explorers in the cloud, building applications such as Google Drive, Gmail, and the Chrome web browser in an effort to create a completely virtual operating environment. A fully functioning operating environment would enable users to sign in on any computer and have "their" computer setup (desktop configurations and images, programs, files, and other personalized settings) display. Additionally, cloud computing would reduce the need for all of us to have the fastest computers with the most memory and storage capabilities. Instead, we could all have simple front-end terminals with basic input and output devices because the computers on the back end will be providing all the computing muscle.

The Chromebook is Google's first attempt at a notebook where all the applications and files are stored on the web. Little is installed or saved to a hard drive, not even the operating system! All programs are accessed and all work is done through the web-based browser, so sending e-mail, editing photos, and working on documents are all done via web-based applications. Because the Chromebook requires an Internet connection to get most tasks done, users must be near a Wi-Fi connection or pay for a data plan.

There are some considerations with cloud computing:

- *Security and privacy:* Right now, the security of information stored on the web is built on trusting that the passwords we set and

**Figure 3.6** There are two sides to cloud computing: the side we see as users and the banks of computers and servers that house the files and programs we access. *(godshutter/ Shutterstock; SFIO CRACHO/Shutterstock; Yakobchuk Viacheslav/Shutterstock Ferenc Szelepcsenyi/ Shutterstock; Anatolii Babii/Alamy Stock Photo; Alamy; rvlsoft/Shutterstock; Digitallife/Alamy Stock Photo; Used with Permission from Dropbox Inc; Courtesy of Google Inc.; PhotoEdit/Alamy Stock Photo)*

the security systems that the data centers put in place are able to keep our information away from unauthorized users. Caution is always warranted, as nothing is completely safe and private.

- *Backup:* Because even the devices in these large data centers and server farms inevitably will break down, the cloud computing systems have redundant systems to provide backup. However, for critical files that you must have, it might be a good idea not to completely rely on the cloud, but to have your own offline backup system as well.
- *Access issues:* With cloud computing, you access your files and programs only through the Internet. If you couldn't access the Internet due to a power failure or system failure with your Internet service provider, you wouldn't be able to access your files. Storing your most critical files and programs offline will help reduce the inconvenience and loss of productivity while access to the Internet is being restored.

Before relying on cloud computing, weigh the above concerns against the convenience of having your information when and where you want it and the ability to promote better collaboration.

important guidelines to follow to ensure your online shopping experience is a safe one (see Table 3.4):

- Look for visual indicators that the website is secure. Check that the beginning of the URL changes from "http://" to "https://"—with the s standing for secure, indicating that the secure sockets layer protocol has been applied to manage the security of the website. Also, look for a small icon of a closed padlock in the address bar (in both Microsoft Edge and Firefox) and a green-colored text or a green address bar—indications that the site may be secure. (However, note that even if a site has these indicators, it still might not be safe. Consider the validity of the site before making a purchase.)

- Shop at well-known, reputable sites. If you aren't familiar with a site, investigate it with the Better Business Bureau or at Bizrate. Make sure the company has a phone number and street address in addition to a website. You can also look for third-party verification such as that from TrustArc or the Better Business Bureau. But let common sense prevail. Online deals that seem too good to be true are generally just that—and may be pirated software or illegal distributions.

- Pay by credit card, not debit card. Federal laws protect credit card users, but debit card users don't have the same level of protection. If possible, reserve one credit card for Internet purchases only; even better, use a prepaid credit card that has a small credit limit. For an extra layer

### Table 3.4 Online Shopping Precautions

| | | | |
|---|---|---|---|
|  |  |  |  |
| When shopping at home, use a firewall and antivirus software for general computer protection. | Don't shop on public Wi-Fi networks, as they may contain spyware. | Check for visual indicators such as https:// in the URL, a closed padlock icon, and green text or a green address bar. | Look for third-party verification from TrustArc or the Better Business Bureau symbol. |
|  |  |  |  |
| Use a credit card, not a debit card, to protect transactions, or use a third-party payer such as PayPal or Apple Pay. | Create a strong password for all online accounts (one that includes numbers and other symbols such as @). | Deals that are too good to be true are usually just that. | Read and understand the fine print on warranties, return policies, and the retailer's privacy statements. |

*(Beboy/Shutterstock; Photoinnovation/Shutterstock; Roy Wylam/Alamy Stock Photo; Ferenc Szelepcsenyi/Shutterstock; Maxx-Studio/Shutterstock; Isak55/Shutterstock; Alhovik/Shutterstock; Shutterstock)*

of security, find out if your credit card company has a service that confirms your identity with an extra password or code that only you know to use when making an online transaction or that offers a one-time-use credit card number. Also, consider using a third-party payment processor such as PayPal or Apple Pay. PayPal also offers a security key that provides additional security to your PayPal account.

- When you place an order, check the return policy, save a copy of the order, and make sure you receive a confirmation number. Make sure you read and understand warranties, return policies, and the retailer's privacy statements. If the site disappears overnight, this information may help you in filing a dispute or reporting a problem to a site such as the Better Business Bureau.
- Avoid making online transactions when using public computers. Public computers may have spyware installed, which are programs that track and log your keystrokes and can retrieve your private information. Similarly, unless you have specific protection on your mobile device, avoid making wireless transactions on public hotspots.

Whether you're doing business or collaborating and communicating with friends or colleagues, the Internet makes these activities more accessible. The Internet can potentially make these experiences and activities more enriched as well, although you must take precautions for the safest of experiences.

**Helpdesk**   **MyLab IT**

**Doing Business Online**

In this Helpdesk, you will play the role of a helpdesk staffer, fielding questions about e-commerce and e-commerce safeguards.

## Bits&Bytes   Bitcoin: A Form of Virtual Currency

Bitcoin is a form of virtual currency (also known as cryptocurrency) that eliminates intermediaries or banks to conduct transactions, thus enabling direct anonymous transactions between users (see Figure 3.7). Payments are sent peer-to-peer from the payee to the recipient with no transaction fees and without the need to supply personal information. The time and amount of every finalized bitcoin transaction are kept on a massive public online ledger known as the *blockchain*. The public nature of the blockchain makes it difficult for bitcoin transactions to be manipulated by anyone. However, the value of the currency is extremely volatile and can fluctuate widely within hours of a day. If you want to

hold and spend bitcoins, you must create a bitcoin wallet, which stores the information needed to complete bitcoin transactions. The security of bitcoin wallets is evolving, but there is a real risk of a wallet being hacked and the contents of the wallet stolen. Although the anonymity of the currency initially encouraged illicit transactions, the use of bitcoins for legitimate purposes is taking hold. Mainstream retailers such as Home Depot, Microsoft, Expedia, and *Overstock.com* are accepting bitcoins, as are many small businesses. Although Bitcoin has the largest user base and market capitalization, it's not the only virtual currency. Alternatives include Litecoin, Ethereum, Zcash, Dash, Ripple, and Monero.

**Figure 3.7** Bitcoin is a type of virtual currency. (*Zapp2Photo/Shutterstock*)

**Before moving on to Part 2:**

1. ▶ Watch Chapter Overview Video 3.1.

2. Then take the Check Your Understanding quiz.

# Check Your Understanding // Review & Practice

For a quick review to see what you've learned so far, answer the following questions.

## multiple choice

1. Which is NOT an event associated with the beginning of the Internet?

   a. Vinton Cerf helped to develop the Internet communications protocol.

   b. *Amazon.com* was one of the first websites on the Internet.

   c. "Login" was intended to be the first network transmission

   d. The U.S. Department of Defense creates ARPANET.

2. Which of the following best describes the transmission lines with the fastest speeds?

   a. Internet backbone

   b. Main Internet

   c. Main backbone

   d. Primary backbone

3. Which category of social networking do Instagram and YouTube fit into?

   a. Information Sharing

   b. Social Commerce

   c. Media Sharing

   d. Business Collaboration

4. Which of the following does not describe a desktop e-mail client?

   a. The e-mail program is installed on your computer.

   b. E-mail is downloaded when the program is opened.

   c. Sending e-mails is not dependent on an Internet connection.

   d. Can access e-mail from any Internet-connected device.

5. Which of the following would be an example of a B2B business?

   a. BestBuy

   b. Target

   c. Google

   d. Omaha Paper

**chew on this**

E-commerce businesses collect purchase data and web-browsing data from customers. They use it to give you more personalized services. You may receive special offers based on your interests, for example. Some view this as invasions of privacy however. Where do you stand?

**MyLab IT**  Go to **MyLab IT** to take an autograded version of the *Check Your Understanding* review and to find all media resources for the chapter.

**For the IT Simulation for this chapter, see MyLab IT.**

# Try This

## Use OneDrive to Store and Share Your Files in the Cloud

You may use a USB drive or use e-mail to access files when away from your computer. However, if you've updated the file on multiple devices or at different times there can be confusion as to which is the most current version. You can also lose the file completely by misplacing your USB drive or deleting the e-mail attachment.

Instead, use a web-based storage and sharing service such as OneDrive, Dropbox, or Google Drive. In this Try This, we'll explore OneDrive. You can access OneDrive through Microsoft's Office Online or with an Office 365 subscription. For more step-by-step instructions, watch the Chapter 3 Try This video on MyLab IT.

**Step 1** **Sign in to OneDrive:** Go to **onedrive.com**. Sign in with your Microsoft account. If you don't have a Microsoft account, creating one is easy.

**Step 2** **Create a Folder and Add Files:** Once in OneDrive, you can create a folder or begin to add files to OneDrive.

- To create a folder: Click **New** at the top of the page, click **Folder**, and then give your new folder a name. Click **Create**, and then select the new folder to open it.
- To add a file: Click **Upload** at the top of the page, select **Files**, and then locate the file on your local computer and click **Open**. To upload more than one file, press and hold **Ctrl** while you select each file.

*(Courtesy of Microsoft Corp.)*

**Step 3** **Share a File or Folder:** To share a file or folder, complete the following steps:

1. Right-click the file or folder that you want to share and click **Share** or click **Share** in the top menu after selecting the desired file or folder.
2. Click **Get a link** to generate a hyperlink you can copy and send to others or click **Email** to send an e-mail message containing the hyperlink.
3. Editing privileges are established by default, so if you want to restrict editing privileges, click to **uncheck** the **Allow editing** box.
4. To see what files that have been shared with you, click **Shared** in the left menu.

*(Courtesy of Microsoft Corp.)*

## A Web-Capable App

Want your app to be able to display a web page?

In this exercise, you will continue your mobile app development by adding a new power to your apps: web browsing.

It is as easy as using the WebViewer component in **App Inventor**. Drag a WebViewer component onto your Designer screen; then control it with the Blocks for WebViewer. These allow you to go back, forward, to the home page, or to any specific URL.

The WebViewer component allows you to control a live browser inside your mobile app.

*(Copyright MIT, used with permission.)*

*(Copyright MIT, used with permission.)*

To create this app for iOS, go to Thunkable.com, a programming platform based on App Inventor.
**For the instructions for this exercise, go to MyLab IT.**

# Using the Web Effectively

**Learning Outcome 3.2** **You will be able to describe the tools and techniques required to navigate and search the web.**

You no doubt know how to use the web—to buy products, send e-mail, visit Facebook, and use Google—but do you know how to use it effectively? In this section, we'll look at ways to make your online experience more enjoyable, more productive, and more efficient.

# Accessing and Moving Around the Web

Can you imagine a day without accessing the Internet? While internet usage is virtually ubiquitous and essential to some, others still don't have the ability or the desire to access the Internet. It's no surprise that results from studies conducted by Pew Research Center found that people with high levels of income and education are the top users of the Internet. As shown in Figure 3.8, location also makes a difference in that those living in rural areas use the Internet the least. Regardless, of how little or how often we access the Internet, none of our online activities could happen without an important software application: a web browser.

## Web Browsers

**Objective 3.7** *Explain what web browsers are, and describe their common features.*

**What is a web browser exactly?** A web browser is software that lets you locate, view, and navigate the web. Most browsers today are graphical browsers, meaning they can display pictures (graphics) in addition to text and other forms of multimedia such as sound and video. The most common browsers are displayed in Figure 3.9.

**What features do web browsers offer?** The most popular browsers share similar features that make the user experience more efficient (see Figure 3.10). For example, browsers include an omnibox, a combined search and address bar, so you can both type a website URL or search the web from the address bar. Other common features include the following:

- **Tabbed browsing:** Web pages are loaded in "tabs" within the same browser window. Rather than having to switch among web pages in several open windows, you can flip between the tabs in one window. You may also save a group of tabs as a Favorites group if there are several tabs you often open at the same time.

- **Pinned tabs:** You can "pin" tabs to lock your most used tabs to the left of the tab bar. Pinned tabs are smaller in size and can't be closed by accident. They will display automatically when the browser opens.

- **Tear-off tabs:** An opened tab can be dragged or moved away from its current window so it's then opened in a new window.

- **Thumbnail previews:** Another convenient navigation tool that most browsers share is providing thumbnail previews of all web pages in open tabs. Microsoft Edge also enables you to display newsfeed items as well.

- **Tab isolation:** With this feature, tabs are independent of each other, so if one crashes, it does not affect the other tabs.

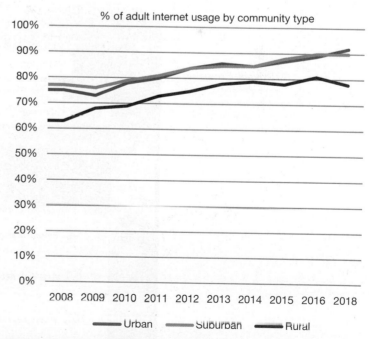

**Figure 3.8** Internet usage is greater in urban and suburban areas of the country. *Data from Pew Research Center (http://www.pewinternet.org/fact-sheet/internet-broadband/)*

**Figure 3.9** Common Web Browsers *(Tommy (Louth)/Alamy; Courtesy of Microsoft Corporation, Courtesy of Microsoft Corporation; Lucia Lanpur/ Alamy; 2020WEB/Alamy)*

**Google Chrome**
Most popular browser
Can run on any device and with any OS

**Microsoft Edge**
Available only with Windows 10 and
Microsoft account

**Firefox**
Open source

**Safari**
Developed by Apple for Macs
Has a Windows version for PCs

- **SmartScreen filter:** Most browsers offer built-in protection against phishing, malware, and other web-based threats.
- **Privacy browsing:** Privacy features (such as InPrivate Browsing in Microsoft Edge or Incognito in Chrome) let you browse the web without retaining a history trail, temporary Internet files, cookies, or usernames and passwords. These features are especially helpful when you use public computers at school or the public library, for example.

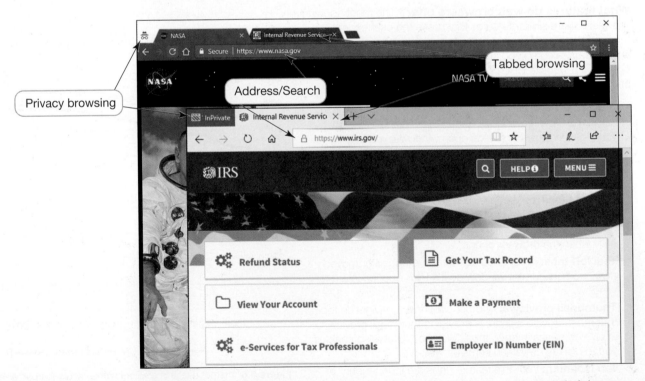

**Figure 3.10** Tabbed and privacy browsing and an address bar that doubles as a search bar are common features in today's browsers. *(Homepage, Internal Revenue Service, Homepage, Aeronautics and Space Administration; Courtesy of Google Inc.)*

- **Add-ons and extensions:** Add-ons (also known as extensions) are small programs that customize and increase the functionality of the browser. Examples include Video DownloadHelper, which converts web videos like those found on YouTube to files you can save, as well as a Facebook toolbar that integrates Facebook functionality into your browser.
- **Session Restore:** Brings back all your active web pages if the browser or system shuts down unexpectedly.

**Are there features in each browser that differentiate one from the other?** Although Chrome, Edge, Firefox, and Safari share many similar features, each browser has features that are less universally common. For example, Google Chrome, with the largest market share of mobile and desktop web browsers, enables you to set up individual profiles if you have multiple people using Chrome on the same device. This allows each user to maintain his or her own bookmarks and browsing preferences. Additionally, Chrome has many custom extensions that let you do things like control your music, take screenshots, and share sites with friends. You can even customize Chrome with your own theme.

Microsoft Edge has some unique features as well. You can make "Webnotes" by annotating a web page and then share them using Onenote or Evernote or save them for later use. Edge is also integrated with Microsoft's personal assistant Cortana, which shares web content with you based on your indicated preferences and interests. Finally, you can save online content to read later, and if the "noise" of a web page is distracting to you, you can use Reading View for a cleaner, simpler layout.

**Can I have the same browser experience on any computer I use?** It's not uncommon for users to have access to, and use, several different computers in their work, school, and personal lives. At a bare minimum, many users switch between a set of personal devices, including a laptop, smartphone, or tablet. Chrome and Firefox are accessible on any device and operate well with any operating system. Each lets you sync personal information and open tabs and bookmarks between different computers, so you have access to the same information on any device.

## URLs, Protocols, and Domain Names

**Objective 3.8** *Explain what a URL is and discuss its main parts.*

**What do all the parts of a URL mean?** You gain initial access to a particular website by typing its unique address, or Uniform Resource Locator (URL, pronounced "you-are-ell"), in your browser. A website comprises many different web pages, each of which is a separate document with its own unique URL. Like a regular street address, a URL is made up of several parts that help identify the web document it stands for (see Figure 3.11):

- the *protocol* (set of rules) used to retrieve the document;
- the domain name; which includes the *top-level domain*
- the *path* or subdirectory.

**Figure 3.11** The Parts of a URL

**What's the protocol?** You're probably most familiar with URLs that begin with http, which is short for Hypertext Transfer Protocol (HTTP). HTTP is the protocol that allows files to be transferred from a web server—a computer that hosts the website you're requesting—so that you can see it on your computer. The HTTP protocol is what the web is based on. Since it is so universal, most current browsers no longer require you to enter the http:// protocol or the "www."

**Is HTTP the only protocol I need to use?** HTTP is the most common protocol, but it's not the only one. HTTP is part of the Internet protocol suite, a group of protocols that govern how information is exchanged on a network. Another protocol in that group is the File Transfer Protocol (FTP). As its name implies, FTP was originally designed to transfer files from a computer to a web server. Today, FTP is often used when you have large files to upload or download. To connect to most FTP servers, you need a user ID and password. To upload and download files from FTP sites, you can use a browser or file transfer software such as CuteFTP or FileZilla.

BitTorrent, like FTP, is a protocol used to transfer files, though it's not part of the Internet protocol suite. To use BitTorrent, you install a software client program. It uses a peer-to-peer networking system so that sharing occurs between connected computers that also have the BitTorrent client installed. BitTorrent is popular especially among users who want to

**Table 3.5  Common Top-Level Domains and Their Authorized Users**

| Domain Name | Who Can Use It |
| --- | --- |
| .biz | Businesses |
| .com | Originally for commercial sites, but now can be used by anyone |
| .edu | Degree-granting institutions |
| .gov | Local, state, and federal U.S. governments |
| .info | Information service providers |
| .mil | U.S. military |
| .net | Originally for networking organizations, but no longer restricted |
| .org | Organizations (often not-for-profits) |

share music, movies, and games. Use caution, however, when accessing BitTorrent content. Because it is a peer-to-peer system, it's possible for copyrighted material to be shared illegally.

**What's in a domain name?** The domain name identifies the site's host, the location that maintains the computers that store the website files. For example, www.berkeley.edu is the domain name for the University of California at Berkeley website. The suffix in the domain name after the dot (such as "com" or "edu") is called the top-level domain. This suffix indicates the kind of organization to which the host belongs. Some browsers don't require you to enter the domain if it is a .com—the browser enters the domain automatically. For example, you can just type in Amazon in any browser and the browser automatically fills in the .com. Table 3.5 lists the most frequently used top-level domains.

Each country has its own top-level domain. These are two-letter designations such as .za for South Africa, and .de for Germany. A sampling of country codes is shown in Table 3.6. Within a country-specific domain, further subdivisions can be made for regions or states. For instance, the .us domain contains subdomains for each state, using the two-letter abbreviation of the state.

**What's the information after the domain name that I sometimes see?** When the URL is the domain name, such as *www.nytimes.com*, you're requesting a site's home page. However, sometimes a forward slash and additional text follow the domain name, such as in *www.nytimes.com/section/technology*. The information after each slash indicates a particular file or path (or subdirectory) within the website. Using the URL in Figure 3.11 you would connect to the technology section on the *New York Times* site.

## Navigating the Web

**Objective 3.9** *Describe tools used to navigate the web.*

**What's the best way to get around in a website?** As its name implies, the web is a series of interconnected paths, or links. You've no doubt moved around the web by clicking on hyperlinks, specially coded elements that let you go from one web page to another within the same website or to another site altogether (see Figure 3.12). Generally, text that operates as a hyperlink appears in a different color (often blue) and is usually underlined, but sometimes images also act as hyperlinks. When you hover your cursor over a hyperlink, the cursor changes to a hand with a finger pointing upward.

**Table 3.6  Examples of Country Codes**

| Country Code | Country |
| --- | --- |
| .au | Australia |
| .ca | Canada |
| .jp | Japan |
| .uk | United Kingdom |

Note: For a full listing of country codes, refer to *www.iana.org/domains/root/db/*.

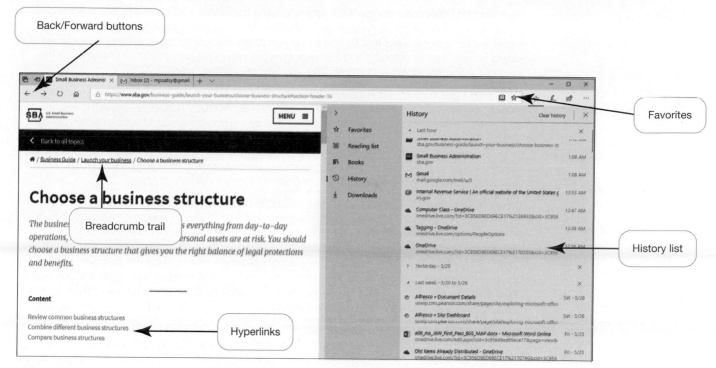

**Figure 3.12** Navigating a Web Page *(U.S. Small Business Administration; Courtesy of Google Inc.)*

**What other tools can I use to navigate a website?** To move back or forward one page at a time, you can use the browser's Back and Forward buttons (see Figure 3.12).

To help navigate more quickly through a website, some sites provide a breadcrumb trail—a navigation aid that shows users the path they have taken to get to a web page, or where the page is located within the website. It usually appears at the top of a page. Figure 3.12 shows an example of a breadcrumb trail. By clicking on earlier links in a breadcrumb trail, you can go directly to a previously visited web page without having to use the Back button to navigate back through the website.

Most browsers offer caret browsing, which lets you use your keyboard to grab text instead of swiping across with a mouse. To activate caret browsing in Microsoft Edge, press F7 on your keyboard while you have the browser open. In Google Chrome you will need to add an extension and in Firefox you will need to enable a preference before you can activate caret browsing. Then, you can use your mouse pointer as an insertion pointer (similar to working in Word) and the arrow keys to move around. Press Shift and an arrow key to select text. Press F7 again to turn off caret browsing. This method offers more precise text selection and is very handy when you frequently copy and paste text from web pages.

**What's the best way to mark a site so I can return to it later?** If you want an easy way to return to a specific web page, you can use your browser's Bookmarks feature (Microsoft Edge calls this feature Favorites). This feature places a marker of the site's URL in an easily retrievable list in your browser's toolbar. To organize the sites into categories, most browsers offer tools to create folders.

## Bits&Bytes   Maintain Your Privacy While Searching the Web

Privacy is important to many people, but creating a private online experience is not always an easy task. Although you can use the privacy or incognito mode in some web browsers, these only disable your browsing history and web cache so that data generated from your searches can't be retrieved later. DuckDuckGo is different—this search engine doesn't collect your personal browsing information to share with third parties for marketing purposes. And although most search engines sell your search term information to third parties, which then use that information to generate display ads and recommendations on pages you visit, DuckDuckGo doesn't sell your search terms to other sites. Moreover, DuckDuckGo doesn't save your search history. Using DuckDuckGo eliminates third-party sharing of your personal information.

Favorites and Bookmarks are great for quickly locating those sites you use most, but they're accessible to you only when you're on your own computer. Most browsers provide features that let you export the list of bookmarks to a file you can import to another computer or another browser. Another way to access your Bookmarks and Favorites from any computer is to use MyBookmarks—a free Internet service that stores your Bookmarks and Favorites online.

**How can I get to a site if it hasn't been bookmarked?** If you forget to add a site as a bookmark or favorite but would like to return to a site you've previously visited, try using the History list. A browser's History list shows all the websites and pages you have visited over a certain period of time. These sites are organized according to date and can go back several months, depending on your browsing activity. To access the History list in Microsoft Edge or Chrome, click the three horizontal lines in the upper right-hand corner of the browser window (often referred to as the hamburger) and then click History in Chrome or Search History in Microsoft Edge.

**What is tagging?** Tagging (also known as social bookmarking) is like bookmarking your favorite website, but instead of saving it to your browser for only you to see, you're saving it to a social bookmarking site so that you can share it with others. A *social bookmark* or *tag* is a term that you assign to a web page, digital image, or video. A tag can be something you create to describe the digital content, or it can be a suggested term provided by the website. For example, if you came across a web page with an article on places to go for spring break, you might tag the article *vacations*. Others on the same social bookmarking site who are looking for websites about vacations may use *vacations* as the search term and find the article you tagged.

You can use sites like Pocket (*getpocket.com*) to save interesting web content such as articles, videos, and images to view or review at a more convenient time. Giving each article you save a tag helps to categorize your content in a meaningful way. When you're ready to access your saved content, you can do so from any device, online or offline. In addition to your content, you can also access trending articles and content based on others' tags.

Other social bookmarking sites include Reddit, StumbleUpon, and Pinterest. Reddit encourages its community to vote on links and stories, so the most popular rise to the top. StumbleUpon offers a Stumble! button that, when clicked, provides new web content that you can like or dislike, which eventually contours the Stumble results more to your interests. Unlike other social bookmarking sites, Pinterest enables you to share only images. You can post images that you find online or that you directly upload.

 Searching the Web Effectively

You've most likely "Googled" something today, and if you did, your search is one of over 5 billion daily searches. Let's look at how to search the web effectively.

### Using Search Engines

**Objective 3.10** *Describe the types of tools used to search the web and summarize strategies used to refine search results.*

**How do search engines work?** Google is the world's most popular search engine—a set of programs that searches the web for keywords (specific words you wish to look for or *query*) and then returns a list of the sites on which those keywords are found. Search engines have three components:

1. The first component is a program called a *spider*, which constantly collects data on the web, following links in websites and reading web pages. Spiders get their name because they crawl over the web using multiple "legs" to visit many sites simultaneously.

2. As the spider collects data, the second component of the search engine, an *indexer program*, organizes the data into a large database.

3. When you use a search engine, you interact with the third component: the *search engine software*. This software searches the indexed data, pulling out relevant information according to your search.

The resulting list appears in your web browser as a list of hits—sites that match your search.

**Why don't I get the same results from all search engines?** Each search engine uses a unique program, or algorithm, to formulate the search and create the resulting index of related sites. In addition, search engines differ in how they rank the search results. Most search engines rank search results based on the frequency of the appearance and location of the queried keywords in websites. This means that sites that include the keywords in their URL or site name will most likely appear at the top of the results list. An important part of a company's marketing strategy is search engine optimization (SEO), which is designing the website to ensure it ranks near the top of search results.

**Are there search engines that offer more specialized results?** Search engines also differ as to which sites they search. For instance, Google and Bing search nearly the entire web, whereas specialty search engines search only sites that are relevant to a particular topic or industry. Specialty search engines exist for almost every industry or interest. DailyStocks is a search engine used primarily by investors that searches for corporate information. Search Engine Watch has a list of many specialty search engines, organized by industry. Google also has several specialized search engines, as shown in Figure 3.13. These can be accessed by clicking on the Google Apps button in Google's main page, then clicking More from Google options. Google's specialized search options include the following:

- *Shopping* lets you search by product rather than by company. So if you're interested in buying a digital camera, Shopping lists cameras by popularity and provides information on the stores that carry the cameras, along with the average price.
- *Finance* gives you access to real-time stock quotes and charts as well as financial news. You can also track your portfolio holdings.
- *Books* features a comprehensive index of full-text books. You can create different bookshelves for your Google Books and magazines.

If you can't decide which search engine is best, you may want to try a metasearch engine. Metasearch engines, such as Dogpile, search other search engines rather than individual websites.

**Figure 3.13** Google's Specialized Search Tools *(Courtesy Google Inc.)*

**Can I use a search engine to search just for images and videos?** With the increasing popularity of multimedia, search engines let you search the web for digital images and audio and video files. After putting in your search term, select Video from Google's top menu to display only the search results that are videos. You can further narrow down the video selection by using the filtering tools. 360Daily is a video search engine that helps you sift through videos posted on the web.

**How else can I customize my searches?** Many other specialty search strategies and services are available. Both Google and Bing have menus at the top of each site to search specifically for movies, videos, maps, and more. In addition, both search engines allow you to restrict search results by time. Google provides additional search customization capabilities providing specific searches for Books, Flights, and Apps. The Search Tools feature in Google provides additional search functionality specific to the type of search being conducted (see Figure 3.14a). For example, when searching for videos, you can continue to customize by time, quality, or duration; if searching for images, Search Tools enables you to restrict the search by Size, Color, Type, Time, or Usage rights. By clicking on the Settings link on Google's search page, you can access an Advanced Search form (see Figure 3.14b) through which you can narrow your search results by language, region, specific terms, usage rights, or file type. Although many of the features in Advanced Search can be found elsewhere in Google's search tools, it's often convenient to have them located in one spot.

**Can I refine my key terms for better results?** You've probably searched for something on Google and gotten back a list of hits that includes thousands—even millions—of web pages that have no relevance to the topic you're interested in. Initially, Boolean operators were needed to help refine a search. Boolean operators are words such as *AND*, *NOT*, and *OR* that describe the

**Figure 3.14** (a) Google Search tools and (b) Advanced Search form offer ways to narrow search results. *(Courtesy Google Inc.)*

relationships between keywords in a search. With the simple addition of a few words or constraints, you can narrow your search results to a more manageable and more meaningful list. Other strategies can help refine your searches when entering your search keywords:

- **Search for a phrase.** To search for an exact phrase, place quotation marks around your keywords. The search engine will look for only those websites that contain the words in that exact order. For example, if you want information on the movie *Captain America: Civil War* and you type these words without quotation marks, your search results will contain pages that include any of the words captain, America, civil, or war, although not necessarily in that order. Typing "Captain America: Civil War" in quotation marks guarantees that search results will include this exact phrase.

- **Search within a specific website.** To search just a specific website, you can use the search keyword, then site: followed by the website's URL. For example, searching with *processor site: www.wired.com* returns results about processors from the Wired magazine website. The same method works for entire classes of sites in a given top-level domain or country code.

- **Use a wild card.** The asterisk (*) is a wild card, or placeholder, feature that is helpful when you need to search with unknown terms. Another way to think about the wild card search feature is as a "fill in the blank." For example, searching with *Congress voted * on the * bill* might bring up an article about the members of Congress who voted no on the healthcare bill or a different article about the members of Congress who voted yes on the energy bill.

## Evaluating Websites

**Objective 3.11** *Describe how to evaluate a website to ensure it is appropriate to use for research purposes.*

**How can I make sure a website is appropriate to use for research?** When you're using the Internet for research, you shouldn't assume that every web article you find is accurate and appropriate to use. The following is a list of questions to consider before you use an Internet resource; the answers to these questions will help you decide whether you should consider a website to be a good source of information:

- **Authority:** Who is the author of the article or the sponsor of the site? If the author is well known or the site is published by a reputable news source (such as *The New York Times*), then you can feel more confident using it as a source than if you are unable to locate such information. Note: Some sites include a page with information about the author or the site's sponsor.

- **Bias:** Is the site biased? The purpose of many websites is to sell products or services or to persuade rather than inform. These sites, though useful in some situations, present a biased point of view. Look for sites that offer several sets of facts or consider opinions from several sources.

- **Relevance:** Is the information on the site current? Material can last a long time on the web. Some research projects (such as historical accounts) depend on older records. However, if you're writing about cutting-edge technologies, you need to look for the most recent sources. Therefore, look for a date on information to make sure it's current.

- **Audience:** For what audience is the site intended? Ensure that the content, tone, and style of the site match your needs. You probably wouldn't want to use information from a site geared toward teens if you're writing for adults, nor would you use a site that has a casual style and tone for serious research.

- **Links:** Are the links available and appropriate? Check out the links provided on the site to determine whether they're still working and appropriate for your needs. Don't assume that the links provided are the only additional sources of information. Investigate other sites on your topic as well. You should also be able to find the same information on at least three different websites to help verify the information is accurate.

If you are still unsure as to whether an article or website is legitimate, you can fact check article details by using sites such as Factcheck.org, Snopes, and Politifact. If you want to check whether an image has been altered in any way to represent something untrue, try using Google's reverse image search (images. google.com) as shown in Figure 3.15.

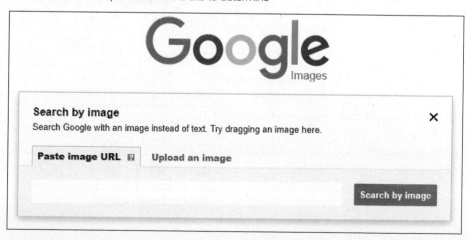

**Figure 3.15** Google's Reverse Image Search *(Courtesy of Google Inc.)*

Think about all the types of data on the web that you access manually, such as appointment times, transportation and entertainment schedules, and store locations and hours. This type of data is referred to as *structured data*—data that can be defined by a particular category (or field) and a specific data type (such as number, text, or date). Structured data is easily entered, stored, queried, and analyzed and is usually found in databases.

However, the web currently is not set up to directly manipulate the structured data that resides on web pages. Initially, the web was set up to link documents together and for people to read web pages. Right now, search engines function by recognizing keywords such as *office hours* and *dentist*, but they can't determine, for example, in which office and on what days Dr. Smith works and what his available appointment times are. The capacity to have linked data, data that is formally defined and that can be expressed in relationships, is beginning to be available, especially using digital assistants as intermediaries.

The Linking Open Data project is an ongoing effort to convert existing data into a usable format and link them together. The process ensures that the same categorization structures are used so that similar information shares the same attributes, ensuring consistency of metadata throughout the web. The project began with formatting and linking the structured information from Wikipedia but has begun to broaden the sources of data as the project continues to evolve. This web of linked data has been coined as the semantic web. The semantic web is an evolving extension of the web in which data is defined in such a way to make it more easily processed by computers. Ultimately, each website would have text and pictures (for people to read) and metadata (for computers to read) describing the information on the web (see Figure 3.16).

With the assistance of a virtual agent, computers would find relevant metadata, coordinate it with your schedules and preferences, and then make appointments for you. Linked data will also assist you in comparing products, prices, and shipping options by finding the best product option based on specified criteria and then placing the order for you. Eventually, the agent could record the financial transaction into your personal bookkeeping software and arrange for a technician to help install the software, if needed.

Although some of the semantic web's functionalities are beginning to emerge in technologies such as the digital assistants Siri, Google Now, and Cortana, much of its functionality and implementation are still in development. The greatest challenge has been the recoding of all the data currently available on the web into the type of metadata that computers can recognize. But as more data is converted, and the capabilities of digital assistants continue to be enhanced, we are closer than ever to realizing the full capabilities of the semantic web and linked data.

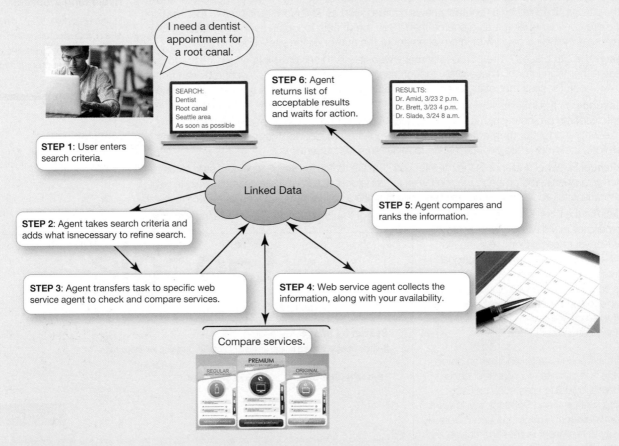

**Figure 3.16** Linked Data and the Semantic Web *(Mangostar/Shutterstock; Kaitshot/Shutterstock; Lfor/Shutterstock)*

# Using the Web Ethically

As you've read in this chapter, the web offers a vast array of opportunities for business, communication, and collaboration. It also poses some temptations for inappropriate behavior, often to seek gain at another's expense. In this section, we'll explore several ethical issues that are challenging how we use the web.

## Digital Activism

**Objective 3.12** *Demonstrate an understanding of the ethical issues regarding digital activism.*

**What is digital activism?** Digital activism describes the use of hashtags and posts to raise awareness and foster discussion about specific issues and causes via social media. You're probably familiar with many hashtag campaigns and their causes:

- The #IceBucketChallenge hashtag campaign raised awareness for Lou Gehrig's disease (ALS) and resulted in raising over $110 million in an 8-week period, a nearly 35 percent increase in donations for the cause.

- In an effort to offset the rampant consumerism that kicks off the pre-holiday buying frenzy starting with Black Friday, Small Business Saturday, and Cyber Monday, the Tuesday after Thanksgiving was designated #GivingTuesday. GivingTuesday is a time for consumers to encourage each other through social media to donate their time, talents, or cash to a cause or an organization. The hashtag campaign has amassed over 3 million users since its inception. The cause has also expanded beyond U.S. borders, with people around the world making millions of contributions in a 24-hour period.

- Movements such as #MeToo, and #TimesUp center on sexual harassment and abuse. The #MeToo campaign has promoted awareness, while the #TimesUp campaign has shifted the conversation into actively solving the problem.

- #TakeAKnee began when NFL quarterback Colin Kaepernick knelt during the playing of the national anthem prior to the start of football games to protest police brutality, especially within the black communities.

Each of these hashtag campaigns was very successful, depending on how you define success. What was the initial goal of each of these campaigns? Was it to bring awareness to an issue, to instigate action, or to produce some other effect? Often, when digital campaigns go viral, people can join in simply by liking a post on Facebook. Proponents of digital activism celebrate the ability of such hashtag campaigns to raise money and awareness, magnify voices that might not otherwise be heard, and effect change.

## Table 3.7  Point/Counterpoint: Digital Activism

| Issue: Digital Activism | Ethical Question: Is digital activism effective or does it foster a false sense of involvement? |
|---|---|
|  Point | • Digital activism raises awareness and enables individuals who otherwise might not be heard to have a voice.<br>• Digital activism initiates conversations and generates attention that otherwise might not happen on any other platform.<br>• Digital activism can spur actions such as donations or political involvement. |
|  Counterpoint | • Digital activism has a limited impact due to the fad-like nature of individuals who participate but have little or no vested interest in the cause.<br>• Digital activism generates attention, but the initial cause or reason may become distorted in the fervor.<br>• Digital activism limits true involvement because people associate passive online actions as "support." |

However, critics of hashtag activism claim the campaigns foster a false sense of involvement, allowing Facebook and Twitter users to feel they have done something when in reality their social media posts will have no tangible impact. Such critics claim that hashtag campaigns quickly fade from public consciousness in part because they're often initially embraced by people who are following a trend and have little or no true interest in the cause. Table 3.7 lists different views on the issue of digital activism. Where do your views fall?

## Geolocation

**Objective 3.13** *Demonstrate an understanding of the ethical issues regarding location tracking applications and devices.*

**What is geolocation and what privacy risks does it pose?** "Where are you?" is the burning social networking question these days, and your smartphone probably has the answer, since all mobile devices have a GPS chip that can calculate your exact position. Geolocation, or the act of targeting consumers by their location, has become a valuable technique that allows businesses to analyze and sculpt customer behaviors and to increase consumer traffic and ultimately revenues. Customers benefit when retailers use geolocation to push ads and coupons to those who have downloaded the store app, are connected with their mobile device, and are within proximity to the business. Additionally, the massive amounts of geolocation data that are generated and analyzed are being used to improve the customer experience. Starbucks, Snapchat, and Uber are just a handful of companies that have apps that have the capacity to track and use your location, with your permission.

Why is this an issue? User location data is often shared with third-party advertising networks and even with law enforcement agencies. Although you can modify or turn off the location aspects in most mobile apps, these measures can't guarantee that data will not be shared with third parties because the location data is "leaked" in other ways.

Even with app location tracking turned off, your location can be captured when your device is turned on. This feature has been useful to pinpoint users in emergency situations, but the data, if placed in the wrong hands or used for the wrong purposes, can be a violation of your privacy. Retrospectively, historical location data can be discerned from service provider records, and additionally, Wi-Fi hotspots can be used to track mobile devices. Moreover, other features of a smartphone, such as the camera and phone, can capture a user's geolocation data. Therefore, the privacy implications still remain. Although legislation has been initiated, no specific law has been passed to address the privacy concerns of location tracking devices and applications. Although most mobile device users are aware of location data collection practices, they're not aware of what was being collected and how it is, and can be, used. Table 3.8 lists different views on the issue of geolocation. What do you think?

## Table 3.8  Point/Counterpoint: Geolocation

| Issue: Geolocation | Ethical Question: Are geolocation applications and devices a threat to privacy? |
| --- | --- |
|  Point | • The social norm has shifted and people have become comfortable with sharing more information, including their location.<br>• Many businesses incorporate geolocation as a primary marketing strategy; the loss of privacy is outweighed by the benefit to consumers.<br>• Society may need to reevaluate its expectations as to the amount of privacy in people's digital lives. |
|  Counterpoint | • The threats and potential risks of using geolocation devices and applications are too great to ignore.<br>• Privacy settings on apps and GPS devices should be more restrictive.<br>• Businesses are responsible for educating consumers about how the data they gather through geolocation is used so consumers can make informed choices. |

## Bits&Bytes | Human-Implanted Data Chips: Protection or Invasive Nightmare?

Many of us give up quite a bit of our privacy voluntarily via the devices we carry and the apps we use. So why does the thought of implanting a data chip inside the human body cause so much uproar and dissent?

Human-implantable microchips were approved for use by the Food and Drug Administration in 2004. The basic advantages of implanted chips are that they can receive and transmit information and are extremely difficult to counterfeit. An implanted chip could positively identify you when you make a retail transaction, virtually eliminating fraud. A chip could provide instant access to medical records to facilitate treatment for unconscious accident victims, or track lost or missing children or Alzheimer's patients. And law enforcement could track the movement of convicted criminals out on parole.

Despite the benefits, people see great potential for privacy infringement and potential misuse of data. Would you want your parents (or the government) to know where you are at any time? Would someone be able to read the medical information in your chip without your permission and use it against you? In fact, there is so much resistance from the public to implants that some states such as Wisconsin, California, Georgia, and North Dakota have already enacted legislation to prohibit mandatory data chips implants in the future, even though it is not being considered now.

The debate will most likely rage on as technologies continue to be developed that will allow implanted chips to gather and provide even more data. Whether the public embraces this technology remains to be seen. Would you ever be willing to have a data chip implanted in your body?

## Cyber Harassment

While the Internet provides an array of benefits and advantages, a darker side has emerged with a growing epidemic of abusive online behaviors collectively referred to as cyber harassment. Cyber harassment is used to describe the pursuit of individual(s) by an individual with the intention to frighten, embarrass, "teach the victim a lesson," or seek revenge. Cyber harassment includes acts such as cyberbullying, cyberstalking, trolling, and catfishing.

*Cyberbullying* and *cyberstalking* involve the use of digital technologies such as the Internet, cell phones, or video to harass, stalk, or bully another. The distinction between cyberbullying and cyberstalking is primarily age. Cyberbullying is generally used when children and adolescents are involved (see Figure 3.17). Cyberbullying and cyberstalking can include actions such as bombarding a victim with harassing instant messages or text messages, spreading rumors or lies on social networking sites, posting embarrassing photos or videos of a victim on the web, or infecting the victim's computer with malware, usually to spy on that person.

The effects of these violations can be devastating. Infamous cases of cyberbullying include Hannah Smith, the English girl who at 14 committed suicide after being repeatedly taunted on social networking sites, and Tyler Clementi, a Rutgers freshman who committed suicide after his roommate showed fellow students videos of him having sex. There are plentiful examples of workplace bullying and celebrity cyberstalking, but often these cases are not as publicized as those involving children.

Trolling is the act of posting inflammatory remarks online for the sheer pleasure of soliciting an angry or negative response. Although both trolling and cyberbullying are generally done with the intention of inflicting fear or anger, the main difference between trolling and cyberbullying is that a troll generally does not personally know his or her target. Trolls derive pleasure from annoying others, and when they are confronted about their behavior, they often shrug off the incident, claiming it was all in good fun. Trolls are more interested in the reaction than the personal confrontation that cyberbullies and cyberstalkers seek. When confronted by a troll, the best thing to do is to not react at all and to leave the conversation as quickly as possible.

Catfishing is another type of Internet harassment where some individual scams others into a false romantic relationship.

**Figure 3.17** Cyberbullying involves the use of digital technologies both to bully and to disseminate acts of bullying. *(Antonio Guillem/Shutterstock)*

Catfishers create fake profiles and trick others into thinking they are someone else entirely. The fabricated relationships are developed through online and phone interactions, but never in person. One of the most public catfish scams involved Notre Dame football player Manti Te'o, who fell in love with a fictitious girl. The resulting tragic realization of the scam played out in public for Te'o. "Catfish," a documentary that highlights a true catfishing situation, and a reality TV series of that same name continues to bring attention to this type of scam.

There is currently no federal law prohibiting cyberbullying, but a recently passed law against cyberstalking may cover this area. According to the Cyberbullying Research Center (cyberbullying.org), currently all states have anti-bullying laws or policies on the books. However, only 48 state laws cover electronic harassment, and a mere 22 state laws cover cyberbullying. Many legislatures are reluctant to pass laws that instruct parents on how to raise their children because this tends to raise issues about personal freedom. Therefore, anti-cyberbullying laws tend to place the burden of detection on the schools or the workplace. For instance, the Massachusetts law requires schools to provide age-appropriate education on bullying to students, to train school employees in detection and prevention of bullying, and to have plans developed for detecting and reporting bullying.

---

### Before moving on to the Chapter Review:

1. ▶ Watch Chapter Overview Video 3.2.
2. Then take the Check Your Understanding quiz.

# Check Your Understanding // Review & Practice

For a quick review to see what you've learned so far, answer the following questions.

## multiple choice

1. Which feature of a browser enables you to separate a browser tab into its own window?

   a. tabbed browsing

   b. pinned tabs

   c. tear-off tabs

   d. tab isolation

2. Which of the following is not an Internet protocol?

   a. HTTP

   b. FTP

   c. BitTorrent

   d. ARPANET

3. What is the navigation aid that shows users the path they have taken to get to a web page located within a website?

   a. Favorites

   b. breadcrumb trail

   c. Bookmarks

   d. social bookmarks

4. Which search strategy should you use to search for a specific phrase?

   a. Use quotation marks around the phrase.

   b. Include Boolean operators in the phrase.

   c. Use asterisks around the phrase.

   d. Use a wild card around the phrase.

5. Which of the following is not true when evaluating web articles for research?

   a. You should not use an article if there is not an author listed.

   b. You should evaluate web articles for bias and relevance.

   c. You can assume everything with an author listed is accurate and appropriate.

   d. You should check any links in a web article to see if they are timely and relevant.

**chew on this**

Google is the largest and most popular search engine. Because of its size and popularity, Google can have enormous power to influence a web user's search experience solely by its website-ranking processes. Read some articles about search engine optimization (SEO) and discuss how SEO works and why it can be so important to a company's success.

**MyLab IT** Go to **MyLab IT** to take an autograded version of the *Check Your Understanding* review and to find all media resources for the chapter.

> **For the IT Simulation for this chapter, see MyLab IT.**

# 3 Chapter Review

## Summary

**Learning Outcome 3.1**   You will be able to explain how the Internet works and how it is used for collaboration, communication, commerce, and entertainment purposes.

### The Internet and How It Works

**Objective 3.1**   *Describe how the Internet got its start.*

- The Internet is the largest computer network in the world, connecting millions of computers.
- Government and military officials developed the early Internet as a reliable way to communicate in the event of war. Eventually, scientists and educators used the Internet to exchange research.
- Today, we use the Internet and the web (which is a part of the Internet) to shop, research, communicate, and entertain ourselves.

**Objective 3.2**   *Explain how data travels on the Internet.*

- A computer (or other device) connected to the Internet acts as either a client (a computer that asks for information) or a server (a computer that receives the request and returns the information to the client).
- Data travels between clients and servers along a system of communication lines or pathways. The largest and fastest of these pathways form the Internet backbone.
- To ensure that data is sent to the correct computer along the pathways, IP addresses (unique ID numbers) are assigned to all computers connected to the Internet.

### Collaborating and Communicating on the Web

**Objective 3.3**   *Evaluate the tools and technologies used to collaborate on the web.*

- Collaboration on the web uses technologies broadly described as Web 2.0. Web 2.0 communication tools are known as social media and include social networking, project collaboration and file sharing tools, blogs, podcasts, webcasts, and media sharing.

- Social networking enables you to communicate and share information with friends as well as meet and connect with others.
- File sharing tools, such as web-based document products, promote online collaboration. A wiki is a document created collaboratively by multiple users, resulting in an emergent common output.
- Project management tools incorporate texting, tasks, and calendar features for individual team members as well as for the project.
- Other useful web tools for group collaboration online are screen sharing and videoconferencing applications.
- Blogs are journal entries posted to the web that are generally organized by a topic or area of interest and are publicly available.
- Video logs are personal journals that use video as the primary content in addition to text, images, and audio.
- Podcasts are audio or video content available over the Internet. Users subscribe to receive updates to podcasts.
- Webcasts are live broadcasts of audio or video content over the Internet.
- Media sharing platforms enable users to create, store, and share multimedia.

**Objective 3.4**   *Summarize the technologies used to communicate over the web.*

- E-mail allows users to communicate electronically without the parties involved being available at the same time.
- Instant-messaging services are programs that enable you to communicate in real time with others who are online.

### Conducting Business on the Web

**Objective 3.5**   *Describe how business is conducted using the Internet.*

- E-commerce is the business of conducting business online.

- E-commerce includes transactions between businesses (B2B), between consumers (C2C), and between businesses and consumers (B2C).

**Objective 3.6**  *Summarize precautions you should take when doing business online.*

- Precautions include using firewalls and up-to-date antivirus software and employing strong passwords for online accounts.

- Check to see if the website is secure, shop at reputable websites, pay by credit card not debit card, check the return policy and save a copy of the receipt, and avoid making online transactions on public computers.

# Part 2
## Using the Web Effectively

**Learning Outcome 3.2**   **You will be able to describe the tools and techniques required to navigate and search the web.**

##  Accessing and Moving Around the Web

**Objective 3.7**  *Explain what web browsers are and describe their common features.*

- Once you are connected to the Internet, in order to locate, navigate to, and view web pages, you need software called a web browser.
- The most common web browsers are Google Chrome, Microsoft Edge, Firefox, and Safari.

**Objective 3.8**  *Explain what a URL is and discuss its main parts.*

- You gain access to a website by typing in its address, called a Uniform Resource Locator (URL).
- A URL is composed of several parts, including the protocol, the domain, the top-level domain, and paths (or subdirectories).

**Objective 3.9**  *Describe tools used to navigate the web.*

- One unique aspect of the web is that you can jump from place to place by clicking on specially formatted pieces of text or images called hyperlinks.
- You can also use the Back and Forward buttons, History lists, and breadcrumb trails to navigate the web.
- Favorites, live bookmarks, and social bookmarking help you return to specific web pages without having to type in the URL and help you organize the web content that is most important to you.

##  Searching the Web Effectively

**Objective 3.10**  *Describe the types of tools used to search the web and summarize strategies used to refine search results.*

- A search engine is a set of programs that searches the web using specific keywords you wish to query and then returns a list of the websites on which those keywords are found.

- Search engines can be used to search for images, podcasts, and videos in addition to traditional text-based web content.
- Metasearch engines search other search engines.

**Objective 3.11**  *Describe how to evaluate a website to ensure it is appropriate to use for research purposes.*

- To evaluate whether it is appropriate to use a website as a resource, determine whether the author of the site is reputable, whether the site is intended for your particular needs, that the site content is not biased, that the information on the site is current, and that all the links on the site are available and appropriate.
- Use reverse image search to check whether an image has been falsified through alterations or tampering.

##  Using the Web Ethically

**Objective 3.12**  *Demonstrate an understanding of the ethical issues regarding digital activism.*

- Digital activism describes the use of hashtags and posts to raise awareness and foster discussion about specific issues and causes on social media.
- Digital activism can be useful to raise awareness and enable people to voice their opinions.
- Digital activist causes can become popular more often because of the immediate fervor rather than the underlying cause.

**Objective 3.13**  *Demonstrate an understanding of the ethical issues regarding location tracking applications and devices.*

- Privacy is the right to be left alone, but it is often difficult to achieve with social media.
- Apps with geolocation technology garner much information about your location. Users should be aware of why companies need to track a user's location, and what the companies will do with that location data.

**MyLab IT**   Be sure to check out **MyLab IT** for additional materials to help you review and learn. And don't forget to watch the Chapter Overview Videos. ▶

# Key Terms

# Chapter Quiz // Assessment

For a quick review to see what you've learned, answer the following questions. Submit the quiz as requested by your instructor. If you are using **MyLab IT**, the quiz is also available there.

## multiple choice

1. Which statement is *not* true about the web?
   a. The web was based on a protocol developed by Tim Berners-Lee.
   b. Special links are used to navigate from page to page on the web
   c. The web is based on the WWW protocol
   d. The web is a subset of the Internet

2. Which of the following describes an IP address?
   a. It is referred to as a dotted quad.
   b. It identifies any computer connecting to the Internet.
   c. It identifies a website.
   d. all of the above

3. Ordering a mocha latte and paying for it from the Starbucks smartphone app is using what type of Internet commerce?
   a. B2B
   b. C2C
   c. social commerce
   d. mobile commerce

4. What web browser feature would be particularly useful when using public computers?
   a. pinned tabs
   b. privacy browsing
   c. session restore
   d. all of the above

5. In the URL **http://www.whitehouse.gov/blog**, which part is considered the top-level domain name?
   a. .gov
   b. www.whitehouse.gov
   c. http
   d. /blog

6. Which of the following is *not* a component of a search engine?
   a. spider
   b. indexer program
   c. search assistant
   d. search engine software

7. Which feature in Google Chrome enables you to restrict search results by Size, Color, Type, Time, or Usage rights?
   a. Search Tools
   b. Custom Search
   c. Favorites
   d. History

8. Ensuring that website content is not slanted in its point of view is checking for:
   a. Audience
   b. Authority
   c. Bias
   d. Relevance

9. Which of the following is a good precaution to take when making online purchases?
   a. use the same strong password for all online accounts
   b. pay by debit card
   c. make sure http: and an open padlock displays in the address bar
   d. use a private browser when purchasing items from a public computer

10. You want to search the web for information on the movie *Captain America: Civil War*. What would be the best way to enter the key terms to get the most specific results?
    a. Captain America *
    b. "Captain America: Civil War"
    c. * Civil War
    d. Captain America Civil War

## true/false

_____ 1. Your location can be captured from your mobile device even if app location tracking is turned off.

_____ 2. Podcasts can only be created by professional organizations.

_____ 3. The "S" in HTTPS stands for secure and indicates that the secure sockets layer protocol has been applied to the website.

_____ 4. Catfishing is posting inflammatory remarks online to generate negative responses.

_____ 5. Google Docs is an example of a wiki.

## What do you think now?

Clickbait is used to generate interest and ultimately revenues. Many might argue that although clickbait is annoying, it is relatively harmless. But is it? Explore and discuss the dangers of clickbait.

# Team Time

## Collaborating with Technology

### problem

Collaborating on projects with team members is a regular part of business and academia. Many great tools are available that facilitate online collaboration, and it's important to be familiar with them. In this Team Time, each team will create a group report on a specific topic, using online collaboration tools, and compare and rate the tools and the collaboration process.

### process

Split your group into teams. To appreciate fully the benefits of online collaboration, each team should have at least five

or six members. Each group will create a team report on a topic that is approved by your instructor. As part of the report, one group member should record the process the group took to create the report, including a review of the tools used and reflections on the difficulties encountered by the group.

1. Conduct a virtual meeting. Agree on an online meeting and video collaboration tool such as Skype, Google Hangouts, or FaceTime and conduct a group chat. In this phase, outline your group project strategy and delegate work responsibilities.

2. Share documents and collaborate online. Your group must create one document that is accessible to every member at all times. Explore document-sharing sites such as Google Drive, Evernote, OneDrive, or Dropbox and collaboratively create your group document. All members are responsible for reviewing the entire document.

## conclusion

After all the team group reports have been completed and shared, discuss the following with your class: What is the benefit of using online collaboration technology to create group projects? How did collaboration technologies help or hinder the team process?

# Ethics Project

## Internet Privacy

In this exercise, you'll research a complicated ethical situation. The position you are asked to take may or may not match your own personal beliefs, but your research and use of logic will enable you to represent whichever view is assigned. Together the team will agree on an ethical solution.

### problem

Our smartphones and other devices that connect to the Internet enable us to share our information, such as where we are, what we've eaten, who we're friends with, when we've exercised, and what we're interested in. In essence, we've become a very public society. And studies show that for the most part, we don't care about being so open. But, should we? It's not just our friends and family that we're sharing this information with. Governments and companies are listening, too, and we've learned that often they can't be trusted in how they collect and use our data. In many cases, we agree to privacy terms when we want to use a device or software. We've come to accept that there is a tradeoff between being able to use a device or software and giving up some level of privacy. But is this the way it should be? Can we have smart devices that offer us great conveniences while preserving our fundamental right to privacy? Who is ultimately responsible for controlling our privacy: we or the companies that make the devices?

### research areas to consider

- Internet privacy
- Internet of Things
- Geolocation
- Social media and privacy

### process

1. Divide the class into teams and assign each team a device that is connected to the Internet or an app that is used to share information. Each team is to research the aspect of privacy from the perspective of digital device or software owners who enjoy the social networking feature of the device/software, and from the perspective of business management who has developed the device/software and is collecting and using the owners' location, usage, and other data.
2. Team members should write a summary of the position their team assumes, outlining the pros and cons of their position.
3. Team members should present their case to the class or submit a PowerPoint presentation for review by the rest of the class, along with the summary and resolution they developed.

### conclusion

As the use of social media and the Internet of Things becomes more prevalent, our definition of privacy and need for privacy may begin to erode. Being able to determine the benefits and potential sacrifices to our privacy is important in this Internet-connected society in which we live.

## Create a Report: Conducting Research on the Web

You and a partner have been asked to write a report on alternatives to using the Google search engine, as well as how to evaluate a website for a research paper. The paper needs to cite references within the body of the text, and include a list of your works cited at the end of the report. Your partner has begun the report. You are going to modify what has been started.

You will use the following skills as you complete this activity:

- Use Find and Replace
- Format Bulleted Lists
- Insert SmartArt

- Insert a Hyperlink
- Add Sources
- Insert Citations and Bibliography

## Instructions

1. Start Word. Open *TIA_Ch03_Start.docx* and save it as **TIA_Ch03_LastFirst.docx**, using your last and first name.
2. Using Find and Replace, find all instances of *meta-search* and replace them with **metasearch**.
3. At the blank paragraph after the end of the second paragraph of text under *Alternative Search Engines*, insert a Vertical Box List SmartArt graphic. Open the text pane, if necessary. With the cursor active in the first bullet, type **Google Scholar**. (Do not include the period.) Press **Enter**, press **Tab**, and then type **Searches scholarly literature**. (Do not include the period.)

   Repeat these steps to add the following information for the next two bullets:

   **Dogpile**
   > **Metasearch engine that searches Google, Yahoo!, and Bing**

   **Specialty Search Engines**
   > **Search only sites that are relevant to a topic or industry**

   Hint: To insert a SmartArt graphic, on the Insert tab, in the Illustrations group, click SmartArt.

4. Change the SmartArt graphic colors to Colorful—Accent Colors. Move the Google Scholar box and bullet point to the bottom of the SmartArt. Change the SmartArt Style to Intense Effect.

   Hint: To change the colors, on the SmartArt Tools Design tab, in the SmartArt Styles group, click Colors. To move the box and bullet point, select the content, then in the Create Graphic group, click Move Down. To change the style, in the SmartArt Styles group, click the more button for Styles.

5. In the second to last sentence of the first paragraph in the *Alternative Search Engines* section, select the text *specialty search engines*. Then, create a hyperlink to the web page **http://bestonlineuniversities.com/2011/20-useful-specialty-search-engines-for-college-students/**.

6. At the end of the first paragraph in the *Evaluating Websites* section, immediately to the left of the period, insert a citation to a new website. Before entering information, click the check box for Show All Bibliography Fields. Use the following information:

   Author: **Kapoun, Jim**
   Name of Web Page: **Five criteria for evaluating Web pages**
   Name of Web Site: **Olin & Uris Libraries, Cornell University**
   Year: **2010**
   Month: **May**
   Day: **10**
   URL: **http://olinuris.library.cornell.edu/ref/research/webcrit.html**

7. In the Evaluating Websites section, create a bulleted list with the five points beginning with *Authority, Bias or Objectivity, Relevance, Audience,* and *Coverage.* Use a checkmark as the bullet point.
8. Press Ctrl+End to go to the end of the document, press **Enter** twice, and then insert a Works Cited Bibliography. Change the citation style to **APA Sixth Edition**.
9. Save the document, and then close Word.
10. Submit the document as directed.

# 4 Application Software: Programs That Let You Work and Play

 For a chapter overview, watch the **Chapter Overview Videos**.

---

---

**MyLab IT** All media accompanying this chapter can be found here.

 **Make This** A More Powerful App on **page 132**

*(Ronstik/123RF; Rawpixel.com/Shutterstock; Rawpixel.com/Shutterstock; Laurent Davoust/123RF)*

# What do you think?

Now that it's effortless to use technology from almost anywhere, more of us are becoming **dependent on the tiny computers** we carry. So, it's no surprise that health experts are seeing a **rise in addictive tendencies** that involve technology. Some researchers say that people who use their phones or stay online for many hours a day experience a similar "high" as with other addictions. They also **feel withdrawal when cut off**. It's not just the amount of time spent with technology that defines addiction, but how excessive use adversely affects one's mental and physical health, daily life, relationships, and academic or job performance.

Apple is adding tools to help limit phone use in response to concerns about phone addiction. A new **activity report will track how much time** you're spending on your mobile device. Apple is also enabling you to see which apps are sending the most notifications, so you can **set your own limits**, such as one hour a day for Instagram.

Keep a technology-use diary for one week and note the amount of time you spend using technology.

- *Less than 4 hours*
- *Between 4 and 8 hours*
- *Between 9 and 12 hours*
- *More than 12 hours*

*See the end of the chapter for a follow-up question.*    (Ollyy/Shutterstock)    **121**

# Accessing, Using, and Managing Software

**Learning Outcome 4.1**   You will be able to explain the ways to access and use software and describe how to best manage your software.

Although a computer's hardware is critical, a computer system does nothing without software. In this section, we'll discuss the way software operates and how you can manage your software to make sure it is current and being used legally.

## Software Basics

It's important to understand what software is, how it's created, and the different models used to distribute it.

### Application vs. System Software

**Objective 4.1**   *Compare application software and system software.*

**What is software?** Technically speaking, the term software refers to a set of instructions that tells the computer what to do. An instruction set, also called a program, provides a means for us to interact with and use the computer, even if we lack specialized programming skills.

**What is the difference between application and system software?** Your computer has two main types of software. Application software is the software you use to do tasks at home, school, and work. System software is software that helps run the computer and coordinate instructions between application software and the computer's hardware devices. System software includes the operating system (such as Windows and macOS) and utility programs (programs in the operating system that help manage system resources). We discuss system software in detail in Chapter 5.

Other types of software, such as web browsers, virus protection, and backup and recovery software, are used every day. We'll discuss these types of software elsewhere in this book. In this chapter, we'll discuss productivity software and other types of software that you use to get things done.

### Distributing Software

**Objective 4.2**   *Explain the differences between commercial software and open source software and describe models for software distribution.*

**How is software created?** There are two main ways software is created. Proprietary (or commercial) software is created by companies for profit and then sold to you. Adobe Photoshop is an example of proprietary software. Open source software is software that is available free of charge and with few licensing and copyright restrictions. One advantage of open source software is that changes are made fairly quickly by community users, rather than having to go through a set process that is required by commercial software developers. However, unlike proprietary applications, open source applications offer little or no formal support. Instead, they're supported from their community of users across websites and newsgroups. Table 4.1 illustrates how some specific software products fit into each of these categories.

**How is software distributed?** Software is distributed in three main ways:

1. **Local installation:** With locally installed software (often referred to as *perpetual-license software*), you pay a one-time fee for either an electronic download or a disc of the software, which you then install on your device. Because the software resides on your hard drive, you can run the software anytime, whether you're connected to the Internet or not. You'll have the option to upgrade to a new version as it's released and you'll likely need to pay again to purchase the upgraded version. Desktop tax preparation software is an example of software distributed in this way.

2. **SaaS:** With Software as a Service (SaaS), the vendor hosts the software online and you access and use the software over the Internet without having to install it on your computer's

**Table 4.1  Open Source vs. Commercial Software**

| | System Software | | Application Software | |
|---|---|---|---|---|
| **Open Source** | Linux | | Gimp | LibreOffice |
| **Commercial** | macOS | Windows | Microsoft Office | Adobe Photoshop CC |

*(Stanislaw Mikulski/Shutterstock; Wikimedia; Wikimedia; Stanislaw Mikulski/Shutterstock; Courtesy of Microsoft Corp; Courtesy of Microsoft Corp; PixieMe/Shutterstock)*

hard drive. Because the program resides on a company's server and you run the program through your browser, you can run the program only when you're connected to the Internet. However, because the manufacturer updates the program on its server, you don't have to worry about manually upgrading the software yourself. Google Docs and Microsoft Office Online are examples of programs that are distributed in this way. SaaS programs are often free of charge but not as full featured as locally installed versions.

3. **Subscription:** With subscription software, you pay a fee to use the software for a certain time period. It is then available for you to download and install on your computer. As soon as updates are available, the manufacturer pushes these new features to you. You can use the software without being on the Internet but can only receive updates when you're connected to the Internet. The Adobe Creative Cloud applications and the Microsoft Office 365 subscription service are examples of software distributed in this way.

---

## Bits&Bytes  Finding Alternative Software

Free open source software products that are very similar to commercially sold versions are often available. But how do you find them? The site AlternativeTo (*alternativeto.net*) can help. Whether you're looking for mobile apps or software for any of the major operating systems, AlternativeTo can help you find the latest and best reviewed software options.

---

# Managing Your Software

It's important to know how to choose the best software for your computing device, how to get it onto your computer correctly, and how to remove it. We discuss all these topics next.

## Purchasing Software

**Objective 4.3**  *Explain the different options for purchasing software.*

**Where is the best place to buy software?** Depending on which device you're purchasing software for, there are many different software outlets. If you have a machine with an optical drive (a DVD or Blu-ray reader), you may want to go to a brick and mortar store for your software. Software for gaming consoles is still sold on discs, for example. However, the most popular way to purchase software is through an online download. Manufacturers' websites offer their full product line as electronic downloads. Software for mobile devices is sold electronically through centralized stores for each operating system. Apple runs the iTunes store, and Google administers the Google Play site. These sites see over 78 billion downloads a year (see Figure 4.1).

**Figure 4.1** Software for mobile devices is sold electronically through centralized stores like iTunes or Google Play. *(Bloomicon/Shutterstock)*

**Is discounted software for students available?** If you're a student, you can buy substantially discounted software that is no different from regularly priced software. Campus computer stores and college bookstores offer discounted prices to students who possess a valid student ID. Online software suppliers such as Journey Education Marketing (*journeyed.com*) and Academic Superstore (*academicsuperstore.com*) also offer popular software to students at reduced prices. Software developers, such as Microsoft and Adobe, also often offer their products to students at a discount, so it's always good to check a manufacturer's website before purchasing software or hardware. In addition, be sure to check with your college or school. Many times they have agreements with large vendors like Microsoft for free or reduced pricing for students.

**Can I get software for free legally?** In addition to open source software, freeware is copyrighted software that you can use for free. Explore sites like FileHippo (*filehippo. com*) to see how many good freeware programs are available. However, while much legitimate freeware exists, some unscrupulous people use freeware to distribute viruses and malware. Be cautious when installing freeware, especially if you're unsure of the provider's legitimacy.

New models for freely distributing software are also appearing. For example, if you use Amazon devices like the Fire tablet, you can get free applications through Amazon Underground. Developers are paid by Amazon for every minute each app is used.

**Can I try new software before it's released?** Some software developers offer beta versions of their software free of charge. A beta version is an application that is still under development. By distributing free beta versions, developers hope users will report errors, or bugs, they find in their programs. Many beta versions are available for a limited trial period and are used to help developers respond to issues before they launch the software on the market.

**Are there risks associated with installing beta versions?** By their very nature, beta products are unlikely to be bug free, so you always run the risk of something going awry with your system by installing and using beta versions. Unless you're willing to deal with potential problems, it may be best to wait until the last beta version is released—often referred to as the *gold version*. By that time, most of the serious bugs have been worked out.

As a precaution, you should be comfortable with the reliability of the source before downloading a beta version of software. If it's a reliable developer whose software you're familiar with, you can be

---

## Trends in IT    Mobile Payment Apps: The Power of M-Commerce

Most people own a mobile device, so it's no surprise that companies regard *mobile commerce* (or m-commerce)—using applications on smartphones and tablets to buy and sell products—as a trend that shouldn't be ignored.

Although mobile commerce hasn't taken over traditional methods of e-commerce just yet, the number of purchases from mobile devices continues to rise. The emergence of tablets and better functioning m-commerce apps has improved the mobile shopping experience.

The ability to make mobile payments is driving m-commerce. Mobile payment apps, such as Android Pay, Apple Pay, and Samsung Pay, make it convenient to pay just by waving your smartphone at an NFC-compatible terminal. (Near field communication, or NFC, is a set of protocols that facilitate communication between two devices.) Mobile payment apps have been available for several years, but why have they been slow to catch on?

People initially feared that the mobile payment apps were less secure than paying with a conventional credit/debit card. But with the large data breaches occurring at such retail stores as Target, conventional payment methods are no longer viewed

as more secure. And most mobile payment apps use *tokenization*, which substitutes *tokens*, one-use-only numbers, for your credit card numbers to process retail transactions. This makes them more secure than just swiping your credit card. Your credit card number remains safe, even if the retailer's system is hacked, because the retailer never actually has your credit card number.

Aside from general payment apps like Apple Pay, many merchants create their own mobile apps, which, in addition to paying for services, can be used to manage coupons, gift cards, and customer loyalty programs (see Figure 4.2). Some merchant apps also use tokenization to safeguard your information.

So wave that phone with confidence when buying your next latte. Your data should be safer than when you swipe your credit card.

**Figure 4.2** Merchant apps allow you to pay for products and manage loyalty rewards. *(Anna Hoychuk/Shutterstock)*

more certain that a serious bug or virus isn't hiding in the software. Similarly, you should be sure that the software you're downloading is meant for your system and that your system has met all the necessary hardware and operating system requirements.

## Installing and Uninstalling Software

**Objective 4.4** *Describe how to install and uninstall software.*

**How do I know the software I buy will work on my computer?** If you're buying software, it's your responsibility to check for compatibility with your system. Every software program has a set of system requirements that specify the minimum recommended standards for the operating system, processor, primary memory (random access memory, or RAM), and storage. These requirements are printed on the software packaging or are available at the manufacturer's website.

**What steps should I take before installing a new program?** Before installing any software, make sure your virus protection software is up to date. It's equally important to back up your system and create a restore point. A restore point doesn't affect your personal data files but saves all the apps, updates, drivers, and information needed to restore your computer system to the exact way it's configured at that time. That way, if something does go wrong, you can return your system to the way it was before the problem occurred. You can create a restore point by using Windows 10 System protection tools. To create a restore point, type *restore point* in the Cortana search box and select *Create a Restore Point Control Panel* to display the System Properties dialog box. On the System Protection tab, click the *Create* button, type a description for the restore point (such as "Before installing [name of software]"), and click *Create*. You will be notified when the restore point is created.

**What's the difference between a custom installation and a full installation?** The exact installation process will differ slightly depending on whether you're installing the software from a disc, purchasing it from an app marketplace, or downloading it from the web. If you're using an option that requires files to be installed locally, the installation wizard will ask you to decide between a full installation and a custom installation. A full installation (sometimes referred to as a typical installation) copies all the most commonly used files and programs to your computer's hard drive. By selecting custom installation, you can decide which features you want installed, which saves space on your hard drive.

**How do I uninstall a program?** An application contains many files—library files, help files, and other text files—in addition to the main file that runs the program. By deleting only the main file, you're not ridding your system of all the programs. Windows 10 makes it easy to uninstall a program: On the Start menu, right-click the app and select *Uninstall*.

**If my computer crashes, can I get the preinstalled software back?** Although some preinstalled software is not necessary to replace if your computer crashes, other software such as the

**Buying and Installing Software**

In this Helpdesk, you'll play the role of a helpdesk staffer, fielding questions about how to best purchase software or to get it for free, how to install and uninstall software, and where you can go for help when you have a problem with your software.

operating system is critical to reinstall. Most manufacturers use a separate partition on the hard drive to hold an image, or copy, of the preinstalled software. However, it's not always possible to reboot from the partitioned hard drive, especially when your computer crashes, so one of the first things you should do after you purchase a new computer is create a recovery drive. A recovery drive contains all the information needed to reinstall your operating system if it should become corrupted. Often the manufacturer will have placed a utility on your system to create this.

You can also use the Recovery utility included in Windows to create a recovery drive. You access these tools in Windows 10 by typing *Recovery* in the Cortana search box, and then selecting *Create a recovery drive*. When the Recovery Drive dialog box opens, click Next. Then insert a blank flash drive into a USB port and follow the steps in the wizard. Once the recovery drive has been made, label the flash drive and put it away in a safe place.

## Upgrading Software

**Objective 4.5** *Explain the considerations around the decision to upgrade your software.*

**When do I need to upgrade software?** Periodically, software developers improve the functionality of their software by releasing a software upgrade. When software is sold by subscription or using the cloud-based SaaS model, you don't need to worry about upgrading because

---

## Dig Deeper    How Number Systems Work

As we discussed in Chapter 2, to process data into information, computers need to work in a language they understand. This language, called *binary language*, consists of two digits: 0 and 1. Everything a computer does, including running the applications we've been discussing, is broken down into a series of 0s and 1s. *Electrical switches* are the devices inside the computer that are flipped between the two states of 1 and 0, signifying on and off. How can simple switches be organized so that they let you use a computer to pay your bills online or write an essay? Let's look at how number systems work.

A **number system** is an organized plan for representing a number. Although you may not realize it, you're already familiar with one number system. The **base-10 number system**, also known as **decimal notation**, is the system you use to represent the numeric values you use each day. It's called base 10 because it uses 10 digits—0 through 9—to represent any value.

To represent a number in base 10, you break the number down into groups of ones, tens, hundreds, thousands, and so on. Each digit has a place value depending on where it appears in the number. For example, using base 10, in the whole number 6,954, there are 6 sets of thousands, 9 sets of hundreds, 5 sets of tens, and 4 sets of ones. Working from right to left, each place in a number represents an increasing power of 10, as follows:

$$6,954 = (6 * 1,000) + (9 * 100) + (5 * 10) + (4 * 1)$$
$$= (6 * 10^3) + (9 * 10^2) + (5 * 10^1) + (4 * 10^0)$$

Note that in this equation, the final digit 4 is represented as $4 * 10^0$ because any number raised to the zero power is equal to 1.

Anthropologists theorize that humans developed a base-10 number system because we have 10 fingers. However, computer systems are not well suited to thinking about numbers in groups of 10. Instead, computers describe a number in powers of 2 because each switch can be in one of two positions: on or off. This numbering system is referred to as the **binary number system** (or **base-2 number system**). In the base-10 number system, a whole number is represented as the sum of 1s, 10s, 100s, and 1,000s—that is, sums of powers of 10. The binary number system works in the same way but describes a value as the sum of groups of 1s, 2s, 4s, 8s, 16s, 32s, 64s, and so on—that is, powers of 2.

Let's look at the number 67. In base 10, the number 67 would be six sets of 10s and seven sets of 1s, as follows:

$$67_{\text{Base 10}} = (6 * 10^1) + (7 * 10^0)$$

One way to figure out how 67 is represented in base 2 is to find the largest possible power of 2 that could be in the number 67. Two to the seventh power is 128, which is bigger than 67. Two to the sixth power is 64, which is less than 67 meaning there is a group of 64 inside a group of 67.

| 67 has | 1 | group of | 64 | That leaves 3 and |
|--------|---|----------|----|----|
| 3 has | 0 | groups of | 32 | |
| | 0 | groups of | 16 | |
| | 0 | groups of | 8 | |
| | 0 | groups of | 4 | |
| | 1 | group of | 2 | That leaves 1 and |
| 1 has | 1 | group of | 1 | Now nothing is left. |

it's handled automatically. Software purchased through mobile app stores also updates automatically. However, if you're using software that was installed locally to your hard drive, you'll need to make the upgrade decision yourself. Before upgrading, it's important to understand what's included in the upgrade and how stable the new software version is. Depending on the software, some upgrades may not be sufficiently different from the previous version to make it cost-effective for you to buy the newest version. Unless the upgrade adds features that are important to you, you may be better off waiting to upgrade. You also should consider whether you use the software frequently enough to justify an upgrade and whether your current system can handle the new system requirements of the upgraded version. In between upgrades, developers will make available software updates (sometimes referred to as software patches). Updates are usually downloaded automatically and provide smaller enhancements to the software or fix program bugs.

## Software Licenses

**Objective 4.6**  *Explain how software licenses function.*

**Don't I own the software I buy?** Unlike most other items you purchase, the software you buy doesn't belong to you. What you're actually purchasing is a license that gives you the right to use the software for your own purpose.

So, the binary number for 67 is written as 1000011 in base 2:

$$67_{Base\ 10} = 64 + 0 + 0 + 0 + 0 + 2 + 1$$
$$= (1 * 2^6) + (0 * 2^5) + (0 * 2^4) + (0 * 2^3) +$$
$$(0 * 2^2) + (1 * 2^1) + (1 * 2^0)$$
$$= 1000011_{Base\ 2}$$

A large integer value becomes a very long string of 1s and 0s in binary. For convenience, programmers often use hexadecimal notation to make these expressions easier to use. Hexadecimal is a base-16 number system, meaning it uses 16 digits to represent numbers instead of the 10 digits used in base 10 or the 2 digits used in base 2. The 16 digits it uses are the 10 numeric digits, 0 to 9, plus six extra symbols: A, B, C, D, E, and F. Each of the letters A through F corresponds to a numeric value, so that A equals 10, B equals 11, and so on. Therefore, the value 67 in decimal notation is 1000011, or 43 (= 4 * 16 + 3 * 1) in hexadecimal notation. It is much easier for computer scientists to use the 2-digit 43 than the 7-digit string 1000011.

We've just been converting integers from base 10, which we understand, to base 2 (binary state), which the computer understands. Similarly, we need a system that converts letters and other symbols that we understand to a binary state the computer understands. To provide a consistent means for representing letters and other characters, certain codes dictate how to represent characters in binary format. Most of today's personal computers use the American National Standards Institute (ANSI, pronounced "AN-see") standard code, called the American Standard Code for Information Interchange (ASCII, pronounced "AS-key"), to represent each letter or character as an 8-bit (or 1-byte) binary code.

When you convert a base 10 number to binary format, the binary format has no standard length. For example, the binary format for the number 2 is two digits (10), whereas for the number 10 it is four digits (1010). Although binary numbers can have more or fewer than 8 bits, each single alphabetic or special character is 1 byte (or 8 bits) of data. The ASCII code uses 8 bits to represent each of the 26 uppercase letters and 26 lowercase letters used in the English language, along with many punctuation symbols and other special characters. Because the ASCII code represents letters and characters using only 8 bits, it can assign only 256 (or $2^8$) different codes. Although this is enough to represent English and many other characters found in the world's languages, the ASCII code can't represent all languages and symbols. Thus, an encoding scheme, called Unicode, was created. By using 16 bits instead of 8 bits, Unicode can represent nearly 1,115,000 code points and currently assigns more than 128,000 unique character symbols. As we continue to become a more global society, it is anticipated that Unicode will replace ASCII as the standard character formatting code.

 **Sound Byte**  MyLab IT

**Where Does Binary Show Up?**

This Sound Byte helps remove the mystery around binary numbers. You'll learn about base conversion between decimal, binary, and hexadecimal numbers using colors, sounds, and images.

A software license, also known as an End User License Agreement (EULA), is an agreement between you, the user, and the software company (see Figure 4.3). You accept this agreement before installing the software on your machine. It's a legal contract that outlines the acceptable uses of the program and any actions that violate the agreement. Generally, the agreement states who the ultimate owner of the software is, under what circumstances copies of the software can be made, and whether the software can be installed on any other computing device. Finally, the license agreement states what, if any, warranty comes with the software.

**Does a license only cover one installation?** Some software comes with a single license that covers only one person's use on a single device. You can't share these licenses, and you can't "extend" the license to install the software on more than one of your devices. Many manufacturers are allowing a single copy to be installed on several devices. For example, Apple offers a Family Pack Software License Agreement that permits a user to install the purchased software legally on as many as five computers in the same household, and some versions of Microsoft Office come with a license that allows the installation of the software on multiple computers.

Businesses and educational institutions often buy multiuser licenses that allow more than one person to use the software. Some multiuser licenses are per-seat and limit the number of users overall, whereas others, called concurrent licenses, limit the number of users accessing the software at any given time.

**Does open source software require a license?** Anyone using open source software has access to the program's code. Therefore, open source software programs can be tweaked by another user and redistributed. A free software license, the GNU General Public License, is required and grants the recipients the right to modify and redistribute the software. Without such a license, the recipient would be in violation of copyright laws. This concept of redistributing modified open source software under the same terms as the original software is known as copyleft. Thus, all enhancements, additions, and other changes to copyleft software must also be distributed as free software.

**Figure 4.3** You must accept the terms of the software license before using the product. *(Courtesy of Microsoft Corp.)*

# Ethics in IT

## Can I Borrow Software That I Don't Own?

As noted earlier, when you purchase software, you're purchasing a license to use it rather than purchasing the actual software. That license tells you how many times you can install the software, so it's important to read it. If you use, copy, or distribute more copies of the software than the license permits, you're participating in software piracy (see Figure 4.4).

Historically, the most common way software has been pirated has been by borrowing installation discs and installing the software on other computers. Larger-scale illegal duplication and distribution by counterfeiters are common as well. In addition, the Internet provides ways to copy and distribute pirated software illegally.

Is it a big deal to copy a program or two? As reported by the Business Software Alliance, over one third of all software used is pirated. Not only is pirating software unethical and illegal, the practice has financial impacts on all software consumers. The financial loss to the software industry is estimated to be over $62 billion a year. This loss decreases the amount of money available for further software research and development, while increasing the up-front costs to legitimate consumers.

To determine whether you have a pirated copy of software installed on your computer, conduct a software audit. The Business Software Alliance website (*bsa.org*) has several free third-party software audit tools that help you identify and track software installed on your computer and networks. These programs check the serial numbers of the software installed on your computer against software manufacturer databases of officially licensed copies and known fraudulent copies. Any suspicious software installations are flagged for your attention.

So far, there's no such thing as an official software police force, but if you're caught with pirated software, severe penalties do exist. A company or individual can pay up to $150,000 for each software title copied. In addition, you can be criminally prosecuted for copyright infringement, which carries a fine of up to $250,000, a five-year jail sentence, or both.

**Figure 4.4** Making more copies than the software license permits is pirating and is illegal. *(Alexskopje/123RF)*

Efforts to stop groups involved with counterfeit software are in full force. Software manufacturers also are becoming more aggressive in programming mechanisms into software to prevent illegal installations. For instance, with many products, installation requires you to activate the serial number of your software with a database maintained by the software manufacturer. Failure to activate your serial number or attempting to activate a serial number used previously results in the software going into a "reduced functionality mode" after a certain number of uses. This usually precludes you from doing useful things like saving files created with the software.

---

### Before moving on to Part 2:

1.  Watch Chapter Overview Video 4.1.
2. Then take the Check Your Understanding quiz.

# Check Your Understanding // Review & Practice

For a quick review to see what you've learned so far, answer the following questions.

## multiple choice

1. Microsoft Office is an example of which type of software?

   a. Open source system software

   b. Proprietary application software

   c. Open source application software

   d. Proprietary system software

2. Beta software is never

   a. system software.

   b. the final finished version of the software.

   c. open source software.

   d. application software.

3. Choosing which features of software you want to install is what kind of installation?

   a. Custom installation

   b. Full installation

   c. Restore installation

   d. Single installation

4. Which type of software is not upgraded automatically?

   a. Software as a service

   b. Mobile apps

   c. Locally installed

   d. Subscription based

5. Which best describes copyleft?

   a. A single license covering a single user on a single device

   b. A license that grants users the right to modify and redistribute the software

   c. A license covering one user with multiple installations

   d. A family pack license

---

**chew on this**

Because app marketplaces work so well with mobile devices, it is difficult to find alternate sources of software.

a. Will this end software piracy, since mobile apps are not distributed on discs and must be purchased at one specified place?

b. Should software for laptops and desktops be distributed only through app marketplaces to prevent piracy?

c. What else might be done to combat software piracy? Explain your answers.

---

**MyLab IT**

Go to **MyLab IT** to take an autograded version of the *Check Your Understanding* review and to find all media resources for the chapter.

---

> **For the IT Simulation for this chapter, see MyLab IT.**

# Try This

## Citing Website Sources

You've been assigned a research paper, and your instructor requires citations. In the past, you might have used websites such as Son of Citation Machine (*citationmachine.net*) to create your citations. As you'll see in this Try This, there are tools built right into Microsoft Word that do the same thing. (Note: For more step-by-step instructions and also for information on how to build a bibliography, watch the Try This video on MyLab IT.)

**Step 1** Click at the end of the sentence or phrase that you want to cite. On the References tab, in the Citations & Bibliography group, set the Bibliography style to the format you wish to follow, for example MLA or APA. Click **Insert Citation**. To add a source, click **Add New Source**.

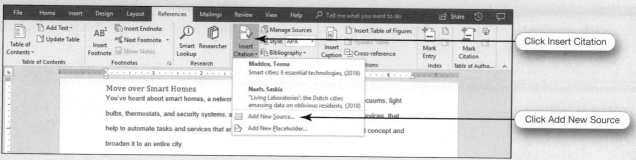

*(Courtesy of Microsoft Corp.)*

Note: To create a citation and fill in the source information later, click **Add New Placeholder**.

**Step 2** Click the arrow next to Type of Source and begin to fill in the source information. Click OK when you're done.

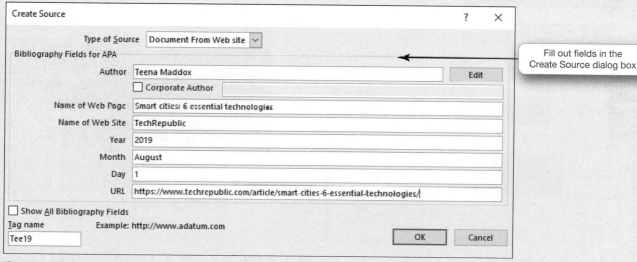

*(Courtesy of Microsoft Corp.)*

**Step 3** The citation will appear in your document.

*(Courtesy of Microsoft Corp.)*

## A More Powerful App

Want your app to be able to open a file from the SD card on your phone, fire up the YouTube app, or display a location in the Maps app?

In this exercise, you'll use ActivityStarter to incorporate the software already on your device into your mobile app.

It's as easy as using the Connectivity drawer of the Designer. Drag the ActivityStarter component onto your Designer screen, and then control it with the Blocks for ActivityStarter. Your apps now have the power of all the software on your device behind them!

The ActivityStarter component allows you to use the existing software on your device from within your mobile app.

*(Copyright MIT, used with permission.)*

*(Copyright MIT, used with permission.)*

*(Copyright MIT, used with permission.)*

To create this app for iOS, go to *Thunkable.com*, a programming platform based on App Inventor.
**For the instructions for this exercise, go to MyLab IT.**

# Application Software

One reason computers are invaluable is that they make it easier to complete daily tasks. While many programs help you be more productive, there are also programs that entertain you with audio, video, and images, as well as games, animations, and movies.

In this section, we'll look at applications that help enhance your productivity, support your business projects, and let you create multimedia.

# Productivity and Business Software

Let's start by looking at productivity and business software.

## Productivity Software

**Objective 4.7**   *Categorize the types of application software used to enhance productivity and describe their uses and features.*

**What is productivity software?** Productivity software lets you perform various tasks required at home, school, and business. The main types of productivity software include programs for word processing, spreadsheet analysis, presentations, database management, note-taking, and personal information management. In addition, financial planning software and tax preparation software are available for personal use.

**How do I choose among the many different programs available?** When you're looking for a specific product, say, a word processing program, you have many choices. As discussed earlier, you can choose between commercial products and open source products or choose to install the program on your local device or use it purely online. Table 4.2 guides you through these many choices.

Microsoft Office is a very successful set of productivity programs and is offered as installed software (Office 2019) or as software as a service (Office 365). A fully online version, Microsoft Office Online, is also available. Google Docs is a strong competitor for purely online products. The open source option LibreOffice is free to download and install and is supported by an active community.

Next, we'll examine each type of program to understand its key features.

**Table 4.2** Productivity Software

| PROGRAM | WORD PROCESSING | SPREADSHEET | PRESENTATION | DATABASE | NOTE-TAKING | PIM/E-MAIL |
|---|---|---|---|---|---|---|
| **Installed: Proprietary** | | | | | | |
| **Microsoft Office** | Word | Excel | PowerPoint | Access | OneNote | Outlook |
| **Apple iWork** | Pages | Numbers | Keynote | | | |
| **Installed: Open Source** | | | | | | |
| **LibreOffice** | Writer | Calc | Impress | Base | | |
| **Web-Based** | | | | | | |
| **Microsoft Office Online** | Word | Excel | PowerPoint | | OneNote | Outlook |
| **Google Docs** | Docs | Sheets | Slides | | | Gmail |
| **Zoho** | Writer | Sheet, Books | Show | Creator | Notebook | |
| **ThinkFree** | Write | Calc | Show | | Note | |

### Word Processing Software

**What are the most common word processing applications?** You've probably used word processing software to create and edit documents such as research papers, class notes, and résumés. Microsoft Word is the most popular word processing program that you can buy and install on your computer. If you're looking for a more affordable alternative, you might want to try an open source program such as Writer, from LibreOffice (*libreoffice.org*). When saving a document in Writer, the default file format has an OpenDocument (.odt) file extension. However, by using the Save As command, you can save files in other formats, such as .docx for Word.

**What are the special features of word processing programs?** Word processors come with basic tools such as spelling and grammar checking, a thesaurus, and language translator. There are tools to format bibliographical references and organize them into a database so you can reuse them in other papers quickly. You can also enhance the look of your document by creating an interesting background, inserting images, or by adding a theme of coordinated colors and styles (see Figure 4.5).

## Bits&Bytes   How to Open Unknown File Types

Normally, when you double-click a file to open it, the program associated with the file opens automatically. For example, when you double-click a file with a .doc or .docx extension, the file opens in Microsoft Word. However, if the file has no extension or Windows has no application associated with that file type, a *How do you want to open this file?* dialog box appears and asks what program you want to use to open the file. In other cases, a document may open with a program other than the one you want to use. This is because many applications can open several file types, and the program you expected the file to open in isn't the program currently associated with that file type. To assign a program to a file type or to change the program to open a particular file type, follow these instructions:

1. Use the search and navigation tools in File Explorer to locate the file you want to change. (For example, you can search for all Word files by searching for *.doc or *.docx.) Right-click on the file, and then point to **Open with**.
2. A list of programs installed on your computer appears. Click the program you want to use to open this file type. If you're sure the selected program is the one that should always be used for this file type, select **Choose another app,** which opens the **How do you want to open this file?** dialog box. Check the **Always use this app to open [extension] files**, and click the default program from the list.

When you open the file in the future, the file will open in the program you selected.

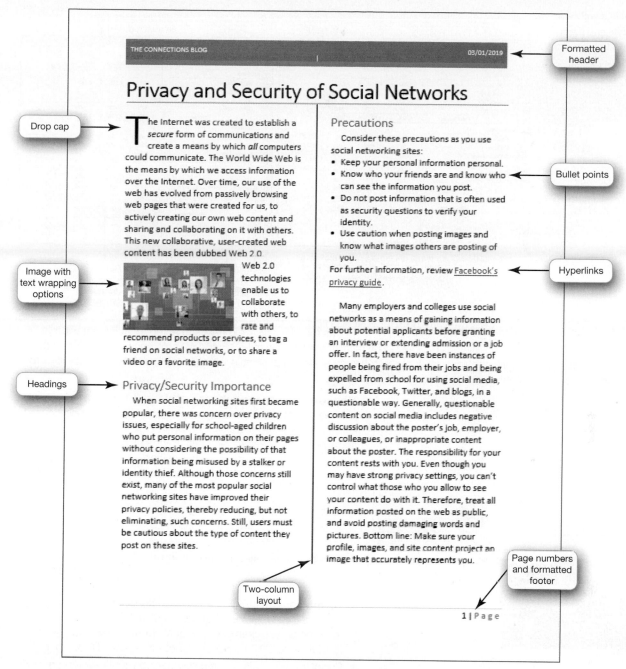

The figure contains the following labeled callouts and document text:

**Callouts:**
- Formatted header
- Drop cap
- Image with text wrapping options
- Headings
- Bullet points
- Hyperlinks
- Page numbers and formatted footer
- Two-column layout

**Document text within figure:**

# Privacy and Security of Social Networks

The Internet was created to establish a *secure* form of communications and create a means by which *all* computers could communicate. The World Wide Web is the means by which we access information over the Internet. Over time, our use of the web has evolved from passively browsing web pages that were created for us, to actively creating our own web content and sharing and collaborating on it with others. This new collaborative, user-created web content has been dubbed Web 2.0.

Web 2.0 technologies enable us to collaborate with others, to rate and recommend products or services, to tag a friend on social networks, or to share a video or a favorite image.

## Privacy/Security Importance

When social networking sites first became popular, there was concern over privacy issues, especially for school-aged children who put personal information on their pages without considering the possibility of that information being misused by a stalker or identity thief. Although those concerns still exist, many of the most popular social networking sites have improved their privacy policies, thereby reducing, but not eliminating, such concerns. Still, users must be cautious about the type of content they post on these sites.

## Precautions

Consider these precautions as you use social networking sites:
- Keep your personal information personal.
- Know who your friends are and know who can see the information you post.
- Do not post information that is often used as security questions to verify your identity.
- Use caution when posting images and know what images others are posting of you.

For further information, review Facebook's privacy guide.

Many employers and colleges use social networks as a means of gaining information about potential applicants before granting an interview or extending admission or a job offer. In fact, there have been instances of people being fired from their jobs and being expelled from school for using social media, such as Facebook, Twitter, and blogs, in a questionable way. Generally, questionable content on social media includes negative discussion about the poster's job, employer, or colleagues, or inappropriate content about the poster. The responsibility for your content rests with you. Even though you may have strong privacy settings, you can't control what those who you allow to see your content do with it. Therefore, treat all information posted on the web as public, and avoid posting damaging words and pictures. Bottom line: Make sure your profile, images, and site content project an image that accurately represents you.

1 | P a g e

**Figure 4.5** Nearly every word processing application has formatting features that let you give your documents a professional look. *(Courtesy of Microsoft Corp.)*

## Spreadsheet Software

**Why would I use spreadsheet software?** Spreadsheet software lets you make calculations and perform numerical analyses. For example, you can use it to create a simple budget, as shown in Figure 4.6a. Microsoft Excel and LibreOffice Calc are two examples of spreadsheet software. (Web-based options are available within Google Docs and Office Online.) One benefit of spreadsheet software is that it can automatically recalculate all formulas and functions in a spreadsheet when values for some of the inputs change. For example, as shown in Figure 4.6b, you can insert an additional row in your budget ("Membership") and change a value (for September Financial aid), and the results for "Total Expenses" and "Net Income" recalculate automatically.

Because automatic recalculation lets you immediately see the effects different options have on your spreadsheet, you can quickly test different assumptions. This is called *what-if analysis*. Look again

**Figure 4.6** Spreadsheet software lets you easily calculate and manipulate numerical data with the use of built-in formulas. *(Courtesy of Microsoft Corp.)*

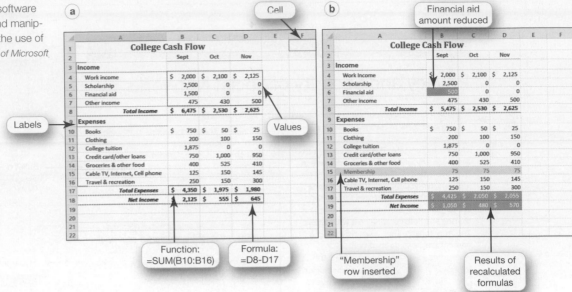

at Figure 4.6b and ask, "If I don't get as much financial aid next semester, what impact will that have on my total budget?" The recalculated cells in rows 18 and 19 help answer your question. In addition to financial analysis, many spreadsheet applications have limited database capabilities to chart, sort, filter, and group data.

**How do I use spreadsheet software?** The basic element in a spreadsheet program is the *worksheet*, which is a grid consisting of columns and rows. As shown in Figure 4.6a, the columns and rows form boxes called *cells*. Each cell can be identified according to its column and row position. For example, the cell in column A, row 1 is cell A1. You can enter several types of data into a cell:

- **Text:** Any combination of letters, numbers, symbols, and spaces. Text is often used as labels to identify the contents of a worksheet or chart.
- **Values and dates (numerical data):** These values can represent a quantity or a date/time and are often the basis for calculations.
- **Formulas:** Equations that use addition, subtraction, multiplication, and division operators, as well as values and cell references. For example, in Figure 4.6a, you would use the formula =D8-D17 to calculate net income for November.
- **Functions:** Functions help develop formulas. Adding a group of numbers (SUM) or determining the monthly loan payment (PMT) can be done using built-in functions. Functions free you from needing to know the math behind the calculation. In Figure 4.6a, to calculate the total expenses for September, you could use the built-in summation function =SUM(B10:B16).

**Figure 4.7** (a) Column charts show comparisons. (b) Pie charts show how parts contribute to the whole. (c) Line charts show trends over time. *(Courtesy of Microsoft Corp.)*

**What kinds of graphs and charts can I create with spreadsheet software?** Most spreadsheet applications let you create a variety of charts, including basic column charts, pie charts, and line charts, with or without 3D effects (see Figure 4.7). In addition, you can make stock charts (for investment analysis) and scatter charts (for statistical analysis) or create custom charts. Another feature in Excel is *sparklines*—charts that fit into a single cell and make it easy to show data trends (see Figure 4.8a). To analyze very large data sets, Excel has added newer chart types like treemaps, sunbursts, and waterfall charts (see Figure 4.8b).

## Presentation Software

**How can software help with my presentations?** You've no doubt sat through presentations where the speaker used presentation software such as Microsoft PowerPoint (see Figure 4.9) or Apple's Keynote or Google Slides to create a slide show. Because these applications are simple to use, you can produce high-quality presentations without a lot of training. You can embed videos, add effects, and trim video clips without separate video-editing programs. You can also integrate quizzes, voice, and video into your PowerPoint presentations to make them more interactive.

**What are some tips to make a great presentation?** Some standard guidelines will help improve your presentation but not interfere with your creativity:

- **Use images:** Images can convey a thought or illustrate a point. Make sure any text over an image can be read easily.
- **Be careful with color:** Choose dark text on a light background or light text on a dark background. Avoid using text and background colors that clash.
- **Use bullets for key points:** Use no more than four to six bulleted points per slide. Avoid full sentences and paragraphs.
- **Consider font size and style:** Keep the font size large enough to read from the back of the room. Avoid script or fancy font styles. Use only one or two font styles per presentation.
- **Keep animations and/or background audio to a minimum:** They can be distracting.

(a) Sparklines

(b)

**Figure 4.8** (a) Sparklines and (b) sunbursts are two of many charting tools in Excel. *(Courtesy of Microsoft Corp.)*

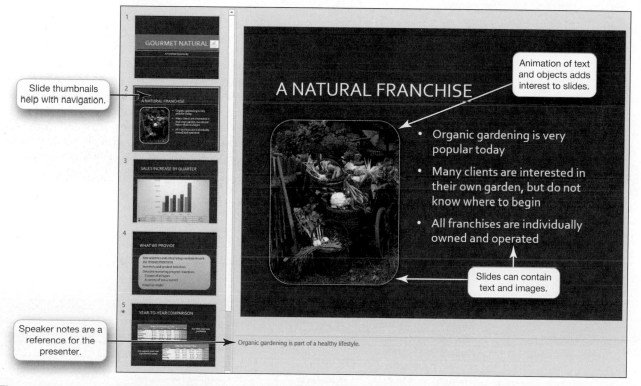

Slide thumbnails help with navigation.

A NATURAL FRANCHISE

Animation of text and objects adds interest to slides.

- Organic gardening is very popular today
- Many clients are interested in their own garden, but do not know where to begin
- All franchises are individually owned and operated

Slides can contain text and images.

Speaker notes are a reference for the presenter.

Organic gardening is part of a healthy lifestyle.

**Figure 4.9** You can use presentation software to create dynamic slide shows. *(Courtesy of Microsoft Corp.; Picture Alliance)*

Several applications offer an alternative to PowerPoint. One option is Prezi. Rather than using a set of slides, Prezi uses a canvas in which you connect ideas. PowToon provides a library of cartoon-like characters that are easily animated to give your presentations more of a "storytelling" aspect. Sway is a stand-alone app from Microsoft that allows you to create presentations that are stored in the cloud and linked to your Microsoft account. Sway facilitates importing content from a variety of sources to allow you to tell a story and is designed primarily for creating web-based presentations. (see Figure 4.10).

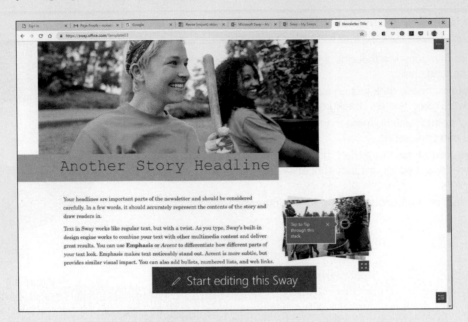

**Figure 4.10** Sway is used to create web-based presentations. *(Courtesy of Microsoft Corp.; Sway.com/Template08)*

## Database Software

**Why is database software useful?** Database software such as Oracle, MySQL, and Microsoft Access are applications that let you store and organize data. Spreadsheet applications have limited database functionalities for simple tasks such as sorting, filtering, and organizing data. However, you need to use a more robust, fully featured database application to manage larger and more complicated data that is organized in more than one table; to group, sort, and retrieve data; and to generate reports. Traditional databases are organized into *fields*, *records*, and *tables*, as shown in Figure 4.11.

**Figure 4.11** In databases, information is organized into fields, records, and tables. *(Courtesy of Microsoft Corp.)*

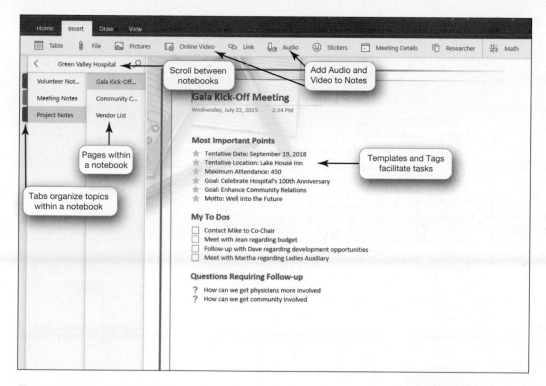

**Figure 4.12** Microsoft OneNote is a great way to collect and organize notes and other information. The files are readily searchable and easy to share. *(Courtesy of Microsoft Corp.)*

**How do businesses use database software?** Most websites rely on databases to keep track of products, clients, invoices, and personnel information. Often, some of that information is available to a home computer user. For example, at Amazon, you can access the history of all the purchases you've made on the site. Shipping companies let you search their online databases for tracking numbers, allowing you to get information on your package status.

### Note-Taking Software

**Is there software to help me take notes?** Microsoft OneNote is a note-taking and organizational tool you can use for research, brainstorming, and collaboration, as well as organizing information. Using OneNote, you can organize your notes into tabbed sections (see Figure 4.12). In addition, you can access your OneNote notes from other Microsoft Office applications. For example, if you're writing a research paper in Word, click the OneNote icon in the Word ribbon to open OneNote, where you can add your notes—perhaps a reference to a website. Later, if you open OneNote and click on that reference, it will bring you to the spot in the Word document where you made the reference.

You can also add audio or video recordings of lectures to OneNote, and you can search for a term across all the digital notebooks you created during the semester to find common ideas, such as key points that might appear on a test. There is also a OneNote mobile app.

Several free online note-taking options are also available to help you take notes or to jot down a quick reminder. Evernote, for example, lets you take notes via the web, your phone, or your computer and then syncs your notes between your devices. You can then share your notes with other Evernote users for easy collaboration. Table 4.3 lists some other popular alternative note-taking applications.

**Table 4.3  Beyond Microsoft OneNote: Alternative Note-Taking Applications**

**Evernote (evernote.com)**
- Web-based
- Notes can be shared for easy collaboration
- Syncs notes between all devices

**AudioNote (luminantsoftware.com)**
- Synchronized note taking and audio recording
- Allows text or handwritten notes
- Highlights notes during playback

**Simplenote (simplenote.com)**
- Web-based, open source
- Notes organized by tags
- Mobile apps available

**Notability (gingerlabs.com)**
- PDF annotations
- Advanced word processing
- Linked audio recordings to notes
- Auto-sync notes between devices

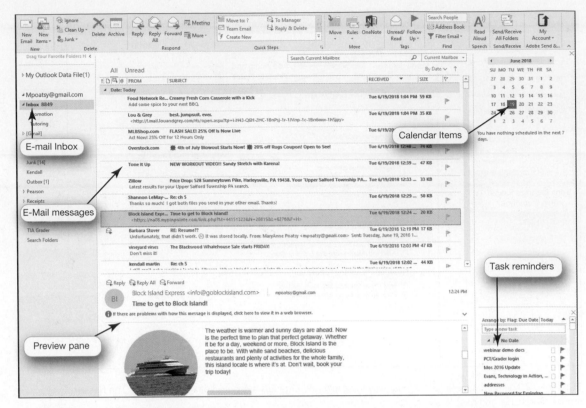

Labels on figure:
Calendar Items
E-mail Inbox
E-Mail messages
Task reminders
Preview pane

**Figure 4.13** Microsoft Outlook includes common PIM features, such as a summary of appointments, a list of tasks, and e-mail messages. *(Courtesy of Microsoft Corp.)*

### Personal Information Manager Software

**How can software help me manage my e-mail, time, contact lists, and tasks?** Most people need some form of personal information manager (PIM) software to help manage e-mail, contacts, calendars, and tasks in one place. Microsoft Outlook (see Figure 4.13) is a widely used PIM program. If you share a network and are using the same PIM software as others on a common network, a PIM program simplifies sharing calendars and scheduling meetings.

Many web-based e-mail clients, such as Yahoo! and Google, also include coordinating calendar and contacts similar to those of Microsoft Outlook. Google's calendar and contacts sync with Outlook so you can access your Outlook calendar information by logging into Google. This gives you access to your schedule anywhere you have access to a computer and an Internet connection.

A wide variety of other to-do lists and simple organizers work with mobile and computing devices. For example, Toodledo is a free program that coordinates well with Microsoft Outlook, and OmniFocus 3 is a more full-featured option for Mac devices, including a slick interface for Apple Watch.

### Productivity Software Features

**What tools can help me work more efficiently with productivity software?** Whether you're working on a word processing document, spreadsheet, database, or slide presentation, you can make use of several tools to increase your efficiency:

**Sound Byte** MyLab IT

**Programming for End Users**

In this Sound Byte, you'll be guided through the creation of a macro in Microsoft Office. You'll learn how Office enables you to program with macros in order to customize and extend the capabilities it offers.

- A wizard walks you through the steps necessary to complete a task. At each step, the wizard asks you questions. Based on your responses, the wizard helps you complete that portion of the task. When you install software, you're often guided by a wizard.
- A template is a predesigned form. Templates are included in many productivity applications. They provide the basic structure for a particular kind of document, spreadsheet, database, or presentation and are designed to be customized to fit specific needs. Templates can include page layout designs, formatting, and styles relevant to that particular document, and automated tasks (macros).
- A macro is a small program that groups a series of commands so that they will run as a single command. Macros are best used to automate a routine task or a complex series of commands that must be run frequently. For example, a teacher may write a macro to sort the grades in her

**Figure 4.14** Mint (*mint.com*) is an online financial management tool. An extensive online community provides helpful tips and discussions with other people in similar situations. *(Reprinted with permission © Intuit Inc. All rights reserved.)*

gradebook in descending order and to highlight grades that add up to less than a C average. Every time she adds the results of an assignment or a test, she can set up the macro to run through this series of steps.

### Personal Financial Software

**How can I use software to keep track of my finances?** Financial planning software helps you manage your daily finances. Financial planning programs include electronic checkbook registers and bill payment tools. With these features, you can make recurring monthly payments, such as rent or student loans, with automatically scheduled online payments. The software records all transactions in the checkbook register. In addition, you can assign categories to each transaction and use these categories to create budgets and analyze your spending patterns.

Intuit's installed and web-based products, Quicken and Mint (*mint.com*), are the market leaders in financial planning software (see Figure 4.14). Both track and analyze your spending habits and offer advice on how to better manage your finances. With either, you also can track your investment portfolio. With Mint, you can monitor and update your finances from any computer with a private and secure setting. You can also access Mint on a smartphone or tablet, so access to your financial information is convenient. Mint also provides access to a network of other users with whom to exchange tips and advice.

**What software can I use to prepare my taxes?** Tax preparation software, such as Intuit TurboTax and H&R Block Tax Software, lets you prepare your state and federal taxes on your own. Both programs offer tax forms and instructions, as well as videos with expert advice on how to complete each form. Each company also offers free web-based versions of federal forms and instructions. In addition, error-checking features are built into the programs to catch mistakes as well as provide audit alerts. Both programs allow you to file your return electronically and offer financial planning guidance to help you plan and manage your financial resources in the following year (see Figure 4.15).

Some financial planning applications also coordinate with tax preparation software. Both Quicken and Mint, for example, integrate with TurboTax, so you never have to go through your debit card

**Figure 4.15** Tax preparation software lets you prepare and file your taxes on mobile devices. *(pkphotograhy/123RF)*

statements and bills to find tax deductions, tax-related income, or expenses. Many banks and credit card companies also offer online services that download a detailed monthly statement into Quicken and Mint. Remember, however, that the tax code changes annually, so you must obtain an updated version of the software each year.

## Business Software

**Objective 4.8** *Summarize the types of software that large and small businesses use.*

**Do businesses use different kinds of software than individuals?** Many businesses rely on the types of software we've discussed so far in the chapter. In addition, specialized software is used in both large and small businesses.

### Small Business Software

**What kinds of software are helpful for small business owners?** If you have a small business or a hobby that produces income, you know the importance of keeping good records and tracking your expenses and income. Accounting software helps small business owners manage their finances more efficiently by providing tools for tracking accounts receivable and accounts payable. In addition, these applications offer inventory management, payroll, and billing tools. Intuit QuickBooks is an example of an accounting application. It includes templates for invoices, statements, and financial reports so that small business owners can create common forms and reports.

If your business requires the need for newsletters, catalogs, annual reports, or other large publications, consider using desktop publishing (DTP) software. Although many word processing applications include many features that are hallmarks of desktop publishing, specialized DTP software, such as Adobe InDesign, allows professionals to design books and other publications that require complex layouts.

**What software do I use to create a web page?** Web authoring software allows even novices to design interactive web pages without knowing any HTML code. Web authoring applications often include wizards, templates, and reference materials to help novices complete most web authoring tasks. More experienced users can take advantage of these applications' advanced features to make the web content current, interactive, and interesting. Adobe Dreamweaver is an installed program that both professionals and casual web page designers use. Squarespace is an online-based option that is full featured and easy to use.

Note that if you need to produce only the occasional web page, you'll find that many applications include features that let you convert your document into a web page. For example, in some Microsoft Office applications, you can choose to save a file as a web page.

### Software for Large and Specialized Businesses

**What types of software do large businesses use?** An application exists for almost every aspect of business. Table 4.4 lists many of the common types of business-related software. Some applications are tailored to the specific needs of a particular company or industry. Software designed for a specific industry, such as property management software for real estate professionals, is called vertical market software.

**What software is used to make 3D models?** Engineers use computer-aided design (CAD) programs such as Autodesk's AutoCAD to create automated designs, technical drawings, and 3D model visualizations. Here are some cool applications of CAD software:

- Architects use CAD software to build virtual models of their plans and readily visualize all aspects of design before actual construction.
- Engineers use CAD software to design everything from factory components to bridges. The 3D nature of these programs lets engineers rotate their models and adjust their designs if necessary, eliminating costly building errors.
- CAD software (and other 3D modeling software) is used to generate designs for objects that will be printed using 3D printers.
- The medical engineering community uses CAD software to create anatomically accurate solid models of the human body, developing medical implants quickly and accurately.

## Table 4.4 Common Types of Large Business-Related Software

| Project Management | Customer Relationship Management (CRM) | Enterprise Resource Planning (ERP) |
|---|---|---|
|  Creates scheduling charts to plan and track specific tasks and to coordinate resources |  Stores sales and client contact information in one central database |  Controls many "back office" operations and processing functions such as billing, production, inventory management, and human resources management |

| E-Commerce | Computer-Aided Design (CAD) | Vertical Market |
|---|---|---|
| Facilitates website creation and hosting services, shopping cart setup, and credit card–processing services | Creates automated designs, technical drawings, and 3D model visualizations for architecture, automotive, aerospace, and medical engineering industries | Addresses the needs of businesses in a specific industry or market such as the real estate, banking, and automotive industries |

(Golden Sikorka/Shutterstock; Macrovector/Shutterstock; Macrovector/Shutterstock; Khanisorn Chalermchan/123RF; Science Photo Library/Alamy Stock Photo; Nmedia/Shutterstock)

The list of CAD applications keeps growing as more and more industries realize the benefits CAD can bring to their product development and manufacturing processes.

**What kind of software can be used for home or landscape planning?** Many software packages enable users to plan the layout of homes and landscapes. A simple, web-based, 3D modeling application is Trimble's SketchUp. SketchUp lets you create a 3D image of your dream home (see Figure 4.16).

**Figure 4.16** SketchUp is a web-based 3D modeling application that can be used for home and landscape design. *(Shutterstock)*

You're part of a group working together on a project and need to keep track of project goals and achievements, as well as communicate with your team members. What should you do? Consider using some of these collaboration software tools (see Figure 4.17):

- UberConference is an app that facilitates group conference calls. You can share your screen with others in the conference, add another person during the conference, record the conference, and mute callers. You can see everyone on the call and even view their social networking profiles. The free version accommodates up to 10 callers.
- Slack is a messaging app that lets you organize your conversations into channels. You can also link to files that are stored in cloud services like Google Drive and Dropbox instead of attaching the files separately in an email or sharing them outside of the Slack platform. The files you link into the conversation are searchable along with your conversations. It runs on mobile apps as well as in a web browser so you can stay in touch anywhere you work.
- Trello is a visually oriented app used for managing projects. Unlike traditional project management apps, it features a board filled with lists, and each list is filled with cards representing tasks to be completed. It is easy to add checklists and due dates to cards as well as upload files to them. You can transfer cards between lists to show progress on various aspects of a project. You can invite as many people to your board as you want. You can then assign people to cards to divide up work tasks. You can also see an overview of your project by glancing at your Trello board. The free version of the app offers a powerful feature set.
- Scribblar (*scribblar.com*) is a multiuser whiteboard with live audio chat, which is great for holding virtual brainstorm sessions.

**Figure 4.17** Collaboration tools make it easier to work effectively as a team. *(Bakhtiar Zein/Shutterstock)*

# Multimedia and Educational Software

While many programs help you increase your productivity, there are also programs that entertain you with audio, video, and digital images and through games, animations, and movies. This section discusses multimedia and educational software, both for your mobile devices and for professional projects (see Figure 4.18).

## Digital Multimedia Software

**Objective 4.9** *Describe the uses and features of digital multimedia software.*

**What is multimedia software?** Multimedia software includes digital image- and video-editing software, digital audio software, and other specialty software required to produce computer games, animations, and movies (see Figure 4.19). Many mobile and desktop software programs allow everyone, from beginner to professional, to create animations, videos, audio clips, and images.

**What software enables you to take and edit photographs?** Mobile devices come with an installed camera app. These apps give you control over standard elements like the use of flash, filtering options, and useful modes like panorama or virtual 360 shots. By purchasing specialized

**Figure 4.18** There are many varieties of multimedia and educational software.

camera apps, you can use additional features like the ability to create a video collage or apply selective focus.

Editing is an important part of creating appealing photo images. Each camera app has editing features that remove red eye and adjust qualities like saturation, contrast, and hue. Specialized apps like Snapseed or Enlight let you do even more. You can merge images, add artistic effects like a pencil sketch look, or apply a filter to make the image look like a watercolor on canvas.

Professionals and advanced amateur photographers often use fully featured image-editing desktop software like Adobe Photoshop and Corel PaintShop Pro. A free alternative is Gimp (*gimp.org*), a download that has most of the features offered by the commercial applications. Desktop photo-editing software offers sophisticated tools (see Figure 4.19) for tasks like layering and masking images (hiding parts of layers to create effects such as collages). Designers use these more sophisticated tools to create the enhanced digital images found commercially in logos and advertisements.

**How do I organize all the photos I take?** Each mobile operating system has a photo app that stores and sorts images by date, by location, and by tags. These apps can be taught the faces of people you know and then automatically identify and group photos by people. Some apps go further and let you search your photo collection. So searching on "food" will let you pull together all photos of any meals you've photographed.

You may want to consider moving your photos and videos from your mobile device and storing them in a cloud storage system. Each mobile OS is designed to work smoothly with a specific cloud system (Apple devices use iCloud and Android devices automatically save to Google Photos), but you can use any cloud service you like. Tools like If This Then That (IFTTT) allow you to easily create recipes that will automatically backup your mobile images to Dropbox, for example. (To learn more about using If This Then That, see the Make This activity in Chapter 1.)

**Figure 4.19** You can create collages of your favorite images using Google Photos. *(Courtesy of Google, Inc.)*

**What software do I need to create and edit digital videos?** The same camera apps that come preinstalled on mobile devices record video. They typically include features that let you record in slow motion, in fast motion, and in time lapse. While it's easy to upload videos directly to YouTube or Facebook unedited, you can use digital video-editing software to refine your videos. Although the most expensive products (such as Adobe Premiere Pro and Apple's Final Cut Pro) offer the widest range of special effects and tools, more moderately priced video-editing programs often have enough features to keep the casual user happy. Apple iMovie and VivaVideo, for example, both have intuitive drag-and-drop features and numerous templates and effects that make it simple to create professional-quality movies with little or no training (see Figure 4.20).

**What kind of software should I use to create illustrations?** Drawing (or illustration) software lets you create and edit 2D, line-based drawings. You can use it to create technical diagrams or original nonphotographic drawings and illustrations using software versions of traditional artistic tools such as pens, pencils, and paintbrushes. You also can drag geometric objects from a toolbar onto the canvas area to create images and can use paint bucket, eyedropper, and spray can tools to add color and special effects to the drawings.

**Figure 4.20** Video editing programs such as Apple iMovie make it easy to create and edit movies to then share on social media. *(Anthony Devlin/AP Images)*

Adobe Illustrator (see Figure 4.21) includes tools that let you create professional-quality creative and technical illustrations such as muscle structures in the human body. Its warping tool allows you to bend, stretch, and twist portions of your image or text. Because of its many tools and features, Illustrator is the preferred drawing software program of most graphic artists. Be sure to also explore Inkscape, an open source program similar to Illustrator. For touch-based devices there is a great collection of software for creating vector art. Apps like Paper and Concepts turn your tablet into a terrific tool for creating illustrations.

## Digital Audio Software

**Objective 4.10** *Describe the uses and features of digital audio software.*

**What's the difference between all the digital audio file types on my computer?** You probably have a variety of digital audio files stored on your computer, such as downloaded music files, audiobooks, and podcasts. These types of audio files have been compressed so they're more manageable to transfer to and from your computer and over the Internet. MP3, short for MPEG-1 Audio Layer 3, is the most common digital audio compression format, but there are other compressed audio formats, such as AAC and WMA.

**Figure 4.21** Adobe Illustrator is the industry standard for creating vector art and illustrations. *(Courtesy Adobe Systems, Inc.)*

You may also see uncompressed audio files on your computer, such as WAV or AIFF files. Uncompressed files—the files found on audio CDs, for example—have not had any data removed, so the quality is a perfect representation of the audio as it was recorded. Unfortunately, the file size is much larger than that of compressed files. Compressed formats remove data such as high frequencies that the human ear does not hear in order to make the files smaller and easier to download and store. MP3 format, for example, makes it possible to transfer and play back music on smartphones and other music players. A typical CD stores between 10 and 15 songs in uncompressed format, but with files in MP3 format, the same CD can store between 100 and 180 songs. The smaller file size not only lets you store and play music in less space but also allows quick and easy distribution over the Internet. Ogg Vorbis (or just Ogg) is a free, open source audio compression format alternative to MP3. Some say that Ogg produces a better sound quality than MP3.

**What do I use to create my own audio files?** Many digital audio applications let you create and record your own audio files. Digital audio workstation software (DAWs) lets you create individual tracks to build songs or soundtracks with virtual instruments, voice recorders, synthesizers, and special audio effects, and these will end up as uncompressed MIDI (Musical Instrument Digital Interface) files. Examples of DAWs include Apple GarageBand and Ableton Live. You can use these programs to record audio from live sources as well, such as riffs from your electric guitar or vocals.

**How do I edit audio files?** Audio-editing software includes tools that make editing audio files as easy as editing text files. Software such as the open source Audacity (*audacity.sourceforge.net*) lets you perform basic editing tasks like cutting dead air space from the beginning or end of a song or clipping a portion from the middle. You can also add special sound effects, such as reverb or bass boost, and remove static or hiss from MP3 files. These applications support recording sound files from a microphone or any source you can connect through the input line of a sound card.

## App Creation Software

**Objective 4.11**  *Describe the features of app creation software.*

**I'm not a programmer, but could I build my own mobile app?** Yes, there are many types of app creation software, programming environments that can produce apps that run on various mobile devices. Many are approachable for beginners. MIT's App Inventor open source web application and Thunkable (which are used in the Make This exercises in this book) make it easy

▶ Helpdesk   **MyLab IT**

**Choosing Software**

In this Helpdesk, you'll play the role of a helpdesk staffer, fielding questions about the different kinds of multimedia software, educational and reference software, and entertainment software.

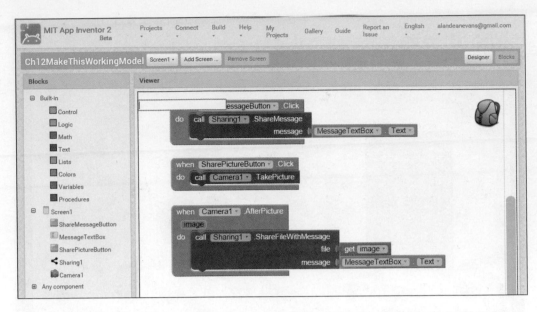

**Figure 4.22** MIT's App Inventor is an open source web application that enables beginners to create apps. *(Copyright MIT, used with permission.)*

for beginners to create functional apps for Android and Apple mobile devices (see Figure 4.22). Featuring a drag-and-drop interface, these applications enable users to quickly begin developing powerful apps without actually knowing how to write program code.

Scratch is another MIT programming environment that facilitates the creation of interactive stories, games, and animations that you can then share with an online community. The programming interface of Scratch is somewhat similar to that of App Inventor. Many elementary schools use Scratch to introduce young children to the ideas behind computer programming.

Corona SDK (*coronalabs.com*) is a powerful, free programming environment that has been used to develop games and business apps. Corona comes with a large library of application programming interfaces (APIs) that can be used as building blocks to make writing computer code less time-consuming (although you will have to learn the Lua programming language). The Composer GUI is a visual editor for Corona, which makes it even easier to create apps without doing as much actual coding. Corona supports both iOS and Android.

Apple also has a powerful development environment for iOS, macOS, and watchOS, called Swift. Swift uses more concise code than some other programming environments. It has a feature that allows you to visually see the results of each line of code as you write it. Many professional developers like using Swift because the code works side-by-side with Objective-C, which is a major programming language used in many businesses.

To get started in Swift, download the Swift Playgrounds app. There is a fun set of puzzles, games, and challenges that guide you into the world of programming for iOS. Despite the power of the Swift environment, it's still very approachable for beginners.

**I just want to make video games. Is that a reasonable goal?** Yes, video games represent an industry that generates billions in revenue each year, so designing and creating video games is a desirable career path. Professionally created video games involve artistic storytelling and design, as well as sophisticated programming. Major production houses such as Electronic Arts use applications not easily available to the casual home enthusiast. However, you can use the editors and game engines available for games such as EverQuest, Oblivion, and Unreal Tournament to create custom levels and characters to extend the games.

If you want to try your hand at creating your own video games right now at home, multimedia applications such as Unity and RPG Maker provide the tools you need to explore game design and creation. The program GameMaker (*yoyogames.com*) is a free product that lets you build a game without any programming; you drag and drop key elements of the new game creation into place. Alice (*alice.org*) is another free environment to check out; it lets you easily create 3D animations and simple games.

## Educational and Reference Software

**Objective 4.12** *Categorize educational and reference software and explain their features.*

**What fun educational and reference software should I check out?** If you want to learn more about a subject, you can turn to the web for many instructional videos and documents. But sometimes, it's best to use software for more complete or detailed instructions. Educational and reference software is available to help you master, study, design, create, or plan. As shown in Table 4.5, there are software products that teach new skills such as typing, languages, cooking, and playing the guitar.

Students who will be taking standardized tests like the SAT often use test preparation software. In addition, many computer and online brain-training games and programs are designed to improve the health and function of your brain. Lumosity (*lumosity.com*) is one such site that has a specific "workout" program that you can play on your PC or smartphone. Brain Age (*brainage.com*) has software for the Nintendo DS and is designed for players of all ages.

### Table 4.5  Educational and Reference Software: A Sample of What's Available

| Test Preparation | Simulation | Instructional | Trip Planning |
|---|---|---|---|
|  |  |  |  |
| Designed to improve your performance on standardized tests | Allows you to experience a real situation through a virtual environment | Designed to teach you almost anything from playing a musical instrument to learning a language or cooking | Generates maps and provides driving instructions; some incorporate hotel, restaurant, and other trip information |
| **Home Design/Improvement** | **Course Management** | **Brain Training** | **Genealogy** |
|  |  |  | |
| Provides 2D or 3D templates and images to let you better visualize indoor and outdoor remodeling projects and landscaping ideas | Web-based software system that creates a virtual learning experience, including course materials, tests, and discussion boards | Features games and activities to exercise your brain to improve your memory, processing speed, attention, and multitasking capabilities | Helps chart the relationships between family members through multiple generations |

(Aduchinootonosama/123RF; Greg Pease/The Image Bank/Getty Images; iQoncept/Shutterstock; ALMAGAMI/Shutterstock; Zack C/Shutterstock; Scott Maxwell LuMaxArt/ Shutterstock; Vlad Kochelaevskiy/Shutterstock; Alfazet Chronicles/Shutterstock)

**What types of programs are available to train people to use software or special machines?** Many programs provide tutorials for popular computer applications (you may even use one in your course provided with MyLab IT). These programs use illustrated systematic instructions, known as simulation programs, to guide users through unfamiliar skills in an environment that acts like the actual software, without the software actually being installed.

Simulation programs allow you to experience or control the software as if it were an actual event. Such simulation programs include commercial and military flight training, surgical instrument training, and machine operation training. One benefit of simulated training programs is that they safely allow you to experience potentially dangerous situations such as flying a helicopter during high winds. Consequently, users of these training programs are more likely to take risks and learn from their mistakes—something they could not afford to do in real life. Simulated training programs also help prevent costly errors. Should something go awry, the only cost of the error is restarting the simulation program.

**Do I need special software to take courses online?** Although some courses are run from an individually developed website, many online courses are run using course management software such as Blackboard, Moodle, and Canvas. In addition to traditional classroom tools such as calendars and grade books, these programs provide special areas for students and instructors to exchange ideas and information through chat rooms, discussion forums, and e-mail. Collaboration tools such as whiteboards and desktop sharing facilitate virtual office hour sessions. Depending on the content and course materials, you may need a password or special plug-ins to view certain videos or demos.

---

**Before moving on to the Chapter Review:**

1. ▶ Watch Chapter Overview Video 4.2.
2. Then take the Check Your Understanding quiz.

---

# Check Your Understanding // Review & Practice

For a quick review to see what you've learned so far, answer the following questions.

## multiple choice

1. Which type of productivity software would you most likely use to do calculations and what-if analyses?
   a. Database
   b. Tax Preparation
   c. Spreadsheet
   d. Financial Planning

2. The software that allows you to edit digital images, videos, as well as digital audio is called
   a. multimedia software.
   b. encryption algorithms.
   c. distributed software.
   d. productivity software.

3. Which of the following is an uncompressed audio file format?
   a. WAV
   b. AAC
   c. MP3
   d. WMA

4. Which of the following software packages would not be used to create mobile applications?
   a. Scratch
   b. App Engine
   c. Thunkable
   d. App Inventor

5. Which of the following is considered a benefit of using simulation programs?
   a. They allow users to experience potentially dangerous situations without risk.
   b. They help to prevent costly errors.
   c. They allow users to experience or control the software as if it were an actual event.
   d. All of the above

**chew on this**

Cloud computing is becoming more popular, and many users are working from the cloud and not even realizing it. Open Google Docs and Office Online and compare these applications with an installed counterpart (e.g., Excel Online and Google Sheets versus Excel). What similarities and differences do you find between the online applications and the installed version? Envision a time when all software is web-based and describe how being totally on the cloud might be an advantage. What disadvantages might a cloud-based environment present?

**MyLab IT**  Go to **MyLab IT** to take an autograded version of the *Check Your Understanding* review and to find all media resources for the chapter.

**For the IT Simulation for this chapter, see MyLab IT..**

# 4 Chapter Review

## Summary

**Learning Outcome 4.1** You will be able to explain the ways to access and use software and describe how to best manage your software.

### Software Basics

**Objective 4.1** *Compare application software and system software.*

- The term *software* refers to a set of instructions that tells the computer what to do.
- *Application software* is the software you use to do everyday tasks at home, school, and work. Microsoft Word and the Edge browser are examples of application software.
- *System software* is the software that helps run the computer and coordinates instructions between application software and the computer's hardware devices. System software includes the operating system and utility programs.

**Objective 4.2** *Explain the differences between commercial software and open source software and describe models for software distribution.*

- There are two basic types of software that you can install on your computer:
  - *Proprietary (or commercial) software* is software you buy.
  - *Open source software* is program code that is free and publicly available with few licensing and copyright restrictions. The code can be copied, distributed, or changed without the stringent copyright protections of software products you purchase
- Software is delivered in three main ways:
  - *Local installation* means that software is installed on your computing device. These programs generally do not require an Internet connection to function.
  - *SaaS* (Software as a Service) is a model for delivery of software whereby the vendor hosts the software online and you access and use the software over the Internet without having to install it on your computer's hard drive.

- *Subscription* is a model whereby the user pays a fee to use the software. The software is downloaded and installed locally but is routinely updated by connection to the manufacturer's server.

### Managing Your Software

**Objective 4.3** *Explain the different options for purchasing software.*

- Although most software today is downloaded from the web, it can also be purchased at retail stores or directly from software developers.
- *Freeware* is copyrighted software that you can use for free.
- *Beta software* comprises apps that are still under development but are released to the public to gather feedback on design features and errors.

**Objective 4.4** *Describe how to install and uninstall software.*

- When installing software, you're often given the choice between a full (typical) or custom installation. Before installing any software, it's important that you back up your system as well as create a *restore point*.
- When uninstalling software, it's best to use the uninstall feature that comes with the operating system. To uninstall an app in Windows 10, on the Start menu, right-click the app and select Uninstall.

**Objective 4.5** *Explain the considerations around the decision to upgrade your software.*

- Before installing software on your computer, ensure that your system setup meets the *system requirements*. System requirements specify the minimum recommended standards for the operating system, processor, primary memory (RAM), and hard drive capacity.

**Objective 4.6**  *Explain how software licenses function.*

- A *software license*, also known as an *End User License Agreement (EULA)*, is an agreement between you, the user, and the software company that owns the software.

- When you purchase software, you're actually purchasing the license to use it and therefore must abide by the terms of the licensing agreement you accept when installing the program.
- Software licenses permit installation on a specific number of devices.

## Part 2

## Application Software

**Learning Outcome 4.2**  **Describe the different types of application software used for productivity and multimedia.**

 ### Productivity and Business Software

**Objective 4.7**  *Categorize the types of application software used to enhance productivity and describe their uses and features.*

- *Productivity software* programs include the following:
  - Word processing: to create and edit written documents
  - Spreadsheet: to do calculations and numerical and what-if analyses easily
  - Presentation: to create slide presentations
  - Database: to store and organize data
  - Note-taking: to take notes and easily organize and search them
  - Personal information manager (PIM): to keep you organized by putting a calendar, address book, notepad, and to-do lists within your computer
- *Financial planning software* helps you manage your daily finances. Examples include Quicken and Mint.
- *Tax preparation software*, such as Intuit TurboTax and H&R Block Tax Software, lets you prepare your state and federal taxes on your own instead of hiring a professional.

**Objective 4.8**  *Summarize the types of software that large and small businesses use.*

- *Accounting software* helps small business owners manage their finances more efficiently by providing tools for tracking accounts receivable and accounts payable.
- *Desktop publishing (DTP) software* is used to create newsletters, catalogs, annual reports, or other large, complicated publications.
- *Web authoring software* allows even novices to design interesting and interactive web pages without knowing any HTML code.
- There are also specialized programs for project management software, customer relationship management (CRM), enterprise resource planning (ERP), e-commerce, marketing and sales, finance, point of sale, security, networking, data management, and human resources, to name just a few.

 ### Multimedia and Educational Software

**Objective 4.9**  *Describe the uses and features of digital multimedia software.*

- *Image-editing desktop software* includes tools for basic modifications to digital photos, such as removing red eye; modifying contrast, sharpness, and color casts; or removing scratches or rips from scanned images of old photos.
- *Digital video-editing software* is used to apply special effects, change the sequence of scenes, or combine separate video clips into one movie.
- *Drawing (or illustration) software* facilitates the creation and editing of 2-D, line-based drawings. It is used for the creation of technical diagrams and original non-photographic drawings.

**Objective 4.10**  *Describe the uses and features of digital audio software.*

- *Digital audio workstation software* (DAWs) lets you create individual tracks to build songs or soundtracks with virtual instruments, voice recorders, synthesizers, and special audio effects, that will end up as uncompressed MIDI files.
- *Audio-editing software* includes tools that make editing audio files as easy as editing text files.

**Objective 4.11**  *Describe the features of app creation software.*

- *App creation software* provides professionals and novices alike with the ability to create their own apps.
- Although used widely in game development, app creation software can be used to create many other types of apps that have business applications.

**Objective 4.12** *Categorize education and reference software and explain their features.*

- *Test preparation software* is designed to improve your performance on standardized tests.
- *Simulation software* allows you to experience or control the software as if it were an actual event. Often this allows you to experience dangerous situations safely.

- *Course management software* creates a virtual learning experience for students and houses course materials, tests, and discussion boards.

**MyLab IT** — Be sure to check out **MyLab IT** for additional materials to help you review and learn. And don't forget to watch the Chapter Overview Videos. ▶

# Key Terms

accounting software **142**

American Standard Code for Information Interchange **127**

app creation software **147**

application software **122**

audio-editing software **147**

base-10 number system (decimal notation) **126**

beta version **124**

binary number system (base-2 number system) **126**

computer-aided design (CAD) **142**

copyleft **128**

course management software **150**

custom installation **125**

database software **138**

desktop publishing (DTP) software **142**

digital audio workstation software (DAWs) **147**

digital video-editing software **146**

drawing (or illustration) software **146**

End User License Agreement (EULA) **128**

financial planning software **141**

freeware **124**

full installation **125**

hexadecimal notation **127**

image-editing desktop software **145**

locally installed software **122**

macro **140**

multimedia software **144**

number system **126**

open source software **122**

personal information manager (PIM) software **140**

presentation software **137**

productivity software **133**

program **122**

proprietary (commercial) software **122**

recovery drive **126**

restore point **125**

simulation programs **150**

software **122**

Software as a Service (SaaS) **122**

software license **128**

software piracy **129**

spreadsheet software **135**

subscription software **123**

system requirements **125**

system software **122**

tax preparation software **141**

template **140**

Unicode **127**

vertical market software **142**

web authoring software **142**

wizard **140**

word processing software **134**

# Chapter Quiz // Assessment

For a quick review to see what you've learned, answer the following questions. Submit the quiz as requested by your instructor. If you are using **MyLab IT**, the quiz is also available there.

## multiple choice

1. Software that is hosted by the vendor and accessed online is called
   a. application software.
   b. productivity software.
   c. Software as a Service (SaaS).
   d. open source software.

2. LibreOffice is an example of which type of software?
   a. freeware
   b. open source software
   c. beta software
   d. Software as a Service (SaaS)

3. Beta software is made available because
   a. new programmers have been hired.
   b. wireless networking must be added.
   c. a company is making an early release to test bugs.
   d. the company needs more profits.

4. When you install all the most commonly used files and programs to your computer's hard drive, you have completed which kind of software installation?
   a. custom
   b. full
   c. complete
   d. common

5. The minimum recommended standards for the operating system, processor, primary memory (RAM), and storage capacity for certain software are called
   a. redistributing standards.
   b. system requirements.
   c. hardware.
   d. minimum standards

6. Ginny downloads and modifies an open source software program, then uploads the program with a different name. Which type of software license is she most likely to be working under?
   a. Copyleft
   b. GNU General Public License
   c. Open Source License
   d. No licence is necessary

7. Calendars, tasks, and e-mail can be found in which application?
   a. Excel
   b. Outlook
   c. OneNote
   d. Access

8. Which of the following is an example of financial management software?
   a. Lumosity
   b. AudioAcrobat
   c. Photos
   d. Quicken

9. Image-editing software allows you to
   a. compute complex formulas.
   b. remove red eye.
   c. create drafting blueprints.
   d. conduct product simulations.

10. Digital audio software can be used to
    a. compute complex formulas.
    b. compose songs or soundtracks with virtual instruments.
    c. create drafting blueprints.
    d. perform mathematical simulations.

## true/false

_____ 1. Google Docs is an example of Software as a Service.

_____ 2. App creation software includes tools like Adobe Photoshop.

_____ 3. Course management software creates a virtual learning experience for students and houses course materials, tests, and discussion boards.

_____ 4. When you subscribe to software, no license is necessary.

_____ 5. A macro is a program released early to the public for testing and evaluation.

## What do you think now?

After reviewing your technology use diary, determine whether you are spending too much time with your devices. Describe the signs of technology addiction and a plan to help reduce tech dependency.

# Team Time

## Software for Startups

### problem

You and your friends have decided to start Recycle Technology, a not-for-profit organization that would recycle and donate used computer equipment. In the first planning session, your group recognizes the need for certain software to help you with various parts of the business, such as tracking inventory, designing notices, mapping addresses for pickup and delivery, and soliciting residents by phone or e-mail about recycling events, to name a few.

### task

Split your class into as many groups of four or five as possible. Make some groups responsible for locating free or web-based software solutions and other groups responsible for finding proprietary solutions. Another group could be responsible for finding mobile app solutions. The groups will present and compare results with each other at the end of the project.

### process

1. Identify a team leader who will coordinate the project and record and present results.
2. Each team is to identify the various kinds of software that Recycle Technology needs. Consider software that will be needed for all the various tasks required to run the organization, such as communication, marketing, tracking, inventory management, and finance.
3. Create a detailed and organized list of required software applications. Depending on your team, you will specify either proprietary software or open source software.

### conclusion

Most organizations require a variety of software applications to accomplish different tasks. Compare your results with those of other team members. Were there applications that you didn't think about, but that other members did? How expensive is it to ensure that even the smallest company has all the software required to carry out daily activities, or can the needs be met with free, open source products?

# Ethics Project

## Open Source Software

Ethical conduct is a stream of decisions you make all day long. In this exercise, you'll research and then role-play a complicated ethical situation. The role you play might or might not match your own personal beliefs, but your research and use of logic will enable you to represent the view assigned. An arbitrator will watch and comment on both sides of the arguments, and together, the team will agree on an ethical solution.

### topic: proprietary software vs. open source software

Proprietary software has set restrictions on use and can be very expensive, whereas open source software is freely available to use as is or to change, improve, and redistribute. Open source software has become acceptable as a cost-effective alternative to proprietary software—so much so that it's reported that the increased adoption of open source software has caused a drop in revenue to the proprietary software industry. But determining which software to use involves more than just reviewing the IT budget.

### research areas to consider

- Open source software
- Proprietary software
- Copyright licensing
- Open source development

### process

1. Divide the class into teams.
2. Research the areas cited above and devise a scenario in which someone is a proponent for open source software but is being rebuffed by someone who feels that "you get what you pay for" and is a big proponent of using proprietary software.
3. Team members should write a summary that provides background information for their character—for example: open source proponent, proprietary developer, or arbitrator—and that details their character's behaviors, to set the stage for the role-playing event. Then, team members should create an outline to use during the role-playing event.
4. Team members should present their case to the class or submit a PowerPoint presentation for review by the rest of the class, along with the summary and resolution they developed.

### conclusion

As technology becomes ever more prevalent and integrated into our lives, more and more ethical dilemmas will present themselves. Being able to understand and evaluate both sides of the argument, while responding in a personally or socially ethical manner, will be an important skill.

## Analyzing Benchmark Data

You work for a design firm that uses many of the software applications in the Adobe Creative Suite, especially Photoshop, Illustrator, and InDesign. You have been asked to evaluate whether it would be worthwhile to upgrade the software to the latest version. In addition to reviewing any new or revised features, you also want to provide an analysis on any improvements in product efficiency and performance, so you have repeated doing the same skills with the current and new data and have recorded the results. Now you just need to analyze it.

You will use the following skills as you complete this activity:

- AutoFill Data
- Insert AVERAGE Function
- Add Borders
- Align and Wrap Text
- Apply Conditional Formatting
- Create Bar Chart

## Instructions

1. Open *TIA_Ch04_Start.xlsx* and save as **TIA_Ch04_LastFirst.xlsx**.
2. In **cell F1**, type **Current Average**, and in cell J1, type **New Average**.
3. In **cell F2**, use the **AVERAGE function** to compute the average of **range C2:E2**. In **cell J2**, use the **AVERAGE function** to compute the average of **range G2:I2**.
4. Select **cell F2**, then drag the Fill Handle to cell F13. Select **cell J2**, then drag the Fill Handle to cell J13.
5. Select the **cells C2:J13**, then format the cell contents with **Number format with one decimal**.
6. Select **cell A2**, and **Merge and Center** across cells A2:A5. Then adjust the orientation of the text to **Rotate Text Up (90 degrees)**. **Middle Align** cell contents and **Bold** text.
7. Use Format Painter to copy these formats to cell A6 and cell A10.
8. Select range **A2:J5**, then apply **Thick Outside Borders**. Repeat with ranges **A6:J9** and **A10:J13**.
9. Select range **F1:F13**, then apply **Thick Outside Borders**. Repeat with range **J1:J13**.
10. Select **J2:J13**, then apply a **Conditional Format** that will format cells that are Less Than those cells in range F2:F13 with Green Fill and Dark Green Text.
    Hint: In the Format cells that are LESS THAN box, enter =F2 (*not* $F$2). The rest of the cells in the range will update automatically.
11. Create a **Clustered Bar Chart** using ranges B1:B13, F1:F13, and J1:J13.
    Hint: Hold down the Ctrl button as you select ranges F1:F13 and J1:J13.
12. Add the title **Benchmark Comparison**: **New and Current Versions of CS Software** to the Clustered Bar Chart, and add a Horizontal Axis title and type **Seconds**. **Position and resize** the chart so it fills range A16:J34.
13. Save the workbook and submit based on your instructor's directions.

**Chapter**

# 5

# System Software: The Operating System, Utility Programs, and File Management

 For a chapter overview, watch the **Chapter Overview videos**.

 **MyLab IT** All media accompanying this chapter can be found here.

**Make This**  A Notification Alert on **page 175**

*(Dizain/Fotolia; Dsplay intermaya/Fotolia; Revers/Shutterstock; Courtesy of Microsoft Corp.; Stanislav Popov/Shutterstock; Reji/Fotolia)*

# What do you think?

Think of the **private information on your smartphone**—your texts, contact lists, and emails. If someone has your phone and can log in to it, could they read your information? Not if it were encrypted. *Encryption* **takes the data stored on your device and changes it using a secret key**. When you log in to an encrypted phone, it automatically unencrypts the data for you to read. Without the encryption key, the data is just garbled nonsense.

And **if your phone is stolen, even without the means to login, the new "owner" could still get information off of it**. They could plug the SD card into a computer or could use software to read the data stored on the phone memory. But not if your operating system encrypted it.

Almost all **modern smartphones offer encryption**. However, tech companies have faced legal action from government agencies when, for example, the FBI wants to break into the phone of a suspect to look for evidence of crime. **Law enforcement wants tech companies to work on a way to defeat the encryption installed in the device** or to add a "backdoor" that would allow the companies to defeat the encryption any time they are asked to. The debate over how much privacy you should expect is an important one.

> **?** We need to balance the privacy rights of individuals against the need for security. Which position should tech companies take?
>
> - *Produce products that support full encryption that can't be broken by anyone – even the tech company*
> - *Produce products that support encryption but enable the tech company to defeat it if asked to by authorities*
> - *Produce products that do not support encryption so that law enforcement can access the data*

*See the end of the chapter for a follow-up question.* *(Wutzkohphoto/Shutterstock)*

# Understanding System Software

**Learning Outcome 5.1** **You will be able to explain the types and functions of operating systems and explain the steps in the boot process.**

Your computer uses two basic types of software: application software and system software. *Application software* is the software you use to do everyday tasks at home and at work. *System software* is the set of programs that helps run the computer and coordinates instructions between application software and the computer's hardware devices. From the moment you turn on your computer to the time you shut it down, you're interacting with system software.

## Operating System Fundamentals

Every computer, from smartphones to supercomputers, has an operating system. Even game consoles, cars, and some appliances have operating systems. The role of the operating system is critical; a computer can't operate without it.

### Operating System Basics

**Objective 5.1** *Discuss the functions of the operating system.*

**What does the operating system do?** System software consists of two primary types of programs: the *operating system* and *utility programs*. The operating system (OS) is a group of programs that controls how your computer functions. The operating system has three primary functions:

- **Managing hardware,** including the processor, memory, and storage devices, as well as peripheral devices such as the printer.
- **Managing software**, which allows application software to work with the central processing unit (CPU).
- **Managing tasks,** such as scheduling and coordinating processes (like reading strokes from the keyboard) and managing network resources.

You interact with your OS through the user interface—the *desktop*, *icons*, and *menus* that let you communicate with your computer.

**How many operating systems are there?** There are several operating systems in the marketplace. Microsoft Windows and Apple's macOS are the most common on desktops and laptops. In terms of mobile devices, operating systems must be designed to manage power and use the limited screen space efficiently. Apple created iOS for use on its tablets, watchOS for use on its Apple Watch, and tvOS for use on its Apple TV product. Meanwhile, Windows 10 is able to run on desktops, laptops, and mobile devices. As devices continue to converge in functionality, developers are making mobile and desktop operating systems that have similar functionality (such as macOS and iOS) or single operating systems (such as Windows 10) that can run on a variety of devices. Table 5.1 lists some popular operating systems.

**How are operating systems categorized?** Early operating systems were designed for one person performing one task at a time. These are named *single-user, single-task operating systems*. Modern operating systems allow a single user to multitask—to perform more than one process at a time. And operating systems such as Windows and macOS provide networking capabilities as well, essentially making them *multiuser, multitasking operating systems*.

Operating systems can also be categorized by the type of device in which they're installed, such as mobile devices, personal computers, robots or mainframes, and network computers.

### Operating Systems for Personal Use

**Objective 5.2** *Explain the most popular operating systems for personal use.*

**What are the most popular operating systems for personal computers?** Microsoft Windows, Apple macOS, and Linux (an open source OS) are popular operating systems for personal computers. Google's Chrome OS is used on the Chromebook series of devices. Although each OS has unique features, they share many features as well.

**Table 5.1   Popular Operating Systems**

| Operating System Name | Windows | macOS | iOS | Android | Linux | Chrome OS |
|---|---|---|---|---|---|---|
| | Windows 10 | macOS | iOS | | | |
| **Developed By** | Microsoft | Apple | Apple | Google | Open source | Google |
| **Available On** | Laptops, tablets, desktops, all-in-ones, smartphones | Laptops, desktops, all-in-ones | Tablets, iPhones, iPod touches | Smartphones, tablets | Laptops, desktops, tablets | Chromebooks |

(Top Photo Corporation/Alamy Stock Photo;  David Paul Morris/Bloomberg/Getty Images; YAY Media AS/Alamy Stock Vector; tibbbb/Fotolia; rvlsoft/123Rf)

**What common features are found in personal computer operating systems?** All personal computer operating systems include a window based interface with icons and other graphics that facilitate point-and-click commands. They also include many utility programs. A utility program is a small program that performs many of the general housekeeping tasks for your computer, to help the computer run more efficiently. Utilities include such things as virus protection, backup and restore software, and system management tools. A set of utility programs is bundled with each OS, but you can also buy stand-alone utility programs that often provide more features.

Other features operating systems incorporate include natural language search capability as well as virtual desktops. They support Bluetooth and WiFi connectivity. Although macOS doesn't have touchscreen capabilities like Windows, iOS offers this capability for iPhones and iPads.

**What kind of OS do mobile devices use?** Smartphones and tablets use a mobile operating system. Android is the mobile OS for devices designed by Google, Samsung, and other companies. The main OS for Apple mobile devices is iOS. Both iOS and Android support devices like cameras, the sensors built into mobile devices, touch screen displays, and multiple types of connectivity (WiFi, Bluetooth, NFC). They also support mobile payment systems, on-screen note taking, and voice recognition.

**Are any operating systems web-based?** Google Chrome OS (see Figure 5.1), is a web-based OS. With the Chrome OS, very few files are installed on your computing device. Rather, the main functionality of the OS is provided through a web browser. Chrome OS is only available on certain devices called *Chromebooks* from Google and Google's manufacturing partners. Chrome OS should not be confused with the Google Chrome browser. The browser is application software that can run on many different operating systems.

**How do other operating systems use the "cloud"?** Operating systems have features that are tied to cloud computing. Using your Microsoft account, Windows 10 stores your settings so you can see your familiar desktop and applications on any device you log into. You can access and store files online from OneDrive, Windows' cloud-based storage system. Similarly, macOS allows you to sign in to any Apple device with your Apple ID, which provides access to Apple's iCloud system. Both systems store your content online and automatically push it out to all your associated devices. There are third-party products that do the same thing (for example Dropbox) but a product built into the OS by the manufacturer is often more tightly integrated into the operating system.

**What is Linux?** Linux is a free open source OS designed for use on personal computers and web servers. Open source software is available for anyone to use or modify. Linux began in 1991 as a project of Finnish university student Linus Torvalds. It has since been tweaked by scores of programmers as part of the Free Software Foundation GNU Project (*gnu.org*).

Linux has a reputation as a stable OS, one that is not subject to crashes. Because the code is available to anyone, Linux can be updated quickly by programmers around the world.

**Where can I get Linux?** Linux is available for download in various packages known as distributions or distros. Distros include the underlying Linux kernel (the code that provides an operating system's basic functionality) and special modifications to the OS, and may also include additional open source software (such as Apache OpenOffice). A good place to start researching

**Figure 5.1** The Google Chrome OS is web-based and has a very minimalist look. *(Courtesy of Google, Inc.)*

Proprietary software such as Windows and macOS is developed by corporations and sold for profit. Open source software, such as Linux, is free, and because users have access to the source code, they can make any changes they want. In fact, the community of open source software users responds to bugs and problems so quickly that the program is relatively bug-free.

So, if an OS such as Linux is free and relatively stable, why do proprietary OSs, which users must pay for, have such a huge market share?

One reason is that corporations and individuals have grown accustomed to having technical support. Some proprietary forms of Linux do provide support. Red Hat offers a free, open source OS called Fedora, but they also have modified the original Linux source code and market a version, Red Hat Enterprise Linux, as a proprietary program. Purchasers of Red Hat Enterprise Linux receive a warranty and technical support.

distros is *distrowatch.com*. This site tracks Linux distros and provides helpful tips for beginners on choosing one.

**Does it matter what OS is on my computer?** Most application software is OS dependent. You need to make sure you get the correct version of software, matched to your OS. Although you might find the same app in Google Play, the Windows store, or the Apple store, you must download and install the app from the specific store that works with your OS.

**Can I have more than one OS on my computer?** Yes, many people run more than one OS on their computer. Windows and Linux can run on most of the hardware being sold today. And, although macOS and iOS run only on Apple equipment, Apple devices can support Windows and Linux as well. Your choice of an OS is mostly a matter of price and personal preference.

Note that Mac users might install Windows on their computers so they can install and run a program they like that is only available on Windows. A Mac computer can boot up into either Windows or macOS using the utility included in macOS named Boot Camp. You can also run both macOS and Windows at the same time, using software such as Parallels or VMware Fusion.

In Windows, you can create a separate section of your hard drive (called a *partition*) and install Linux on it while leaving your original Windows installation untouched. After installing Linux, when your computer starts, you're offered a choice of which OS to use.

**How do I update my OS?** Microsoft Windows delivers automatic OS updates, including new features, apps, and patches, as necessary. You can manage your update settings through the Update & Security section of Settings. Advanced options let you choose to automatically download updates or to defer a feature update for a certain amount of time.

Apple releases periodic new versions of its desktop and mobile operating systems. The newest versions as of this writing are iOS 12 and macOS Mojave. These versions for Apple mobile and desktop OSs are pushed to the user, and the user can decide whether to install the updates.

Updates to the mobile Android OS get pushed to users but at the discretion of the device manufacturer. For example, when a new version of Android is released, Samsung may release it immediately for the Galaxy smartphone but may not release it for another Samsung device, whereas LG may choose to delay the release for all its smartphones. If having the latest update on your Android device is important to you, consider purchasing Google hardware since the updates come to Google devices first.

Have you thought about having an operating system for your home? Smart home devices are becoming more inexpensive and powerful. These devices include light switches, alarm systems, doorbell cameras, door locks, garage door openers, and smoke detectors—each connected to the Internet. Having a central controller for your home to manage them all and to provide a consistent interface is important.

Amazon's Echo and Google's Home are two candidates for organizing and controlling your smart home. These devices have operating systems that respond to voice commands and can run your smart devices, as well as send text messages or place or receive phone calls. There are also open source solutions like openHAB (*openhab.org*) that can run on inexpensive hardware like the Raspberry Pi. Explore making your home smarter!

# Operating Systems for Machinery, Networks, and Business

**Objective 5.3** *Explain the different kinds of operating systems for machines, networks, and business.*

**Why do machines with built-in computers need an OS?** Machinery that performs a repetitive series of specific tasks in an exact amount of time requires a real-time operating system (RTOS). Also referred to as *embedded systems*, RTOSs require minimal user interaction. This type of OS is a program with a specific purpose, and it must guarantee certain response times for certain computing tasks; otherwise, the machine is useless. The programs are written specifically for the needs of the devices and their functions. Devices that must perform regimented tasks or record precise results require RTOSs. Examples include a pacemaker or the anti-lock braking system in your car.

You also encounter RTOSs every day in devices such as point of sale systems, fuel-injection systems in car engines, as well as some common appliances. RTOSs are also found in many types of robotic equipment, such as the robotic cameras television stations use that glide across a suspended cable system to record sports events from many angles (see Figure 5.2).

**What kind of operating systems do networks use?** A multiuser operating system (or network operating system) lets more than one user access the computer system at a time by handling and prioritizing requests from multiple users. Networks (groups of computers connected to each other so that they can communicate and share resources) need a multiuser OS because many users simultaneously access the server (the computer that manages network resources such as printing and communications). The latest versions of Windows and macOS can be considered network operating systems because they enable multiple computers in a home or small business to connect to each other and share resources.

**Figure 5.2** Real-time operating systems can be found in devices such as TV sky cameras, cars, medical equipment, and point of sale machines. *(Cal Sport Media/Newscom; Syda Productions/Shutterstock; Elfstrom/Getty Images; Sergiy Zavgorodny/Shutterstock)*

## The Great Debate: Is macOS Safer Than Windows?

Many Mac users feel they're impervious to viruses and malware (software that can disable or interfere with the use of a device) because those are "just Windows problems." This means that Mac users often run their computers with only the basic protection provided by Apple in its operating system software. Are Mac users wild risk takers, or are they safe from hackers? As with many issues, it's a little bit of both.

### Threats Are Out There

Windows users have been bombarded by malware and virus attacks for decades. When you bought your last Windows device, it came with a Windows Defender security solution built into Windows. Manufacturers also often include trial versions of third-party antivirus/anti-malware software. Running a Windows computer without antivirus/anti-malware software is just asking for trouble.

However, over the past several years, the attacks against Macs have increased. Why weren't Macs attacked frequently in the past? Most malware is designed to steal sensitive information such as credit card numbers. When thieves expend the time, money, and effort to develop malware, they want to ensure that it targets the largest population of potential victims. As macOS gains market share, Mac users are becoming a larger group of potential targets. In fact, in many affluent nations, Mac ownership has reached 20% of the market. And since Macs tend to cost more than Windows machines, it can be argued that Mac users may have more disposable income than other computer buyers. And wealthy people always make attractive targets for thieves.

### But Isn't macOS Safer Than Windows by Design?

To a certain extent, this is true. macOS does have certain design features that tend to prevent the installation and spread of malware. Apple has also designed current versions of iOS and macOS to prevent the installation of unapproved software (i.e., software not available on Apple's approved online outlets like the App Store). In addition, apps sold on the App Store are required to be designed using the access control technology known as *App Sandbox*.

When most software programs or apps are running, they have broad latitude to interact with the OS. Usually, they have all the rights that the user has over the OS. So if hackers can design an exploit that takes advantage of a security flaw in an app, they can potentially gain extensive control over the computer using the access that the user has to the OS. As noted, Apple requires all approved apps to be "sandboxed." When an app is sandboxed, the developer defines what the app needs to do in order to interact with the OS. The OS then grants only those specific rights and privileges to the app and nothing else. By doing this, it severely limits what hackers can do in an OS if they breach the security of an app. It's like being in a high-walled sandbox as a child. You can play within the confines of your space, but you can't make mischief outside certain limits.

### So I'll Buy a Mac and Be Safe Forever, Right?

Although it's more difficult to design exploits for macOS and iOS, it's not impossible. And a great deal of cybercrime relies on social engineering techniques like those used in scareware scams. *Scareware* is software designed to make it seem as if there is something wrong with your computer. The author of the scareware program then "persuades" you to buy a solution to the problem, acquiring your credit card number in the process. Scareware victims can be both Mac and PC users, so even if you own a Mac, you need to be aware of such scams and avoid falling prey to them (see Chapter 9).

### The Solution: Extra Security Precautions

The current versions of macOS, iOS, and Windows all include security tools. Here are a few additional things you should do to protect yourself:

1. **Make sure your software is set to download and install updates automatically.** As OS developers discover holes in their software's security, they provide updates to repair these problems.
2. **Consider using third-party antivirus/anti-malware software (even on a Mac).** Although no product will detect 100% of malware, detecting some is better than detecting none.
3. **Be aware of social engineering techniques.** Use vigilance when surfing the Internet so you don't fall prey to scams.

So, no OS is 100% safe. But if you're informed and proceed with caution, you can avoid a lot of schemes perpetrated by hackers and thieves.

---

In larger networks, a more robust network OS is required to support workstations and the sharing of databases, applications, files, and printers among multiple computers in the network. This network OS is installed on servers and manages all user requests. For example, on a network where users share a printer, the network OS ensures that the printer prints only one document at a time in the order the requests were made. Examples of network operating systems include Windows Server, Linux, and UNIX.

**What is UNIX?** UNIX is a multiuser, multitasking OS that's used as a network OS, although it can also be found on PCs. Developed in 1969 by Ken Thompson and Dennis Ritchie of AT&T's Bell Labs, the UNIX code was initially not proprietary—no one company owned it. Rather, any programmer could use the code and modify it to meet their needs. UNIX is now a brand that belongs to the company The Open Group, but any vendor that meets the testing requirements and pays a fee can use the UNIX name. Individual vendors then modify the UNIX code to run specifically on their hardware.

**What other kinds of computers require a multiuser OS?** Mainframes and supercomputers also require multiuser operating systems. Mainframes routinely support hundreds or thousands of users at a time, and supercomputers are often accessed by multiple people working on complex calculations. Examples of mainframe operating systems include UNIX, Linux on System z, and IBM's z/OS, whereas the clear majority of supercomputers use Linux.

# What the Operating System Does

As shown in Figure 5.3, the OS is like an orchestra's conductor. It coordinates and directs the flow of data and information through the computer system. In this section, we explore the operations of the OS in detail.

Manages computer hardware and peripherals

Provides a user interface

Provides a consistent interaction between applications and the CPU

The Operating System

Manages memory and storage

Manages the processor

**Figure 5.3** The OS is the orchestra conductor of your computer, coordinating its many activities and devices. *(StockPhotosArt/Shutterstock; Ra2studio/Shutterstock; Shutterstock; Ragnarock/Shutterstock; Arno van Dulmen/Shutterstock; Pearson Education, Inc. Shcherbakov Roman/Shutterstock)*

**Figure 5.4** (a) A command-driven interface. (b) A menu-driven interface. *(Courtesy of Microsoft Corp.)*

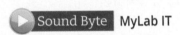

**Sound Byte** MyLab IT

**Using Windows Task Manager to Evaluate System Performance**

In this Sound Byte, you'll learn how to use the utilities provided by Windows to evaluate system performance. You'll also learn about shareware utilities that expand on the capabilities the Task Manager utility provides.

# The User Interface

**Objective 5.4** *Explain how the operating system provides a means for users to interact with the computer.*

**How does the OS control how I interact with my computer?** The OS provides a user interface that lets you interact with your device. Early personal computers used the *Microsoft Disk Operating System* (*MS-DOS* or just *DOS*), which had a command-driven interface, as shown in Figure 5.4a. A command-driven interface is one in which you enter commands to communicate with the computer system. The DOS commands were not always easy to understand and the interface proved to be complicated.

The command-driven interface was later improved by incorporating a menu-driven interface, as shown in Figure 5.4b. A menu-driven interface is one in which you choose commands from menus displayed on the screen. Menu-driven interfaces eliminated the need for users to know every command because they could select from a menu. However, they still were not intuitive for most people.

**What kind of interface do operating systems use today?** Current computer and mobile operating systems such as Microsoft Windows and macOS use a graphical user interface, or GUI (pronounced "gooey"). Unlike command- and menu-driven interfaces, GUIs display graphics and use the point-and-click technology of the mouse and cursor (or human finger), making them much more user-friendly.

With Linux-based operating systems, users are free to choose among many commercially available and free interfaces, such as GNOME and KDE, each of which provides a different look and feel.

# Hardware Coordination

**Objective 5.5** *Explain how the operating system helps manage hardware such as the processor, memory, storage, and peripheral devices.*

## Processor Management

**Why does the OS have to manage the processor?** When you use your computer, you're usually asking the processor, or CPU, to perform several tasks at once. You might be creating a PowerPoint presentation, have a Word document printing out, and be streaming music from Spotify—all at the same time, or at least what appears to be at the same time. But although the CPU is powerful, it needs the OS to arrange the execution of all these activities so it can work on them one at a time but so quickly that you think it is happening simultaneously.

**How does the OS coordinate all the activities?** The OS assigns a slice of its time to each activity that requires the processor's attention. The OS then switches between different processes billions of times per second to make it appear that all the processes are running at the same time.

Every keystroke and every mouse click creates an action, or event, in the respective device (keyboard, mouse, etc.) to which the OS responds. Sometimes these events occur one after another (such as when you type characters on the keyboard), but other events involve multiple devices working at the same time (such as the printer printing while you type and stream music). When you tell your computer to print your document, the printer generates a unique signal called an interrupt that tells the OS that it's in need of immediate attention. Every device has its own type of interrupt, which is associated with an interrupt handler, a special numerical code that prioritizes the requests. These requests are placed in the interrupt table in the computer's primary memory (RAM). The OS runs the task with a higher priority before running a task assigned a lower priority. This is called preemptive multitasking.

In our example, when the OS receives the interrupt from the printer, it suspends the CPU's typing activity and the next command Spotify needs to run and puts a "memo" in a special location in RAM called a *stack*. The memo is a reminder of what the CPU was doing before it started to work on the printer request. The CPU then retrieves the printer request from the interrupt table and begins to process it. On completion of the printer request, the CPU goes back to the stack, retrieves the memo it placed about the keystroke or Spotify, and returns to that task until it is interrupted again, in a very quick and seamless fashion, as shown in Figure 5.5.

**What happens if many processes need the same resources?** When the processor receives a request to send information to the printer, it first checks with the OS to ensure that the printer is not already in use. If it is, the OS puts the request in another temporary storage area in RAM, called the *buffer*. The request then waits in the buffer until the spooler, a program that helps coordinate all print

**STEP 2:** CPU receives an interrupt request from the printer.

**STEP 1:** CPU is streaming music.

**STEP 4:** CPU executes printing.

**STEP 6:** CPU continues streaming music.

CPU Processing Activity

**STEP 3:** Note written to stack that remembers where we were in streaming.

Stack

**STEP 5:** Note retrieved from stack so we can resume streaming music.

RAM

**Figure 5.5** How preemptive multitasking works.

jobs currently being sent to the printer, indicates the printer is available. If more than one print job is waiting, a line (or *queue*) is formed so that the printer can process the requests in order.

### Memory and Storage Management

**How does the OS manage the computer's memory?** As the OS coordinates the activities of the processor, it uses RAM as a temporary storage area for instructions and data the processor needs. The processor then accesses these instructions and data from RAM when it's ready to process them. So the OS is responsible for coordinating the space allocations in RAM, making sure there is enough space for all the pending instructions and data. The OS then clears the items from RAM when the processor no longer needs them.

**What happens if the applications I'm using require more RAM than what's installed?** Any system has a fixed amount of RAM installed. When there isn't enough RAM for the OS to store the required data and instructions, the OS borrows from the more spacious hard drive. This process of optimizing RAM storage by borrowing hard drive space is called virtual memory. As shown in Figure 5.6, when more RAM is needed, the OS swaps out from RAM the data or instructions that haven't recently been used and moves them to a temporary storage area on the hard drive called the swap file (or page file). If the data or instructions in the swap file are needed later, the OS swaps them back into active RAM and replaces them in the hard drive's swap file with less active data or instructions. This process of swapping is known as paging.

**Can I ever run out of virtual memory?** Only a portion of the hard drive is allocated to virtual memory. You can manually change this setting to increase the amount of hard drive space allocated, but eventually your computer will become sluggish as it is forced to page more often. This condition of excessive paging is called thrashing. The solution to this problem is to increase the amount of RAM in your computer, if there is excess capacity available. If you increase the RAM, it won't be necessary to send data and instructions to virtual memory.

**How does the OS manage files?** All of the details of how a file is stored, retrieved, named, compressed—all of the things we do with files—are the responsibility of the operating system. Different operating systems allow different naming schemes and have different tools for searching and optimizing file access. One operating system, say Windows, can even support different file systems. Some Windows versions support FAT file architecture and some NTFS. Before you format a disk drive make sure you know which file system you want plan to use with it.

**Figure 5.6** Virtual memory borrows excess storage capacity from the hard drive when there isn't enough capacity in RAM. *(Ragnarock/ Shutterstock; Tim Dobbs/Shutterstock)*

RAM

Data and instructions not recently used.

Operating System

Data and instructions needed now.

Hard drive's swap file

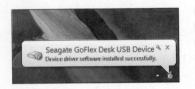

**Figure 5.7** A Windows message showing a successful driver installation the first time an external hard drive was connected to the computer. *(Courtesy of Microsoft Corp.)*

### Hardware and Peripheral Management

**How does the OS manage the hardware and peripheral devices?** Each device attached to your computer comes with a special program called a device driver that facilitates communication between the device and the OS. Because the OS must be able to communicate with every device in the computer system, the device driver translates the device's specialized commands into commands the OS can understand, and vice versa. Devices wouldn't function without the proper device drivers because the OS wouldn't know how to communicate with them.

**Do I always need to install drivers?** Today, most devices, such as flash drives, mice, keyboards, and digital cameras, come with the driver already installed in Windows. The devices whose drivers are included in Windows are called Plug and Play devices. Plug and Play (PnP) is a software and hardware standard designed to facilitate the installation of new hardware in PCs by including in the OS the drivers these devices need in order to run. Because the OS includes this software, incorporating a new device into your computer system seems automatic. PnP lets you plug a new device into your computer, turn it on, and immediately use the device (see Figure 5.7).

**What happens if the device is not PnP?** Sometimes you may have a device, such as a printer, that does not have a driver incorporated into Windows. You'll then be prompted to install or download from the Internet the driver required for that device. If you obtain a device secondhand without the device driver, or if you're required to update the device driver, you can often download the necessary driver from the manufacturer's website. You can also go to websites such as Driver-Zone (*driverzone.com*) to locate drivers.

**Can I damage my system by installing a device driver?** Occasionally, when you install a driver, your system may become unstable. Programs may stop responding, certain actions may cause a crash, or the device or the entire system may stop working. Although this is uncommon, it can happen. Fortunately, to remedy the problem, Windows has a Roll Back Driver feature that removes a newly installed driver and replaces it with the last one that worked (see Figure 5.8).

### Software Application Coordination

**Objective 5.6** *Explain how the operating system interacts with application software.*

**How does the OS help application software run on the computer?** Every computer program, no matter what its type or manufacturer, needs to interact with the CPU using computer code. For programs to work with the CPU, they must contain code the CPU recognizes. Some operations that happen are common to so many programs that the operating system includes these blocks of code. These are called an application programming interface (API). Microsoft DirectX, for example, is a group of multimedia APIs built into the Windows OS that improves graphics and sounds when you're playing games or watching videos on your PC.

**What are the advantages of APIs?** To create applications that can communicate with the OS, software programmers need only refer to the API code when they write an application. This standardizes the code and save developers time. APIs not only prevent redundancies in software code but also make it easier for software developers to respond to changes in the OS. Software companies also take advantage of APIs to ensure applications in software suites (such as Microsoft Office) have a similar interface and functionality. And since these applications share common APIs, data exchange is facilitated between two programs, such as inserting a chart from Excel into a Word document.

**Figure 5.8** The Roll Back Driver feature in Windows removes a newly installed driver and replaces it with the last one that worked.
> To access Device Manager, right-click the **Start** button and select **Device Manager**. To display the Properties dialog box, double-click on a device. Click the **Driver** tab. *(Courtesy of Microsoft Corp.)*

## Trends in IT    Are Personal Computers Becoming More Human?

Watch nearly any sci-fi movie or show and you'll see that making computers more human-like has long been a dream. Now, that dream is becoming a reality with advances in the field of artificial intelligence. For example, IBM's artificial intelligence supercomputer Watson was put to the test in a *Jeopardy* challenge and beat two of the show's greatest human champions. Although we've grown to expect great processing capabilities from computers, the *Jeopardy* challenge was different. Watson, like its human competitors, needed to discern specific pieces of data from complex questions in the *Jeopardy* game. Computers hadn't been capable of processing these types of complex situations previously.

What's behind Watson's abilities? The computer's ability to generate answers from complex questions is a matter of synthesizing large amounts of unstructured data with natural language processing and machine learning. Natural language processing is a field of artificial intelligence that uses software to analyze, understand, and generate human languages naturally, enabling users to communicate with computers as if they were humans. Machine learning is another form of artificial intelligence that provides computers with the ability to learn without being explicitly programmed. In other words, machine learning enables computer programs to grow and adapt when exposed to new data (much like human brains). Machine

learning uses data to detect patterns and adjust programmed actions accordingly.

Familiar systems are beginning to use these advanced forms of artificial intelligence. Facebook, for example, personalizes News Feeds based on how users react to posts. Modern operating systems now incorporate personal digital assistants (Siri, Cortana, and Google Assistant) to facilitate searches using voice commands. Amazon's Echo is a stand-alone device that uses natural language processing to receive and respond to voice commands. In doing so, Echo can coordinate smart-home devices, fire up playlists, or read your daily to-do list. The Watson technology is also being leveraged to discern personalities from Twitter posts and to translate multi-language conversations in real time.

Google has made great advances in using machine learning with photo recognition. A program called PlaNet is able to recognize where a photo was taken just by the details in the photo. Obviously, it's easy to determine the location of photos that include the Golden Gate Bridge or Wrigley Field, but PlaNet is able to determine the location of photos without such distinctive landmarks, such as an image of an open field or a random tree-lined street, with relative accuracy. If you want to challenge yourself to a similar task, visit GeoGuessr (*geoguessr.com*) and you'll quickly realize how difficult a task this is (see Figure 5.9).

While PlaNet is still in its infancy, Google currently uses natural language processing to enable you to search your stored photos based on characteristics. For example, typing "my photos of birds" brings up all the images from your Google photos that contain an image of a bird—without you having to previously tag the image. Finding images based on a characteristic, such as "tree" or "bird," is a conceptual task that computers haven't been able to handle before. The next step, however, goes further, using facial recognition to bring up photos of "Uncle Ted" or "grandpa." With this type of intelligence built into computers, the futuristic visions of sci-fi are not so futuristic anymore.

**Figure 5.9** Can you guess the location of this photo? Google is creating a program to do just that. You can try your hand at how hard this is by playing GeoGuessr. *(Courtesy of Google, Inc.)*

# Starting Your Computer

Many things happen quickly between the time you turn on your computer and the time it's ready for you to start using it. Data and instructions, including the OS, are stored in RAM while your computer is on. When you turn off your computer, RAM is wiped clean of all its data, including the OS. How does the computer know what to do when you turn it on if there is nothing in RAM? It runs through a *boot process,* a special start-up procedure that loads the OS into RAM.

## The Boot Process

**Objective 5.7** *Discuss the process the operating system uses to start up the computer and how errors in the boot process are handled.*

**What are the steps involved in the boot process?** As illustrated in Figure 5.10, the boot process consists of four basic steps. The term *boot,* from *bootstrap loader* (a small program used to start a larger program), alludes to the straps of leather, called *bootstraps,* that people used to use to help them pull on their boots. This is also the source of the expression "pull yourself up by your bootstraps." Let's look at each step of the boot process in detail.

### Step 1: Activating BIOS

**What's the first thing that happens after I turn on my computer?** In the first step of the boot process, the CPU activates the basic input/output system (BIOS). BIOS is a program that manages the exchange of data between the OS and all the input and output devices attached to the system. BIOS is also responsible for loading the OS into RAM from its permanent location on the hard drive. BIOS itself is stored on a read-only memory (ROM) chip on the motherboard. Unlike data stored in RAM, data stored in ROM is permanent and is not erased when the power is turned off.

### Step 2: Performing the Power-On Self-Test

**How does the computer determine whether the hardware is working properly?** The first job BIOS performs is to ensure that essential peripheral devices are attached and operational—a process called the power-on self-test (POST). The BIOS compares the results of the POST with the various hardware configurations permanently stored in CMOS (pronounced "see-moss"). CMOS,

**STEP 1:** CPU activates BIOS.
- Basic input/output system
- Stored permanently in ROM

CPU

ROM chip

**STEP 2:** Power-on self-test (POST).
- Tests components of the computer
- Compares results with configuration information in CMOS

**STEP 3:** Load OS to RAM.
- OS loaded from hard drive
- Kernel is *memory resident*

**STEP 4:** Configuration and customization settings checked and Start screen displays.

**Figure 5.10** The Boot Process *(Pearson Education; Pearson Education; Ragnarock/Shutterstock; Arno van Dulmen/Shutterstock)*

which stands for *complementary metal-oxide semiconductor*, is a special kind of memory that uses almost no power. A small battery provides enough power so that the CMOS contents won't be lost after the computer is turned off. CMOS contains information about the system's memory, types of disk drives, and other essential input and output hardware components. If the results of the POST compare favorably with the hardware configurations stored in CMOS, the boot process continues.

### Step 3: Loading the OS

**How does the OS get loaded into RAM?** Next, BIOS goes through a preconfigured list of devices in its search for the drive that contains the system files, the main files of the OS. When the system files are located, they load into RAM.

Once the system files are loaded into RAM, the kernel is loaded. The kernel is the essential component of the OS. It's responsible for managing the processor and all other components of the computer system. Because it stays in RAM the entire time your computer is powered on, the kernel is said to be *memory resident*. Other, less critical, parts of the OS stay on the hard drive and are copied over to RAM on an as-needed basis so that RAM is managed more efficiently. These programs are referred to as *nonresident*. Once the kernel is loaded, the OS takes over control of the computer's functions.

### Step 4: Checking Further Configurations and Customizations

**Is that it?** Finally, the OS checks the registry for the configuration of other system components. The registry contains all the different configurations (settings) used by the OS and by other applications. It contains the customized settings you put into place, such as mouse speed, as well as instructions as to which programs should be loaded first.

**How do I know if the boot process is successful?** The entire boot process takes only a few minutes to complete. If the entire system is checked out and loaded properly, the process completes by displaying the lock screen. After logging in, the computer system is now ready to accept your first command.

**Starting the Computer: The Boot Process**

In this Helpdesk, you'll play the role of a helpdesk staffer, fielding questions about how the operating system helps the computer start up.

**Why do I sometimes need to enter a login name and password at the end of the boot process?** The verification of your login name and password is called authentication. The authentication process blocks unauthorized users from entering the system. You may have your home computer set up for authentication, especially if you have multiple users accessing it. All large networked environments, like your college, require user authentication for access.

### Handling Errors in the Boot Process

**What should I do if my computer doesn't boot properly?** Sometimes during the boot process, BIOS skips a device (such as a keyboard) or improperly identifies it. Your only indication that this problem has occurred is that the device won't respond after the system has been booted. Try one of the following suggestions:

1. Power the computer off and on again.
2. If you've recently installed new software or hardware, try uninstalling it. Make sure you uninstall software using Windows *Apps & features*. From the Settings app, select Apps then select the program you wish to uninstall to remove the software.
3. Try accessing the Windows Advanced Options Menu (accessible by pressing the F8 key during the boot process). If Windows detects a problem in the boot process, it will add Last Known Good Configuration to the Windows Advanced Options Menu. Every time your computer boots successfully, a configuration of the boot process is saved. When you choose to boot with the Last Known Good Configuration, the OS starts your computer by using the registry information that was saved during the last successful shut down.
4. Try resetting your computer from the Update & Security Settings screen. It's recommended that you back up your PC prior to resetting it as a precautionary measure. Reset this PC is a utility program in Windows 10 that attempts to diagnose and fix errors in your Windows system files that are causing your computer to behave improperly (see Figure 5.11). When a PC is reset, your data files and personalization settings are not changed. Apps that you have downloaded from the Windows Store are kept intact but apps that you have downloaded from the Internet will be removed from your PC. Therefore, you'll need to reinstall them after the reset.
5. Finally, try *Go back to an earlier build* to revert to a past configuration. System Recovery is covered in more detail later in this chapter.

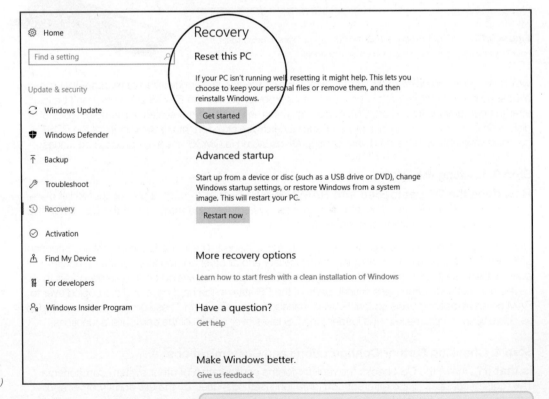

**Figure 5.11** The Recovery screen in Windows 10 provides access to the Reset this PC option.
> *To access the Recovery control, from the Start menu click **Settings**, then click **Update & security**. On the Update & security screen, select **Recovery**. (Courtesy of Microsoft Corp.)*

**Before moving on to Part 2:**

1.  Watch Chapter Overview Video 5.1.
2. Then take the Check Your Understanding quiz.

# Check Your Understanding // Review & Practice

For a quick review to see what you've learned so far, answer the following questions.

## multiple choice

1. Which is NOT an example of a mobile operating system?
   a. iOS
   b. Windows 10
   c. Android
   d. macOS

2. You're most likely to find an RTOS
   a. on an iPad.
   b. in a robotic camera.
   c. on a supercomputer.
   d. on a mainframe.

3. Operating systems that have windows and icons have which type of user interface?
   a. command-driven
   b. menu-driven
   c. graphical
   d. magnetic tape–based

4. The OS can optimize RAM storage by using
   a. virtual memory.
   b. thrashing.
   c. an interrupt handler.
   d. a spooler.

5. BIOS stands for
   a. bundled input output software
   b. billable input output services
   c. basic input output system.
   d. basic in order services

**chew on this**

As more devices and appliances make use of RTOSs, protecting them from hackers becomes increasingly critical. Developers are working to improve the security of the software and to safeguard communications between such devices. How concerned are you about the security of RTOSs in cars, smart homes, and wearable technology? Is enough being done to ensure the safety of these devices? What else can be done?

**MyLab IT**   Go to **MyLab IT** to take an autograded version of the *Check Your Understanding* review and to find all media resources for the chapter.

> **For the IT Simulation for this chapter, see MyLab IT.**

## Using Virtual Desktops in Windows 10

*Virtual desktops* are a great way to organize your working space into different displays when you're multitasking between projects. This exercise will walk you through the process of organizing your files into virtual desktops. Have several applications open at the same time before you begin. For more detail, watch the Try This video.

**Step 1** Click **Task View** on the taskbar to bring up the Task View interface. This consists of a display area that shows large thumbnails of all open windows running on your system. You haven't created any virtual desktops yet, so you will only see a button + New Desktop in the upper left corner. To organize open windows into specific groups, we will make a virtual desktop.

**Step 2** While in Task View, click + **New desktop** in the upper left corner. This adds a virtual desktop, named Desktop 2.

*(Courtesy of Microsoft, Corp.)*

**Step 3** Hover over Desktop 1 and you will see the programs and files you were working on earlier. Click on any of them and drag it into Desktop 2.

Note: You can also use the timeline to go back in time to retrieve things you were working on days ago.

**Step 4** Now to move between desktops, press **Ctrl + Windows key + an arrow key**. You can quickly move between desktops customized to specific projects now.

*(Courtesy of Microsoft, Corp.)*

## A Notification Alert

Does your app need to communicate with or provide feedback to the user? With the Notifier component of **App Inventor**, you can make your program generate message boxes or ask for a response from the user.

In this exercise, you'll use the Notifier component of **App Inventor** to show a message box, post a user choice with two buttons for response, or post an alert. Your apps can now use more of the features of the operating system to communicate!

The Notifier component allows you to communicate with alerts, message boxes, and text choice popups within your mobile app.

*(Courtesy of MIT, used with permission.)*

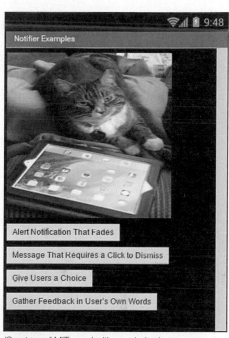

*(Courtesy of MIT, used with permission.)*

To create this app for iOS, go to *Thunkable.com*, a programming platform based on App Inventor.
**For the detailed instructions for this exercise, go to MyLab IT.**

# Using System Software

> **Learning Outcome 5.2** You will be able to describe how to use system software, including the user interface, file management capabilities, and utility programs.

Now that you know how system software works, let's explore how specific operating systems and their tools function.

# The Windows Interface

One of the functions of the operating system is to provide a user interface that lets you communicate with your computer. Today's operating systems use a graphical user interface. We describe the Windows 10 user interface in this section, but it's very similar to the user interfaces for the macOS and Linux operating systems.

## Using Windows 10

**Objective 5.8** *Describe the main features of the Windows interface.*

**What are the main features of the Windows 10 desktop?** After logging into your Microsoft account by entering or confirming your e-mail address and entering a password, you're brought to the primary working area: the desktop. At the bottom of the Windows 10 desktop is the taskbar, which displays open and favorite applications for easy access. You can point to an icon to preview windows of open files or programs, or you can move your mouse over a thumbnail to preview a full-screen image. You can also right-click an icon to view a Jump List—a list of the most recently or commonly used files or commands for that application.

**How do I find and open applications?** The Start menu provides access to all applications and apps installed on your device as well as access to settings and power options. You open the Start menu by clicking the Windows icon (or Start button) on the far left side of the taskbar or by pressing the Windows key on the keyboard.

**Figure 5.12** The Windows 10 Start menu provides access to your most used programs and apps. You can customize the Start menu by adding, resizing, and grouping tiles. *(Courtesy of Microsoft, Corp.)*

The Start menu is divided into two sections (see Figure 5.12). The right side has block tiles that provide easy access to your most frequently used software and Windows apps (such as Weather, Mail, and Photos). In addition to programs, tiles can represent files and folders. If there are more tiles on the Start menu than displayed, a scroll bar becomes available. The left side of the Start menu provides access to your most used programs as well as to Documents, Pictures, Settings, Power, and a list of all the installed apps and programs on your computer.

**Can I modify the Start menu?** You can customize the Start menu to meet your needs (refer to Figure 5.12). It's easy to add, remove, resize, move, and group application tiles on the Start menu. You can choose which applications are tiles on the Start menu through a process called pinning. Just right-click any application in the app list or in the Most used list, and choose Pin to Start.

Once on the Start menu, a tile can be resized by right-clicking the tile, pointing to Resize, and then selecting Small, Medium, Wide, or Large. You can rearrange apps on the Start menu by dragging them to a new location. You can also arrange several tiles near each other to create a group. Point to the top of the group to display a name box where you can type a group name. If there is a tile on the Start menu you don't need, just right-click it (or touch and hold), and select Unpin from Start.

You can also customize the left section of the Start menu. Right-click any app in the Most used section to get Pin to Start, More, and Uninstall options. If you click on More, Pin to taskbar and other options that vary by app appear. Go to Settings, Personalization and click Start, and you can determine which folders display on the left side of the Start menu. The default is Documents and Settings, but there are others to choose from, including Music, Pictures, or Downloads.

Because of the potential for customization, the Start menu on your computer will most likely be different from your friend's Start menu. However, because your Windows 10 settings and preferences are saved in your Microsoft account, you'll see your own personal settings, preferences, and applications reflected on the Start menu when you log on to any Windows 10 computer.

**How can I change the appearance of my desktop and lock screen?** You can also personalize the desktop and lock screen (the screen where you enter a password to resume using your computer) to suit your tastes. You can choose to have a picture, a slide show, or a single-color display on the desktop and lock screen. You can also determine whether you'd like other information to display on the lock screen, such as the weather, time, or your e-mail or calendar. Choosing a theme sets a color and font scheme for your entire system.

**How can I organize more than one window on my screen at a time?** You can "snap" windows—fixing open programs into place on either the left or the right side of the screen, to easily display two apps at the same time. Once you snap a window into place, you see thumbnails of all the other open windows. Clicking any thumbnail will snap that window into place. You can also snap windows to the corners, thus having up to four windows displayed at the same time.

**How can I see open windows and quickly move between them?** Task View allows you to view all the tasks you're working on in one glance. To see all open windows at once, click Task View on the taskbar. This is similar to using Alt+Tab.

**Can I group my open programs and windows into task-specific groups?** When faced with situations in which you're working with multiple documents for multiple projects, it might be easier to group the sets of documents together for each project and just switch between projects. You can do that now in Windows 10 with a feature called virtual desktops, which allow you to organize groups of windows into different displays (see Figure 5.13). For example, you can put an open Word document, web browser, and PowerPoint presentation that you need for your business class in one desktop, and, in a second desktop, you can put a Word document and an Excel spreadsheet for a project you're working on for your job. There is no limit as to the number

## Bits&Bytes    The Snipping Tool

The Snipping Tool is a Windows tool found in the Windows Accessories folder in the apps list that enables you to capture, or snip, a screen display so that you can save, annotate, or share it. You can capture screen elements as a rectangular snip, free-form snip, window snip, or as a full-screen snip. You can also draw on or annotate the screen capture, then save it, or send it to others. The Snipping Tool also has a delay timer so you can pause the capturing process for up to five seconds to set up screenshots of dialog boxes, menus, or other features that don't stay displayed when you initiate the Snipping Tool.

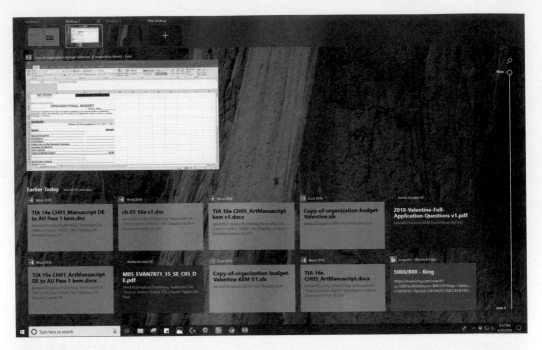

**Figure 5.13** Virtual desktops enable you to organize your open files into separate working spaces. *(Courtesy of Microsoft, Corp.)*

of desktops you can create. You can see all virtual desktops by clicking Task View. For more information on how to work with virtual desktops in Windows 10, see the Try This on page 176.

### User Interfaces for Other OSs

**How does the Mac user interface compare with that of Windows?** Although macOS and the Windows operating systems aren't compatible, they're extremely similar in terms of functionality. macOS programs appear in resizable windows and use menus and icons, just like Windows. Although macOS doesn't have a Start menu, it features a Dock with icons for your most popular programs (see Figure 5.14), very similar to the Windows taskbar.

Apple offers operating systems for different categories of devices: macOS for desktops and laptops, iOS for the iPhone and iPad, and watchOS for the Apple watch. macOS features a tight integration between the desktop and portable devices running iOS. With the macOS desktop, you can take and make phone calls, receive and send text messages, and easily transfer files with iOS devices. Windows 10 can run on mobile devices, like Windows phones, but has such a small market share that it isn't a key advantage for that OS.

**Is a Linux user interface similar to that of macOS and Windows?** Different distros of Linux feature different user interfaces. But most of them, like Ubuntu (see Figure 5.15), are based on familiar Windows and macOS paradigms, such as using icons to launch programs and having apps run in a window environment.

**Figure 5.14** macOS Mojave is Apple's latest operating system for desktop and laptop computers. *(shutterstock)*

**Figure 5.15** The Ubuntu Linux user interface resembles the Windows desktop. *(Ubuntu is a trademark of Canonical Limited and is used with the permission of Canonical Limited. Pearson is not endorsed by or affiliated with Canonical Limited or the Ubuntu project.)*

# File Management

So far we've discussed how the OS manages the processor, memory, storage, and devices, and how it provides a way for applications and users to interact with the computer. An additional function of the OS is to enable file management, which provides an organizational structure to your computer's contents. In this section, we discuss how you can use this feature to make your computer more organized and efficient.

## Organizing Your Files

**Objective 5.9** *Summarize how the operating system helps keep your computer organized and manages files and folders.*

**How does the OS organize computer contents?** Windows organizes the contents of your computer in a hierarchical directory structure composed of *drives*, *libraries*, *folders*, *subfolders*, and *files*. The hard drive, represented as the C: drive, is where you permanently store most of your files. Each additional storage drive, such as an optical drive, flash drive, or external hard drive, is given a unique letter (*D, E, F*, and so on). The C: drive is like a large filing cabinet in which all files are stored. The C: drive is the top of the filing structure of your computer and is referred to as the root directory. All other folders and files are organized within the root directory. There are areas in the root directory that the OS has filled with files and folders holding special OS files. The programs within these files help run the computer and generally shouldn't be accessed. In addition, sometimes the manufacturer will store files used to reinstate your computer back to the original factory state. Those files should not be accessed unless necessary.

**What exactly are files, folders, and libraries?** In an OS, a file is a collection of program instructions or data that is stored and treated as a single unit. Files can be generated from an application such as a Word document or an Excel workbook. In addition, files can represent an entire application, a web page, a set of sounds, an image, or a video. Files can be stored on the hard drive, a flash drive, online, or on any other permanent storage medium. As the number of files you save increases, it becomes more important to keep them organized in folders and libraries. A folder is a collection of files.

**How can I easily locate and see the contents of my computer?** In Windows, File Explorer is the main tool for finding, viewing, and managing the contents of your computer. It shows the location and contents of every drive, folder, and file. As illustrated in Figure 5.16, File Explorer is divided into two panes or sections:

1. The *Navigation pane* on the left shows the contents of your computer. It displays commonly accessed files and folders in the Quick Access area, files stored online in OneDrive, and other storage areas in This PC such as Documents, Music, Pictures, and Videos.

2. When you select a folder, drive, or library from the Navigation pane, the contents of that particular area are displayed in the *File list* on the right.

For those folders that have been shared with others using an online storage system such as OneDrive or Dropbox, Windows 10 displays a shared icon instead of the traditional yellow folder icon.

When you save a file for the first time, you give the file a name and designate where you want to save it. For easy reference, the OS includes libraries where files are saved unless you specify otherwise. In Windows, the default libraries are Documents for document files, Music for audio files, Pictures for graphics files, and Videos for video files. These are in the This PC section of File Explorer.

You can determine the location of a file by its file path. The file path starts with the drive in which the file is located and includes all folders, subfolders (if any), the file name, and the extension. For example, if you were saving a picture of Andrew Carnegie for a term paper for a U.S. History course, the file path might be C:\Documents\HIS182\Term Paper\Illustrations\ACarnegie.jpg.

As shown in Figure 5.17, "C:" is the drive on which the file is stored (in this case, the hard drive), and "Documents" is the file's primary folder. "HIS182," "Term Paper," and "Illustrations" are

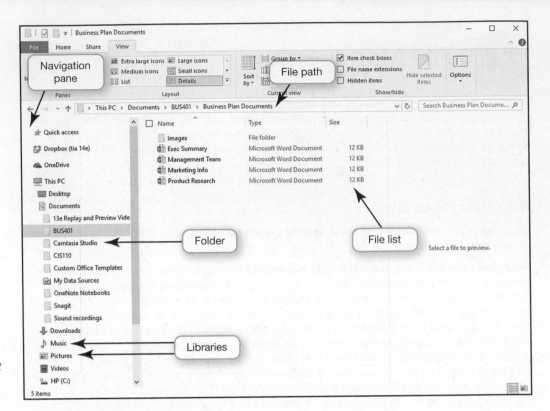

**Figure 5.16** File Explorer lets you see the contents of your computer. > Click **File Explorer** from the Start menu or from the taskbar. (Courtesy of Microsoft Corp.)

successive subfolders within the "Documents" main folder. Last comes the file name, "ACarnegie," separated from the file extension (in this case, "jpg") by a period. The backslash character (\), used by Windows, is referred to as a path separator. macOS files use a colon (:), whereas UNIX and Linux files use the forward slash (/) as the path separator.

**Are there different ways I can view and sort my files and folders?** Clicking on the View tab in File Explorer offers you different ways to view the folders and files.

1. **Details view:** This is the most interactive view. Files and folders are displayed in list form, and the additional file information is displayed in columns alongside the name of the file. You can sort and display the contents of the folder by clicking any of the column headings, so you can sort the contents alphabetically by name or type or hierarchically by date last modified or file size. Right-click the column heading area to modify the display of columns.

2. **Icons view:** There are a number of icon views that display files and folders in sizes ranging from small to extra-large. In most icon views, the folders are displayed as *Live Icons*. Live Icons allow you to preview the actual contents of a specific folder without opening the folder. Large Icons view, as shown in Figure 5.19, is the best view to use if your folder contains picture files because you can see a bit of the actual images peeking out of the folder. It's also good to use if your folder contains PowerPoint presentations because the title slide of the presentation will display, making it easier for you to distinguish among presentations.

You can change the views by using the controls in the Layout group on the View tab, or by clicking between Details view and Large Icons view from the bottom right corner of File Explorer. The View tab also enables you to display a Preview pane or a Details pane. The Preview pane displays the first page of the selected document, and the Details pane displays the file or folder's properties.

**Figure 5.17** Understanding File Paths

Save Files in the Cloud

If you're still using a flash drive, consider saving to the cloud instead. Cloud storage sites such as Microsoft's OneDrive, Google Drive, and Dropbox provide easy solutions. The advantage of saving files to the cloud is that your files are accessible from any Internet-connected device—including your smartphone. Using cloud storage will ensure the availability of your files when you need them (see Figure 5.18). Moreover, files and folders stored in the cloud are easily shared with others to facilitate collaboration. OneDrive and iCloud are proprietary cloud storage systems for Windows and macOS, respectively. Google Drive is another popular cloud storage system that also integrates with a suite of cloud-based productivity applications. Dropbox integrates with Windows and macOS as well as on Apple and Android mobile devices.

**Figure 5.18** OneDrive and Dropbox are integrated in Windows File Explorer for easy cloud-based file storage. *(Courtesy of Microsoft Corp.)*

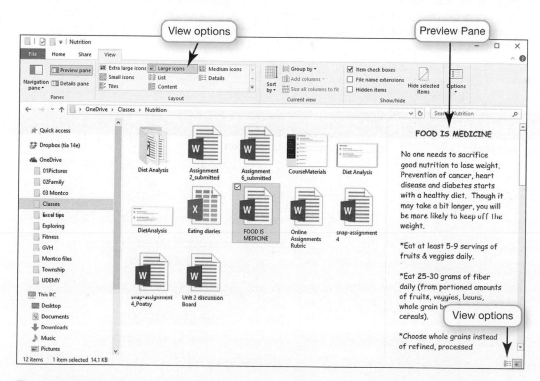

**Figure 5.19** The View tab in File Explorer enables you to use different views to display the contents of files and folders. The Preview pane on the right lets you see the first page of your document without first opening it. *(Courtesy of Microsoft Corp.)*

Creating folders is the key to organizing files because folders keep related documents together. For example, you might create one folder called "Classes" to hold your class work. Inside the "Classes" folder, you could create subfolders for each of your classes (such as ENG 325 and BUS 401). Inside each of those subfolders, you could create further subfolders for each class's assignments, homework, and so on.

Grouping related files into folders makes it easier for you to identify and find files. Which would be easier—going to the BUS 401 folder to find a file or searching through the hundreds of individual files in the Documents library hoping to find the right one? Grouping files in a folder also allows you to move files more efficiently, so you can quickly transfer critical files needing frequent backup, for instance.

### Naming Files

**Are there special rules I have to follow when I name files?** The first part of a file, or the file name, is generally the name you assign to the file when you save it. For example, "bioreport" may be the name you assign a report you have completed for a biology class.

In a Windows application, an extension, or file type, follows the file name and a period or dot (.). Like a last name, this extension identifies what kind of family of files the file belongs to, or which application should be used to read the file. For example, if "bioreport" is a spreadsheet created in Microsoft Excel, it has an .xlsx extension and its name is "bioreport.xlsx." You can choose to display file extensions by checking or unchecking the File name extensions box in the Show/hide group on the View tab in File Explorer.

Table 5.2 lists some common file extensions and the types of documents they indicate.

**Why is it important to know the file extension?** When you save a file created in most applications running under the Windows OS, you don't need to add the extension to the file name; it is added automatically for you. Mac and Linux operating systems don't require file extensions. This is because the information as to the type of application the computer should use to open the file is stored inside the file itself. However, if you're using the Mac or Linux OS and will be sending files to Windows users, you should add an extension to your file name so that Windows can more easily open your files.

| Table 5.2 | Common File Name Extensions | |
|---|---|---|
| **Extension** | **Type of Document** | **Application** |
| .docx | Word processing document | Microsoft Word 2007 and later |
| .xlsx | Workbook | Microsoft Excel 2007 and later |
| .accdb | Database | Microsoft Access 2007 and later |
| .pptx | Presentation | Microsoft PowerPoint 2007 and later |
| .pdf | Portable Document Format | Adobe Acrobat or Adobe Reader |
| .rtf | Text (Rich Text Format) | Any program that can read text documents |
| .txt | Text | Any program that can read text documents |
| .htm or .html | HyperText Markup Language (HTML) for a web page | Any program that can read HTML |
| .jpg | Joint Photographic Experts Group (JPEG) image | Most programs capable of displaying images |
| .zip | Compressed file | Various file compression programs |

If you try to open a file with an unknown extension, Windows 10 displays a dialog box that offers several suggested programs that can be used (see Figure 5.20). If you're certain of the type of file you're opening and know the program you'll want to use in the future to open similar types of files, select the option to always use the selected program. However, if you're at all unsure of the program to use or don't want to set a default program for this type of file, make sure that option is not selected.

**Are there things I shouldn't do when naming my files?** It's important that you name your files so that you can easily identify them. File names can have as many as 255 characters, so don't be afraid to use as many characters as you need. A file name such as "BIO 101 Research Paper First Draft.docx" makes it very clear what that file contains.

Keep in mind, however, that all files must be uniquely identified, unless you save them in different folders or in different locations. Therefore, although files may share the same file name (such as "bioreport.docx" or "bioreport.xlsx") or share the same extension ("bioreport.xlsx" or "budget.xlsx"), no two files stored in the same folder can share *both* the same filename and the same file extension. In addition, some characters can't be used in a file name, such as a quotation mark, and the file will not be saved until the file name is modified.

### Copying, Moving, and Deleting Files and Folders

**How can I move and copy files and folders?** You can move or copy a file or folder to another location using the Cut or Copy commands, respectively, on the ribbon or by right-clicking the file and selecting an option from the shortcut menu. After selecting Cut or Copy, select the new location, and then select Paste from the ribbon or right-click the new location folder and select Paste. Alternatively, you can drag and drop a file or folder to a new location. One method is to open two File Explorer windows side by side and drag a file or folder from one window to the other. Another method is to drag a file or folder from the File list to a new location displayed in the Navigation pane. When dragging a file or folder, the default action is to move the file or folder. If you'd rather make a copy, press Ctrl while you drag the file or folder to its new location.

**Where do deleted files go?** The Recycle Bin is a folder on the desktop, represented by an icon that looks like a recycling bin, where files deleted from the hard drive reside until you permanently purge them from your system. Unfortunately, files deleted from other storage locations or files stored in the cloud don't go to the Recycle Bin but are deleted from the system immediately.

Mac systems have something similar to the Recycle Bin, called Trash, which is represented by a wastebasket icon. To delete files on a Mac, drag the files to the Trash icon.

**How do I permanently delete files from the Recycle Bin?** Files placed in the Recycle Bin or the Trash remain in the system until they're permanently deleted. To delete files from the Recycle Bin permanently, select Empty Recycle Bin after right-clicking the desktop icon. On Macs, select Empty Trash from the Finder menu in macOS.

**What happens if I need to recover a deleted file?** Getting a file back after the Recycle Bin has been emptied still may be possible using one of two methods:

- File History is a Windows 10 utility that automatically backs up files and saves previous versions of files to a designated drive (such as an external hard drive). If you're using File History, you can restore previously deleted files or even previous versions of files you've changed. (We'll discuss File History in more detail later in the chapter.)
- Additionally, OneDrive and other cloud-based storage systems, such as Dropbox and Google Drive, maintain histories of files and you can not only recover a deleted file, but also roll back files edit by edit.

When the Recycle Bin is emptied, only the reference to the file is deleted permanently, so the OS has no easy way to find the file. The file data actually remains on the hard drive until it's written over by another file. You may be able to use a program such as FarStone's RestoreIT or Norton Online Backup to try to retrieve files you think you've permanently deleted. These programs reveal files that are still intact on the hard drive and help you recover them.

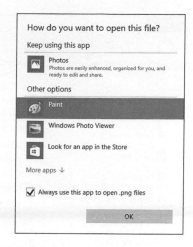

**Figure 5.20** When you open a file with an unknown file type, you can choose the app you want to use.
*(Courtesy of Microsoft Corp.)*

**Organizing Your Computer: File Management**

In this Helpdesk, you'll play the role of a helpdesk staffer, fielding questions about the desktop, window features, and how the OS helps keep the computer organized.

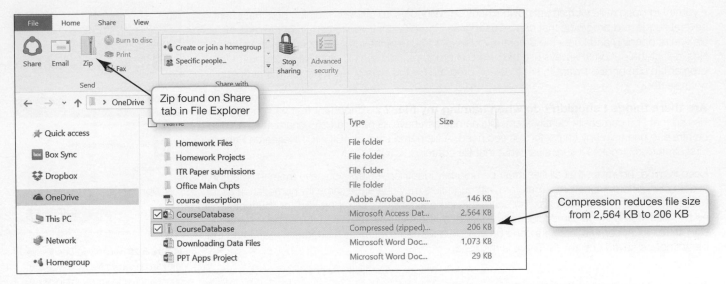

**Figure 5.21** File compression is a built-in utility of the Windows OS. Compressing the file reduces the size from 2,564 KB to 206 KB.
> *To compress a file or folder, open File Explorer, click the* **Share** *tab, and then click Zip. (Courtesy of Microsoft Corp.)*

### File Compression

**Why would I want to compress a file?** File compression makes a large file more compact, making it easier and faster for you to send large attachments by e-mail, upload them to the web, or save them onto a flash drive or other storage medium. You can also compress a group of files together, so you can manage one compressed folder rather than manipulating individual files. As shown in Figure 5.21, Windows has a built-in file compression utility that can be accessed through File Explorer. You can also obtain several stand-alone freeware and shareware programs, such as WinZip (for Windows) and StuffIt (for Windows or Mac), to compress your files. Often file compression is referred to as "zipping" a file.

**How does file compression work?** Compression takes out redundancies in a file to reduce the file size. Most compression programs look for repeated patterns of letters and replace these patterns with a shorter placeholder. The repeated patterns and the associated placeholder are cataloged and stored temporarily in a separate file called the *dictionary*. For example, in the following sentence, you can easily see the repeated patterns of letters.

**The rain in Spain falls mainly on the plain.**

Although this example contains obvious repeated patterns (ain and the), in a large document, the repeated patterns will be more complex. The compression program's algorithm (a set of instructions designed to complete a solution in a step-by-step manner), therefore, runs through the file several times to determine the optimal repeated patterns needed to obtain the greatest compression.

**How effective are file compression programs?** Current compression programs can reduce text files by 50% or more, depending on the file. However, some files, such as PDF files, already contain a form of compression, so they don't need to be compressed further. Image files such as JPEG, GIF, and PNG files discard small variations in color that the human eye might not pick up. Likewise, MP3 files permanently discard sounds that the human ear can't hear. These graphic and audio files don't need further compression.

**How do I restore a file I've compressed?** When you want to restore the file to its original state, you need to *decompress* the file. In File Explorer, when you click on a Compressed (or zipped) folder, the Compressed Folder Tools tab displays (see Figure 5.22). Click Extract all to open the Extract Compressed (Zipped) Folders dialog box. Browse to locate where you want to save the extracted files, or just click Extract to accept the default location (which is generally the location of the zipped folder).

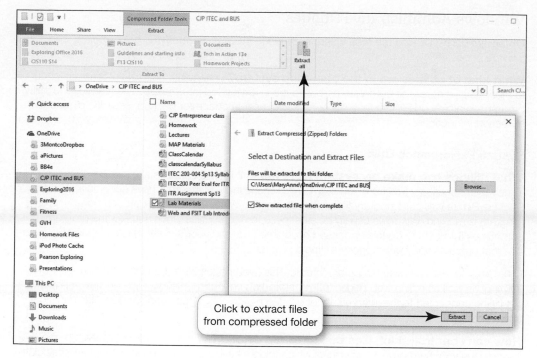

**Figure 5.22** Extracting files from a zipped folder is simply done through the Extract all feature in File Explorer.
*(Courtesy of Microsoft Corp.)*

# Utility Programs

The main component of system software is the operating system. However, *utility programs*—small applications that perform special functions on the computer—are also an essential part of system software. Utility programs come in three flavors:

1. Those included with the OS (such as System Restore)
2. Those sold as stand-alone programs (such as Norton AntiVirus)
3. Those offered as freeware (such as anti-malware software like Ad-Aware from Lavasoft)

Table 5.3 lists some of the various types of utility programs available within Windows as well as some alternatives available as stand-alone programs.

**Table 5.3   Utility Programs Available Within Windows and as Stand-Alone Programs**

| Windows Utility Program | Stand-Alone Alternatives | What It Does |
| --- | --- | --- |
| Disk Cleanup | CCleaner | Removes unnecessary files from your hard drive |
| Defragment and Optimize Drives | Norton Utilities, iDefrag | Rearranges files on your hard drive to allow for faster access of files |
| Task Manager and Resource Monitor | Process Explorer | Displays performance measures for processes; provides information on programs and processes running on your computer |
| File History, File Recovery | Acronis True Image, Norton Online Backup | Backs up important files, makes a complete mirror image of your current computer setup |
| System Restore | Acronis True Image | Restores your system to a previous, stable state |

# Windows Administrative Utilities

**Objective 5.10** *Outline the tools used to enhance system productivity, back up files, and provide accessibility.*

**What kind of utilities are in the operating system?** In general, the basic utilities designed to manage and tune your computer hardware are incorporated into the OS. The stand-alone utility programs typically offer more features or an easier user interface for backup, security, diagnostic, or recovery functions.

### System Performance Utilities

**What utilities can make my system work faster?** Disk Cleanup is a Windows utility that removes unnecessary files from your hard drive. These include files that have accumulated in the Recycle Bin as well as temporary files—files created by Windows to store data temporarily while a program is running. Windows usually deletes these temporary files when you exit the program, but sometimes it forgets to do this or doesn't have time because your system freezes or incurs a problem that prevents you from properly exiting a program.

Disk Cleanup also removes temporary Internet files (web pages stored on your hard drive for quick viewing) as well as offline web pages (pages stored on your computer so you can view them without being connected to the Internet). If not deleted periodically, these unnecessary files can slow down your computer.

**How can I control which files Disk Cleanup deletes?** When you run Disk Cleanup, the program scans your hard drive to determine which folders have files that can be deleted and calculates the amount of hard drive space that will be freed up by doing so. You check off which type of files you would like to delete, as shown in Figure 5.23.

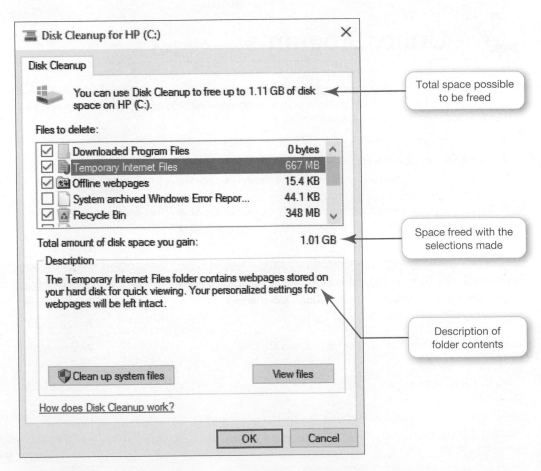

**Figure 5.23** Using Disk Cleanup will help free space on your hard drive. *(Courtesy of Microsoft Corp.)*
> *To access Disk Cleanup, click the **Start** button, scroll to **Windows Administrative Tools**, and click **Disk Cleanup**.*

**Figure 5.24** You can use Task Manager to close nonresponsive programs. *(Courtesy of Microsoft Corp.)*
> *To access Task Manager, right-click the taskbar and select* **Task Manager**.

**How can I check on a program that's stopped running?** If a program has stopped working, you can use the Windows Task Manager utility (see Figure 5.24) to check on the program or to exit the nonresponsive program. The Processes tab of Task Manager lists all the programs you're using and indicates their status. "Not responding" will be shown next to a program that stopped improperly. You can terminate programs that aren't responding by right-clicking the app name and selecting End task from the shortcut menu.

If you're working on a Mac, Force Quit can help you close out nonresponsive applications. You can access Force Quit by clicking the Apple menu, or simply by pressing Command + Option + Esc. Alternatively, you can press and hold the Option and Ctrl keys and click the nonresponsive program's icon on the dock.

**How can I improve my computer's performance?** After you have used your computer for a while, uploading, creating, changing, and deleting content, the hard drive becomes fragmented: Parts of files get scattered (fragmented) around the hard disk, making the hard disk do extra work, which can slow down your computer. Disk defragmentation rearranges fragmented data so that related file pieces are unified. The Defragment and Optimize Drives utility is found in the Windows Administrative Tools folder in the apps list. Before you defragment your hard drive, you should first determine if the disk needs to be defragmented by selecting Analyze. If your disk is more than 10% fragmented, you should run the disk defragmenter utility. Note that disk defragmentation doesn't apply to solid state drives (SSDs) because they don't have sectors. See the Dig Deeper *How Disk Defragmenting Utilities Work* for more information.

Disk defragmenting programs group together related pieces of files on the hard drive, allowing the OS to work more efficiently. To understand how disk defragmenting utilities work, you first need to understand the basics of how a hard disk drive stores files. A hard disk drive is composed of several platters, or round, thin plates of metal, covered with a special magnetic coating that records the data. The platters are about 3.5 inches in diameter and are stacked onto a spindle. There are usually two or three platters in any hard disk drive, with data stored on one or both sides. Data is recorded on hard disks in concentric circles called tracks. Each track is further broken down into pie-shaped wedges, each called a sector (see Figure 5.25). The data is further identified by clusters, which are the smallest segments within the sectors.

When you want to save (or write) a file, the bits that make up your file are recorded onto one or more clusters of the drive. To keep track of which clusters hold which files, the drive also stores an index of all sector numbers in a table. To save a file, the computer looks in the table for clusters that aren't already being used. It then records the file information on those clusters. When you open (or read) a file, the computer searches through the table for the clusters that hold the desired file and reads that file. Similarly, when you delete a file, you're actually not deleting the file itself but rather the reference in the table to the file.

So, how does a disk become fragmented? When only part of an older file is deleted, the deleted section of the file creates a gap in the sector of the disk where the data was originally stored. In the same way, when new information is added to an older file, there may not be space to save the new information sequentially near where the file was originally saved. In that case, the system writes the added part of the file to the next available location on the disk, and a reference is made in the table as to the location of this file fragment. Over time, as files are saved, deleted, and modified, the bits of information for various files fall out of order and the disk becomes fragmented.

Disk fragmentation is a problem because the OS isn't as efficient when a disk is fragmented. It takes longer to locate a whole file because more of the disk must be searched for the various pieces, slowing down your computer.

Defragmenting tools take the hard drive through a defragmentation process in which pieces of files scattered over the disk are placed together and arranged sequentially on it. Also, any unused portions of clusters that were too small to save data in before are grouped, increasing the available storage space on the disk. Figure 5.26 shows before and after shots of a fragmented disk that has gone through the defragmentation process. The Defragment and Optimize Drives utility in Windows 10 is set by default to automatically defragment the hard drive on a regular basis. Macs don't have a defragmentation utility built into the system. Those users who feel the need to defragment their Mac can use iDefrag, an external program from Coriolis Systems.

For more about hard disks and defragmenting, check out the Sound Byte "Hard Disk Anatomy."

**Figure 5.25** On a hard disk platter, data is recorded onto tracks, which are further divided into sectors and clusters.

**Figure 5.26** Defragmenting the hard drive arranges file fragments so that they are located next to each other. This makes the hard drive run more efficiently.

---

**Hard Disk Anatomy**

In this Sound Byte, you'll watch a series of animations that show various aspects of a hard drive, including the anatomy of a hard drive, how a computer reads and writes data to a hard drive, and the fragmenting and defragmenting of a hard drive.

**File and System Backup Utilities**

**How can I protect my data in the event something malfunctions in my system?** As noted earlier, when you use the File History utility, you can have Windows automatically create a duplicate of your libraries, desktop, contacts, and website favorites and copy it to another storage device, such as an external hard drive (see Figure 5.27). A backup copy protects your data in the event your hard drive fails or files are accidentally erased. File History also keeps copies of different versions of your files. This means that if you need to go back to the second draft of your history term paper, even though you are now on your fifth draft, File History should allow you to recover it. File History needs to be turned on by the user and requires an external hard drive (or network drive) that is always connected to the computer to function. You can choose to back up all folders on the C: drive, or select certain ones that you use most often or contain the most sensitive files to back up.

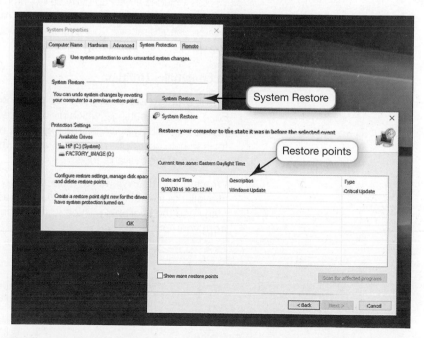

**Figure 5.27** File History backs up files to an external hard drive.
*> To turn on File History, choose Settings, select Update & security, and then select Backup. To modify File History and Backup settings, click More options. (Courtesy of Microsoft Corp.)*

Windows 10 also includes recovery tools that allow you to complete backups of your entire system (system image) that you can later restore in the event of a major hard drive crash.

**How can I recover my entire system?** Suppose you've just installed a new software program and your computer freezes. After rebooting the computer, when you try to start the application, the system freezes once again. You uninstall the new program, but your computer continues to freeze after rebooting. What can you do now?

Windows has a utility called System Restore that lets you roll your system settings back to a specific date when everything was working properly. A system restore point, which is a snapshot of your entire system's settings, is generated prior to certain events, such as installing or updating software, or automatically once a week if no other restore points were created in that time. You also can create a restore point manually at any time.

Should problems occur, if the computer was running just fine before you installed new software or a hardware device, you could restore your computer to the settings that were in effect before the software or hardware installation (see Figure 5.28). System Restore doesn't affect your personal data files (such as Word documents or e-mail), so you won't lose changes made to these files.

**Figure 5.28** The System Restore Wizard shows restore points set manually by a user and automatically by Windows when updates were installed. Setting a restore point is good practice before installing any hardware or software.
*> To access System Restore, search for "System restore" in the Windows 10 search box and select "Create a restore point." The System Restore Wizard displays, with the restore points shown on the second page of the Wizard. (Courtesy of Microsoft Corp.)*

## Table 5.4 Windows Ease of Access Tools

**Magnifier**

- Creates a separate window that displays a magnified portion of the screen

**Narrator**

- Reads what is on screen
- Can read the contents of a window, menu options, or text you have typed

**Speech Recognition**

- Allows you to dictate text and control your computer by voice

**On-Screen Keyboard**

- Allows you to type with a pointing device

**High Contrast**

- Provides color schemes that invert screen colors for vision-impaired individuals

*To locate Ease of Access, click the **Start** button, click **Settings**, then select **Ease of Access.*** *(Imagery Majestic/Fotolia; Anatoly Maslennikov/Fotolia; iqoncept/123RF; Pockgallery/Shutterstock; Courtesy of Microsoft Corp.; Pearson Education)*

macOS includes a backup utility called Time Machine that automatically backs up your files to a specified location. Because Time Machine makes a complete image copy of your system, it can also be used to recover your system in the case of a fatal error. (For more information on backing up your files, see Chapter 9.)

### Accessibility Utilities

**What utilities are designed for users with special needs?** Microsoft Windows includes Ease of Access settings, which provide a centralized location for assistive technology and tools to adjust accessibility settings. The Ease of Access tools, which are accessible from Settings, include tools to help users with disabilities, as shown in Table 5.4. The tools shown in the table are just a sampling of the available tools.

Whether you use Windows, macOS, Linux, or another operating system, a fully featured OS is available to meet your needs. As long as you keep the operating system updated and regularly use the available utilities to fine-tune your system, you should experience little trouble from your OS.

---

### Before moving on to the Chapter Review:

1. ▶ Watch Chapter Overview Video 5.2.
2. Then take the Check Your Understanding quiz.

# Check Your Understanding // Review & Practice

For a quick review to see what you've learned so far, answer the following questions.

## multiple choice

1. The process of adding a Windows 10 app to the Start menu is known as
   a. clipping.
   b. pinning.
   c. visualizing.
   d. screening.

2. The Windows app used for locating files and folders is
   a. Disk Manager.
   b. Finder.
   c. Library Explorer.
   d. File Explorer.

3. Which view in File Explorer can you use to sort files by column heading?
   a. Details
   b. Small icons
   c. Tiles
   d. Large icons

4. Which of the following is used to reduce the file size of a file or folder?
   a. defragmenter
   b. extraction
   c. compression
   d. shrinker

5. Which utility is used to exit from a nonresponsive program?
   a. System Refresh
   b. Disk Cleanup
   c. Task Manager
   d. File Explorer

**chew on this**

Windows and macOS both include a number of features and utilities designed for users with special needs. Compare the offerings of each OS. Are there options offered by one OS that are not available in the other? Which OS do you think has the best selection? Can you think of any areas that have not been addressed by this assistive technology? Research software from third-party developers to see if there are other tools that would also be useful. Should these tools be included in the OS? Why or why not?

**MyLab IT** Go to **MyLab IT** to take an autograded version of the *Check Your Understanding* review and to find all media resources for the chapter.

> **For the IT Simulation for this chapter, see MyLab IT.**

# 5 Chapter Review

## Summary

**Learning Outcome 5.1** You will be able to explain the types and functions of operating systems and explain the steps in the boot process.

 **Operating System Fundamentals**

**Objective 5.1** *Discuss the functions of the operating system.*

- System software is the set of software programs that helps run the computer and coordinates instructions between application software and hardware devices. It consists of the operating system (OS) and utility programs.
- The OS controls how your computer system functions. It manages the computer's hardware, provides a means for application software to work with the CPU, and is responsible for the management, scheduling, and coordination of tasks.
- Utility programs perform general housekeeping tasks for the computer, such as system maintenance and file compression.
- Modern operating systems allow for multitasking—performing more than one process at a time.

**Objective 5.2** *Explain the most popular operating systems for personal use.*

- Microsoft Windows is the most popular OS. The most recent release is Windows 10. macOS is designed to work on Apple computers, and Linux is an open source OS based on UNIX and designed primarily for use on personal computers.
- Some operating systems allow interaction with touch-screen interfaces. All personal use operating systems incorporate elements to share and store files on the Internet.
- An OS is designed to run on specific CPUs. Application software is OS dependent.
- Smartphones and tablets have their own specific mobile operating systems, which allow the user to multitask.

**Objective 5.3** *Explain the different kinds of operating systems for machines, networks, and business.*

- Real-time operating systems (RTOSs) require no user intervention.
- A multiuser operating system (network operating system) provides access to a computer system by more than one user at a time.
- UNIX is a multiuser, multitasking OS that is used as a network OS, though it can be used on PCs.
- Mainframes and supercomputers are specialty computers that require mainframe operating systems.

 **What the Operating System Does**

**Objective 5.4** *Explain how the operating system provides a means for users to interact with the computer.*

- The OS provides a user interface that enables users to interact with the computer.
- Most OSs today use a graphical user interface (GUI). Common features of GUIs include windows, menus, and icons.

**Objective 5.5** *Explain how the operating system helps manage hardware such as the processor, memory, storage, and peripheral devices.*

- When the OS allows you to perform more than one task at a time, it is multitasking. To provide for seamless multitasking, the OS controls the timing of the events on which the processor works.
- As the OS coordinates the activities of the processor, it uses RAM as a temporary storage area for instructions and data the processor needs. The OS coordinates the space allocations in RAM to ensure that there is enough space for the waiting instructions and data. If there isn't sufficient space in RAM for all the data and instructions, then the OS allocates the least necessary files to temporary storage on the hard drive, called *virtual memory*.

- The OS manages storage by providing a file management system that keeps track of the names and locations of files and programs.
- Programs called *device drivers* facilitate communication between devices attached to the computer and the OS.

**Objective 5.6** *Explain how the operating system interacts with application software.*

- All software applications need to interact with the CPU. For programs to work with the CPU, they must contain code that the CPU recognizes.
- Rather than having the same blocks of code appear in each application, the OS includes the blocks of code to which software applications refer. These blocks of code are called *application programming interfaces* (APIs).

 **Starting Your Computer**

**Objective 5.7** *Discuss the process the operating system uses to start up the computer and how errors in the boot process are handled.*

- When you start your computer, it runs through a special process called the *boot process.*
- The boot process consists of four basic steps: (1) The basic input/output system (BIOS) is activated when the user powers on the CPU. (2) In the POST check, the BIOS verifies that all attached devices are in place. (3) The OS is loaded into RAM. (4) Configuration and customization settings are checked.
- An authentication process occurs at the end of the boot process to ensure an authorized user is entering the system.
- Sometimes errors occur in the boot process. Try rebooting the computer or resetting the computer if the problem persists.

# Part 2
## Using System Software

**Learning Outcome 5.2** **You will be able to describe how to use system software, including the user interface, file management capabilities, and utility programs.**

 **The Windows Interface**

**Objective 5.8** *Describe the main features of the Windows interface.*

- In Windows 10, the Start menu provides access to your computer's apps, tools, and commonly used programs, and the desktop is the main working area.
- You can customize the Start menu by pinning and resizing tiles and organizing tiles into groups.
- Virtual desktops are used to organize open programs into different working areas.

 **File Management**

**Objective 5.9** *Summarize how the operating system helps keep your computer organized and manages files and folders.*

- Files and folders are organized in a hierarchical directory structure composed of drives, libraries, folders, subfolders, and files.
- The C: drive represents the hard drive and is where most programs and files are stored.
- File Explorer is the main tool for finding, viewing, and managing the contents of your computer.
- File Explorer helps you manage your files and folders by showing the location and contents of every drive, folder, and file on your computer.

- There are specific rules to follow when naming files.
- The Recycle Bin is the temporary storage location for deleted files from the hard drive.
- File compression reduces the size of a file by temporarily storing components of a file, and then when the file is extracted (uncompressed) the removed components are brought back into the file.

 **Utility Programs**

**Objective 5.10** *Outline the tools used to enhance system productivity, back up files, and provide accessibility.*

- Task Manager is used to exit nonresponsive programs.
- Disk Cleanup removes unnecessary files from your hard drive. If not deleted periodically, these unnecessary files can slow down your computer.
- Disk defragmentation utilities rearrange fragmented data so that related file pieces are unified. When a disk is fragmented, it can slow down your computer.
- File History automatically creates a duplicate of your hard drive (or parts of your hard drive) and copies it to another storage device, such as an external hard drive. You can use File History to recover deleted or corrupted files.

- System Restore lets you roll your system settings back to a specific date (restore point) when everything was working properly.

- Windows Ease of Access settings include tools that help adjust computer settings for those users with disabilities.

 Be sure to check out **MyLab IT** for additional materials to help you review and learn. And don't forget to watch the Chapter Overview Videos. ▶

# Key Terms

Android **161**

application programming interface (API) **168**

authentication **172**

basic input/output system (BIOS) **170**

boot process **170**

cluster **188**

CMOS **170**

command-driven interface **166**

desktop **176**

device driver **168**

directory **179**

Disk Cleanup **186**

disk defragmentation **187**

distributions (distros) **161**

event **166**

extension (file type) **182**

file **179**

file compression utility **184**

File Explorer **179**

File History **188**

file management **179**

file name **182**

file path **179**

folder **179**

Google Chrome OS **161**

graphical user interface (GUI) **166**

interrupt **166**

interrupt handler **166**

iOS **161**

kernel **161**

Linux **161**

machine learning **169**

macOS **160**

menu-driven interface **166**

Microsoft account **177**

mobile operating system **161**

multitask **160**

multiuser operating system (network operating system) **163**

natural language processing **169**

operating system (OS) **160**

paging **167**

path separator **180**

pinning **177**

Plug and Play (PnP) **168**

power-on self-test (POST) **170**

preemptive multitasking **166**

real-time operating system (RTOS) **163**

Recycle Bin **183**

registry **171**

Reset this PC **172**

root directory **179**

sector **188**

spooler **166**

Start menu **176**

swap file (page file) **167**

system files **171**

System Restore **189**

system restore point **189**

Task Manager **187**

taskbar **176**

thrashing **167**

track **188**

UNIX **164**

user interface **160**

utility program **161**

virtual desktops **177**

virtual memory **167**

Windows **160**

# Chapter Quiz // Assessment

For a quick review to see what you've learned, answer the following questions. Submit the quiz as requested by your instructor. If you are using **MyLab IT**, the quiz is also available there.

## multiple choice

1. Which of the following would you NOT see on a Windows 10 Start menu?
   a. Task View
   b. Power
   c. apps list
   d. tiles

2. When an OS processes tasks in a priority order, it is known as
   a. preemptive interrupting.
   b. interruptive multitasking.
   c. multitasking handling.
   d. preemptive multitasking.

3. An example of an open source OS is
   a. Linux.
   b. macOS.
   c. Windows.
   d. DOS.

4. Which of the following is not considered an accessibility utility?
   a. Magnifier
   b. System Restore
   c. Narrator
   d. Speech Recognition

5. Which of the following devices would use a real-time operating system?
   a. iPhone
   b. Roomba Vacuum
   c. Microsoft Surface tablet
   d. all of the above

6. Device drivers are
   a. are no longer used because of Plug and Play.
   b. often bundled with the operating system.
   c. always installed from a CD.
   d. mapping programs to generate driving instructions.

7. A GUI user interface is special because
   a. it uses a very small set of commands.
   b. the menus are organized well.
   c. there is a set of icons that represent the OS tasks.
   d. it uses voice commands to run tasks.

8. A feature in Windows 10 that is used to organize open windows into task-specific groups is called
   a. Program Manager.
   b. Virtual View.
   c. Snap Assist.
   d. Virtual Desktops.

9. When a printer receives a command, it generates a unique signal to the OS, which is called a(n)
   a. interrupt.
   b. event.
   c. slice.
   d. none of the above.

10. The C: drive on a Windows PC is like a large filing cabinet and is referred to as the
    a. main directory.
    b. root directory.
    c. library directory.
    d. main path.

## true/false

_____ 1. Different versions of Linux are known as distros.

_____ 2. Modern desktop operating systems are considered single-user multitasking operating systems.

_____ 3. The power-on self-test ensures all peripheral devices are attached and operational.

_____ 4. System restore points can only be created by Windows automatically on a regular schedule.

_____ 5. Once files are placed in the Recycle Bin they cannot be recovered.

## What do you think now?

1. Is your data safe enough if law enforcement agencies can have access to it?

2. Should the government be able to demand that tech companies create algorithms that engineers themselves are opposed to creating?

# Team Time

## Choosing the Best OS

### problem

You're the owner of a technology consulting firm. Your current assignments include advising start-up clients on their technology requirements. The companies include a nonprofit social service organization, a small interior design firm, and a social media advertising agency. One of the critical decisions for each company is the choice of OS.

### task

Recommend the appropriate OS for each company.

### process

1. Break up into teams that represent the three primary operating systems: Windows, macOS, or Linux.
2. As a team, research the pros and cons of your OS. What features does it have that would benefit each company?

What features does it not have that each company would need? Discuss why your OS would be the appropriate (or inappropriate) choice for each company.
3. Develop a presentation that states your position with regard to your OS. Your presentation should have a recommendation and include facts to back it up.
4. As a class, decide which OS would be the best choice for each company.

### conclusion

Because the OS is the most critical piece of software in the computer system, the selection should not be taken lightly. The OS that is best for a nonprofit social service organization may not be best for an interior design firm. A social media advertising agency may have different needs altogether. To ensure a good fit, it's important to make sure you consider all aspects of the work environment and the type of work being done.

# Ethics Project

## Upgrade Your World

In this exercise, you'll research and then role-play a complicated ethical situation. The role you play may or may not match your own personal beliefs, but your research and use of logic will enable you to represent whichever view is assigned.

### problem

With the release of Windows 10, Microsoft began the "Upgrade Your World" project, to work with 10 global nonprofit groups and 100 local nonprofits (10 in 10 countries). The organizations were selected because they addressed a key societal issue and had demonstrated a consistent record of creating meaningful change in their community and the world. Each local nonprofit will receive a $50,000 cash investment plus technology from Microsoft. If Microsoft decided to extend the program to another local nonprofit, which nonprofit organization in your area would you choose and why?

### research areas to consider

- Windows 10 features
- Upgrade Your World project
- The global and local Upgrade Your World nonprofits

### process

1. Divide the class into teams.
2. Research the areas cited above and determine a local nonprofit that you think would be deserving of an Upgrade Your World grant.
3. Team members should write a summary that provides background information for their nonprofit suggestion.
4. The team members will present their case to the class or submit a PowerPoint presentation for review by the rest of the class, along with the summary and resolution they developed. The class should determine the pros and cons of awarding the local nonprofit nominee the Upgrade Your World grant, and reach an agreeable conclusion as to which nonprofit would be the best choice to suggest to Microsoft.

### conclusion

As deserving as most nonprofits seem to be, some may benefit more than others and ultimately serve the community better than others after receiving a substantial grant such as that from Upgrade Your World. Being able to understand and evaluate a decision, while responding in a personally or socially ethical manner, will be an important skill.

## Operating Systems: Analyzing Market Share

As a sector analyst for one of the regional banks, you are responsible for reviewing and analyzing data to determine trends. Your analyses are used by bankers to inform prospective and current clients of possible investment opportunities. Currently, you are looking at the market trends of operating systems and have obtained historical market share data for mobile/tablet operating systems in the U.S., global market share data for desktop and table operating systems, and market share data for all operating systems for select countries around the world. You will chart the data to determine trends.

You will use the following skills as you complete this activity:

- Create an Area Chart
- Create a Map Chart
- Create Sparklines

- Add a Shape to a Chart
- Create a 2-D Pie Chart
- Apply Formats and Filters to Charts

## Instructions

1. Open *TIA_Ch5_Start* and save as **TIA_Ch5_LastFirst**.

2. Create a 2-D Area chart using data in the range A3:G7.
   Hint: Charts are on the Insert tab in the Chart group. Click Insert Line or Area Chart.

3. Modify the chart as follows:
   a. Position the chart so it fills cells **J2:S19**
   b. Add a title: **Change in Mobile OS Market Share 2013–2018**. Place 2013-2018 on a separate line.
      Hint: Place insertion point before 2013 and press Shift + Enter to place dates on separate line.
   c. Change the font size of 2013–2018 to **10**.
   d. Filter out the **Others** and **Windows** data so only Android and iOS data displays.
      Hint: Use the Chart Filters icon (the Funnel) on the right of the chart. Uncheck Windows and Others. Click Apply.

4. Add a **Callout: Line shape** to the chart with the line pointing at the top of the orange area between 2014 and 2015.
   Hint: Callout: Line is in the Callouts section in the Insert Shape group on the Format Chart Tools tab.

5. Add text to the callout: **Android Market Share Takes Off!**

6. Format the callout with **Subtle Effect - Gold, Accent 4 Shape Style.**

7. Create a **2-D Pie chart** using the ranges **A15:A21** and **G15:G21**.
   Hint: Select A15:A21, then press the **Ctrl key** while selecting G15:G21.

8. Modify the chart as follows:
   a. Add a title: **Operating System 2018 Global Market Share**
   b. Use **Quick Layout 1** to add data % and Series data labels to each data point.
      Hint: Quick Layouts are on the Chart Tools Design tab in the Chart Layouts group.
   c. Move the chart so it is on its own worksheet. Label the worksheet **Global OS.**
      Hint: Use Move Chart on the Chart Tools Design Tab. Do not copy and paste.

9. On the Data worksheet, add a **Column Sparkline** to cell range **H16:H21** using the data in range **B16:G21**. Increase the width of column H to **12**.

10. Create a Filled Map Chart from the data in ranges **A26:A39** and **D26:D39**. Place the chart to fill the range **I26:S45**. Add a title: **2018 Android Market Share by Country**
    a. Click **Chart Elements** and add **Data Labels**.

11. Save the document and submit based on your instructor's directions.

# 6 Understanding and Assessing Hardware: Evaluating Your System

 For a chapter overview, watch the **Chapter Overview Videos**.

 All media accompanying this chapter can be found here.

 **Make This** A Location-Aware App on **page 216**

*(WavebreakmediaMicro/Fotolia; Crstrbrt/123RF; Joppo/Shutterstock; Aeksanderdn/123RF; Leigh Prather/Shutterstock; Ivelin Radkov/Alamy Stock Photo)*

# What do you think?

As **self-driving cars become more commonplace**, society may face real dilemmas about how the **artificial intelligence (AI) in these vehicles responds to emergency situations**. Suppose a car comes over a hill and faces a stopped school bus. What should the AI do? Swerve into the woods to the right side to avoid the bus but thereby endanger the occupants of the car? Collide with the bus since the danger to the car occupants is minimal in a rear-end collision? Swerve left into oncoming traffic to avoid the bus, but possibly causing a fatal head-on collision with another vehicle? **How the vehicle responds depends on how the car's AI is programmed**.

Should cars always be programmed to minimize loss of human life, or should they always afford maximum protection for their occupants? **Who should make this decision?** What system provides the best benefit for society?

Who should be responsible for the ethics of the AI in self-driving cars?

- *Manufacturers best understand the cars so they should assume responsibility.*
- *Consumers should be able to choose the ethical standards of the AIs in their vehicles.*
- *A government agency should be responsible for setting standards to ensure fairness.*

*See the end of the chapter for a follow-up question.*          (Rico Ploeg/Alamy Stock Photo)

# Evaluating Key Subsystems

> **Learning Outcome 6.1** You will be able to evaluate your computer system's hardware functioning, including the CPU and memory subsystems.

It can be tough to know if your computer is the best match for your needs. New technologies emerge so quickly, and it's hard to determine whether they're expensive extras or tools you need. Do you need USB 3.1 instead of Thunderbolt? Doesn't it always seem as though your friend's computer is faster than yours? Maybe you could get more out of newer technologies, but should you upgrade the system you have or buy a new machine? In this chapter, you learn how to measure your system's performance and gauge your needs so that you end up with a system you love.

## Your Ideal Computing Device

There never seems to be a perfect time to buy a new computer. It seems that if you can just wait a year, computers will be faster and cost less. But is this actually true?

### Moore's Law

**Objective 6.1** *Describe the changes in CPU performance over the past several decades.*

**How quickly does computer performance improve?** As it turns out, it is true that if you wait just a while, computers will be faster and cost less. In fact, a rule of thumb often cited in the computer industry, called Moore's Law, describes the pace at which central processing units (CPUs) improve. Named for Gordon Moore, the cofounder of the CPU chip manufacturer Intel, this rule predicts that the number of transistors inside a CPU will increase so fast that CPU processing power will double about every two years. (The number of transistors on a CPU chip helps determine how fast it can process data.)

This rule of thumb has held true for over 50 years. Figure 6.1 shows a way to visualize this kind of exponential growth. If CPU capacity were put into terms of population growth, a group of 2,300 people at the start of CPU development would now be a country of over 1 billion!

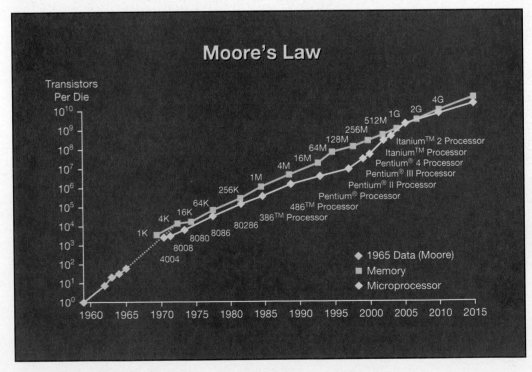

**Figure 6.1** Moore's Law illustrates the amazing pace of growth in CPU capabilities.

In addition to the CPU becoming faster, other system components also continue to improve dramatically. For example, the capacity of memory chips such as dynamic random access memory (DRAM)—the most common form of memory found in personal computers—increases about 60% every year. Meanwhile, hard drives have been growing in storage capacity by some 50% each year.

**Will Moore's Law always be true?** Probably not. Moore himself has predicted that in the future, CPU chips will be manufactured in a different way, thus changing or eliminating the effects of Moore's Law altogether. The scale to which reliable functioning transistors can be produced with silicon has limits (both functional and monetary). Intel is currently producing chips with features just 14 nanometers (nm) wide. It has postponed a switch to a 10-nm width in part due to the costs of constructing the fabrication facilities. Intel and other chip companies are investigating alternative elements for chips such as carbon (in both nanotube and graphene form), indium antimonide (InSb), and indium gallium arsenide (InGaAs). The main advantage with these substances is that they offer higher switching speeds than silicon, at lower power consumption rates. Therefore, the goal may shift toward better performing transistors rather than sheer quantity.

With technology demands switching to mobile devices and the Internet of Things, the goals of computing chip design have also changed. The drive for conventional CPUs used to be all about increasing computing capacity. Now chip designers are more concerned about low power processors (to conserve battery power) and integrating components such as RAM, cellular, Wi-Fi, and sensors (like accelerometers) into chips. So, although Moore's Law isn't quite obsolete, the way the industry looks at increases in computing power and functionality of chips is changing.

## Selecting a Computing Device

**Objective 6.2**  *Compare and contrast a variety of computing devices.*

**OK, things change fast. How do I know which device is best for me?** Consider what kind of user you are and what needs you have. For example, are you a power user who wants a machine for doing video editing and high-end gaming? Or are you a more casual user, mainly using a device for word processing and Internet access? Or are you on the move and need to bring your computer with you everywhere? Figure 6.2 shows a few different types of users—which type (or types) are you?

Now ask yourself, does your current computer match your needs? As we evaluate the pieces of your system in this chapter, it'll become clear whether your current device will need a few upgrades or whether you may need to acquire a new machine.

**What are the main types of devices available?** As we discussed in Chapter 2, a huge number of choices are on the market (see Figure 6.3):

- Smartphones
- Tablets (like the iPad or Galaxy)
- Ultrabooks (like the MacBook Air)
- 2-in-1s (which can serve as a tablet but also have a full keyboard)
- Laptops (or notebooks)
- Desktops

The main distinction among the available options is based on your need for mobility versus your need for processing power. If you're on the move all the time, don't use keyboard-intensive apps (like word processing), just need to check e-mail and the Internet, and want to have the lightest solution possible, a smartphone may be best for you. But if you use productivity software and need the convenience of a larger screen and a physical keyboard, you might want an ultrabook. At less than three pounds, they're great on weight but don't include as much storage space as conventional laptops. Even lighter are tablets like the iPad, but they have less processing power and, again, may not be able to run all the software you need.

**Figure 6.2   What kind of technology user are you?**

**Casual User**
- Uses the computer primarily for Internet access
- Uses some software applications locally, like Microsoft Office
- Uses videos and software but does not create them

**Power User**
- Needs fast, powerful processing
- Needs fast storage and lots of it
- Creates videos and software programs

**Mobile User**
- Needs a lightweight device
- Needs a long battery life
- Is happy to sacrifice some capabilities for less weight

*(Ilaszlo/Shutterstock, ColorBlind Images/The Image Bank/Getty Images, Ollyy/Shutterstock)*

Figure 6.3 Range of Computing Devices

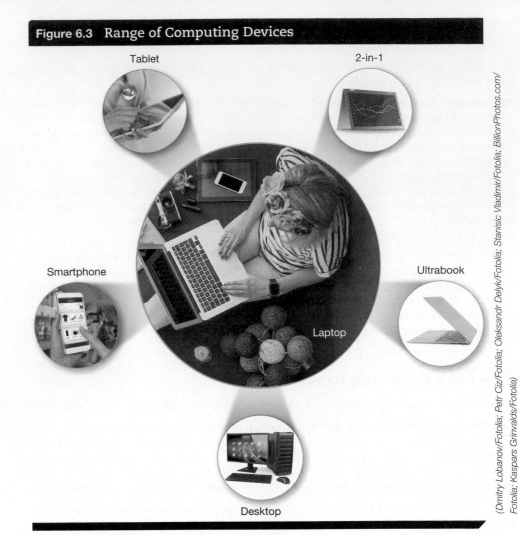

Tablet

2-in-1

Smartphone

Ultrabook

Laptop

Desktop

*(Dmitry Lobanov/Fotolia; Petr Ciz/Fotolia; Oleksandr Delyk/Fotolia; Stanisic Vladimir/Fotolia; BillionPhotos.com/ Fotolia; Kaspars Grinvalds/Fotolia)*

**Why would anyone consider buying a desktop?** Desktop systems are invariably a better value than lighter, more mobile computers. You'll find you get more computing power for your dollar, and you'll have more opportunity to upgrade parts of your system later. In addition, desktops often ship with a 24-inch or larger monitor, whereas portable computers offer screens between 10 and 17 inches.

Desktop systems are also more reliable. Because of the vibration that a mobile device experiences and the added exposure to dust, water, and temperature fluctuations that portability brings, mobile devices often have a shorter lifespan than stationary computers. You'll have less worry over theft or loss with a desktop, too. Manufacturers do offer extended warranty plans that cover mobile devices for accidental damage and theft; however, such plans can be costly.

**How long should I plan on keeping my computing device?** You should be able to count on two years, and maybe even four or five years. The answer depends in part on how easy it is to upgrade your system. Take note of the maximum amount of memory you can install in your device. Also, check whether you can upgrade your device's graphics capabilities down the road. In this chapter, we focus primarily on laptops and desktops, as they provide you with the most options for upgrading a current device without replacing it.

**How do I evaluate the performance of my current device?** We'll begin by conducting a system evaluation. To do this, we'll look at your computer's subsystems (see Figure 6.4), see what they do, and check how they perform during your typical workday. Then we'll compare that with what is available on the market, and the path forward for you will become clearer. Even if you're not in the market for a new computer, conducting a system evaluation will help you understand what you might want down the road.

**Figure 6.4 Computer Subsystems**

CPU

Memory

Storage

Media (video and sound)

*(Maxim_Kazmin/Fotolia; Destina/Fotolia; Maxim_Kazmin/ Fotolia; BillionPhotos.com/Fotolia)*

# Evaluating the CPU Subsystem

Let's start by considering your system's processor, or CPU. The CPU is located on the system motherboard and is responsible for processing instructions, performing calculations, and managing the flow of information through your computer. The dominant processors on the market are the Core family from Intel, featuring the i9, i7, i5, and i3 (see Figure 6.5).

## How the CPU Works

**Objective 6.3**   *Describe how a CPU is designed and how it operates.*

**How can I find out what CPU my computer has?** If you're running Windows, the System About window will show you the type of CPU you have installed. For example, the computer in Figure 6.6 has an Intel i7 CPU running at 2.2 GHz. AMD is another popular manufacturer of CPUs; you may have one of its processors, such as the Ryzen or the FX series. More detailed information about your CPU, such as its number of cores and amount of cache memory, is not shown on this screen. Let's dive into that.

**How does the CPU process data?** Any program you run on your computer is a long series of binary code describing a specific set of commands the CPU must perform. These commands may be coming from a user's actions or may be instructions fed from a program while it executes. Each CPU is somewhat different in the exact steps it follows to perform its tasks, but all CPUs must

**Figure 6.5**   The Intel i9, i7, i5, and i3 CPU chips run many of the laptop and desktop offerings on the market today. *(David Caudery/ PC Format Magazine/Future Publishing/Getty Images)*

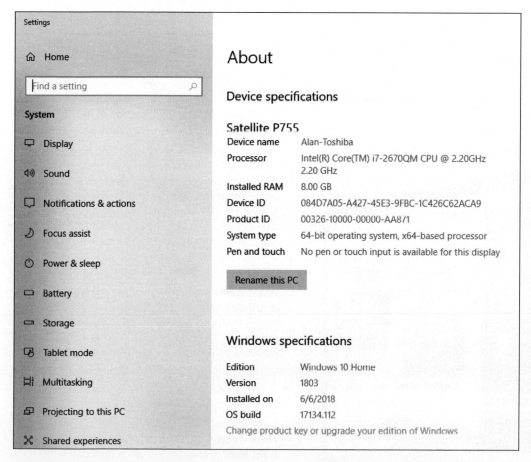

**Figure 6.6** The System About window identifies your computer's CPU as well as its speed. This computer has an Intel i7 running at 2.2 GHz. *(Courtesy of Microsoft Corp.)*
> *To view the system window, right-click the* **Start** *button. From the menu that displays, choose* **System**.

perform a series of similar general steps. Every time the CPU performs a program instruction, it goes through this series of steps:

1. **Fetch.** When any program begins to run, the 1s and 0s that make up the program's binary code must be "fetched" from their temporary storage location in random access memory (RAM) and moved to the CPU before they can be executed.

2. **Decode.** Once the program's binary code is in the CPU, it is decoded into commands the CPU understands.

3. **Execute.** Next, the CPU performs the work described in the commands. Specialized hardware on the CPU performs addition, subtraction, multiplication, division, and other mathematical and logical operations.

4. **Store.** The result is stored in one of the registers, special memory storage areas built into the CPU, which are the most expensive, fastest memory in your computer. The CPU is then ready to fetch the next set of bits encoding the next instruction.

The above process is called a machine cycle (see Figure 6.7). No matter what program you're running and no matter how many programs you're using at one time, the CPU performs these four steps over and over at incredibly high speeds. (We discuss the machine cycle steps in more detail in the Dig Deeper feature in this chapter.)

**What are the main components within a CPU?** The CPU is composed of two units: the arithmetic logic unit (ALU) and the control unit. The ALU is responsible for performing all the arithmetic calculations (addition, subtraction, multiplication, and division). It also makes logic and comparison decisions, such as comparing items to determine if one is greater than, less than, or equal to another.

The control unit of the CPU manages the switches inside the CPU. The CPU, like any part of the computer system, is designed from a collection of switches. How can the simple on/off switches of the CPU "remember" the fetch–decode–execute–store sequence of the machine cycle? It is programmed by CPU designers to remember the sequence of processing stages for that CPU and how each switch in the CPU should be set (i.e., on or off) for each stage. With each beat of the system clock, the control unit moves each switch to the correct on or off setting and then performs the work of that stage.

To move from one stage of the machine cycle to the next, the motherboard uses a built-in system clock. This internal clock is a special crystal that acts like a metronome, keeping a steady beat and controlling when the CPU moves to the next stage of processing.

These steady beats or "ticks" of the system clock, known as the clock cycle, set the pace by which the computer moves from process to process. The pace, known as clock speed, is measured in hertz (Hz), which describes how many times something happens per second. Today's system clocks are measured in gigahertz (GHz), or a billion clock ticks per second. Therefore, in a 3-GHz system, there are three billion clock ticks each second.

**What makes one CPU different from another?** You pay more for a computer with an Intel i9 than one with an Intel i7 because of its increased processing power. A CPU's processing power is determined by the following:

- Its clock speed
- How many cores it has
- Its amount of cache memory

**How does a CPU with a higher clock speed help me?** The faster the clock speed, the more quickly the next instruction is processed. CPUs currently have clock speeds of up to 4 GHz (or more).

**Figure 6.7** The CPU machine cycle.

Some users push their hardware to perform faster, overclocking their processor. Overclocking means that you run the CPU at a faster speed than the manufacturer recommends. It produces more heat, meaning a shorter lifespan for the CPU, and usually voids any warranty, but in gaming systems, you'll see this done quite often.

**How does increasing the number of cores in a CPU help me?** A core on a CPU contains the parts of the CPU required for processing an instruction. With multiple-core technology, two or more complete processors live on the same chip, enabling the independent execution of two or more sets of instructions at the same time.

If you had clones of yourself sitting next to you working, you could get twice as much (or more) done: That is the idea of multi-core processing. With multi-core processing, applications that are always running behind the scenes, such as virus protection software and your operating system (OS), can have their own dedicated processor, freeing the other processors to run other applications more efficiently. This results in faster processing and smoother multitasking. Chips with quad-core processing capabilities (see Figure 6.8) have four separate parallel processing paths inside them, so they're almost as fast as four separate CPUs. It's not quite four times as fast because the system must do some extra work to decide which processor will work on which part of the problem and to recombine the results each CPU produces.

**Figure 6.8** Intel Quad Core processors have four cores that are able to run four programs simultaneously.

Eighteen-core processors, like the Intel Core i9-7980XE, are now available and feature 18 separate processing paths. Multi-processor systems are often used when intensive computational problems need to be solved in such areas as computer simulations, video production, and graphics processing. Extreme gamers also use them in home computers.

**Are multi-core CPUs the only way to handle simultaneous processing?** Certain types of problems are well suited to a parallel-processing environment, although this approach is not used in personal computing. In parallel processing, there is a large network of computers, with each computer working on a portion of the same problem simultaneously. To be a good candidate for parallel processing, a problem must be able to be divided into a set of tasks that can be run simultaneously. For example, a problem where millions of faces are being compared with a target image for recognition is easily adapted to a parallel setting. The target face can be compared with many hundreds of faces at the same time. But if the next step of an algorithm can be started only after the results of the previous step have been computed, parallel processing will present no advantages.

**What other factors can affect processing speed?** The CPU's cache memory is a form of RAM that gets data to the CPU for processing much faster than bringing the data in from the computer's RAM. There are three levels of cache memory, defined by their proximity to the CPU:

- Level 1 cache is a block of memory built on the CPU chip itself for storage of data or commands that have just been used. That gets the data to the CPU blindingly fast!
- Level 2 cache is located on the CPU chip but is slightly farther away and so takes somewhat longer to access than Level 1 cache. It contains more storage area than Level 1 cache.
- Level 3 cache is also located on the CPU chip itself but is slower to reach and larger in size than Level 2 cache.

Generally, the more expensive the CPU, the more cache memory it will have. As an end user of computer programs, you do nothing special to use cache memory. Unfortunately, because it's built into the CPU chip or motherboard, you can't upgrade cache; it's part of the original design of the CPU. Therefore, as with RAM, when buying a computer, it's important to consider the one with the most cache memory, everything else being equal.

**Besides multiple cores and cache memory, what else can be done to increase the processing power of a CPU?** As an instruction is processed, the CPU runs sequentially through the four stages of processing: fetch, decode, execute, and store. Pipelining is a technique that allows the CPU to work on more than one instruction (or stage of processing) at the same time, thereby boosting CPU performance.

For example, without pipelining, it may take four clock cycles to complete one instruction (one clock cycle for each of the four processing stages). However, with a four-stage pipeline, the computer can process four instructions at the same time. The ticks of the system clock (the clock cycle)

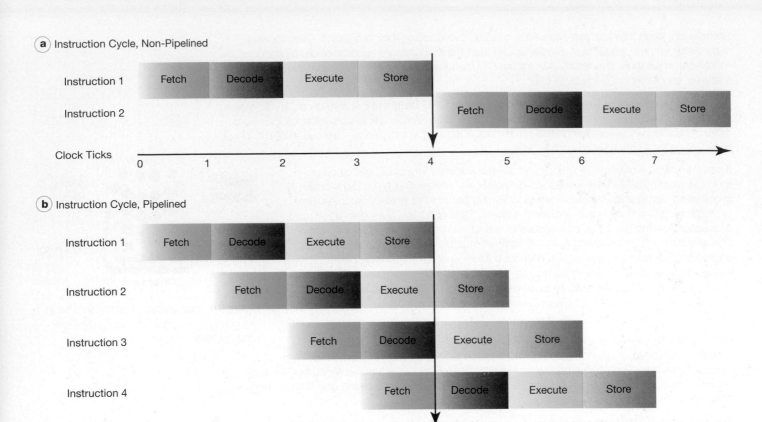

**a** Instruction Cycle, Non-Pipelined

Instruction 1 | Fetch | Decode | Execute | Store

Instruction 2 | Fetch | Decode | Execute | Store

Clock Ticks    0    1    2    3    4    5    6    7

**b** Instruction Cycle, Pipelined

Instruction 1 | Fetch | Decode | Execute | Store

Instruction 2 | Fetch | Decode | Execute | Store

Instruction 3 | Fetch | Decode | Execute | Store

Instruction 4 | Fetch | Decode | Execute | Store

Clock Ticks    0    1    2    3    4    5    6    7

**Figure 6.9**   Instead of (a) waiting for each instruction to complete, (b) pipelining allows the system to work on more than one set of instructions at one time.

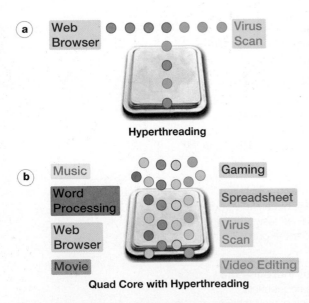

**Figure 6.10**   (a) Hyperthreading allows work on two processes to happen in one core at the same time. (b) So, a four-core hyperthreaded processor can be working on eight programs at one time.

indicate when all instructions move to the next process. Using pipelining, a four-stage processor can potentially run up to four times faster because some instruction is finishing every clock cycle rather than waiting four cycles for each instruction to finish. In Figure 6.9a, a nonpipelined instruction takes four clock cycles to be completed, whereas in Figure 6.9b, the four instructions have been completed in the same time using pipelining.

There is a cost to pipelining a CPU, however. The CPU must be designed so that each stage (fetch, decode, execute, and store) is independent. This means that each stage must be able to run while the other three stages are running. This requires more transistors and a more complicated hardware design.

CPUs began to expand their processing power further when hyperthreading was introduced in 2002. Hyperthreading provides quicker processing of information by enabling a new set of instructions in a different program (or thread) to start executing before the previous set has finished. This process takes advantage of certain delays that occur in reading and writing memory to registers with pipelining. As shown in Figure 6.10a, hyperthreading allows two different programs to be processed at one time, but they're sharing the computing resources of the chip.

All of the Intel Core processors have multiple cores *and* hyperthreading (see Figure 6.10b). The Intel i9-7980XE has 18 cores, each one using hyperthreading, so it simulates having 36 processors!

A critical aspect of the design of a computer system is to manage how the heat will be removed. One approach is to water-cool the system (see Figure 6.11). A tube containing liquid is placed in contact with heat-producing parts of the system, such as the CPU. The liquid picks up heat and carries it to a radiator, just as in a car. A fan blows across the fins of the radiator and efficiently disperses the heat. High-performance computers like the Aventum from Digital Storm feature complex water-cooling systems because of the massive amount of heat they generate. Want to try water cooling in a computer you're building but nervous about water inside your system? Sealed water-cooling solutions are also available so you never have to pour water near the inside of your computer.

**Figure 6.11** PC with liquid cooling system. *(Raw Group/Shutterstock)*

## Measuring CPU Performance

**Objective 6.4** *Describe tools used to measure and evaluate CPU performance.*

**So how do I compare different CPUs?** You'll often see models of the same computer with just a different CPU varying in cost by $200 or more. Is the price difference worth it? It's hard to know because so many factors influence CPU performance. Picking the best CPU for the kind of work you do is easier if you research some performance benchmarks. CPU benchmarks are measurements used to compare performance between processors. Benchmarks are generated by running software programs specifically designed to push the limits of CPU performance. Articles are often published comparing CPUs, or complete systems, based on their benchmark performance. Investigate a few, using sites like *cpubenchmark.net*, before you select the chip that's best for you.

**How can I tell whether my current CPU is meeting my needs?** One way to determine whether your CPU is right for you is to watch how busy it is as you work. You can do this by checking out your CPU usage—the percentage of time your CPU is working.

Your computer's OS has utilities that measure CPU usage. These are incredibly useful, both for considering whether you should upgrade and for investigating if your computer's performance suddenly seems to drop off for no apparent reason.

On Windows systems, the Task Manager utility lets you access this data (see Figure 6.12). The CPU usage graph records your CPU usage for the past minute. (Note that if you have multiple cores and hyperthreading, you'll see only one physical processor listed, but it will show that you have several virtual processors.) Of course, there will be periodic peaks of high CPU usage, but if your CPU usage levels are greater than 90% during most of your work session, a faster CPU will contribute a great deal to your system's performance.

To walk through using the Task Manager, check out the Try This on page 215. macOS has a similar utility named Activity Monitor located in the Utilities folder in the Applications subfolder.

**How often should I watch the CPU load?** Keep in mind that the workload your CPU experiences depends on how many programs are running at one time. Even though the CPU may meet the specs for each program separately, how you use your machine during a typical day may tax

**Figure 6.12** The Performance tab of the Windows Task Manager utility shows you how busy your CPU is. *(Courtesy of Microsoft Corp.)*
*> To access the Performance tab, right-click the **Start** button. From the menu, select **Task Manager**, click **more details** (if necessary), and then click the **Performance** tab.*

## Figure 6.13 Evaluating the CPU

**Clock Speed**
- Power users: Clock speed is very important; consider whether overclocking is worth sacrificing CPU longevity
- Casual/Mobile users: Clock speed is not as important

**Multiple Cores**
- Power users: Get as many cores as possible
- Casual users: Fewer cores is acceptable
- Mobile users: Low power draw is more critical than number of cores

**Cache Memory**
- Power users: Paying for more cache memory is a good investment
- Casual/Mobile users: Save your money

**CPU Benchmark**
- Use benchmarks to get an exact measure of the difference between two CPUs

*(Maxim_Kazmin/Fotolia)*

the CPU. If you're having slow response times or decide to measure CPU performance as a check, open the Task Manager and leave it open for a full day. Check in at points when you have a lot of open windows and when you have a lot of networking or disk-usage demand.

**So a better CPU means a better-performing system?** Your CPU affects only the processing portion of the system performance, not how quickly data can move to or from the CPU. Your system's overall performance depends on many factors, including the amount of RAM installed as well as hard drive speed. Your selection of CPU may not offer significant improvements to your system's performance if there is a bottleneck in processing because of insufficient RAM or hard drive performance, so you need to make sure the system is designed in a balanced way. Figure 6.13 lists factors to consider as you decide which specific CPU is right for you.

As you learned earlier, the *machine cycle* refers to the four stages performed by the CPU to process and store data. In this Dig Deeper, we take an in-depth look at each of these stages.

### Stage 1: The Fetch Stage

The data and program instructions the CPU needs are stored in different areas in the computer system. Data and program instructions move between these areas as they're needed by the CPU for processing. Programs are permanently stored on the hard drive because it offers nonvolatile storage. However, when you launch a program, it—or sometimes only its essential parts—is transferred from the hard drive into RAM.

(mdorottya/123RF)

The program moves to RAM because the CPU can access the data and program instructions stored in RAM more than 1 million times faster than if they're left on the hard drive. In part, this is because RAM is much closer to the CPU than the hard drive is. Another reason for the delay in transmission of data and program instructions from the hard drive to the CPU is the relatively slow speed of mechanical hard drives. The read/write heads must sweep over the spinning platters, which takes time. Even nonmechanical *solid-state drives* have slower access speeds than RAM. RAM is a type of memory that gives very fast direct access to data.

As specific instructions from the program are needed, they're moved from RAM into registers (the special storage areas located on the CPU itself), where they wait to be executed.

The CPU's storage area isn't big enough to hold everything it needs to process at the same time. If enough memory were located on the CPU chip itself, an entire program could be copied to the CPU from RAM before it was executed. This would add to the computer's speed and efficiency because there would be no delay while the CPU stopped processing operations to fetch instructions from RAM to the CPU. However, including so much memory on a CPU chip would make these chips extremely expensive. In addition, CPU design is so complex that only a limited amount of storage space is available on the CPU itself.

However, the CPU doesn't need to fetch every instruction from RAM each time it goes through a cycle. Another layer of storage, called *cache memory*, has even faster access to the CPU than RAM. Cache memory blocks are holding places for recently or frequently used instructions or data that the CPU needs the most. When these instructions or data are stored in cache memory, the CPU can retrieve them more quickly than if it had to access them in RAM. The CPU first looks for the instructions or data in Level 1 cache. If it doesn't find them there, it looks in Level 2 or Level 3 cache. If the needed information is not found in cache, the CPU retrieves it from RAM.

### Stage 2: The Decode Stage

The main goal of the decode stage is for the CPU's control unit to translate (or decode) the program's instructions into commands the CPU can understand. The collection of commands that a specific CPU can execute is called

(Andrea Danti/Fotolia)

the instruction set for that system. Each CPU has its own unique instruction set. The control unit interprets the code's bits according to the instruction set the CPU designers laid out for that particular CPU. The control unit then knows how to set up all the switches on the CPU so that the proper operation will occur.

Because humans are the ones who write the initial instructions, all the commands in an instruction set are written in a language called *assembly language*, which is easier for humans to work with than binary language. Many CPUs have similar assembly commands in their instruction sets. CPUs differ in the choice of additional assembly language commands selected for the instruction set. Each CPU design team works to develop an instruction set that is both powerful and speedy.

However, because the CPU knows and recognizes only patterns of 0s and 1s, it can't understand assembly language directly, so these human-readable instructions are translated into binary code. The control unit uses these long strings of binary code, called *machine language*, to set up the hardware in the CPU for the rest of the operations it needs to perform. Machine language is a binary code for computer instructions. Like each letter or character having its own unique combination of 0s and 1s assigned to it, a CPU has a table of codes consisting of combinations of 0s and 1s for each of its commands. If the CPU sees a particular pattern of bits arrive, it knows the work it must do. Table 6.1 shows a few commands in both assembly language and machine language.

| Table 6.1    Representations of Sample CPU Commands | | |
| --- | --- | --- |
| Human Language for Command | CPU Command in Assembly Language (Language Used by Programmers) | CPU Command in Machine Language (Language Used in the CPU's Instruction Set) |
| Add | ADD | 1110 1010 |
| Subtract | SUB | 0001 0101 |
| Multiply | MUL | 1111 0000 |
| Divide | DIV | 0000 1111 |

### Stage 3: The Execute Stage

The arithmetic logic unit (ALU) is the part of the CPU designed to perform mathematical operations such as addition, subtraction, multiplication, and division and to test the comparison of values such as greater than, less than, and equal to. For example, in calculating an average, the ALU is where the addition and division operations would take place.

*(Taras Livyy/Fotolia)*

The ALU also performs logical OR, AND, and NOT operations. For example, in determining whether a student can graduate, the ALU would need to ascertain whether the student had taken all required courses AND obtained a passing grade in each of them. The ALU is specially designed to execute such calculations flawlessly and with incredible speed.

The ALU is fed data from the CPU's registers. The amount of data a CPU can process at a time is based in part on the amount of data each register can hold. The number of bits a computer can work with at a time is referred to as its *word size*. Therefore, a 64-bit processor can process more information faster than a 32-bit processor.

### Stage 4: The Store Stage

In the final stage, the result produced by the ALU is stored back in the registers. The instruction itself will explain which register should be used to store the answer.

Once the entire instruction has been completed, the next instruction will be fetched, and the fetch–decode–execute–store sequence will begin again.

*(John Takai/Fotolia)*

# Evaluating the Memory Subsystem

Let's now take a peek at the memory subsystem of your computer. The memory subsystem can have a terrific impact on your system's processing speed if it is well matched to the power of your CPU. In this section, we look at how to measure that and how to upgrade if you need to.

## Random Access Memory

**Objective 6.5** *Discuss how RAM is used in a computer system.*

**What is RAM?** Random access memory (RAM) is your computer's temporary storage space. It really is the computer's short-term memory. When the computer is running, the RAM remembers everything that the computer needs to process data, such as data that has been entered and software instructions. But when the power is off, the data stored in RAM disappears. So, RAM is an example of volatile storage. Therefore systems always include both RAM and nonvolatile storage devices for permanent storage of instructions and data. For example, read-only memory (ROM) is a type of nonvolatile storage that holds the critical startup instructions. Hard drives provide the largest nonvolatile storage capacity in the computer system in laptops and desktops. In mobile devices that lack hard drives, memory chips function as nonvolatile storage.

**Why not use a hard drive to store the data and instructions?** It's about 1 million times faster for the CPU to retrieve a piece of data from RAM than from a mechanical hard drive. The time it takes the CPU to grab data from RAM is measured in nanoseconds (billionths of seconds), whereas pulling data from a fast mechanical hard drive takes an average of 10 milliseconds (ms), or thousandths of seconds. Even if you are using a solid-state hard drive (SSD), which is about eight times faster than a conventional hard drive, it is still much faster to retrieve data from RAM.

Figure 6.14 shows the various types of memory and storage distributed throughout your system: memory that is part of the CPU (such as CPU registers and cache), RAM, virtual memory, SSDs, and mechanical hard drives. Each of these has its own tradeoff of speed versus price. Because the fastest memory is so much more expensive, systems are designed with much less of it. This principle is influential in the design of a balanced computer system and can have a tremendous impact on system performance.

**Figure 6.14** A computer system's memory has many different levels, ranging from the small amounts in the CPU to the much slower but more plentiful storage of a mechanical hard drive. *(Pearson Education)*

**Are there different types of RAM?** Yes, but in most lower-end systems, the type of RAM used is double data rate 3 (DDR3) memory modules. High-performance systems use DDR4 memory, available in several different speeds (2400 MHz, 2800 MHz, and 3200 MHz). The higher the speed, the better the performance. High-performance video graphics cards often use GDDR5 memory, which has an even faster data transfer rate.

RAM appears in the system on memory modules (or memory cards), small circuit boards that hold a series of RAM chips and fit into special slots on the motherboard. Most memory modules in today's systems are packaged as a dual inline memory module (DIMM), a small circuit board that holds several memory chips (see Figure 6.15).

**How can I tell how much RAM is installed in my computer?** The amount of RAM actually sitting on memory modules in your computer is your computer's physical memory. The easiest way to see how much RAM you have is to look in the System window. (On a Mac, choose the Apple menu and then About This Mac.) This is the same window you looked in to determine your system's CPU type and speed and is shown in Figure 6.5. RAM capacity is measured in gigabytes (GB), and most machines sold today have at least 4 GB of RAM.

**How can I tell how my RAM is being used?** To see exactly how your RAM is being used, open the Resource Monitor and click on the Memory tab (see Figure 6.16). The Resource Monitor gives additional details on CPU, disk, network, and memory usage inside your system, and you can use it to see how you're using all the RAM you paid for.

Windows uses a memory-management technique known as SuperFetch. SuperFetch monitors the applications you use the most and preloads them into your system memory so that they'll be ready to be used when you want them. For example, if you have Microsoft Word running, Windows stores as much of the information related to Word in RAM as it can, which speeds up how fast your application responds. This is because pulling information from RAM is much faster than pulling it from the hard drive. You can watch this process at work using the Resource Monitor. Figure 6.16 shows how the 4 GB of installed RAM is being used:

- 1.1 GB is reserved to run the hardware systems.
- 0.98 GB is running programs.
- 1.7 GB is holding cached data and files ready for quick access.
- 0.2 GB is currently unused.

This is a system that would most likely benefit from additional memory.

**Figure 6.15** A DIMM memory module holds a series of RAM chips and is wrapped with an aluminum heatsink plate to pull away heat. *(Scanrail/123RF)*

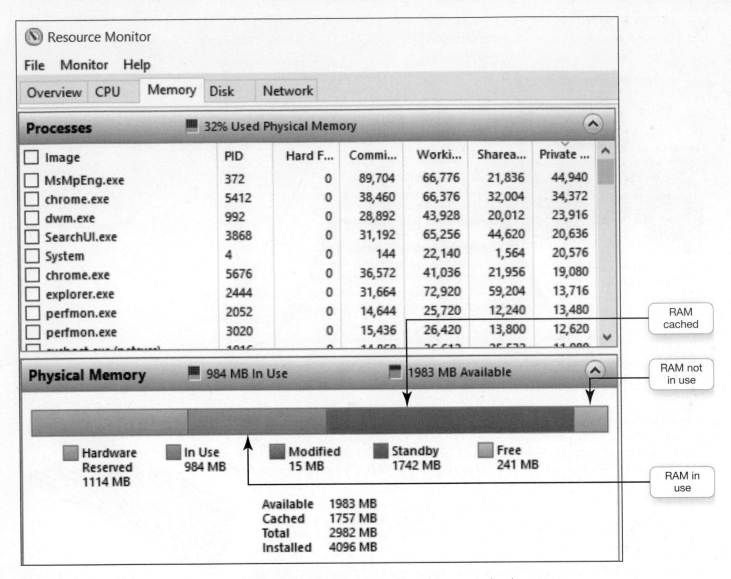

**Figure 6.16** The Resource Monitor's Memory tab shows a detailed breakdown of how the computer is using memory.
> *To access the Resource Monitor, type resource monitor in the **Start** search box, then select it from the list that appears. (Courtesy of Microsoft Corp.)*

**How much RAM do I need?** At a minimum, your system needs enough RAM to run the OS. Running the 64-bit version of Windows requires a minimum of 2 GB of RAM. However, because you run more applications at one time than just the OS, you'll want to have more RAM than just what's needed for the OS. For example, Table 6.2 shows how much RAM is recommended for the OS, a web browser, and some software.

It's a good idea to have more than the minimum amount of RAM you need now so you can use more programs in the future. Remember, too, that "required" means these are the minimum values recommended by manufacturers; having more RAM often helps programs run more efficiently. High-end systems can come with 64 GB of RAM. The rule of thumb: When buying a new computer, buy as much RAM as you can afford.

## Adding RAM

**Objective 6.6** *Evaluate whether adding RAM to a system is desirable.*

**Is there a limit to how much RAM I can add to my computer?** The motherboard is designed with a specific number of slots into which the memory cards fit, and each slot has a limit on the amount of RAM it can hold. Some systems ship with the maximum amount of RAM installed, whereas others have room for additional RAM. To determine your specific system limits,

## Table 6.2 Sample RAM Allocation

| Application | RAM Recommended |
| --- | --- |
| Windows 10 (high resolution) | 2 GB |
| Microsoft Office Professional 2019 | 2 GB |
| Microsoft Edge | 1 GB |
| iTunes 12 | 2 GB |
| Adobe Photoshop Elements 2018 | 4 GB |
| **Total RAM recommended to run all programs simultaneously** | **11 GB** |

check the system manufacturer's website. Also, memory seller sites like Crucial (*crucial.com*) can also help you determine how much RAM your computer model contains, whether you can add more, and the type of memory to add.

In addition, the OS running on your machine imposes its own RAM limit. For example, the maximum amount of RAM for the 32-bit version of Windows 10 Home is 4 GB, whereas the maximum memory limit using the 64-bit version of Windows 10 Pro is 2 TB.

**Is it difficult or expensive to add RAM?** Adding RAM is easy (see Figure 6.17). Be sure that you purchase a memory module that's compatible with your computer. Also, be sure to follow the installation instructions that come with the RAM module. Typically, you simply line up the notches and gently push the memory module in place.

RAM is a relatively inexpensive system upgrade. The cost of RAM does fluctuate in the marketplace as much as 400% over time, though, so if you're considering adding RAM, you should watch the prices of memory in advertisements.

### Sound Byte

**Installing RAM**

In this Sound Byte, you learn how to select the appropriate type of memory to purchase, how to order memory online, and how to install it yourself. As you'll discover, the procedure is a simple one and can add great performance benefits to your system.

**Figure 6.17** Adding RAM to a computer is quite simple and relatively inexpensive. On a laptop, you often gain access through a panel on the bottom. *(Editorial Image, LLC/Alamy Stock Photo; Editorial Image, LLC/Alamy Stock Photo)*

### Before moving on to Part 2:

1. ▶ Watch Chapter Overview Video 6.1.
2. Then take the Check Your Understanding quiz.

# Check Your Understanding // Review & Practice

For a quick review to see what you've learned so far, answer the following questions.

## multiple choice

1. Moore's Law describes the pace at which _____ improve.

    a. RAM chips

    b. clock cycles

    c. CPUs

    d. cache modules

2. Which of the following is a stage in the machine cycle?

    a. Fetch

    b. Calculate

    c. Decrypt

    d. Save

3. CPU _____ are measurements used to compare performance between processors.

    a. RAM speeds

    b. usage graphs

    c. cache cycles

    d. benchmarks

4. The limit to how much RAM you can add to your system

    a. depends on the design of the motherboard.

    b. depends on the operating system running on your system.

    c. depends on the amount of memory each memory card slot supports.

    d. all of the above

5. Adding RAM to your computer

    a. won't improve its performance.

    b. is not limited by the operating system installed.

    c. is relatively easy for most people to do.

    d. is not limited by how much RAM the computer can accommodate.

---

**chew on this**

Briefly describe the way you would evaluate whether the CPU and memory of your system were meeting your needs. What tools would you need? What operating system programs help you evaluate performance?

---

**MyLab IT**  Go to **MyLab IT** to take an autograded version of the *Check Your Understanding* review and to find all media resources for the chapter.

For the IT Simulation for this chapter, see MyLab IT.

# Try This

## Measure Your System Performance

Using the Windows Task Manager and the Resource Monitor can provide you with a lot of useful information about your computer system. Let's make sure you can use these Windows tools to keep an eye on your system performance. For more step-by-step instructions, watch the Try This video on MyLab IT.

**Step 1**  Hold the **Windows key** and press **X**. From the pop-up menu, select **Task Manager**. Click **More Details (if necessary)**, and then click the **Processes tab**.

**Step 2**  If you leave this window open while you work, you can pop in and check the history of how your CPU, disk, memory, and network are performing. Let's start by clicking on the **Performance tab**, and then looking at CPU utilization. This computer is only occasionally going over 30%, so the system isn't limited by CPU performance.

**Step 3**  Clicking on **Memory** in the left panel shows that we have 8 GB of DDR3 memory installed in this computer. Notice that memory usage is consistent at about 3.6 GB. We have memory available, so this system isn't limited by memory capacity with its current workload.

**Step 4**  Clicking on **Disk** in the left panel shows that here we have one disk drive, a 1 TB internal hard drive. The lower graph shows the history of data moving back and forth to the disk, the disk transfer rate. The larger upper graph shows how active the disk is—what percentage of time it is reading and writing. This system was not doing any disk-intensive operations when the screenshot was captured. If the active time is consistently high, upgrading to a faster, larger disk will have a big performance impact.

*(Courtesy of Microsoft Corp.)*

*(Courtesy of Microsoft Corp.)*

*(Courtesy of Microsoft Corp.)*

## A Location-Aware App

Your smartphone comes equipped with many built-in sensors that can, for example, read accelerations (to tell if your phone is shaking), location (using GPS satellites), and even atmospheric pressure. App Inventor can work with sensor data and supports a wide set of sensors used in the Lego Mindstorms kits to recognize color or respond to touch and sound.

*(Copyright MIT, used with permission.)*

In this exercise, you'll use the LocationSensor component in App Inventor to combine information about your environment into your apps.

The LocationSensor component allows you to work with live GPS data within your mobile app.

*(Copyright MIT, used with permission.)*

To create this app for iOS, go to *Thunkable.com*, a programming platform based on App Inventor.
**For the instructions for this exercise, go to MyLab IT.**

# Evaluating Other Subsystems and Making a Decision

**Learning Outcome 6.2**   **You will be able to evaluate your computer system's storage subsystem, media subsystem, and reliability and decide whether to purchase a new system or upgrade an existing one.**

The audio and video subsystems of your computer affect much of your enjoyment of the machine. Equally important is the storage subsystem, which allows you to save all that content you're generating. Let's evaluate those subsystems and consider what state-of-the-art audio/video would add to your computing experience. Then let's consider how to make sure your system is reliable—nothing interferes with enjoying technology like a misbehaving computer!

# Evaluating the Storage Subsystem

Remember, there are two ways data is stored on your computer: temporary storage and permanent storage. RAM is a form of temporary (or volatile) storage. It's critical to have the means to store data and software applications permanently, which we discuss in this section.

## Types of Storage Drives

**Objective 6.7**   *Classify and describe the major types of nonvolatile storage drives.*

Permanent storage options include mechanical hard drives, solid-state hard drives, solid-state hybrid drives, and external hard drives. When you turn off your computer, the data that has been written to these devices will be available the next time the machine is powered on. These devices therefore provide nonvolatile storage.

Today, most desktop system units are designed to support more than one internal hard drive. The Apple Mac Pro has room for four hard drives, and the Thermaltake Level 10 can support six hard drives. Each one simply slides into place when you want to add more storage. To save weight, most laptops have space for only one hard drive.

### Mechanical Hard Drives

**What makes the hard drive such a popular storage device?** With storage capacities exceeding 8 terabytes (TB), a mechanical hard drive has the largest capacity of any storage device. And because it offers the most storage per dollar, the mechanical hard drive is also a more economical device than other options.

**How is data stored on a hard drive?** A mechanical hard drive is composed of several coated, round, thin plates of metal stacked on a spindle. Each plate is called a platter. When data is saved to a hard drive platter, a pattern of magnetized spots is created on the iron oxide coating of each platter. When the spots are aligned in one direction, they represent a 1; when they're aligned in the other direction, they represent a 0. These 0s and 1s are bits (or binary digits) and are the smallest pieces of data that computers can understand. When data stored on the hard drive platter is retrieved (or read), your computer translates these patterns of magnetized spots into the data you have saved.

**How quickly does a hard drive find information?** The hard drive's access time, the time it takes a storage device to locate its stored data and make it available for processing, are measured in milliseconds (ms). For large-capacity drives, access times of approximately 12–13 milliseconds are typical.

**Figure 6.18** The new M.2 form factor allows the production of very fast, thin, and light SSD drives that resemble a stick of chewing gum. *(Andrush/Shutterstock)*

### Solid-State Drives

**Do mechanical hard drives have the fastest access times?** A solid-state drive (SSD) uses electronic memory and has no mechanical motors or moving parts. Having no mechanical motors allows SSDs to offer incredibly fast access times, reaching data in only a 10th of a millisecond (0.1 ms). That's about 100 times faster than mechanical hard drives. SSDs also have a great advantage when booting up because a mechanical hard drive must wait for motors to bring the platters up to the final rotation speed. The startup time of SSDs is so fast, in fact, that most desktop and laptop systems offer an option to use at least one SSD. This "system drive" may only be 20 GB, but it holds the operating system and means the wake-up time for the system will be very fast. In addition, SSDs run with no noise, generate very little heat, and require very little power, making them a popular option in laptops.

Storage capacities for SSDs now range up to around 15 TB, but such a large SSD is very expensive. Typical systems now often offer an SSD of 256 GB or 512 GB and then a mechanical hard drive, or two, to provide TBs of inexpensive slower storage space. But with prices of SSD drives continuing to fall, perhaps soon just having a single SSD drive may be affordable and provide the storage you need.

In the quest for ever thinner and lighter laptops, the newest type of SSD drive is in the M.2 form factor. First-generation SSD drives were contained in relatively large (2.5- or 3.5-inch) cases to fit the industry-standard hard drive bays in desktops and laptops. But inside these SSD cases was mostly empty space. Now newer motherboards use the M.2 connector (see Figure 6.18) and the drives that connect to it are only about 22 mm wide and range in length from 42 to 80 mm. The drives look like sticks of chewing gum that have sprouted memory modules and a controller chip. This allows the SSD drives to be integrated into the motherboard, which saves space and weight and allows tablet computers to feature SSD drives. In addition, the M.2 drives have even faster data transfer rates than the previous generation of drives.

**Solid-State Hybrid Drives** Another relatively new storage option is the solid-state hybrid drive (SSHD). An SSHD drive is a combination of both a mechanical hard drive and an SSD into a single device (see Figure 6.19). SSHD drives offer a small amount of SSD storage space, perhaps 8 GB. If it is enough to store the operating system, however, it can have a huge impact on the system boot time. For laptops that will accept only one drive, these drives are a great option if you need large amounts of affordable storage space, as they're currently less expensive than SSD drives.

Cover
Interface Connector
Magnetic Platters
Spindle
Actuator Arm with Read/Write Heads

Logic Board with Controller Circuits
Actuator

SSD Controller Chip
Drive Cache Memory Chips
SSD NAND Memory Chips

Logic Board

Bottom Cover

**Figure 6.19** The SSHD is a single unit that contains both an SSD electronic drive and a mechanical hard drive. *(Zern Liew/Shutterstock)*

The thin metal platters that make up a mechanical hard drive are covered with a special magnetic coating that enables the data to be recorded onto one or both sides of the platter. Hard drive manufacturers prepare the disks to hold data through a process called *low-level formatting*. In this process, concentric circles, each called a track, and pie-shaped wedges, each called a sector, are created in the magnetized surface of each platter, setting up a gridlike pattern that identifies file locations on the hard drive. A separate process called *high-level formatting* establishes the catalog that the computer uses to keep track of where each file is located on the hard drive. (More detail on this process is presented in the Dig Deeper feature in Chapter 5.)

Hard drive platters spin at a high rate of speed, some as fast as 15,000 revolutions per minute (rpm). Sitting between the platters are special "arms" that contain read/write heads (see Figure 6.20).

A read/write head moves from the outer edge of the spinning platter to the center, as frequently as 50 times per second, to retrieve (read) and record (write) the magnetic data to and from the hard drive platter. As noted earlier, the average total time it takes for the read/write head to locate the data on the platter and return it to the CPU for processing is called its access time. A new hard drive should have an average access time of approximately 12 ms.

Access time is mostly the sum of two factors—seek time and latency:

1. The time it takes for the read/write heads to move over the surface of the disk, moving to the correct track, is called the seek time. (Sometimes people incorrectly refer to this as access time.)
2. Once the read/write head locates the correct track, it may need to wait for the correct sector to spin to the read/write head. This waiting time is called latency (or rotational delay).

The faster the platters spin (or the faster the rpm), the less time you'll have to wait for your data to be accessed. Currently, most hard drives for home systems spin at 7,200 rpm.

The read/write heads don't touch the platters of the hard drive; rather, they float above them on a thin cushion of air at a height of 0.5 microinch. As a matter of comparison, a human hair is 2,000 microinches thick and a particle of dust is larger than a human hair. Therefore, it's critical to keep your hard drive free from all dust and dirt because even the smallest particle could find its way between the read/write head and the disk platter, causing a head crash—a stoppage of the hard drive that often results in data loss.

**Figure 6.20** A mechanical hard drive is a stack of platters enclosed in a sealed case. Special arms fit between each platter. The read/write heads at the end of each arm read data from and save data to the platters. *(Skaljac/Shutterstock)*

SSDs free you from worry about head crashes at all. The memory inside an SSD is constructed with electronic transistors, meaning there are no platters, no motors, and no read/write arms. Instead, a series of cells are constructed in the silicon wafers. If high voltage is applied, electrons move in and you have one state. Reverse the voltage and the electrons flow in another direction, marking the cell as storing a different value. The limiting factor for an SSD's lifespan is how many times data can be written to a cell. But the current generation of SSDs is proving to have very strong performance over time. Intel, one manufacturer of SSDs, says its drives will last five years when being written to heavily (20 GB per day).

However, the higher cost of SSD drives means they can only provide smaller amounts of storage. One compromise solution is the SSHD, a single drive that has both a small (perhaps 8 GB) SSD as well as a high-capacity mechanical hard drive. The faster SSD space can be used to store the operating system so that boot-up times are greatly reduced. These drives will continue to be popular as a cost-effective combination of nonvolatile storage.

Capacities for mechanical hard drives can exceed 8,000 GB (8 TB), and SSD drives are now capable of storing 15 TB (although they are very expensive at that capacity). Increasing the amount of data stored in mechanical drives is achieved either by adding more platters or by increasing the amount of data stored on each platter. SSD capacities continue to increase as the density of transistors on silicon wafers increases. And the new M.2 form factor allows for the production of very thin SSD drives. Modern technology continues to increase the quantities of data that can be stored in small places.

# Storage Needs

**Objective 6.8** *Evaluate the amount and type of storage needed for a system.*

**How do I know how much storage capacity I have?** Typically, hard drive capacity is measured in gigabytes (GB) or terabytes (1 TB = 1,000 GB). Accessing This PC from File Explorer will display the hard drives, their capacity, and usage information, as shown in Figure 6.21. To get a slightly more detailed view, select a drive and then right-click and choose Properties.

**How much storage do I need?** You need enough space to store the following:

* The OS
* The software applications you use, such as Microsoft Office, music players, and games
* Your data files
* Your digital music library, photos, videos of television shows and movies, and so on

Table 6.3 shows an example of storage calculation. If you plan to have a system backup on the same drive, be sure to budget for that room as well. However, note that if you're going to store your data files only online instead of on your computer, you may not need much hard drive space. For example, if you stream all the movies you watch from Netflix, keep all your data files in Microsoft OneDrive, and use online software like Google Docs to edit, you may need very little hard drive space.

If you still need more local storage than your internal hard drive provides, you can also add an external hard drive to your system. These use a USB port to connect. If you're looking to buy an external hard drive, the USB 3.1 standard is about 10 times faster than USB 2.0, so if your system supports USB 3.1, that's the better choice.

**What is RAID technology?** A redundant array of independent disks (RAID) is a set of strategies for using more than one drive in a system (see Figure 6.22). RAID 0 and RAID 1 are the most popular options for consumer machines. If you purchase two smaller drives, you can combine them using RAID technology.

**Figure 6.21** In Windows, the free and used capacity of each device in the computer system is shown in the This PC window. The General tab of the Properties dialog box gives you more detailed information.
> To view storage device details, launch File Explorer, and then click **This PC**. To view more details, right-click the **C drive**, and select **Properties**. (Courtesy of Microsoft Corp.)

Table 6.3 Sample Hard Drive Space Requirements

| Application/Data | Hard Drive Space Required | Heavy Cloud Storage User |
|---|---|---|
| Windows 10 | 20 GB | 20 GB |
| Microsoft Office 2019 | 3.5 GB | 3.5 GB |
| Adobe Photoshop Elements 2018 | 4 GB | 4 GB |
| Adobe Premiere Pro CC | 10 GB | 10 GB |
| Video library of movies | 80 GB (about 40 HD movies) | Streamed through online services |
| Music library | 50 GB (about 7,000 songs) | Stored in cloud (iCloud or Amazon Cloud Drive) |
| Photographs | 5 GB | Stored in iCloud or Dropbox |
| **Total storage in use** | **172.5 GB** | **37.5 GB** |
| Full backup | 172.5 GB | Stored in cloud using Carbonite |
| **Total required** | **345 GB** | **37.5 GB** |

If disk performance is very important—for example, when you're doing video editing or sound recording—using two files in RAID 0 could be desirable. RAID 0 is faster because every time data is written to a hard drive, it's spread across the two physical drives (see Figure 6.21a). The write begins on the first drive, and while the system is waiting for that write to be completed, the system jumps ahead and begins to write the next block of data to the second drive. This makes writing information to disk almost twice as fast as using just one hard drive. The downside is that if either of these disks fails, you lose all your data because part of each file is on each drive. So RAID 0 is for those most concerned with performance.

**Figure 6.22** (a) A RAID 0 configuration speeds up file read/write time. (b) A RAID 1 configuration gives you an instant backup. (Sergey Nivens/Fotolia; Ragnarock/Shutterstock)

No matter what kind of device you purchase, you'll have to decide how much storage you're willing to pay for. Does your Nexus 10 tablet need 16 GB? 32 GB? Should the SSD drive in your ultrabook be 128 GB? 256 GB? 512 GB? When you make your decision, keep in mind three factors:

- Check whether you can add storage later using an SD card. If you can use a few SD cards to store music or photos, that will be a cheaper option.

- Check how much usable storage is available in the device. For example, a 128-GB drive might offer less than 90 GB of available storage space after the operating system, the manufacturer software, and backup storage space are accounted for.
- Even though you can use cloud storage to expand your options, keep in mind that you need a base amount of local storage for installing apps. If you need to use a large variety of apps, make sure you'll have room to install them all.

If you're really paranoid about losing data, you should consider having two drives in RAID 1. In a RAID 1 configuration, all the data written to one drive is instantly perfectly mirrored and written to a second drive (see Figure 6.22b). This provides you with a perfect, instant-by-instant backup of all your work. It also means that if you buy two 1-TB drives, you only have room to store 1 TB of data because the second 1-TB drive is being used as the "mirror."

RAID 0 and RAID 1 configurations are available on many desktop systems and are even beginning to appear on laptop computers.

**So how do my storage devices measure up?** Figure 6.23 summarizes the factors you should consider in evaluating your storage subsystem. Don't forget that you can always extend the storage subsystem in your Internet-connected devices by utilizing cloud storage options. If you constantly switch between devices, cloud storage is most likely your best option.

**Figure 6.23 Evaluating Storage**

**Mechanical Hard Drive**
- How much storage space do you need?
- Do you need a RAID 0 configuration for better performance?
- Do you want a RAID 1 configuration for immediate constant backup?

**Solid-State Drive**
- Do you want a very fast start-up of the system at boot-up and from sleep mode?
- Are you okay having a second hard disk drive for larger storage space?

**Solid-State Hybrid Drive**
- Do you want the speed advantage at boot-up of an SSD, the large storage capacity of a mechanical hard drive, and only one drive?

**Cloud Storage**
- Do you need access to your files from multiple devices?
- Do you need to access your files when you travel?

Storage

(Maxim_Kazmin/Fotolia)

# Evaluating the Media Subsystems

Enjoying interactive media through your computer demands both good video processing hardware and good audio processing hardware. Video quality depends on two components: your video card and your monitor. If you're considering using your computer to display complex graphics, edit high-definition videos, or play graphics-rich games with a lot of fast action, you may want to consider upgrading your video subsystem. Let's start our look at the media subsystems by examining video cards.

## Video Cards

**Objective 6.9** *Describe the features of video cards.*

**What exactly is a video card?** A video card (or video adapter) is an expansion card that's installed inside the system unit to translate binary data into the images you view on your monitor. Modern video cards like the ones shown in Figure 6.24 let you connect video equipment using several different ports:

- HDMI ports for high-definition TVs, Blu-ray players, or gaming consoles
- DVI ports for digital LCD monitors
- DisplayPorts for digital monitors or projectors

**How much memory does my video card need?** All video systems include their own RAM, called video memory. Several standards of video memory are available, including graphics double data rate 3 (GDDR3) memory and the newer graphics double data rate 5 (GDDR5) memory. Newer GDDR5X video memory chips offer faster data rates (twice as fast) than earlier chips and improvements in energy efficiency.

**Figure 6.24** Video cards require their own fan for cooling. They support multiple monitors and multiple styles of ports like HDMI, DVI, and DisplayPort. *(YamabikaY/Shutterstock)*

The amount of video memory on your video card makes a big impact on the resolution the system can support and on how smoothly and quickly it can render video. Most new laptop computers come with video cards equipped with a minimum of 1 GB of video memory. For the serious gamer, 2 GB or more is essential, and cards with 16 GB are available (at very high prices). These high-end video cards allow games to generate smoother animations and more sophisticated shading and texture.

**How can I tell how much memory my video card has?** You'll find information about your system's video card in the Advanced Display Settings of the Screen Resolution window. On a Windows computer, to get to the Screen Resolution window, right click on your desktop and select Display settings. Click the Advanced display settings link, and then click the Display adapter properties link. A dialog box will appear that shows you the type of video card installed in your system, as well as its memory capacity.

**How does the CPU handle intensive video calculations?** Because displaying graphics demands a lot of computational work from the CPU, video cards come with their own graphics processing unit (GPU). The GPU is a separate processing chip specialized to handle 3D graphics and image and video processing with incredible efficiency and speed. When the CPU is asked to process graphics, it redirects those tasks to the GPU, significantly speeding up graphics processing. Figure 6.25 shows how the CPU can run much more efficiently when a GPU does all the graphics computations.

**Without a GPU**

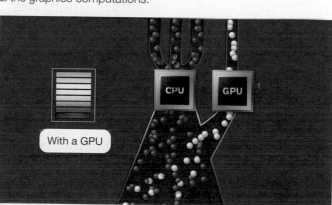

**With a GPU**

**Figure 6.25** The GPU is specialized to handle processing of photos, videos, and video game images. It frees up the CPU to work on other system demands.

In addition, special lighting effects can be achieved with a modern GPU. Designers can change the type of light, the texture, and the color of objects based on complex interactions. Some GPU designs incorporate dedicated hardware to allow high-definition movies to be decoded or special physics engines to model water, gravity, and rigid body movements.

**Why do some people use more than one video card in the same system?** For users who are primarily doing text-based work, one video card is usually enough. Computer gamers and users of high-end visualization software, however, often take advantage of the ability to install more than one video card. Two or even three video cards can be used in one system. When the system is running at very high video resolutions, such as 1920 × 1200 or higher, multiple video cards working together provide the ultimate in performance.

The two major video chip set manufacturers, NVIDIA and AMD, have each developed their own standards supporting the combining of multiple video cards. For NVIDIA, this standard is named SLI; for AMD, it is called CrossFireX. If you're buying a new desktop system and might be interested in employing multiple video cards, be sure to check whether the motherboard supports SLI or CrossFireX.

**Can I run a few monitors from one video card?** Working with multiple monitors is useful if you often have more than one application running at a time (see Figure 6.26) or even if you just want to expand your gaming experience. Some video cards can support up to six monitors from a single card. The AMD Radeon graphics cards, for example, let you merge all six monitors to work as one screen or to combine them into any subset—for example, displaying a movie on two combined screens, Excel on one monitor, Word on another, and a browser spread across the final two.

**Can I have a 3D experience from a computer monitor?** 3D panels are available for desktop monitors and for some laptops. The 3D wireless vision glasses included with the panels make existing games or 3D movies display in stereoscopic 3D.

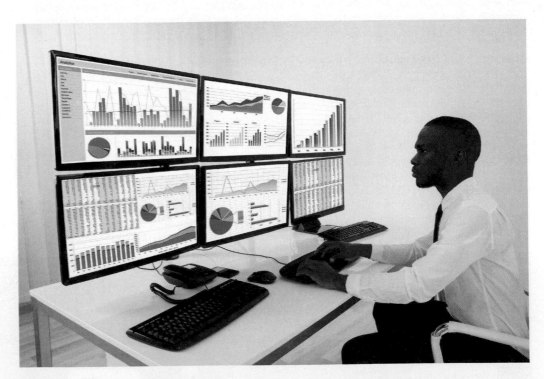

**Figure 6.26** AMD Radeon technology supports six monitors, which can be combined in any way.
(Andriy Popov/123Rf)

Rendering graphics for digital movies like *The Incredibles 2* by Pixar is very processor intensive. Pixar maintains a huge collection of computers, called a *render farm*, just for the purpose of rendering the graphics. Rendering means generating the graphics in final full-color form for viewing. Even with a render farm, it still takes 20–29 hours to render a single frame of a movie. Depending on their format, movies run at 24–60 frames per second. Therefore, it currently takes years of render farm time to render a movie in final form.

AMD answered demand by releasing the Radeon Pro SSG video card, which allows owners to install up to 1 TB of NAND flash memory directly into the graphics card. This essentially combines an SSD with a video card. This design allows massive amounts of data to be processed locally on the video card without having to use system RAM. This provides a huge performance boost in high-resolution rendering work required by the movie industry. However, you probably won't find them in most home computers, as they cost around $4,400. With the demand for animated movies on the rise, you can bet that movie studios like Pixar are upgrading their render farms with these cards.

**How do I know if I'm putting too much demand on my video card?** If your monitor takes a while to refresh when you're editing photos or playing a graphics-rich game, then the video card could be short on memory or the GPU is being taxed beyond its capacity. You can evaluate this precisely using the software that came with your card. For example, AMD OverDrive software monitors the GPU usage level, the current temperature, and the fan speed.

Review the considerations listed in Figure 6.27 to see if it might be time to upgrade your video card. On a desktop computer, replacing a video card is fairly simple: Just insert the new video card in the correct expansion slot on the motherboard. For laptop computers, it's usually not practical (or even possible in some cases) to upgrade the video card, as it's integrated directly into the motherboard. Usually your best option is to purchase a new laptop that has a more powerful video card.

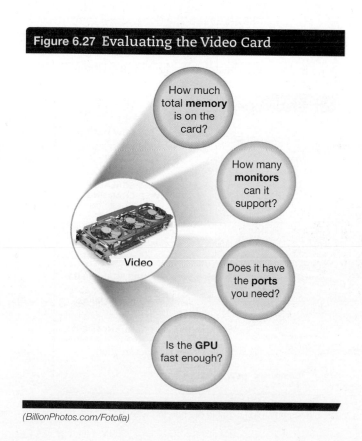

**Figure 6.27 Evaluating the Video Card**

How much total **memory** is on the card?

How many **monitors** can it support?

Video

Does it have the **ports** you need?

Is the **GPU** fast enough?

*(BillionPhotos.com/Fotolia)*

When the USB standard was introduced, many different ports began to fade from use. With USB, one port could be used to connect a keyboard, a mouse, a flash drive, an external hard drive, and a camera. For sure, USB seemed to be the perfect standard.

But as the need for larger file transfers grew with larger HD video files and higher-resolution image files, the USB standard needed to keep improving to offer faster data transfer rates. The USB connector also needed to be redesigned to different sizes so it could be used in phones, cameras, and thinner ultrabooks. This resulted in a collection of USB 1.0, 2.0, and 3.0 devices along with USB 1.0 and 2.0 ports, blue USB 3.0 ports, tiny mini USB ports, and even tinier micro USB ports. And, of course, each connector was oriented in a certain way, so we found ourselves spinning the cable around to try to find the right orientation to actually fit the connector into the port.

The USB standard faced competition as well, with the Thunderbolt technology appearing on Apple products. Thunderbolt 3 supports fast transfer rates of 40 Gb/s, zooming past the limit of the USB 3.0, which is 4.8 Gb/s. How fast is that? Intel, the company that developed the technology, claims that Thunderbolt can transfer a full-length HD movie in under 30 seconds, or copy in just 10 minutes a library of music that would take a solid year to play through.

Intel used fiber optics—the transmission of digital data through pure glass cable as thin as human hair—to develop Thunderbolt. And Thunderbolt supplies much more power to devices than the USB 3.0 standard allows. It also has a very slim connector design, allowing laptop designers to make their systems even thinner. And Thunderbolt can be used to connect displays!

But the most recent release of the USB standard, USB 3.1, solved many problems as it addressed many of these issues. The USB 3.1 speed limit matches the 10 Gb/s of Thunderbolt 1, making

**Figure 6.29** The Google Pixel computer has one USB-C port on each side but also includes two USB 3.0 ports. *(Jeff Chiu/AP Images)*

it twice as fast as USB 3.0. It can also transfer up to 100 watts of power, compared to just 10 watts for USB 3.0. This means a USB 3.1 port could be used to replace even the power charging port of a laptop. If the USB 3.1 standard is implemented using a USB-C connector, then we have the best of all worlds. The USB-C connector, shown in Figure 6.28, is thin, small, and reversible, so the connector will slide into the port in either an up or down orientation.

What does this mean to laptop designers? Computer designers can now create computers with a radical port layout: a single USB 3.1 C port. The Google Pixel computer still has two of the familiar USB 3.0 ports, but it has added a USB 3.1 C port to each side of the machine (see Figure 6.29). Look for a USB 3.1 C port on your next phone, camera, and laptop!

**Figure 6.28** USB-C brings a reversible, durable plug capable of charging with 100 watts of power.
*(Crystal Eye Studio/Shutterstock)*

# Sound Cards

**Objective 6.10** *Describe the features of sound cards.*

**What does the sound card do?** A sound card is an expansion card that enables the computer to drive the speaker system. Sound cards are now routinely integrated into the motherboard on most computers and provide excellent quality sound for most users. However, if you often use your computer to play games, music, and video, you may want to upgrade your speakers or add a higher-quality sound card (which is usually only an option in a desktop computer).

**Why do I get such good-quality sound from today's sound cards?** Most computers include a 3D sound card. 3D sound technology is better at convincing the human ear that sound is omnidirectional, meaning that you can't tell from which direction the sound is coming. This tends to produce a fuller, richer sound than stereo sound. However, 3D sound is not surround sound.

**What is surround sound, then?** Surround sound is a type of audio processing that makes the listener experience sound as if it were coming from all directions by using multiple speakers. The current surround-sound standard is from Dolby. There are many formats available, including Dolby Digital EX and Dolby Digital Plus for high-definition audio. Dolby TrueHD is the newest standard. It features high-definition and lossless technology, which means that no information is lost in the compression process.

To create surround sound, another standard, Dolby Digital 7.1, takes digital sound from a medium (such as a streaming movie) and reproduces it in eight channels. Seven channels cover the listening field with placement to the left front, right front, left rear, right rear, and center of the audio stage, as well as two extra speakers to the side, as shown in Figure 6.30. The eighth channel holds extremely low-frequency (LFE) sound data and is sent to a subwoofer, which can be placed anywhere in the room.

The name 7.1 surround indicates that there are seven speakers reproducing the full audio spectrum and one speaker handling just lower-frequency bass sounds. There is also a 5.1 surround-sound standard, which has a total of six speakers—one subwoofer, a center speaker, and four speakers for right/left in the front and the back. If you have a larger space or want precise location of sounds, use the newer 7.1 system.

To set up surround sound on your computer, you need two things: a set of surround-sound speakers and, for the greatest surround-sound experience, a sound card that is Dolby Digital compatible.

**What if I don't like the sound from my laptop speakers?** The limited size for speakers in a laptop and the added weight of circuitry to drive them means most people use headphones or ear buds for great audio instead of speakers. However, some laptops have built-in higher-quality speakers, like the HP series offering Bang and Olufsen speakers.

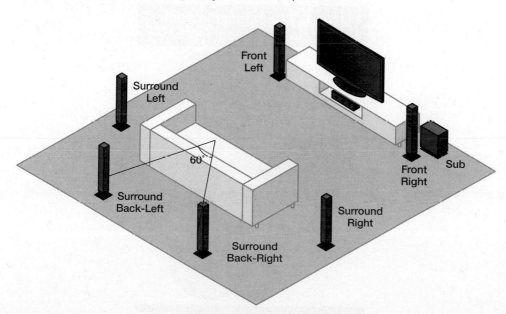

**Figure 6.30** Dolby Digital 7.1 surround sound gives you a better quality audio output. *(Zern Liew/Shutterstock)*

**Figure 6.31** Sample home recording studio setup. *(AbsentAnna/Fotolia; Sashkin/Fotolia; Nakov/Fotolia; Aleksangel/ Fotolia; Mariusz Blach/Fotolia; Maksym Yemelyanov/Fotolia; Fotolia)*

**What setup do I need if I want to use my computer for recording my band?** You can connect MIDI instruments, high-quality microphones, and recording equipment to your computer through an audio MIDI interface box. MIDI is an electronics standard that allows different kinds of electronic instruments to communicate with each other and with computers. The audio interface box attaches to your computer through a USB port and adds jacks for connecting guitars and microphones. You can edit and mix tracks through many different software packages, like Ableton Live or GarageBand. Figure 6.31 shows a simple home recording studio setup.

Figure 6.32 lists the factors to consider when deciding whether your audio subsystem meets your needs.

**Figure 6.32 Evaluating the Audio Subsystem**

Do you want to upgrade your **speaker** quality?

Do you need an **audio MIDI interface** box?

Do you want **surround sound**?

Audio

*(Gonin/Fotolia)*

# Evaluating System Reliability and Moving On

Many computer users decide to buy a new system because they're experiencing problems such as slow performance, freezes, and crashes. Over time, even normal use can cause your computer to build up excess files and to become internally disorganized. This excess, clutter, and disorganization can lead to deteriorating performance or system failure, but fortunately can usually be easily fixed. If you think your system is unreliable, see if the problem is one you can fix before you buy a new machine. Proper upkeep and maintenance also may postpone an expensive system upgrade or replacement.

## Maintaining System Reliability

**Objective 6.11**  *Describe steps you can take to optimize your system's reliability.*

**What can I do to ensure my system stays reliable?** Here are several procedures you can follow to ensure your system performs reliably (see also Table 6.4):

- **Install a reliable antivirus package.** Make sure it's set to update itself automatically and to run a full system scan frequently.

- **Run spyware and adware removal programs.** These often detect and remove different pests and should be used in addition to your regular antivirus package.

- **Clear out unnecessary files.** Temporary Internet files can accumulate quickly on your hard drive, taking up unnecessary space. Running the Disk Cleanup utility is a quick and easy way to ensure your temporary Internet files don't take up precious hard drive space. Likewise, you should delete any unnecessary files from your hard drive regularly because they can make your hard drive run more slowly.

- **Run the Disk Defragmenter utility on your hard drive.** When your hard drive becomes fragmented, its storage capacity is negatively affected. When you defragment (defrag) your hard drive, files are reorganized, making the hard drive work more efficiently. But remember that this only makes sense for mechanical drives. There is no need to defrag an SSD drive.

- **Automate the key utilities.** The utilities that need to be run more than once—like Disk Cleanup, Disk Defragmenter, and the antivirus, adware, and spyware programs—can be configured to run automatically at any time interval you want. You can use Windows Task Scheduler or third-party programs like Norton Security Suite to set up a sequence of programs to run one after the other every evening while you sleep, so you can wake up each day to a reliable, secure system.

**What can I do when my system crashes?** Computer systems are complex. It's not unusual to have your system stop responding occasionally. If rebooting the computer doesn't help, you'll need to begin troubleshooting:

1. **If your system isn't responding, try a System Restore.** Windows automatically creates restore points before any major change to the system takes place, such as when you install a new program or change a device driver. Type Restore Point in the search box, select Create a restore point, and then click the Create button to manually create a restore point at any time. You can then select any restore point and bring your system back to the state it was in at that point. From the System Properties dialog box (accessed through the instructions above), select System Restore on the System Protection tab to learn more about restoring your system.

## Table 6.4  Utilities to Keep Your System Reliable

| To Avoid This Problem | Use This Tool | For More Info |
|---|---|---|
| Your hard drive is running low on space, making it run slowly | Disk Cleanup utility | Chapter 5 |
| Your system is slowing down; browsers or other programs are behaving strangely | Antivirus software; spyware and adware removal software | Chapter 9 |
| Files are spread across many spots on the hard drive, making the hard drive run slowly | Disk Defragmenter utility | Chapter 5 |
| System not responding | Windows Reset | Chapter 5 |

For Mac systems, the macOS Time Machine provides automatic backup and enables you to look through and restore (if necessary) files, folders, libraries, or the entire system.

2. **Check that you have enough RAM.** You learned how to do this in the "Evaluating the Memory Subsystem" section earlier in this chapter. Systems with insufficient RAM often crash.

3. **If you see an error code in Windows, visit the Microsoft Knowledge Base** (*support.microsoft.com*). This online resource helps users resolve problems with Microsoft products. For example, it can help you determine what an error code indicates and how you may be able to solve the problem.

4. **Search with Google.** If you don't find a satisfactory answer in the Knowledge Base, try copying the entire error message into Google and searching the larger community for solutions.

5. **As a last resort, consider a Windows Reset on your system.** This Windows utility, shown in Figure 6.33, removes all the changes you've made to the system and brings it back to the state it came to you from the factory. It removes all the applications from third-party vendors, but it gives you the option to keep or remove personal files like your music, documents, or videos. Make sure you select the correct option so you don't lose all your personal files!

**Can my software affect system reliability?** Having the latest version of software makes your system much more reliable. You should upgrade or update your OS, browser software, and application software as often as new patches (or updates) are reported for resolving errors. Sometimes these errors are performance related; sometimes they're potential system security breaches.

If you're having a software problem that can be replicated, use the Steps Recorder to capture the exact steps that lead to it. In Windows, type "steps" in the search box and select the Steps Recorder desktop app. Now run the Steps Recorder and go through the exact actions that create the problem you're having. At any particular step, you can click the Add Comment button and add a comment about any part of the screen. The Steps Recorder then produces a documented report, complete with images of your screen and descriptions of each mouse movement you made. You can then e-mail this report to customer support to help technicians resolve the problem.

**How do I know whether updates are available for my software?** You can configure Windows so that it automatically checks for, downloads, and installs any available updates for itself, the Microsoft Edge browser, and other Microsoft applications such as Microsoft Office. Type "update" in the search box and select Check for updates in System Settings. Click *Advanced options* and customize your update strategy.

Many other applications now also include the ability to check for updates. For instance, in Microsoft Office, click the File tab and select Account. Then click Update Options.

**So is it time to buy a new computer?** Now that you've evaluated your computer system, you need to shift to questions of value. How close does your system come to meeting your needs? Can you even upgrade your existing system (tablets and phones usually have very few upgrade options)? How

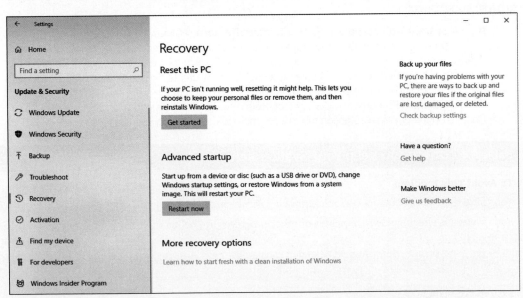

**Figure 6.33** The Reset this PC feature in Windows can help when your computer stops responding.
> *To access Recovery, from **Settings**, select **Update & security**, then select **Recovery**. (Courtesy of Microsoft Corp.)*

much would it cost to upgrade your current system to match what you'd ideally like your computer to do, not only today but also a few years from now? How much would it cost to purchase a new system that meets these specifications?

To know whether upgrading or buying a new system would have better value for you, you need to price both scenarios. Conduct a thorough system evaluation (see Figure 6.34) to gather the data to help you decide. Purchasing a new system is an important investment of your resources, and you want to make a well-reasoned, well-supported decision.

## Getting Rid of Your Old Computer

**Objective 6.12** *Discuss how to recycle, donate, or dispose of an older computer.*

**What should I do with my old computer?** If the result of your system evaluation is that you need a new computer, you're probably thinking of your next new system with excitement. But what can you do with your old machine? You have options. If your old system still works, be sure to consider what benefit you might obtain by having two systems. Would you have a use for the older system?

Also, before you decide to throw it away, consider the environmental impact (see Figure 6.35). Mercury in LCD screens, cadmium in batteries and circuit boards, and flame retardants in plastic housings are all toxic. An alarming, emerging trend is that discarded machines are beginning to create an e-waste crisis.

**So how can I recycle my old computer?** Instead of throwing your computer away, you may be able to donate it to a nonprofit organization. Here are a few ways to do this:

- Many manufacturers, such as Dell, offer recycling programs and have formed alliances with nonprofit organizations to help distribute your old technology to those who need it.
- Sites like Computers with Causes (*computerswithcauses.org*) organize donations of both working and nonworking computers, printers, and mice.
- You can also take your computer to an authorized computer recycling center in your area. The Telecommunications Industry Association provides an e-cycling information site you can use to find a local e-cycling center (*ecyclingcentral.com*).

## Figure 6.34 Key Items in System Evaluation

**CPU**
- What is your CPU usage level?

**RAM**
- Do you have at least 4 GB?

**Storage**
- Do you need an SSD drive for fast start-up?
- Do you have a fast-access mechanical drive for large storage space?
- Do you need RAID 0 or RAID 1 storage drives for extra-fast performance or mirroring?

**Video**
- Do you have enough graphics memory?
- Is your GPU powerful enough?
- Do you have HDMI ports?
- How many monitors do you need to run simultaneously?

**Audio**
- Do you have 7.1 or 5.1 surround sound?

*(Oleksandr Delyk/Fotolia; Hugh Threlfall/Alamy Stock Photo; Nikkytok/Shutterstock; Fotolia)*

**Figure 6.35** An electronics garbage dump can cause environmental concerns like the leaching of lead, mercury, and other hazardous substances into the ground. *(Dzejdi/Shutterstock)*

# Ethics in IT

## Free Hardware for All

The open-source software movement has flourished over the past decade. In response to increasing prices and the limitations placed on commercially available software, programmers began to donate time to design, develop, and support software systems. These products, like Gimp (a photo-editing tool), were then made freely available.

In the world of hardware, a similar but different approach called the open-source hardware movement has flourished. Because hardware projects require materials and tools to assemble, products distributed as open source are not free in terms of cost, but they are free from any restrictions on how you modify them. Inexpensive hardware devices now span the range from the Digispark, an $8 microcontroller the size of a quarter, to the

$40 Raspberry Pi, a full Linux-based computer the size of a credit card. Sample open-source hardware projects include video game systems, 3D printers, and even do-it-yourself medical devices.

Is open hardware good for the world? Does it undermine the intellectual property of others who want to create hardware resources and sell them for a profit? What is the impact on developing countries if they have immediate access to hardware designs instead of being required to purchase these items from a for-profit company? Follow the future of open-source hardware by keeping an eye on ezines like Make (*makezine.com*), developer and supplier sites like Adafruit (*adafruit.com*), and tutorial head-quarters like Instructables (*instructables.com*).

For companies that need to retire large quantities of computers, the risk of creating an environmental hazard is serious. Firms like GigaBiter (*gigabiter.com*) offer a solution. GigaBiter eliminates security and environmental risks associated with electronic destruction by first delaminating the hard drive and then breaking down the computer e-waste into recyclable products. The result of the final step is a sandlike substance that is 100% recyclable.

**Can I donate a computer safely, without worrying about my personal data?** Before donating or recycling a computer, make sure you carefully remove all data from your hard drive. Built into Windows is an option to help with this. In the search box, type Reset and select Reset this PC. Upon clicking the Get started button, you will have the option to keep or remove your files and then reinstall Windows.

Becoming a victim of identity theft is a serious risk. Credit card numbers, bank information, Social Security numbers, tax records, passwords, and personal identification numbers (PINs) are just some of the types of sensitive information that we casually record to our computers' hard drives. Just deleting files that contain proprietary personal information is not protection enough. Likewise, reformatting or erasing your hard drive does not totally remove data, as was proved by two MIT graduate students. They bought more than 150 used hard drives from various sources. Although some of the hard drives had been reformatted or damaged so that the data was supposedly nonrecoverable, the two students were able to retrieve medical records, financial information, pornography, personal e-mails, and more than 5,000 credit card numbers!

The U.S. Department of Defense suggests a seven-layer overwrite for a "secure erase." This means that you fill your hard drive seven times over with a random series of 1s and 0s. Fortunately, several programs exist for doing this. For PCs running Windows, look for utility programs like File Shredder or Eraser. Wipe is available for Linux, and ShredIt X can be used for macOS. These programs provide secure hard drive erasures, either of specific files on your hard drive or of the entire hard drive.

**What if my hard drive isn't functional? How can I ensure the data won't be recovered?** Physical destruction of your hard drive is the best solution. Many computer recycling centers offer hard drive destruction as a service where the drive is tossed into an industrial-strength shredder and is rendered totally unrepairable/usable.

> **Before moving on to the Chapter Review:**
>
> 1. ▶ Watch Chapter Overview Video 6.2.
> 2. Then take the Check Your Understanding quiz.

# Check Your Understanding // Review & Practice

For a quick review to see what you've learned so far, answer the following questions.

## multiple choice

1. Hard drives are classified as which type of storage?
   a. Volatile
   b. GPU
   c. Nonvolatile
   d. Cache

2. When would you want to consider RAID 0 technology?
   a. When you need the fastest solution for writing data
   b. If you think that SSDs are too expensive
   c. When you need an instant backup of your work
   d. When you want to have only one hard disk drive

3. Which is *not* a type of video port?
   a. HDMI
   b. DVI
   c. GPU
   d. DisplayPort

4. Dolby Digital 7.1 creates
   a. ultra-sharp high-definition video.
   b. a digital signal from an audio input.
   c. seven-channel surround sound.
   d. eight-channel surround sound.

5. Your Windows computer can be brought to the state it was in before problems began occurring by using a utility called Windows
   a. Return.
   b. Refresh.
   c. Reset.
   d. Reboot.

**chew on this**

Review the impacts on the environment of your computer during its entire life cycle. How do the production, transportation, and use of the computer affect the increase of greenhouse gas emissions? How does the selection of materials and packaging impact the environment? What restricted substances (like lead, mercury, cadmium, and PVC) are found in your machine? Could substitute materials be used? How would the ultimate "green machine" be designed?

**MyLab IT**    Go to **MyLab IT** to take an autograded version of the *Check Your Understanding* review and to find all media resources for the chapter.

**For the IT Simulation for this chapter, see MyLab IT.**

# 6 Chapter Review

## Summary

### Part 1
### Evaluating Key Subsystems

**Learning Outcome 6.1    You will be able to evaluate your computer system's hardware functioning, including the CPU and memory subsystems.**

### Your Ideal Computing Device

**Objective 6.1**    *Describe the changes in CPU performance over the past several decades.*

- Moore's Law describes the pace at which CPUs improve by holding more transistors. This rule predicts that the number of transistors inside a CPU will double about every two years.

**Objective 6.2**    *Compare and contrast a variety of computing devices.*

- A huge number of computing choices are on the market, including smartphones, tablets, ultrabooks, netbooks, 2-in-1s, laptops, and desktops.
- The kind of technology user you are will determine what kind of device you need.

### Evaluating the CPU Subsystem

**Objective 6.3**    *Describe how a CPU is designed and how it operates.*

- The CPU is composed of two units: the control unit and the arithmetic logic unit (ALU). The control unit coordinates the activities of all the other computer components. The ALU is responsible for performing all the arithmetic calculations (addition, subtraction, multiplication, and division). Every time the CPU performs a program instruction, it goes through the same series of steps (a machine cycle): fetch, decode, execute, and store.
- The clock speed of a CPU dictates how many instructions the CPU can process each second.
- A core contains the parts of the CPU required for processing. Modern CPUs have multiple cores.
- Hyperthreading allows two sets of instructions to be run by a single CPU core.

- Pipelining is a technique that allows the CPU to work on more than one instruction (or stage of processing) at the same time, thereby boosting CPU performance.
- The CPU's cache memory is a form of RAM that is part of the CPU chip itself, so retrieving data is much faster than bringing the data in from the computer's RAM.

**Objective 6.4**    *Describe tools used to measure and evaluate CPU performance.*

- CPU benchmarks are measurements used to compare performance between processors.
- CPU usage is the percentage of time the CPU is busy doing work.
- On Windows systems, the Task Manager utility lets you access this data.

### Evaluating the Memory Subsystem

**Objective 6.5**    *Discuss how RAM is used in a computer system.*

- Random access memory (RAM) is your computer's temporary storage space. RAM is an example of volatile storage. RAM appears in the system on memory modules. There are several types of RAM, including DDR3 and DDR4.
- Physical memory is the amount of RAM installed in the system.
- The Resource Monitor shows how much memory is in use at any time.

**Objective 6.6**    *Evaluate whether adding RAM to a system is desirable.*

- Adding RAM is simple to do and relatively inexpensive. However, there is a limit to how much RAM can be installed in a device.

## Part 2
# Evaluating Other Subsystems and Making a Decision

**Learning Outcome 6.2**  You will be able to evaluate your computer system's storage subsystem, media subsystem, and reliability and decide whether to purchase a new system or upgrade an existing one.

## Evaluating the Storage Subsystem

**Objective 6.7**  *Classify and describe the major types of nonvolatile storage drives.*

- Major types of nonvolatile storage include mechanical hard drives, SSDs, and SSHDs.
- Mechanical hard drives are the least expensive and the slowest to access information.
- SSD drives are electronic, so they have no moving parts, produce no heat, and are many times faster than hard drives. However, they are more expensive.
- An SSHD drive is a combination of both a mechanical hard drive and an SSD into a single device.

**Objective 6.8**  *Evaluate the amount and type of storage needed for a system.*

- Your storage needs will depend on the number and types of programs and data you use. Your local storage needs may be significantly reduced if you utilize cloud storage for your data files.
- It may be better to have several drives connected, either in RAID 0 for more speed or in RAID 1 for instantaneous backup protection.

## Evaluating the Media Subsystems

**Objective 6.9**  *Describe the features of video cards.*

- A video card translates binary data into images that are displayed on a monitor.
- A video card has specialized video memory that is very fast. Some systems have multiple video cards for even greater performance.
- A video card has a graphics processing unit (GPU), which helps the CPU by handling the graphics workload.
- Certain individual video cards can support multiple monitors.

**Objective 6.10**  *Describe the features of sound cards.*

- A sound card can support 3D sound as well as surround sound like Dolby 7.1.
- Dolby 7.1 surround sound has one speaker for low-frequency tones and seven additional speakers for a full, immersive experience.
- An audio MIDI interface unit allows you to connect musical instruments, microphones, and headphones to your computer.

## Evaluating System Reliability and Moving On

**Objective 6.11**  *Describe steps you can take to optimize your system's reliability.*

- There are many regular maintenance steps you should take to keep your system reliable. They include using an antivirus program, adware removal software, clearing out unnecessary files, and running a disk defragmenter.

**Objective 6.12**  *Discuss how to recycle, donate, or dispose of an older computer.*

- A used computer can be recycled through several manufacturers or through nonprofit organizations.
- To safely recycle or donate a computer, you must first remove all applications and personal data. There are options in Windows to help with this.

**MyLab IT**  Be sure to check out **MyLab IT** for additional materials to help you review and learn. And don't forget to watch the Chapter Overview Videos. ▶

# Key Terms

# Chapter Quiz // Assessment

For a quick review to see what you've learned, answer the following questions. Submit the quiz as requested by your instructor. If you are using **MyLab IT**, the quiz is also available there.

## multiple choice

1. Moore's Law refers to the
   a. amount of memory on a memory chip.
   b. overall system processing capability.
   c. speed of DRAM.
   d. pace at which CPUs improve.

2. When the binary code is retrieved from RAM and moved to the CPU, this stage is known as
   a. fetch.
   b. decode.
   c. store.
   d. execute.

3. RAM is
   a. volatile memory.
   b. nonvolatile memory.
   c. neither volatile nor nonvolatile memory.
   d. both volatile and nonvolatile memory.

4. A good way to assess your CPU usage is to
   a. check the Performance tab of the Task Manager.
   b. listen for the sound of a spinning hard disk drive.
   c. check the number reported by the system defrag utility.
   d. feel the temperature of the CPU with your hand.

5. _____ is a set of strategies for using more than one drive in a system.
   a. A machine cycle
   b. GPU
   c. RAID
   d. VPU

6. A special processing chip found on video cards is the
   a. ROM.
   b. HDMI.
   c. CPU.
   d. GPU.

7. If you want to use your computer for recording your band, you would benefit most from a(n)
   a. HDMI interface.
   b. MIDI interface.
   c. RAID interface.
   d. overclocking interface.

8. Before donating your Windows computer, you should perform a Windows
   a. Restore.
   b. Refresh.
   c. Reclaim.
   d. Reset.

9. Data can be retrieved fastest from
   a. registers.
   b. cache memory.
   c. RAM.
   d. HDMI.

10. Windows creates "restore points" so that you can
    a. return your system to the way it was before you installed new software.
    b. add additional hard disk storage space.
    c. extend your warranty.
    d. protect your system from hackers.

## true/false

_____ 1. Desktop systems are invariably a better value than lighter, more mobile computers.

_____ 2. Conventional hard drives are preferable to SSD drives because they transfer data more quickly.

_____ 3. In Windows, if you experience unreliable behavior, try a System Restore before doing a Windows Reset.

_____ 4. There is no limit to how much RAM you can add to modern computers.

_____ 5. Moore's Law describes the pace at which RAM modules improve.

## What do you think now?

Although we don't have self-driving vehicles yet, many vehicles are available with AI-controlled safety features (such as collision-avoidance systems). Recently, there have been a number of accidents involving cars with intelligent safety features. Studies of these accidents have revealed that in many cases, the car occupants did not understand how the safety systems were designed to function and that they overestimated the protection provided by these systems.

What do you think is the best way to educate consumers about vehicle safety systems? Who should be responsible for this education?

# Team Time

## Many Different Devices for Many Different Needs

### problem

Even within one discipline, there are needs for a variety of types of computing solutions. Consider the communications department in a large university. There are some groups involved in video production, some groups producing digital music, and some groups creating scripts.

### process

1. Split the class into teams. Select one segment of the communications department that your team will represent: video production, digital music, or scripting. The video production team requires its labs to be able to support the recording, editing, and final production and distribution of digital video. The digital music group wants to establish a recording studio (after the model of the Drexel University recording label, Mad Dragon Music Group, at *maddragonmusic.com*). The scripting group needs to support a collaborative community of writers and voice-over actors.

2. Analyze the computing needs of that segment, with particular focus on how it needs to outfit its computer labs.

3. Price the systems you would recommend and explain how they will be used. What decisions have you made in order to guarantee they will still be useful in three years?

4. Write a report that summarizes your findings. Document the resources you used and generate as much enthusiasm as you can for your recommendations.

### conclusion

Being able to evaluate a computer system and match it to the current needs of its users is an important skill.

# Ethics Project

## Benchmarking

In this exercise, you'll research and then role-play a complicated ethical situation. The role you play might not match your own personal beliefs; regardless, your research and use of logic will enable you to represent the view assigned. An arbitrator will watch and comment on both sides of the arguments, and, together, the team will agree on an ethical solution.

## problem

We've seen that for complex systems like computers, performance is often determined by using benchmarks, software suites that test a full area of performance. The results of these tests become a major force in marketing and selling the product.

There have been a number of claims of unethical conduct in the area of benchmarking. Companies have been accused of using out-of-date testing software to skew their results. Some companies have manipulated the settings on the machine to artificially raise their score (for example, turning off the display before testing for battery life). Some companies make sure the systems sent out to magazines and other evaluators have better-performing components than you might get off the shelf. Where is the line between gaining a competitive edge and lying when it comes to hardware assessment?

## research areas to consider

- BAPCo
- MobileMark
- 2009 Nobel Prize for Physics

## process

1. Divide the class into teams. Research the areas cited above from the perspective of either an Intel engineer working on a new CPU, an engineer working on a competing CPU, or a benchmark designer.
2. Team members should write a summary that provides documentation for the positions their character takes on the issue of equitable testing of hardware. Then, team members should create an outline to use during the role-playing event.
3. Team members should present their case to the class or submit a PowerPoint presentation for review, along with the summary they developed.

## conclusion

As technology becomes ever more prevalent and integrated into our lives, more and more ethical dilemmas will present themselves. Being able to understand and evaluate both sides of the argument, while responding in a personally or socially ethical manner, will be an important skill.

## Solve This   MyLab IT Grader

### Laptop Alternatives

You are in need of a new laptop that is lightweight, but that has enough power to edit the videos you produce for your You-Tube channel. You have asked a few of your friends for some suggestions. One friend put together a list of possible computers in an Excel workbook; the other friend created a list as a text file. You will import the text file into the Excel table, sort the data, then filter the data to display only those computers you are interested in. Using Excel you will use tables to sort, filter, and display data.

You will use the following skills as you complete this activity:

- Format as Table
- Sort Data

- Apply Filters
- Change Cell Fill Color

### Instructions:

1. Open *TIA_Ch6_Start.xlsx*, and save as **TIA_Ch6_ LastFirst.xlsx**.

2. **Format range A1:M41 as a table**, with Blue, **Table Style Medium 9**. Select **Yes** when asked to convert the selection to a table and remove all external connections.
   Hint: To format a range as a table, on the Home tab, in the Styles group, select Format as Table, then select the desired style. Ensure *My table has headers* checkbox is selected.

3. **Sort** the data by multiple levels: **Style (A to Z), Processor Speed (Largest to Smallest)**, and **RAM (Largest to Smallest)**.
   Hint: To Sort data with multiple levels, on the Data tab, in the Sort & Filter group, click Sort, then click Add level. Select the desired column in each sort drop down list.

4. **Filter** the data to display Intel i7 processors, and 12 and 16 GB RAM.
   Hint: To Filter data, ensure Filter is selected on the Data tab, in the Sort & Filter group. Then click the arrow for each column to be filtered, and then add or delete checkmarks for the desired category.

5. **Copy** the header row and four rows that display after all filters have been applied. Open a new worksheet, and paste the copied data in cell A1. Rename the new worksheet **Choices**. Click the **Data worksheet** and press **Esc** to clear the selection.

6. Click the **Choices worksheet**, change the width of **columns C, G, H, I, J, K, L** to **9**, and change the width of **columns D, E, G, and M** to **12**. Select **cells A1:M1** and **Wrap Text**.
   Hint: To change the width of non-adjacent columns, select the first column heading, then hold down Ctrl while selecting the remaining column headings. Click Format in the Cells group and then select Column Width.

7. Select **cells A3:M3**, and change the Fill Color to **Yellow**.

8. In cell A8, type **The Toshiba Ultrabook is my choice as it has the most RAM, greatest storage capacity, and the best wireless standard of the four choices.**

9. Save the workbook and submit based on your instructor's directions.

**Chapter**

# 7 Networking: Connecting Computing Devices

 For a chapter overview, watch the **Chapter Overview Videos**.

---

**PART 1**

## How Networks Function

| Learning Outcome 7.1 | You will be able to explain the basics of networking, including the components needed to create a network, and describe the different ways a network can connect to the Internet. |

**PART 2**

## Your Home Network

| Learning Outcome 7.2 | You will be able to describe what is necessary to install and configure a home network and how to manage and secure a wireless network. |

---

 **Networking Fundamentals** 242

**Objective 7.1**  *Describe computer networks and their pros and cons.*
**Helpdesk:** Understanding Networking

 **Network Architectures** 244

**Objective 7.2**  *Explain the different ways networks are defined.*

 **Network Components** 247

**Objective 7.3**  *Describe the types of transmission media used in networks.*
**Objective 7.4**  *Describe the basic hardware devices necessary for networks.*
**Objective 7.5**  *Describe the type of software necessary for networks.*
**Sound Byte:** Installing a Home Computer Network

 **Connecting to the Internet** 251

**Objective 7.6**  *Summarize the broadband options available to access the Internet.*
**Objective 7.7**  *Summarize how to access the Internet wirelessly.*

 **Installing and Configuring Home Networks** 257

**Objective 7.8**  *Explain what should be considered before creating a home network.*
**Objective 7.9**  *Describe how to set up a home network.*

 **Managing and Securing Wireless Networks** 262

**Objective 7.10**  *Describe the potential problems with wireless networks and the means to avoid them.*
**Objective 7.11**  *Describe how to secure wireless home networks.*
**Sound Byte:** Securing Wireless Networks
**Helpdesk:** Managing and Securing Your Wireless Network

---

**MyLab IT**  All media accompanying this chapter can be found here.

**Make This**   Networked Devices on **page 256**

*(Number168/123RF; Anton Shaparenko/Shutterstock; Arcady31/123RF; Leo Blanchette/123RF;Nata-Lia/Shutterstock; McCarony/Shutterstock)*

# What do you think?

Since **DNA sequencing has become more affordable,** many are spitting into a tube to learn about their genetic makeup and receive a glimpse into their ancestry. Now, companies are emerging that will enable people to choose from different apps that offer **personalized and customized services and products based on their DNA results.** For example, once you have your DNA results, you can order a **customized nutrition or fitness plan** or determine if you're at risk for inherited heart problems. Other apps will use DNA results for less serious products such as **determining your wine preferences** or creating a scarf or socks that have been printed with your DNA code. There are **questions as to the long-term risk of devaluing DNA tests** that are medically necessary to determine inherited diseases, as well as the risk to a person's overall privacy. And yet, the lure of owning a product or service that is unique to just you may make some think the risks are worth taking.

Which DNA-generated products would you consider purchasing (check all that apply)?

- *An image of what a future baby may look like (requires your partner's DNA)*
- *A wine app that suggests customized varietals*
- *A personalized fitness or diet plan*
- *I would not have my DNA used for any reason*

*See the end of the chapter for a follow-up question*

# How Networks Function

> **Learning Outcome 7.1** **You will be able to explain the basics of networking, including the components needed to create a network, and describe the different ways a network can connect to the Internet.**

You access wired and wireless networks all the time—when you use an ATM, print out a document, or use the Internet (the world's largest network). It's important to understand the fundamentals of networking, such as how networks are set up, what devices are necessary to establish a network, and how you can access a network so that you can share, collaborate, and exchange information.

# Networking Fundamentals

A typical family engages in many activities that involve sharing and accessing files over and from the Internet and using a variety of Internet-connected devices (see Figure 7.1). What makes all this technology transfer and sharing possible? A computer network!

## Understanding Networks

**Objective 7.1** *Describe computer networks and their pros and cons.*

**What is a network?** A computer network is simply two or more computers that are connected via software and hardware so they can communicate with each other. Each device connected to a network is referred to as a node. A node can be a computer, a peripheral such as a printer or a game console, or a network device such as a router (see Figure 7.2).

**What are the benefits of networks?** There are several benefits to having computers networked:

- **Sharing an Internet connection.** Probably the primary reason to set up a network is to share an Internet connection. For example, networks with wireless Internet make connecting "smart" home devices possible and also enable laptops and other portable devices to connect to the Internet wirelessly.

- **Sharing printers and other peripherals.** Networks let you share printers and other peripheral devices. For example, to print a document from a laptop that's not connected to a network, you

Jackie watches a video she took while on vacation.

Andy plays PlayStation online and uploads a video he made for school.

Mom watches a lecture from her online course while she prepares a snack.

Dad watches a streaming movie and checks fantasy football scores on his iPad.

Andrea takes pictures of her dog and uploads them directly to Facebook.

**Figure 7.1** With a home network, all family members can connect their computing devices whenever and wherever they want.

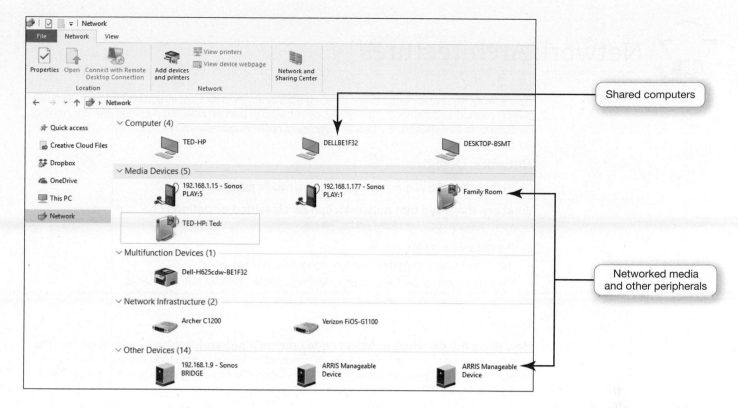

**Shared computers**

**Networked media and other peripherals**

**Figure 7.2** File Explorer shows computers, media, and other devices (such as set-top boxes) that are networked for sharing. *(Courtesy of Microsoft Corp.)*

would need to transfer the file to a connected computer using a flash drive or another device that's connected to the printer or carry your laptop to the printer and connect your laptop to it. With a network, you can print directly from your device even if it's not physically connected to the printer.

- **Sharing files.** In many businesses, employees share files between networked computers without having to use portable storage devices such as flash drives to transfer the files. At home, you can set sharing options in Windows or macOS so files can be shared between networked computers. In addition to connecting to home, local, or wide area networks, you can also use services such as OneDrive, Dropbox, and Google Drive to share files that are connected to the Internet (keeping in mind that the Internet is the largest network).

- **Online gaming and home entertainment.** Many popular computer games have modes where multiple players can play together if they have their computers networked. Smart TVs, music systems, and other entertainment devices also support wired or wireless networks.

- **Telephone.** For those still with a landline, you can make and receive phone calls through your home network across the Internet with Voice over IP (VoIP) services.

- **Common communications.** Devices running different operating systems can communicate on the same network.

**Are there disadvantages to setting up networks?** A disadvantage of setting up a network is the initial time it takes to set it up. Once it's set up, however, there is very little ongoing maintenance and administration for a home network. In addition, since networks involve passing data between two points, security liabilities exist on protecting that data. Additionally, large networks involve an initial purchase of equipment to set them up. They also need to be administered, which can be costly and time-consuming. Network administration involves tasks such as:

- Installing new computers and devices
- Monitoring the network to ensure it is performing efficiently
- Updating and installing new software on the network
- Configuring, or setting up, proper security for a network

**How fast does data move through networks?** Data transfer rate (also called bandwidth) is the maximum speed at which data can be transmitted between two nodes on a network. Throughput is the actual speed of data transfer that is achieved. Throughput is always less than or equal to the data transfer rate. Data transfer rate and throughput are usually measured in megabits per second (Mbps) or gigabits per second (Gbps). One of the main factors that determine how fast data moves is the type of network, which we discuss later in this chapter.

**Helpdesk**   **MyLab IT**

**Understanding Networking**

In this Helpdesk, you'll play the role of a helpdesk staffer, fielding questions about home networks—their advantages, their main components, and the most common types—as well as about wireless networks and how they're created.

# Network Architectures

The network you have in your home differs greatly in terms of its size, structure, and cost from the one on your college campus. This difference is based in part on how the networks are designed or configured. In this section, we look at a variety of network classifications.

## Network Designs

**Objective 7.2** *Explain the different ways networks are defined.*

**What are the ways that networks can be classified or defined?** Network architectures, or network designs, can be classified by the following:

- The distance between nodes
- The way in which the network is managed (or administered)
- The set of rules (or protocol) used to exchange data between network nodes

### Distance

**How does the distance between nodes define a network?** Networks can range from the smallest network of just one person, in one room with multiple connected devices, to the largest network that spans between cities and even the world. The following are common types of networks (see Figure 7.3):

- A personal area network (PAN) is a network used for communication among devices close to one person, such as smartphones and tablets using wireless technologies such as Bluetooth and Wi-Fi.

**WAN**
Wide Area
Network

**MAN**
Metropolitan
Area Network

**HAN**
Home Area
Network

**LAN**
Local Area
Network

**PAN**
Personal Area
Network

**Figure 7.3** Networks can be classified by the distance between their nodes. *(Fenton one/Shutterstock; CataVic/Shutterstock; SiuWing/Shutterstock; Lucadp/Shutterstock)*

- A local area network (LAN) is a network in which the nodes are located within a small geographical area. Examples include a network in a computer lab at school or at a fast-food restaurant.
- A home area network (HAN) is a specific type of LAN located in a home. HANs are used to connect all of a home's digital devices, such as computers, peripherals, phones, gaming devices, digital video recorders (DVRs), and televisions.
- A metropolitan area network (MAN) is a large network designed to provide access to a specific geographical area, such as an entire city. Many U.S. cities are now deploying MANs to provide Internet access to residents and tourists. Some MANs employ WiMAX wireless technology that extends local Wi-Fi networks across greater distances.
- A wide area network (WAN) spans a large physical distance. The Internet is the largest WAN, covering the globe. A WAN is also a networked collection of LANs. If a school has multiple campuses located in different towns, each with its own LAN, connecting the LANs of each campus by telecommunications lines allows the users of the LANs to communicate. All the connected LANs would be described as a single WAN.

### Levels of Administration

**How does the level of administration define a network?** A network can be administered, or managed, in two main ways—centrally or locally (see Figure 7.4):

- *Central administration*: In a centrally administered network, tasks performed from one computer can affect the other computers on the network. A client/server network is an example. In a client/server network, a client is a computer on which users accomplish tasks and make requests, whereas the server is the computer that provides information or resources to the client computers as well as central administration for network functions such as printing. Most networks that have 10 or more nodes are client/server networks.

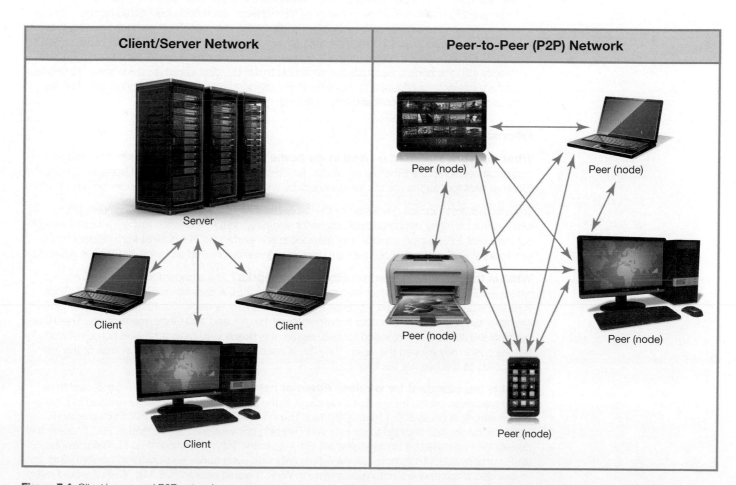

**Figure 7.4** Client/server and P2P networks. *(Sashkin/Fotolia, Tuulijumala/Fotolia, Scanrail/Fotolia, Scanrail/Fotolia, Maksym Dykha/Fotolia, Scanrail/Fotolia)*

The process of users transferring files between computers is referred to as peer-to-peer (P2P) sharing (see Figure 7.5). Any kind of file can be made available to share with others. Often media files, songs, and movies are made easily obtainable on P2P sites. These sites don't have a central computer acting to index all this information. Instead, they operate in a true P2P sharing environment in which computers connect directly to other computers. This makes them a prime source of unwanted viruses and spyware.

Some blame peer-to-peer networks for the growth of piracy on the Internet. As more sites have made it easier to illegally download music using P2P networks, music sales have dropped significantly. The recording industry is still trying to counter losing these sales. The heavy amount of traffic on P2P sites also played into the debate on Internet neutrality. Internet service providers like Comcast were choosing to throttle, or limit, the speed of data transfer for P2P file exchanges. Users complained this was an illegal use of a public resource and all data should be treated equally by such Internet service providers.

P2P networks defend their legality in that they don't run a central server but only facilitate connections between users. Therefore, they have no control over what the users choose to trade. There are legitimate uses of these new avenues of distribution. For example, *BitTorrent (BT) Bundles* are packages of free audio, video, and print content provided for download by musicians through BitTorrent. You can unlock additional content by paying or supplying your e-mail address. Tracks that are easy to remix are provided so fans can create and share their own extensions to the work.

**Figure 7.5** Peer-to-peer (P2P) networks do not have a central computer distributing information but instead send information between each member.
*(So47/Fotolia)*

- *Local administration*: In a locally administered network, the configuration and maintenance of the network must be performed on each individual computer attached to the network. A peer-to-peer (P2P) network is an example. In a P2P network, each node connected on the network can communicate directly with every other node on the network. Thus, all nodes on this type of network are peers (equals). When printing, for example, a computer on a P2P network doesn't have to go through the computer that's connected to the printer. Instead, it can communicate directly with the printer. Because they're simple to set up, cost less than client/server networks, and are easier to configure and maintain, P2P networks are the most common type of home network. Very small schools and offices may also use P2P networks.

### Ethernet Protocols

**What network standard is used in my home network?** The vast majority of home and corporate networks are Ethernet networks. An Ethernet network is so named because it uses the Ethernet protocol as the means (or standard) by which the nodes on the network communicate.

The Ethernet protocol was developed by the Institute of Electrical and Electronics Engineers (IEEE), which develops many standard specifications for electronic data transmission that are adopted throughout the world. Establishing standards for networking is important so that devices from different manufacturers will work well together. There are different standards for wired and wireless Ethernet networks.

**What is the standard for wired Ethernet networks?** The standard for wired Ethernet networks is IEEE 802.3, also known as gigabit Ethernet (GbE). A data transfer rate of up to 1 Gbps is possible using this standard. For even faster data transfer speeds, 10, 40, and even 100 GbE is available, providing maximum data transfer rates of 10, 40, and 100 Gbps, respectively. The 10 and certainly the 40 GbE are intended for businesses. It is possible to have a 10 GbE home network, but the costs may exceed the need. 100 GbE is used for the major transmission lines of the Internet known as the Internet backbone.

**What is the standard for wireless Ethernet networks?** Wireless networks (referred to as Wi-Fi) are based on the IEEE 802.11 standard. In the past, Wi-Fi versions were referred to by one or two letters, such as 802.11n or 802.11ac. The Wi-Fi Alliance, the group that manages Wi-Fi implementation, has decided to simplify Wi-Fi naming conventions. So, instead of 802.11ac as the current Wi-Fi standard, it is now called Wi-Fi 5—as in the fifth generation of Wi-Fi. The previous Wi-Fi version, 802.11n, is now called Wi-Fi 4. Although even earlier versions aren't really being re-branded since they are not in use anymore, Wi-Fi 3 would refer to 802.11g, Wi-Fi 2 would refer to 802.11a, and Wi-Fi 1 would refer to 802.11b.

**How is Wi-Fi 5 different from previous versions?** The newer wireless Ethernet standard, Wi-Fi 5, is faster and has a better signal range than Wi-Fi 4. Wi-Fi 4, often referred to as *dual band*, operates at either a 2.4 GHz or a 5 GHz frequency. Prior standards operated only at the 2.4 GHz frequency and often competed with the many other wireless devices (such as wireless landline phones) that run on the same frequency. Wi-Fi 5 operates at a 5 GHz frequency. This means Wi-Fi 5 is more resistant to signal interference from other wireless devices in the home.

**Are there new and emerging wireless standards?** WiGig is a wireless option that delivers speeds up to 7 gigabits per second (Gbps) at 60 GHz frequencies. However, WiGig won't replace Wi-Fi because it works for short distances. Wi-Fi 5 and WiGig are best when put to work in tandem: WiGig providing very fast transmission speeds for a room-sized area—perfect for delivering streaming media or quick data transfers between devices—and Wi-Fi 5 for all other wireless transmissions. Two other standards, Wi-Fi 6 and HaLow or Low-Power Wi-Fi, help accommodate the continued dependence on wireless devices. Unlike Wi-Fi, HaLow can connect many devices without the signal diminishing. HaLow has twice the range of current Wi-Fi and is also more robust to easily penetrate walls or other barriers, which is perfect for connecting the smaller Internet of Things (IoT) devices throughout a home.

**Will devices using older Wi-Fi standards still work on a newer network?** Devices using older standards will still work with newer network devices. The ability of current devices to use earlier standards in addition to the current standard is known as backward compatibility. It's important to note that the speed of a network connection is determined by the slowest speed of any network device, so while an older Wi-Fi device might work, it will operate with slower data transfer rates and may run into some frequency interference. If you haven't replaced the router in your home network and are noticing slower speeds, you might need to upgrade the router to a newer standard. If the router only supports Wi-Fi 4, for example, all your devices will run at that speed—even if they are capable of working with the Wi-Fi 5.

# Network Components

To function, all networks must include:

- A means to connect the nodes on the network (transmission media)
- Special hardware devices that allow the nodes to communicate with each other and to send data
- Software that allows the network to run (see Figure 7.6)

## Transmission Media

**Objective 7.3** *Describe the types of transmission media used in networks.*

**How do nodes connect to each other?** All network nodes are connected to each other and to the network by transmission media. Transmission media establish a communications channel between the nodes on a network. They can be either wired or wireless. The media used depend on the requirements of a network and its users.

**What wired transmission media is used on a network?** Wired networks use various types of cable (wire) to connect nodes. As shown in Figure 7.7, the type of network and the distance between nodes determine the type of cable used:

- Unshielded twisted-pair (UTP) cable is composed of four pairs of wires twisted around each other to reduce electrical interference. UTP is slightly different from twisted-pair cable, which is what is used for telephone cable. Twisted-pair cable is made up of copper wires that are twisted around each other and surrounded by a plastic jacket.
- Coaxial cable consists of a single copper wire surrounded by layers of plastic. If you have cable TV, the cable running into your TV or cable box is most likely coaxial cable.
- Fiber-optic cable is made up of plastic or glass fibers that transmit data at extremely fast speeds.

**Sound Byte** MyLab IT

**Installing a Home Computer Network**

Installing a network is relatively easy if you watch someone else do it. In this Sound Byte, you'll learn how to install the hardware and to configure Windows for a wired or wireless home network.

**Figure 7.6** Network components. *(RealVector/Shutterstock, Doomu/Fotolia, Ifong/Shutterstock, Adrian Lyon/Alamy Stock Photo, Norman Chan/Shutterstock)*

**What type of transmission media is most common in wired home networks?** The most popular transmission media option for wired Ethernet home networks is UTP cable. You can buy UTP cable in varying lengths with Ethernet connectors (called RJ-45 connectors) already attached. Ethernet connectors resemble standard phone connectors (called RJ-11 connectors) but are slightly larger and have contacts for eight wires (four pairs) instead of four wires.

**Is there just one kind of UTP cable?** There are several types of UTP cable commonly found in wired Ethernet networks (see Table 7.1). Cat 5e and Cat 6 cable are more common in home networks, while Cat 6a and Cat 7 are designed for bigger networks that require more speed. However, with the proliferation of IoT devices in the home, it may not be uncommon to see these types of cables used for home networks.

**Figure 7.7** Wired transmission media. (a) Unshielded twisted-pair cable. (b) Coaxial cable. (c) Fiber-optic cable. *(Deepspacedave/Shutterstock, Zwola Fasola/Shutterstock, Zentilia/Shutterstock)*

| Table 7.1 | UTP Cable Types |
|---|---|
| Cat 5e | Cat 5e cable is the cheapest and is sufficient for many home networking tasks. It is designed for 100 Mbps–wired Ethernet networks that were popular before gigabit Ethernet networks became the standard. |
| Cat 6 | Cat 6 cable is designed to achieve data transfer rates that support a 1 GbE network. Although using Cat 5e cable is sufficient, using Cat 6 cable is probably the better choice for home networking cable, though it's slightly more expensive and more difficult to work with than Cat 5e cable. |
| Cat 6a | Cat 6a cable is designed for ultrafast Ethernet networks that run at speeds as fast as 10 Gbps and is the most expensive option. Installing a 10 GbE network in the home may be worth the added expense to accommodate the many Internet-dependent devices as well as the current and anticipated use of today's home applications such as gaming and streaming media. |
| Cat 7 | Cat 7 cable supports 10 GbE networks, with the difference of offering greater throughput than Cat 6a. |

**What transmission media is used on a wireless network?** Wireless (or Wi-Fi) networks use radio waves to connect computing devices to other devices and to the Internet instead of using wires.

**Can the same network have both wired and wireless nodes?** One network can support nodes with both wireless and wired connections. A home network might include a desktop or printer that uses a wired connection, and then use the wireless connection for the host of portable devices such as laptops and smartphones. Wireless connections are also used for stationary devices such as printers, TVs, and some smart home devices such as thermostats and security systems.

**Why might a portable device use a wired connection?** When you want to achieve the highest possible throughput on your portable device, you may want to use a wired connection, if one is available. Wireless signals have slower throughput than wired connections for the following reasons:

- Wireless bandwidth is shared among devices.
- Wireless signals are more susceptible to interference from magnetic and electrical sources.
- Other wireless networks (such as your neighbor's network) can interfere with the signals on your network.
- Certain building materials (such as concrete and cinderblock) and metal (such as a refrigerator) can decrease throughput.
- Throughput varies depending on the distance between your networking equipment.
- Wireless networks usually use specially coded signals to protect their data, whereas wired connections don't protect their signals. This process of coding signals can slightly decrease throughput, although once coded, data travels at usual speeds.

## Basic Network Hardware

**Objective 7.4** *Describe the basic hardware devices necessary for networks.*

**What hardware is needed for different nodes on a network to communicate?** For the different nodes on a network to communicate with each other and access the network, each node needs a network adapter. All desktop and laptop computers as well as smartphones, tablets, and many peripherals sold today contain network adapters. Network adapters included in computing devices today are built for both wired and wireless connections.

**What equipment do I need to connect to the Internet and share data through the network?** A modem connects your network to the Internet to bring the Internet signal to your home. To share that signal with your home network and all the devices in your home, you

**Figure 7.8** Together with network adapters, switches act like traffic signals or traffic cops. They enforce the rules of the data road on an Ethernet network and help prevent data packets from crashing into each other.

need network navigation devices: a router and a switch. A router transfers packets of data between two or more networks such as your home network and the Internet. Today, most routers support wired and wireless connections. To then distribute the Internet signal to the devices in your home, you need a switch. Most routers include a built-in switch. A switch acts like a traffic signal on a network (see Figure 7.8). Switches receive data packets and send them to their intended nodes on the same network. During the transmission process, data packets can suffer collisions; subsequently, the data in them is damaged or lost and the network doesn't function efficiently. The switch keeps track of the data packets and, in conjunction with network adapters, helps the data packets find their destinations without running into each other. The switch also keeps track of all the nodes on the network and sends the data packets directly to the node for which they're headed. This keeps the network running efficiently.

Most modern network equipment has simplified to one device that combines a modem and a router with integrated switches. The specific type of modem will depend on the type of broadband service you have. Your Internet service provider will rent the appropriate modem to you or specify what type of modem you have to buy to work properly with the Internet service provider's technology. Your Internet service provider will usually provide you with a device that supports the most recent wireless protocol, but if you haven't changed your Internet service in a while, it may be time for a router/modem upgrade to ensure you're receiving the fastest connection.

## Network Software

**Objective 7.5** *Describe the type of software necessary for networks.*

**What network software do home networks require?** Because home networks are P2P networks, they need operating system software that supports P2P networking. Windows, macOS, and Linux all support P2P networking. You can connect computers running any of these operating systems to the same home network.

**Is the same network software used in client/server networks?** No, nodes on client/server networks are different than P2P networks. They communicate through a centralized server instead of communicating directly with each other. Communicating through a server is more efficient in a network with many nodes, but more complex network software is necessary. Therefore, network operating system (NOS) software is installed on the servers in client/server networks. This software handles requests for information, Internet access, and the use of peripherals for the rest of the network nodes. Examples of NOS software include Windows Server and SUSE Linux Enterprise Server.

The concept of a smart home—where devices and appliances are automated or controlled by apps installed on your smartphone or tablet (see Figure 7.9)—is in full play today, thanks to the power and availability of strong wireless networks and Bluetooth.

With smart home automation, you can dictate how and when a device should engage or respond. For some devices and appliances, just set a schedule and the rest is automated. Other devices and appliances work using some type of sensor and react to changes in their surrounding environment, such as motion, light, or temperature. For example, some smart home thermostats learn your habits (such as waking and sleeping patterns) and heating and cooling preferences over time and create automatic settings. Some smart home draperies and blinds open and close in reaction to the timing of sunrise and sunset using geolocation settings.

Smart home automation can also alert you to unpredictable events, such as water leaks and unexpected visitors to your home. But smart home technology isn't only about security and efficiency. It's also used to help control your entertainment devices as well.

At the heart of many smart homes are hubs that are used to control a variety of devices from different manufacturers. A hub receives different wireless signals from smart devices and then translates those into one Wi-Fi signal that your router can understand. In addition, the hub consolidates the controls required by each device and provides one single app for you to interact with, thus simplifying your experience. Other hubs, such as the Belkin WeMo, control devices more locally. Plug a device (e.g., a lamp or coffee maker) into the WeMo and you can control it from your phone or tablet. An alternative to a hub is a single home automation platform, such as those offered by Google, Microsoft, Samsung, and AT&T.

You can create your own automation by using the IFTTT (If This Then That) app (*IFTTT.com*) or the open-source application

**Figure 7.9** You can remotely monitor your home through a dashboard on your mobile device with smart home technology. *(Scyther5/123RF)*

openHAB and an IoT device (such as a WeMo motion detector, Nest thermostat, or Philips light bulb).

As of yet, no single standard has been adopted for home automation. Some devices work on Wi-Fi, while others work on Bluetooth. Some smart devices interact with apps on mobile devices, whereas others interact with each other directly. There have been some attempts at single platforms, such as Google's Android@ Home platform and Microsoft's Home 2.0 program, but neither of these programs, nor anything else, has been accepted as the standard. Also, while costs have come down significantly on many smart home devices, the overall cost is not completely affordable to most, especially as a complete smart home solution.

Still, the smart home technology industry is estimated to increase to $100 billion by 2020. The smart home is here to stay.

# Connecting to the Internet

One of the main reasons for setting up a network is to share an Internet connection. Broadband is the preferred way to access the Internet, but in some situations, other connections may be necessary.

## Broadband Internet Connections

**Objective 7.6**   *Summarize the broadband options available to access the Internet.*

**What exactly is broadband Internet access?** Broadband, often referred to as high-speed Internet, refers to a type of connection that offers a means to connect to the Internet with fast throughput. Broadband has a data transmission rate that ranges from 1 to 500 Mbps. Some businesses and large organizations have a dedicated connection to the Internet, but most homeowners and small businesses purchase Internet access from Internet service providers (ISPs). ISPs may be specialized providers, like Juno, or companies like Comcast that provide additional services, such as phone and cable TV.

**What types of broadband are available?** As shown in Table 7.2, the standard wired broadband technologies in most areas are cable, DSL (digital subscriber line), and fiber-optic service. Satellite broadband is used mostly in rural or mountain areas where DSL, cable, or fiber-optic service is unavailable or very costly.

## Table 7.2 Comparing Common Wired Broadband Internet Connection Options

| Broadband Type | Transmission Medium | Speed Considerations | Average and Maximum Download Speeds |
|---|---|---|---|
| Cable | Coaxial cable, similar to cable TV wire | Cable connections are shared, so speed can drop during high-usage periods | Average speed of 10 Mbps, with maximum of 30 Mbps |
| DSL (digital subscriber line) | Copper wire phone line | Speed drops as distance from the main signal source increases | Average speed of 3.7 Mbps, with maximum of 15 Mbps |
| Fiber-optic | Strands of optically pure glass or plastic | Transmits data via light signals, which do not degrade over long distances | Average speed of 50 Mbps, with maximum of 950 Mbps |

**How does cable Internet work?** Cable Internet is a broadband service that transmits data over the coaxial cables that also transmit cable television signals; however, cable TV and cable Internet are separate services. Cable TV is a one-way service in which the cable company feeds programming signals to your television. To bring two-way Internet connections to homes, cable companies had to upgrade their networks with two-way data-transmission capabilities.

**How does DSL work?** DSL (digital subscriber line) uses twisted-pair cable, the same as that is used for regular telephones, to connect your computer to the Internet. The bandwidth of the wires is split into three sections, like a three-lane highway. One lane is used to carry voice data. DSL uses the remaining two lanes to send and receive data separately at much higher frequencies than voice data.

**How does fiber-optic service work?** Fiber-optic service uses fiber-optic cable to transmit data via light signals over long distances. Because light travels so quickly, this technology transmits an enormous amount of data at superfast speeds. When the data reaches your house, it's converted to electrical pulses that transmit digital signals your computer can "read." Note that fiber-optic cable is not usually run inside the home. On a fiber-optic network, twisted-pair or coaxial cable is still used inside the home to transport the network signals.

**How does satellite Internet work?** To take advantage of satellite Internet, you need a satellite dish placed outside your home and connected to your router/modem with coaxial cable. Data from your computer is transmitted between your personal satellite dish and the satellite company's receiving satellite dish by a satellite that sits in geosynchronous orbit thousands of miles above Earth (see Figure 7.10).

**How do I choose which broadband connection option is best for me?** Depending on where you live, you might not have a choice of the broadband connection available. Check with your local Internet service provider to determine what broadband options are available and what the transfer rates are in your area. Often, the most difficult decision is choosing between high-speed plans that include varying levels of Internet speeds, TV packages, and phone services.

**Figure 7.10** Internet data is transmitted between your personal satellite dish and the satellite company's receiving satellite dish by a satellite that sits in geosynchronous orbit thousands of miles above Earth. *(Rendeeplumia/Fotolia)*

## Bits&Bytes  Net Neutrality

Until recently, small Web-based businesses had the same opportunity of being accessed on the Internet as a new on-demand movie from Verizon or an online sale at Target. This is because of *net neutrality*, where Internet access was not differentiated by the type of user, the content being uploaded, or the mode of communication. In 2018, the U.S. Federal Communications Commission (FCC) voted to repeal net neutrality and put in place a tiered structure for Internet access: a premium tier with priority access to a faster Internet and a lower tier with less priority and slower speeds. Access to the faster tier would be costlier than access to the lower tier. In this new structure, big Internet service providers like Comcast and Spectrum could charge large Internet content companies, like Netflix or Facebook, a fee to avoid being given slower access speeds for their customers. Smaller users who might not be able to afford the better access would have less priority and slower access, thus putting them at a disadvantage. There is still much controversy around the 2018 FCC decision. Proponents claim that a tiered priority system will promote competition and innovation. Opponents claim that paying for faster access will put small Internet startups at a disadvantage and ultimately stifle innovation. What are your thoughts on net neutrality?

Although about 90% of Internet users in the United States use high-speed Internet connections such as DSL, cable, or fiber-optic, there are still those who use dial-up because of lack of access to high-speed Internet or because high-speed Internet is too expensive. In addition, the use of home broadband has declined over the past few years. Nearly 20 percent only use their cellular plans and public Wi-Fi to connect to the Internet, forgoing the need to obtain broadband Internet at home.

## Wireless Internet Access

**Objective 7.7**   *Summarize how to access the Internet wirelessly.*

**How can I access the Internet wirelessly at home?** As mentioned earlier, to access the Internet wirelessly at home you need to establish Wi-Fi on your home network by using a router that features wireless capabilities. Virtually all laptops, smartphones, game systems, and personal media players sold today are Wi-Fi enabled and come with wireless capability built in.

**How can I access Wi-Fi when I'm away from home?** When you're away from home, you need to find a Wi-Fi hotspot. Many public places, such as libraries, hotels, and fast-food shops, offer free Wi-Fi access. Websites like Wi-Fi-FreeSpot or apps such as WiFiGet help you locate a free hotspot wherever you're planning to go. Your ISP may also provide free hotspot service.

Alternatively, you can connect to the Internet using a mobile hotspot. Mobile hotspots let you tether, or connect, more than one device to the Internet but require access to a data plan. Although you can buy a separate mobile hotspot device, most smartphones have built-in functionality, enabling you to turn your smartphone into a mobile hotspot (see Figure 7.11).

When you're not within range of a Wi-Fi hotspot but still need to access the Internet, you may want to consider mobile broadband. Mobile broadband connects you to the Internet through a cellular network to get Internet access.

**How do I get mobile broadband?** Just as you have an ISP for Internet access for your desktop or laptop computer, you must have a wireless Internet service provider (or wireless ISP) such as T-Mobile, Verizon, or AT&T to connect your smartphone to the Internet.

Mobile broadband technologies are categorized in generations. 4G (fourth generation) is the most current service standard. 5G (or fifth generation) wireless data is being rolled out as the latest mobile data service and also as a home Internet service (instead of fiber-optic, cable, or DSL). 5G will deliver improved wireless service over the current 4G technologies, transmitting data up to 1 Gbps, which, for example, would allow you to download a full-length high-definition movie in seconds. Because 5G will have incredibly fast speeds to push more data more quickly, as a home Internet service 5G will enable video streaming to be seamless and online games to be played in real time. 5G will also be able to connect more devices at once and without a reduction in speeds as currently experienced with Wi-Fi. Additionally, 5G could save up to 90% on energy consumption over current standards.

**How am I charged for mobile broadband?** Mobile broadband providers measure your Internet usage according to how much data you download and upload. A mobile Internet connectivity plan is known as a data plan. You pay a monthly price and are allowed data transfers up to some fixed limit per month, such as 2 GB or 5 GB. If you exceed your monthly data limit, additional data access is provided at an extra cost. You can limit the amount of your mobile data usage by using Wi-Fi whenever possible.

Mobile Hotspot

**Figure 7.11** You can turn your smartphone into a mobile hotspot. *(Courtesy of Google Inc.)*

**Before moving on to Part 2:**

1. ▶ Watch Chapter Overview Video 7.1.

2. Then take the Check Your Understanding quiz.

# Check Your Understanding // Review & Practice

For a quick review to see what you've learned so far, answer the following questions.

## multiple choice

1. Which of the following transmission media is used most often for wired connections within a home?
   a. Twisted-pair cable
   b. Coaxial cable
   c. Fiber-optic cable
   d. Unshielded twisted-pair cable

2. The type of network used for communication among a laptop and smartphone using Bluetooth is a
   a. PAN.
   b. MAN.
   c. LAN.
   d. WAN.

3. Which of the following is not part of a combined device that brings and distributes Internet to home devices?
   a. Switch
   b. Modem
   c. Home network server
   d. Router

4. The fastest broadband Internet service is usually
   a. DSL.
   b. fiber-optic.
   c. cable.
   d. satellite.

5. Which of the following allows you to connect to the Internet wirelessly without needing a cellular plan?
   a. Wi-Fi
   b. 4G
   c. DSL
   d. Mobile broadband

**chew on this**

Today, more than just computers are connected to the Internet. The Internet of Things (IoT) relates to the many "smart" objects that are dependent on a wireless connection to the Internet to receive and transmit data. In healthcare, IoT or smart devices are popping up to help keep patients safe through better monitoring and also to help doctors deliver care. However, challenges such as data security and data management can make the costs outweigh the benefits. Think about some healthcare-related IoT devices and discuss the benefits and related concerns of those devices.

**MyLab IT**  Go to **MyLab IT** to take an autograded version of the *Check Your Understanding* review and to find all media resources for the chapter.

> **For the IT Simulation for this chapter, see MyLab IT.**

# Try This

## Testing Your Internet Connection Speed

Your ISP may have promised you certain download and upload data speeds. How can you tell if you're getting what was promised? Numerous sites on the Internet, such as SpeedOf.Me and speedtest.net, test the speed of your Internet connection. In this Try This, we will test your Internet connection speed using SpeedOf.Me. For more step-by-step instructions, watch the Try This video on MyLab IT.

**Step 1** Type *SpeedOf.Me* in any browser. SpeedOf.Me is an HTML5 Internet speed test, so it will work on PCs, Apple, and Android devices. Click Start Test to begin.

**Step 2** SpeedOf.Me tests upload and download speeds using sample files of varying sizes, starting with a 128 KB sample until it reaches a sample size that takes more than 8 seconds to upload or download (with the largest possible sample size being 128 MB). The results are based on the last sample file. As the test runs, graphics illustrate the process, with the final results displaying when the test is finished.

**Step 3** A history chart displays at the bottom of the screen, showing the results of any previous tests you have run on that device. If you want to share your results, you can use the Share button to post them to a social media site or by e-mail.

**Download Speed:** Time taken to move data from the server to your computer

**Upload Speed:** Time taken to move data from your computer to the server

Bands represent series of sample files sent

*(Courtesy of SpeedOf.Me)*

### Networked Devices

One of the nice features of App Inventor is that, using Wi-Fi, you can instantly see changes on your target device that you make on your PC while programming. But what is going on behind the scenes to allow this connection?

In this exercise, you explore how the AI Companion software works with the App Inventor program to connect your systems. You'll see how networking utilities like Ping and Telnet are used to investigate how network firewalls are set up.

The App Inventor Companion app and program communicate across Wi-Fi to make your programming easier.

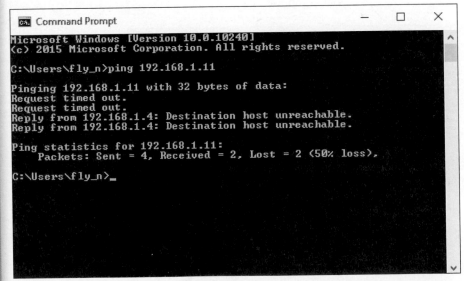

**For the instructions for this exercise, go to MyLab IT.**

# Your Home Network

You know what a network is and the advantages of having one. In this section, we look at installing or updating a home network and keeping it safe.

## Installing and Configuring Home Networks

Now that you understand the basic components of a network and your Internet connection options, you're ready to install a network in your home. If you already have a network in your home, it's useful to examine your network settings and configuration to make sure they're still meeting your needs, especially if you've added new devices.

Only a few years ago, most home networks included just a few computers and a printer. However, a network that can manage those devices is often very different from one that can support the smartphones, gaming consoles, tablets, smart TVs, and IoT devices many homes now have connected to their networks. If you're using any of these additional devices and you haven't updated your network equipment or setup in a while, it may be time to do so.

### Planning Your Home Network

**Objective 7.8**   *Explain what should be considered before creating a home network.*

**Where do I start?** One of the first things you should do to evaluate your network is list all the devices that will connect to it. Consider not only the obvious devices, such as computers, laptops, tablets, and printers, but also smartphones, DVR boxes, smart TVs, wireless stereo equipment, and any other appliance that connects to the Internet wirelessly. You might be surprised at how many devices you list. Then include any devices you think you may add. Once you have a complete list, determine whether your router can support all your devices.

**What wireless Ethernet standard should my network be using?** For a home network to run most efficiently and to provide the fastest experience, it's best that all network nodes—computers, network adapters, routers, and so on—use the latest wireless Ethernet standard. If you have the fastest Wi-Fi 5 network adapter in your device but the router is the slower Wi-Fi 4, then data will be sent at the speeds supported by the lower standard. For networks that will support more than 15 connected devices, you should have at least an a Wi-Fi 5 router. If you haven't updated your router in a while, you may want to consider getting a Wi-Fi 5 router (see Figure 7.12) to get the fastest connection speeds. Most new routers that offer Wi-Fi 5 also support WiGig. WiGig is used for speedy short-range connections between devices, and Wi-Fi is necessary for longer-range wireless connections.

**How can I tell what wireless standard my router supports?** You may be able to tell what standard your router is supporting just by looking at it. Many routers have the wireless standard indicated on the device. If you're still not sure, you can search for more information on your router by entering the model number into a search engine. If your router is provided by your ISP and it's an older standard, you should consider having your ISP provide you with a new router.

**Figure 7.12** Wi-Fi 5 wireless routers offer the fastest connection speeds and a greater wireless signal range. *(AlexLMX/Shutterstock)*

**How can I tell what network adapters are installed in my computer?** To see which network adapters are installed in your Windows computer, use the Device Manager utility (see Figure 7.13), which lists all the adapters. If you can't tell which wireless standard the adapter supports from the list, search the Internet for information on your specific adapter to determine its capability. The Device Manager can also alert you if there's a problem with the adapter.

## Power Your Devices—Wirelessly

Think of when you've been unable to use your mobile phone, smartwatch, Bluetooth speaker, or other device because it's out of power and you don't have access to a charger or the time to wait while the device charges. Wouldn't it be great to always have access to charging power without needing to plug in your device or wait while it charges?

Cota—short for charging over the air—is an emerging technology that will bring wireless power to devices without cables, batteries, or charging pads. Cota technology sends power to mobile devices the same way a wireless router sends data, by

flowing through the 2.45-GHz spectrum band. A device would have an embedded Cota receiver (a tiny silicon chip). That receiver would send a low-power beacon signal to a Cota transmitter indicating what kind of charging is needed. When the transmitter gets the signal, it sends power back to the receiver. The Cota beacon can bounce off walls and objects, so power is delivered even while the device is in motion. Cota wireless power technology will fit into a wide range of industries and applications, eventually enabling everyone to never need a charging cord again.

**Figure 7.13** The Windows Device Manager shows the wireless and wired network adapters installed on a computer.
> *To access Device Manager, right-click the Windows **Start** button on the taskbar and select **Device Manager.** (Courtesy of Microsoft Corp.)*

## Connecting Devices to a Network

**Objective 7.9** *Describe how to set up a home network.*

### How should a basic home network be set up?

Because most newer modems have integrated routers, and only a few wired connections may be needed, setting up a home network is fairly straightforward. As shown in Figure 7.14, the modem/router is the central device of a home network. The router is best placed in a centralized location to increase the wireless signal throughout the home. To reduce interference, the router should be placed away from large metal objects, appliances, and obstructing walls (such as those made of brick). An Ethernet cable connects directly to the modem/router using the WAN or Internet port. Then, all computer devices—such as laptops, tablets, smartphones, HDTVs, gaming consoles, and printers—are connected to the modem/router wirelessly or via wired connections to the LAN ports.

**How do I set up a Windows home network for the first time?** The process of setting up a network is fairly automated, especially if you're using the same version of Windows on all your computers. The examples in this section assume all computers are running Windows 10.

Before configuring the computers to the network, do the following:

1. Establish a broadband Internet account with a local ISP and either obtain a modem/router from the ISP or purchase a compatible modem/router.

2. Make sure the modem/router is connected to the Internet. If you have separate devices, then make sure that your modem is connected to the Internet and that the router is connected to the modem.

3. For any wired connections, plug all devices using Ethernet cables into the router or switch.

4. Turn on your equipment in the following order:
   a. Your modem/router (or if individual devices, the modem and then the router, allowing each device about one minute each to power up)
   b. All computers and peripherals (printers, scanners, and so on)

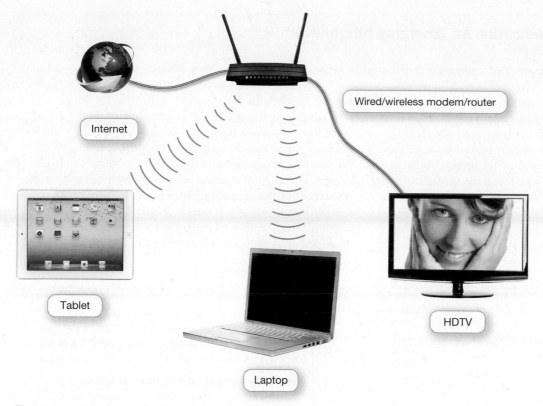

**Figure 7.14** A small network with a wired/wireless modem/router attached. *(Laurentiu Iordache/Fotolia, Beboy/ Shutterstock, Oleksiy Maksymenko/Alamy, Sergey Peterman/Shutterstock, Iko/Shutterstock)*

Internet

Wired/wireless modem/router

Tablet

HDTV

Laptop

If your computer has a wired connection to the network, you should automatically be connected. You should give the network the same secured name you give to your router (see the "Troubleshooting Wireless Network Problems" section in this chapter).

5. To connect wireless devices, ensure that your Wi-Fi is turned on by selecting Wi-Fi in the Network & Internet group in Settings. Then, from the Notification area on the taskbar, click Internet access. A panel opens, displaying the network options. You'll need to enter your security passphrase to connect to your wireless network initially. For unsecure networks, you don't need a password. Checking the "Remember this network" check box makes any network a preferred network, enabling the computer to connect to the network automatically when that network is available.

**Is there a limit to the number of wired devices I can have in my network?** Most home routers have three or four LAN ports on the back to support wired connections. This is usually sufficient for the general house that has at least one computer, maybe a printer, and perhaps some entertainment devices that are connected directly to the router. If you need more LAN ports for wired connections, you can buy a stand-alone switch and plug it into one of the ports on your router (see Figure 7.15). Usually a networking switch with an additional five to eight ports will suffice, but you can find switches with many more ports, if needed.

**How many wireless devices can connect to a router in a home network?** Most home wireless routers can support up to 253 wireless connections at the same time, although most home networks have far fewer. Regardless of how many devices your home network has, keep in mind that they all share bandwidth when they're connected to a router. Therefore, the more devices connected to a single router that are actively transmitting data, the smaller the portion of the router's bandwidth each device receives. So, for example, when eight wireless devices are all connected to the network, each device has less bandwidth than it would if only six devices were connected to the network.

**Are wireless routers for Windows and macOS networks different?** All routers that support Wi-Fi 4 and the newer Wi-Fi 5 should work with computers running the more recent versions of Windows or macOS. However, Apple has routers that are optimized for working with Apple computers. So, if you're connecting Apple computers to a larger home network, you may want to use the Apple AirPort Extreme router, which is Wi-Fi 5 compatible. For smaller home networks using

Router

Switch

**Figure 7.15** You can add ports to your network by connecting a switch to your router. *(Alarich/ Shutterstock; Lexan/Shutterstock)*

Have you ever heard of a *mesh network*? This emerging technology uses small radio transmitters instead of wireless routers as its network nodes. What is so great about mesh networks is that only one node needs to physically connect to a network connection, and then all other nodes can share wirelessly with each other. This connection-sharing between nodes can extend almost endlessly, since one wired node can share its Internet connection wirelessly with other nearby nodes, and then those nodes can share their connection wirelessly with nodes closest to them—thus creating a "mesh" of connectivity. The truly wireless aspect of mesh networks poses several advantages to the wireless networks that are in place today: They're easier to install because fewer wires need to be run; they can accommodate more nodes; and they enable wireless networks to be created in outdoor and unstructured venues.

In developing nations as well as in some areas in the United States, mesh networks have helped provide access to the Internet in a more timely and inexpensive manner than waiting for the physical connections to be established. Mesh networks can also help promote cellular communications during times of disasters when traditional communications are halted. And if you have an Android mobile phone, you can participate in the Serval Mesh, which allows users to send and receive information without depending on established cellular networks.

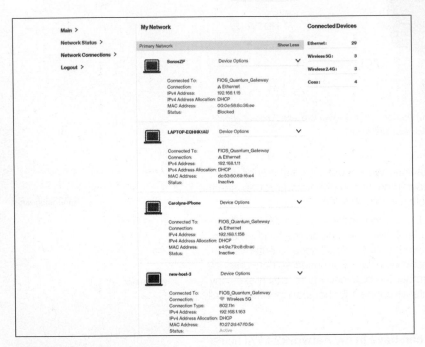

**Figure 7.16** Wired and wireless connections can use the same router. *(Courtesy of Microsoft Corp.)*

Apple devices, consider using the AirPort Express, which is 802.11n compatible. Windows devices can also connect to either router, so it's a great choice for households with both Apples and PCs.

**How do I know what's connected to my router?** To determine what's connected to your router, you need to log in to an account associated with your router's IP address. You can find your router's IP address on the router manufacturer's website. Once you know it, type it into a Web browser. You may need to enter a user name and password, but eventually you'll get to a configuration page that lists what wired and wireless devices are in your network. You may be surprised at all the various devices associated with your network.

Figure 7.16 shows a router network listing with wired (desktop computer) and wireless (DVR, laptop, iPhone, and iPad) devices connected in a home network. You'll notice that each device also has an IP address. You can think of your network as an apartment building. The router's IP address is the building's street address, while the IP addresses of the individual devices connected to the router are the apartment numbers. Each device needs an IP address so the router knows to which device to send information.

**Figure 7.17** A network-attached storage device provides centralized data storage and access. *(Leslie Wilk/Alamy Stock Photo)*

### Specialized Home Networking Devices

**What can I attach to my network to facilitate file sharing and backup of data?** Network-attached storage (NAS) devices are specialized devices designed to store and manage all network data. Although data can always be stored on individual hard drives in computers on a network, NAS devices provide for centralized data storage and access.

Popular for years on business networks, NAS devices are available for home networks (see Figure 7.17). You can think of them as specialized external hard drives. NAS devices connect directly to the network via a wired Ethernet connection to a router or switch. Specialized software is installed on all computers on the network to ensure that data saved to an individual computer is also stored on the NAS device as a backup.

For Apple computers, the AirPort Time Capsule serves as a NAS device as well as a wireless router. The AirPort Time Capsule works in conjunction with the Time Machine backup feature of macOS.

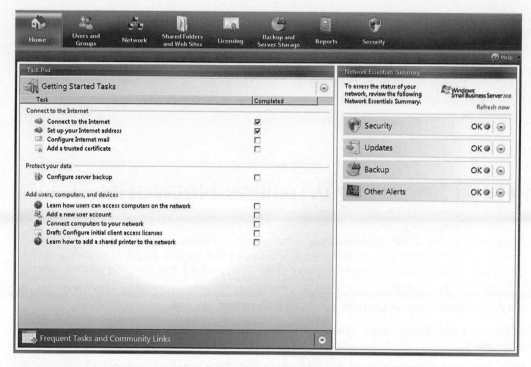

**Figure 7.18** Home network servers are often configured with software such as Windows Server. (*Courtesy of Microsoft Corp.*)

**What other storage devices could I use on a home network?** As its name implies, network-attached storage devices are meant specifically for providing a central location for file storage, sharing, and backup. Similar to a NAS, a home network server provides centralized file storage and sharing, as well as more sophisticated functionality. A home network server uses a server operating system such as Windows Server or macOS Server (see Figure 7.18). Think of a home network server as another computer on the network, but one that just holds centralized files and applications and is not capable of user interaction like a PC. As such, a home network server can do the following:

- Authenticate and authorize all users and computers on the network
- Provide file storage, sharing, and collaboration tools
- Share applications between connected computers

Note that even though these devices are servers, they don't convert a home P2P network into a client/server network because these servers don't perform all the functions performed on client/server networks.

**Why should I connect digital entertainment devices to my network?**
One reason for connecting entertainment devices to your network is to access and share digital content between devices. Connecting these devices to your network also connects them to the Internet so you can access online entertainment content, including movies, videos, and music.

You can also use gaming devices to play multiplayer games with players in the next room or all over the world. The content you access is either downloaded or streamed to your devices. Newer smart TVs and other smart devices (such as Blu-ray players, game consoles, and home theater systems) are continually adding apps and video services so that you can play games, view on-demand and online videos, listen to Internet radio, and access social networking sites (see Figure 7.19). Some smart devices also feature an integrated Web browser that lets you access the Web directly, without the use of apps.

**What if I don't have a smart TV?** You can use streaming media devices such as Apple TV, Google Chromecast, or Roku that enable you to send Internet-based media to your traditional TV. Alternatively, you can access online entertainment from game consoles and Blu-ray players. Most set-top boxes also allow you to switch from live TV to an online entertainment service.

**Figure 7.19** Smart TVs have their own apps and let you directly access the Web. (*Scanrail/123RF*)

# Managing and Securing Wireless Networks

All networks require some maintenance and management, but wireless networks require additional installation, maintenance, and security measures. In this section, we look at how to troubleshoot typical wireless network problems and how to protect wireless networks from common security threats.

## Troubleshooting Wireless Network Problems

**Objective 7.10**    *Describe the potential problems with wireless networks and the means to avoid them.*

**What types of problems can I run into when installing wireless networks?** The maximum range of Wi-Fi 4 or Wi-Fi 5 wireless devices is about 350 feet. But as you go farther away from your router, the throughput you achieve decreases. Obstacles between wireless nodes also decrease throughput. Walls, floors, and large metal objects (such as refrigerators) are the most common sources of interference with wireless signals.

**What if a node on the network seems slow?** Repositioning the node within the same room (sometimes even just a few inches from the original position) can affect communication between nodes. If this doesn't work, move the device closer to the router or to another room in your house. You might also try repositioning the antennas on your router. If these solutions don't work, consider adding additional equipment to your network.

**What equipment will help improve a wireless signal throughout the network?** There are two types of devices that you can use to amplify or to extend the wireless signal to parts of your home that are experiencing poor connectivity: access points and extenders. An access point connects to the router with an Ethernet cable and creates a wireless signal at the location of the access point. Therefore, an access point should be placed in the location where the original Wi-Fi signal becomes weaker. However, because an access point requires a wired connection with the router, given the distance between access point and router, using an access point to improve connectivity may not always be possible.

Alternatively, consider using a wireless range extender, which repeats or amplifies the wireless signal from the router. Because Wi-Fi signals have limited ranges, wireless range extenders work by receiving the Wi-Fi signal near the end of the range and transmitting it a second time to extend the range of the network. For example, as shown in Figure 7.20, Laptop C on the back porch can't connect to the wireless network, even though Computer B in the den can. By placing a wireless range extender in the den, where there is still good connectivity to the wireless network, the wireless signal is amplified and beamed farther out to the back porch. This allows Laptop C to make a good connection to the network. The downside of using an extender over an access point is that it shares the wireless connection and can potentially slow the entire network.

## Securing Wireless Networks

**Objective 7.11**    *Describe how to secure wireless home networks.*

**Why is a wireless network more vulnerable than a wired network?** Packets of information on a wireless network are broadcast through the airwaves. Savvy hackers can intercept and decode information from your transmissions that may allow them to bypass standard protections, such as a firewall, that you have set up on your network. All computers that connect to the Internet need to be secured from intruders. This is usually accomplished by using a firewall, which is a

Computer A with
wireless network adapter

Computer B with
wireless range extender

Laptop C with
wireless network adapter

**Figure 7.20** Because a wireless range extender is installed in the den, Laptop C on the back porch can now connect to the wireless network.

hardware or software solution that helps shield your network from prying eyes. (We discuss firewalls at length in Chapter 9.)

Wireless networks present special vulnerabilities; therefore, you should take additional steps to keep your wireless network safe. Wireless networks with strong signals have wide ranges that may extend outside your house. This makes it possible for someone to access your network without your knowledge. Hackers are known to take advantage of these vulnerabilities, but in areas where residences are close together, wireless signals can reach a neighbor's residence, enticing someone to "borrow" your wireless signal rather than getting one of their own. Piggybacking is connecting to a wireless network without the permission of the owner. This practice is illegal in many jurisdictions.

**Why should I be worried about someone logging onto my wireless network without my permission?** If your neighbor is using your network connection, his or her usage could be slowing down your connection speed. Some neighbors might even be computer savvy enough to penetrate your unprotected wireless network and steal personal information, just as any hacker could. Any cyberattack or illegal behavior a hacker initiates from your wireless network could get you in trouble with the authorities. Therefore, to prevent unwanted users gaining access to your wireless network, it's important to take measures to secure it.

**How can I secure my wireless network?** To secure a wireless network, take the additional precautions described as follows:

1. **Use encryption and security protocols.** Most routers ship with security protocols such as Wired Equivalent Privacy (WEP), Wi-Fi Protected Access (WPA), or Wi-Fi Protected Access Version 2 (WPA2). Each use encryption (a method of translating your data into code) to protect data in your wireless transmissions. WPA2 is the most secure, but WPA may be compatible with more client devices. WEP still offers protection but offers the least protection of the three.

2. **Change your network name (SSID).** Each wireless network has its own name to identify it, known as the service set identifier (SSID). Unless you change this name when you set up your router, the router uses a default network name that all routers from that manufacturer use (such as "Wireless" or "Netgear"). Hackers know the default names and access codes for routers. If you haven't changed the SSID, it's advertising the fact that you probably haven't changed any of the other default settings for your router either.

3. **Disable SSID broadcast.** Most routers are set up to broadcast their SSIDs so that other wireless devices can find them. Disable SSID broadcasting, if your router supports doing so. This makes it more difficult for a hacker to detect your network and nearly impossible for a neighbor to inadvertently connect to your network. Keep in mind that you will have to re-enable this setting when adding new components to the network.

4. **Change the default password on your router.** Routers have default user names and passwords. Hackers can use these to access your router and break into your network. Change the password on your router to something hard to guess. Use at least 12 characters that are a combination of letters, symbols, and numbers.

5. **Use a passphrase.** When you attempt to connect a node to a security-enabled network for the first time, you're required to enter the security key. The security key or passphrase (see

| Wireless Status | |
|---|---|
| Radio Enabled: | Yes |
| SSID: | K5SKF |
| Channel: | Automatic |
| Security Enabled: | Yes |
| WEP 64-bit: | N/A |
| WEP 802.1x: | N/A |
| WPA2: | 5XKJ598SRHMX5TN2 |
| SSID Broadcast: | Enabled |
| MAC Authentication: | Disabled |
| Wireless Mode: | Compatibility Mode (802.11b/g/n) |
| WMM: | Enabled |
| WPS: | Enabled |
| WPS BUTTON: | Off |
| Received Packets: | 2153 |
| Sent Packets: | 3554 |

Unique SSID name

Create hard to guess passphrase

Security protocol in use

Disable for extra protection

**Figure 7.21** By accessing your router, you can configure the security protocols available on your router and change the SSID. (*Courtesy of Microsoft Corp.*)

**Sound Byte** MyLab IT

**Securing Wireless Networks**

In this Sound Byte, you learn some simple steps to secure your wireless network against intruders.

**Helpdesk** MyLab IT

**Managing and Securing Your Wireless Network**

In this Helpdesk, you'll play the role of a helpdesk staffer, fielding questions about ways to manage and secure wireless networks.

Figure 7.21) is the code that computers on your network need to decrypt (decode) data transmissions. Without this key, it's extremely difficult, if not impossible, to decrypt the data transmissions from your network. Usually the manufacturer assigns a passphrase to the router. You can find the passphrase printed on a sticker on the side of your router. You can keep that passphrase or create a passphrase that is more meaningful and easier for you to remember. Keep in mind, however, that you should take similar precautions when creating a passphrase as you do when creating any password. Using upper- and lowercase letters, numbers, and special characters helps to create a passphrase that is hard to guess by intruders.

6. **Implement media access control.** Each network adapter on your network has a unique number (like a serial number) assigned to it by the manufacturer. This is called a *media access control (MAC)* address, and it's a number printed right on the network adapter. Many routers allow you to restrict access to the network to only certain MAC addresses. This helps ensure that only authorized devices can connect to your network.

7. **Limit your signal range.** Many routers allow you to adjust the transmitting power to low, medium, or high. Cutting down the power to low or medium could prevent your signal from reaching too far away from your home, making it tougher for interlopers to poach your signal.

8. **Apply firmware upgrades.** Your router has read-only memory that has software written to it. This software is known as firmware. As bugs are found in the firmware (which hackers might exploit), manufacturers issue patches, just as the makers of operating system software do. Periodically check the manufacturer's website and apply any necessary upgrades to your firmware.

9. **Disable remote access.** Some routers have a setting to allow remote access. This makes it easier for the manufacturer to offer technical support. However, hackers can use this to get into your home network. You can always turn on this feature when needed.

If you follow these steps, you'll greatly improve the security of your wireless network. In Chapter 9, we continue to explore many other ways to keep your computer safe from malicious individuals on the Internet and ensure that your digital information is secure.

**Before moving on to the Chapter Review:**

1. ▶ Watch Chapter Overview Video 7.2.

2. Then take the Check Your Understanding quiz.

# Check Your Understanding // Review & Practice

For a quick review to see what you've learned so far, answer the following questions.

## multiple choice

1. Which is the central device to a home network?
   a. Modem/router
   b. Wired-connected PC
   c. Network range extender
   d. Network interface card

2. When planning a network, which devices should be considered?
   a. Only the computers that will have a wired connection
   b. Just the computers and printers that will have a wired connection
   c. Just PCs connected with a wired connection and any laptop or tablet connected wirelessly
   d. All devices that will connect with a wired or wireless connection

3. Which of the following might cause a potential problem on a wireless network?
   a. Devices too close to the router
   b. Interference from walls, floors, and large objects
   c. A router using the Wi-Fi 5 standard
   d. A unique password created for the network

4. Which of the following would help improve a wireless signal throughout a network?
   a. Network Internet card
   b. Access point
   c. Network switch
   d. Wireless router

5. Which is a precaution to be taken when setting up a wireless network?
   a. Disable the passphrase.
   b. Keep the default network name.
   c. Keep the default network password.
   d. Use WPA2 encryption.

**chew on this**

Networks facilitate the sharing of files between connected computers. Online storage systems such as Dropbox, Google Drive, and OneDrive take advantage of using the Internet to share files. Alternatively, people still use flash drives to physically transport files from one location to another. Discuss advantages and disadvantages of the various options of sharing and transporting files between devices.

**MyLab IT**  Go to **MyLab IT** to take an autograded version of the *Check Your Understanding* review and to find all media resources for the chapter.

> **For the IT Simulation for this chapter, see MyLab IT.**

# 7 Chapter Review

## Summary

**Learning Outcome 7.1** **You will be able to explain the basics of networking, including the components needed to create a network, and describe the different ways a network can connect to the Internet.**

### Networking Fundamentals

**Objective 7.1** *Describe computer networks and their pros and cons.*

- A computer network is simply two or more computers that are connected using software and hardware so they can communicate.
- Advantages of networks include allowing users to share an Internet connection, share printers and other peripheral devices, share files, and communicate with computers regardless of their operating system.
- Disadvantages for larger networks are that they require administration and that they may require costly equipment.

### Network Architectures

**Objective 7.2** *Explain the different ways networks are defined.*

- Networks can be defined by the distance between nodes:
  - A personal area network (PAN) is used for communication among personal mobile devices using Bluetooth or Wi-Fi wireless technologies.
  - A local area network (LAN) connects nodes that are located in a small geographical area.
  - A home area network (HAN) is a specific type of LAN located in a home.
  - A metropolitan area network (MAN) is a large network in a specific geographical area.
  - A wide area network (WAN) spans a large physical distance.
- Networks can also be defined by the level of administration:
  - **Central:** A client/server network contains two types of computers: a client computer on which

users perform specific tasks and a server computer that provides resources to the clients and central control for the network. Most networks that have 10 or more nodes are client/server networks.
  - **Local:** Peer-to-peer (P2P) networks enable each node connected to the network to communicate directly with every other node. Most home networks are P2P networks.
- Ethernet networks are the most common networks used in home networking. Most Ethernet networks use a combination of wired and wireless connections, depending on the data throughput required. Wired connections usually achieve higher throughput than wireless connections. Wired Ethernet home networks use the gigabit Ethernet standard.
- Wireless Ethernet networks are identified by a protocol standard: 802.11a/b/g/n/ac. 802.11ac is the newest standard. WiGig (802.11ad) is a wireless link between devices. WiGig is like Bluetooth, but faster. 802.11af (Super Wi-Fi or White-Fi) and 802.11ah (HaLow or Low-Power Wi-Fi) help accommodate the continued dependence on wireless devices.

### Network Components

**Objective 7.3** *Describe the types of transmission media used in networks.*

- Wired networks use various types of cable to connect nodes, including unshielded twisted-pair cable, coaxial cable, and fiber-optic cable. The type of network and the distance between the nodes determine the type of cable used.
- Wireless networks use radio waves.

**Objective 7.4** *Describe the basic hardware devices necessary for networks.*

- All devices must have a network adapter. Network adapters may be used for both wired and wireless connections.

- Network navigation devices, such as routers and switches, are necessary for computers to communicate in a network.

**Objective 7.5**  *Describe the type of software necessary for networks.*

- Home networks need operating system software that supports peer-to-peer networking. Windows, macOS, and Linux all support P2P networking.
- Servers on client/server networks use network operating systems (NOS).

## Connecting to the Internet

**Objective 7.6**  *Summarize the broadband options available to access the Internet.*

- Broadband connections include the following types:
  - Cable transmits data over coaxial cable, which is also used for cable television.
  - DSL uses twisted-pair wire, similar to that used for telephones.
  - Fiber-optic cable uses glass or plastic strands to transmit data via light signals.
  - Satellite is a connection option for those who do not have access to faster broadband technologies. Data is transmitted between a satellite dish and a satellite that is in a geosynchronous orbit.

**Objective 7.7**  *Summarize how to access the Internet wirelessly.*

- Wi-Fi allows users to connect to the Internet wirelessly but is not as fast as a wired connection.
- Mobile broadband is a service delivered by cell-phone networks.

---

# Part 2
## Your Home Network

**Learning Outcome 7.2**  **You will be able to describe what is necessary to install and configure a home network and how to manage and secure a wireless network.**

## Installing and Configuring Home Networks

**Objective 7.8**  *Explain what should be considered before creating a home network.*

- Most home network routers should support both wireless and wired access to the Internet.
- For a home network to run efficiently, all connected devices and routers should use the same Ethernet standard.
- The Device Manager utility in Windows lists all adapters installed on your computer.

**Objective 7.9**  *Describe how to set up a home network.*

- All devices are connected to your router, either wirelessly or with a wired connection. Wired connections deliver better throughput than wireless.
- To add additional ports to your network, you can connect a switch to your router.
- Network-attached storage (NAS) devices let you store and share data files such as movies and music, as well as provide a central place for file backups.
- Home network servers can be used instead of a NAS device if your needs require more sophisticated functionality.
- The latest versions of Windows make it easy to set up wired and wireless networks.

- Devices such as gaming consoles each have their own setup procedures for connecting to wireless networks but usually require the same information as that needed for connecting a computer to a secured wireless network.

## Managing and Securing Wireless Networks

**Objective 7.10**  *Describe the potential problems with wireless networks and the means to avoid them.*

- Wireless connections have less throughput, therefore, you may need to consider a wired connection for certain devices.
- Distance from the router, as well as walls, floors, and large metal objects between a device and the router, can interfere with wireless connectivity.
- Access points or wireless range extenders can amplify signals to improve connectivity in areas of poor signal strength.

**Objective 7.11**  *Describe how to secure wireless home networks.*

- Wireless networks are even more susceptible to hacking than wired networks because the signals of most wireless networks extend beyond the walls of your home.

- To prevent unwanted intrusions into your network, you should change the default password on your router to make it tougher for hackers to gain access, use a hard-to-guess SSID (network name), disable SSID broadcasting to make it harder for outsiders to detect your network, enable security protocols such as WPA2, WPA or WEP, create a network passphrase, implement media access control, limit your signal range, and apply firmware upgrades.

**MyLab IT**  Be sure to check out **MyLab IT** for additional materials to help you review and learn. And don't forget to watch the Chapter Overview Videos. ▶

# Key Terms

| | | |
|---|---|---|
| 4G  **253** | gigabit Ethernet (GbE)  **246** | peer-to-peer (P2P) network  **246** |
| 5G  **253** | home area network (HAN)  **245** | peer-to-peer (P2P) sharing  **246** |
| access point  **262** | home network server  **261** | personal area network (PAN)  **244** |
| backward compatibility  **247** | Internet service provider (ISP)  **251** | piggybacking  **263** |
| broadband  **251** | local area network (LAN)  **245** | router  **250** |
| cable Internet  **252** | metropolitan area network (MAN)  **245** | satellite Internet  **252** |
| Cat 5e cable  **248** | mobile broadband  **253** | service set identifier (SSID)  **263** |
| Cat 6 cable  **248** | mobile hotspot  **253** | smart home  **251** |
| Cat 6a cable  **248** | modem  **249** | switch  **250** |
| Cat 7 cable  **248** | network  **242** | throughput  **243** |
| client/server network  **245** | network adapter  **249** | transmission media  **247** |
| coaxial cable  **247** | network administration  **243** | twisted-pair cable  **247** |
| data plan  **253** | network architecture  **244** | unshielded twisted-pair (UTP) cable  **247** |
| data transfer rate (bandwidth)  **243** | network-attached storage (NAS) device  **260** | wide area network (WAN)  **245** |
| DSL (digital subscriber line)  **252** | network navigation device  **250** | Wi-Fi  **246** |
| Ethernet network  **246** | network operating system (NOS)  **250** | wireless Internet service provider (wireless ISP)  **253** |
| fiber-optic cable  **247** | node  **242** | wireless range extender  **262** |
| fiber-optic service  **252** | | |
| firmware  **264** | | |

# Chapter Quiz // Assessment

For a quick review to see what you've learned, answer the following questions. Submit the quiz as requested by your instructor. If you're using MyLab IT, the quiz is also available there.

## multiple choice

1. Which of the following would *not* be a benefit of networking computers?
   a. Sharing an Internet connection
   b. Sharing software licenses
   c. Sharing printers and other peripherals
   d. Sharing files

2. Bethany is in her home, watching a video she took on vacation, while her brother is playing FIFA Soccer on his Xbox and her dad is checking stock quotes on his iPad. What kind of network does this family most likely have?
   a. Client/server network
   b. P2P network
   c. Both a and b
   d. Neither a nor b

3. What two devices are often combined into one device to connect the network to the Internet and to share the connection between devices on the network?
   a. Router hub and switch
   b. Switch and hub
   c. Router and switch
   d. Modem and router

4. Which of the following does *not* describe mobile broadband?
   a. 4G or 5G
   b. A cellular service that brings Internet access to mobile devices
   c. A wireless hotspot
   d. Requires a wireless ISP

5. Which of the following should you *not* do to secure a wireless network?
   a. Implement media access control.
   b. Disable SSID broadcasting.
   c. Create a security encryption passphrase.
   d. Keep the default network name and router password.

6. Which type of broadband Internet offers connections nearing the speed of light?
   a. Cable
   b. Satellite
   c. DSL
   d. Fiber-optic

7. Which of the following would *not* cause interference or poor connectivity between nodes on a wireless network?
   a. Concrete walls
   b. A wireless extender
   c. Some appliances
   d. Nodes that are too far apart

8. Which of the following is the most secure security protocol used with routers?
   a. WPA2
   b. WPA
   c. WEP2
   d. WEP

9. The type of network that would be necessary to connect the networks of two college campuses would be:
   a. LAN
   b. MAN
   c. WAN
   d. PAN

10. Which of the following describes fiber-optic broadband?
    a. It uses strands of pure glass or plastic.
    b. It connects via an orbiting satellite.
    c. It connects with coaxial cable.
    d. Speed drops as the distance from the main signal source increases.

## true/false

_____ 1. You can attach more than four wired devices to a network by using a switch.

_____ 2. P2P networks require specialized network operating system software.

_____ 3. Actual data throughput is usually higher on wireless networks than on wired networks.

_____ 4. A network-attached storage device is like a network-connected hard drive.

_____ 5. Cat 5e and Cat 6 are types of twisted-pair cable.

## What do you think now?

Your genetic data is uniquely yours, so before spitting into a tube with the hopes of getting a personalized wine list, consider the risks involved. Research the privacy risks of sharing your DNA with testing companies and explain why you would be likely or unlikely to submit your DNA for testing.

# Team Time

## Providing Wireless Internet Access to the Needy

### problem

Not everyone can afford wireless Internet access, and this can put families, especially ones with school-age children, at a disadvantage.

### task

You're volunteering for a charity that wants to install wireless networks in the homes of needy families. The project is funded by charitable grants, with the objective of providing basic broadband Internet access and networking capabilities at no cost to the recipients.

### process

Break the class into three teams. Each team will be responsible for investigating one of the following issues:

1. **Internet service providers:** Research broadband Internet service providers that serve the town where your school is located. Compare maximum upload and download speeds as well as costs. Be sure to consider the cost of the modems—whether they're purchased or rented. Select what your group considers the best deal.

2. **Networking equipment and network-ready peripherals:** Each home needs to be provided with an 802.11ac-capable wireless router (or modem/router) and a network-ready all-in-one printer. Research three options for these devices, considering price as well as functionality.

3. **Security:** Work in conjunction with the group researching routers to determine the best router to purchase, since it needs to support a security protocol such as WPA2. Consider other types of protection needed, such as antivirus software and firewalls.

Present your findings to your class and come to a consensus about the solution you would propose for the charity.

### conclusion

Providing technology to underserved populations on a cost-effective basis will go a long way toward closing the digital divide.

# Ethics Project

## Firing Employees for Expressing Views on Social Media Sites

In this exercise, you'll research and then role-play a complicated ethical situation. The role you play may or may not match your own personal beliefs; regardless, your research and use of logic will enable you to represent the view assigned. An arbitrator will watch and comment on both sides of the arguments, and together the team will agree on an ethical solution.

### problem

Employers are often intolerant of employees who express negative opinions or expose inside information about their employers on social media sites. Given that most jurisdictions in the United States use the doctrine of employment at will (employees can be fired at any time for any reason), many employers are quick to discipline or terminate employees who express opinions with which the company disagrees. When such cases come to court, the courts often find in favor of the employers.

### research areas to consider

- Ellen Simonetti and Delta Airlines
- Fired for blogging about work
- Free speech
- Joyce Park or Michael Tunison

### process

1. Divide the class into teams. Research the areas above and devise a scenario in which someone has complained about an employee blogging about a sensitive company issue, such as cleanliness at a food manufacturing facility.

2. Team members should assume the role of an employee or a human resources manager that represents each side of this scenario. Another team member can opt to be an arbitrator who would present an objective point of view for each character. To set the stage for the role-playing event, each team member should write a summary that provides background information for their role and that details their character's behaviors.

3. Team members should present their case to the class or submit a PowerPoint presentation for review, along with the summary and resolution they developed.

### conclusion

As technology becomes ever more prevalent and integrated into our lives, more and more ethical dilemmas will present themselves. Being able to understand and evaluate both sides of the argument, while responding in a personally or socially ethical manner, will be an important skill.

## Home Networking Guide

You write a newsletter, **The Everyday Technologist**, which specializes in technology tips and tricks for the casual everyday technology user. Your current newsletter is a guide to home networks. The basic document has been created, and now using Microsoft Word you need to add formatting and images to make the guide more visually appealing.

You will use the following skills as you complete this activity:

- Apply Text Effects
- Insert Word Art
- Insert Columns
- Insert Section Breaks

- Insert Column Break
- Insert Images
- Apply Text Wrapping
- Use Custom Margins

## Instructions

1. Open *TIA_Ch7_Start.docx*, and save as **TIA_Ch7_ LastFirst.docx**.

2. Select the title Home Networking Guide and convert the text to a **Word Art Object** using **Fill: Gold, Accent color 4; Soft Bevel**.

3. With the WordArt object still selected, click **Layout Options**, and select **Top and Bottom**. Then, click **See more** . . . at the bottom of the Layout Options window, and in the Layout dialog box, in the Horizontal section, select **Alignment**, and then choose **Centered** from the drop-down box.

4. Apply the **Fill: Blue, Accent Color 2, Shadow Text Effect** to the three headings: Hardware, Wireless vs. Wired, and Powerline Adapters. Increase the font size of each heading to 18.

5. Create **custom margins** so all margins are **.7"**.

6. Position the cursor before the heading Hardware. Insert a **Section Break (Continuous)**, and then apply **Two Column** formatting.

7. Place the cursor at the end of the second bullet point paragraph in the Hardware section. Insert the image *TIA_Ch7_ Modem Router.jpg*. Change the Layout Option of the image to **Square**. Resize the image so the height is **.9"** and the width is **1.2"**, then move the image so that the two top lines of the Router paragraph display above the image and the left side of the image is flush with the left margin.

8. Place the cursor at the beginning of the Powerline Adapters paragraph. Insert the image *TIA_Ch7_Powerline.jpg*. Change the Layout Option to **Tight**. Change the height of the image to **1"**, and then move the image so the right side is flush with the right margin of the document and centered vertically in the Powerline Adapter paragraph.

9. Place the cursor at the beginning of Current Wireless (Wi-Fi) Standards. Insert a **Column Break**. Format the heading with **Bold** and **Italics**.

10. Save and submit for grading.

# 8 Managing Your Digital Lifestyle: Challenges and Ethics

  For a chapter overview, watch the **Chapter Overview Videos**.

 **MyLab IT**   All media accompanying this chapter can be found here.

 Make This   A Video-Playing App on **page 296**

*(Kuroji/Fotolia, Tetra Image/Getty Images; Kevin Nixon/Future Music Magazine/Getty Images; olly/Fotolia; Sebastien Decoret/123rf; Jakub Jirsák/Fotolia; John Williams RUS/Shutterstock)*

# What do you think?

**Autonomous (self-driving) vehicles** are fast becoming a reality. Proponents of these vehicles tout the **increased levels of safety and decline of accidents** as AIs working together with each other will result in lower speeds for the same traffic volume and **better decision making than humans can achieve**. But it may take a while to achieve this Utopia.

Theoretically, having an AI make the same decisions based on the same set of circumstances should result in less accidents than relying on individual humans to make the best decisions in stressful situations. But **the AI is programmed by humans and therefore is subject to errors**. Also, automobiles operate in a very complex environment where many different things could happen at any time. Accidents (including fatalities) have occurred while testing the prototypes of autonomous vehicles. **Is it possible to program an AI to handle every possible situation it might encounter?**

And once autonomous vehicles are deemed sufficiently developed to be permitted on public roads, they won't suddenly replace all human-driven vehicles. Developers are concerned that human drivers may "bully" autonomous vehicles by driving aggressively (such as cutting them off in traffic), if they believe the autonomous vehicles' AI will always err on the side of caution. **Integrating autonomous vehicles onto our streets might be tougher than we first thought**.

 Which of the following statements do you agree with?

- *I'd never feel comfortable using a driverless car.*
- *I might feel comfortable putting my car in autonomous mode if I knew I could take control of it.*
- *Autonomous vehicles are safer than human drivers so I'd feel fine using a driverless car.*

*See the end of the chapter for a follow-up question.*

# The Impact of Digital Information

> **Learning Outcome 8.1** **You will be able to describe the nature of digital signals; how digital technology is used to produce and distribute digital texts, music, and video; and the challenges in managing a digital lifestyle.**

Do you realize how many revolutionary changes are happening in all kinds of media as we continue to use digital formats? The entertainment industry has become an all-digital field. The publishing, music, photography, and film industries have all seen radical changes in how content is created and distributed to an audience. In this section, we examine what digital really is and explore how digital technology has changed the production and distribution of media.

## Digital Basics

How did we end up in a world in which we're all connected to our devices and able to communicate with each other whenever and almost wherever we want? Part of the story relates to the concept of *digital convergence*, as we explore in this section.

### Digital Convergence and the Internet of Things

**Objective 8.1** *Describe how digital convergence and the Internet of Things have evolved.*

**What is digital convergence?** Digital convergence refers to our ability to use a single device to meet all of our media, Internet, entertainment, and phone needs. For example, you see digital convergence in the evolution of smartphones, which now let you do just about anything a computer can do. You can also see the push to digital convergence in the migration of digital devices into environments like the cabin of cars (see Figure 8.1a). In fact, devices are beginning to converge so much that an organization—the Digital Living Network Alliance (*dlna.org*)—exists to standardize them.

Even some refrigerators, like the one shown in Figure 8.1b, include LCD touch-screen displays and network adapters so that they can display recipes from websites as well as place a call to the service center and schedule their own repair visit for you. These devices are all a part of the so-called *Internet of Things*.

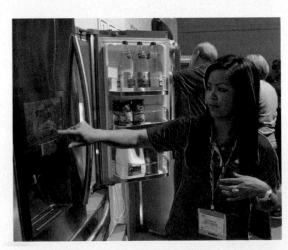

(a)

(b)

**Figure 8.1** (a) Auto electronics have now converged with tablet technology. The Tesla S features a 17-inch touch-screen display that controls all of the car's electronics systems, providing Internet access, mobile communications, and navigation features, including sensors that detect vehicles in your blind spot. (b) Some refrigerators are now equipped with touch screens that connect to the Internet. *(David Paul Morris/Bloomberg/Getty Images, Steve Marcus/Reuters/Alamy Stock Photo)*

## Figure 8.2 The Internet of Things

### The Things You Can Do

**Home entertainment.** The DVR is just for starters.

**Security cameras.** Watch your house with cameras in each room.

**Appliances.** Trigger or time any function, or set it to alert you.

**Security locks.** Let people into your home remotely.

**Lighting.** Turn lights on or off remotely, for hands-free safety.

**Smoke detector.** Get a fire alert on your phone.

**Thermostat.** Heat choices when you want, for energy savings.

**Irrigation.** Program lawn sprinklers for best times of the day.

2000

2004

2008

2012

2016

2020 (projected)

**Each "thing" on the Internet has its own unique address.**

It's called an IP (Internet Protocol) address. As more things people own will have IP addresses — not just computers and smart phones, but the above kinds of devices — there'll be more IP addresses assigned.

**This graph shows the number of things with an IP address, for each person on the planet (not just online).**

**That's how many IP addresses are used. So how many IP addresses *can there be*?**

Since the beginning of the internet, they've been using a method called IPv4: four clumps of digits, broken up with periods. That method let us have a total of

**4,294,967,296**

IP addresses, or about 1 for every 2 people on the planet (not just online) in 2016.

But soon, it was clear there were way too few combinations. So on June 16, 2012, they established IPv6, which is six clumps of digits.

With that new standard, the potential number of IP addresses is now

**340,282,366,920,938,463,463, 374,607,431,768,211,456**

...or, **over 45 octillion** ($45 \times 10^{27}$) for each person on the planet (not just online) in 2016.

← And we'll only use enough for **seven per person** by 2020! Think we'll run out, ever?

The Internet of Things (IoT) is defined as the interconnection of uniquely identifiable embedded computing devices that transfer data over a network without requiring human-to-human or human-to-computer interaction (see Figure 8.2). "Things" can be anything—machines, appliances, buildings, vehicles, even animals, people, plants, and soil. In addition to all the smart TVs, refrigerators, and thermostats we hear so much about, a thing can be a heart monitor implant that can warn of an oncoming problem or a device in an automobile that monitors driving behaviors so insurance companies can better assess risk. Ultimately, the Internet of Things is about connecting companies, people, and technology in real time via an extension of the Internet into the physical world. By the year 2020, there will be an estimated 30 billion connected devices.

As our appliances, cars, and homes become designed to communicate over a common network, how we manage our media, control our living spaces, and communicate with others will continue to change. Let's start by looking at the foundation for all our computing devices: digital signals.

# Digital versus Analog

**Objective 8.2** *Explain the differences between digital and analog signals.*

**What does it mean to be "digital"?** Any kind of information can be digitized—measured and converted to a stream of numerical values. Consider sound. It's carried to your ears by sound waves, which are actually patterns of pressure changes in the air. Images are our interpretation of the changing intensity of light waves around us. These sound and light waves are called analog waves or continuous waves. They illustrate the loudness of a sound or the brightness of the colors in an image at a given time. They're continuous signals because you would never have to lift your pencil off the page to draw them; they're just long, continuous lines.

First-generation recording devices such as vinyl records and analog television broadcasts were designed to reproduce these sound and light waves. A needle in the groove of a vinyl record vibrates in the same pattern as the original sound wave. Analog television signals are actually waves that tell an analog TV how to display the same color and brightness as is seen in the production studio.

However, it's difficult to describe a wave, even mathematically. The simplest sounds, such as that of middle C on a piano, have the simplest shapes, like the one shown in Figure 8.3a. However, something like the word *hello* generates a highly complex pattern, like the one shown in Figure 8.3b.

**What advantages do digital formats have over analog ones?** Digital formats describe signals as long strings of numbers. This digital representation gives us a simple way to describe sound and light waves exactly so that sounds and images can be reproduced perfectly any time they're wanted. In addition, we already have easy ways to distribute digital information, such as streaming movies or sending photos in a text message. Digital information can be reproduced exactly and distributed easily. These reasons give digital advantages over an analog format.

When the market for communication devices for entertainment media—like photos, music, and video—switched to a digital standard, we began to have products with new capabilities. Small devices can now hold huge collections of a variety of information. Users can create their own digital assets instead of just being consumers of digital media. We can interact with our information any time we like in ways that, prior to the conversion to digital media, had been too expensive or too difficult to learn. The implications of the shift to digital media are continually evolving.

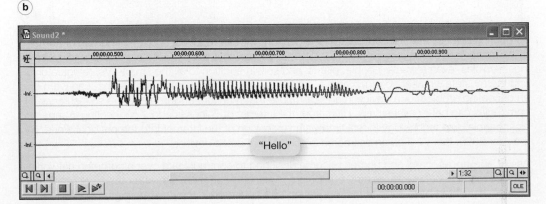

**Figure 8.3** (a) An analog wave showing the simple, pure sound of a piano playing middle C. (b) The complex wave produced when a person says "Hello." *(Courtesy of Microsoft Corp.)*

## Table 8.1  Analog versus Digital Entertainment

| | Analog | Digital |
|---|---|---|
| **Publishing** | Magazines, books | E-books, e-zines |
| **Music** | Vinyl record albums and cassette tapes | CDs, MP3 files, and streaming music stations |
| **Photography** | 35-mm single-lens reflex (SLR) cameras<br>Photos stored on film | Digital cameras, including digital SLRs<br>Photos stored as digital files |
| **Video** | 8-mm, VHS, and Hi8 camcorders<br>Film stored on tapes | HD digital video (DV) cameras<br>Film stored as digital files; distributed on DVD and Blu-ray discs and streamed |
| **Radio** | AM/FM radio | HD Radio, SiriusXM satellite radio |
| **Television** | Analog TV broadcast | High-definition digital television (HDTV), 4K Ultra HD (UHD) television |

**So how has digital impacted entertainment?** Today, all forms of entertainment have migrated to the digital domain (see Table 8.1).

Phone systems and TV signals are now digital streams of data. MP3 files encode digital forms of music, and cameras and video equipment are all digital. In Hollywood, feature films are shot with digital equipment. Movie theaters receive a hard drive storing a copy of a new release to show using digital projection equipment. Satellite radio systems such as SiriusXM and HD Radio are broadcast in digital formats.

**How is analog converted to digital?** The answer is provided by a process called *analog-to-digital conversion*. In analog-to-digital conversion, the incoming analog signal is measured many times each second. The strength of the signal at each measurement is recorded as a simple number. The series of numbers produced by the analog-to-digital conversion process gives us the digital form of the wave. Figure 8.4 shows analog and digital versions of the same wave. In Figure 8.4a, you see the original, continuous analog wave. You could draw that wave without lifting your pencil. In Figure 8.4b, the wave has been digitized and is no longer a single line; instead, it's represented as a series of points or numbers.

In the next sections, we discuss different types of digital media you interact with or create.

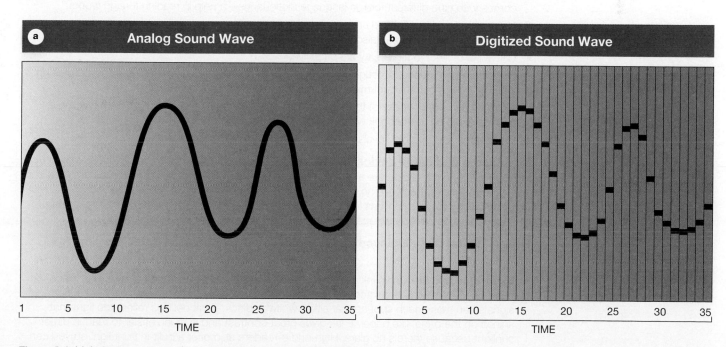

**Figure 8.4** (a) A simple analog wave. (b) A digitized version of the same wave.

# Digital Publishing

**Figure 8.5** e-Readers are popularizing the digital e-book.
*(Kristoffer Tripplaar/Alamy Stock Photo)*

The publishing industry is migrating to digital materials. How does this impact books?

## e-Readers

**Objective 8.3** *Describe the different types of e-readers.*

**Are printed books dead?** Electronic text (e-text) is textual information captured digitally so that it can be stored, manipulated, and transmitted by electronic devices. With the increasing usage of e-text, the market for printed materials is changing. In fact, Amazon now sells more Kindle e-books than printed books each year. Mainstream authors who traditionally relied on print publishing, such as Stieg Larsson and James Patterson, have each sold over 1 million e-books. John Locke, a self-published author, has also sold over 1 million e-books, giving hope to fledgling writers everywhere. But the conversion to digital books is not a 100% shift. Globally, e-books are now accounting for approximately 25% of total book sales.

**What electronic devices are trying to replace books?** e-Readers (see Figure 8.5) are devices that display e-text and have supporting tools, like note-taking, bookmarks, and integrated dictionaries. They're selling at a brisk pace with a range of offerings on the market, including versions of the Amazon Kindle and the Barnes & Noble NOOK.

Tablets, like the Amazon Fire, are also helping to popularize the e-book and electronic versions of magazines and newspapers. And while traditional print publishers' sales are falling (including their e-book sales), independently published e-book sales are rising at a fast pace.

**What features make digital text and e-readers popular?** One big allure of digital publishing is distribution. Even a 1,000-page book can be delivered to your e-reader in under a minute. An array of titles is available—over six million books in the Amazon Kindle store alone. In addition, millions of texts without copyright are available for free.

The basic features of e-readers offer many advantages over paper books:

- Integrated dictionaries pull up a definition when you highlight a word. The Kindle, for example, comes with nine different foreign language dictionaries—a help in reading foreign works.
- Note-taking and highlighting are supported, and you can search the text for your own notes or for specific terms. You can also share the notes you make with others.
- URL links or links to a glossary are often live.
- Bookmarks are pushed through cloud technology so you can read on one device and pick up with your most current bookmark on another.
- e-Books and audio books of the same title can be linked, so you can switch from reading a book to listening to the book without losing your place.
- For comics and graphic novels, you can magnify panels to read them fully.

**Do I need a dedicated device just for reading e-texts?** Free software download versions of the Kindle and the NOOK are available that run on either Windows or Apple computers. You can also download texts that have no copyrights and read them directly on a computer either as a PDF file or by using browser add-ons like MagicScroll Web Reader for Google Chrome. In fact, MagicScroll can display any web page in e-book format for easier reading.

**How is digital text displayed?** Two popular technologies are used for representing digital text:

- **Electronic ink:** Electronic ink (E ink) is a sharp grayscale representation of text. The "page" is composed of millions of microcapsules with white and black particles in a clear fluid. Electronic signals can make each spot appear either white or black. E ink devices reflect the light that shines on the page, like paper. E ink gives great contrast and is much easier to read in direct sunlight because there's no glare. High-end e-readers also offer a built-in front light so you can

(a)  (b)

**Figure 8.6** The two main technologies for e-text display are (a) E ink grayscale displays, like on the Amazon Kindle, and (b) high-resolution backlit color screens, like on the Amazon Fire. *(David McNew/Getty Images News/Getty Images, Oleksiy Maksymenko Photography/Alamy Stock Photo)*

read in any light. Examples of devices using E ink include the Amazon Kindle Paperwhite (see Figure 8.6a).

- **Backlit monitors:** Another option is the high-resolution backlit monitors seen in tablets like the Amazon Fire (see Figure 8.6b). These screens illuminate themselves instead of depending on room lighting. They display color materials, like magazines, with clarity. The glass does reflect glare, though, which makes them hard to use in direct sunlight. Some people experience more eye fatigue when reading from a backlit device than when using E ink. Also note that E ink readers have a battery life of a month or two on a charge, whereas high-resolution color readers hold a charge for 8 to 10 hours.

**What kinds of file formats are used in electronic publishing?** Digital formats for publishing vary. Amazon uses a proprietary format (.azw extension), so books purchased for a Kindle aren't transportable to a device that isn't running Kindle software. An open format, ePub, is also supported by some e-readers, and ePub reader extensions (plug-ins) exist for all major browsers, as well as stand-alone ePub reader apps.

## Using e-Texts

**Objective 8.4**  *Explain how to purchase, borrow, and publish e-texts.*

**Where do I buy e-books?** Many vendors are associated with e-reader devices:

- Amazon Kindle devices connect directly to the Amazon Kindle store.
- Barnes & Noble NOOK devices work with the Barnes & Noble e-bookstore.
- Many publishers sell e-books online that can be read on any kind of device.
- Textbooks can be purchased in e-book format directly from the publisher. Another option is a company like VitalSource, which offers subscriptions to digital texts. When the subscription ends, the book disappears from your device.

**What if I just want to borrow a book from a library?** Libraries now offer e-books and audio books (see Figure 8.7). There is never a late fee; the book just times out and disappears from your device when the borrowing period expires. Software like the Libby app (*libbyapp.com*) lets you search to find which area library has the book you want. Libraries have a specific number of copies of

▶ **Helpdesk**  **MyLab IT**

**Managing Digital Media**

In this Helpdesk, you'll play the role of a helpdesk staffer, fielding questions about e-readers and e-texts.

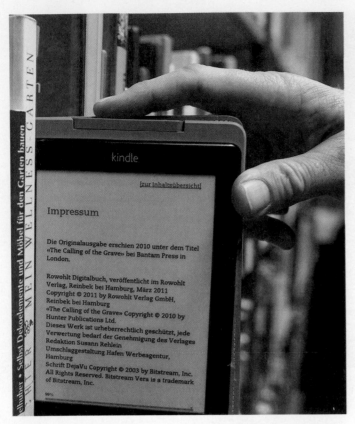

each e-book title available, so you may be added to a wait list if all the copies are checked out. However, friction exists between publishers and libraries on how to handle lending electronically. It's so convenient that some publishers are refusing to allow their e-books to be distributed through libraries.

**Can I borrow an e-book from a friend?** Lending of e-books is becoming a popular feature of e-reader systems. Both Barnes & Noble and Amazon support lending books for up to two weeks.

**Where can I find free e-books?** A great source of free reading is Project Gutenberg (*gutenberg.org*), a collection of over 57,000 free books in ePub, Kindle, and PDF format. It contains books that are free in the United States because their copyrights have expired. The catalog includes many classic titles like *Moby Dick* by Herman Melville or science fiction novels by H. G. Wells.

**How can I publish my own works?** Self-publishing is much easier in the age of digital texts. Many options are available:

- Self-publish into the Amazon Kindle Store in a matter of minutes and earn up to 70% royalty on sales. The Kindle Direct Publishing site (*kdp.amazon.com*) has information on self-publishing using the Kindle format.
- Use a company like Smashwords (*smashwords.com*). It accepts a Microsoft Word document from you and then makes your book available through many vendors like the Apple iBooks store and the Barnes & Noble e-store. Your book can also be distributed as an app to mobile marketplaces like Google Play or the Apple App Store.

**Figure 8.7** e-Books and audio books can be borrowed for free at most public libraries. *(Alex Ehlers/DPA/Picture-alliance/Newscom)*

- Use a site like Lulu (*lulu.com*) to learn about social media marketing and other techniques for promoting your book. In addition, it offers services from editors, designers, and marketers and can also allow you to offer your e-book for sale as a physical book.

# Digital Music

Digital music has upended the recording industry, with new models of distributing music, streaming services, and issues of copyright protection. In this section, we look at the mechanics of creating and distributing digital music.

## Creating and Storing Digital Music

**Objective 8.5** *Describe how digital music is created and stored.*

**How is digital music created?** To record digital music, the sound waves created by instruments need to be turned into a string of digital information. Figure 8.8 shows the process of digitally recording a song:

1. Playing music creates analog waves.
2. A microphone feeds the sound waves into a chip called an *analog-to-digital converter (ADC)* inside the recording device.
3. The ADC digitizes the waves into a series of numbers.
4. This series of numbers can be saved in a file and then recorded onto digital media or sent electronically.
5. On the receiving end, a playback device such as a mobile device or a DVD player is fed that same series of numbers. Inside the playback device is a *digital-to-analog converter (DAC)*, a chip that converts the digital numbers to a continuous analog wave.
6. That analog wave tells the receiver how to move the speaker cones to reproduce the original waves, resulting in the same sound as the original.

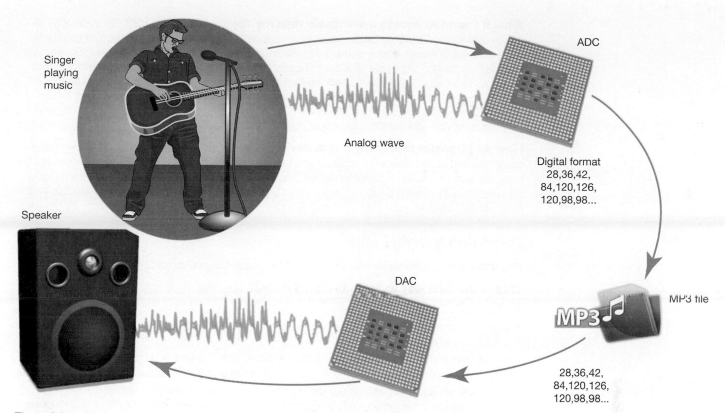

**Figure 8.8** During the complete recording process, information changes from analog form to digital data and then back again to analog sound waves.

More precisely, the digital wave will be *close* to exact. How accurate it is, or how close the digitized wave is in shape to the original analog wave, depends on the sampling rate of the ADC. The sampling rate specifies the number of times the analog wave is measured each second. The higher the sampling rate, the more accurately the original wave can be recreated. The improved sound quality higher sampling can afford also depends on the quality of the output device and speakers, of course. However, higher sampling rates also produce more data and therefore result in bigger files. For example, sound waves on CDs are sampled at a rate of approximately 44,000 times a second. This produces a huge list of numbers for even a single minute of a song.

**What file types store digital music?** You're no doubt familiar with the MP3 format used to store digital music, but many others exist, such as AAC and WMA. If you buy a song from the iTunes Store, for example, you receive an AAC-format file (although these files can be converted to other formats within iTunes). Many formats—such as DivX, MPEG-4 (which usually has an .mp4 extension), WMV, and Xvid—hold both video and audio information. All file formats compete on sound and video quality and *compression*, which relates to how small the file can be and still provide high-quality playback. Check what kind of files your audio device understands before you store music on it.

**How do I know how much digital media my device can hold?** The number of songs or hours of video your device can hold depends on how much storage space it has. Some mobile devices also use flash memory or SD cards storing from 2 to over 256 GB.

Another factor that determines how much music a player can hold is the quality of the MP3 files. The size of an MP3 file depends on the digital sampling of the song. The same song could be sampled at a rate anywhere between 64 kbps and 320 kbps. The size of the song file will be five times larger if it's sampled at 320 kbps rather than 64 kbps. The higher the sampling rate, the better quality the sound—but the larger the file.

**How do you control the size of an MP3 file?** If you're *ripping*, or converting, a song from a CD to a digital MP3 file, you can select the sampling rate yourself. You decide by considering what quality sound you want as well as how many songs you want to fit onto your device. For example, 1 GB of storage could hold about 700 minutes of music if you've ripped songs at 192 kbps. The same 1 GB could store three times as much music if it were sampled at 64 kbps.

**What if I want to access more music than my device has room for?** Some devices allow you to add storage capacity by purchasing removable flash memory or SD cards. You could also choose to use a service that streams the music to you over Wi-Fi or 3G/4G networks. Spotify, Google Play Music, and Apple Music are subscription services that let you listen to tracks in their catalogs. The music isn't yours to own, however—if you cancel your subscription, you no longer have access to the music. But because it's streamed to you, it doesn't take up space on your device. Some streaming services offer options that let you download music so that you can still play the songs on your playlist even if you don't have Internet access.

**How do I transfer files to my music device?** To move large volumes of data between your computer and music device, you can connect the devices using a USB port. Cloud services automatically push music to your mobile device. For example, when you purchase a song from iTunes, it's automatically pushed to all your registered iTunes devices—your Mac, your Windows computer (with iTunes installed), your iPad, and your iPhone.

## Distributing Digital Music

**Objective 8.6**   *Summarize how to listen to and publish digital music.*

**What's the best way to listen to digital music?** You have many options for listening to music other than with headphones:

- Many audio receivers come with a port or dock so you can connect a mobile device to them as an audio input source.
- Networked audio/video receivers have the hardware and software required to connect to your home network and use streaming services like Pandora or Spotify to play music (see Figure 8.9).
- New cars are equipped with an auxiliary input to the speaker system to support connecting a mobile device; others have a fully integrated software system (like Apple CarPlay) that displays and runs your playlists, connecting wirelessly to your device over Bluetooth.
- Systems like Sonos (see Figure 8.10) can mate wirelessly with a mobile device and broadcast sound throughout the house.

**If I don't pay for a music download, is it illegal?** Although you're required to pay for most music you download, some artists post songs for free. Business models are evolving as artists and recording companies try to meet audience needs while also protecting their intellectual property rights. Several approaches exist. One is to deliver *tethered downloads*, in which you pay for the music and own it but are subject to restrictions on its use. Another approach is to offer *DRM-free* music, which is music without any digital rights management (DRM). DRM is a system of access control that allows only limited use of material that's been legally purchased. It may be that the song can run only on certain devices or a movie can be viewed only a certain number of times. A DRM-free song can be placed on as many computers or players as you wish.

**Will streaming music services eliminate radio stations?** The Internet allows artists to release new songs to their fans (on sites such as SoundCloud) without relying on radio airtime. This opens up channels for artists to reach an audience and changes the amount of power radio stations have in the promotion of music. Many radio stations have increased listenership by making their stations available through Internet sites and by broadcasting in high-definition quality.

**Figure 8.9** Networked audio receivers can run Internet streaming services like Spotify and can connect to home servers.
*(Anton Mishchenko/123RF)*

**Figure 8.10** Sonos is a multi-room system that streams music wirelessly throughout your home.
*(Robert Schlesinger/DPA/Picture-alliance/ Newscom)*

**What if I want to publicize my band's music?** Digital music has made the distribution of recordings simple using sites like SoundCloud (*soundcloud.com*), CD Baby (*cdbaby.com*), and ReverbNation (*reverbnation.com*). You can quickly create a web page for your band, post songs, and start building a fan base through social media. ReverbNation sends you reports detailing who's listening to your music and what they're saying about it. ReverbNation is also a way to connect with independent recording labels and to find places that want to book your band.

**How can I get my band's music on streaming sites like Spotify?** Streaming sites usually use artist aggregators like TuneCore and CD Baby rather than dealing with independent artists. Once your music is uploaded to the aggregator, it can be made available to fans on streaming media services at no cost to you.

# Digital Media

Photography and video have also moved to digital formats, impacting the movie industry and creating new styles of visual performance.

## Digital Photography

**Objective 8.7** *Explain how best to create, print, and share digital photos.*

**What is analog photography?** Before digital cameras hit the market, most people used 35-mm single-lens reflex (SLR) cameras. When you take a picture using a traditional SLR camera, a shutter opens, creating an aperture (a small window) that allows light to hit the film inside. Chemicals coating the film react when exposed to light. Later, additional chemicals develop the image on the film, and it's printed on special light-sensitive paper. A variety of lenses and processing techniques, equipment, and filters are needed to create printed photos taken with traditional SLR cameras.

**What's different about digital photography?** Digital cameras don't use film. Instead, they capture images on electronic sensors called charge-coupled device (CCD) arrays and then convert those images to digital data, series of numbers that represent the color and brightness of millions of points in the image. Unlike traditional cameras, digital cameras allow you to see your images the instant you shoot them. Most camera models can now record digital video as well as digital photos. Images and video are usually stored on flash memory cards in the camera.

**Don't most people use the camera on their smartphone to take photos?** For casual photos, the answer is yes. The cameras on smartphones have improved significantly in resolution. But for taking high-quality photos, phone cameras fall short because they often employ smaller image sensors and inferior lenses compared to stand-alone cameras. In addition, many features that serious photographers rely on aren't available in smartphone cameras, such as different types of autofocus and image stabilization algorithms. So, if you're a serious amateur photographer or want to sell your work, invest in a digital stand-alone camera.

**How do I select a digital camera?** If you want a stand-alone digital camera, you have a number of camera models from which to choose. Some digital cameras are *fixed-lens cameras*, meaning they come with one lens that you can't change. However, digital SLRs let you switch among different lenses, as shown in Figure 8.11.

In addition to allowing you to switch lenses, the size of the image sensor that actually captures the light is critical. Larger sensors demand larger cameras and lenses. Professional digital SLR cameras use a full-frame sensor, whereas smartphones use a compact sensor and use a wider-angle lens to capture the full scene, making them less powerful.

**Figure 8.11** Digital SLR cameras can accommodate a range of separate auto-focus lenses. *(B@rmaley/ Fotolia)*

Although having such flexibility in selection of lenses and a larger sensor are great advantages, most digital SLR cameras are larger, heavier, and use more battery power than fixed-lens models. Think about how you'll be using your camera and decide which model will serve you best. One resource is Digital Photography Review (*dpreview.com*), a site that compares cameras (including those in phones) and provides feedback from owners.

**What determines the quality of a digital image?** The overall image quality is determined by many factors:

- Lens quality
- Image sensor size
- File format and compression used
- Color management software included
- The camera's resolution

A digital camera's resolution, or the number of data points it records for each image captured, is measured in megapixels (MP). The word *pixel* is short for *picture element*, which is a single dot in a digital image. Point-and-shoot models typically offer resolutions from 12 to 20 MP. Professional digital SLR cameras, such as the Canon EOS 5DS, can take photos at resolutions as high as 50.6 MP.

If you're interested in making only 5" × 7" or 8" × 10" prints, a lower-resolution camera is fine. However, low-resolution images become grainy and pixelated when pushed to larger sizes. For example, if you tried to print an 11" × 14" enlargement from an 8 MP image taken using your smartphone camera, you'd see individual dots of color instead of a sharp image. The 16- to 24-MP cameras on the market have plenty of resolution to guarantee sharp images even with enlargements as big as 11" × 14".

**What file formats are used for digital images?** Digital cameras let you choose from several file types in order to compress the image data into less memory space. When you choose to compress your images, you'll lose some of the detail, but in return you'll be able to fit more images on your flash card. The most common file types supported by digital cameras are raw uncompressed data (RAW) and Joint Photographic Experts Group (JPEG):

- *RAW files* have different formats and extensions, depending on the camera manufacturer. The RAW file records all the original image information, so it's larger than a compressed JPEG file.
- *JPEG files* can be compressed just a bit, keeping most of the details, or compressed a great deal, losing some detail. Most cameras let you select from a few JPEG compression levels.

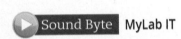

**Enhancing Photos with Image-Editing Software**

In this Sound Byte, you learn tips on how to best use image-editing software. You learn how to remove red eye from photos and how to incorporate borders, frames, and other enhancements.

Often, cameras also support a very low-resolution option that produces images that aren't useful for printing but are so small that they're easy to e-mail or download quickly. Low-resolution images are often used on mobile-friendly websites because the expectation is that the images will be viewed on smaller screens and need to download quickly to save on data.

**What's the best way to transfer photos from my stand-alone camera to my computer?** Most cameras support wireless connections so you can transfer images without connecting cables. If that isn't available, you can connect the camera to your computer through a USB port or transfer the flash card from your camera directly to a built-in memory card reader on your computer.

**How do I share my photos?** You've probably shared photos on Snapchat or Instagram. Both iOS and Android have photo-sharing features that provide access to photos or video you capture from your devices. iCloud Photo Sharing is an option within Apple's iCloud storage that allows you to organize photos and videos into albums and share them. Google Photos (*photos.google.com*) is an even better option. The Google Photos app (available for Android, iOS, Windows, and macOS) automatically uploads photos from your device to the Google Photos website and syncs them to all your other devices. From the website, you can easily share photos. This is especially handy when you upgrade to new devices because you can maintain access to all the images captured with your old devices.

**Can I make my old photos digital?** You can use an all-in-one printer, which contains a flat-bed scanner, to turn your old photos into digital files. If lower resolution is acceptable, scanning apps are available that use your phone camera. Most scanner software lets you store the converted images as TIFF files or in compressed JPEG files. Some scanners include hardware that lets you scan film negatives or slides as well, or even insert a stack of photos to be scanned in sequence.

**What are the best options for printing digital photos?** If you want to print photos, you have two main options:

1. **Use a photo printer.** The most popular and inexpensive ones are inkjet printers. Some inkjet printers can print high-quality color photos, although they vary in speed, quality, and features. Dye-sublimation printers are another option for printing only photos. However, some models print only specific sizes, such as 4" × 6" prints, so be sure the printer you buy fits your needs.

2. **Use a photo-printing service.** Most photo-printing labs, including film-processing departments at stores such as Target, offer digital printing services. The paper and ink used at these labs are higher quality than what's available for home use and produce heavier, glossier prints that won't fade. You can send your photos directly to local merchants such as CVS for printing using the merchant's websites that allow uploading from your device or Facebook. Online services, such as Flickr (*flickr.com*), store your images and allow you to create hard-copy prints, greeting cards, photo books, calendars, and gifts (like mugs and T-shirts).

## Digital Video

**Objective 8.8**  *Describe how to create, edit, and distribute digital video.*

**What devices, sites, and other sources provide digital video content?** Digital video surrounds us:

- Television is broadcast in digitally formatted signals.
- The Internet delivers digital video through YouTube, communities like Vimeo (*vimeo.com*), and webcasting sites like IBM Cloud Video (*video.ibm.com*).
- Many pay services are available to deliver digital video. These include on-demand streaming from Internet providers, iTunes, Netflix, Hulu, and Amazon.

**How do I record my own digital video?** Although you can buy dedicated digital camcorders to record digital video, most smartphones now record HD video. Webcams (integrated into laptops) also work as inexpensive devices for creating digital video. You can transfer video files to your computer and, using video-editing software, edit the video at home. You can write your final product to a disc or upload it to a web-based video channel.

**What if I decide to add special effects and a soundtrack?** Video-editing software such as Adobe Premiere presents a storyboard or timeline you can use to manipulate your video file, as shown in Figure 8.12. You can review your clips frame by frame or trim them at any point. You can add titles, audio tracks, and animations; order each segment on the timeline; and correct segments for color balance, brightness, or contrast. Examine online tutorial resources such as Izzy Video podcasts (*izzyvideo.com*) and No Film School (*nofilmschool.com*) to learn how to make the most impact with the editing and effects you apply to your video footage.

**What kinds of files will I end up with?** Once you're done editing your video, you can save or export it in a variety of formats. Table 8.2 shows some of the popular video file formats in use, along with their file extensions.

Your choice of file format for your video will depend on what you want to do with it. For example, the QuickTime streaming file format is a great choice if your file is large and you plan to post it on the Web. The Microsoft AVI format is a good choice if you're sending your file to a wide range of users because it's the standard video format for Windows and is recognized by most popular free media players used in Windows 10 like 5KPlayer and GOM Player.

Different compression algorithms will have different results on your particular video. Try several to see which one does a better job of compressing your file. A codec (compression/decompression) is a rule, implemented in either software or hardware, that squeezes the same audio and video information into less space. Some information will be lost using compression, and there are several different codecs to choose from, each claiming better performance than its competitors. Commonly used codecs include MPEG-4, H.264, and DivX. There's no one codec that's always superior—a codec that works well for a simple interview may not do a good job compressing a live-action scene.

**What's the quickest way to get my video out to viewers?** Webcasting, or broadcasting your video live to an audience, is a simple option. Use either your phone or a compact camera

**Figure 8.12** Adobe Premiere allows you to build a movie from video clips (and still photos) and add soundtracks and special effects. *(Courtesy of Adobe Premiere)*

like a GoPro (see Figure 8.13) and apps like Meerkat and Periscope to stream live video. Snapchat Stories is also a popular option for distributing casual videos. These apps have features like interactive chat next to the video feed so viewers can interact with you while you're live. On many apps, both the chat and video can be captured and archived for viewers who missed the live broadcast.

### Table 8.2 Typical File Formats for Digital Video

| Format | File Extension | Notes |
|---|---|---|
| QuickTime | .qt<br>.mov | You can download the QuickTime player without charge from *apple.com/quicktime*. The Pro version allows you to build your own QuickTime files. |
| Moving Picture Experts Group (MPEG) | .mpg<br>.mpeg<br>.mp4 | The MPEG-4 video standard was adopted internationally in 2000; it's recognized by most video player software. |
| Windows Media Video | .wmv | This is a Microsoft file format recognized by Windows Media Player (included with the Windows OS). |
| Microsoft Video for Windows | .avi | This is a Microsoft file format recognized by Windows Media Player (included with the Windows OS). |

You can upload to video-sharing sites like YouTube or Vimeo. Of course, it's illegal for you to upload videos you don't own. You also can't take a piece of a copyrighted video and post it publicly. The second part of this chapter presents legal and ethical situations that are important for you to be aware of as a content creator in the digital age.

**How is HD different from "plain" digital?** HD stands for high definition. It's a standard of digital television signal that guarantees a specific level of resolution and a specific *aspect ratio*, the ratio of the width of an image to its height. For example, an aspect ratio of 16:9 might mean an image is 16" wide and 9" high. A 1080p HDTV displays 1,920 vertical lines and 1,080 horizontal lines of video on the screen, which is over six times as many pixels as a standard-definition TV. The popular standard, UHDTV (ultra-high-definition television), is also known as 4K or 2160p. A 2160p UHDTV has a resolution of 3840 × 2160 pixels. The aspect ratio used is 16:9 in both formats, which makes the screen wider than it is tall, giving it the same proportions as the rectangular shape of a movie screen (see Figure 8.14). This allows televisions to play movies in widescreen format instead of "letterboxing" the film with black bars on the top and bottom. Another format is starting to become available: 8K. Featuring resolution of 7680 × 4320 pixels, it might eventually overtake 4K as the popular standard.

**Figure 8.13** Compact cameras like the GoPro are small enough to make them part of any activity. *(Cyrus McCrimmon/The Denver Post/ Getty Images)*

**Figure 8.14** (a) Standard-definition TV has a more "square" aspect ratio, whereas (b) HDTV and UHDTV matches the 16:9 ratio used in the motion picture industry without the need for (c) letterboxing. *(Dmitry Pichugin Shutterstock)*

Some companies routinely generate valuable digital assets. Managing these assets to ensure they're being properly monetized is now a full-time job. *Digital asset management (DAM)* is an up-and-coming field for media-savvy graduates.

The creative industries were the first to realize they needed DAM. Photographers and graphic designers generate a tremendous amount of content in various formats. Images may need to be saved in different file formats and at different resolutions. The rights granted to third parties for the use of images needs to be tracked. Creation of new digital assets needs to be managed.

However, many other businesses realize the need for DAM as they roll out cohesive brand strategies that need consistency in imagery both on the Web and in printed media. Organizing,

cataloging, tracking, and sharing image and video files are often done with DAM software, such as Webdam and Libris.

So what skills does it take to become a digital asset manager? Obviously, an understanding of the creation process of digital assets is the first step. Experience managing projects and workflows is also important. The ability to work well with different types of people in the creative, IT, and marketing departments is also a plus. And because many assets are created with Adobe Creative Cloud products, experience with these software packages would make your transition into the job much easier.

So, if you enjoy working with digital content creators and have the ability to organize complex workflows, your next job might just be a lot of DAM fun.

**What types of connectivity are provided on modern TV sets?** A typical HDTV or UHDTV set has multiple HDMI connectors, allowing game consoles, Blu-ray players, computing devices, and cable boxes to be connected and to produce the highest-quality output. HDMI is a single cable that carries all the video and audio information.

You can also connect your devices to your TV wirelessly. Roku, Apple TV, Amazon Fire TV, and Google Chromecast let you view content from your device or stream content from the Internet on the big screen without connecting cables.

**Can I record the digital video that comes over my TV?** A variety of digital video recorders (DVRs) are available, provided by cable companies and independent vendors. You can also install personal video recording (PVR) software on your computer. Programs like Kodi (*kodi.tv*), an open-source software media center, let you use your computer to view the program guide, select shows to record, and then watch them from anywhere you have Internet access. Unlike Netflix or other streaming services, Kodi doesn't include content; rather, it depends on sources of free content or content from services you may already have.

**Can I get digital video to watch on my portable device?** Most cable providers have apps, like FiOS TV to Go from Verizon, that facilitate watching TV shows on your mobile devices. Most DVR units let you transfer recorded shows to files on your PC and format them for viewing on a mobile device. Devices like Slingbox take the video from your TV and broadcast it to you over the Internet. With Slingbox, you can be in another room, or another country, and control and watch your home TV on your laptop or smartphone (see Figure 8.15).

**Figure 8.15** Slingbox can send your digital television content to your tablet, notebook, or phone, wherever you may be. *(Handout/MCT/Newscom)*

## Managing Your Digital Lifestyle

As technology has become more integrated into our daily lives, we continue to face challenges of seamlessly using technology and protecting our privacy. In this section, we discuss some of the challenges faced in managing an active digital lifestyle.

# Digital Challenges and Dilemmas

**Objective 8.9**  *Discuss the challenges in managing an active digital lifestyle.*

### Keeping Data (and Conversations) Private

**What are some challenges presented by technology being so integral to our lives?**
We interact with the IoT—knowingly and sometimes unknowingly—in many aspects of our lives.
As we become more connected to the Internet through our vast array of devices, we also become
part of the information infrastructure, each of us essentially acting as nodes on the IoT. Although
the interconnectivity of the IoT brings with it many benefits, it also poses ethical concerns, including
those related to privacy and equal access.

**What privacy issues are raised by participation in the IoT?** As we use our Internet-connected devices, we generate huge amounts of data. Many organizations are acquiring and using that data to help with decision making, resource allocation, and operations.
Although we may be used to having Internet advertisers take our search data and send us
targeted advertising, how would you feel about companies using information gleaned from
an IoT-connected device? For example, say you wear a fitness tracker, such as a Fitbit or an
Apple Watch. The sensors in these activity monitors are connected wirelessly to smartphones
and to the Internet to enable users to track their workout activities. How would you feel if the
data collected by your Fitbit or Apple Watch was then shared by your mobile phone carrier with
a third-party marketer? How would you feel if you were in a restaurant or grocery store and
received text messages providing discounts or coupons for low-calorie offerings from those
third-party marketers, simply because your behavior implied that weight loss is one of your
goals? Although some might welcome these opportunities, others might consider the offerings
an invasion of their privacy.

Also consider the digital assistants (like Alexa) being deployed in IoT devices like the Amazon
Echo (see Figure 8.16). Some privacy advocates have voiced concerns about privacy being
invaded when the digital assistants are "listening" a nd possibly storing conversations. Glitches
in the devices have occurred. For example, a woman's conversations were secretly recorded by
her device and then sent to a random person in another city. Reports of Amazon Echos randomly
laughing have been attributed to a fault in the listening software, but eerie occurrences like these
don't exactly give comfort that our privacy is being safeguarded.

**How does the IoT raise issues of equal access?** The Internet of Things also adds to the
ethical dilemma of the *digital divide*—the technological gap between those who can and cannot
afford to own these devices. At the very core of the dilemma is the ability for users to access the
Internet at all. Significant work has been done to provide developing countries with access to
the Internet. But now, the IoT adds new considerations, not only discriminating against certain
groups of people who do not have access to the Internet but also those who cannot afford IoT
devices. There have been discussions about providing free nationwide wireless Internet access
to bridge this gap, but the creation and delivery of that type of service is complicated and
fraught with political and corporate debate, preventing any type of public access anytime soon.

**Is anything being done to protect our privacy?** Fortunately, states are beginning to realize
that consumers need their data to be protected from misuse. In June 2018, California became
the first state to pass a sweeping data protection law
that takes effect in January 2020. Until this point,
there have been very few laws enacted in the United
States that protect consumer data that is gathered by companies. Under this law, consumers are
granted the right to be informed about the data that
companies are collecting about them, the reasons
the data is being collected, and with whom the company is sharing the data. California consumers now
gain the right to force companies to delete the information gathered about them as well as the option
to prevent the sharing and selling of their data. The
law also restricts the collection and sharing of information about children under age 16. Although this
is not quite as stringent as laws enacted in Europe,
it is expected that this law will be a model for laws
passed in other states.

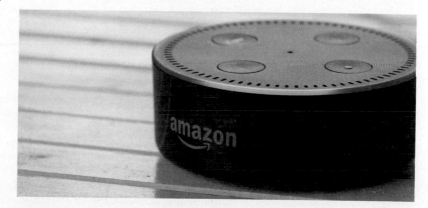

**Figure 8.16** Digital assistants are standing by for our queries, but are they listening
when we don't expect them to be? *(Mahathir Mohd Yasin/Shutterstock)*

**Deep Web versus Dark Web: Are There Places You Shouldn't Go?**

Just as in real life, there are places on the Internet you just shouldn't go because they can be dangerous! But let's separate fact from fiction regarding the so-called Deep Web and Dark Web.

You are probably in and out of different areas of the Deep Web every day even though you don't realize it. The **Deep Web** is any part of the Internet that you can't find by using a search engine. This would be any areas that are gated off from the open Internet, such as areas protected by a password (such as your bank account) or a paywall (content available on Netflix by subscription). Anything that is not located on the "surface" of the Internet (easily found by an unrestricted URL) is considered in the Deep Web.

Obviously, there is nothing scary about accessing your bank account, but you certainly wouldn't want it laying around on the surface of the Web where anyone could see it. We need secure areas of the Web to protect sensitive information from unauthorized access, hence the Deep Web. Unfortunately, people often confuse the Deep Web with the Dark Web, even incorrectly using these terms interchangeably. While there is nothing scary about the Deep Web, the Dark Web can be extremely frightening. The **Dark Web** (see Figure 8.17) is actually part of the Deep Web; however, it is a very well-concealed part of it. You can't locate the Dark Web through a search engine and you can't even access it with a regular web browser. Consider it analogous to the back room at a seedy bar where an illegal gambling game is being played. It is definitely not someplace you want to explore.

The Dark Web consists of anonymously hosted websites that are mostly used for illegal activities or by people who are very concerned about privacy. In most countries it is not illegal to surf the Dark Web, but many of the activities you can engage in on Dark Web sites (like buying and selling drugs) are definitely illegal. Criminals prefer the security of the Dark Web because most sites on it use sophisticated encryption tools like Tor or Freenet. You need special tools to find the Dark Web and use the sites on it. So fortunately, you won't stumble onto the Dark Web accidentally.

One app used to access the Dark Web is the **Tor (The Onion Router) Browser**, which allows you to locate hidden websites in the

**Figure 8.17** The Dark Web is mostly used for illegal activities. Fortunately, you won't stumble into the Dark Web accidentally! *(Leo Lintang/123RF)*

**.onion** domain. The name is a play on the structure of an onion that has layers that can be peeled away, reminiscent of the layers of security on the Dark Web. Estimates are that the Tor Browser is used less than 6% of the time to access the Dark Web. Most users of Tor are using it to surf the surface Web anonymously because of its many security features. Unfortunately, these layers of security come at a price: the Tor Browser tends to provide much slower response times than conventional browsers.

The interfaces on the Dark Web remind some users of the early days on the Internet. Sites are simple and unsophisticated. Sites often go down or disappear altogether. It can also be difficult to navigate the Dark Web. Although you won't have search engines to help you navigate, directories on the Dark Web such as the Hidden Wiki maintain lists of sites.

So, we need the Deep Web to protect personal privacy and proprietary assets on the Internet. The Dark Web we could certainly do without—and it's an excellent place to avoid. Although you can use the Tor Browser to protect your privacy when surfing the surface Web, other tools such as VPNs provide protection without sacrificing response speed.

### Cryptocurrency: Should You Use It?

**What is cryptocurrency?** In Chapter 3 we introduced cryptocurrency (also called virtual, cyber, or digital currency). Cryptocurrency attempts to eliminate intermediaries or banks to conduct transactions, thus enabling direct anonymous transactions between users. Payments are sent peer-to-peer from the payee to the recipient without the need to supply personal information; therefore, it is an anonymous way to send money. The "currency" is not U.S. dollars or Euros, but a new currency specifically created for the purpose of making payments. Bitcoin is the most well-known cryptocurrency, but many other types exist, such as Litecoin, Ethereum, Zcash, Dash, Ripple, and Monero (see Figure 8.18).

**What makes cryptocurrency different from regular currencies?** Unlike regular currencies, cryptocurrencies are not under the regulation of governments nor are they issued by central banks of governments. However, cryptocurrencies still function like regular currency as you can use them to pay for goods and services wherever a particular cryptocurrency is accepted. Also, you can make cryptocurrency payments anonymously. Not having to reveal details of your identity during a transaction makes it virtually impossible for identity theft to occur. This also makes transactions quicker to process.

**If banks aren't involved, how are cryptocurrency transactions tracked?** The time and amount of every finalized cryptocurrency transaction is kept on a massive public online ledger known as a blockchain. The public nature of the blockchain makes it difficult for cryptocurrency transactions to be manipulated by anyone. Unlike traditional banks and financial institutions that tend to keep transactions relatively private, the blockchain ledger is much more transparent to users and forms the permanent record of a particular cryptocurrency's transactions.

**Where do you store cryptocurrency?** If you want to hold and spend cryptocurrency, you must create a digital wallet, which stores the information needed to complete cryptocurrency transactions. There are two types of wallets: *hot wallets* and *cold wallets*. Hot wallets are digital wallets that are constantly connected to the Internet. Cold wallets are disconnected from the Internet. A hot wallet is analogous to a checking account: you keep small amounts of money in it for making purchases. A cold wallet is more like a savings account, where you keep most of your money safe and secure. Cold wallets are much safer than hot wallets because disconnection from the Internet means hackers can't get to your cryptocurrency.

**Figure 8.18** Although cryptocurrencies like Bitcoin and Ethereum are proliferating, they still have some major disadvantages of which users need to be aware.
*(Steven Heap/123RF)*

---

Wearable technology, as its name indicates, is technology incorporated into things you wear. The devices become a part of your personal area network (PAN) as they transfer data via Bluetooth to a mobile app or your computer. Popular wearable devices include fitness trackers, such as those from Garmin and Fitbit, and interactive digital fabrics, such as Athos Gear, which have built-in sensors that monitor specific activity as well as your heart rate while you're working out. In addition to health and fitness monitoring, some wearable devices, such as the Apple Watch, let you connect to your e-mail and calendar, among other personal productivity tools (see Figure 8.19). The medical industry is also implementing wearable devices, such as those used to monitor cardiac patients for heart rate and blood pressure. Nearly 50% of American adults already own some form of a wearable device, and the trend is increasing at a remarkable rate. Do you have any wearable technology as a part of your PAN?

**Figure 8.19** Smartwatches are a form of wearable technology that can monitor your activity and let you connect to personal productivity tools like your e-mail and calendar, as well as sync to your mobile device.
*(DMstudio House/Shutterstock)*

**Why isn't cryptocurrency in more widespread use?** Anonymous, fast, and secure—what could be better? As good as it sounds, there are still disadvantages to cryptocurrency:

- **You can't reverse transactions.** Although a benefit for payees who are ensured their money, this is a drawback for payors.
- **Loss of wallet means loss of currency.** If your digital wallet is inadvertently lost or destroyed, your currency is gone.
- **No insurance.** Unlike deposits in banks, your deposits with cryptocurrency exchanges are not protected. Cryptocurrency exchanges have been hacked, so your money could be lost.
- **Value fluctuates.** Unlike standard currencies whose values tend to remain relatively stable, cryptocurrency values can fluctuate wildly.
- **Its largely unregulated.** Therefore consumers have very little protection and recourse if something goes amiss.
- **Not widely accepted.** Most merchants do not accept cryptocurrency at this point.

Until some of these disadvantages are mitigated, you should exercise caution when using or investing in any cryptocurrency.

### Streaming Media: Where Should I Buy It?

Until recently, most people in the United States bought their television media from cable television providers. But with the proliferation of streaming media companies, cable TV companies are becoming less popular than they once were. Many people are "cutting the cord" and opting out of cable television altogether.

**What does "cutting the cord" mean?** Cutting the cord refers to dropping cable television service and obtaining television programs a different way (Figure 8.20). There are some straightforward steps you can follow to arrive at your own cord-cutting strategy.

Step 1 is to assess how you watch TV. Do you mostly watch television at home on a TV set or do you prefer to watch television on your portable computing devices? Step 2, if you like to use mobile devices, is to assess your data plan with your phone provider.

**Figure 8.20** Many people save money by "cutting the cord" and replacing cable television services with Internet streaming services. *(Kristin Chiasson/Shutterstock)*

**What size data plan should I buy?** Before subscribing to or changing a data plan, you should assess your needs. When you are out of reach of a Wi-Fi network, how often do you:

- download apps, stream music, or play online games?
- watch streaming video?
- download files attached to e-mails or from a website?
- use apps that are communicating with the Internet?

Begin by estimating how much data you transfer up and down from the Internet each month. To do so, you can use an online estimator supplied by your provider like the one shown in Figure 8.21.

The Android OS allows you to see a graph of your data usage and set alarms at specific levels. iOS keeps track of your cellular data usage too. This feature resets automatically each month so you know how much data transfer you have left. Most mobile operating systems keep track of data usage for you.

Be sure you select a data plan that provides adequate service at a good price. There are plans that allow a group of people to share data and pull from a single pool. Some plans transfer unused data over to the next month, some do not. Shop carefully.

**What should I do to watch TV at home on a television without cable?** Step 3 in your cord-cutting strategy is to buy a digital TV antenna. These inexpensive antennas attach to the antenna port on your television and are designed to pick up the digital broadcast signals transmitted through the public airwaves. Depending on where you live, you may receive many television channels for free.

For step 4, assess your current television. If you have smart televisions, you can access television programming over your Internet connection without a cable TV subscription. If you have a TV that isn't "smart," an option is to attach a media streaming device (such as a Roku, Amazon Firestick, or

Google Chromecast) to your television. These devices, in conjunction with an Internet connection, allow you to receive streaming media from the Internet. Not all streaming media is free, but you may be able to save money by not subscribing to a standard cable TV package. Make a list of the channels that you watch regularly. There is no sense in subscribing to channels you rarely (or never) watch.

The final step is to decide which streaming services to subscribe to based on the channels you like to watch. There are many streaming services such as Netflix, Hulu, Amazon Prime, Crackle, Vudu, and YouTube, and all offer different channels and programming content. Make sure to check that your chosen options will work for you before canceling your cable TV subscription. And of course you may still need to get your Internet service from your cable provider.

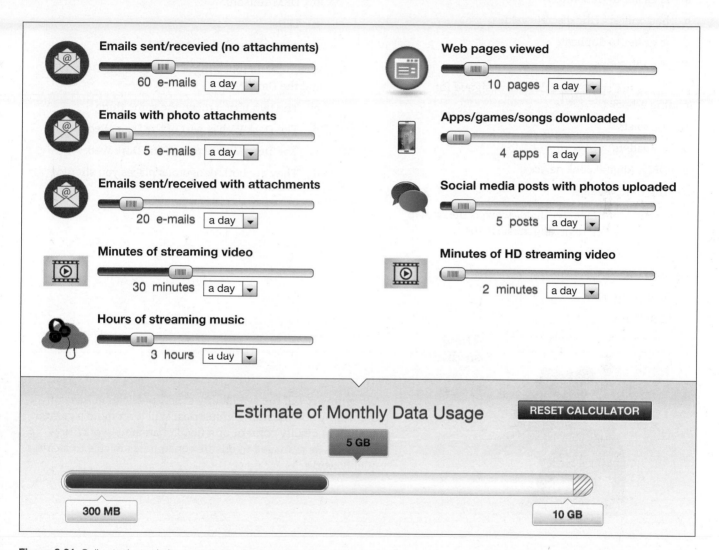

**Figure 8.21** Online tools can help you estimate your monthly data usage.

**Before moving on to Part 2:**

1.  ▶ Watch Chapter Overview Video 8.1.
2.  Then take the Check Your Understanding quiz.

# Check Your Understanding // Review & Practice

For a quick review to see what you've learned so far, answer the following questions.

## multiple choice

1. An analog signal is different from a digital signal because it
   a. is easier to transmit.
   b. has only specific discrete values.
   c. is easier to duplicate.
   d. is continuous.

2. _____ are specialized devices designed for reading e-books.
   a. e-Tablets
   b. e-Readers
   c. DBDs (digital book devices)
   d. Digitized readers

3. The number of times the analog wave is measured each second when digitizing music is the
   a. MP3 rate.
   b. bit rate.
   c. sampling rate.
   d. DRM rate.

4. Digital cameras capture images using
   a. digital film.
   b. DRM sensors.
   c. LEDs.
   d. charge-coupled device (CCD) arrays.

5. Which of the following is *true* about the Deep Web and the Dark Web?
   a. The two terms mean the same thing.
   b. The Dark Web is part of the Deep Web.
   c. The Deep Web is part of the Dark Web.
   d. They are both dangerous places you should avoid.

**chew on this**

What impact will the availability of self-publication have on the writing and recording industries? Will it promote a greater amount of quality content or a flood of amateur work? How could this be managed to ensure consumers are able to locate quality works?

**MyLab IT**  Go to **MyLab IT** to take an autograded version of the *Check Your Understanding* review and to find all media resources for the chapter.

> For the IT Simulation for this chapter, see MyLab IT.

# Try This

## Creating and Publishing a Movie

You've just taken some video and photos at the zoo, and you'd like to organize the media and put it on your YouTube channel. What should you do? In this Try This, we explore Ezvid. For more step-by-step instructions, watch the Chapter 8 Try This video in MyLab IT. Before starting, do the following:

1. Make sure you have video clips and photos available. If you don't have any, you can find free images and video clips at sites like *videezy.com*.

2. Download Ezvid, a free video editor, from *ezvid.com*. Click on the **Ezvid for Windows** link, then click the **Download** button. Once installed, type **Ezvid** in the search box to launch.

**Step 1** Click the **add pictures or video** button. In the dialog box that displays, browse to where your media files are saved, select the files you wish to import, and then click the **Open** button. The files you've selected will appear on the Media timeline.

**Step 2** Click and drag your media to the spot in the timeline where you want it to appear.

**Step 3** To create a text slide, click the **add text** button. In the dialog box that displays, type the text you want to appear; change the text color, background color, and font; and then click the **finish** button to add the text slide to your timeline. Click and drag the text slide where you want it to appear.

*(Courtesy of Ezvid)*

*(Courtesy of Ezvid)*

**Step 4** To adjust the length of time a piece of media displays, click the media and then adjust the width of the clip. Add a video title, description, and category in the appropriate boxes. Select a music track from the ones provided or use your own.

**Step 5** To preview your movie, click **Play**. When you're satisfied, click the **save video** button. If you start a new project or close Ezvid, your project will automatically be saved.

*(Courtesy of Ezvid)*

## A Video-Playing App

Do you want to run video clips inside your app?

In this exercise, you'll continue your mobile app development by using the Video Player component in App Inventor (or Thunkable) to run video clips inside your app. Using the component, you can play clips stored on your device, clips that you've recorded with the built-in camera, or clips on the Internet.

The Video Player has controls to pause, play, and fast forward or rewind and lets you manipulate the size of the video screen as well as the volume. So decide how you will make your applications more media-intensive using the Video Player component in App Inventor!

The Video Player component allows you to display video inside your app.

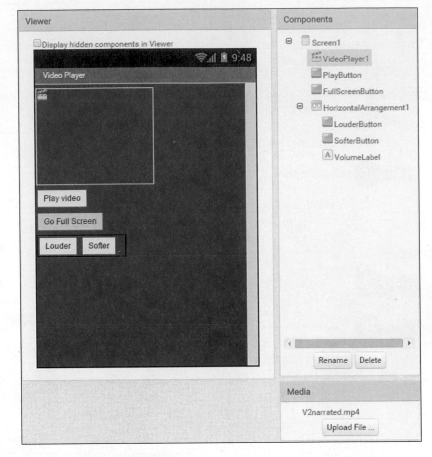

*(Copyright MIT, used with permission.)*

*(Copyright MIT, used with permission.)*

To create this app for iOS, go to *Thunkable.com*, a programming platform based on App Inventor.
**For the instructions for this exercise, go to MyLab IT.**

# Ethical Issues of Living in the Digital Age

**Learning Outcome 8.2**   **You will be able to describe how to respect digital property and use it in ways that maintain your digital reputation.**

In Part 1 of this chapter, you learned about ways to create digital assets. Unfortunately, the proliferation of the digital lifestyle has made it easier to misuse or misappropriate another's digital property. In the following sections, you learn how to protect your digital rights and how to avoid infringing on the rights of others.

## Protection of Digital Property

You can easily locate a picture of almost anything by searching Google Images. If you have to prepare a research paper on global warming, you can find millions of sources on the subject, including professionally written articles. Does that mean you can freely use all these resources you locate? No, you can't, because they're most likely someone else's property. Just as you wouldn't take someone's bike parked outside your dorm, you can't just take property you find on the Internet.

Property comes in two general types: real and personal. Real property is considered immoveable, such as land or a home, and it's often called *real estate*. Personal property, which is stuff you own, comes in two types: tangible and intangible. We're all familiar with tangible personal property, which is something that has substance like your smartphone or car. Intangible personal property can't be touched—or potentially even seen—yet it still has value. If someone steals your iPad, the action is easily recognizable as theft. However, what if someone tries to steal your ideas? This action moves into the realm of one of the biggest problems in cyberspace: the theft of intangible personal property or intellectual property.

## Intellectual Property

**Objective 8.10**   *Describe the various types of intellectual property.*

**What is intellectual property?** Intellectual property (IP) is a product of a person's mind and is usually considered an expression of human creativity. Examples of IP are books (or any type of writing), art, music, songs, movies (or any type of video), patents for inventions, formulas (or methods of production), and computer software. IP is considered intangible personal property.

It's important to distinguish intellectual property from the physical medium that carries it. A music CD is not IP. The music that is contained on a CD is the IP, whereas the CD itself is merely a delivery device. Likewise, a poem is IP, but the piece of paper on which it's written is not.

### Types of Intellectual Property

**How is intellectual property categorized?** IP is divided into five broad categories: *copyright*, *patents*, *trademarks*, *service marks*, and *trade dress*. Each category has its own laws of protection.

Copyright protection can be granted to creators of "original works of authorship." In the United States, copyrightable works include:

- Literary works, including computer software
- Musical works, including any accompanying words
- Dramatic works, including any accompanying music
- Pantomimes and choreographic works
- Pictorial, graphic, and sculptural works
- Motion pictures and other audiovisual works
- Sound recordings
- Architectural works

Patents grant inventors the right to stop others from manufacturing, using, or selling (including importing) their inventions for a period of 20 years from the date the patent is filed. Generally, patents aren't renewable but may be extended under certain circumstances.

A trademark is a word, phrase, symbol, or design—or a combination of these—that uniquely identifies and differentiates the goods of one party from those of another. A service mark is essentially the same as a trademark, but it applies to a service as opposed to a product. The Nike swoosh and McDonald's Golden Arches are trademarks, whereas the FedEx logo is a service mark.

Similar to a trademark, a *trade dress* applies to the visual appearance of a product or its packaging. The unique shape of the iconic Coca Cola bottle is an example of trade dress.

Most digital assets you create will be protected by copyright. In this section, we discuss the basic tenets of copyright and how it protects you.

## Copyright Basics

**Objective 8.11**  *Explain how copyright is obtained and the rights granted to the owners.*

**When does copyright protection begin?** Copyright begins when a work is created and fixed into a digital or physical form. For example, if you record a video of your cat, as soon as you save the video to your phone, the video is subject to copyright protection. There is no need for the video to be registered or even published for it to be protected by copyright.

**If I own copyright to a work I created, what exactly do I own?** Copyright holders own rights that grant them the ability to exclusively do things with the copyrighted work. U.S. law grants these rights to a copyright holder:

- **Reproducing the work.** Applies to copying the entire work or just part of the work. For instance, you might sell prints of one of your paintings on Etsy.
- **Preparing derivative works based on the original work.** This means developing any media based on the original work regardless of what form the original is in. *Iron Man* was originally a character in a Marvel comic book, but he now appears in movies and video games.
- **Distributing the work to the public.** This usually involves selling the work. However, the copyright holder could also loan, rent, or give away the work.
- **Public performance of the work.** This applies to any audiovisual work such as plays, movies, and songs. In the case of audio recordings, this also means digital audio transmission.
- **Public display of the work.** This right usually applies to works of art such as paintings, photographs, and sculptures, but this also includes posting images on the Internet.

Figure 8.22 shows ways you could capitalize on a video of your band that you created by exercising your rights granted by copyright.

**Can I copyright anything I create?** U.S. copyright law does not protect all ideas, but rather the *unique expression* of an idea. You can't copyright common phrases, such as "bad boy" or "good girl"; discoverable facts, such as water boils at 212 degrees Fahrenheit; or old proverbs, such as "To err is human, to forgive divine." However, you can copyright a creative twist on the proverb, such as the one in Figure 8.23.

Generic settings and themes of a story also can't be copyrighted. J. R. R. Tolkien wrote *The Lord of the Rings* trilogy, which is about a person who overcomes hardships to save the world from an evil being. In an e-book or video game you create, you're not allowed to use the same characters and plot lines Tolkien used, but you could write about the basic idea of a lone individual overcoming the forces of evil.

**How long does copyright last?** Current U.S. law grants copyright for the life of the author (creator) plus 70 years for original works. After you die, any copyrights you own are transferred to your heirs. Therefore, if you write a best-selling e-book in 2022 and die in 2092, your heirs can continue to earn money from the book until the year 2162.

**Figure 8.22 Exercising Your Rights with a Video of Your Band**

**Public Performance**

- Post the video on YouTube

**Reproduction**

- Burn DVDs

**Distribution to the Public**

- Sell DVDs at your concerts

**Derivative Work**

- Capture audio tracks from the video soundtrack

**Public Display**

- Place a still image from the video on a poster

(Ipopba/Fotolia, Denis Dryashkin/Fotolia, Pixelrobot/Fotolia, Djvstock/Fotolia, Log88off/Fotolia)

**Figure 8.23** You can copyright this clever twist on an old proverb.
(Quote by Tim Falconer)

**Can rights to a copyrighted work be sold?** Rights can be sold or granted for free to various individuals or entities in perpetuity or for a limited time. For instance, if your band is going to appear at a bar, you might grant the bar owner the right to play your band video in his bar for a specific period of time leading up to your performance. Or, you might grant the right to produce and sell DVDs of your performance to a distributor such as CD Baby (*cdbaby.com*).

**If I work for a company and develop intellectual property, do I own it?** The answer to this question depends on the terms of your employment contract. *Works made for hire* or *works of corporate authorship* occur when a company or person pays you to create a work and the company or person owns the copyright when it's completed. Most companies in which IP is developed require employees to sign agreements that any IP developed while working for the company becomes the company's property.

**Is buying a copyrighted work the same as buying the copyright?** Usually you only buy a physical or digital copy, not the actual copyright. When you buy software, usually what you've purchased is a license to install the software and use it on a specific number of devices. When you purchase music, you've bought the right to listen to the music in a private setting, such as on your phone. When you download a movie or subscribe to Netflix, again you've purchased the right to view the content privately.

However, buying copyrighted works is covered by a rule of law known as the *first sale doctrine*. You have the right to sell, lend, give away, or otherwise dispose of the item you purchase. This principle gives you the right to sell your book to another student at the end of the semester.

**Are all works protected by copyright?** Works without copyright protection are considered to be in the public domain. Works in the public domain are considered public property and therefore, anyone can modify, distribute, copy, or sell them for profit. Some works that were created never had a copyright holder. Examples are traditional folk songs or stories, the origins of which are unknown and can't be attributed to a specific individual. Copyrighted works can lose their copyright protection after their term of protection expires.

It can be difficult to determine when works enter the public domain. Therefore, you should probably consider a work to be in the public domain only if there is provable, objective evidence that it's in the public domain or it's clearly identified as being in the public domain. The safest assumption is that all intellectual property you find on the Internet is protected by copyright, *unless otherwise stated*.

## Protecting Your Work with Copyrights

As we discussed in Part 1 of this chapter, you're potentially creating intellectual property on a regular basis. If your work is valuable and you're using it to earn a living, you definitely want to take appropriate steps to protect your copyright.

**Isn't copyright protection automatic?** Copyright does accrue as soon as you create the intellectual property and set it down in digital or physical form. However, registering copyright provides certain advantages, including the ability to sue someone for violating your copyright.

**How do I register works for copyright protection?** Instructions and forms for registering work for copyright protection can be found on the U.S. Copyright Office website (*copyright.gov*). Registration can be done online and requires payment of a small fee. Although you can file online, the Library of Congress might still require you to submit a hard copy of your work. It can take up to eight months to receive your notice of registration, but your registration is effective when the Copyright Office receives your registration form.

Posting a copyright notice with your work is also a deterrent to copyright infringement, as it establishes the work is copyrighted. A simple format is to use the word copyright (or the copyright symbol ©), the year the work was first published, the copyright holder's name, and optionally, the location of the copyright holder.

**Do I have to pay to register each photo in my portfolio?** A copyright registration form can be filed for a collection of works. The stipulation is that the works must be published as a collection. A group of related images, songs, videos, poems, or short stories or a collection of blog postings prior to registration meets this criterion.

**What if I don't mind people using my work, but I don't want to constantly answer permission requests?** Copyleft—a play on the word *copyright*—is a term for various licensing plans that enable copyright holders to grant certain rights to the work while retaining other rights.

## License Conditions

Creators choose a set of conditions they wish to apply to their work.

**(i) Attribution (by)**

All CC licenses require that others who use your work in any way must give you credit the way you request, but not in a way that suggests you endorse them or their use. If they want to use your work without giving you credit or for endorsement purposes, they must get your permission first.

**(⟳) ShareAlike (sa)**

You let others copy, distribute, display, perform, and modify your work, as long as they distribute any modified work on the same terms. If they want to distribute modified works under other terms, they must get your permission first.

**($) NonCommercial (nc)**

You let others copy, distribute, display, perform, and (unless you have chosen NoDerivatives) modify and use your work for any purpose other than commercially unless they get your permission first.

**(=) NoDerivatives (nd)**

You let others copy, distribute, display and perform only original copies of your work. If they want to modify your work, they must get your permission first.

**Figure 8.24** The Creative Commons has a variety of licenses, one of which should be right for you.
*(Courtesy of Creative Commons)*

Usually, the rights (such as modifying or copying a work) are granted with the stipulation that when users redistribute their work (based on the original work), they agree to be bound by the same terms of the copyleft plan used by the original copyright holder. The General Public License (GNU) is a popular copyleft license used for software. For other works, the Creative Commons, a nonprofit organization, has developed a range of licenses that can be used to control rights to works (see Figure 8.24). It provides a simple algorithm to assist you with selecting the proper license for your work (*creativecommons.org/share-your-work*).

**What are the advantages and drawbacks of licenses designed by Creative Commons?**
The advantage to using Creative Commons licenses is that people won't constantly send you permission requests to use your work. The licenses explain how your work can be used. Also, many advocates of copyleft policies feel that creativity is encouraged when people are free to modify other people's work instead of worrying about infringing on copyright.

Opponents of Creative Commons licenses complain that the licenses have affected their livelihoods. If millions of images are on Google Photos with Creative Commons licenses that permit free commercial use, professional photographers might have a tougher time selling their work. Furthermore, Creative Commons licenses are irrevocable. If you make a mistake and select the wrong license for your work, or you later find out a work is valuable and you've already selected a license that allows commercial use, you're out of luck.

Understanding the meaning of copyright, and copyleft, is important so that you respect the rights of others and so that you can simplify your life in granting permission rights to the works you create.

 **Helpdesk**     MyLab IT

**Understanding Intellectual Property and Copyright**

In this Helpdesk, you'll play the role of a helpdesk staffer, fielding questions about the basics of intellectual property and how individuals can protect their digital assets with copyright.

# Copyright Infringement

**Objective 8.12** *Explain copyright infringement, summarize the potential consequences, and describe situations in which you can legally use copyrighted material.*

**What happens if you use copyrighted material without permission of the copyright holder?** A violation of the holder's rights is known as copyright infringement. Illegally copying or using software, music, video, and photos tops the list of digital rights violations on the Internet. Here are a few examples of copyright infringement that you may recognize:

- Taking someone else's photo from the Internet and posting it on Instagram
- Copying a CD of someone else's music and giving it to a friend
- Using a peer-to-peer file sharing service or torrent to download a movie
- Copying a copyrighted software app and giving it to a coworker

**What happens to people who infringe on someone's copyright?** Infringing on copyright risks a potentially long and costly legal battle. At best, you might receive a slap on the wrist, but worst-case scenarios involve large fines and prison terms. Penalties vary depending on the type of property being infringed and the country whose laws are in effect.

**Is posting a picture on a social media site really copyright infringement?** If you don't own the copyright to the picture or the rights to display a copyrighted image, then it's copyright infringement. Although you may not have read a social media site's user agreement, most sites, like Pinterest, have users agree not to post material to which they don't own copyright. Of course, if a website provides a Pinterest link for you to share material, you could argue that they're giving you implicit permission to share their material.

**How do courts decide when copyright has been infringed?** When judges consider cases of infringement, they generally examine the extent to which there is a substantial similarity between the copyrighted work and the infringing work. Obviously, if you copy an image from the Internet or burn a copy of a music CD, that is an exact copy and is clearly infringement. What if you wrote a story with a similar plot to an episode of your favorite TV show? The courts will have to determine how similar the characters and plot are to the copyrighted work and if infringement exists.

**Why would anyone risk copyright infringement?** Severe monetary penalties exist for copyright infringement, so why take a chance? Here are a few reasons people have indicated they risk copyright infringement:

- **Low likelihood of getting caught.** If you download three songs from a file-sharing website, are you likely to get caught? Probably not, but that doesn't make it ethical. You're still depriving an artist of his or her livelihood. However, some people commit such acts if they think they can escape notice.
- **Everyone is doing it.** If people think "everyone else does it so why shouldn't I?", they might take a chance, especially if the likelihood of getting caught is low.
- **No one would come after an individual.** Many people believe that only large corporations are sued for copyright infringement. But thousands of individuals have been sued by the record and motion picture industries for illegal file sharing. Most of these cases were settled out of court for amounts ranging from $3,000 to $4,000, but court awards have gone higher. The Recording Industry Association of America (RIAA) and movie studios tend to target *supernodes*—people who offer thousands of music or video files on P2P networks for sharing—for their legal action, but they can just as easily target you for downloading a movie or a CD of songs.
- **I'm only downloading one song, picture, etc.—it isn't worth that much.** Whether you're stealing one candy bar from a convenience store or a box of them from a truck, they're both crimes. Because copyright infringement is prohibited by law, copying one song is still stealing.

**Is putting a URL that points to a copyrighted website on my social media page copyright infringement?** A URL is a direction for finding a specific page on the Internet. It isn't debatable or open to interpretation; therefore, it's considered a fact. Because facts can't be copyrighted, you can list all the textual URLs you want on your website without committing copyright infringement. However, be sure you don't take copyrighted material, such as a logo or character, to use as a visual link to a website. For instance, using a picture of Mickey Mouse to link to the Disney website may constitute infringement.

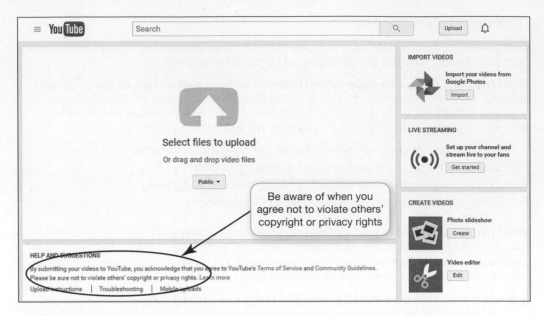

**Figure 8.25** Although you might have missed it, when you upload videos to YouTube, you agree to respect copyright and privacy. *(Courtesy of You Tube)*

## Music and Video Issues

**I uploaded clips from TV shows to YouTube. Could I be liable for copyright infringement?** Although many people think that YouTube would be responsible for any infringement, anyone who uploads copyrighted material could be held responsible. Although you might not pay attention when uploading videos, you agree not to infringe on copyright when uploading the files, as shown in Figure 8.25. Therefore, YouTube has potential legal recourse to recover damages from users who ignore the terms of use on its website. If you've uploaded copyrighted material without permission to YouTube or any other file-sharing site, you should remove it immediately.

**Why would a band object to uploading a music video to YouTube? Wouldn't it be free publicity for them?** Each time someone plays a video that's uploaded illegally to a website, the performer (singer or band), the songwriter, and the music publisher potentially lose money. A song played on a website is considered a live performance. Songwriters and music publishers are entitled to a royalty every time a song is played live, on the radio, on a streaming service (like Spotify), or anywhere on the Internet. Normally, radio stations and streaming services pay royalty fees to performing rights organizations (PROs). The PROs then forward the royalties to the songwriters, music publishers, and other copyright holders. Because you're not paying royalties to a PRO when you view the video on YouTube, someone is losing money.

**How significant is the loss of revenue from music and video infringement?** A recent study from Columbia University concluded that 45% of U.S. citizens pirate movies on a regular basis. Many popular movies are illegally downloaded tens of millions of times. If everyone pays $4 to watch the movie from a legitimate streaming source, the movie studio could have earned millions of more dollars. Clearly, illegal file swapping is costing people and companies a significant amount of revenue.

## Software Issues

**How are the rights of software copyright holders usually violated?** Illegally using copyrighted software is known as software piracy. If you've ever given a friend a copy of a copyrighted software program or downloaded copyrighted software from a file-sharing site, you've committed infringement.

You need to exercise caution when buying software online to ensure that it's a real, fully licensed copy. Otherwise you might not be able to use the software you bought. Most modern software requires a serial number or product key for installation. Typically, the first time you launch the software after installation, this serial number is checked against a database to ensure the software hasn't been installed on more computers than the license allows. This is a form of digital rights management (DRM). If you're buying illegally copied software on the Internet, you might not be able to activate it because too many other people have already used the same serial number.

Copying and downloading software aren't the only acts of software piracy. The Business Software Alliance (*bsa.org*), an organization that has among its goals the prevention of software piracy, provides a few other examples:

- Taking advantage of upgrade offers without possessing a required older version of the software
- Using software designed specifically for academic or noncommercial use for commercial purposes

- Installing a licensed copy of software on more computers than the license permits
- Counterfeiting software (copying it for the purpose of selling it as if it were the real, licensed product)
- Selling computers preloaded with illegal copies of software already installed

**How widespread is software piracy?** In some countries, such as Indonesia and China, software piracy is rampant. Piracy rates approach 90% in some areas of the world. Although less of a problem in the United States on a percentage basis, the United States still leads the world in lost revenue from software piracy.

## Photographic Issues

**Why is photographic infringement widespread on the Internet?** Because it's so easy! Need a picture of the Eiffel Tower for your presentation? Google's image search makes it simple to find a picture. Copy and paste it into your presentation and you're done. Congratulations, you've probably just infringed on someone's copyright!

**Who owns the copyright to a photo?** When the photo is taken, the photographer owns the copyright, assuming the photographer was taking photos in a public place or had permission from the property owner. If the photographer was working on a "work for hire" basis, usually the copyright belongs to his or her employer.

**Do people in the photo have any rights?** Being photographed without your consent generally falls under the realm of privacy. The Fourth Amendment to the U.S. Constitution and various other laws and court cases have recognized Americans' rights to certain amounts of privacy. Usually, if a photographer includes you in a photo (see Figure 8.26) that he or she intends to sell for publication, you'll be asked to sign a model release, which usually grants the photographer the right to use an image of the model (or subject of the photo) commercially.

If a picture of you is published without your consent, you might have the basis for a lawsuit. However, be aware that there are times when you agree to allow your photo to be taken and used commercially (usually for publicity), such as when you enter a contest, buy a ticket for an amusement park, or enter an event such as a marathon. So read the conditions on sign-up forms and tickets to ensure you understand any rights you're surrendering.

**How do you know if a photo on the Internet is copyrighted?** Usually information is attached to a photo to indicate it's copyrighted, in the public domain, or that all rights are reserved. If there's no information attached, the safest course of action is to assume that the photo is protected by copyright and you'd need permission to use the photo. Figure 8.27 shows an example of copyright information for a photo on the Flickr website.

**Figure 8.26** There is no problem taking a picture of this statue of Abraham Lincoln on display in a public park. But if you want to use the photo for commercial purposes, you need to obtain a model release from the man chatting with Lincoln. *(Alan Evans)*

## Using Copyrighted Material Legally

**Under what circumstances can I use copyrighted material?** Many websites that contain copyrighted material also contain lengthy legal documents that delineate the terms of use for the material that you download from the site (see Figure 8.28). It's important to read the terms of use *before* using any copyrighted material on the site. Failure to read the terms of use doesn't absolve you from liability for using copyrighted material without permission.

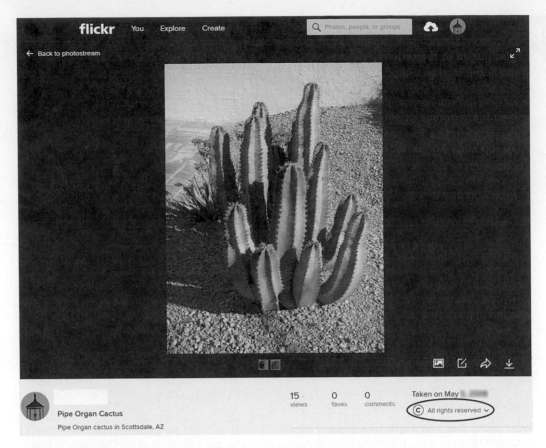

**Pipe Organ Cactus**
Pipe Organ cactus in Scottsdale, AZ

**Figure 8.27** Although you can download this photo from Flickr, all rights are reserved so you cannot use it without obtaining permission. *(Courtesy of Flickr)*

**What if a website does not have terms of use?** Ferreting out the terms of use on a site can sometimes be tricky. Look for links that say Terms of Use, Restrictions, Copyright, Rules, Media Room, Usage Guidelines, FAQ, or Contact Us. Sometimes, the usage terms aren't displayed until you attempt to download copyrighted material. If you've done a thorough search and can't find them, contact the organization that maintains the website and ask about the site's terms of use.

**Can I use copyrighted material if it isn't permitted in the terms of use or there are no terms of use?** Copyright holders can always grant permission to use copyrighted material to an individual or organization. Depending on the material used and the specific nature of the usage, a payment may be required to secure the rights to the copyrighted work. Sometimes, though, simply asking permission is enough to get you the rights to use the work for a specific purpose free of charge.

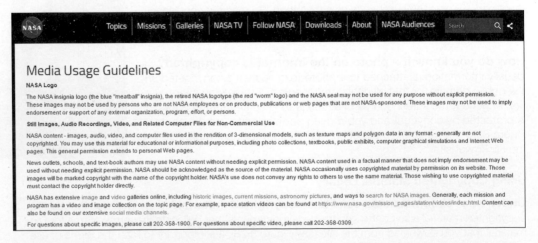

**Figure 8.28** The terms of use page from nasa.gov clearly spells out your rights regarding photos downloaded from its website. NASA's media usage guidelines are very generous. *(Courtesy of NASA)*

Need an image or a video but don't want to pay for it? Many (if not all) images posted on U.S. government websites have generous usage guidelines. Need a V-2 rocket photo (see Figure 8.29)? Head to *nasa.gov*. NASA's collection of media is free to use for educational and informational purposes without explicit permission. You can even use NASA media for commercial purposes if it doesn't imply endorsement of your product or company by NASA. Need a photo of Arches National Park? Check out the U.S. Geological Survey site (*library.usgs.gov/photo*). Any images posted on the site generated by employees of the USGS are considered in the public domain. Picture of a grizzly bear? The U.S. Fish and Wildlife Service can help you out (*digitalmedia.fws.gov*). So make your tax dollars work for you by saving money on permissions fees for media!

**Figure 8.29** U.S. government websites have a wealth of media, like this rocket, that is free to use. *(NASA)*

**Whom do I contact for permission?** Identifying the appropriate contact from which to obtain permission depends on the nature of the intellectual property. Sometimes it can be difficult to tell who actually owns the copyright, or the particular rights you need, to a piece of media. The creator may not be the copyright holder any longer. He or she may have sold the rights to another party. Figure 8.30 provides suggestions about permission contacts.

**What information should I provide in a permission request?** Be sure to include these points:

- **Who you are.** Include your contact information (name, address, phone number, and e-mail) and whether you're requesting permission personally or on behalf of an organization.
- **Which work you're requesting permission to use.** Describe the work completely as well as how much of the work you'll be using.
- **Complete details of your usage of the work.** Indicate why you're using the work, if the work is being used as part of a money-making project, where the work will be used (website, book, magazine, etc.), how frequently the work will be used, and if you're making modifications to the work.
- **The timing of the request.** Indicate the date you intend to begin using the work and suggest a deadline for responding to the request.

Be sure you receive a written response to your request authorizing the usage you requested. Never assume that a lack of response indicates a tacit approval on the part of the copyright holder. Remember, copyright holders are under no obligation to grant your request or even to respond to it.

### Figure 8.30 Contacts for Various Types of Media

**Books and Periodicals**
- Author or publisher

**Website Content**
- Webmaster, website owner, or author

**Photos, Sculpture, Paintings, or Other Art**
- Artist or photographer, publisher (print media), gallery management (on display)

**Movies or Video**
- Uploader (original video on website), production company, film distributor, screenwriter

*(Monticellllo/Fotolia, Bannosuke/Fotolia, Sakunee9///Fotolia, Vikivector/Fotolia)*

### Fair Use

**Are there any instances in which I can use copyrighted work without permission of the copyright holder?** Fair use provides for people to use portions of a copyrighted work for specific purposes without receiving prior permission from the copyright holder. However, there are no specific rules on exactly what amount of use constitutes fair use, which means each case has to be decided on its own merits.

**What types of activities constitute fair use?** The following are examples of fair-use activities permitted in the United States:

- Quotation of excerpts in a review or criticism
- Summary of an address or article, with brief quotations, in a news report
- Reproduction by a teacher or student of a small part of a work to illustrate a lesson; this is commonly known as educational fair use

## Table 8.3 Suggested Educational Fair-Use Guidelines

| Media | Quantity |
|---|---|
| Motion media | Up to 10% or 3 minutes, whichever is less |
| Text material | Up to 10% or 1,000 words, whichever is less |
| Music, lyrics, and music videos | Up to 10%, but in no event more than 30 seconds, of the music and lyrics from an individual musical work (or in the aggregate of extracts from an individual work) |
| Illustrations and photographs | a. One artist: No more than five images<br>b. Collections of works: No more than 10% or 15 images, whichever is less |
| Numerical data sets (databases and spreadsheets) | Up to 10% or 2,500 fields or cell entries, whichever is less |

**Does being a student who uses educational (academic) fair use give me a defense for using any copyrighted material I want?** Because there are no fixed guidelines on the quantity of material that can be used and still be considered fair use, guidelines have been developed to assist teachers and students. The Consortium of College and University Media Centers developed suggested guidelines for various types of media, excerpts of which are summarized in Table 8.3.

Again, these are only suggested guidelines and depending on the individual case, you may be able to make a successful argument under the fair use doctrine to use a greater percentage of a given work. Many educational institutions publish their own guidelines, so inquire about your school's guidelines.

# Living Ethically in the Digital Era

The rise of digital technology provides new challenges to us all. In this section, we'll explore some of the ethical choices you might be confronted with as you navigate the digital world.

## Plagiarism

**Objective 8.13** *Explain plagiarism and strategies for avoiding it.*

**What exactly is plagiarism?** Plagiarism is the act of copying text or ideas from someone else and claiming them as your own. Using ideas from other sources and integrating them into your work is acceptable only if you clearly indicate the content being used (such as through quotation marks) and attribute your source. Changing a few words but keeping the essence of someone else's idea is still plagiarism even if you don't copy the text exactly. Although the following examples don't involve copying words or ideas without attribution, they're still examples of plagiarism under the academic definition:

- **Turning in work that someone else did for you.** Copying the Excel file that was due for homework in your computer literacy class from a classmate is still plagiarism, even though the file isn't a text file.
- **Failing to identify a direct quotation with quotation marks.**
- **Copying too much material from other sources.** If a work consists mostly of quotes and ideas from other sources, even though the source has been identified, it's difficult to justify it as original, creative work.

Plagiarism is usually considered an academic offense of dishonesty and isn't punishable under U.S. civil law. Plagiarism is prohibited by almost all academic institutions, and the penalties usually are severe, ranging from receiving a failing grade on the assignment to receiving a failing grade for the course to being dismissed from the institution. Although plagiarism isn't technically copyright infringement, it can easily turn into copyright infringement if too much material is stolen from other sources, such as an entire chapter of a book or an entire research paper. The author may choose to sue you if the market for his or her intellectual property is damaged.

**Why is plagiarism such a big issue today when it has been a problem for centuries?** Quick access to information on the Internet has made it easier than ever to commit plagiarism. It's possible to copy and paste large quantities of information with just a few mouse clicks.

Another huge problem today is presented by paper mills—websites that sell prewritten or custom-written research papers to students. For custom work, you can even specify what type of grade you would like to get. Some students choose to buy papers to earn them a grade of "C" if they think that it's less likely to arouse suspicion from their instructor. It's illegal in most states to sell essays that will be turned in by students as their own work, but the mills get around this by putting disclaimers on their websites that the papers should be used only for research purposes and not as the student's work. Fortunately, tools are available to instructors for detecting this type of plagiarism.

**What can my instructor do to detect plagiarism?** Sometimes, just reading a student's work is a giveaway. If the level of writing improves dramatically from earlier assignments, most instructors become suspicious. Most colleges allow instructors to test students orally on the content of papers they suspect aren't the student's own work. If a student is unfamiliar with the content of the paper and the sources used, charges of academic dishonesty can be brought against the student.

Typing suspicious phrases from a paper into a search engine is an effective way to find uncredited sources. Also, most school libraries subscribe to searchable databases of periodicals that contain the full text of published articles. This aids instructors in ferreting out plagiarism from printed sources.

Educational institutions also often subscribe to specialized electronic tools such as Turnitin (*turnitin. com*). The subscription enables instructors to upload student papers, which are then checked against databases of published journals and periodicals, previously submitted student papers, and websites—both current sites and archived sites that are no longer live. Customized reports, such as the one shown in Figure 8.31, are generated to determine the amount of suspected plagiarism in the paper. Instructors have the option of letting students upload their papers to check them for inadvertent plagiarism to give them a chance to cite uncredited sources before turning in their final product.

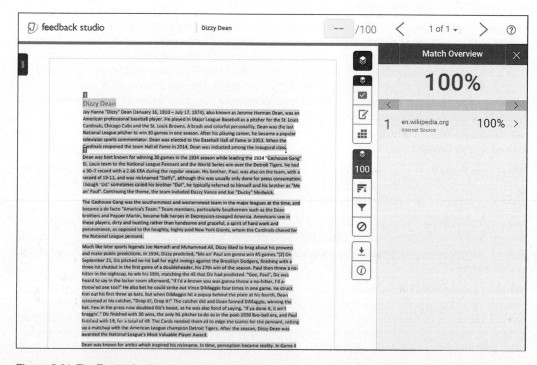

**Figure 8.31** The Turnitin feedback report for this paper clearly shows that it was plagiarized directly from Wikipedia. *(Courtesy of Turnitin USA)*

**How can I avoid committing plagiarism?** Learn to follow this simple maxim: *When in doubt, cite your source*. If you're taking an exact quote from a work, cite the source. If you're paraphrasing someone else's idea but still retaining the essence of their original, creative idea, cite the source.

**How do I cite a printed source properly?** Many different styles of citations have been developed by organizations such as the American Psychological Association (APA) and the Modern Language Association (MLA). Ask your instructor which style is preferred. Regardless of the style, readers of your work need enough information to find the sources you cite. Microsoft Word has built-in features that make creating citations easy (see the Try This feature in Chapter 4 for more information).

So if plagiarism isn't illegal, why do professors get so upset about it? A summary of the issues follows in Table 8.4.

**Table 8.4   Point/Counterpoint: Plagiarism**

| Issue: Plagiarism | Ethical Question: Is plagiarism wrong? |
|---|---|
|  Point | • Taking credit for another's work is always unethical.<br>• Plagiarizing published work (implying it's a higher-quality product) puts an unfair burden on other students who have to compete with the plagiarizer.<br>• Creators of intellectual property deserve full credit for their work. |
|  Counterpoint | • There are no laws in the United States that make plagiarism a crime.<br>• Only academics frown on plagiarism. The "real world" is more concerned with results.<br>• Today's culture fosters an environment of collaborating and sharing. Therefore, how can accessing published information and using it be wrong? |

## Hoaxes and Digital Manipulation

**Objective 8.14**   *Describe hoaxes and digital manipulation.*

Everyone seems to post social media stories warning about a variety of issues, such as the police in your state giving out speeding tickets or the plight of sick children with one last wish. Because anyone can put up a web page on any subject, post to social media, or send off a quick e-mail, how can you distinguish fact from fiction? Determining the reliability of information you encounter in cyberspace can be a challenge, but it's important when you use the Internet as a source of scholarly research. Your professor would not be impressed if you gave a presentation on the illusive North American Jackalope (see Figure 8.32).

### Hoaxes and Other Lies

**What is a hoax?** A hoax is anything designed to deceive another person either as a practical joke or for financial gain. Hoaxes perpetrated in cyberspace for financial gain are classified as *cybercrimes*. Hoaxes are most often perpetrated by e-mail and postings on social media.

Many hoaxes become so well known that they're incorporated into society as true events even though they're false. Once this happens, they're known as urban legends. An example of an urban legend is the story about a man who wakes up in a bathtub full of ice water to discover he's had his kidney removed.

**What is fake news?** Fake news is a type of hoax. Fake news refers to stories that are invented and are intended to spread misinformation rather than being factual. Fake news is most often spread through social media, but it has also made its way into traditional news media. The purpose of fake news is to mislead individuals in order to damage or disparage groups of people, companies, agencies, or governments. Fake news is also propagated for political or financial gain.

**How can I tell if something on social media is a hoax or fake news?** Many hoaxes are well written and crafted in such a way that they sound real. Before sharing the post, check it out at

# International Jackalope Foundation

## The world's foremost authority on this illusive and beautiful creature!

| Our Mission | Recent Sightings | Photo Archive | Get Involved |

**Figure 8.32** Hoax websites often look real and are used in computer fluency classes to teach people the value of fact checking.
*(Patti McConville/Alamy Stock Photo)*

sites such as Snopes (*snopes.com*), Hoax-Slayer (*hoax-slayer.com*), or the Museum of Hoaxes (*hoaxes.org*). These sites are searchable, so you can enter a few keywords from the item you suspect may be a hoax and find similar items with an explanation of whether they're true or false. Regarding fake news, there are many fact-checking websites such as *FactCheck.org* (run by the Annenberg Public Policy Center) that specialize in helping identify fake news stories and helping individuals separate fact from fiction.

**How do I know if something in Wikipedia is true?** Wikipedia entries are reviewed by editors, so there's some control over the accuracy of content. But, just as with any other source of information, articles in Wikipedia need to be evaluated based on the criteria described in Chapter 3. Many articles on Wikipedia have extensive footnotes and lists of sources, making it possible to investigate the reliability of the source material. So treat Wikipedia as you would any other web page you might want to rely on; evaluate the content thoroughly before relying on it.

**Is there a resource for finding quality sites for scholarly research?** Several resources on the Internet, many of which are created (or maintained) by librarians, can be useful for locating websites and scholarly publications that are considered reliable, current, and suitable for academic research. Some of the more popular ones are described in Figure 8.33. Using these sites doesn't mean you don't have to check facts, but it does provide you with an excellent starting point for your research.

## Figure 8.33 Resources for Conducting Scholarly Research

**Google Scholar** (scholar.google.com)
- Specialty search engine that returns results from scholarly sources

**Academia** (academia.edu)
- A free site where users share scholarly research and follow the research of others

**BASE** (base-search.net)
- Operated by Bielefeld University Library—included information is carefully selected and reviewed

**RefSeek** (refseek.com)
- Searches over 1 billion documents such as books, encyclopedias, newspapers, professional journals, and websites

## Table 8.5 Point/Counterpoint: Posting False Information

| Issue: Posting False Information | Ethical Question: Is it unethical to post false information on the Internet? |
|---|---|
|  Point | • Creating stories for the purposes of deceiving people is always unethical.<br>• Inaccurate content might be used as the basis for the creation of new content, thereby spreading the contamination even further.<br>• Spreading false information for monetary gain is illegal. |
|  Counterpoint | • Writers create works of fiction every day. Why is creating hoaxes and rumors any different?<br>• People should be able to judge for themselves and do research to figure out when authors are creating false information for amusement or satire.<br>• Advertisers constantly exaggerate about product attributes. Hoaxes help foster healthy skepticism in the public. |

Because anyone can post anything to the Internet, what's the harm in posting something that is false (see Table 8.5)? Not passing on information that is false is part of being an ethical Internet user. It takes more effort to check potential hoaxes and the accuracy of websites. But think of all the time you'll save your friends and family by not sending out endless streams of bogus information. And certainly your research papers will benefit from using accurate information sources.

### Digital Manipulation

**What is digital manipulation?** Now that we have computer apps that can generate lifelike images for movies and alter photographs, can we believe anything we see? Digital manipulation involves altering media so that the images captured are changed from the way they were originally seen by the human eye.

**So manipulation of images started when Photoshop was invented?** Hoaxes perpetrated via photographic manipulation have been around since photography was invented. Multiple exposures, compositing negatives, and cutting-and-pasting multiple photos and then reshooting were common methods of manipulation clever photographers used in the past (see Figure 8.34). It was once common practice for images of family members to be cut and pasted into the same photo to make it seem as though they were together for a family portrait when in fact they never had been.

**So when is manipulating a photograph or a video unethical?** If changes are made to an image for the purpose of deceiving someone or to alter perceptions of reality, this crosses the boundaries into unethical behavior. For instance, there was a famous image floating around the Internet of George W. Bush reading to elementary school children and the book he was holding was made to appear upside down through digital manipulation. It didn't really happen, but many people believed it did!

Some adjustments that photographers make are purely for aesthetic reasons. *Aesthetics* deals with making things pleasing in appearance. When you use a flash, people in the photo often have red eyes. Eliminating the red eye and changing the brightness and contrast of a photo are things you can do right from your camera app. This doesn't alter the reality of the photo; it just improves the appearance. Therefore, this type of digital manipulation isn't considered unethical because it only involves enhancing the photo's aesthetics.

**Aren't photos and videos often submitted as evidence in courts?** Quite frequently they are and this presents new dilemmas. If a photo or video can be altered, can you rely on it as evidence? Videos are often enhanced for bringing out details that are obscured under normal circumstances. Is this fabrication of evidence or just improving aesthetics? Most photos and videos submitted as evidence are examined to determine whether they have been altered. But the techniques for manipulating images are advancing, and soon it may be difficult, if not impossible, to determine whether an image has been altered. Courts are now beginning to wrestle with these issues.

**Figure 8.34** Over 100 years before the invention of Photoshop, photo manipulation was alive and well. This purported photo of General Ulysses S. Grant at City Point is a composite of three different photographs. *(Library of Congress (Photoduplication))*

## Table 8.6 Point/Counterpoint: Digital Manipulation

| Issue: Digital Manipulation | Ethical Question: Is digital manipulation unethical? |
|---|---|
|  Point | • Images and videos are meant to represent what happened in the real world and therefore should not be subject to alteration.<br>• Photographic and video evidence in court cases would be useless unless we're able to determine whether they've been altered. |
|  Counterpoint | • Artists and photographers need to be free to alter the aesthetics of images for artistic purposes.<br>• People should be able to tell when images have been purposely distorted for satirical purposes. Isn't it obvious there is no such thing as an 80-pound housecat? |

So should you engage in digital manipulation? We explore both sides of the argument in Table 8.6. But as with any other type of information you find on the Internet, be sure to validate the accuracy of photos and videos before relying on them.

## Protecting Your Online Reputation

**Objective 8.15**  *Describe what comprises your online reputation and how to protect it.*

There is already quite a bit of information about you on the Internet. Chances are you've put most of it out there yourself through sites such as Facebook, Instagram, and Twitter. Most people strive to maintain a good reputation in the real world, but in the twenty-first century, your online reputation is just as important as your real-life one.

**What is my online reputation?** Your online reputation consists of the information available about you in cyberspace that can influence people's opinions of you in the real world. Your online reputation is an extension of your real-life reputation—the view held by the community, the general public, friends, family, and others of your general character. Are you considered an honest person? Do you always speak your mind regardless of the consequences? Are you known for defending the rights of less fortunate individuals? These are examples of factors that contribute to society's view of the type of individual you are.

Information is constantly added to the Internet about many of us, even by people we don't know. It can be challenging to control the information that contributes to your online reputation. If you go to a party and guests take pictures of you, they may post their pictures to sites and identify (or tag) you in them. Your friends might write about you on their Facebook or Twitter feed. No matter whether this information is true, false, misleading, embarrassing, or disturbing, it's part of your online reputation.

**Why is it so important to protect my online reputation?** If you say something or do something you wish you hadn't done in real life, most people will forget about it eventually. However, given the persistence of information on the Internet, pictures, videos, and narratives about you might never disappear. Even if you delete something, it probably still exists somewhere. There are numerous examples of politicians tweeting something they later regret and deleting it from their Twitter feed, only to find many people have captured and saved their tweet already.

Sites such as the Internet Archive (*archive.org*) feature utilities such as the Wayback Machine that show you what a website looked like at a previous point in time. Ever wonder what Yahoo! looked like in the early days? A search on the Wayback Machine shows you that in 1996 it looked like Figure 8.35.

Of course, your reputation varies depending on who is interpreting the cyberspace information about you. Your friends might laugh at that picture on Facebook of you at a recent party, but employers routinely browse through social networking sites to evaluate job applicants as part of their hiring decision process. And just keeping your information private isn't a good solution. Many employers don't interview candidates for whom they find a lack of social information online because

Yahoo! Deutschland — CLICK HERE TO VISIT THE STARS **LOS ANGELES** Weekly Picks

[ Search ] [ Options ]

Yellow Pages - People Search - City Maps -- News Headlines - Stock Quotes - Sports Scores

- **Arts** - - *Humanities, Photography, Architecture, ...*
- **Business and Economy [Xtra!]** - - *Directory, Investments, Classifieds, ...*
- **Computers and Internet [Xtra!]** - - *Internet, WWW, Software, Multimedia, ...*
- **Education** - - *Universities, K-12, Courses, ...*
- **Entertainment [Xtra!]** - - *TV, Movies, Music, Magazines, ...*
- **Government** - - *Politics [Xtra!], Agencies, Law, Military, ...*
- **Health [Xtra!]** - - *Medicine, Drugs, Diseases, Fitness, ...*
- **News [Xtra!]** - - *World [Xtra!], Daily, Current Events, ...*
- **Recreation and Sports [Xtra!]** - - *Sports, Games, Travel, Autos, Outdoors, ...*
- **Reference** - - *Libraries, Dictionaries, Phone Numbers, ...*
- **Regional** - - *Countries, Regions, U.S. States, ...*
- **Science** - - *CS, Biology, Astronomy, Engineering, ...*
- **Social Science** - - *Anthropology, Sociology, Economics, ...*
- **Society and Culture** - - *People, Environment, Religion, ...*

Yahoo! New York - Yahoo! Shop - Yahooligans!

Yahoo! Japan - Yahoo! Internet Life - Yahoo! San Francisco

**Figure 8.35** A much simpler Yahoo! home page is preserved for posterity in the Internet Archive. Your web pages might live on forever also. *(Courtesy of Yahoo)*

they view this as a negative or at least a potential concern. Even after you're hired, if your employer finds things that he or she doesn't like on your sites, you might be fired because of it. According to CareerBuilder, 18% of employers surveyed have fired employees due to social media posts.

**Figure 8.36** You have the right to protest, but your employer's social media policy may prohibit you from posting a picture of yourself wearing a company T-shirt while attending the event. *(Photographee.eu/Fotolia)*

**How can an employer fire me for writing something on my own time?** In the majority of states, the employment at-will principle governs the firing of employees. *Employment at-will* means that unless you're covered by an employment contract or a collective bargaining agreement, such as a union contract, employers can fire you at any time for any reason, unless the reason violates a legal statute such as race or age discrimination. Your employer is not required to provide you with a reason for the firing but can simply tell you not to report for work any longer.

You do have a constitutional right to free speech. However, that doesn't mean your employer is going to agree with your opinions. Therefore, it's a good idea to familiarize yourself with your employer's social media policies. Many employers now have such policies, and they usually prevent you from saying disparaging things about your employer, work environment, customers, and coworkers on social media sites. Also, giving the appearance that your employer supports an activity or political agenda is usually prohibited (see Figure 8.36), so make sure you're aware of the rules at your workplace.

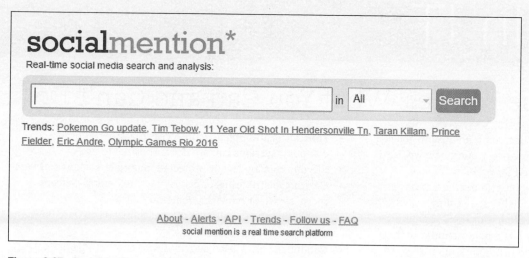

**Figure 8.37** SocialMention.com aggregates content from social media sites so you can keep up with any person, topic, or business—even yourself! *(Courtesy of Social mention)*

**What steps should I take to protect my online reputation?** There are many things you can do if you're proactive:

- **Improve and update your personal profiles.** Make sure your profiles on social media sites are accurate. Update them with new information.
- **Create content on relevant sites.** For instance, if you're an up-and-coming interior designer, post positive comments on relevant sites that assist people with some aspect of design. Make sure your name is associated with things people feel good about reading.
- **Post frequently.** Posting frequently helps minimize negative information, as newer information tends to come up first in search engine results.
- **Be vigilant.** Contact people who've posted negative things about you and see if you can get them to modify or delete them.

You need to examine your own reputation periodically. Google yourself and see what information about you is available on the Internet. If you see something that displeases you, ask the poster or the webmaster to remove the offending material. Don't have time to constantly monitor your reputation? Sites such as *SocialMention.com* (see Figure 8.37) and Trackur (*trackur.com*) provide tools to conduct searches and generate updates regarding information posted about you on social media sites. These tools can also be used to track mentions about specific topics or businesses that interest you.

Keeping your online reputation accurate and not damaging other people's reputations unfairly are integral parts of being an ethical cyber-citizen.

## Bits&Bytes    Celebrity Photographic Rights

How do paparazzi get away with photographing celebrities without their consent? By the nature of being a celebrity, courts have decided that these individuals surrender a certain amount of privacy. In the United States, photos that are taken for editorial use in a public place generally enjoy constitutional protection under the right of free speech. Paparazzi are free to photograph celebrities in public places for the purposes of selling their photos to news outlets and news publications. However, paparazzi can't sneak into a celebrity's backyard and photograph them through a window.

There are several exceptions to the free speech doctrine, however. Photos can't have captions that imply something false or libelous about the person in the photo. If they do, then they aren't legally protected free speech. Also, photos of a celebrity can't be used to promote any goods or services without permission of the celebrity. This is because celebrities have the right of publicity, which grants them control of the commercial use of their name, image, likeness, and other unequivocal aspects of their identity.

# Ethics in IT

## Acceptable Use Policies: What You Can and Can't Do

With computers and the Internet becoming ubiquitous tools, more and more ethical decisions revolve around how we use technology. Because of the potential for problems related to misuse of technology, most schools and businesses have adopted acceptable use policies—guidelines regarding usage of computer systems—relating to the use of their computing resources. Your school most likely has a policy similar to that shown in Figure 8.38 with which you should familiarize yourself. You can usually find it on your institution's website, either under the Information Technology department section or the Student Policies section. If you can't locate it, check with the helpdesk personnel at your school; they can likely direct you to the appropriate web page. Among other things, these policies usually cover the following:

- Keeping your account access (logon ID and password) secure from others
- Not running a side business with college/business assets

- Prohibiting attempts to gain access to portions of the computer systems you are not authorized to use
- Illegally copying legally protected materials, such as software
- Creating, distributing, or displaying threatening, obscene, racist, sexist, or harassing material
- Prohibiting the installation of unauthorized software on the institution's computers
- Conducting any illegal activities with computing systems

If you have a job, you should also familiarize yourself with your employer's policy because it may differ from your school's policy. For instance, most schools consider any work products—such as research papers, poems, musical compositions, and so forth—generated with school computing resources to be the property of the students who created them, unless the students were paid to create the works. With many employers, any work products created using company-provided computing resources are deemed to be the property of the company, not the employees who created them.

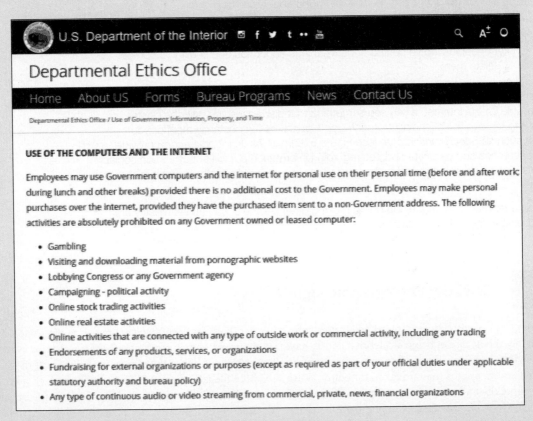

**Figure 8.38** A typical acceptable use policy. *(Courtesy of U.S. Department of the Interior)*

## Figure 8.39 The Ten Commandments of Computer Ethics

Thou shalt not use a computer to harm other people

Thou shalt not interfere with other people's computer work

Thou shalt not snoop around in other people's computer files

Thou shalt not use a computer to steal

Thou shalt not use a computer to bear false witness

Thou shalt not copy or use proprietary software for which you have not paid

Thou shalt not use other people's computer resources without authorization or proper compensation

Thou shalt not appropriate other people's intellectual output

Thou shalt think about the social consequences of the program you are writing or the system you are designing

Thou shalt always use a computer in ways that ensure consideration and respect for your fellow humans

If your school or employer doesn't have an acceptable use policy, the Computer Ethics Institute (*computerethicsinstitute.org*) has developed a well-known set of guidelines you can follow. They are known as the Ten Commandments of Computer Ethics (see Figure 8.39).

In the absence of clear policies, following the Ten Commandments of Computer Ethics should help you steer clear of most unethical behavior.

### Before moving on to Chapter Review:

1. ▶ Watch Chapter Overview Video 8.2.
2. Then take the Check Your Understanding quiz.

# Check Your Understanding // Review & Practice

For a quick review to see what you've learned so far, answer the following questions.

## multiple choice

1. Which of the following is considered intellectual property?

    a. A song

    b. A sculpture

    c. A movie

    d. All of the above

2. Copyright

    a. protects you from having others use your work.

    b. is a term for a set of licensing plans.

    c. legalizes unlimited copying of digital music.

    d. all of the above

3. When is posting a picture on social media considered copyright infringement?

    a. When you don't own the copyright to the photo

    b. When you don't have permission from the copyright holder to post the photo

    c. Neither A nor B

    d. Both A and B

4. Fake news is

    a. illegal under U.S civil law.

    b. a type of hoax.

    c. not unethical.

    d. not a big problem on social media.

5. Altering a picture so that it doesn't reflect the reality of what is being shown is known as

    a. digital interpretation.

    b. pixel manipulation.

    c. digital manipulation.

    d. digital intervention.

---

**chew on this**

Although copyright accrues without registration, there are additional benefits to having your copyright registered. Visit *copyright.gov* and prepare a summary of the advantages of registration and explain how registration would help you pursue an infringement action.

---

**MyLab IT**  Go to **MyLab IT** to take an autograded version of the *Check Your Understanding* review and to find all media resources for the chapter.

**For the IT Simulation for this chapter, see MyLab IT.**

# 8 Chapter Review

## Summary

### Part 1
### The Impact of Digital Information

**Learning Outcome 8.1** **You will be able to describe the nature of digital signals; how digital technology is used to produce and distribute digital texts, music, and video; and the challenges in managing a digital lifestyle.**

### Digital Basics

**Objective 8.1** *Describe how digital convergence and the Internet of Things have evolved.*

- Digital convergence has brought us single devices with the capabilities that used to require four or five separate tools. With more computing power in a mobile processor, a single device can perform a wider range of tasks.
- The Internet of Things (IoT) is embedded computing devices that transfer data over a network without requiring outside interaction. The IoT is integral to the development of smart homes.

**Objective 8.2** *Explain the differences between digital and analog signals.*

- Digital media is based on a series of numerical data—that is, number values that were measured from the original analog waveform. As a string of numbers, a digital photo or video file can be easily processed by modern computers.

### Digital Publishing

**Objective 8.3** *Describe the different types of e-readers.*

- e-Readers are devices that store, manipulate, and transmit textual information digitally. Some use electronic ink for a sharp grayscale representation of text. Others use backlit monitors.

**Objective 8.4** *Explain how to purchase, borrow, and publish e-texts.*

- There are a variety of formats for e-text files, including .azw and ePub. e-Texts can be purchased from many publishers directly or from online stores. Libraries also loan e-texts You can easily publish your own books using services such as the Amazon Kindle Store, Smashwords, or Lulu.

### Digital Music

**Objective 8.5** *Describe how digital music is created and stored.*

- Digital music is created by combining pure digital sounds with samples of analog sounds. It has meant changes for the recording industry, for performers, and for music listeners. It's now inexpensive to carry a music library, to create new songs, and to distribute them worldwide. The sampling rate determines the fidelity of the final recorded digital sound.

**Objective 8.6** *Summarize how to listen to and publish digital music.*

- Digital rights management is a system of access control to digital music. Many services, such as SoundCloud, CD Baby, and ReverbNation, are available for openly sharing and streaming your own content.

### Digital Media

**Objective 8.7** *Explain how best to create, print, and share digital photos.*

- Digital cameras allow you to instantly capture and transfer images to your devices, computers, and cloud storage sites. The camera's resolution is important, as it tells the number of data points recorded for each image captured.

**Objective 8.8** *Describe how to create, edit, and distribute digital video.*

- Using software for video production, you can create polished videos with titles, transitions, a sound track, and special effects.
- A codec is a compression/decompression rule, implemented in either software or hardware, that squeezes the same audio and video information into less space.
- You can also use a webcam to stream live video to sites that will "broadcast" it over the Internet.

## Managing Your Digital Lifestyle

**Objective 8.9** *Discuss the challenges in managing an active digital lifestyle.*

- Although the interconnectivity of the IoT brings with it many benefits, it also poses ethical concerns, including those related to privacy and equal access.

- Although cryptocurrency provides many advantages such as anonymity, speed, and security, there are still drawbacks like the inability to reverse transactions, value fluctuations, and lack of insurance on deposits.
- Vast choices in streaming media allow savvy consumers to "cut the cord" and save money by ceasing purchasing their television media from cable TV companies.

## Part 2
## Ethical Issues of Living in the Digital Age

**Learning Outcome 8.2**   **You will be able to describe how to respect digital property and use it in ways that maintain your digital reputation.**

## Protection of Digital Property

**Objective 8.10** *Describe the various types of intellectual property.*

- Intellectual property (IP) is a product of a person's mind. Types of IP include copyrights, patents, trademarks, service marks, and trade dress. Copyright protection can be granted to creators of "original works of authorship."

**Objective 8.11** *Explain how copyright is obtained and the rights granted to the owners.*

- Copyright begins when a work is created and fixed into a digital or physical form. Copyright can also be registered. Copyright includes the rights to sell, reproduce, and display (or perform) the work publicly.

**Objective 8.12** *Explain copyright infringement, summarize the potential consequences, and describe situations in which you can legally use copyrighted material.*

- Using someone's copyrighted work without permission is copyright infringement. Consequences include lawsuits and fines. You can use copyrighted material if you obtain permission from the copyright holder, adhere to terms of use, or qualify under a *fair use* exception.

## Living Ethically in the Digital Era

**Objective 8.13** *Explain plagiarism and strategies for avoiding it.*

- Plagiarism is the act of copying text or ideas from someone else and claiming them as your own. Citing your sources will help you avoid plagiarism.

**Objective 8.14** *Describe hoaxes and digital manipulation.*

- A *hoax* is anything designed to deceive another person as a practical joke or for financial gain. *Digital manipulation* involves altering media so that the images are changed from the way they were originally seen by the human eye.

**Objective 8.15** *Describe what comprises your online reputation and how to protect it.*

- Your online reputation is information available about you online that can influence opinions of you in the real world. Keeping content current, being vigilant, and frequently creating content can help you protect your digital reputation.

   Be sure to check out **MyLab IT** for additional materials to help you review and learn. And don't forget to watch the Chapter Overview Videos. ▶

# Key Terms

# Chapter Quiz // Assessment

For a quick review to see what you've learned, answer the following questions. Submit the quiz as requested by your instructor. If you're using **MyLab IT**, the quiz is also available there.

## multiple choice

1. The combination of media, Internet, entertainment, and phone services into a single device illustrates the principal of
   a. digital collusion.
   b. digital cohesion.
   c. digital combination.
   d. digital convergence.

2. Which of the following is an *open* electronic publishing format?
   a. PDF    b. azw    c. ePub    d. SMS

3. When analog data is measured and converted to a stream of numerical values, this is referred to as _____ the data.
   a. compressing
   b. streamlining
   c. digitizing
   d. upstreaming

4. Reducing the sampling rate when digitizing a file has which effect on the file?
   a. It increases the file size
   b. It decreases the file size
   c. It neither increases nor decreases the file size
   d. It depends on the codec used to digitize the file

5. Which of the following does *not* determine the quality of a digital image?
   a. Resolution of the camera
   b. Image sensor size
   c. File format and compression used
   d. The number of pixels in the camera lens

6. Which of the following is *not* a digital video file format?
   a. MPEG-4    c. AVI
   b. PDF    d. WMV

7. Which of the following is *not* a category of intellectual property?
   a. Copyright    c. Patent
   b. Imprint    d. Trade dress

8. Using copyrighted works without permission of the copyright holder
   a. is never possible.
   b. is possible under the "fair use" doctrine.
   c. only applies to proprietary software.
   d. is only possible for photographs of public places.

9. A type of journalism where stories are invented and intended to spread misinformation rather than being factual is known as
   a. a public domain tale.
   b. a persistence of information story.
   c. fake news.
   d. an urban legend.

10. It is important to maintain your online reputation
    a. because of the persistence of information.
    b. because employers often review social media before hiring employees.
    c. to ensure information about you is accurate.
    d. all of the above

## true/false

_____ 1. Analog signals are continuous.

_____ 2. Plagiarism is technically not illegal in the United States.

_____ 3. Digital rights management (DRM) is a system of access control that allows only limited use of the material.

_____ 4. Copyright lasts for only 50 years in the United States.

_____ 5. Copying a music CD and giving it to a friend is "fair use."

## What do you think now?

Engineers who design self-driving cars may make decisions about sacrificing speed for controlled acceleration, turns, and braking that result in better fuel economy and less pollution. What is more important? Travel efficiency or environmental impact? Who should make these decisions—you or the car's designer? Explain your answers.

# Team Time

## "And One Will Rule Them All"

### problem

*Digital convergence* posits the dream of one device that can do it all, for everyone. But there are so many different mobile devices saturating the market that many people are left confused.

### task

For each scenario described as follows, the group will select the *minimum* set of devices that would support and enhance the client's life.

### process

1. Consider the following three clients:
   - A retired couple who now travels for pleasure a great deal. They want to be involved in their grandchildren's lives and need support for their health, finances, and personal care as they age.
   - A young family with two children, two working parents, and a tight budget.
   - A couple in which each individual is a physician and each adores technology.
2. Make two recommendations for your clients in terms of digital technologies that will enhance their business or their lifestyle. Discuss the advantages and disadvantages of each technology. Consider value, reliability, computing needs, training required, and communication needs as well as expandability for the future.
3. As a group, prepare a final report that considers the recommendations you've made for your clients.

### conclusion

With so many digital solutions on the market, recommending options needs to focus on converging to the minimum set of tools that will enhance life without adding complication to it.

# Ethics Project

## When Everyone Has a Voice

In this exercise, you research and then role-play a complicated ethical situation. The role you play might or might not match your own personal beliefs; in either case, your research and use of logic will enable you to represent the view assigned. An arbitrator will watch and comment on both sides of the arguments, and together the team will agree on an ethical solution.

### background

Much of the world's population is now equipped with Internet-ready camera phones. Sensors on these phones could measure for viruses or compute pollution indexes, while the cameras could be used to document a range of human behavior. This could create changes in political movements, art, and culture as everyone's experience is documented and shared.

### research areas to consider

- Evgeny Morozov RSA Animate
- Smart Insights mobile marketing statistics
- The Witness Project
- Center for Embedded Networked Sensing

### process

1. Divide the class into teams.
2. Research the areas cited above and devise a scenario in which mobile access could make an impact politically or environmentally, positively or negatively.
3. To set the stage for the role-playing event, team members should write a summary that provides background information for their character—for example, business owner, politician, reporter, or arbitrator—and that details their character's behaviors. Then team members should create an outline to use during the role-playing event.
4. Team members should arrange a mutually convenient time to meet for the exchange, using a virtual meeting tool or by meeting in person.
5. Team members should present their case to the class or submit a PowerPoint presentation for review by the rest of the class, along with the summary and resolution they developed.

### conclusion

As technology becomes ever more prevalent and integrated into our lives, more and more ethical dilemmas will present themselves. Being able to understand and evaluate both sides of the argument, while responding in a personally or socially ethical manner, will be an important skill.

# Intellectual Property and Copyright Basics

You have been asked to make a presentation about intellectual property and copyright basics as they apply to digital images. The presentation is almost done, but you need to make a few adjustments. In addition, you'll need to add a few images from a website and give credit to the source.

You'll use the following PowerPoint skills as you complete this activity:

- Apply Theme
- Create and Modify SmartArt
- Add and Modify Text
- Add New Slide
- Add Zoom Summary Slide
- Insert Images from Web Page
- Apply Design Ideas
- Rearrange Slides
- Apply Slide Transition

1. Open *TIA_Ch8_Start.pptx*, and save as **TIA_Ch8_LastFirst.pptx**. Select slide 1, and add your first and last names as the subtitle.

2. Apply the **Berlin Theme** to the entire presentation.
   Hint: Click the Berlin Theme from the Themes group on the Design tab.

3. Select **Slide 2**. Click just before the second sentence beginning with *IP is considered*, and press **Enter** to create a new bullet point.

4. Create a **New Slide using Title and Content layout** (new slide becomes slide 3). Using the Text Pane, enter **Examples of Intellectual Property** as the title. Insert a **Basic Block List SmartArt** diagram, and enter the following as individual items: **Books, Art, Photographs, Music and Songs, Movies and Videos, Patents, Formulas**, and **Computer Software**.
   Hint: Click the arrow to the left of the SmartArt diagram to open the SmartArt Text Pane to enter text more easily.

5. Change the color of the SmartArt to **Gradient Loop - Accent 2**, and change the color of the font to **Black, Background 1.**

6. Select **Slide 4**. Reposition the second bullet so it becomes the first bullet. Create a sub-bullet for the new second bullet and type **This includes photographs and videos posted to the Internet.** Select copyright infringement in the third bullet, and format with **Bold** and **Italics**.

7. Select **Slide 5**. Enter **Copyright Infringement and Social Media** as the slide title. Increase the font size of the bulleted text to **32**.

8. Select **Slide 6**. Change the title of the slide to **Photographic Copyrights**.

9. Move **Slide 8** so that it becomes Slide 9.

10. Select **Slide 9**. Using any browser, go to **Nasa.gov**. Click **Galleries** from the top menu, then select **Image Galleries**. Click **NASA Images** then type **rocket** in the search box (uncheck videos and audio to only search for images). Right-click any photo of a rocket and select **Copy image**. Click **Slide 9**, click the **Paste arrow**, and select **Picture**. Repeat the procedure with a second rocket image.

11. Select an appealing layout from the **Design Ideas pane**.
    Hint: If the Design Ideas pane does not automatically display, click Design Ideas from the Designer group on the Design tab.

12. On Slide 9, insert a **Text Box** and type **Images courtesy of Nasa.gov** in the text box. Change the font to **Arial Narrow** and font size to **16**. Place the text box near the photos.

13. Apply the **Wipe** transition and the **From Left** effect option to **all slides**.

14. Click **Slide 1**. Insert a **Summary Zoom** slide, selecting **Slides 2** and **4**. Change the slide layout to **Blank**.
    Hint: Summary Zoom is on the Insert Tab in the Links group.

15. Run through the presentation in Slide Show mode.

16. Save the file and submit for grading.

Chapter

# 9 Securing Your System: Protecting Your Digital Data and Devices

 For a chapter overview, watch the **Chapter Overview Videos**.

## PART 1

### Threats to Your Digital Assets

**Learning Outcome 9.1** You will be able to describe hackers, viruses, and other online annoyances and the threats they pose to your digital security.

 **Identity Theft and Hackers** 324

**Objective 9.1** Describe how identity theft is committed and the types of scams identity thieves perpetrate.

**Objective 9.2** Describe the different types of hackers and the tools they use.

 **Computer Viruses** 329

**Objective 9.3** Explain what a computer virus is, why it is a threat to your security, how a computing device catches a virus, and the symptoms it may display.

**Objective 9.4** List the different categories of computer viruses, and describe their behaviors.

**Sound Byte:** Protecting Your Computer

 **Online Annoyances and Social Engineering** 332

**Objective 9.5** Explain what malware, spam, and cookies are and how they impact your security.

**Objective 9.6** Describe social engineering techniques, and explain strategies to avoid falling prey to them.

**Helpdesk:** Threats to Your Digital Life

## PART 2

### Protecting Your Digital Property

**Learning Outcome 9.2** Describe various ways to protect your digital property and data from theft and corruption.

 **Restricting Access to Your Digital Assets** 343

**Objective 9.7** Explain what a firewall is and how a firewall protects your computer from hackers.

**Objective 9.8** Explain how to protect your computer from virus infection.

**Objective 9.9** Describe how passwords and biometric characteristics can be used for user authentication.

**Objective 9.10** Describe ways to surf the Web anonymously.

**Helpdesk:** Understanding Firewalls

 **Keeping Your Data Safe** 352

**Objective 9.11** Describe the types of information you should never share online.

**Objective 9.12** List the various types of backups you can perform on your computing devices, and explain the various places you can store backup files.

**Sound Byte:** Managing Computer Security with Windows Tools

 **Protecting Your Physical Computing Assets** 357

**Objective 9.13** Explain the negative effects environment and power surges can have on computing devices.

**Objective 9.14** Describe the major concerns when a device is stolen and strategies for solving the problems.

 **MyLab IT** All media accompanying this chapter can be found here.

 **Make This** A Password Generator on **page 342**

*(Robert Mizerek/Fotolia; wk1003mike/Shutterstock; Carlos Amarillo/Shutterstock; James Thew/Fotolia; Ymgerman/Fotolia; Graja/Shutterstock)*

# What do you think?

In the Information Age, **data is valuable**. Your private information—your Social Security number, credit card information, address, and passwords—has great value to companies trying to market you things or to criminals trying to exploit your information for gain. The **number of ways that your data could be exposed** is growing all the time. Even one hack of a major company could be enough to expose your data. The 2017 data breach at the credit-reporting agency Equifax alone affected over 148 million people. As society struggles to create laws that keep up with the many ways your privacy can be compromised, **you need to stay informed and protect your information yourself**.

**?** Which of the following has happened to you? (Choose all that apply.)

- *I got a letter notifying me that a company with my credit card info had been hacked.*
- *I logged on to a website from a link sent to me in an e-mail.*
- *I worried about opening an e-mail because it might infect my computer.*
- *I worried my social media settings let too many people see my information.*

*See the end of the chapter for a follow-up question.*

*(Maxim Filipchuk / Alamy Stock Photo)*

# Threats to Your Digital Assets

**Learning Outcome 9.1**    **You will be able to describe hackers, viruses, and other online annoyances and the threats they pose to your digital security.**

The media is full of stories about malicious computer programs damaging computers, criminals stealing people's identities online, and attacks on corporate websites bringing major corporations to a standstill. These are examples of cybercrime—any criminal action perpetrated primarily through the use of a computer. Cybercriminals are individuals who use computers, networks, and the Internet to perpetrate crime. In this part of the chapter, we discuss the most serious types of cybercrime you need to worry about as well as some online annoyances to avoid.

## Identity Theft and Hackers

Every year, the Internet Crime Complaint Center (IC3)—a partnership between the FBI and the National White Collar Crime Center (NW3C)—receives hundreds of thousands of complaints related to Internet crime. *Government impersonation scams* involve people pretending to represent official organizations—such as the FBI, the IRS, or Homeland Security—to defraud. *Nonauction/nondelivery scams* involve running auctions (or sales) of merchandise that does not really exist, wherein the perpetrators just collect funds and disappear without delivering the promised goods. *Advance fee fraud* involves convincing individuals to send money as a "good-faith" gesture to enable them to receive larger payments in return. The scammers then disappear with the advance fees. *Identity theft* involves the stealing of someone's personal information for financial gain. Other complaints received involve equally serious matters such as computer intrusions (hacking), extortion, and blackmail. Figure 9.1 shows that all kinds of industries are having trouble staying current with their security measures. In this section, we look at both identity theft and hacking in more detail.

**Figure 9.1  How prepared is industry for cybercrimes?**

**Industries Respond to the Threat**

■ has strong cybersecurity
■ compliant with OWASP Top 10 Policies

| Manufacturing | Financial Services | Retail and Hospitality |
| 35% | 42% | 30% |
| 81% | 65% | 60% |

| Technology | Healthcare | Government |
| 32% | 31% | 24% |
| 50% | 43% | 27% |

*(Robert Mizerek/123RF)*

# Identity Theft

**Objective 9.1** *Describe how identity theft is committed and the types of scams identity thieves perpetrate.*

**What is identity theft?** Identity theft occurs when a thief steals personal information and poses as you in financial or legal transactions. They may use your name, address, Social Security number, birth date, bank account number, or credit card information in pretending to be you. Many victims of identity theft spend months, or even years, trying to repair their credit and eliminate fraudulent debts.

**What types of scams do identity thieves perpetrate?** The nefarious acts cover a wide range:

- Counterfeiting your existing credit and debit cards
- Requesting changes of address on your bank and credit card statements, which makes detecting fraudulent charges take longer
- Opening new credit cards and bank accounts in your name and then writing bad checks and not paying off the credit card balances (ruining your credit rating in the process)
- Obtaining medical services under your name, potentially causing you to later lose coverage if the thief's treatment exceeds the limits of your policy's covered services
- Buying a home with a mortgage in your name, then reselling the house and absconding with the money (leaving you with the debt)

Many people believe that the only way your identity can be stolen is by using a computer, but you need to protect your information away from the computer as well. Remember to:

- Keep purses and wallets safe to protect ATM and credit cards
- Protect bank statements and credit card bills, shredding before you dispose of them
- Never reveal sensitive information over the phone
- Be vigilant at ATM machines so that account numbers and passcodes are secure

Although foolproof protection methods don't exist, there are precautions that will help you minimize your risk.

# Hacking

**Objective 9.2** *Describe the different types of hackers and the tools they use.*

**What defines a hacker?** A hacker is most commonly defined as anyone who unlawfully breaks into a computer system—either an individual computer or a network (see Figure 9.2).

**Are there different kinds of hackers?** Not all hackers have criminal intent. There are several categories of hackers:

- White-hat hackers (or ethical hackers) break in to systems for nonmalicious reasons, such as to test system security vulnerabilities or to expose undisclosed weaknesses. They believe in making security vulnerabilities known either to the company that owns the system or software or to the general public, often to embarrass a company into fixing a problem.
- Black-hat hackers break into systems to destroy information or for illegal gain. The terms *white hat* and *black hat* are references to old Western movies in which the heroes wore white hats and the outlaws wore black hats.
- Gray-hat hackers are a bit of a cross between black and white—they often illegally break into systems merely to flaunt their expertise to the administrator of the system they penetrated or to attempt to sell their services in repairing security breaches.

The laws in the United States consider *any* unauthorized access to computer systems a crime.

**Figure 9.2** Hackers use a number of techniques to gain access to private information and systems.
*(Macrovector/Shutterstock)*

**Could a hacker steal my debit card or bank account number?** Hackers often try to break in to computers or websites that contain credit card information. If you perform financial transactions online, such as banking or buying goods and services, you probably do so using a credit or debit card. Credit card and bank account information can thus reside on your hard drive or an online business's hard drive and may be detectable by a hacker.

Aside from your home computer, you have personal data stored on various websites. For example, many sites require that you provide a login ID and password to gain access. Even if this data isn't stored on your computer, a hacker may be able to capture it when you're online by using a *packet analyzer (sniffer)* or a *keylogger* (a program that captures all keystrokes made on a computer).

**What's a packet analyzer?** Data travels through the Internet in small pieces called packets. The packets are identified with an Internet protocol (IP) address, in part to help identify the computer to which they are being sent. Once the packets reach their destination, they're reassembled into cohesive messages. A packet analyzer (sniffer) is a program deployed by hackers that examines each packet and can read its contents. A packet analyzer can grab all packets coming across a particular network—not just those addressed to a particular computer. For example, a hacker might sit in a coffee shop and run a packet sniffer to capture credit card numbers from patrons using the coffee shop's free wireless network.

Wireless networks (see Chapter 7) can be set to use encryption to protect against this. Encrypting data packets protects from this risk because the data is transformed with a complex algorithm before it is sent. The data is then decoded at its destination. A sniffer could only steal the encoded data.

**What do hackers do with your information?** Once hackers have your debit/credit card information, they can use it to purchase items illegally or can sell the number to someone who will. If hackers steal the login ID and password to an account where you have your bankcard information stored, they can also use your account to buy items and have them shipped to him- or herself instead of to you. If hackers can gather enough information in conjunction with your credit card information, they may be able to commit identity theft.

Although this sounds scary, you can easily protect yourself from packet sniffing by installing a firewall and using a personal VPN to secure all the data you exchange over the Internet. (We discuss these topics later in this chapter.)

### Trojan Horses and Rootkits

**What other problems can hackers cause if they break into my computer?** Hackers often use individuals' computers as a staging area for mischief. To commit widespread computer attacks, for example, hackers need to control many computers at the same time. To this end, hackers often use Trojan horses to install other programs on computers. A Trojan horse is a program that appears to be something useful or desirable, like a game or a screen saver, but while it runs it does something malicious in the background without your knowledge (see Figure 9.3).

**What damage can Trojan horses do?** Often, the malicious activity perpetrated by a Trojan horse program is the installation of a backdoor program or a rootkit. Backdoor programs and rootkits are programs that allow hackers to gain access to your computer and take almost complete control of it without your knowledge. Using a backdoor program, hackers can access and delete all the files on your computer, send e-mail, run programs, and do just about anything else you can do with your computer. A rootkit is a program that gives an outsider remote control over a computer. A computer that a hacker controls in this manner is referred to as a zombie. Zombies are often used to launch denial-of-service attacks on other computers.

**Figure 9.3** The term *Trojan horse* derives from Greek mythology and refers to the wooden horse that the Greeks used to sneak into the city of Troy and conquer it. Computer programs that contain a hidden, and usually dreadful, "surprise" are referred to as Trojan horses. *(Ralf Kraft/Fotolia)*

## Denial-of-Service Attacks

**What are denial-of-service attacks?** In a denial-of-service (DoS) attack, legitimate users are denied access to a computer system because hackers are repeatedly making requests of that computer system through a computer they have taken over as a zombie. A computer system can handle only a certain number of requests for information at one time. When it's flooded with requests in a DoS attack, it shuts down and refuses to answer any requests, even if the requests are from a legitimate user. Thus, the computer is so busy responding to the bogus requests for information that authorized users can't gain access.

**Could a DoS attack be traced back to the computer that launched it?** Yes, launching a DoS attack on a computer system from a single computer is easy to trace. Therefore, most savvy hackers use a distributed denial-of-service (DDoS) attack, which launches DoS attacks from more than one zombie (sometimes thousands of zombies) at the same time.

Figure 9.4 illustrates how a DDoS attack works. A hacker creates many zombies and coordinates them so that they begin sending bogus requests to the same computer at the same time. Administrators of the victim computer often have a great deal of difficulty stopping the attack because it comes from so many computers. Often, the attacks are coordinated automatically by botnets. A botnet is a large group of devices that have been infected by software programs (called *robots* or *bots*) that runs autonomously. Some botnets have been known to span millions of computers.

Because many commercial websites receive revenue from users, either directly (such as via subscriptions to online games) or indirectly (such as when web surfers click on advertisements), DDoS attacks can be financially distressing for the owners of the affected websites.

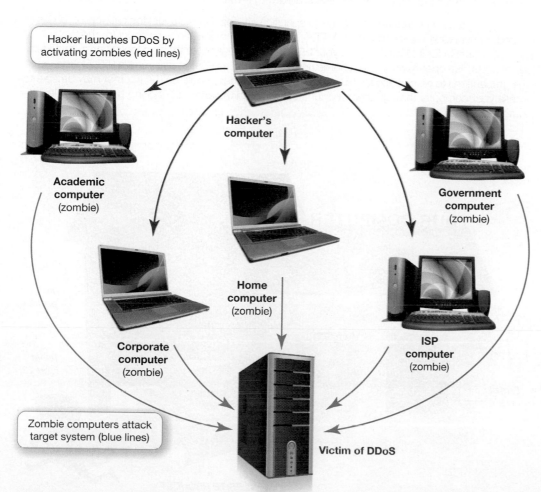

Hacker launches DDoS by activating zombies (red lines)

Hacker's computer

Academic computer (zombie)

Government computer (zombie)

Home computer (zombie)

Corporate computer (zombie)

ISP computer (zombie)

Zombie computers attack target system (blue lines)

Victim of DDoS

**Figure 9.4** Zombie computers are used to facilitate a DDoS attack. *(Vovan/Shutterstock; nico_blue/E+/Getty Images; Juffin/Getty images)*

### How Hackers Gain Computer Access

**How does a hacker gain access to a computer?** Hackers can gain access to computers directly or indirectly. Direct access involves sitting down at a computer and installing hacking software. It's unlikely that such an attack would occur in your home, but it's always a wise precaution to set up your computer so that it requires a password for a user to gain access.

Indirect access involves subtler methods. Many professional hackers use exploit kits. Exploit kits are software programs that run on servers and search for vulnerabilities of computers that visit the server. Exploit kits look for security holes in browsers and operating systems that haven't yet been patched by the users. When they detect a vulnerability, they can deliver spyware, bots, backdoor programs, or other malicious software to your computer. Fortunately, most exploit kits take advantage of known vulnerabilities, so if your antivirus software and operating system are up to date, you should be secure.

Hackers also can access a computer indirectly through its Internet connection. Many people forget that their Internet connection is a two-way street. Not only can you access the Internet, but also people on the Internet can access your computer. Think of your computer as a house. Common sense tells you to lock your home's doors and windows to deter theft when you aren't there. Hooking your computer up to the Internet without protection is like leaving the front door to your house wide open. Your computer obviously doesn't have doors and windows, but it does have logical ports.

**What are logical ports?** You already know what physical ports are: You use them to attach peripherals, as when you plug your USB flash drive into a USB port. Logical ports are virtual—that is, not physical—communications paths. Unlike physical ports, you can't see or touch a logical port; it's part of a computer's internal organization. Logical ports allow a computer to organize requests for information. So all information arriving from another computer or network that's related to e-mail will be sent to the logical port associated with e-mail.

Logical ports are numbered and assigned to specific services. For instance, logical port 80 is designated for hypertext transfer protocol (HTTP), the main communications protocol for the Web. Thus, all requests for information from your browser to the Web flow through logical port 80. Open logical ports, like open windows in a home, invite intruders, as illustrated in Figure 9.5. Unless you take precautions to restrict access to your logical ports, other people on the Internet may be able to access your computer through them. Fortunately, you can thwart most hacking problems by installing a firewall.

**Figure 9.5** Open logical ports are an invitation to hackers.

# Computer Viruses

Creating and disseminating computer viruses is one of the most widespread types of cybercrimes. Some viruses cause only minor annoyances, whereas others cause destruction or theft of data.

## Virus Basics

**Objective 9.3**  *Explain what a computer virus is, why it is a threat to your security, how a computing device catches a virus, and the symptoms it may display.*

**What is a computer virus?** A computer virus is a computer program that attaches itself to another computer program (known as the *host* program) and attempts to spread to other computers when files are exchanged. That behavior is very similar to how biological viruses spread, giving this type of threat its name.

**What does a computer virus do?** A computer virus's main purpose is to replicate itself and copy its code into as many other host files as possible. This gives the virus a greater chance of being copied to another computer system so that it can spread its infection. However, computer viruses require human interaction to spread. Although there might be a virus in a file on your computer, a virus normally can't infect your computer until the infected file is opened or executed.

**Why are viruses such a threat to my security?** Although virus replication can slow down networks, it's not usually the main threat. The majority of viruses have secondary objectives or side effects, ranging from displaying annoying messages on the computer screen to destroying files or the contents of entire hard drives.

Computer viruses are engineered to evade detection. Viruses normally attempt to hide within the code of a host program to avoid detection. And viruses are not just limited to computers. Smartphones, tablet computers, and other devices can be infected with viruses. Viruses exist that trick users into downloading an infected file to their phones, and then steal their online banking information.

**How does my computer catch a virus?** If your computer is exposed to a file infected with a virus, the virus will try to copy itself and infect a file on your computer.

Downloading infected audio and video files from peer-to-peer file-sharing sites is a major source of virus infections. Shared flash drives are also a common source of virus infection, as is e-mail. Just opening an e-mail message usually won't infect your computer with a virus, although some new viruses are launched when viewed in the preview pane of your e-mail software. Downloading and executing a file that's attached to the e-mail are common ways that your computer becomes infected. Thus, be extremely wary of e-mail attachments, especially if you don't know the sender. Figure 9.6 illustrates the steps by which computer viruses are often passed from one computer to the next:

1. An individual writes a virus program, attaches it to a music file, and posts the file to a file-sharing site.
2. Unsuspecting Tony downloads the "music file" and infects his computer when he listens to the song.
3. Tony sends his friend Amit an e-mail with the infected "music file" and contaminates Amit's tablet.
4. Amit syncs his phone with his tablet and infects his phone when he plays the music file.
5. Amit e-mails the file from his phone to Lily, one of his colleagues at work. Everyone who copies files from Lily's infected work computer, or whose computer is networked to Lily's computer, risks spreading the virus.

**I have an Apple computer, so I don't need to worry about viruses, do I?** This is a popular misconception! Everyone, even Apple users, needs to worry about viruses. As the macOS operating system has gained market share, the number of virus attacks against it is on the rise. (For more information, see Chapter 5.)

**STEP 1:** Virus creation

**STEP 2:** Initial virus infection

Hacker's computer

File-sharing server

Tony's computer

**STEP 3:** Virus spreads to another computer

Lily's work computer

Amit's smartphone

Amit's tablet

**STEP 5:** Other computers susceptible to infection

**STEP 4:** Amit infects his cell phone

**Figure 9.6** Computer viruses are passed from one unsuspecting user to the next. *(Stanca Sanda/Alamy Stock Photo; Ian Dagnall/Alamy Stock Photo; Denis Rozhnovsky/Alamy Stock Photo; Vovan/Shutterstock; Juffin/Getty Images)*

**How can I tell if my computer is infected with a virus?** Sometimes it can be difficult to definitively tell whether your computer is infected with a virus. However, if your computer displays any of the following symptoms, it may be infected with a virus:

- Existing program icons or files suddenly disappear. Viruses often delete specific file types or programs.
- You start your browser and it takes you to a home page you didn't set or it has new toolbars.
- Odd messages, pop-ups, or images are displayed on the screen or strange music or sounds play.
- Data files become corrupt. (However, note that files can become corrupt for reasons other than a virus infection.)
- Programs stop working properly, which could be caused by either a corrupted file or a virus.
- Your system shuts down unexpectedly, slows down, or takes a long time to boot up.

**Can I get a virus on my smartphone?** Viruses can indeed infect smartphones. Over half of users say they send confidential e-mails using their phones, and one-third of users access bank account or credit card information on their phones, so smartphones are the next most likely realm of attack by cybercriminals. Although viruses plaguing smartphones have not yet reached the volume of viruses attacking PC operating systems, with the proliferation of mobile devices, virus attacks are expected to increase.

Trend Micro and McAfee are among the leading companies currently providing antivirus software for mobile devices. Products are designed for specific operating systems; for example, Trend Micro Mobile Security has versions for Android phones and tablets and iOS devices. Often, businesses will have their information technology department install and configure an antivirus solution like this for all the phones used in the organization.

If no antivirus program is available for your phone's OS, the best precautions are commonsense ones. Check the phone manufacturer's website frequently to see whether your smartphone needs any software upgrades that could patch security holes. In addition, remember that you shouldn't download ring tones, games, or other software from unfamiliar websites.

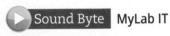

**Sound Byte** MyLab IT

**Protecting Your Computer**

In this Sound Byte, you learn how to use a variety of tools to protect your computer, including antivirus software and Windows utilities.

# Types of Viruses

**Objective 9.4** *List the different categories of computer viruses, and describe their behaviors.*

**What types of viruses exist?** Although thousands of computer viruses and variants exist, they can be grouped into broad categories based on their behavior and method of transmission.

## Boot-Sector Viruses

**What are boot-sector viruses?** A boot-sector virus replicates itself onto a hard drive's master boot record. The master boot record is a program that executes whenever a computer boots up, ensuring that the virus will be loaded into memory immediately, even before some virus protection programs can load. Boot-sector viruses are often transmitted by an infected flash drive left in a USB port. When the computer boots up with the flash drive connected, the computer tries to launch a master boot record from the flash drive, which is usually the trigger for the virus to infect the hard drive.

## Logic Bombs and Time Bombs

**What are logic bombs and time bombs?** A logic bomb is a virus that is triggered when certain logical conditions are met, such as opening a file or starting a program a certain number of times. A time bomb is a virus that is triggered by the passage of time or on a certain date. For example, the Michelangelo virus was a famous time bomb that was set to trigger every year on March 6, Michelangelo's birthday. The effects of logic bombs and time bombs range from the display of annoying messages on the screen to the reformatting of the hard drive, which causes complete data loss.

## Worms

**What is a worm?** Although often called a virus, a worm is subtly different. Viruses require human interaction to spread, whereas worms take advantage of file transport methods, such as e-mail or network connections, to spread on their own. A virus infects a host file and waits until that file is executed to replicate and infect a computer system. A worm, however, works independently of host file execution and is much more active in spreading itself. Some worms even attack peripheral devices such as routers. Worms can generate a lot of data traffic when trying to spread, which can slow down the Internet.

## Script and Macro Viruses

**What are script and macro viruses?** Some viruses are hidden on websites in the form of scripts. A script is a series of commands—actually, a miniprogram—that is executed without your knowledge. Scripts are often used to perform useful, legitimate functions on websites, such as collecting name and address information from customers. However, some scripts are malicious. For example, you might click a link to display a video on a website, which causes a script to run that infects your computer with a virus.

A macro virus is a virus that attaches itself to a document that uses macros. A *macro* is a short series of commands that usually automates repetitive tasks. However, macro languages are now so sophisticated that viruses can be written with them. The Melissa virus became the first major macro virus to cause problems worldwide.

## E-Mail Viruses

**What is an e-mail virus?** In addition to being a macro virus, the Melissa virus was the first practical example of an e-mail virus. E-mail viruses use the address book in the victim's e-mail system to distribute the virus. In the case of the Melissa virus, anyone opening an infected document triggered the virus, which infected other documents on the victim's computer. Once triggered, the Melissa virus sent itself to the first 50 people in the e-mail address book on the infected computer.

## Encryption Viruses

**What are encryption viruses?** When encryption viruses (also called *ransomware*) infect your computer, they run a program that searches for common types of data files, such as

**Table 9.1** Major Categories of Viruses

| Boot-Sector Viruses | Logic Bombs/Time Bombs | Worms |
|---|---|---|
| Execute when a computer boots up | Execute when certain conditions or dates are reached | Spread on their own with no human interaction needed |
| **Script and Macro Viruses** | **E-mail Viruses** | **Encryption Viruses** |
| Series of commands with malicious intent | Spread as attachments to e-mail, often using address books | Hold files "hostage" by encrypting them; ask for ransom to unlock them |

*(Glinskaja Olga/Shutterstock; Oleksandr Delyk/Fotolia; DedMazay/Fotolia; neyro2008/123RF; Beboy/Fotolia; Lukas Gojda/Fotolia)*

Microsoft Word files, and compresses them using a complex encryption key that renders your files unusable. You then receive a message that asks you to send payment to an account if you want to receive the program to decrypt your files. The flaw with this type of virus, which keeps it from being widespread, is that law enforcement officials can trace the payments to an account and may possibly be able to catch the perpetrators. Table 9.1 summarizes the major categories of viruses.

### Additional Virus Classifications

**How else are viruses classified?** Viruses can also be classified by the methods they take to avoid detection by antivirus software:

- A polymorphic virus changes its own code or periodically rewrites itself to avoid detection. Most polymorphic viruses infect a particular type of file such as .exe files, for example.
- A multi-partite virus is designed to infect multiple file types in an effort to fool the antivirus software that is looking for it.
- Stealth viruses temporarily erase their code from the files where they reside and then hide in the active memory of the computer. This helps them avoid detection if only the hard drive is being searched for viruses. Fortunately, current antivirus software scans memory as well as the hard drive.

# Online Annoyances and Social Engineering

Surfing the Web, using social networks, and sending and receiving e-mail have become common parts of most of our lives. Unfortunately, the Web has become fertile ground for people who want to advertise their products, track our browsing behaviors, or even con people into revealing personal information. In this section, we look at ways in which you can manage, if not avoid, these and other online headaches.

# Online Annoyances

**Objective 9.5**    *Explain what malware, spam, and cookies are and how they impact your security.*

## Malware

**What is malware?** Malware is software that has a malicious intent (hence the prefix *mal*). There are three primary forms of malware: adware, spyware, and viruses. Adware and spyware are not physically destructive like viruses and worms, which can destroy data. Known collectively as *grayware*, most malware consists of intrusive, annoying, or objectionable online programs that are downloaded to your computer when you install or use other online content such as a free program, game, or utility.

**What is adware?** Adware is software that displays sponsored advertisements in a section of your browser window or as a pop-up box. It's considered a legitimate, though sometimes annoying, means of generating revenue for those developers who don't charge for their software or information. Fortunately, because web browsers such as Safari, Chrome, and Edge have built-in pop-up blockers, the occurrence of annoying pop-ups has been greatly reduced.

Some pop-ups, however, are legitimate and increase the functionality of the originating site. For example, your account balance may pop up on your bank's website. To control which sites to allow pop-ups on, you can access the pop-up blocker settings in your browser (see Figure 9.7) and add websites for which you allow pop-ups. Whenever a pop-up is blocked, the browser displays an information bar or plays a sound to alert you. If you feel the pop-up is legitimate, you can choose to accept it.

**What is spyware?** Spyware is an unwanted piggyback program that usually downloads with other software you install from the Internet and that runs in the background of your system. Without your knowledge, spyware transmits information about you, such as your Internet-surfing habits, to the owner of the program so that the information can be used for marketing purposes.

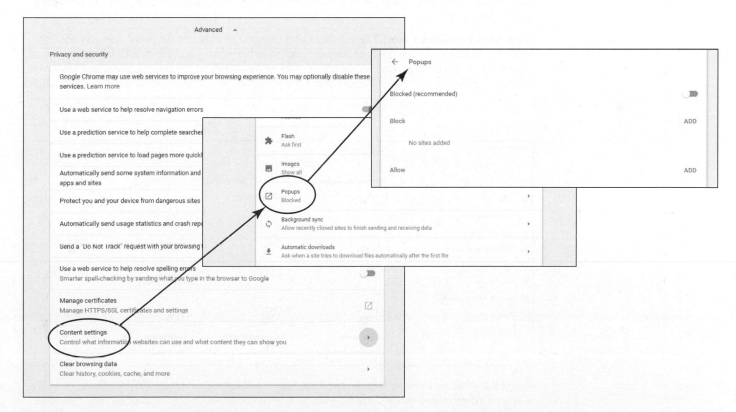

**Figure 9.7** Chrome allows you to customize how you manage pop-ups.
> *To display the pop-up management in Chrome, click* **Settings**, *then click* **Advanced**, *then from the* **Privacy and security** *group, select* **Content settings**, *and customize the choices in* **Popups**. *(Courtesy Google Inc.)*

Many spyware programs use tracking cookies (small text files stored on your computer) to collect information. One type of spyware program known as a keystroke logger (keylogger) monitors keystrokes with the intent of stealing passwords, login IDs, or credit card information.

**Can I prevent spyware from spying on me?** Antispyware software detects unwanted programs and allows you to delete the offending software easily. Most Internet security suites now include antispyware software. Because so many variants of spyware exist, your Internet security software may not detect all types that attempt to install themselves on your computer. Therefore, it's a good idea to install one or two additional stand-alone antispyware programs on your computer.

Because new spyware is created all the time, you should update and run your antispyware software regularly. Windows comes with a program called Windows Defender, which scans your system for spyware and other potentially unwanted software. Malwarebytes Anti-Malware, Ad-Aware, and Spybot—Search & Destroy are other antispyware programs that are easy to install and update. Figure 9.8 shows an example of Windows Defender in action.

### Spam

**How can I best avoid spam?** Companies that send out spam—unwanted or junk e-mail—find your e-mail address either from a list they purchase or with software that looks for e-mail addresses on the Internet. Unsolicited instant messages are also a form of spam, called *spim*. If you've used your e-mail address to purchase anything online, open an online account, or participate in a social network such as Facebook, your e-mail address eventually will appear on one of the lists that spammers get.

One way to avoid spam in your primary account is to create a secondary e-mail address that you use only when you fill out forms or buy items on the Web. If your secondary e-mail account is saturated with spam, you can abandon that account with little inconvenience. It's much less convenient to abandon your primary e-mail address.

Another way to avoid spam is to filter it. A spam filter is an option you can select in your e-mail account that places known or suspected spam messages into a special folder (called "Spam" or "Junk Mail"). Most e-mail services, such as Gmail and Outlook, offer spam filters (see Figure 9.9).

**How do spam filters work?** Spam filters and filtering software can catch as much as 95% of spam by checking incoming e-mail subject headers and senders' addresses against databases of known spam. Spam filters also check your e-mail for frequently used spam patterns and keywords, such as "for free" and "over 21." Spam filters aren't perfect, and you should check the spam folder

**Figure 9.8** Windows Defender Security Center will help you establish secure computing practices.
> *To open the Windows Defender Security Center, go to the Windows search box and type "Security" then select Windows Defender Security Center. (Courtesy of Microsoft Corp.)*

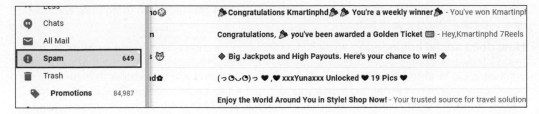

**Figure 9.9** In Gmail, messages identified as spam are directed into a folder called "Spam" for review and dele-tion. *(Courtesy Google Inc.)*

before deleting its contents because legitimate e-mail might end up there by mistake. Most pro-grams let you reclassify e-mails that have been misidentified as spam.

**How else can I prevent spam?** Before registering on a website, read its privacy policy to see how it uses your e-mail address. Don't give the site permission to pass on your e-mail address to third parties. Another strategy is to make sure you don't reply to spam to remove yourself from the spam list. By reply-ing, you're confirming that your e-mail address is active. Instead of stopping spam, you may receive more.

## Cookies

**What are cookies?** Cookies are small text files that some websites automatically store on your hard drive when you visit them. When you log on to a website that uses cookies, a cookie file assigns an ID number to your computer. The unique ID is intended to make your return visit to a website more efficient and better geared to your interests. The next time you log on to that site, the site marks your visit and keeps track of it in its database.

**What do websites do with cookie information?** Cookies can provide websites with informa-tion about your browsing habits, such as the ads you've opened, the products you've looked at, and the time and duration of your visits. Companies use this information to determine the traffic flowing through their website and the effectiveness of their marketing strategy and placement on websites. By tracking such information, cookies enable companies to identify different users' preferences.

**Can companies get my personal information when I visit their sites?** Cookies do not go through your hard drive in search of personal information such as passwords or financial data. The only personal information a cookie obtains is the information you supply when you fill out forms online.

**Do privacy risks exist with cookies?** Some sites sell the personal information their cookies collect to web advertisers who are building huge databases of consumer preferences and habits, col-lecting personal and business information such as phone numbers, credit reports, and the like. The main concern is that advertisers will use this information indiscriminately, thus invading your privacy. And you may feel your privacy is being violated by cookies that monitor where you go on a website.

**Should I delete cookies from my hard drive?** Cookies pose no security threat because it's vir-tually impossible to hide a virus or malicious software program in a cookie. Because they take up little room on your hard drive and offer you small conveniences on return visits to websites, there is no great reason to delete them. Deleting your cookie files could actually cause you the inconvenience of reentering data you've already entered into website forms. However, if you're uncomfortable with the accessibility of your personal information, you can periodically delete cookies or configure your browser to block certain types of cookies (as shown in Figure 9.10).

## Social Engineering

**Objective 9.6** *Describe social engineering techniques, and explain strategies to avoid falling prey to them.*

**What is social engineering?** Social engineering is any technique that uses social skills to generate human interaction that entices individuals to reveal sensitive information. Social engineering often doesn't involve the use of a computer or face-to-face interaction. For example, telephone

**Figure 9.10** Tools are available in your browser (Chrome is shown here) to distinguish between cookies you want to keep and cookies you don't want on your system.
> *From Chrome **Settings**, click **Advanced**. Then in the **Privacy and security** block, click **Content settings**. The **Cookies** block allows you to set cookie-handling preferences. (Courtesy Google Inc.)*

scams are a common form of social engineering because it's often easier to manipulate someone when you don't have to look at them.

**How does social engineering work?** Most social engineering schemes use a pretext to lure their victims. Pretexting involves creating a scenario that sounds legitimate enough that someone will trust you. For example, you might receive a phone call during which the caller says he is from your bank and that someone tried to use your account without authorization. The caller then tells you he needs to confirm a few personal details such as your birth date, Social Security number, bank account number, and whatever other information he can get out of you. The information he obtains can then be used to empty your bank account or commit some other form of fraud. The most common form of pretexting in cyberspace is phishing.

### Phishing and Pharming

**How are phishing schemes conducted?** Phishing (pronounced "fishing") lures Internet users to reveal personal information such as credit card numbers, Social Security numbers, or passwords that could lead to identity theft. The scammers send e-mail messages that look like they're from a legitimate business such as a bank. The e-mail usually states that the recipient needs to update or confirm his or her account information. When the recipient clicks on the provided link, they go to a website. The site looks like a legitimate site but is really a fraudulent copy that the scammer has created. Once the e-mail recipient enters his or her personal information, the scammers capture it and can begin using it.

**Is pharming a type of phishing scam?** Pharming is much more insidious than phishing. Phishing requires a positive action by the person being scammed, such as going to a website mentioned in an e-mail and typing in personal information. Pharming occurs when malicious code is planted on your computer, either by viruses or by your visiting malicious websites, which then alters your browser's ability to find web addresses. Users are directed to bogus websites even when they enter the correct address of the real website. You end up at a fake website that looks legitimate but is expressly set up for the purpose of gathering information.

**How can I avoid being caught by phishing and pharming scams?** Follow these guidelines to avoid falling prey to such schemes:

- Never reply directly to any e-mail asking you for personal information.
- Don't click on a link in an e-mail to go to a website. Instead, type the website address in the browser.
- Check with the company asking for the information and only give the information if you're certain it's needed.
- Never give personal information over the Internet unless you know the site is secure. Look for the closed padlock, https, or a certification seal such as Norton Secured to help reassure you that the site is secure.
- Use phishing filters. The latest versions of Safari, Chrome, and Edge have phishing filters built in, so each time you access a website, the phishing filter checks for the site's legitimacy and warns you of possible web forgeries.
- Use Internet security software on your computer that's constantly being updated.

---

## Bits&Bytes    I Received a Data Breach Letter . . . Now What?

Data breaches are becoming more common, and companies that are the subject of data breaches now routinely notify customers of them—usually by physical letter, but sometimes via e-mail. Here's what you should do if you receive such a letter:

1. Take it seriously. Quite often the recipients of these letters become the victim of identity theft.
2. Contact one of the three big credit bureaus (Equifax, Experian, and TransUnion) and have a fraud alert put on your credit report. This alerts people accessing your credit report that your identity information has been stolen and that the person who is applying for credit in your name might be an imposter.

3. For even better security, contact all three credit bureaus and have a credit freeze put on your credit reports. This prevents anyone (even you) from getting credit in your name. You can always unfreeze your accounts later if you need to apply for credit yourself.
4. Review your credit reports regularly. You are entitled to one free credit report per year from each of the three big agencies. Go to *annualcreditreport.com* and request a report from one of the agencies. Repeat the process every four months from a different agency. Review the reports for any suspicious activity.

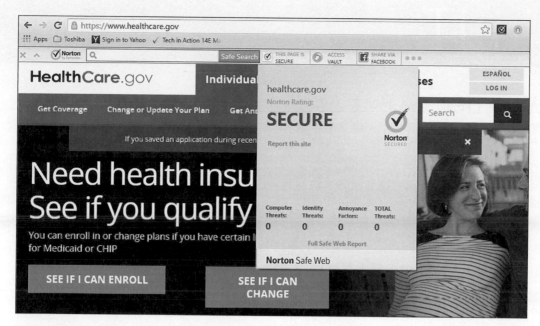

Figure 9.11 Not sure whether you're on the Healthcare.gov website or a cleverly disguised phishing site? Anti-virus software can reassure you all is well. *(U.S. Centers for Medicare & Medicaid Services)*

Most Internet security packages can detect and prevent pharming attacks. The major Internet security packages—for example, McAfee and Norton (see Figure 9.11)—also offer phishing-protection tools. When you have the Norton Toolbar displayed in your browser, you're constantly informed about the legitimacy of the site you are visiting.

## Scareware

**What is scareware?** Scareware is a type of malware that downloads onto your computer and tries to convince you that your computer is infected with a virus or other type of malware. Pop-ups, banners, or other annoying types of messages will flash on your screen, saying frightening things like "Your computer is infected with a virus . . . immediate removal is required." You're then directed to a website where you can buy fake removal or antivirus tools that provide little or no value. Some scareware even goes so far as to encrypt your files and then demand that you pay to have them unencrypted, which is essentially extortion. In 2017, an international cyberattack like this hit hospitals and businesses in 99 countries at the same time (see Figure 9.12).

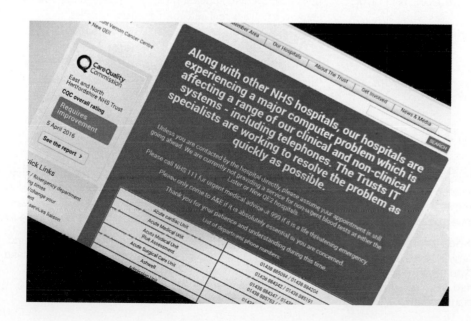

Figure 9.12 In 2017, a massive ransomware attack hit hospitals, businesses, and universities in 99 countries. *(Jeffrey Blackler/Alamy Stock Photo)*

# Ethics in IT

## You're Being Watched ... But Are You Aware You're Being Watched?

Think you aren't being closely watched by your employer? Think again. A recent survey of employers by the American Management Association and the ePolicy Institute revealed that, of the employers surveyed:

- 73% monitored e-mail messages
- 66% monitored web surfing
- 48% monitored activities using video surveillance
- 45% monitored keystrokes and keyboard time
- 43% monitored computer files in some other fashion

As you can see, there is a high probability that you're being monitored while you work and when you access the Internet via your employer's Internet connection.

The two most frequently cited reasons for employee monitoring are to prevent theft and to measure productivity. Monitoring for theft isn't new—monitoring cameras have been around for years, and productivity monitoring has been used for assembly-line workers for decades. However, the Internet has led to a new type of productivity drain of concern to employers. Cyberloafing (or cyberslacking) means using your computer for non-work activities while you're being paid to do your job. Examples of cyberloafing activities include playing games and using social networks. Some employees even do multiple nonwork tasks at the same time, which is known as *multi-shirking*. Estimates of business productivity losses due to cyberloafing top $50 billion annually.

Do you have a right to privacy in the workplace? Laws such as the 1986 Electronic Communications Privacy Act (ECPA), which prohibits unauthorized monitoring of electronic communications, have been interpreted by the courts in favor of employers. The bottom line is that employers who pay for equipment and software have the *legal* right to monitor their usage (see Figure 9.13).

So, is it *ethical* for employers to monitor their employees? Certainly, it seems fair that employers ensure they're not the

**Figure 9.13** It's legal for employers to monitor your computer usage. *(Beatriz J Gascon/Shutterstock)*

victims of theft and that they're getting a fair day's work from their employees, just as employees have an obligation to provide a fair effort for a fair wage. The ethical issue is whether employees are adequately informed of monitoring policies. Employers have an ethical responsibility (and a legal one as well, depending on the jurisdiction) not to place monitoring devices in sensitive locations such as bathrooms and dressing areas. However, in many states, the employer does not legally need to inform employees in advance that they're being monitored. Conscientious employers include monitoring disclosures in published employee policies to avoid confusion and conflict.

The bottom line? Because employers may have a legal right to monitor you in the workplace, operate under the assumption that everything you do on your work computer is subject to scrutiny and behave accordingly.

---

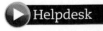 **Helpdesk** MyLab IT

**Threats to Your Digital Life**

In this Helpdesk, you'll play the role of a helpdesk staffer, fielding calls about identity theft, computer viruses, and malware.

Scareware is a social engineering technique because it uses people's fear of computer viruses to convince them to part with their money. Scareware is often designed to be extremely difficult to remove from your computer and to interfere with the operation of legitimate security software. Scareware is usually downloaded onto your computer from infected websites or Trojan horse files.

**How do I protect myself against scareware?** Most Internet security suites, antivirus, and antimalware software packages now detect and prevent the installation of scareware. But make sure you never click on website banners or pop-up boxes that say "Your computer might be infected, click here to scan your files" because these are often the starting points for installing malicious scareware files on your computer.

Most people have vast amounts of personal data residing in the databases of the various companies with which they conduct business. *Amazon.com* has your credit card and address information. Your bank has your Social Security number, birth date, and financial records. Your local supermarket probably has your e-mail address from when you joined its loyalty club to receive grocery discounts. All this data in various places puts you at risk when companies responsible for keeping your data confidential suffer a data breach.

A data breach occurs when sensitive or confidential information is copied, transmitted, or viewed by an individual who isn't authorized to handle the data. Data breaches can be intentional or unintentional. Intentional data breaches occur when hackers break into digital systems to steal sensitive data. Unintentional data breaches occur when companies controlling data inadvertently allow it to be seen by unauthorized parties, usually due to some breakdown in security procedures or precautions.

Unfortunately, data breaches appear to be quite common, as there always seems to be another one in the news. Thousands of data breaches a year are reported by U.S. companies. Over a hundred million records are exposed in a typical year. These breaches pose serious risks to the individuals whose data has been compromised, even if financial data is not involved. The data thieves now have the basis with which to launch targeted social engineering attacks even if they just have contact information, such as e-mail addresses.

With regular phishing techniques, cybercriminals just send out e-mails to a wide list of e-mail addresses, whether they have a relationship with the company or not. For example, a criminal might send out a general phishing e-mail claiming that a person's Citibank checking account had been breached. People receiving this e-mail who don't have any accounts at Citibank should immediately realize this is a phishing attack and ignore the instructions to divulge sensitive data.

But when cybercriminals obtain data on individuals that includes information about which companies those individuals have a relationship with, they can engage in much more targeted attacks known as spear phishing (see Figure 9.14). Spear phishing e-mails are sent to people known to be customers of a company and have a much greater chance of successfully getting individuals to reveal sensitive data. If cybercriminals obtain a list of

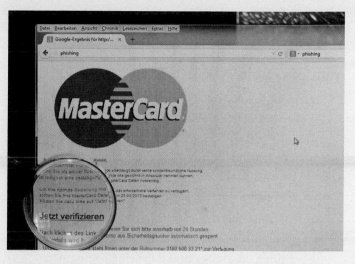

**Figure 9.14** Spear phishing is a targeted type of social engineering. *(Schoening Berlin/Arco Images GmbH/Alamy Stock Photo)*

e-mail addresses of customers from Barclays Bank, for example, they can ensure that the spear phishing e-mails purport to come from Barclays and will include the customer's full name. This type of attack is much more likely to succeed in fooling people than just random e-mails sent out to thousands of people who might not have a relationship with the company mentioned in the phishing letter.

So how can you protect yourself after a data breach? You need to be extra suspicious of any e-mail correspondence from companies involved in the data breach. Companies usually never contact you by e-mail or phone asking you to reveal sensitive information or reactivate your online account by entering confidential information. Usually, these requests come via regular snail mail.

If you receive any e-mails or phone calls from companies you deal with purporting to have problems with your accounts, your best course of action is to delete the e-mail or hang up the phone. Then contact the company that supposedly has the problem by a phone number that you look up yourself either in legitimate correspondence from the company (say, the toll-free number on your credit card statement) or in the phone book. The representatives from your company can quickly tell if a real problem exists or if you were about to be the victim of a scam.

---

### Before moving on to Part 2:

1. ▶ Watch Chapter Overview Video 9.1.
2. Then take the Check Your Understanding quiz.

# Check Your Understanding // Review & Practice

For a quick review to see what you've learned so far, answer the following questions.

## multiple choice

1. When a hacker steals personal information with the intent of impersonating another individual to commit fraud, it is known as

   a. impersonation theft.

   b. identity theft.

   c. scareware theft.

   d. malware theft.

2. An attack that renders a computer unable to respond to legitimate users because it is being bombarded with data requests is known as a _____ attack.

   a. stealth

   b. backdoor

   c. denial-of-service

   d. scareware

3. Some spyware catches your private information by using

   a. a spam filter.

   b. botnets.

   c. a keystroke logger.

   d. a data breach.

4. A series of commands that are executed without your knowledge is a typical attribute of a(n) _____ virus.

   a. script

   b. boot-sector

   c. time bomb

   d. encryption

5. Software that pretends your computer is infected with a virus to entice you into spending money on a solution is known as

   a. trackingware.

   b. spyware.

   c. adware.

   d. scareware.

### chew on this

You most likely have provided personal information to many websites and companies. What information do you wish you had never disclosed? What types of information have companies asked you to provide that you believe was unnecessary? List specific companies and examples of the extraneous information.

**MyLab IT**  Go to **MyLab IT** to take an autograded version of the *Check Your Understanding* review and to find all media resources for the chapter.

**For the IT Simulation for this chapter, see MyLab IT.**

# Try This

## Testing Your Network Security

A properly installed firewall should keep you relatively safe from hackers. But how do you know if your computer system is safe? Many websites help test your security. In this exercise, we use tools provided by Gibson Research Corporation (*grc.com*) to test the strength of your protection.

**Step 1** Open a web browser and navigate to *grc.com*. From the pull-down Services menu at the top of the screen, select **ShieldsUP!** On the ShieldsUP! welcome screen, click the **Proceed button**.

**Step 2** Click the **Common Ports link** to begin the security test. It will take a few moments for the results to appear, depending on the speed of your Internet connection.

**Step 3** You'll now see a report showing your computer's status on the TruStealth analysis test. If you passed, it means that your computer is very safe from attack. However, don't panic if your results say **Failed for TruStealth Analysis**. Consider these common issues:

- A common failure on the TruStealth test is ping reply. This means GRC attempted to contact your computer using a method called ping and it replied to the GRC computer. This is not a serious problem. It just means it's a little easier for a hacker to tell your computer network exists, but that doesn't mean that a hacker can break in. Often, your ISP will insist that your home modem be configured to reply to ping requests to help them run remote diagnostics if there is ever a problem with your modem. As long as your ports are closed (or stealthed), your system should still be secure.

- As long as all ports are either stealth or closed, you're well protected. For the TruStealth analysis, though, if ports are only closed (not stealthed) the report will result in a failure. Only if some ports report as being open do you have to worry that your computer is exposed to hackers. Consult your firewall documentation to resolve the problem.

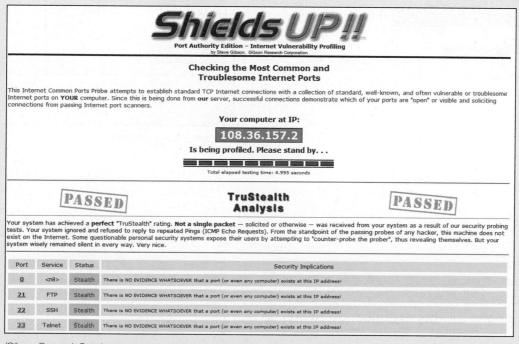

*(Gibson Research Corp.)*

### A Password Generator

Want to make sure your passwords are randomly selected so they are more secure, but afraid you'll forget what you chose?

In this exercise, you continue your mobile app development by using the TinyDB component in App Inventor to store information on your phone so it can be recalled by your application the next time it runs. This is called *data persistence*, and as you'll see, it is very easy to do!

The TinyDB component allows you to store data on your device to use the next time the app opens.

*(Copyright MIT, used with permission.)*

*(Copyright MIT, used with permission.)*

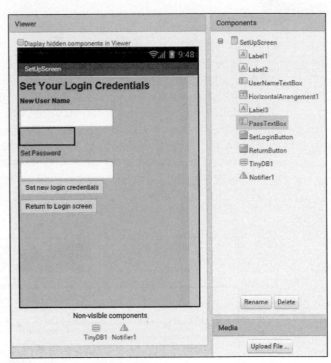

*(Copyright MIT, used with permission.)*

To create this app for iOS, go to *Thunkable.com*, a programming platform based on App Inventor.

**For the instructions for this exercise, go to MyLab IT.**

# Protecting Your Digital Property

**Learning Outcome 9.2**  **Describe various ways to protect your digital property and data from theft and corruption.**

Often, we can be our own worst enemies when using computing devices. If you're not careful, you might be taken in by thieves or scam artists who want to steal your digital and physical assets. As we discuss in this section, protecting yourself is key, and there are many relatively easy measures you can take to increase your level of security.

## Restricting Access to Your Digital Assets

Keeping hackers and viruses at bay is often a matter of keeping them out. You can achieve this by:

- Preventing hackers from accessing your computer (usually through your Internet connection)
- Using techniques to prevent virus infections from reaching your computer
- Protecting your digital information in such a way that it can't be accessed (by using passwords, for example)
- Hiding your activities from prying eyes

In this section, we explore strategies for protecting access to your digital assets and keeping your Internet-surfing activities private.

### Firewalls

**Objective 9.7**  *Explain what a firewall is and how a firewall protects your computer from hackers.*

**What is a firewall?** A firewall is a software program or hardware device designed to protect computers from hackers. It's named after a housing construction feature that slows the spread of fires from house to house. A firewall designed specifically for home networks is called a personal firewall. By using a personal firewall, you can close open logical ports and make your computer invisible to other computers on the Internet.

**Which is better, a software firewall or a hardware firewall?** One type isn't better than the other. Both hardware and software firewalls will protect you from hackers. Although installing either a software or a hardware firewall on your home network is probably sufficient, you should consider installing both for maximum protection. This will provide you with additional safety.

### Types of Firewalls

**What software firewalls are there?** Both Windows and macOS include reliable firewalls. The Windows Action Center is a good source of information about the security status of your computer. The status of your Windows Firewall is shown in the Windows Firewall screen (see Figure 9.15). Security packages such as Norton Security Suite and Trend Micro Internet Security also include firewall software. Although the firewalls that come with Windows and macOS will protect your computer, firewalls included in security suites often come with additional features such as monitoring systems that alert you if your computer is under attack.

If you're using a security suite that includes a firewall, the suite should disable the firewall that came with your OS. Two software firewalls running at the same time can conflict with each other and cause your computer to slow down or freeze up.

**What are hardware firewalls?** You can also buy and configure hardware firewall devices, although most routers sold for home networks include firewall protection. Just like software firewalls, the setup for hardware firewalls is designed for novices, and the default configuration on most routers keeps unused logical ports closed. Documentation accompanying routers can assist more experienced users in adjusting the settings to allow access to specific ports, if needed.

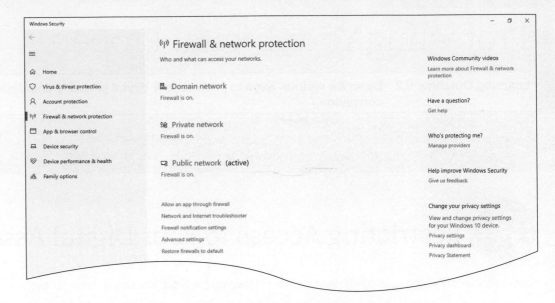

**Figure 9.15** The Windows Firewall screen provides the status of your firewall. *(Courtesy of Microsoft Corp.)*
> *To view the Windows Firewall screen, access **Settings**, select **Network & Internet**, and then click the **Windows Firewall** link.*

### How Firewalls Work

**How do firewalls protect you from hackers?** Firewalls are designed to restrict access to a network and its computers. Firewalls protect you in two major ways: (1) by blocking access to logical ports and (2) by keeping your computer's network address secure.

**How do firewalls block access to your logical ports?** Recall that logical ports are virtual communications paths that allow a computer to organize requests for information from other networks or computers. See Table 9.2 for some logical port numbers and the services they are associated with.

Certain logical ports are very popular in hacker attacks. For example, logical port number 1337 is often used because it looks close to the word "leet," which is hacker talk for "elite," so hackers think it's fun to go after that port.

To block access to logical ports, firewalls examine data packets that your computer sends and receives. Data packets contain the address of the sending and receiving computers and the logical port that the packet will use. Firewalls can be configured so that they filter out packets sent to specific logical ports in a process known as packet filtering.

Firewalls can also be configured to completely refuse requests from the Internet asking for access to specific ports. That process is referred to as logical port blocking. By using filtering and blocking, firewalls help keep hackers from accessing your computer (see Figure 9.16).

**Table 9.2  Common Logical Ports**

| Port Number | Protocol Using the Port |
|---|---|
| 21 | FTP (File Transfer Protocol) control |
| 23 | Telnet (unencrypted text communications) |
| 25 | SMTP (Simple Mail Transfer Protocol) |
| 53 | DNS (domain name system) |
| 80 | HTTP (Hypertext Transfer Protocol) |
| 443 | HTTPS (HTTP with Transport Layer Security [TLS] encryption) |

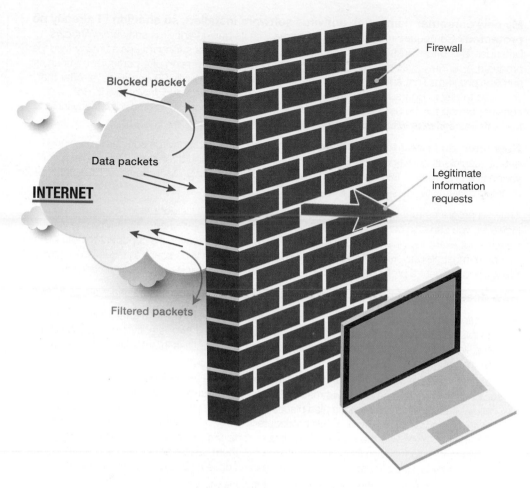

Figure 9.16 Firewalls use filtering and blocking to keep out unwanted data on specific logical ports. That keeps your network safe.

**How do firewalls keep your network address secure?** Every computer connected to the Internet has a unique address called an *Internet protocol address* (IP address). Data is routed to the correct computer on the Internet based on the IP address. This is similar to how a letter finds its way to your mailbox. You have a unique postal address for your home. If a hacker finds out the IP address of your computer, they can locate it on the Internet and try to break into it.

Your IP address for your home network is assigned to your router by your Internet service provider (ISP). Then each device on your home network has its own IP address. Firewalls use a process called network address translation (NAT) to assign internal IP addresses on a network. The internal IP addresses are used only on the internal network and therefore can't be detected by hackers. For hackers to access your computer, they must know your computer's internal IP address. With a NAT-capable router/firewall installed on your network, hackers are unable to access the internal IP address assigned to your computer, so your computer is safe. Most routers sold for home use are configured as firewalls and feature NAT.

## Preventing Virus Infections

**Objective 9.8** *Explain how to protect your computer from virus infection.*

**What is the best way to protect my devices from viruses?** There are two main ways to protect your computer from viruses: by installing antivirus software and by keeping your software up to date.

### Antivirus Software

**What antivirus software do I need?** Antivirus software is specifically designed to detect viruses and protect your computer and files from harm. Symantec, Trend Micro, and Avast are among the companies that offer highly rated antivirus software packages. Antivirus protection is also included in comprehensive Internet security packages such as Norton Security Suite or Trend Micro Internet Security. These software packages also help protect you from threats other than computer viruses.

▶ Helpdesk  MyLab IT

**Understanding Firewalls**

In this Helpdesk, you'll play the role of a helpdesk staffer, fielding questions about how hackers can attack networks and what harm they can cause as well as what a firewall does to keep a computer safe from hackers.

**My new computer came with antivirus software installed, so shouldn't I already be protected?** Computers running Windows come with its built-in antivirus software, Windows Defender. This offers built-in virus protection but does not get as strong ratings as many third-party products. Your new system will probably also come with a trial version of a particular company's antivirus program. That software is free only for a limited time, usually 90 or 180 days. After that, you have to pay to upgrade to the full version of the product if you decide you like it. Before you consider paying for the upgrade though, check with your Internet service provider. Many include free antivirus software with your monthly service plan.

**How often do I need to run antivirus software?** Although antivirus software is designed to detect suspicious activity on your computer at all times, you should run an active virus scan on your entire system at least once a week. By doing so, all files on your computer will be checked for undetected viruses.

Antivirus programs run scans in the background when your CPU is not being heavily utilized. However, you can also configure the software to run scans at times when you aren't using your system—for example, when you're asleep (see Figure 9.17). (However, it's important to note that your computer must be powered on and not in sleep mode for these virus scans to take place.) Alternatively, if you suspect a problem, you can launch a scan manually and have it run immediately.

**How does antivirus software work?** The main functions of antivirus software are as follows:

- *Detection.* Antivirus software looks for virus signatures in files. A virus signature is a portion of the virus code that's unique to a particular computer virus. Antivirus software scans files for these signatures when they're opened or executed and identifies infected files and the type of virus infecting them.
- *Stopping virus execution.* If the antivirus software detects a virus signature or suspicious activity, such as the launch of an unknown macro, it stops the execution of the file and virus and notifies you that it has detected a virus. It also places the virus in a secure area on your hard drive so that it won't spread to other files; this procedure is known as quarantining. Usually, the antivirus software then gives you the choice of deleting or repairing the infected file. Unfortunately, antivirus programs can't always fix infected files to make them usable again. You should keep backup copies of critical files so that you can restore them in case a virus damages them irreparably.
- *Prevention of future infection.* Most antivirus software will also attempt to prevent infection by inoculating key files on your computer. In inoculation, the antivirus software records key attributes about your computer files, such as file size and date created, and keeps these statistics

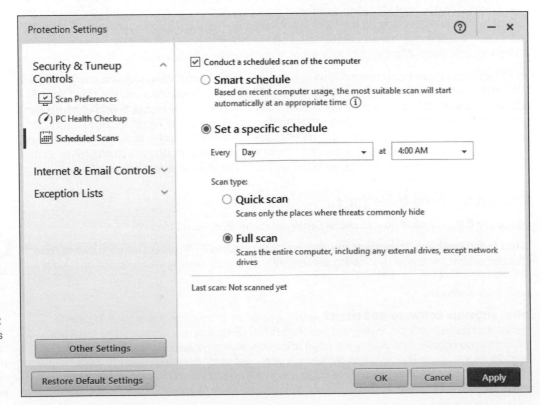

**Figure 9.17** In Trend Micro Internet Security, you can set up virus scans to run automatically based on your usage or on a specific schedule.
*(Reprinted courtesy of Trend Micro Incorporated)*

in a safe place on your hard drive. When scanning for viruses, the antivirus software compares the attributes of the files with the attributes it previously recorded to help detect attempts by virus programs to modify your files.

**Does antivirus software stop all viruses?** Antivirus software catches known viruses effectively; however, new viruses are written all the time. To combat unknown viruses, modern antivirus programs search for suspicious virus-like activities as well as virus signatures. To minimize your risk, you should keep your antivirus software up to date.

**How do I make sure my antivirus software is up to date?** Most antivirus programs have an automatic update feature that downloads updates for virus signature files every time you go online. Also, the antivirus software usually shows the status of your update subscription so that you can see how much time you have remaining until you need to buy another version of your software. Many Internet security packages offer bonus features such as cloud storage scanners and password managers (see Figure 9.18) to provide you with extra protection.

**What should I do if I think my computer is infected with a virus?** If you see suspicious behavior from your system, run a complete virus scan. If viruses are detected, you may want to research the situation further to determine whether your antivirus software will eradicate them completely or whether you'll need to take additional manual steps to eliminate the viruses. Most antivirus company websites contain archives of information on viruses and provide step-by-step solutions for removing them if they're particularly stubborn.

**How do I protect my phone from viruses?** Because smartphones and other mobile devices run operating systems and contain files, they are susceptible to infection by viruses. Cybercriminals hide viruses in legitimate-looking apps for download to mobile devices. Most antivirus software companies now offer antivirus software specifically designed for mobile devices. The Google Play store offers effective free products to protect your Android devices such as 360 Security and Avast Mobile Security.

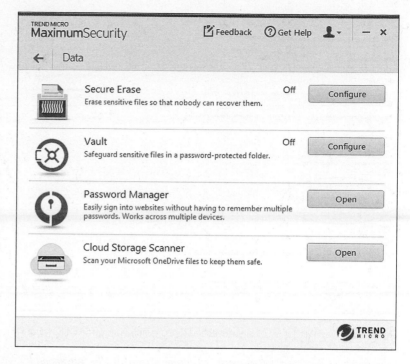

**Figure 9.18** Many protection packages, such as Trend Micro Internet Security, offer other types of security features besides basic malware protection. *(Courtesy of Trend Micro Incorporated)*

### Software Updates

**Why does updating my operating system (OS) software help protect me from viruses?** Many viruses exploit weaknesses in operating systems. Malicious websites can be set up to attack your computer by downloading harmful software onto your computer. According to research conducted by Google, this type of attack, known as a drive-by download, affects almost 1 in 1,000 web pages. To combat these threats, make sure your OS is up to date and contains the latest security patches.

**Do OS updates only happen automatically?** Prior to the release of Windows 10, you updated your Windows OS with an automatic update utility called Windows Update. You had the ability to decide when to download updates and when to install them. (macOS has a similar utility for gathering updates.) With Windows 10, however, you no longer have as many choices. Updates are now downloaded automatically whenever they're provided by Microsoft. You do have the choice to allow Windows to automatically schedule a restart of your computer to apply the updates or pick a more convenient restart time manually (see Figure 9.19).

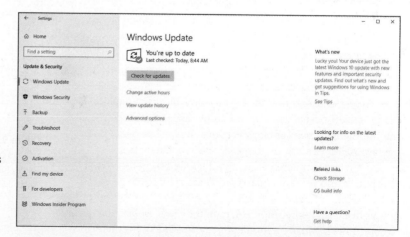

**Figure 9.19** The Windows Update screen makes it easy for users to stay abreast of software updates and manage restarts. *(Courtesy of Microsoft Corp.)*
> *To access the Windows Update screen, access **Settings**, select **Update & security**, then select **Windows Update**. (Windows 10, Microsoft Corporation)*

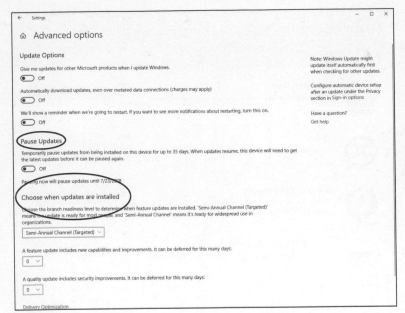

**Figure 9.20** The Windows Update Advanced Options screen provides a few more user-controlled update options.

> *To access the Windows Update Advanced options screen, click the* **Advanced options** *link of the Windows Update screen (Figure 9.19). (Courtesy of Microsoft Corp.)*

The Advanced Options screen for Windows Update provides a few other options (see Figure 9.20). The most notable is the ability to receive updates for other Microsoft products like Microsoft Office.

## Authentication: Passwords and Biometrics

**Objective 9.9** *Describe how passwords and biometric characteristics can be used for user authentication.*

**How do I restrict access to my device?** Windows, macOS, and most other operating systems have built-in password protection for files as well as the entire device. After a certain period of idle time, the device is automatically locked. This provides excellent protection from casual snooping if you need to walk away for a period of time. It's a good idea to use login security on mobile devices because this provides protection of your data if your device is lost or stolen.

**How can I best use passwords to protect my computer?** You no doubt have many passwords you need to remember to access your digital life. However, creating strong passwords—ones that are difficult for hackers to guess—is an essential piece of security that people sometimes overlook. Password-cracking programs have become very sophisticated. In fact, some commonly available programs can test more than 1 million password combinations per second! Creating a secure password is therefore more important than ever.

When you are creating a password, be mindful that many sites or organizations have rules you must obey. Typically the password must be at least eight characters and use uppercase, lowercase, numeric, and symbol characters. Longer passwords are more difficult to break, so using a passphrase is a good idea—a sentence that you can easily remember and type quickly.

Websites that need to be very secure, such as those for financial institutions, usually have strong defenses to prevent hackers from cracking passwords. But sites that need less security, such as casual gaming or social networking sites, might have less protection. Hackers attack poorly defended sites for passwords because many people use the same password for every

---

**Bits&Bytes** · CAPTCHA: Keeping Websites Safe from Bots

Automated programs called *bots* (or web robots) are used to make tasks easier on the Internet. For example, search engines use bots to search and index web pages. Unfortunately, bots can also be used for malicious or illegal purposes because they can perform some computing tasks faster than humans. For example, bots can be used on ticket-ordering sites to buy large blocks of high-demand concert tickets. They are also often used to post spam in the comment sections of blogs. Fortunately, website owners can deploy CAPTCHA software to prevent such bot activities.

CAPTCHA (Completely Automated Public Turing test to tell Computers and Humans Apart) programs are used to generate distorted text and require that it be typed into a box. Newer programs, like Google's reCAPTCHA, monitor users' website behavior to determine if you are a human or a bot. reCAPTCHA merely asks you to click a check box and if it displays a green check (see Figure 9.21a), you have passed the bot test. If the app isn't sure if you are a human, it may ask you to type in some distorted text

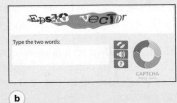

**Figure 9.21** (a) CAPTCHA programs like reCAPTCHA monitor a user's website behavior and can often determine if a user is human just by having the user check a box. If a green check mark appears, you are human! (b) If the app isn't sure if you're a bot, you may be asked to enter some text. *(Metrue/Shutterstock)*

(see Figure 9.21b) just like older versions of the program did. If you want to try integrating a CAPTCHA program into your website (to protect your e-mail address), go to *google.com/recaptcha*, which offers free CAPTCHA tools to help you protect your data.

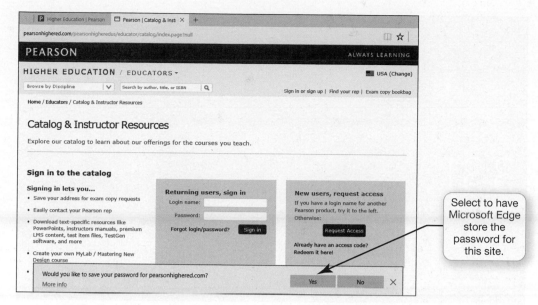

**Figure 9.22** The password dialog box in Microsoft Edge displays whenever you type in a password for a website for which Microsoft Edge hasn't yet stored the password. *(Courtesy of Pearson Higher Education website)*

site they use. Don't let a hacker get your password from a poorly secured gaming site, and then be able to access your bank account with the same password!

**How do I manage so many passwords?** Products like Dashlane (*Dashlane.com*) are available to both generate strong passwords and store them for you. You need only one key to open Dashlane and then it fills in all your passwords automatically.

If you don't want to purchase an additional product, web browsers provide password-management tools. When you go to a website that requires a login, the browser will display a dialog box asking if you want the browser to remember the password for the site (see Figure 9.22). The next time you return to the site, it will automatically fill in the information for you. Consider combining this with two-factor authentication of access to your browser account to be most secure.

**What other ways are there to secure login to your device?** There are a number of security options beyond typing a password. Windows allows you to use gestures on touchscreen devices. You select a picture and then draw three gestures on it—either straight lines, circles, or taps to access your device).

A biometric authentication device is a device that reads a unique personal characteristic such as a fingerprint or the iris pattern in your eye and converts its pattern to a digital code (see Figure 9.23).

**Figure 9.23** Modern mobile devices include iris scanning as an option for securing your device. *(Titima Ongkantong/Shutterstock)*

**Figure 9.24** Windows Hello brings facial recognition for login to laptops and mobile devices that have an integrated camera.
> *From the* **Start** *menu, select* **Settings**. *Go to* **Accounts**, *then select* **Sign-in options**. *Under* **Windows Hello**, *select* **Set Up**. *(Courtesy of Microsoft Corp.)*

Because fingerprints and iris patterns are unique, these devices provide a high level of security. They also eliminate the human error that can occur in password protection. You might forget your password, but you won't forget to bring your fingerprints when you're working on your computer!

Biometric verification is available on most devices now. Many smartphones include fingerprint readers and facial recognition systems. Windows 10 offers facial recognition for login, called Hello, in laptops (see Figure 9.24) and tablets that have integrated cameras. Table 9.3 summarizes security measures in the marketplace.

## Anonymous Web Surfing: Hiding from Prying Eyes

**Objective 9.10**    *Describe ways to surf the Web anonymously.*

**Should I be concerned about surfing the Internet on public computers?** If you use shared computers in public places, such as libraries or coffee shops, you never know what nefarious tools have been installed by hackers. When you browse the Internet, traces of your activity are left behind on that computer, often as temporary files. A wily hacker can glean sensitive information long after you've finished your surfing session. In addition, many employers routinely review the Internet browsing history of employees to ensure workers are spending their time on the Internet productively.

**Table 9.3    Security Measures**

| Style | Devices | Advantages | Disadvantages |
|---|---|---|---|
| Password | Any | Can be long personal phrase | Takes time to type; must be updated often |
| Fingerprint | Smartphones, tablets | Unique; cannot be forgotten | Could possibly be lifted and used by another person |
| Gesture | Windows 10 devices, many mobile devices | Quick; hard to forget | Can be compromised if someone watches you log in |
| Facial recognition | iOS and Android devices; Windows | Quick; no need to remember anything | Some algorithms have trouble matching faces of people of certain ethnic groups |
| Iris scan | Android | Quick; unique; difficult to steal | Can be difficult if user wears eyeglasses |

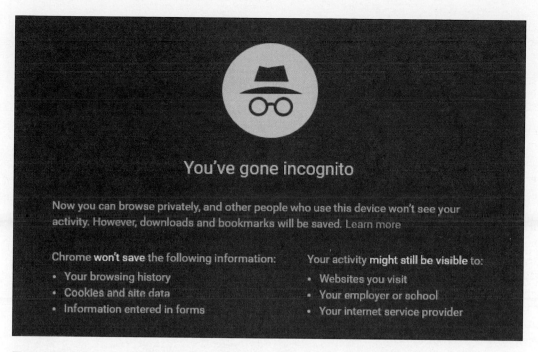

**Figure 9.25** Modern browsers include privacy tools to support anonymous web surfing. *(Courtesy of Google Inc.)*

**What tools can I use to keep my browsing activities private when surfing the Internet?**
The current versions of Mozilla Firefox, Microsoft Edge, and Google Chrome include privacy tools (called Private Browsing, InPrivate, and Incognito, respectively) that help you surf the Web anonymously (see Figure 9.25). When you choose to surf anonymously, all three browsers open special versions of their browser windows that are enhanced for privacy. When surfing in these windows, records of websites you visit and files you download don't appear in the web browser's history files. Furthermore, any temporary files generated in that browsing session are deleted when you exit the special window.

**Are there any other tools I could use to protect my privacy?** Portable privacy devices, such as the Kingston Personal Flash Drives (*kingston.com*), provide an even higher level of surfing privacy. Simply plug the device into an available USB port on the machine on which you'll be working. All sensitive Internet files, such as cookies, passwords, Internet history, and browser caches, will be stored on the privacy device, not on the computer you're using. Privacy devices such as these often come preloaded with software designed to shield your IP address from prying eyes, making it difficult for hackers to tell where you're surfing on the Internet. These privacy devices also have password-management tools that store all of your login information and encrypt it so it will be safe if your privacy device falls into someone else's hands.

**Is there anything else I can do to keep my data safe on shared computers?** Another free practical solution is to take the Linux OS with you on a flash drive and avoid using the public or work computer's OS. The interfaces of many Linux distros look almost exactly like Windows and are easy to use. There are several advantages to using a Linux-based OS on a public or work computer:

- When you run software from your own storage medium, such as a flash drive, you avoid reading and writing to the hard disk of the computer. This significantly enhances your privacy because you don't leave traces of your activity behind.

- Your risk of picking up viruses and other malicious programs is significantly reduced because booting a computer from a flash drive completely eliminates any interaction with the computer's OS. This, in turn, significantly reduces the chance that your flash drive will become infected by any malware running on the computer.

- Virus and hacking attacks against Linux are far less likely than attacks against Windows. Because Windows has about 90% of the OS market, people who write malware tend to target Windows systems.

Pendrivelinux (*pendrivelinux.com*) is an excellent resource that offers many different versions of Linux for download and includes step-by-step instructions on how to install them on your flash drive. If you're a Mac user, the Elementary OS Luna distro of Linux provides a close approximation of macOS, so you can feel right at home.

Computer system security depends on authentication—proving users are who they say they are. There are three independent authentication factors:

- Knowledge: something the user knows (password, PIN)
- Possession: something the user has (ATM card, mobile phone)
- Inherence: something only the user is (biometric characteristics, such as fingerprints or iris pattern)

Multi-factor authentication requires two of the three above factors be demonstrated before authorization is granted (see Figure 9.26). At your bank's ATM machine, you present an ATM card (something you have) and then use a PIN code (something you know) to access your account.

For online access, multi-factor authentication often relies on the use of mobile phones. For instance, when you register a Google account, you supply your mobile phone number. If you then want to make changes to your account, you supply the password (something you know). The second step of authentication is Google sending an SMS message with a unique code to your mobile phone. Retrieving the code and entering it online proves you have the phone (something the user has) and serves as the second authentication step.

Multi-factor authentication is much safer than single-factor authentication. So make use of it when it is offered to you to enhance your account security.

**Figure 9.26 Multi-factor Authentication**

**Something you KNOW:**
Something the user knows
*(password, PIN)*

**Something you HAVE:**
Something the user has
*(ATM card, mobile phone)*

**Something you ARE:**
Something only the user is
*(fingerprints, iris patterns)*

**Strong Authentication:**
Two of the three factors

*(LoloStock/Fotolia; Jamdesign/Fotolia; jamie/Fotolia; Art Pencil Studio/Shutterstock)*

**How can I protect sensitive data transmissions if I have to use a public wireless network?** Virtual private networks (VPNs) are secure networks that are established using the public Internet infrastructure. Using specialized software, servers, and data transmission protocols, VPNs are used to send information on the public Internet in such a manner that the data is as secure as sending it on a private network. VPNs were only used by businesses, but with public concerns about information security on the rise, many VPN software providers (such as Private Internet Access and NordVPN) are marketing affordable solutions to individuals. So if you routinely transmit sensitive information, you should consider a personal VPN solution.

Make sure to use some of these methods to keep your activities from prying eyes and to restrict access to your digital information.

# Keeping Your Data Safe

 Sound Byte **MyLab IT**

**Managing Computer Security with Windows Tools**

In this Sound Byte, you learn how to monitor and control your computer security using features built into the Windows OS.

People are often too trusting or just plain careless when it comes to protecting private information about themselves or their digital data. In this section, we discuss ways to keep your data safe from damage, either accidental or intentional.

## Protecting Your Personal Information

**Objective 9.11** *Describe the types of information you should never share online.*

If a complete stranger walked up to you on the street and asked you for your address and phone number, would you give it to him or her? Of course you wouldn't! But many people are much less

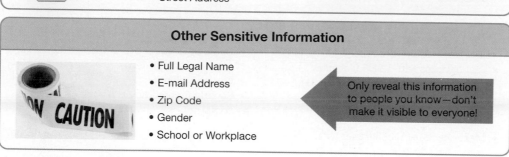

**Information Identity Thieves Crave**

STOP

- Social Security Number
- Full Date of Birth
- Phone Number
- Street Address

Never make this information visible on websites!

**Other Sensitive Information**

CAUTION

- Full Legal Name
- E-mail Address
- Zip Code
- Gender
- School or Workplace

Only reveal this information to people you know—don't make it visible to everyone!

**Figure 9.27** Internet information-sharing precautions *(Mograph/Fotolia, Kevin Largent/Fotolia)*

careful when it comes to sharing sensitive information online. And often people inadvertently share information that they really only intended to share with their friends. With cybercrimes like identity theft rampant, you need to take steps to protect your personal information.

**What information should I never share on websites?** A good rule of thumb is to reveal as little information as possible, especially if the information would be available to everyone. Figure 9.27 gives you some good guidelines.

Your Social Security number, phone number, date of birth, and street address are four key pieces of information that identity thieves use to steal an identity. This information should never be shared in a public area on any website.

**How can I tell who can see my information on a social network?** Social networking sites like Facebook and Instagram make privacy settings available in your profile settings. If you've never changed your default privacy settings, you're probably sharing information more widely than you should.

**How can I protect my information?** To begin, consider changing your privacy settings in your profile from some of the default options. In general, it's a bad idea to make personal information available to the public. It's a good idea to consider using two-factor authorization as well, to reduce the chance of having your account hijacked.

## Backing Up Your Data

**Objective 9.12** *List the various types of backups you can perform on your computing devices, and explain the various places you can store backup files.*

**How might I damage my data?** A hacker can gain access to your computer and steal your data, but a more likely scenario is that you'll lose your data unintentionally. You may accidentally delete files or drop your laptop on the ground, damaging the hard drive. You should have a strategy for backing up your files (see Table 9.4). Backups are copies of files that you can use to replace the originals if they're lost or damaged.

**What types of files do I need to back up?** Two types of files need backups:

1. Data files include files you've created or purchased, such as research papers, spreadsheets, music and photo files, contact lists, address books, e-mail archives, and your Favorites list from your browser.

2. Program files include files used to install software. Most manufacturers allow you to re-download the installation files if you need to reinstall the program, but some don't or charge you an extra fee for that service. Making sure you have your own backup of your system protects you in either case.

**Table 9.4 An Effective Backup Strategy**

**Files to Back Up**

- **Program files:** Installation files for productivity software (i.e., Microsoft Office)
- **Data files:** Files you create (term papers, spreadsheets, etc.)

**Types of Backups**

- **Full backup:** All appliation and data files
- **Image (system):** Snapshot of your entire computer, including system software

**Where to Store Backup Files**

- Online (in the cloud)
- External hard drives
- Network-attached storage devices or home servers

## Table 9.5   A Comparison of Typical Data Backup Locations

| Backup Location | Pros | Cons |
|---|---|---|
| Online (in the cloud)  | • Files stored at a secure, remote location<br>• Files/backups accessible anywhere through a browser | • Most free storage sites don't provide enough space for image backups |
| External hard drive  | • Inexpensive, one-time cost<br>• Fast backups with USB 3.0 devices connected directly to your computer | • Could be destroyed in one event (fire/flood) with your computer<br>• Can be stolen<br>• Slightly more difficult to back up multiple computers with one device |
| Network-attached storage device and home server  | • Makes backups much easier for multiple computing devices | • More expensive than a stand-alone external hard drive<br>• Could be destroyed in one event (fire/flood) with your computer<br>• Can be stolen |

*(Mipan/Fotolia, Prapass Wannapinij/Fotolia, Darkdesigns/Fotolia)*

**What types of backups can I perform?** There are two important types of backups:

1. A full backup means that you create a copy of all your application and data files. This is followed by a schedule of incremental backups (or partial backups). These involve only backing up files that have changed or have been created since the last backup was performed.

2. An image backup (or system backup) means that all system files are backed up, not just the application and data files. An image backup ensures you capture a complete snapshot of everything that makes your computer run—the operating system, the applications, and the data. The idea of imaging is to make an exact copy of the setup of your computer so that in the event of a total hard drive failure, you can copy the image to a new hard drive and have your computer configured exactly the way it was before the crash.

**Where should I store my backups?** You have three main choices for where to back up your files (see Table 9.5).

1. *Online (in the cloud).* To be truly secure, backups should be stored online. Because the information is stored online, it's in a secure, remote location, so data isn't vulnerable to the disasters that could harm data stored in your home. Image backups may not fit within the storage limits offered for free by cloud providers. Look for a service that specifically provides mirror-image backups, which will include a copy of your full operating system. For example, Carbonite (*carbonite.com*) offers certain plans that include online storage of a full system backup.

2. *External hard drives.* External hard drives, or even large-capacity flash drives, are popular backup options. Although convenient and inexpensive, using external hard drives for back-ups still presents the dilemma of keeping the hard drive in a safe location. Also, external hard drives can fail, possibly leading to loss of your backed-up data. Therefore, using an external hard drive for backups is best done in conjunction with an online backup strategy for added safety.

3. *Network-attached storage (NAS) devices and home servers.* NAS devices are essentially large hard drives connected to a network of computers instead of to just one computer, and they can be used to back up multiple computers simultaneously. Home servers also act as high-capacity NAS devices for automatically backing up data and sharing files.

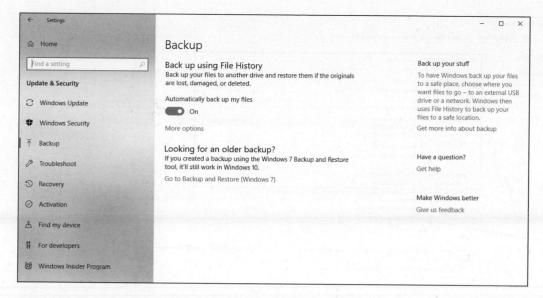

**Figure 9.28** You can use the Windows File History utility to back up files and restore files from a previous backup. > Access **Settings,** select **Update & security,** then click **Backup.** *(Courtesy of Microsoft Corp.)*

**How do I create a backup of my data files?** Use the Windows 10 File History utility (see Figure 9.28). You may want to connect an external hard drive to your computer or a NAS device (or home server) to your network to store your backup or you may just want to back up to a USB flash drive, depending on how much data you have to store. Once configured, your data files will be backed up as often as you indicate. You can also restore files that you've backed up from the File History utility. With a few clicks you can retrieve any file back to your system.

**How often should I back up my data files?** File History can be set to automatically save files you've changed every 10 minutes or every day, whatever you select. File History keeps previous versions of the file on the backup drive so you can revert to an older copy of the file if you need to do so.

**How do I create an image backup?** Windows also includes the System Image backup utility, which provides a quick and easy way to perform image backups. You can access this utility from the Backup and Restore screen (see Figure 9.29a) by clicking *Create a system image*. Before starting this utility, make sure your external drive or NAS device is connected to your computer or network and is powered on. To create the image backup:

1. Click the *Create a system image* link. Select the location (drive) for your backup files and click *Next* to proceed.
2. On the second screen (see Figure 9.29b), you can select the drives (or partitions of drives) from your computer to be backed up. Notice that all the drives/partitions that are required for Windows to run are preselected for you. Windows will back up all data files and system files on all selected drives/partitions. Click (*Next* to proceed.
3. On the third screen, click *Start backup* to start your system image.

After the system image backup runs for the first time, you'll see the results of the last backup and the date of the next scheduled backup on the Backup and Restore (Windows 7) screen (see Figure 9.29a). If the scheduled backup time is not convenient for you, click the *Change settings* link to select an alternative time.

From the Backup and Restore screen, you can also create a system repair disc. A system repair disc contains files that can be used to boot your computer in case of a serious Windows error.

**How often should I create an image backup?** Because your program and OS files don't change as often as your data files, you can perform image backups on a less frequent basis. You might consider scheduling an image backup of your entire system on a weekly basis, but you should definitely perform one after installing new software.

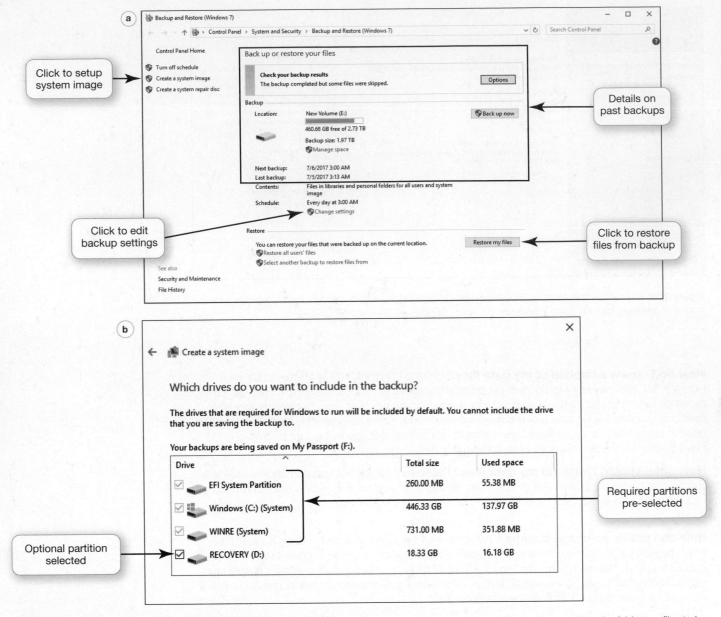

**Figure 9.29** (a) The Backup utility allows you to customize many details of the backup regimen. (b) Restore allows you to select the folders or files to be pulled back from a specific date. *(Courtesy of Microsoft Corp.)*

**What about backing up Apple computers?** For macOS users, backups are very easy to configure. The Time Machine feature in macOS detects when an external hard drive is connected to the computer or a NAS device is connected to your network. You're then asked if you want this to be your backup drive. If you answer yes, all of your files (including OS files) are automatically backed up to the external drive or NAS device.

**Should I back up my files that are stored on my school's network?** If you're allowed to store files on your school's network, most likely these files are backed up regularly. You should check with your school's network administrators to determine how often they're backed up and how you would request that files be restored from the backup if they're damaged or deleted. But don't rely on these network backups to bail you out if your data files are lost or damaged. It may take days for the network administrators to restore your files. It's better to keep backups of your data files yourself, especially homework and project files, so that you can immediately restore them. Storing your school projects in an organized portfolio with a cloud service like Dropbox or Google Drive is the best way to keep safe and to be prepared for creating the resumé you'll need in the future.

# Protecting Your Physical Computing Assets

It's essential to ensure a safe environment for all your computing devices. This includes protecting them from environmental factors, power surges, power outages, and theft.

## Environmental Factors and Power Surges

**Objective 9.13** *Explain the negative effects environment and power surges can have on computing devices.*

**Why is the environment critical to the operation of my computer equipment?** Sudden movements, such as a fall, can damage your computing device's internal components. Make sure that your computer sits on a flat, level surface, and if it's a laptop or a tablet, carry it in a protective case.

Electronic components don't like excessive heat or excessive cold. Don't leave computing devices and phones in a car during especially hot or cold weather because components can be damaged by extreme temperatures. Unfortunately, computers generate a lot of heat, which is why they have fans to cool their internal components. Chill mats that contain cooling fans and sit underneath laptop computers are useful accessories for dissipating heat. Make sure that you place your desktop computer where the fan's intake vents, usually found on the rear of the system unit, are unblocked so air can flow inside.

Naturally, a fan drawing air into a computer also draws in dust and other particles, which can wreak havoc on your system. Therefore, keep the room in which your computer is located as clean as possible. Finally, because food crumbs and liquid can damage keyboards and other computer components, consume food and beverages away from your computer.

**What is a power surge?** Power surges occur when electric current is supplied in excess of normal voltage. Old or faulty wiring, downed power lines, malfunctions at electric company substations, and lightning strikes can all cause power surges. A surge protector is a device that protects your computer against power surges (see Figure 9.30).

Note that you should replace your surge protectors every two to three years. Also, after a major surge, the surge protector will no longer function and must be replaced. And it's wise to buy a surge protector that includes indicator lights, which illuminate when the surge protector is no longer functioning properly. Don't be fooled by old surge protectors—although they can still function as multiple-outlet power strips, they deliver power to your equipment without protecting it from surges.

**Besides my computer, what other devices need to be connected to a surge protector?** All electronic devices in the home that have solid-state components, such as TVs, stereos, printers, and smartphones (when charging), should be connected to a surge protector. However, it can be inconvenient to use individual surge protectors on everything. A more practical method is to install a whole-house surge protector (see Figure 9.31). Whole-house surge protectors function like other surge protectors, but they protect all electrical devices in the house. Typically, you'll need an electrician to install a whole-house surge protector, which costs hundreds of dollars.

**Is my equipment 100% safe when plugged into a surge protector?** No. Lightning strikes can generate such high voltages that they can overwhelm a surge protector. Unplugging electronic devices during an electrical storm is the only way to achieve absolute protection.

## Preventing and Handling Theft

**Objective 9.14** *Describe the major concerns when a device is stolen and strategies for solving the problems.*

**What if my computing device is stolen?** The theft of tablets, smartphones, notebook computers, and other portable computing devices is always a risk. The resale value for used electronic equipment is high, and the equipment can be easily sold online. And because they're portable, laptops, tablets, and phones are easy targets for thieves. The main security concerns with mobile devices are:

1. Keeping them from being stolen
2. Keeping data secure in case they are stolen
3. Finding a device if it is stolen

**Figure 9.30** Surge protectors are critical for protecting your electronic devices. *(JcJq Photography/Fotolia)*

Surge protector

**Figure 9.31** A whole-house surge protector is usually installed at the breaker panel or near the electric meter.

**What type of alarm can I install on my mobile device?** Motion alarm software is a good, inexpensive theft deterrent. Free software such as LAlarm (*lalarm.com*) is effective for laptops. Apps such as Motion Alarm and Alarmomatic help secure your iPad or iPhone. Alarm software either detects motion, as when your device is being picked up, or sounds near your device and then sets off an ear-piercing alarm until you enter the disable code.

**How can I secure the data on my mobile devices?** The easiest way to keep the data secure is to make sure you have a login passcode set for your device. If your device supports biometrics like fingerprint detection for login, that's another way to make sure the contents are safe even if it's stolen.

Even if somehow the thief gets entry into the device, you can protect the data from prying eyes. Encrypting the data on your mobile device can make it practically impossible for thieves to obtain the data. Encryption involves transforming your data using an algorithm that can only be unlocked by a secure passcode. Encrypted data can't be read unless it's decrypted, which requires the passcode. If you encrypt your SD card, for example, then if it is removed and placed in another device, it cannot be read. On both iOS and Android devices, the operating system offers a built-in encryption option.

**How can my device help me recover it when it is stolen?** Software is available that lets your device report back its current location. For iOS devices, Apple offers the Find My iPhone service. Enabling this service provides you with numerous tools to assist you in recovering and protecting your mobile devices. Did you forget where you left your iPad? Just sign in with your Apple ID at the iCloud website to see a map showing the location of your iPad. You can send a message to your device, remotely password-lock the device, or wipe all data from the device to completely protect your privacy. For Android devices, the Android Device Manager offers similar features. You can easily type "Find my phone" into the omnibox (the browser search bar) of Google Chrome, and a map with the location of your Android device will be shown (see Figure 9.32). And for Windows 10 devices, there is a similar Find My Device command located in the Update and Security section of Settings.

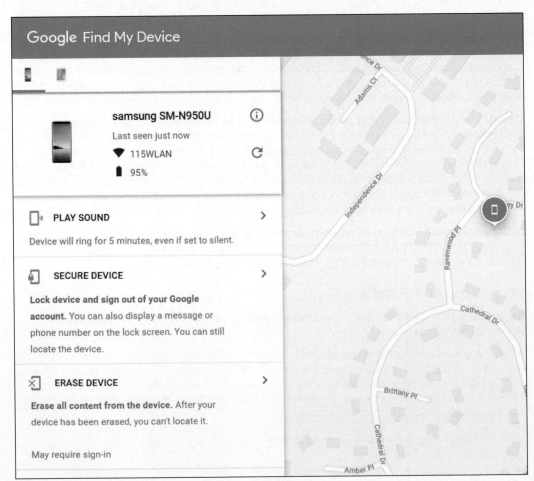

**Figure 9.32** The Android Device Manager lets you locate any Android device and take steps to find and return it to its owner. *(Courtesy of Google Inc.)*

On law enforcement TV shows, you often see computer technicians working on suspects' computers to assist detectives in solving crimes. It may look simple, but the science of computer forensics is a complex, step-by-step process that ensures evidence is collected within the confines of the law.

*Forensic* means that something is suitable for use in a court of law. There are many branches of forensic science. For example, forensic pathologists provide evidence about the nature and manner of death in court cases involving deceased individuals. Computer forensics involves identifying, extracting, preserving, and documenting computer evidence. Computer forensics is performed by individuals known as *computer forensicsscientists*, who rely primarily on specialized software to collect their evidence.

### Phase 1: Obtaining and Securing Computer Devices

The first step in a computer forensics investigation is to seize the computer equipment that law enforcement officials believe contains pertinent evidence. Police are required to obtain a warrant to search an individual's home or place of business. Warrants must be very specific by spelling out exactly where detectives can search for evidence and exactly what type of evidence they're seeking. If a warrant indicates that the police may search an individual's home for his laptop computer, they can't then confiscate a tablet computer they notice in his car. It is important to specify in the warrant all types of storage devices where potential evidence might be stored, such as external hard drives, flash drives, and servers.

Once permission to collect the computers and devices containing possible evidence has been obtained, law enforcement officials must exercise great care when collecting the equipment. They need to ensure that no unauthorized persons are able to access or alter the computers or storage devices. The police must make sure the data and equipment are safe; if the equipment is connected to the Internet, the connection must be severed without data loss or damage. It's also important for law enforcement officials to understand that they may not want to power off equipment because potential evidence contained in RAM may be lost. After the devices are collected and secured, the computer forensic scientists take over the next phase of the investigation.

### Phase 2: Cataloging and Analyzing the Data

It's critical to preserve the data exactly as it was found, or attorneys may argue that the computer evidence was subject to tampering or altering. Because just opening a file can alter it, the first task is to make a copy of all computer systems and storage devices collected (see Figure 9.33). The investigators then work from the copies to ensure that the original data always remains preserved exactly as it was when it was collected.

After obtaining a copy to work from, forensics professionals attempt to find every file on the system, including deleted files. Files on a computer aren't actually deleted, even if you empty the Recycle Bin, until the section of the hard disk they're stored on is overwritten with new data. Therefore, using special forensic software tools such as SANS Investigative Forensic Toolkit (SIFT), the forensic scientists catalog all files found on the system or storage medium and recover as much information from deleted files as they can. Software like the Forensic Toolkit (FTK) can readily detect hidden files and perform procedures to crack encrypted files or access protected files and reveal their contents.

The most important part of the process is documenting every step. Forensic scientists must clearly log every procedure performed because they may be required to provide proof in court that their investigations did not alter or damage information contained on the systems they examined. Detailed reports should list all files found, how the files were laid out on the system, which files were protected or encrypted, and the contents of each file. Finally, computer forensic professionals are often called on to present testimony in court during a trial.

Criminals are getting more sophisticated and are now employing antiforensics techniques to foil computer forensic investigators. Although techniques for hiding or encrypting data are popular, the most insidious antiforensics techniques are programs designed to erase data if unauthorized persons (i.e., not the criminal) access a computer system or if the system detects forensics software in use. When computer forensic investigators detect these countermeasures, they must often use creative methods and custom-designed software programs to retrieve and preserve the data.

Computer forensics is an invaluable tool to law enforcement in many criminal investigations, but only if the correct procedures are followed and the appropriate documentation is prepared.

**Figure 9.33** Portable computer forensic devices make it easy to copy storage devices at crime scenes. *(Lance Mueller/Alamy Stock Photo)*

**How can I ensure that I've covered all aspects of protecting my digital devices?**
Table 9.6 provides a guide to ensure you haven't missed critical aspects of security. If you've addressed all of these issues, you can feel reasonably confident that your data and devices are secure.

| Table 9.6 Computer Security Checklist |
| --- |
| **Firewall** |
| • Do all your computers and tablets have firewall software installed and activated before connecting to the Internet?<br>• Is your router also able to function as a hardware firewall?<br>• Have you tested your firewall security by using the free software available at grc.com? |
| **Virus and Spyware Protection** |
| • Is antivirus and antispyware software installed on all your devices?<br>• Is the antivirus and antispyware software configured to update itself automatically and regularly?<br>• Is the software set to scan your device on a regular basis (at least weekly) for viruses and spyware? |
| **Software Updates** |
| • Have you configured your operating systems (Windows, macOS) to install new software patches and updates automatically?<br>• Is other software installed on your device, such as Microsoft Office or productivity apps, configured for automatic updates?<br>• Is the web browser you're using the latest version? |
| **Protecting Your Devices** |
| • Are all computing devices protected from electrical surges?<br>• Do your mobile devices have alarms or tracking software installed on them? |

---

### Before moving on to the Chapter Review:

1.  Watch Chapter Overview Video 9.2.
2. Then take the Check Your Understanding quiz.

# Check Your Understanding // Review & Practice

For a quick review to see what you've learned so far, answer the following questions.

## multiple choice

1. Firewalls work by closing _____ in your computer.

   a. software gaps

   b. logical ports

   c. logical doors

   d. backdoors

2. Antivirus software looks for _____ to detect viruses in files.

   a. virus signatures

   b. virus artifacts

   c. virus bots

   d. virus VPNs

3. _____ involve using a physical attribute such as a fingerprint for authentication.

   a. Backdoors

   b. Biometrics

   c. Rootkits

   d. Trojan horses

4. When you are surfing the Web anonymously,

   a. the sites you visit are not stored in the browser history.

   b. temporary files created are immediately deleted.

   c. you are using a browser that has privacy tools.

   d. all of the above

5. Once you encrypt your SD card, those files

   a. are illegal.

   b. are compressed and can be stored in less space.

   c. cannot be read if the SD card is put in another phone.

   d. are backed up.

**chew on this**

To keep your data secure you have many choices. How will you structure the combination of multi-factor authentication, biometrics, and password managers to make sure your devices are safe from prying eyes? How would your answer be different if you ran a business of 20 people?

**MyLab IT**  Go to **MyLab IT** to take an autograded version of the *Check Your Understanding* review and to find all media resources for the chapter.

> **For the IT Simulation for this chapter, see MyLab IT.**

# 9  Chapter Review

## Summary

**Learning Outcome 9.1**  You will be able to describe hackers, viruses, and other online annoyances and the threats they pose to your digital security.

### Identity Theft and Hackers

**Objective 9.1**  *Describe how identity theft is committed and the types of scams identity thieves perpetrate.*

- Identity theft occurs when a thief steals personal information about you and runs up debts in your name. Identity thieves can obtain information by stealing mail, searching through trash, or tricking people into revealing information over the phone or via e-mail. Identity thieves counterfeit existing credit cards, open new credit card and bank accounts, change the address on financial statements, obtain medical services, and buy homes with a mortgage in the victim's name.

**Objective 9.2**  *Describe the different types of hackers and the tools they use.*

- White-hat hackers break into systems for nonmalicious reasons such as testing security to expose weaknesses. Black-hat hackers break into systems to destroy information or for illegal gain. Gray-hat hackers often break into systems just for the thrill or to demonstrate their prowess.
- Packet analyzers (sniffers) are programs used to intercept and read data packets, and they travel across a network. Trojan horses are programs that appear to be something else but are really a tool for hackers to access your computer. Backdoor programs and rootkits are tools used by hackers to gain access to and take total control of a computer system. Denial-of-service attacks overwhelm computer systems with so many requests for data that legitimate users can't access the system.

### Computer Viruses

**Objective 9.3**  *Explain what a computer virus is, why it is a threat to your security, how a computing device catches a virus, and the symptoms it may display.*

- A computer virus is a computer program that attaches itself to another computer program and attempts to spread to other computers when files are exchanged.

Computer viruses can display annoying messages, destroy your information, corrupt your files, or gather information about you. Computers catch viruses when exposed to infected files. This can occur from downloading infected files, downloading and running infected e-mail attachments, or sharing flash drives that contain infected files. Symptoms of virus infection include (1) files or app icons disappear; (2) browser is reset to an unusual home page; (3) odd messages, pop-ups, or images are displayed; (4) data files become corrupt; and (5) programs stop working properly.

**Objective 9.4**  *List the different categories of computer viruses, and describe their behaviors.*

- Boot-sector viruses copy themselves onto the master boot record of a computer and execute when the computer is started. Logic bombs and time bombs are viruses triggered by the completion of certain events or by the passage of time. Worms can spread on their own without human intervention, unlike conventional viruses. Macro viruses lurk in documents that use macros (short series of commands that automate repetitive tasks). E-mail viruses access the address book of a victim to spread to the victim's contacts. Encryption viruses render files unusable by compressing them with complex encryption keys. A multi-partite virus is designed to infect multiple file types in an effort to fool the antivirus software that is looking for it. Polymorphic viruses periodically rewrite themselves to avoid detection. Stealth viruses temporarily erase their code and hide in the active memory of the computer.

### Online Annoyances and Social Engineering

**Objective 9.5**  *Explain what malware, spam, and cookies are and how they impact your security.*

- Malware is software that has a malicious intent. Adware is software that displays sponsored advertisements in a section of your browser window or as a pop-up box. Spyware collects information about you, without your knowledge, and transmits it to the owner of the program.

- Spam is unwanted or junk e-mail. Spim is unsolicited instant messages, which is also a form of spam. Spam filters in e-mail systems forward junk mail to their own folder. Never reply to spam or click on unsubscribe links, as this usually just generates more spam.
- Cookies are small text files that some websites automatically store on your hard drive when you visit them. Cookies are usually used to keep track of users and personalize their browsing experience. Cookies do not pose a security threat, although some individuals view them as privacy violations.

**Objective 9.6** *Describe social engineering techniques, and explain strategies to avoid falling prey to them.*

- Social engineering is any technique that uses social skills to generate human interaction that entices individuals to reveal sensitive information. Phishing lures people into revealing personal information via bogus e-mails that appear to be from legitimate sources and direct people to scammer's websites. Pharming occurs when malicious code is planted on your computer, either by viruses or by your visiting malicious websites, which then alters your browser's ability to find web addresses. Scareware attempts to convince you that your computer is infected with a virus and then tries to sell you a "solution." Most Internet security software packages have scareware, phishing, and pharming protection built in.

## Part 2

## Protecting Your Digital Property

**Learning Outcome 9.2** **Describe various ways to protect your digital property and data from theft and corruption.**

### Restricting Access to Your Digital Assets

**Objective 9.7** *Explain what a firewall is and how a firewall protects your computer from hackers.*

- A firewall is a software program or hardware device designed to protect computers from hackers. Firewalls block access to your computer's logical ports and help keep your computer's network address secure. Firewalls use packet filtering to identify packets sent to specific logical ports and discard them. Firewalls use network address translation to assign internal IP addresses on networks. The internal IP addresses are much more difficult for hackers to detect.

**Objective 9.8** *Explain how to protect your computer from virus infection.*

- Antivirus software is specifically designed to detect viruses and protect your computer and files from harm. Antivirus software detects viruses by looking for virus signatures: code that specifically identifies a virus. Antivirus software stops viruses from executing and quarantines infected files in a secure area on the hard drive. Virus software must be constantly updated to remain effective.

**Objective 9.9** *Describe how passwords and biometric characteristics can be used for user authentication.*

- Utilities built into web browsers and Internet security software can be used to manage your passwords.
- A biometric authentication device reads a unique personal characteristic to identify an authorized user.

Fingerprint readers, iris scanners, and facial recognition software are common examples of biometric security devices.

**Objective 9.10** *Describe ways to surf the Web anonymously.*

- Privacy tools built into web browsers help you surf anonymously by not recording your actions in the history files. USB devices containing privacy tools are available that prevent the computer you are using from storing any information about you. Virtual private networks (VPNs) are secure networks that can be used to send information securely across the public Internet.

### Keeping Your Data Safe

**Objective 9.11** *Describe the types of information you should never share online.*

- Reveal as little information as possible about yourself. Your Social Security number, phone number, date of birth, and street address are four key pieces of information that identity thieves need to steal an identity.

**Objective 9.12** *List the various types of backups you can perform on your computing devices, and explain the various places you can store backup files.*

- An incremental backup involves backing up only files that have changed or have been created since the last full backup was performed. An image backup (or system backup) means that all system, application, and data files are backed up, not just the files that changed. You can store backups online (in the cloud), on external hard drives, or on network-attached storage (NAS) devices.

## Protecting Your Physical Computing Assets

**Objective 9.13** *Explain the negative effects environment and power surges can have on computing devices.*

- Computing devices should be kept in clean environments free from dust and other particulates and should not be exposed to extreme temperatures (either hot or cold). You should protect all electronic devices from power surges by hooking them up through surge protectors, which will protect them from most electrical surges that could damage the devices.

**Objective 9.14** *Describe the major concerns when a device is stolen and strategies for solving the problems.*

- The four main security concerns regarding computing devices are (1) keeping them from being stolen, (2) keeping data secure in case they are stolen, (3) finding a device if it is stolen, and (4) remotely recovering and wiping data off a stolen device.
- Software is available for installation on devices that will (1) set off an alarm if the device is moved; (2) help recover the device, if stolen, by reporting the computer's whereabouts when it is connected to the Internet; and (3) allow you to lock or wipe the contents of the device remotely.

 Be sure to check out **MyLab IT** for additional materials to help you review and learn. And don't forget to watch the Chapter Overview Videos. ▶

# Key Terms

adware **333**
antivirus software **345**
backdoor program **326**
backup **353**
biometric authentication device **349**
black-hat hacker **325**
boot-sector virus **331**
botnet **327**
computer forensics **359**
cookie **335**
cybercrime **324**
cyberloafing (cyberslacking) **338**
data breach **339**
data file **353**
denial-of-service (DoS) attack **327**
distributed denial-of-service (DDoS) attack **327**
drive-by download **347**
e-mail virus **331**
encryption virus **331**
exploit kits **328**
firewall **343**
full backup **354**

gray-hat hacker **325**
hacker **325**
identity theft **325**
image backup (system backup) **354**
incremental backup (partial backup) **354**
inoculation **346**
keystroke logger (keylogger) **334**
logic bomb **331**
logical port **328**
logical port blocking **344**
macro virus **331**
malware **333**
master boot record **331**
multi-factor authentication **352**
multi-partite virus **332**
network address translation (NAT) **345**
packet **326**
packet analyzer (sniffer) **326**
packet filtering **344**
personal firewall **343**
pharming **336**
phishing **336**

polymorphic virus **332**
pretexting **336**
program file **353**
quarantining **346**
rootkit **326**
scareware **337**
script **331**
social engineering **335**
spam **334**
spam filter **334**
spear phishing **339**
spyware **333**
stealth virus **332**
surge protector **357**
time bomb **331**
Trojan horse **326**
virtual private network (VPN) **352**
virus **329**
virus signature **346**
white-hat hacker (ethical hacker) **325**
whole-house surge protector **357**
worm **331**
zombie **326**

# Chapter Quiz // Assessment

For a quick review to see what you've learned, answer the following questions. Submit the quiz as requested by your instructor. If you're using MyLab IT, the quiz is also available there.

## multiple choice

1. When someone uses your personal information to pose as you, this is
   a. identity theft.
   b. white-hat hacking.
   c. cybersecurity.
   d. a backdoor rootkit.

2. Viruses that load from USB drives left connected to computers when computers are turned on are known as
   a. script viruses.
   b. polymorphic viruses.
   c. encryption viruses.
   d. boot-sector viruses.

3. A packet analyzer is called a sniffer because
   a. it filters out spam.
   b. it starts a denial-of-service attack.
   c. it captures and reads data inside each packet.
   d. it detects high-speed transmissions.

4. Computer viruses can be spread by
   a. sharing flash drives.
   b. downloading and running a file attached to an e-mail.
   c. downloading a song from a peer-to-peer sharing site.
   d. all of the above

5. A _____ is a program that takes complete control of your computer without your knowledge.
   a. botnet
   b. rootkit
   c. VPN
   d. sniffer

6. A backup of all the data files on your computer can be managed easily using the Windows 10 _____ utility.
   a. Windows Defender
   b. File History
   c. Windows Update
   d. Recovery

7. Authentication techniques that rely on personal biological traits are called
   a. Trojan horses.
   b. scanners.
   c. botnets.
   d. biometrics.

8. Antivirus software prevents infection by recording key attributes about your files and checking to see if they change over time in a process called
   a. updating.
   b. quarantine.
   c. signature.
   d. inoculation.

9. A surge protector may look like just another power strip but it also can
   a. detect viruses.
   b. prevent theft.
   c. save your device if a voltage spike is sent through the electrical system.
   d. help manage heat.

10. Firewalls use a process of _____ to assign IP addresses to the devices internal to the network so hackers will not know what they are.
    a. packet filtering
    b. port blocking
    c. VPN
    d. network address translation (NAT)

## true/false

_____ 1. A 32-character password is an example of using biometrics.

_____ 2. Your Social Security number should never be shared on a website, in an e-mail, or through messaging.

_____ 3. Sending e-mails to lure people into revealing personal information is a technique known as phishing.

_____ 4. Encrypting data is not an appropriate measure for mobile devices such as smartphones.

_____ 5. Virtual private networks make it just as secure to send information across a public network as it is on a secure private network.

## What do you think now?

1. After reading this chapter, are you planning to use two-factor authentication? On which sites or products?

2. Check your mobile devices for the types of bioauthentication they provide. Are you using these in place of traditional passcodes?

# Team Time

## Protecting a Network

### problem

Along with easy access to the Web comes the danger of theft of digital assets.

### task

A school alumnus is in charge of the county government computer department. The network contains computers running Windows 10, Windows 8, Windows 7, and macOS. He asked your instructor for help in ensuring that his computers and network are protected from viruses, malware, and hackers. He is hoping that there may be free software available that can protect his employees' computers.

### process

1. Break the class into three teams. Each team will be responsible for investigating one of the following issues:
   a. **Antivirus software.** Research alternatives that protect computers from viruses. Find three alternatives and support your recommendations with reviews that evaluate free packages.
   b. **Antimalware software.** Research three free antimalware alternatives and determine whether the software can be updated automatically. You may want to recommend that the county purchase software to ensure that a minimum of employee intervention is needed to keep it up to date.
   c. **Firewalls.** Determine if the firewall software provided with Windows 10, Windows 8, Windows 7, and macOS is reliable. If it is, prepare documentation (for all four OSs) for county employees to determine if their firewalls are properly configured. If additional firewall software is needed, research free firewall software and locate three options that can be deployed by the county.
   d. Present your findings to the class and provide your instructor with a report suitable for eventual presentation to the manager of the county office network.

### conclusion

With the proliferation of viruses and malware, it is essential to protect computers and networks. Free alternatives might work, but you should research the best protection solution for your situation.

# Ethics Project

## Content Control: Censorship to Protect Children

In this exercise, you research and then role-play a complicated ethical situation. The role you play might or might not match your own personal beliefs; in either case, your research and use of logic will enable you to represent the view assigned. An arbitrator will watch and comment on both sides of the arguments, and together the team will agree on an ethical solution.

### problem

Many parents use web-filtering software (content-control software) to protect their children from objectionable Internet content. The U.S. government requires libraries to use content-control software as a condition to receiving federal funds. Some states, such as Virginia, have passed laws requiring libraries to install filtering software even if they did not receive federal funds. Upon installation of the software, it's up to the library administrators to decide what content is restricted. Therefore, content restriction can vary widely from library to library.

### research areas to consider

- U.S. Supreme Court case *United States v. American Library Association*
- Content-control software and First Amendment rights
- Violation of children's free speech rights
- Children's Internet Protection Act (CIPA)

### process

1. Divide the class into teams. One team will play the role of parents of elementary school students. Another team will be the library administration and another will be the users of the local town library.
2. Each team will be presenting its position on how access to the Internet should be managed for the local library, where there are many children, as well as adults, using services. The team position needs to be grounded in more than just opinion. Research so your position is supported by specific data, facts, and examples. Consider both the benefits and challenges of your position and how it will impact the other groups' interests.
3. Team members should present their case to the class or submit a PowerPoint presentation for review by the class. Be sure to include a summary statement of your position.

### conclusion

As technology becomes ever more prevalent and integrated into our lives, more and more ethical dilemmas will present themselves. Being able to understand and evaluate both sides of the argument, while responding in a personally or socially ethical manner, will be an important skill.

## Computer Security

You have been asked to prepare a report on computer security using Microsoft Word. You have written the majority of the report, but you have to make some final modifications and refinements such as adding the results of some research of good antivirus software, adding a cover page, and generating a table of contents.

You will use the following skills as you complete this activity:

- Create and Modify Tables
- Insert Tab Stops
- Add Watermark
- Insert Cover Page

- Create and Update Table of Contents
- Add Footnote
- Use Find and Replace

## Instructions

1. Open *TIA_Ch9_Start.docx* and save as **TIA_Ch9_LastFirst.docx**.

2. Find all instances of *e-mail* and replace with **e-mail** (do not apply bold formatting).
   *Hint:* Click Replace in the Editing group on the Home tab. Use e-mail as the Find term, and use e-mail as the Replace term. Click Replace All. You will make four replacements.

3. Find the first instance of malware. Place the cursor after the word *malware* (before the period) and insert the footnote:
   **Malware is defined as software that is intended to gain access to, or damage or disable, computer systems for the purposes of theft or fraud.** Close the Navigation pane.
   *Hint:* Use Find in the Editing group on the **Home** tab to locate malware.
   *Hint:* Click Insert Footnote in the Footnotes group on the References tab.

4. In the section, *Types of Viruses*, highlight the six lines of text that outline the categories of computer viruses and variants. Add a **Right Align Tab Stop** at 2".
   *Hint:* To set the tab stop, display the ruler and select tab stop style from the Select tab box to the left of the ruler, click at the desired position on the ruler.

5. Place cursor at the end of the paragraph in the *Antivirus Software* section. Press **Enter**, then insert a **3×4 Table**. Type **Product Name**, **Description/Review**, and **Cost** in the top three cells. Adjust the width of the Description/Review column to 3.5" and the width of the Cost column to 1".
   *Hint:* Click Table in the Tables group on the Insert tab, and drag to select the desired grid.

6. Add a row at the top of the table, **Merge Cells**, and type **Antivirus Software Reviews** and **Align Center** the contents. Format the table with **Grid Table 4 - Accent 1** style.
   *Hint:* Click Insert above in the Rows & Columns group on the **Table Tools Layout** tab.

7. Open a browser and go to **www.pcmag.com/reviews/antivirus**. Research four antivirus software programs and place the software name, review, and cost of the software in the respective columns in the table.
   *Hint:* Press tab at the end of the third row to add an additional line to the table to accommodate a fourth review.

8. Press **Ctrl+Home**, then insert the **Banded Cover Page**. Ensure *Computer Security* displays as the title and *your name* displays as the Author. **Delete** the Company and Address placeholders.

9. Insert **Page Numbers** at the bottom of the page using the **Plain Number 3** format. Ensure "Different First Page" is checked. Close Header and Footer.

10. On page 2 of the document, insert a **Page Break** before the report title, *Computer Security*.

11. Place the cursor at the top of the new blank page, and insert **Table of Contents** using the Contents format.
    *Hint:* Click Table of Contents in the Table of Contents group on the References tab.

12. Press **Ctrl+End**, scroll up and change the heading style of *Firewalls* to **Heading 2**, change the heading style of *Software Firewalls* and *Hardware Firewalls* to **Heading 3**.

13. **Update** the Table of Contents to reflect the changes in headings; ensure you update the entire table.
    *Hint:* Click anywhere in the Table of Contents, and click Update table, then click Update entire table.

14. Add a **Draft 1 Watermark** to the report.
    *Hint:* Click Watermark in the Page Backgroup group on the Design tab.

15. Save the document and submit based on your instructor's directions.

# The History of the Personal Computer

 For an overview of how the PC got its start, watch the **History of the PC video**.

**Learning Outcome A.1**   **You will be able to describe the history of personal computer hardware and software development.**

Have you ever wondered how big the first personal computer was or how much the first laptop weighed? Computers are such an integral part of our lives that we don't often stop to think about how far they've come or where they got their start. In just over 40 years, computers have evolved from expensive, huge machines that only corporations could own to small, powerful devices that almost anyone can have. In this appendix, we look at the history of the personal computer.

## Early Personal Computers

Our journey through the history of the personal computer starts in 1975. At that time, most people weren't familiar with the mainframes and supercomputers that large corporations and the government owned. With price tags exceeding the cost of buildings, and with few (if any) practical home uses, these monster machines weren't appealing to or attainable by average Americans.

**The Altair 8800**
- Only 256 bytes of memory
- No keyboard or monitor
- Switches on front used to enter data in machine code (1s and 0s)
- Lights on front indicated results of a program

1975

**Commodore PET**
- Featured in *Popular Science* magazine
- Popular in business settings in Europe

October 1977

1976

June 1977

- Had to provide your own keyboard and monitor
- First unit produced was used in a high school math class

**Apple I**

- Featured color monitor, sound, and game paddles
- 4 KB of RAM
- Operating system stored in ROM
- Optional floppy disk to load programs (mostly games)

**Apple II**

**Figure A.1**   Timeline of early personal computer development. *(B Christopher/Alamy Stock Photo; SSPL/The Image Works; Science & Society Picture Library/Getty Images; Photo Researchers, Inc./Science Source)*

# The First Personal Computer: The Altair

**Objective A.1** *Describe the earliest personal computer ever designed.*

In 1975, the first personal computer, the Altair 8800 (see Figure A.1), was born. At around $400 for a do-it-yourself kit or around $600 for a fully assembled unit (about $2,800 in today's dollars), the price was reasonable enough that computer fanatics could finally own their own computers.

The Altair was primitive by today's standards—no keyboard, no monitor, and completely not user friendly. Despite its limitations, computer enthusiasts flocked to the machine. Many who bought it had been taught to program, but until that point, they had access only to big, clumsy computers at their jobs. With the Altair, they could create their own programs at home. Within 3 months, 4,000 orders were placed for the machine.

The release of the Altair marked the start of the personal computer boom. In fact, two men whose names you might have heard were among the first Altair owners—Bill Gates and Paul Allen were so enamored by the "minicomputer" that they wrote a compiling program (a program that translates user commands into commands the computer can understand) for it. The two later convinced the Altair's developer to buy their program, marking the start of a company called Microsoft. We get to that story later. First, let's see what their rivals were up to.

# The Apple I and II

**Objective A.2** *Describe the distinguishing features of the Apple I and Apple II.*

Around the time the Altair was released, Steve Wozniak, an employee at Hewlett-Packard, was dabbling with his own computer design. Steve Jobs, who was working for computer game manufacturer Atari at the time, liked Wozniak's prototypes and made a few suggestions. Together, the two built a personal computer, the Apple I, in Wozniak's garage (see Figure A.1) and formed the Apple Computer Company in 1976.

### TRS-80

- Introduced by Radio Shack
- Monochrome display
- 4 KB of RAM
- Circuitry hidden under keyboard
- Wildly popular with consumers—sold 10,000 units in the first month

November 1977

### IBM PC (5150)

- Marketed to businesses and consumers
- 64 KB to 256 KB of RAM
- Floppy disk drives optional
- Hard disks not supported in early models

August 1981

April 1981

- First "portable" computer
- Weighed 24.5 pounds
- 5-inch screen
- 64 kilobytes of RAM
- Two floppy disk drives
- Preinstalled with spreadsheet and word processing software

### Osborne

*(Interfoto/Alamy Stock Photo; Interfoto/Alamy Stock Photo; Science & Society Picture Library/Getty Images)*

One year later, in 1977, the Apple II was born (see Figure A.1). The Apple II included a color monitor, sound, and game paddles. Priced around $1,300 (about $5,245 in today's dollars), one of its biggest innovations was that the operating system was stored in read-only memory (ROM). Previously, the operating system had to be rewritten every time the computer was turned on. The friendly features of the Apple II operating system encouraged less technically oriented computer enthusiasts to write their own programs.

An instant success, the Apple II would eventually include a spreadsheet program, a word processor, and desktop publishing software. These programs gave personal computers like the Apple functions beyond gaming and special programming and led to their popularity.

# Enter the Competition

Around the time Apple was experiencing success with its computers, a number of competitors entered the market. The largest among them were Commodore, Radio Shack, Osborne, and IBM. The Commodore PET (see Figure A.1) was aimed at the business market and did well in Europe, while Radio Shack's TRS-80 (see Figure A.1) was clearly aimed at the U.S. consumer market. Just 1 month after its release in 1977, it had sold about 10,000 units.

## The Osborne: The Birth of Portable Computing

**Objective A.3**   *Describe the first portable computer.*

The Osborne Computer Corporation introduced the first portable computer, the Osborne, in 1981 (see Figure A.1). Although portable, the computer weighed 24.5 pounds. It featured a minuscule 5-inch screen and carried a price tag of $1,795 (about $4,884 today). The Osborne was an overnight success, and its sales quickly reached 10,000 units per month. However, despite the computer's popularity, the Osborne Computer Corporation eventually closed.

## IBM PCs

**Objective A.4**   *Describe the development of the IBM PC.*

Until 1980, IBM primarily made mainframe computers, which it sold to large corporations, and hadn't taken the personal computer seriously. In 1981, however, IBM released its first personal computer, the IBM PC (see Figure A.1). Because many companies were familiar with IBM mainframes, they adopted the IBM PC. The term *PC* soon became the term used to describe all personal computers.

IBM marketed its PC through retail outlets such as Sears to reach home users, and it quickly dominated that market. In January 1983, *Time* magazine, playing on its annual person of the year issue, named the computer "1982 Machine of the Year."

Between 1975 and the early 1980s, huge advancements were made in personal computer technology so that by the early 1990s, when access to the Internet became readily available to more people, PCs had begun to be a common (and necessary) home device. Technology advancements have continued with devices becoming smaller yet more powerful and faster. Table A.1 lists some devices that were common at the turn of the 21st century but have since been replaced by more advanced technology. How many of these devices do you remember?

## Table A.1 Devices That Have Become Obsolete Since 2000

| Obsolete Device | Use | Replaced by | Obsolete Device | Use | Replaced by |
|---|---|---|---|---|---|
| Floppy disk | External file storage with maximum capacity of 1.44 MB | Online storage and flash drives | Serial port | Connect printers and mice to computer | USB ports and wireless |
| Zip disk | External file storage with maximum capacity of 100 MB–750 MB | Online storage and flash drives | Parallel port / PS/2 port | Connect printers to computer / Connect mice and keyboards to computer | USB ports and Wi-Fi printers / USB ports and wireless mice and keyboards |
| CRT monitor | Output display device | LCD, LED, and OLED displays | Encyclopedia on CD | Comprehensive reference source on CD | Wikipedia |
| Trackball mouse and Rollerball mouse | Input device | Optical mouse | Camcorder | Portable video recording device | Smartphones |
| Trackpoint | Input device for laptops | Touchpad | Sony Walkman | Portable music device | iPod and smartphones |
| PDA | Small mobile device for storing and accessing digital information including contacts, calendars, modified productivity software, songs, games, and photos | Smartphones | Cassette tape and player | Music storage and player | Online streaming services |
| Dot matrix printer | Output device that used tiny hammer-like keys to strike paper through an inked ribbon | Inkjet and laser printers | VCR (video cassette recorder) | Video recorder/ player | DVR, DVD, Blu-ray players |

# Other Important Advancements

It wasn't just personal computer hardware that was changing. At the same time, advances in programming languages and operating systems and the influx of application software were leading to more useful and powerful machines.

## The Importance of BASIC

**Objective A.5**   *Explain why BASIC was an important step in revolutionizing the software industry.*

The software industry began in the 1950s with programming languages such as FORTRAN, ALGOL, and COBOL. These languages were used mainly by businesses to create financial, statistical, and engineering programs. However, in 1964, John Kemeny and Thomas Kurtz designed the Beginner's All-Purpose Symbolic Instruction Code (BASIC) at Dartmouth College and revolutionized the software industry. BASIC was a language that beginning programming students could easily learn. It thus became enormously popular—and the key language of the PC. In fact, Bill Gates and Paul Allen used BASIC to write their program for the Altair, which led to the creation of Microsoft, a company that produced (and continues to produce) computer software.

## The Advent of Operating Systems

**Objective A.6**   *Explain why the development of the operating system was an important step in PC development.*

Because data on the earliest personal computers was stored on audiocassettes, many programs weren't saved or reused. This meant that programs had to be rewritten whenever they were needed. In 1978, Steve Wozniak designed a 5.25-inch floppy disk drive so that programs could be saved easily and operating systems developed.

**Figure A.2** This 1983 Hewlett-Packard computer used an early version of the MS-DOS operating system as well as the Lotus 1-2-3 spreadsheet program. *(Everett Collection/SuperStock)*

Operating systems are written to coordinate with the specific processor chip that controls the computer. At that time, Apple computers ran on a Motorola chip, whereas PCs (IBMs and so on) ran on an Intel chip. The Disk Operating System (DOS), developed by Wozniak (in conjunction with Paul Laughton of Shepardson Microsystems) and introduced in 1977, was the OS that controlled the first Apple computers. The Control Program for Microcomputers (CP/M), developed by Gary Kildall, was the OS designed for the Intel 8080 chip (the processor for PCs).

In 1980, when IBM was entering the personal computer market, it approached Bill Gates at Microsoft to write an OS program for the IBM PC. Gates recommended that IBM investigate the CP/M OS, but IBM couldn't arrange a meeting with the founder, Gary Kildall. Microsoft reconsidered the opportunity to write an OS program and developed MS-DOS for IBM computers. Eventually, virtually all PCs running on the Intel chip used MS-DOS as their OS (see Figure A.2). Microsoft's reign as one of the dominant players in the personal computer landscape had begun.

## The Software Application Explosion: VisiCalc and Beyond

**Objective A.7**   *List early application software that was developed for the PC.*

Because the floppy disk was a convenient way to distribute software, its inclusion in personal computers set off an application software explosion. In 1978, Harvard Business School student Dan Bricklin recognized the potential for a personal computer spreadsheet program. He and his friend Bob Frankston created the program VisiCalc, which became an instant success. Finally, ordinary home users could see the benefit of owning a personal computer. More than 100,000 copies of VisiCalc were sold in its first year.

After VisiCalc, other electronic spreadsheet programs entered the market. Lotus 1-2-3 came on the market in 1983, and Microsoft Excel entered the scene in 1985. These products became so popular that they eventually put VisiCalc out of business.

Meanwhile, word processing software was also gaining a foothold in the industry. Until then, there were separate, dedicated word processing machines; personal computers, it was believed, were

| Table A.2 | Application Software Development |
|-----------|--------------------------------|
| **Year** | **Application** |
| 1978 | **VisiCalc:** First electronic spreadsheet application<br>**WordStar:** First word processing application |
| 1980 | **WordPerfect:** Best DOS-based word processor, was eventually sold to Novell and later acquired by Corel |
| 1983 | **Lotus 1-2-3:** Added integrated charting, plotting, and database capabilities to spreadsheet software<br>**Word for MS-DOS:** Introduced in the pages of *PC World* magazine on the first magazine-inserted demo disk |
| 1985 | **Excel:** One of the first spreadsheets to use a graphical user interface<br>**PageMaker:** The first desktop publishing software |

for computation and data management only. However, once WordStar, the first word processing application, became available for personal computers in 1979, word processing became another important use for the personal computer. Competitors such as Word for MS-DOS (the precursor to Microsoft Word) and WordPerfect soon entered the market. Table A.2 lists some of the important dates in application software development.

# The Graphical User Interface and the Internet Boom

Other important advancements related to personal computers came in the form of the graphical user interface and the Internet.

## Xerox and Apple's Lisa and Macintosh

**Objective A.8** *Describe the features of the Lisa and Macintosh computers and their predecessor, the Xerox Alto.*

A graphical user interface (GUI), which uses icons to represent programs and actions, allows users to interact with the computer more easily. Until that time, users had to use complicated command- or menu-driven interfaces. Apple was the first company to take full commercial advantage of the GUI, but the GUI was not invented by a computer company.

In 1972, a few years before Apple launched its first personal computer, photocopier manufacturer Xerox was designing a personal computer of its own. Named the Alto (see Figure A.3), the computer included a word processor, based on the What You See Is What You Get (WYSIWYG) principle, that incorporated a file management system with directories and folders. It also had a mouse and could connect to a network. None of the other personal computers of the time had these features. For a variety of reasons, Xerox never sold the Alto commercially. Several years later, it developed the Star Office System, which was based on the Alto. Despite its convenient features, the Star never became popular because no one was willing to pay the $17,000 asking price.

Xerox's ideas were ahead of their time, but many of the ideas present in the Alto and Star would soon catch on. In 1983, Apple introduced the Lisa—the first successful personal computer brought to market that used a GUI (see Figure A.4). Legend has it that Jobs had seen the Alto during a visit to Xerox in 1979 and was influenced by its GUI. He therefore incorporated a similar user interface into the Lisa, providing features such as windows, drop-down menus, icons, a file system with folders and files, and a point-and-click device called a *mouse*. The only problem with the Lisa was its price. At $9,995 (about $24,047 in today's dollars), few buyers were willing to take the plunge.

One year later, in 1984, Apple introduced the Macintosh, shown in Figure A.5. The Macintosh was everything the Lisa was and then some, at about a third of the cost. The Macintosh was also the first personal computer to utilize 3.5-inch floppy disks with a hard cover, which were smaller and sturdier than the previous 5.25-inch floppies.

**Figure A.3** The Alto was the first computer to use a GUI, and it provided the basis for the GUI that Apple used. However, because of marketing problems, the Alto never was sold. *(Josie Lepe/MCT/Newscom)*

**Figure A.4** The Lisa was the first computer to introduce a GUI to the market. Priced too high, it never gained the popularity it deserved. *(SSPL/The Image Works)*

**Figure A.5** The Macintosh became one of Apple's best-selling computers, incorporating a GUI along with other innovations such as the 3.5-inch floppy disk drive. *(Interfoto/Alamy Stock Photo)*

## The Internet Boom

**Objective A.9** *List the first successful web browsers.*

The GUI made it easier for users to work on the computer. The Internet provided another reason for people to buy computers. Now people could conduct research and communicate in a new way. In 1993, the web browser Mosaic was introduced. This browser allowed users to view multimedia on the Web, causing Internet traffic to increase by nearly 350%.

Meanwhile, companies discovered the Internet as a means to do business, and computer sales took off. IBM-compatible PCs became the computer system of choice when, in 1995, Microsoft introduced Internet Explorer, a browser that integrated web functionality into Microsoft Office applications, and Windows 95, the first Microsoft OS designed to be principally a GUI OS.

About one year earlier, in 1994, a team of developers launched the Netscape Navigator web browser, which soon became a predominant player in browser software. However, pressures from Microsoft became too strong, and in 1998, Netscape announced it would no longer charge for the product and would make the code available to the public.

# Making the Personal Computer Possible: Early Computers

Billions of personal computers have been sold over the past four decades. But the computer is a compilation of parts, each of which is the result of individual inventions. Let's look at some early machines that helped to create the personal computer we know today.

## The Pascalene Calculator and the Jacquard Loom

**Objective A.10** *Discuss the features of the Pascalene calculator and the Jacquard loom that inspired modern computer elements.*

From the earliest days of humankind, we have been looking for a more systematic way to count and calculate. Thus, the evolution of counting machines led to the development of the computer we know today. The Pascalene (also known as Pascal's calculator) was the first accurate mechanical calculator. This machine, created by French mathematician Blaise Pascal in 1642, used revolutions of gears, like odometers in cars, to count by tens. The Pascalene could be used to add, subtract, multiply, and divide. The basic design of the Pascalene was so sound that it lived on in mechanical calculators for more than 300 years.

Nearly 200 years later, Joseph Jacquard revolutionized the fabric industry by creating a machine that automated the weaving of complex patterns. Although not a counting or calculating machine,

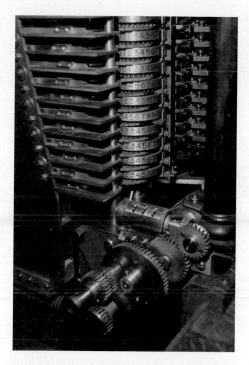

**Figure A.6** The Jacquard loom used holes punched in stiff cards to make complex designs. This technique would later be used in punch cards that controlled the input and output of data in computers. *(Janek Skarzynski/AFP/Getty Images/Alamy Stock Photo)*

**Figure A.7** The Analytical Engine, designed by Charles Babbage, was never fully developed but included components similar to those found in today's computers. *(Chris Howes/Wild Places Photography/Alamy Stock Photo)*

the Jacquard loom (shown in Figure A.6) was significant because it relied on stiff cards with punched holes to automate the weaving process. Much later, this punch-card process would be adopted as a means for computers to record and read data.

## Babbage's Engines and the Hollerith Tabulating Machine

**Objective A.11** *Discuss the contributions of Babbage's engines and the Hollerith Tabulating Machine to modern computing.*

In 1834, Charles Babbage designed the first automatic calculator, called the Analytical Engine (see Figure A.7). The machine was actually based on another machine called the Difference Engine, which was a huge steam-powered mechanical calculator that Babbage designed to print astronomical tables. Although the Analytical Engine was never developed, Babbage's detailed drawings and descriptions of the machine include components similar to those found in today's computers, including the store (akin to RAM) and the mill (a central processing unit) as well as input and output devices. This invention gave Charles Babbage the title of the "father of computing."

Meanwhile, Ada Lovelace, who was the daughter of poet Lord Byron and a student of mathematics (which was unusual for women of the time), was fascinated with Babbage's engines. She translated an Italian paper on Babbage's machine and, at the request of Babbage, added her own extensive notes. Her efforts are thought to be the best description of Babbage's engines.

In 1890, Herman Hollerith, while working for the U.S. Census Bureau, was the first to take Jacquard's punch-card concept and apply it to computing with his Hollerith Tabulating Machine. Until that time, census data had been tabulated manually in a long, laborious process. Hollerith's tabulating machine automatically read data that had been punched onto small punch cards, speeding up the tabulation process. Hollerith's machine became so successful that he left the Census Bureau in 1896 to start the Tabulating Machine Company. His company later changed its name to International Business Machines, or IBM.

## The Z1, the Atanasoff–Berry Computer, and the Harvard Mark I

**Objective A.12** *Discuss the features of the Z1, the Atanasoff–Berry Computer, and the Mark I.*

German inventor Konrad Zuse is credited with a number of computing inventions. His first, in 1936, was a mechanical calculator called the Z1. The Z1 is thought to be the first computer to include certain features integral to today's systems, such as a control unit and separate memory functions.

In 1939, John Atanasoff, a professor at Iowa State University, and his student Clifford Berry built the first electrically powered digital computer, called the Atanasoff–Berry Computer (ABC), shown in Figure A.8. The computer was the first to use vacuum tubes, instead of the mechanical switches used in older computers, to store data. Although revolutionary at the time, the machine weighed 700 pounds, contained a mile of wire, and took about 15 seconds for each calculation. (In comparison, today's personal computers can perform billions of calculations in

**Figure A.8** The Atanasoff–Berry Computer laid the design groundwork for many computers to come. *(Frederick News Post/AP Images)*

15 seconds.) Most importantly, the ABC was the first computer to use the binary system and to have memory that repowered itself upon booting. The design of the ABC would be central to that of future computers.

From the late 1930s to the early 1950s, Howard Aiken and Grace Hopper designed the Mark series of computers used by the U.S. Navy for ballistic and gunnery calculations. Aiken, an electrical engineer and physicist, designed the computer, while Hopper did the programming. The Harvard Mark I, finished in 1944, could add, subtract, multiply, and divide.

However, many believe Hopper's greatest contribution to computing was the invention of the compiler—a program that translates English-language instructions into computer language. The team was also responsible for a common computer-related expression. Hopper was the first to "debug" a computer when she removed a moth that had flown into the Harvard Mark I and had caused the computer to break down (see Figure A.9). After that, problems that caused a computer not to run were called *bugs*.

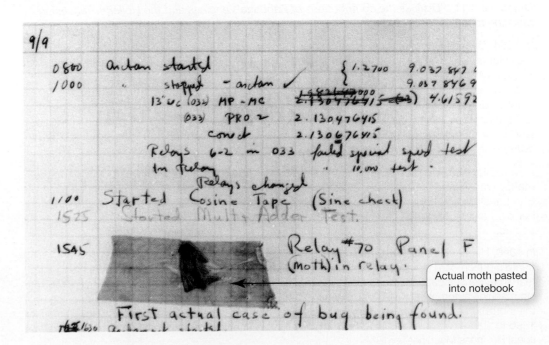

**Figure A.9** Grace Hopper coined the term computer bug when a moth flew into the Harvard Mark I, causing it to break down. *(Claudio Divizia/Shutterstock)*

Actual moth pasted into notebook

**Figure A.10** The ENIAC took up an entire room and required several people to manipulate it. *(Interfoto/History/ Alamy Stock Photo)*

## The Turing Machine, the ENIAC, and the UNIVAC

**Objective A.13** *Discuss the major features of the Turing Machine, the ENIAC, and the UNIVAC.*

Meanwhile, in 1936, British mathematician Alan Turing created an abstract computer model that could perform logical operations. The Turing Machine was not a real machine but rather a hypothetical model that mathematically defined a mechanical procedure (or algorithm). Additionally, Turing's concept described a process by which the machine could read, write, or erase symbols written on squares of an infinite paper tape. This concept of an infinite tape that could be read, written to, and erased was the precursor to today's RAM.

The Electronic Numerical Integrator and Computer (ENIAC), shown in Figure A.10, was another U.S. government–sponsored machine developed to calculate the settings used for weapons. Created by John W. Mauchly and J. Presper Eckert at the University of Pennsylvania, it was put into operation in 1944. Although the ENIAC is generally thought of as the first successful high-speed electronic digital computer, it was big and clumsy. The ENIAC used nearly 18,000 vacuum tubes and filled approximately 1,800 square feet of floor space. Although inconvenient, the ENIAC served its purpose and remained in use until 1955.

**Figure A.11** UNIVACs were the first computers to use magnetic tape for data storage. *(Underwood Archives/ UIG/Shutterstock)*

The Universal Automatic Computer, or UNIVAC, was the first commercially successful electronic digital computer. Completed in 1951, the UNIVAC operated on magnetic tape (see Figure A.11), setting it apart from its competitors, which ran on punch cards. The UNIVAC gained notoriety when, in a 1951 publicity stunt, it was used to predict the outcome of the Stevenson–Eisenhower presidential race. After analyzing only 5% of the popular vote, the UNIVAC correctly identified Dwight D. Eisenhower as the victor. After that, UNIVAC soon became a household word. The UNIVAC and computers like it were considered first-generation computers and were the last to use vacuum tubes.

**Figure A.12** Transistors were one-tenth the size of vacuum tubes, were faster, and produced much less heat. *(Borissos/Fotolia)*

**Figure A.13** Today's microprocessors can contain billions of transistors.

*(Tudor Voinea/Shutterstock)*

## Transistors and Beyond

**Objective A.14** *Describe the milestones that led to each "generation" of computers.*

Only one year after the ENIAC was completed, scientists at the Bell Telephone Laboratories in New Jersey invented the transistor (see Figure A.12). The transistor replaced the bulky vacuum tubes of earlier computers and was smaller and more powerful than tubes. It was used in almost everything, from radios to phones. Computers that used transistors were referred to as second-generation computers. Still, transistors were limited as to how small they could be made.

A few years later, in 1958, Jack Kilby, while working at Texas Instruments, invented the world's first integrated circuit—a small chip capable of containing thousands of transistors. This consolidation in design enabled computers to become smaller and lighter. The computers in this early integrated-circuit generation were considered third-generation computers.

Other innovations in the computer industry further refined the computer's speed, accuracy, and efficiency. However, none was as significant as the 1971 introduction by the Intel Corporation of the microprocessor chip—a small chip containing millions of transistors (see Figure A.13). The microprocessor functions as the CPU, or brains, of the computer. Computers that use a microprocessor chip are called fourth-generation computers. Over time, Intel and Motorola became the leading manufacturers of microprocessors. Today, the Intel Core i9 is one of Intel's most powerful processors.

As you can see, personal computers have come a long way since the Altair and have a number of inventions and people to thank for their amazing popularity. What will the future bring?

# Check Your Understanding // Review & Practice

For a quick review of what you've learned, answer the following questions.

## multiple choice

1. What was the name of the first web browser?
   a. Internet Explorer
   b. Netscape
   c. Mosaic
   d. Firefox

2. Which was the first electronic spreadsheet program?
   a. Excel
   b. Numbers
   c. VisiCalc
   d. Lotus 1-2-3

3. Which invention replaced transistors in computers?
   a. The integrated circuit
   b. Magnetic tape
   c. The microprocessor chip
   d. The vacuum tube

4. Which computer was touted as the first portable personal computer?
   a. Lisa
   b. Commodore PET
   c. Altair
   d. Osborne

5. What was the importance of the Turing machine to today's computers?
   a. It described a system that was a precursor to today's notebook computer.
   b. It described a process to read, write, and erase symbols on a tape and was the precursor to today's RAM.
   c. It was the first computer to have a monitor.
   d. It was the first electronic calculator and a precursor to the computer.

6. Which computer is considered the first commercially successful high-speed electronic digital computer?
   a. ENIAC
   b. Apple I
   c. UNIVAC
   d. Personal Computer

7. Which early programming language was developed for beginning programming students?
   a. BASIC
   b. FORTRAN
   c. COBOL
   d. PASCAL

8. Which was the first personal computer sold as a kit?
   a. Apple I
   b. Altair 8800
   c. TRS-80
   d. Commodore PET

9. What was Grace Hopper best known for?
   a. Creating the first portable computer.
   b. Developing magnetic storage.
   c. Removing a moth from a computer.
   d. Developing the BASIC programming language.

10. Which early personal computer was the first to use 3.5-inch floppy disks for external storage?
    a. Lisa
    b. Apple I
    c. Apple II
    d. Macintosh

# B Careers in IT

**Learning Outcome B.1**   Describe the various categories of IT jobs available, explain why IT jobs are in demand, and discuss various ways to prepare for IT employment.

It's hard to imagine an occupation in which computers aren't used in some fashion. Even such previously low-tech industries as waste disposal and fast food use computers to manage inventories and order commodities. In this appendix, we explore various information technology (IT) career paths open to you.

## Rewards of Working in Information Technology

**Objective B.1**   *List the reasons why IT fields are attractive to students pursuing bachelor's degrees.*

There are many great reasons to work in the exciting, ever-changing field of IT. In this section, we explore some reasons why the IT field is so attractive to graduates looking for entry-level positions.

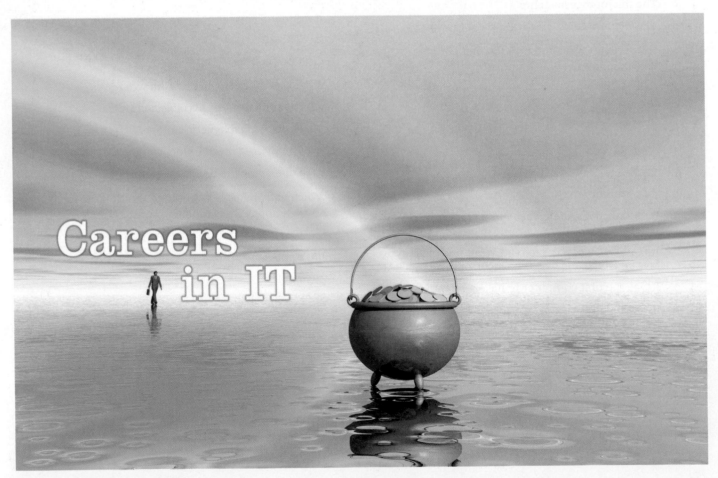

(Carol and Mike Werner/Alamy Stock Photo)

# IT Workers Are in Demand

If you're investigating a career with computers, the first question you may have is, "Will I be able to get a job?" Consider the following:

- According to projections by the U.S. Department of Labor's Bureau of Labor Statistics, computer-related jobs are expected to be among the fastest-growing occupations through 2024 (see Table B.1).
- In 2018, *U.S. News & World Report* published a list of the 100 best careers to consider based on employment opportunity, salary, work–life balance, and job security. Software developer leads the list at number 1, while computer systems analyst, information security analyst, computer systems administrator, database administrator, web developer, computer network architect, computer support specialist, and IT manager were also on the list.
- According to the National Association of Colleges and Employers (NACE) Winter 2018 Salary Survey, the average starting salary for computer science majors with bachelor's degrees was projected to be $66,005 and was the second-highest average salary on the list, just below engineering majors.

The number of students pursuing computer science degrees has also been increasing over the past several years. Fields of specialization such as game development, information security, and mobile app development are very popular. Yet, shortages of computing professionals in the United States are still projected over the next 5–10 years. What does all this mean? In terms of job outlook, now is a perfect time to consider an IT career.

## IT Jobs Pay Well

As you can see from Table B.1, median salaries in IT careers are robust. But what exactly affects your salary in an IT position? Your skill set and your experience level are obvious answers, but the size of an employer and its geographical location are also factors. Large companies tend to pay more, so if you're pursuing a high salary, set your sights on a large corporation. But remember that making a lot of money isn't everything—be sure to consider other quality-of-life issues, such as job satisfaction. Of course, choosing a computer career isn't a guarantee you'll get a high-paying job. Just as in any other profession, you'll need appropriate training and on-the-job experience to earn a high salary.

So how much can you expect to start out earning? Although starting salaries for some IT positions, such as computer support specialists, are more on the modest side ($40,000), starting salaries for students with bachelor's degrees in IT are fairly robust.

## Table B.1 High-Growth IT Jobs

| Occupation | Median Pay ($) | 10-Year Growth Rate (%) | 10-Year Total New Jobs |
|---|---|---|---|
| Information security analysts | 95,510 | 28 | 28,500 |
| Software developers | 103,560 | 24 | 302,500 |
| Computer and information research scientists | 114,520 | 19 | 5,400 |
| Web developers | 67,990 | 15 | 24,400 |
| Database administrators | 87,020 | 11 | 13,700 |
| Computer support specialists | 52,810 | 11 | 88,500 |
| Computer systems analysts | 88,270 | 9 | 54,400 |
| Computer network architects | 104,650 | 6 | 10,500 |
| Network and computer systems administrators | 81,100 | 6 | 24.000 |

Source: *Excerpted from* Occupational Outlook Handbook, *2018 Edition, U.S. Bureau of Labor Statistics.*

**Figure B.1** Although many companies outsource IT jobs to third-party companies, this does not mean the jobs necessarily go offshore. *(Tyler Olson/123RF)*

To obtain the most accurate information, you should research salaries yourself in the geographical area where you expect to work. *Salary.com* provides a free salary wizard to help you determine what IT professionals in your area are making compared with national averages. You can add information such as your degree and the size of the company to your search selection to fine-tune the figures further. Hundreds of IT job titles are listed in *Salary.com*, so you can tailor your search to the specific job, location, and industry in which you're interested.

## IT Jobs Are Not Going "Offshore"

In the global economy in which we now operate, job outlook includes the risk of jobs being outsourced, possibly to other countries. Outsourcing is a process whereby a business hires a third-party firm to provide business services (such as customer-support call centers) that were previously handled by in-house employees (see Figure B.1). Offshoring occurs when the outsourcing firm is located (or uses employees) outside the United States.

India, China, and Romania and other former Eastern Bloc countries are major players in providing outsourcing services for U.S. companies. The big lure of outsourcing and offshoring is cost savings: Considering that the standard of living and salaries are much lower in many countries than they are in the United States, offshoring is an attractive option for many U.S. employers.

However, outsourcing and offshoring don't always deliver the cost savings that CEOs envision. Demand for personnel overseas has led to increased costs (primarily due to wage increases) for service providers in foreign markets. Furthermore, other, less tangible factors can outweigh the cost savings from outsourcing. Communications problems can arise between internal and external employees, for example, and cultural differences between the home country and the country doing the offshoring can result in software code that needs extensive rework by in-house employees. Data can also be less secure in an external environment or during the transfer between the company and an external vendor. Although outsourcing and offshoring won't be going away, companies are approaching these staffing alternatives with more caution and are looking more to U.S. companies to provide resources.

So, many IT jobs are staying in the United States. According to *InformationWeek* magazine, most jobs in the following three categories (see Table B.2) will stay put:

1. **Customer interaction:** jobs that require direct input from customers or that involve systems with which customers interface daily
2. **Enablers:** jobs that involve getting key business projects accomplished, often requiring technical skills beyond the realm of IT and good people skills
3. **Infrastructure:** jobs that are fundamental to moving and storing the information that U.S.-based employees need to do their jobs

**Table B.2    Jobs That Will Likely Remain Onshore**

| Customer Interaction | Enablers | Infrastructure Jobs |
| --- | --- | --- |
| Web application developers | Business process analysts | Network security |
| Web interface designers | Application developers (when customer interaction is critical) | Network installation technicians |
| Database and data warehouse designers/developers | Project managers (for systems with users who are located predominantly in the United States) | Network administrators (engineers) |
| Customer relationship management (CRM) analysts | | Wireless infrastructure managers and technicians |
| Enterprise resource planning (ERP) implementation specialists | | Disaster recovery planners and responders |

In addition, jobs that require specific knowledge of the U.S. marketplace and culture, such as social media managers, are also very likely not to be offshored.

## Women Are in High Demand in IT Departments

Currently, women make up about 26% of the IT workforce (per the National Center for Women and Information Technology). This presents a huge opportunity for women who have IT skills because many IT departments are actively seeking to diversify their workforces. In addition, although a salary gender gap (the difference between what men and women earn for performing the same job) exists in IT careers, it's smaller than in most other professions.

## You Have a Choice of Working Location

In this case, location refers to the setting in which you work. IT jobs can be office based, field based, project based, or home based. Because not every situation is perfect for every individual, you can look for a job that suits your tastes and requirements. Table B.3 summarizes the major job types and their locations.

## You Constantly Meet New Challenges

In IT, the playing field is always changing. New software and hardware are constantly being developed. You'll need to work hard to keep your skills up to date. You'll spend a lot of time in training and self-study, trying to learn new systems and techniques. Many individuals thrive in this type of environment because it keeps their jobs from becoming dull or routine.

## You Work in Teams

When students are asked to describe their ideal jobs, many describe jobs that involve working in teams. Despite what some people think, IT professionals are not locked in lightless cubicles, basking in the glow of their monitors and working alone on projects. Most IT jobs require constant interaction with other workers, usually in team settings. People skills are highly prized by IT departments. If you have good leadership and team-building skills, you'll have the opportunity to exercise them in an IT job.

## You Don't Need to Be a Mathematical Genius

Certain IT careers such as programming involve a fair bit of math. But even if you're not mathematically inclined, you can explore many other IT careers. IT employers also value such attributes as creativity, marketing, and artistic style, especially in jobs that involve working on the Internet or with social media.

### Table B.3 Where Do You Want to Work?

| Type of Job | Location and Hours | Special Considerations |
|---|---|---|
| **Office-Based**  | Report for work to the same location each day and interact with the same people on a regular basis; requires regular hours of attendance (such as 9:00 A.M. to 5:00 P.M.) | May require working beyond "normal" working hours; may also require workers to be on call 24/7 |
| **Field-Based**  | Travel from place to place as needed and perform short-term jobs at each location | Involves a great deal of travel and the ability to work independently |
| **Project-Based**  | Work at client sites on specific projects for extended periods of time (weeks or months) | Can be especially attractive to individuals who like workplace situations that vary on a regular basis |
| **Home-Based (Telecommuting)**  | Work from home | Involves very little day-to-day supervision and requires an individual who is self-disciplined |

*(Rawpixel.com/Shutterstock; Muellek Josef/Shutterstock; Maksym Dykha/Shutterstock; Samuel Borges Photography/Shutterstock)*

### IT Skills Are Transferable

Most computing skills are transferable from industry to industry. A networking job in the clothing manufacturing industry uses the same primary skill set as a networking job for a supermarket chain. Therefore, if something disastrous happens to the industry you're in, you should be able to switch to another industry without having to learn an entirely new skill set. Combining business courses with IT courses will also make you more marketable when changing jobs. For example, as an accounting major, if you minor in IT, employers may be more willing to hire you because working in accounting today means constantly interfacing with management information systems and manipulating data.

# Challenges of IT Careers

**Objective B.2**   *Explain the various challenges of IT careers.*

Although there are many positive aspects of IT careers, there can be some challenges. The discussions that follow aren't meant to discourage you from pursuing an IT career but merely to make you aware of exactly what challenges you might face in an IT department.

### Stress

Most IT jobs are hectic (see Figure B.2). Whereas the average American works 42 hours a week, a survey by *InformationWeek* revealed that the average IT staff person works 45 hours a week and is

**Figure B.2** Stress comes from multiple directions in IT jobs. *(Khakimullin Aleksandr/Shutterstock; Monkey Business Images/Shutterstock; Rawpixel.com/Shutterstock; Torwaistudio/Shutterstock; Ollyy/Shutterstock)*

on call for another 24 hours. On-call time (hours an employee must be available to work in the event of a problem) has been increasing because most IT systems require 24/7 availability.

## Women Are in the Minority

A majority of IT jobs are filled by men, so some women view IT departments as *Dilbert*-like microcosms of antisocial geeks and don't feel as though they would fit in. Unfortunately, it is true that in most IT departments, women are underrepresented. As companies begin to push to address this imbalance, new opportunities are emerging for women with technical skill sets.

## Lifelong Learning Is Required

Although the constantly changing nature of IT can alleviate boredom, keeping up with the changes can also cause some stress. You'll need to take training courses, do self-study, and perhaps take additional college courses, such as getting a graduate degree, to keep up with the vast shifts in technology.

# Choosing Your Realm of IT

**Objective B.3** *List and describe the various IT careers for which you can train.*

Figure B.3 shows an organizational chart for a modern IT department at a large corporation that should help you understand the variety of careers available and how they interrelate. The chief information officer (CIO) has overall responsibility for the development, implementation, and maintenance of information systems and their infrastructure. Usually, the CIO reports to the chief operating officer (COO).

The responsibilities below the CIO are generally grouped into two units:

1. Development and integration (responsible for the development of systems and websites)
2. Technical services (responsible for the day-to-day operations of the company's information infrastructure and network, including all hardware and software deployed)

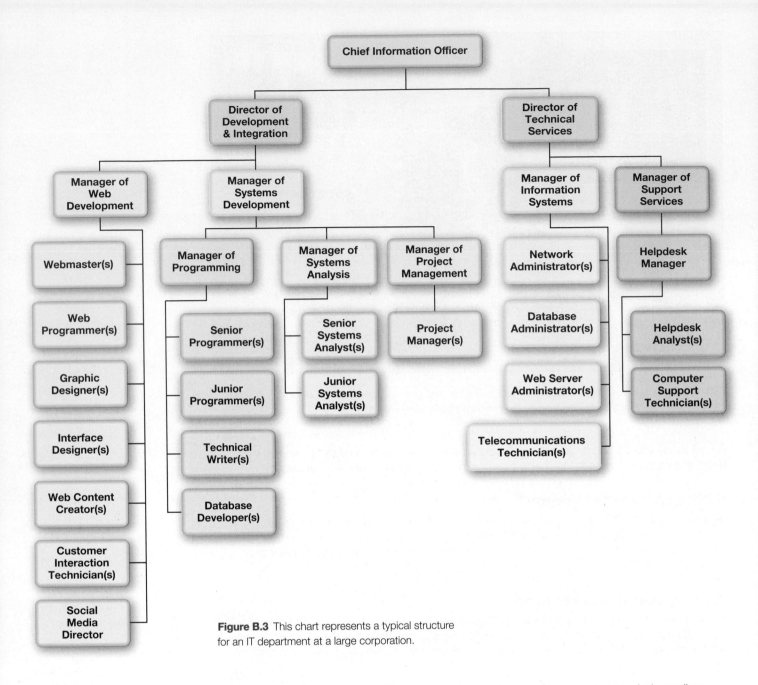

**Figure B.3** This chart represents a typical structure for an IT department at a large corporation.

In large organizations, responsibilities are distinct, and jobs are defined more narrowly. In medium-sized organizations, there can be overlap between position responsibilities. At a small company, you might be the network administrator, database administrator, computer support technician, and social media manager all at the same time. Let's look at the typical jobs found in each department.

## Working in Development and Integration

Two distinct paths exist in this division: web development and systems development. Because everything involves the web today, there's often a great deal of overlap between these paths.

**Web Development.** When most people think of web development careers, they usually equate them with being a webmaster. Webmasters used to be individuals who were solely responsible for all aspects of a company's website. However, today's webmasters are usually supervisors with responsibility for certain aspects of web development. At smaller companies, they may also be responsible for tasks that other individuals in a web development group usually do, such as:

- Web content creators generate the words and images that appear on the Web. Journalists, other writers, editors, and marketing personnel prepare an enormous amount of web content, whereas video producers, graphic designers, and animators create Web-based multimedia. Web content creators have a thorough understanding of their own fields as well as HTML, PHP, and JavaScript.

- Interface designers work with graphic designers and animators to create a look and feel for the site and make it easy to navigate.

- Web programmers build web pages to deploy the materials that the content creators develop. They wield software tools such as Adobe Dreamweaver and InDesign to develop the web pages. They also create links to databases using products such as Oracle and SQL Server to keep information flowing between users and web pages. They must possess a solid understanding of client- and server-side web languages (HTML, XML, Java, JavaScript, ASP, PHP, Silverlight, and Perl) and of development environments such as the Microsoft .NET Framework.

- Customer interaction technicians provide feedback to a website's customers. Major job responsibilities include answering e-mail, sending requested information, funneling questions to appropriate personnel (technical support, sales, and so on), and providing suggestions to web programmers for site improvements. Extensive customer service training is essential to work effectively in this area.

- Social media directors are responsible for directing the strategy of the company on all social media sites where the company maintains a presence. Often, while supervising customer interaction technicians, social media directors make sure that customers have a quality experience while interacting with company employees and customers on sites such as Facebook, Twitter, and Yelp. Responding to comments left on such sites, developing promotional strategies, and designing functionality of the company's social media sites are common job responsibilities.

As you can see in Figure B.4, many different people can work on the same website. Web programming jobs often require a four-year college degree in computer science, whereas graphic designers are often hired with two-year art degrees.

**Figure B.4** It takes a team to create and maintain a website. *(United States Department of Agriculture)*

Trends in technology and business often give clues to up-and-coming IT jobs. Consider these trends when considering your educational choices:

**Drone aircraft.** Drones are making their way from the military to businesses and households. Companies that make or use drones will need drone programmers.

**Cyber spying.** Recent revelations of widespread cyber spying and espionage point to a continued demand for IT security professionals.

**The Internet of Things.** More and more devices are featuring Internet connectivity every year. Companies will need designers for user interfaces and software applications to drive connected devices.

**Driverless cars.** As vehicles become ever more sophisticated, so do their IT systems. Developers of artificial intelligence systems for vehicles and business equipment will be highly sought after.

**Systems Development.** Ask most people what systems developers do and they'll answer "programming." However, programming is only one aspect of systems development. Because large projects involve many people, there are many job opportunities in systems development, most of which require four-year college degrees in computer science or management information systems:

- Systems analysts gather information from end users about problems and existing information systems. They document systems and propose solutions to problems. Having good people skills is essential to success as a systems analyst. In addition, systems analysts work with programmers during the development phase to design appropriate programs to solve the problem at hand. Therefore, many organizations insist on hiring systems analysts who have solid business backgrounds and programming experience (at least at a basic level).

- Programmers attend meetings to document user needs, and they work closely with systems analysts during the design phase of program development. Programmers need excellent written communication skills because they often generate detailed systems documentation for end-user training purposes. Because programming languages are mathematically based, it is essential for programmers to have strong math skills and an ability to think logically.

- Project managers manage the overall systems development process: assigning staff, budgeting, reporting to management, coaching team members, and ensuring deadlines are met. Project managers need excellent time management skills because they're often pulled in several directions at once. They usually have prior experience as programmers or systems analysts. Many project managers obtain master's degrees to supplement their undergraduate degrees.

In addition to these key players, the following people are also involved in the systems development process:

- Technical writers generate systems documentation for end users and for programmers who may make modifications to the system in the future.

- Network administrators help the programmers and analysts design compatible systems because many systems are required to run in certain environments (UNIX or Windows, for instance) and must work in conjunction with other programs.

- Database developers design and build databases to support the software systems being developed.

Large development projects may have all of these team members on the project. Smaller projects may require an overlap of positions, such as a programmer also acting as a systems analyst. As shown in Figure B.5, team members work together to build a system.

## Working in Technical Services

Technical services jobs are vital to keeping IT systems running. The people in these jobs install and maintain the infrastructure behind the IT systems and work with end users to make sure they can interact with the systems effectively. There are two major categories of technical services careers: information systems and support services. Note that these also are the least likely IT jobs to be outsourced because hands-on work with equipment and users is required on a regular basis.

- **Programmers build the software that solves problems.**

- **Systems analysts document systems and propose solutions.**

- **Project managers supervise, organize, and coach team members.**

- **Database developers ensure data is accessible when it's needed.**

**Figure B.5** There are many important team members in systems development. *(Dmitry Nikolaev/Fotolia; Rob/Fotolia; Cheekywemonkey/Fotolia; Trueffelpix/Shutterstock)*

**Information Systems.** The information systems department keeps the networks and telecommunications up and running at all times. Within the department, you'll find a variety of positions.

- **Network administrators** (sometimes called *network engineers*) are involved in every stage of network planning and deployment (see Figure B.6). They decide what equipment to buy and what media to use, determine the network's topology, and help install the network (by supervising contractors or doing it themselves). Network administrators plan disaster-recovery strategies (such as what to do if a fire destroys the server room). When equipment and cables break, network administrators must fix the problem. They also obtain and install updates to network software and evaluate new equipment to determine whether the network should be upgraded. In addition, they monitor the network's performance and often develop policies regarding network usage, security measures, and hardware and software standards.
- Database administrators (DBAs) install and configure database servers and ensure that the servers provide an adequate level of access to all users.
- Web server administrators install, configure, and maintain web servers and ensure that the company maintains Internet connectivity at all times.
- Telecommunications technicians oversee the communications infrastructure, including training employees to use telecommunications equipment. They are often on call 24 hours a day.

**Support Services.** As a member of the support services team, you interface with users (external customers or employees) and troubleshoot their computer problems. Support service positions include:

- Helpdesk analysts staff the phones, respond to Internet live chats, or respond to e-mails and solve problems for customers or employees, either remotely or in person. Often, helpdesk personnel are called on to train users on the latest software and hardware.
- Computer support technicians go to a user's location and fix software and hardware problems. They also often have to chase down and repair faults in the network infrastructure.

As important as these people are, they may receive a great deal of abuse by angry users whose computers are not working. When working in support services, you need to be patient and not be overly sensitive to insults!

**Figure B.6** At smaller companies, network administrators may be fixing a user's computer in the morning, installing and configuring a new network operating system in the afternoon, and troubleshooting a server problem (shown here) in the evening. *(SeventyFour/Shutterstock)*

The video gaming industry in the United States has surpassed the earning power of the Hollywood movie industry. In 2017, the U.S. video game industry brought in sales of $36 billion worth of video game software, hardware, and accessories, whereas Hollywood took in just over $11 billion. Although some aspects of game development, such as scenery design and certain aspects of programming, are being sent offshore, the majority of game development requires a creative team whose members need to work in close proximity. Therefore, it's anticipated that many game development jobs will stay in the United States.

Consoles such as the Xbox and the PlayStation generate demand for large-scale games. The popularity of mobile devices such as smartphones and tablets is driving demand for lower-end, casual game applications. Casual games are games that can be played relatively quickly or occasionally, such as MMO (massively multiplayer online) strategy games like Clash of Clans (see Figure B.7). Demand for family-friendly games without violence, sex, and profanity is on the rise. With all this demand, there are many opportunities for careers in game development.

Game development jobs are usually split along two paths: designers and programmers.

- Game designers tend to be artistic and are responsible for creating 2D and 3D art, game interfaces, video sequences, special effects, game levels, and scenarios. Game designers must master software packages such as Autodesk 3ds Max, Autodesk Maya, NewTek LightWave 3D, Adobe Photoshop, and Adobe Flash.
- Game programmers are responsible for coding the scenarios developed by the designers. Using languages and toolsets such as Objective-C, Unity, Apple Xcode, C, C++, Assembly, and Java, programmers build the game and ensure that it plays accurately.

Aside from programmers and designers, play testers and quality-assurance professionals play the games with the intent of

**Figure B.7** Clash of Clans, which has you build a village and recruit soldiers to fend off neighboring marauders, is an example of a popular casual game available for mobile platforms. *(Kevin Britland/Alamy Stock Photo)*

breaking them or discovering bugs within the game interfaces or worlds. Play testing is an essential part of the game development process because it assists designers in determining which aspects of the game are most intriguing to players and which parts of the game need to be repaired or enhanced.

No matter what job you may pursue in the realm of gaming, you'll need to have a two- or four-year college degree. If you're interested in gaming, look for a school with a solid animation or 3D art program or a computer game–programming curriculum. Programming requires a strong background in math and physics to enable you to realistically program environments that mimic the real world. Proficiency with math (especially geometry) also helps with design careers.

For more information on gaming careers, check out the International Game Developers Association site (*igda.org*) and the Game Career Guide (*gamecareerguide.com*).

---

Technical services jobs often require a two-year college degree or training at a trade school or technical institute. At smaller companies, job duties tend to overlap between the helpdesk and technician jobs. These jobs are in demand and require staffing in local markets, so they are staying onshore. You can't repair a computer's power supply if you are located in another country!

# Preparing for a Job in IT

**Objective B.4**   *Explain the various ways you can prepare for a career in IT.*

A job in IT requires a robust skill set and formal training and preparation. Most employers today have an entry-level requirement of a college degree, a technical institute diploma, appropriate professional certifications, experience in the field, or a combination of these. How can you prepare for a job in IT?

1. **Get educated.** Two and four-year colleges and universities normally offer three degrees to prepare students for IT careers: computer science, management information systems, and information technology (although titles vary). Alternatives to colleges and universities are

privately licensed technical (or trade) schools. Generally, these programs focus on building skill sets rapidly and qualifying for a job in a specific field. The main advantage of technical schools is that their programs usually take less time to complete than college degrees. However, to have a realistic chance of employment in IT fields other than networking or web development, you should attend a degree-granting college or university.

2. **Investigate professional certifications.** Certifications attempt to provide a consistent method of measuring skill levels in specific areas of IT. Hundreds of IT certifications are available, most of which you get by passing a written exam. Software and hardware vendors (such as Microsoft and Cisco) and professional organizations (such as the Computing Technology Industry Association) often establish certification standards. Visit *microsoft.com*, *cisco.com*, *comptia.org*, and *sun.com* for more information on certifications.

3. **Get experience.** In addition to education, employers want you to have experience, even for entry-level jobs. While you're still completing your education, consider getting an internship or part-time job in your field of study. Many schools will help you find internships and allow you to earn credit toward your degree through internships.

4. **Do research.** Find out as much as you can about the company and the industry it's in before going on an interview. Start with the company's website, and then expand your search to business and trade publications such as *Businessweek* and *Inc.* magazines.

# Getting Started in an IT Career

**Objective B.5**    *Explain the various ways you can find a career in IT.*

Training for a career is not useful unless you can find a job at the end of your training. Here are some tips on getting a job:

1. **Use the career resources at your school.** Many employers recruit at schools, and most schools maintain a placement office to help students find jobs. Employees in the placement office can help you with résumé preparation and interviewing skills and can provide you with leads for internships and jobs.

2. **Develop relationships with your instructors.** Many college instructors still work in or previously worked in the IT industry. They can often provide you with valuable advice and industry contacts.

3. **Start networking.** Many jobs are never advertised but instead are filled by word of mouth. Seek out contacts in your field and discuss job prospects with them. Find out what skills you need, and ask them to recommend others in the industry with whom you can speak. Professional organizations such as the Association for Computing Machinery (ACM) offer one way to network. These organizations often have chapters on college campuses and offer reduced membership rates for students. Table B.4 lists major professional organizations you should consider investigating.

   If you're a woman and are thinking about pursuing an IT career, many resources and groups cater to female IT professionals and students (see Table B.5). The oldest and best-known organization is the Association for Women in Computing, founded in 1978.

4. **Check corporate websites for jobs.** Many corporate websites list current job opportunities. For example, Google provides searchable job listings by geographical location. Check the sites of companies in which you are interested and then do a search on the sites for job openings or, if provided, click their employment links.

### Table B.4 Professional Organizations

| Organization Name | Purpose | Website |
|---|---|---|
| Association for Computing Machinery (ACM) | Oldest scientific computing society; maintains a strong focus on programming and systems development | acm.org |
| Association for Information Systems (AIS) | Organization of professionals who work in academia and specialize in information systems | aisnet.org |
| CompTIA Association of Information Technology Professionals (AITP) | Heavy focus on IT education and development of seminars and learning materials | aitp.org |
| Institute of Electrical and Electronics Engineers (IEEE) | Provides leadership and sets engineering standards for all types of network computing devices and protocols | ieee.org |
| Information Systems Security Association (ISSA) | Not-for-profit, international organization of information security professionals and practitioners | issa.org |

### Table B.5 Resources for Women in IT

| Organization Name | Purpose | Website |
|---|---|---|
| Anita Borg Institute | Organization whose aim is to ensure "a future where the teams that imagine and build technology mirror the people and societies for whom they build it." | anitab.org |
| Association for Women in Computing (AWC) | A not-for-profit organization dedicated to promoting the advancement of women in computing professions | awc-hq.org |
| The Center for Women in Technology (CWIT) | An organization dedicated to providing global leadership in achieving women's full participation in all aspects of IT | cwit.umbc.edu |
| Women in Technology International (WITI) | A global trade association for tech-savvy, professional women | witi.com |

5. **Visit online employment sites.** Most of these sites allow you to store your résumé online, and many sites allow employers to browse résumés to find qualified employees. Begin looking at job postings on these sites early in your education because these job postings detail the skill sets employers require. Focusing on coursework that will provide you with desirable skill sets will make you more marketable. Table B.6 lists employment sites as well as sites that offer other career resources.

The outlook for IT jobs should continue to be positive in the future. We wish you luck with your education and job search.

### Table B.6 Resources for IT Employment

| Site Name | URL |
|---|---|
| CareerBuilder | careerbuilder.com |
| ComputerJobs.com | computerjobs.com |
| ComputerWork.com | computerwork.com |
| Dice | dice.com |
| Gamasutra | gamasutra.com |
| JustTechJobs | justtechjobs.com |
| LinkedIn | linkedin.com |
| Monster | monster.com |
| TechCareers | techcareers.com |

# Check Your Understanding // Review & Practice

For a quick review of what you've learned, answer the following questions.

## multiple choice

1. The individuals responsible for generating images for websites are referred to as
   a. network administrators.
   b. web programmers.
   c. graphic designers.
   d. interface designers.

2. What type of job involves working at client sites on specific assignments for extended periods of time?
   a. Home based
   b. Project based
   c. Office based
   d. Field based

3. Which position is typically a part of the information systems department?
   a. Web programmer
   b. Computer support technician
   c. Network administrator
   d. Systems analyst

4. Outsourcing is thought to be an attractive option for many companies because of
   a. the emphasis on employee training.
   b. increased data security.
   c. the cost savings that can be realized.
   d. decreased travel and entertainment costs.

5. Which of the following IT positions is responsible for directing a company's strategy on sites such as Facebook, Twitter, and Yelp?
   a. Project manager
   b. Social media director
   c. Customer interaction technician
   d. Social web analyst

6. Which of the following statements about IT careers is *true*?
   a. Most IT jobs require little interaction with other people.
   b. Women who have IT skills have very few opportunities for securing IT employment.
   c. Many IT jobs are staying in the United States.
   d. IT salaries are declining.

7. Which task is typically performed by a network administrator?
   a. Developing network usage policies
   b. Going to a user's location and fixing software and hardware problems
   c. Web programming
   d. Generating systems documentation for end users

8. Which of the following is *not* a challenge in an IT career?
   a. Stress often accompanies IT jobs.
   b. You usually work alone.
   c. Women are in the minority.
   d. Lifelong learning is the norm.

## true/false

_____ **1.** IT certifications are considered unimportant by most employers.

_____ **2.** Online employment sites can provide guidance as to coursework you should take.

# Glossary

**2-in-1 PC** A laptop computer that can convert into a tablet-like device.

**3D printer** Used to print three-dimensional models.

**3-D sound card** An expansion card that enables a computer to produce omnidirectional or three-dimensional sounds.

**4G** Stands for fourth generation. The current mobile communication standard with faster data transfer rates than 3G.

**5G** Stands for fifth generation. The latest mobile communication standard being rolled out as a mobile data service and also as a home Internet service. 5G will have faster data transfer rates than 4G.

## A

**acceptable use policies** Guidelines regarding usage of computer systems.

**access point** Device that is connected by a cable to the main router that amplifies a wireless signal to otherwise unreachable locations.

**access time** The time it takes a storage device to locate its stored data.

**accounting software** An application program that helps business owners manage their finances more efficiently by providing tools for tracking accounting transactions such as sales, accounts receivable, inventory purchases, and accounts payable.

**adware** A program that downloads on your computer when a user installs a freeware program, game, or utility. Generally, adware enables sponsored advertisements to appear in a section of a browser window or as a pop-up ad.

**affective computing** A type of computing that relates to emotion or that deliberately tries to influence emotion.

**aggregator** A software program that finds and retrieves the latest update of web material (usually podcasts) according to your specifications.

**all-in-one computer** A desktop system unit that houses the computer's processor, memory, and monitor in a single unit.

**all-in-one printer** A device that combines the functions of a printer, scanner, copier, and fax.

**American Standard Code for Information Interchange (ASCII)** The American National Standards Institute's (ANSI, pro-nounced "AN-see") standard code, pronounced "AS-key," to represent each letter or character as an 8-bit (or 1-byte) binary code.

**amoral behavior** When a person has no sense of right and wrong and no interest in the moral consequences of his or her actions.

**analog** Waves that illustrate the loudness of a sound or the brightness of the colors in an image at a given moment in time.

**Android** A mobile operating system designed by Google and used by Samsung, Google, and other manufacturers.

**antivirus software** Software specifically designed to detect viruses and protect a computer and files from harm.

**app creation software** Programming environments that can produce apps that run on various mobile devices.

**application software** The set of programs on a computer that helps a user carry out tasks such as word processing, sending e-mail, balancing a budget, creating presentations, editing photos, taking an online course, and playing games.

**arithmetic logic unit (ALU)** The part of the CPU that performs arithmetical and logic calculations.

**artificial intelligence (AI)** The branch of computer science that deals with the attempt to create computers that think like humans.

**artificial neural networks (ANNs)** Computer systems constructed based on the structure of the human brain using loosely connected artificial neurons.

**aspect ratio** The width-to-height proportion of a monitor.

**assistive (adaptive) technology** Any device, software feature, or app that is designed to improve the functional capabilities for individuals with disabilities.

**audio-editing software** Programs that perform basic editing tasks on audio files such as cutting dead air space from the beginning or end of a song or cutting a portion from the middle.

**audio MIDI interface** Interface technology that allows a user to connect musical instruments and microphones to his or her computer.

**augmented reality** A combination of our normal sense of the objects around us with an overlay of information displayed.

**authentication** The process of identifying a computer user, based on a login or username and password. The computer system determines whether the computer user is authorized and what level of access is to be granted on the network.

## B

**backdoor program** A program that enables a hacker to take complete control of a computer without the legitimate user's knowledge or permission.

**backup** A copy of a computer file that can be used to replace the original if it's lost or damaged.

**backward compatibility** The accommodation of current devices being able to use previously issued software standards in addition to the current standards.

**base-10 number system (decimal notation)** The system you use to represent all of the numeric values you use each day. It's called *base 10* because it uses 10 digits—0 through 9—to represent any value.

**basic input/output system (BIOS)** A program that manages the data between a computer's operating system and all the input and output devices attached to the computer; also responsible for loading the operating system (OS) from its permanent location on the hard drive to random access memory (RAM).

**beta version** A version of the software that's still under development. Many beta versions are available for a limited trial period and are used to help the developers correct any errors before they launch the software on the market.

**Big Data** Very large data sets that are analyzed to reveal patterns, trends, and associations.

**binary digit (bit)** A digit that corresponds to the on and off states of a computer's switches. A bit contains a value of either 0 or 1.

**binary language** The language computers use to process data into information, consisting of only the values 0 and 1.

**binary number system (base-2 number system)** A method of representing a number in powers of 2.

**biometric authentication device** A device that uses some unique characteristic of human biology to identify authorized users.

**black-hat hacker** A hacker who uses his or her knowledge to destroy information or for illegal gain.

**blockchain** A massive public online ledger that keeps track of transactions made in a digital currency.

**blog (weblog)** A personal log or journal posted on the Web; short for *web log*.

**Bluetooth technology** A type of wireless technology that uses radio waves to transmit data over short distances often used to connect peripherals such as printers and keyboards to computers or headsets to cell phones.

**Blu-ray disc (BD)** A method of optical storage for digital data, developed for storing high-definition media. It has the largest storage capacity of all optical storage options.

**Bookmarks** Features in some browsers that place markers of websites' Uniform Resource Locators (URLs) in an easily retrievable list.

**Boolean operators** A word used to refine logical searches. For Internet searches, the words AND, NOT, and OR describe the relationships between keywords in the search.

**boot process** The process for loading the operating system (OS) into random access memory (RAM) when the computer is turned on.

**boot-sector virus** A virus that replicates itself into the master boot record of a flash drive or hard drive.

**bot accounts** Automated programs retweeting news stories and quotes.

**botnet** A large group of software applications (called *robots* or *bots*) that run without user intervention on a large number of computers.

**breadcrumb trail** A navigation aid that shows users the path they have taken to get to a web page or where the page is located within the website; it usually appears at the top of a page.

**broadband** A high-speed Internet connection such as cable, satellite, or digital subscriber line (DSL).

**business-to-business (B2B)** E-commerce transactions between businesses.

**business-to-consumer (B2C)** E-commerce transactions between businesses and consumers.

**byte** Eight binary digits (bits).

## C

**cable Internet** A broadband service that transmits data over coaxial cables.

**cache memory** Small blocks of memory, located directly on and next to the central processing unit (CPU) chip, that act as holding places for recently or frequently used instructions or data that the CPU accesses the most.

**catfishing** A type of Internet harassment where some individual scams others into a false romantic relationship.

**Cat 5e cable** A UTP cable commonly found in wired Ethernet networks, designed for 100 Mbps-wired Ethernet networks.

**Cat 6 cable** A UTP cable that provides more than 1 Gbps of throughput.

**Cat 6a cable** A UTP cable that is designed for ultrafast 10GbE networks.

**Cat 7 cable** A UTP cable that is designed for 10GbE networks and offers greater throughput than Cat 6a cable.

**central processing unit (CPU or processor)** The part of the system unit of a computer that is responsible for data processing; it is the largest and most important chip in the computer. The CPU controls all the functions performed by the computer's other components and processes all the commands issued to it by software instructions.

**charge-coupled device (CCD) arrays** Electronic sensors used to capture images on digital cameras.

**Chromebook** Any laptop or tablet running the Chrome OS as its operating system.

**client** A computer that requests information from a server in a client/server network (such as your computer when you are connected to the Internet).

**client/server network** A type of network that uses servers to deliver services to computers that are requesting them (clients).

**clock cycle** Steady beats or "ticks" of the system clock.

**clock speed** The steady and constant pace at which a computer goes through machine cycles, measured in hertz (Hz).

**cloud computing** The process of storing data, files, and applications on the Web, which allows access to and manipulation of these files and applications from any Internet-connected device.

**cloud-ready printer** Printers that connect directly to the Internet and register themselves with Google Cloud Print.

**cloud storage** A service that keeps files on the Internet (in the "cloud") rather than storing files solely on a local device.

**cluster** The smallest increment in which data is stored on hard disks; hard disks are divided into *tracks*, then *wedges*, then *sectors*, then *clusters*.

**CMYK** A color model in which all colors are described as a mixture of four base colors (cyan, magenta, yellow, and black).

**coaxial cable** A single copper wire surrounded by layers of plastic insulation, metal sheathing, and a plastic jacket; used mainly in cable television and cable Internet service.

**codec** A rule, implemented in either software or hardware, which squeezes a given amount of audio and video information into less space.

**cognitive surplus** The combination of leisure time and the tools to be creative.

**cold boot** The process of starting a computer from a powered-down or off state.

**collaborative consumption** Joining together as a group to use a specific product more efficiently.

**command-driven interface** Interface between user and computer in which the user enters commands to communicate with the computer system.

**computer** A data-processing device that gathers, processes, outputs, and stores data and information.

**computer-aided design (CAD)** A 3-D modeling program used to create automated designs, technical drawings, and model visualizations.

**computer forensics** The application of computer systems and techniques to gather potential legal evidence; a law enforcement specialty used to fight high-tech crime.

**computer literacy** Being familiar enough with computers that a user knows how to use them and understands their capabilities and limitations.

**computer vision** The ability of a computing device to interpret visual information the way humans do.

**connectivity port** A port that enables a computing device to be connected to other devices or systems such as networks, modems, and the Internet.

**consumer-to-consumer (C2C)** E-commerce transactions between consumers through online sites such as eBay.

**control unit** Unit of the CPU that manages the switches inside the CPU.

**cookie** A small text file that some websites automatically store on a client computer's hard drive when a user visits the site.

**copyleft** A simplified licensing scheme that enables copyright holders to grant certain rights to a work while retaining other rights.

**copyright** A creator's exclusive rights to use a work of intellecutal property, such as making copies of it or selling it.

**copyright infringement** Any violation of someone's rights under copyright laws, such as reproducing his or her work without permission.

**core** A complete processing section from a central processing unit, embedded into one physical chip.

**course management software** A program that provides traditional classroom tools, such as calendars and grade books, over the Internet, as well as areas for students to exchange ideas and information in chat rooms, discussion forums, and e-mail.

**CPU benchmarks** Measurements used to compare performance between processors.

**CPU usage** The percentage of time the central processing unit (CPU) is working.

**CPU usage graph** Records central processing unit (CPU) usage and displays it visually.

**crisis-mapping tool** A tool that collects information from e-mails, text messages, blog posts, and Twitter tweets and maps them, making the information publicly available instantly.

**crowdfunding** Asking for small donations from a large number of people, often using the Internet; a style of generating capital to start a business through social media.

**crowdsourcing** Obtaining information or input for a project (such as development of a product) by obtaining the opinions of many different people.

**cryptocurrency (virtual, cyber, or digital currency)** A currency specifically created for the purpose of making payments. Bitcoin is the most well-known cryptocurrency.

**CSMA/CD** The method used on Ethernet networks to avoid data collisions; short for *carrier sense multiple access with collision detection*. A node connected to the network uses carrier sense to verify that no other nodes are currently transmitting data signals.

**cursor** An onscreen icon (often shown by a vertical bar or an arrow) that helps the user keep track of exactly what is active on the display screen

**custom installation** The process of installing only those features of a software program that a user wants on the hard drive.

**cutting the cord** Dropping cable television service and obtaining television programs a different way (using via streaming media services).

**cyber harassment** Using technology to harass or intimidate another individual.

**cybercrime** Any criminal action perpetrated primarily through the use of a computer.

**cyberloafing** Doing anything with a computer that's unrelated to a job (such as playing video games) while one's supposed to be working. Also called *cyberslacking*.

# D

**Dark Web** A very well-concealed part of the Deep Web where many illegal and illicit activities take place.

**data** Numbers, words, pictures, or sounds that represent facts, figures, or ideas; the raw input that users have at the start of a job.

**data breach** When sensitive or confidential information is copied, transmitted, or viewed by an individual who is not authorized to handle the data.

**data file** A file that contains stored data.

**data-flow diagram** Diagrams that trace all data in an information system from the point at which data enters the system to its final resting place (storage or output).

**data mining** The process by which great amounts of data are analyzed and investigated. The objective is to spot significant patterns or trends within the data that would otherwise not be obvious.

**data plan** A connectivity plan or text messaging plan in which data charges are separate from cell phone calling charges and are provided at rates different from those for voice calls.

**data transfer rate (bandwidth)** The maximum speed at which data can be transmitted between two nodes on a network; measured in megabits per second (Mbps) or gigabits per second (Gbps).

**database software** An electronic filing system best used for larger and more complicated groups of data that require more than one table and the ability to group, sort, and retrieve data and generate reports.

**deep learning (DL)** AI systems capable of learning from their mistakes (just as humans do). DL systems therefore improve their accuracy going forward.

**Deep Web** Any part of the Internet that you can't find by using a search engine, such as areas protected by a password or a paywall.

**denial-of-service (DoS) attack** An attack that occurs when legitimate users are denied access to a computer system because a hacker is repeatedly making requests of that computer system that tie up its resources.

**desktop** The primary working area of Windows 10.

**desktop client** A software program that runs on a computer and is used to send and receive e-mail through an Internet service provider's server.

**desktop computer** A computer that is intended for use at a single location. A desktop computer consists of a case that houses the main components of the computer, plus peripheral devices.

**desktop publishing (DTP) software** Programs for incorporating and arranging graphics and text to produce creative documents.

**device driver** Software that facilitates the communication between a device and its operating system.

**digital activism** The use of hashtags and posts to raise awareness and foster discussion about specific issues and causes via social media.

**digital audio workstation software (DAW)** Software used to record and edit music.

**digital convergence** The use of a single unifying device to handle media, Internet, entertainment, and telephony needs.

**digital divide** The discrepancy between those who have access to the opportunities and knowledge that computers and the Internet offer and those who do not.

**digital manipulation** Altering media so that the images captured are changed from the way they were originally seen by the human eye.

**digital rights management (DRM)** A system of access control that allows only limited use of material that has been legally purchased.

**digital video-editing software** A program for editing digital video.

**digital wallet** A software-based storage device that stores the information needed to complete cryptocurrency transactions.

**digitized** Information measured and converted (from analog data) to a stream of numerical values.

**directory** A hierarchical structure that include files, folders, and drives used to create a more organized and efficient computer.

**Disk Cleanup** A Windows utility that removes unnecessary files from the hard drive.

**disk defragmentation** The process of regrouping related pieces of files on the hard drive, enabling faster retrieval of the data.

**display screen (monitor)** A common output device that displays text, graphics, and video as soft copies (copies that can be seen only on screen).

**distributed (grid) computing** A software system in which components located on networked computers interact to achieve a common goal.

**distributed denial-of-service (DDoS) attack** An automated attack that's launched from more than one zombie computer at the same time.

**distributions (distros)** Linux download packages.

**domain name** A part of a Uniform Resource Locator (URL). Domain names consist of two parts: the site's host and a suffix that indicates the type of organization (e.g., popsci.com, where *popsci* is the domain name and *com* is the suffix).

**drawing software (illustration software)** Programs for creating or editing two-dimensional line-based drawings.

**drive bay** A special shelf inside a computer that is designed to hold storage devices.

**drive-by download** The use of malicious software to attack a computer by downloading harmful programs onto a computer, without the user's knowledge, while they are surfing a website.

**DSL (digital subscriber line)** A type of connection that uses telephone lines to connect to the Internet and that allows both phone and data transmissions to share the same line.

# E

**earbuds** Listening devices that connect to computing devices so sound can be heard.

**e-commerce (electronic commerce)** The process of conducting business online for purposes ranging from fund-raising to advertising to selling products.

**educational fair use** Extension of fair use guidelines that grants additional exceptions to copyright infringement for teachers and students when the material is used for educational purposes.

**electronic ink (E Ink)** A very crisp, sharp grayscale representation of text achieved by using millions of microcapsules with white and black particles in a clear fluid.

**electronic text (e-text)** Textual information stored as digital information so that it can be stored, manipulated, and transmitted by electronic devices.

**electrical switches** The devices inside the computer that are flipped between the two states of 1 and 0, signifying on and off.

**e-mail** Internet-based communication in which senders and recipients correspond.

**e-mail virus** A virus transmitted by e-mail that often uses the address book in the victim's e-mail system to distribute itself.

**embedded computer** A specially designed computer chip that resides inside another device, such as a car. These self-contained computer devices have their own programming and typically neither receive input from users nor interact with other systems.

**embodied agents** Robots that look and act like human beings.

**encryption virus** A malicious program that searches for common data files and compresses them into a file using a complex encryption key, thereby rendering the files unusable.

**End User License Agreement (EULA)** An agreement between the user and the software developer that must be accepted before installing the software on a computer.

**e-reader** A device that can display e-text and that has supporting tools, like note taking, bookmarks, and integrated dictionaries.

**ergonomics** How a user sets up his or her computer and other equipment to minimize risk of injury or discomfort.

**Ethernet network** A network that uses the Ethernet protocol as the means (or standard) by which the nodes on the network communicate.

**Ethernet port** A port that transfers data at speeds of up to 10 Gbps; used to connect a computer to a modem or to a network.

**ethics** The study of the general nature of morals and the choices individuals make.

**event** The result of an action—such as a keystroke, mouse click, or signal to the printer—in the respective device (keyboard, mouse, or printer) to which the operating system responds.

**expansion cards (or adapter cards)** A circuit board with specific functions that augment the computer's basic functions and provide connections to other devices; examples include sound cards and video cards.

**expert system** A system that tries to replicate the decision-making processes of human experts in order to solve specific problems.

**exploit kits** A software toolkit used to take advantage of security weaknesses found in apps or operating systems, usually to deploy malware.

**extension (file type)** In a file name, the three letters that follow the user-supplied file name after the dot (.); the extension identifies what kind of family of files the file belongs to, or which application should be used to read the file.

**external hard drive** A hard drive that is enclosed in a protective case to make it portable; the drive is connected to the computer with a data transfer cable and is often used to back up data.

# F

**fair use** Guidelines allowing people to use portions of a copyrighted work for specific purposes without receiving prior permission from the copyright holder.

**fake news** Stories that are invented rather than being factual and that are intended to spread misinformation.

**Favorites** A feature in Microsoft Internet Explorer that places a marker of a website's Uniform Resource Locator (URL) in an easily retrievable list in the browser's toolbar. (Called *Bookmarks* in some browsers.)

**feature phone** Inexpensive cell phones with modest processors, simple interfaces, and, often, no touch screens.

**fiber-optic cable** A cable that transmits data via light waves along glass or plastic fibers.

**fiber-optic service** Internet access that is enabled by transmitting data at the speed of light through glass or plastic fibers.

**file** A collection of related pieces of information stored together for easy reference.

**file compression utility** A program that takes out redundancies in a file in order to reduce the file size.

**File Explorer** The main tool for finding, viewing, and managing the contents of your computer by showing the location and contents of every drive, folder, and file; called Windows Explorer prior to Windows 8.

**File History** A Windows utility that automatically creates a duplicate of your libraries, desktop, contacts, and favorites and copies it to another storage device, such as an external hard drive.

**file management** The process by which humans or computer software provide organizational structure to a computer's contents.

**file name** The first part of the label applied to a file; generally the name a user assigns to the file when saving it.

**file path** The exact location of a file, starting with the drive in which the file is located and including all folders, subfolders (if any), the file name, and the extension (e.g., C:\ Users\username\Documents\ Illustrations\ EBronte.jpg).

**File Transfer Protocol (FTP)** A protocol used to upload and download files from one computer to another over the Internet.

**financial planning software** Programs for managing finances, such as Intuit's Quicken, which include electronic checkbook registers and automatic bill-payment tools.

**firewall** A software program or hardware device designed to prevent unauthorized access to computers or networks.

**firmware** System software that controls hardware devices.

**flash drive (jump drive, USB drive, or thumb drive)** A drive that plugs into a universal serial bus (USB) port on a computer and that stores data digitally.

**flash memory card** A form of portable storage; this removable memory card is often used in digital cameras, smartphones, video cameras, and printers.

**flatbed scanner** Used to create a digital image from a tangible image (like a paper photo).

**folder** A collection of files stored on a computer.

**freeware** Any copyrighted software that can be used for free.

**full backup** A file backup that encompasses all files on a computer regardless of whether they have changed since the last backup.

**full installation** The process of installing all the files and programs from the distribution media to the computer's hard drive.

**G**

**game controllers** Devices such as joysticks, game pads, and steering wheels that function as input devices because they send data to computing devices.

**geolocation** The method of identifying the geographical location of a person or device, usually by utilizing information processed through the Internet.

**gigabit Ethernet (GbE)** The most commonly used wired Ethernet standard deployed in devices designed for home networks; provides bandwidth of up to 1 Gbps.

**gigabyte (GB)** About a billion bytes.

**gigahertz (GHz)** One billion hertz.

**global positioning system (GPS)** A system of 21 satellites (plus three working spares), built and operated by the U.S. military, that constantly orbit the earth. The satellites provide information to GPS-capable devices to pinpoint locations on the earth.

**Google Chrome OS** A Web-based OS.

**graphical user interface (GUI)** Unlike the command- and menu-driven interfaces used in earlier software, GUIs display graphics and use the point-and-click technology of the mouse and cursor, making them much more user friendly.

**graphics double data rate 5 (GDDR5)** A standard of video memory.

**graphics processing unit (GPU)** A specialized logic chip that's dedicated to quickly displaying and calculating visual data such as shadows, textures, and luminosity.

**gray-hat hacker** A cross between black and white—a hacker who will often illegally break into systems merely to flaunt his or her expertise to the administrator of the system he or she penetrated or to attempt to sell his or her services in repairing security breaches.

**green computing (green IT)** A movement that encourages environmentally sustainable computing (or IT).

**H**

**hacker** Anyone who unlawfully breaks into a computer system (whether an individual computer or a network).

**hacktivism** Using computers and computer networks in a subversive way to promote an agenda.

**hard drive** The computer's nonvolatile, primary storage device for permanent storage of software and data.

**hardware** Any part of a computer or computer system you can physically touch.

**head crash** Impact of the read/write head against the magnetic platter of the hard drive; often results in data loss.

**headphones** Devices for listening to sounds on computing devices.

**hexidecimal notation** A base-16 number system, meaning it uses 16 digits to represent numbers instead of the 10 digits used in base 10 or the two digits used in base 2. The 16 digits it uses are the 10 numeric digits, 0 to 9, plus six extra symbols: A, B, C, D, E, and F.

**hibernate** A power-management mode that saves the current state of the current system to the computer's hard drive.

**high definition** A standard of digital TV signal that guarantees a specific level of resolution and a specific *aspect ratio*, which is the rectangular shape of the image.

**high-definition multimedia interface (HDMI) port** A compact audio–video interface standard that carries both high-definition video and uncompressed digital audio.

**hoax** Anything designed to deceive another person either as a practical joke or for financial gain.

**home area network (HAN)** A network located in a home that's used to connect all of its digital devices.

**home network server** A device designed to store media, share media across the network, and back up files on computers connected to a home network.

**host** The portion of a domain name that identifies who maintains a given website. For example, berkeley.edu is the domain name for the University of California at Berkeley, which maintains that site.

**hyperlink** A type of specially coded text that, when clicked, enables a user to jump from one location, or web page, to another within a website or to another website altogether.

**Hypertext Transfer Protocol (HTTP)** The protocol that allows files to be transferred from a web server so that you can see them on your computer by using a browser.

**hyperthreading** A technology that permits quicker processing of information by enabling a new set of instructions to start executing before the previous set has finished.

## I

**identity theft** The process by which someone uses personal information about someone else (such as the victim's name, address, and Social Security number) to assume the victim's identity for the purpose of defrauding another.

**image backup (system backup)** A copy of an entire computer system, created for restoration purposes.

**image-editing software** Programs for editing photographs and other images.

**incremental backup (partial backup)** A type of backup that only backs up files that have changed since the last time files were backed up.

**information** Data that has been organized or presented in a meaningful fashion; the result, or output that users require at the end of a job.

**information technology (IT)** The set of techniques used in processing and retrieving information.

**inkjet printer** A nonimpact printer that sprays tiny drops of ink onto paper.

**inoculation** A process used by antivirus software; compares old and current qualities of files to detect viral activity.

**input device** A hardware device used to enter, or input, data (text, images, and sounds) and instructions (user responses and commands) into a computer.

**instant messaging (IM)** A program that enables users to communicate online in real time with others who are also online.

**instruction set** The collection of commands that a specific CPU can execute. Each CPU has its own unique instruction set.

**intangible personal property** Property that can't be touched—or potentially even seen—yet it still has value.

**integrated circuits (or chips)** Tiny regions of semiconductor material that support a huge number of transistors.

**intellectual property** Refers to products derived from the mind, such as works of art and literature, inventions, and software code.

**intelligence** The ability to acquire and apply knowledge and skills.

**intelligent personal assistant** Software designed to perform tasks or services for individuals.

**interactive white board** An input/output device that projects the computer's display onto a surface, which allows users to interface with the board and computing device.

**internal hard drive** A hard drive that resides within the computer's system unit and that usually holds all permanently stored programs and data.

**Internet** A network of networks that's the largest network in the world, connecting billions of computers globally.

**Internet backbone** The main pathway of high-speed communications lines over which all Internet traffic flows.

**Internet of Things (IoT)** The interconnection of uniquely identifiable embedded computing devices that transfer data over a network without requiring human-to-human or human-to-computer interaction.

**Internet protocol (IP) address** The means by which all computers connected to the Internet identify each other. It consists of a unique set of four numbers separated by dots, such as 123.45.178.91.

**Internet service provider (ISP)** A company that specializes in providing Internet access. ISPs may be specialized providers, like Juno, or companies that provide other services in addition to Internet access (such as phone and cable television).

**interrupt** A signal that tells the operating system that it's in need of immediate attention.

**interrupt handler** A special numerical code that prioritizes requests from various devices. These requests then are placed in the interrupt table in the computer's primary memory.

**iOS** The operating system for Apple mobile devices like the iPhone and iPad.

**IP address** *See Internet protocol address.*

## K

**kernel** The essential component of the operating system that's responsible for managing the processor and all other components of the computer system. Because it stays in random access memory (RAM) the entire time the computer is powered on, the kernel is called *memory resident.*

**keyboard** A hardware device used to enter typed data and commands into a computer.

**keystroke logger (keylogger)** A type of spyware program that monitors keystrokes with the intent of stealing passwords, login IDs, or credit card information.

**keyword** (1) A specific word a user wishes to query (or look for) in an Internet search. (2) A specific word that has a predefined meaning in a particular programming language.

**kilobyte (KB)** A unit of computer storage equal to approximately 1,000 bytes.

**knowledge representation** Encoding information about the world into formats that an AI system can understand.

## L

**laptop (or notebook) computer** A portable computer with a keyboard, a monitor, and other devices integrated into a single compact case.

**large-format printer** A printer that prints on oversized paper. Often used for creating banners and signs.

**laser printer** A nonimpact printer known for quick and quiet production and high-quality printouts.

**latency (rotational delay)** The process that occurs after the read/write head of the hard drive locates the correct track and then waits for the correct sector to spin to the read/write head.

**light-emitting diode (LED)** An energy-efficient technology used in monitors. It may result in better color accuracy and thinner panels than traditional LCD monitors.

**linked data** Data that is formally defined and that can be expressed in relationships.

**Linux** An open-source operating system based on UNIX. Because of the stable nature of this operating system, it's often used on web servers.

**liquid crystal display (LCD)** The technology used in flat-panel computer monitors.

**local area network (LAN)** A network in which the nodes are located within a small geographic area.

**locally installed software** Software that is installed on your device's internal storage.

**logic bomb** A computer virus that runs when a certain set of conditions is met, such as when a program is launched a specific number of times.

**logical port** A virtual communications gateway or path that enables a computer to organize requests for information (such as web page downloads and e-mail routing) from other networks or computers.

**logical port blocking** A condition in which a firewall is configured to ignore all incoming packets that request access to a certain port so that no unwanted requests will get through to the computer.

**M**

**machine cycle** The series of steps a central processing unit goes through when it performs a program instruction.

**machine learning** A form of artificial intelligence that provides computers with the ability to learn without being explicitly programmed.

**macOS** The first commercially available operating system to incorporate a graphical user interface (GUI) with user-friendly point-and-click technology.

**macro virus** A virus that's distributed by hiding it inside a macro.

**mainframe** A large, expensive computer that supports hundreds or thousands of users simultaneously and executes many different programs at the same time.

**malware** Software that's intended to render a system temporarily or permanently useless or to penetrate a computer system completely for purposes of information gathering. Examples include spyware, viruses, worms, and Trojan horses.

**master boot record** A small program that runs whenever a computer boots up.

**megabyte (MB)** A unit of computer storage equal to approximately 1 million bytes.

**memory module (memory card)** A small circuit board that holds a series of random access memory (RAM) chips.

**menu-driven interface** A user interface in which the user chooses a command from menus displayed on the screen.

**metasearch engine** A search engine, such as Dogpile, that searches other search engines rather than individual websites.

**metropolitan area network (MAN)** A wide area network (WAN) that links users in a specific geographic area (such as within a city or county).

**microblog** Social media in which users post short text with usually frequent updates.

**microphone (mic)** A device that allows you to capture sound waves, such as those created by your voice, and to transfer them to digital format on your computer.

**microprocessors** The chips that contain a central processing unit (CPU, or processor).

**Microsoft account** Registered user profile with specific user id and password to log into Windows account from any machine and access familiar desktop and applications.

**mobile broadband** Connection to the Internet through the same cellular network that cell phones use to get 3G or 4G Internet access.

**Mobile commerce (m-commerce)** Conducting commercial transactions online through a smartphone, tablet, or other mobile device.

**mobile hotspot** Devices that enable you to connect more than one device to the Internet; they require access to a data plan. Most smartphones have this capability built-in.

**mobile operating system** An operating system that includes many features of personal computer operating systems but are modified to be more functional on handheld devices.

**model release** A release that usually grants a photographer the right to use an image of the model (or subject of the photo) commercially.

**modem** A device that connects a network to the Internet.

**Moore's Law** A prediction, named after Gordon Moore, the co-founder of Intel; states that the number of transistors on a central processing unit chip will double every two years.

**motherboard** A special circuit board in the system unit that contains the central processing unit, the memory (RAM) chips, and the slots available for expansion cards; all of the other boards (video cards, sound cards, and so on) connect to it to receive power and to communicate.

**mouse** A hardware device used to enter user responses and commands into a computer.

**multi-factor authentication** A process that requires two of the three assigned factors be demonstrated before authentication is granted.

**multimedia software** Programs that include image-, video-, and audio-editing software, animation software, and other specialty software required to produce computer games, animations, and movies.

**multi-partite virus** Literally meaning "multi-part" virus; a type of computer virus that attempts to infect computers using more than one method.

**multi-task** The ability of an operating system to perform more than one process at a time.

**multi-user operating system (network operating system)** An operating system that enables more than one user to access the computer system at one time by efficiently juggling all the requests from multiple users.

**N**

**natural language processing** A feature of AI systems that allows the system to understand written and spoken words and to interact with humans using language.

**near field communication (NFC)** A set of communication protocols that enable devices to communicate with each other when they are held in close proximity. NFC is commonly used for mobile payments.

**network** A group of two or more computers (or nodes) that are configured to share information and resources such as printers, files, and databases.

**network adapter** A device that enables the computer (or peripheral) to communicate with the network using a common data communication language, or protocol.

**network address translation (NAT)** A process that firewalls use to assign internal Internet protocol addresses on a network.

**network administration** Involves tasks such as (1) installing new computers and devices, (2) monitoring the network to ensure it's performing efficiently, (3) updating and installing new software on the network, and (4) configuring, or setting up, proper security for a network.

**network architecture** The design of a computer network; includes both physical and logical design.

**network-attached storage (NAS) device** A specialized computing device designed to store and manage network data.

**network interface card (NIC)** An expansion card that enables a computer to connect other computers or to a cable modem to facilitate a high-speed Internet connection.

**network navigation device** A device on a network such as a router or switch that moves data signals around the network.

**network operating system (NOS)** Software that handles requests for information, Internet access, and the use of peripherals for network nodes, providing the services necessary for the computers on the network to communicate.

**network-ready device** A device (such as a printer or an external hard drive) that can be attached directly to a network instead of needing to attach to a computer on the network.

**node** A device connected to a network such as a computer, a peripheral (such as a printer), or a communications device (such as a modem).

**nonvolatile storage** Permanent storage, as in read-only memory (ROM).

**number system** An organized plan for representing a number.

## O

**omnibox** A combined search and address bar, so you can both type a website URL or search the Web from the address bar.

**online reputation** Information available about you in cyberspace that can influence people's opinions of you in the real world.

**open-source software** Program code made publicly available for free; it can be copied, distributed, or changed without the stringent copyright protections of proprietary software products.

**operating system (OS)** The system software that controls the way in which a computer system functions, including the management of hardware, peripherals, and software.

**optical character recognition (OCR) software** Software that digitizes and saves text in digital form.

**optical mouse** A mouse that uses an internal sensor or laser to control the mouse's movement. The sensor sends signals to the computer, telling it where to move the pointer on the screen.

**organic light-emitting diode (OLED) displays** Displays that use organic compounds to produce light when exposed to an electric current. Unlike LCDs, OLEDs do not require a backlight to function and therefore draw less power and have a much thinner display, sometimes as thin as 3 mm.

**output device** A device that sends processed data and information out of a computer in the form of text, pictures (graphics), sounds (audio), or video.

**overclocking** Running the central processing unit at a speed faster than the manufacturer recommends.

## P

**packet analyzer (sniffer)** A computer hardware device or software program designed to detect and record digital information being transmitted over a network.

**packet filtering** A process in which firewalls are configured so that they filter out packets sent to specific logical ports.

**paging** The process of swapping data or instructions that have been placed in the swap file for later use back into active random access memory (RAM). The contents of the hard drive's swap file then become less active data or instructions.

**paper mills** Websites that sell prewritten or custom-written research papers to students.

**parallel processing** A large network of computers, with each computer working on a portion of the same problem simultaneously

**patents** Grant inventors the right to stop others from manufacturing, using, or selling (including importing) their inventions for a period of 20 years from the date the patent is filed.

**path (subdirectory)** The Information after the slash that indicates a particular file or path (or subdirectory) within the website.

**path separator** The backslash mark (\) used by Microsoft Windows and DOS in file names. Mac files use a colon (:), and UNIX

and Linux use the forward slash (/) as the path separator.

**peer-to-peer (P2P) network** A network in which each node connected to the network can communicate directly with every other node on the network.

**peer-to-peer (P2P) sharing** The process of users transferring files between computers.

**peripheral device** A device such as a monitor, printer, or keyboard that connects to the system unit through a data port.

**persistence of information** The tendency for pictures, videos, and narratives to continue to exist in cyberspace even after you delete them.

**personal area network (PAN)** A network used for communication among devices close to one person, such as smartphones, laptops, and tablets, using wireless technologies such as Bluetooth.

**personal ethics** The set of formal or informal ethical principles that an individual uses to guide their ethical decisions.

**personal firewall** A firewall specifically designed for home networks.

**personal information manager (PIM) software** Programs such as Microsoft Outlook or Lotus Organizer that strive to replace the various management tools found on a traditional desk such as a calendar, address book, notepad, and to-do lists.

**personal property** Things of value that you own (such as a car or laptop).

**petabyte** $10^{15}$ bytes of digital information.

**phablet** Model of phone, with screen sizes of almost 6 inches.

**pharming** Planting malicious code on a computer that alters the browser's ability to find web addresses and that directs users to bogus websites.

**phishing** The process of sending e-mail messages to lure Internet users into revealing personal information such as credit card or Social Security numbers or other sensitive information that could lead to identity theft.

**physical memory** The amount of random access memory (RAM) that's installed in a computer.

**piggybacking** The process of connecting to a wireless network without the permission of the owner of the network.

**pinning** The process through which you choose which applications are visible on the Windows Start screen.

**pipelining** A technique that allows the CPU to work on more than one instruction (or stage of processing) at the same time, thereby boosting CPU performance.

**pixel** A single point that creates the images on a computer monitor. Pixels are illuminated by an electron beam that passes rapidly back and forth across the back of the screen so that the pixels appear to glow continuously.

**plagiarism** The act of copying text or ideas from someone else and claiming them as your own.

**platform** The combination of a computer's operating system and processor. The two most common platform types are the PC and the Apple.

**platter** A thin, round, metallic storage plate stacked onto the hard drive spindle.

**Plug and Play (PnP)** The technology that enables the operating system, once it is booted up, to recognize automatically any new peripherals and to configure them to work with the system.

**podcast** A clip of audio or video content that's broadcast over the Internet using compressed audio or video files in formats such as MP3.

**polymorphic virus** A virus that changes its virus signature (the binary pattern that makes the virus identifiable) every time it infects a new file. This makes it more difficult for antivirus programs to detect the virus.

**port** An interface through which external devices are connected to the computer.

**positive psychology** A field that attempts to discover the causes of happiness rather than to address the treatment of mental dysfunctions.

**power supply** Regulates the wall voltage to the voltages required by computer chips; it's housed inside the system unit.

**power-on self-test (POST)** The first job the basic input/output system (BIOS) performs, ensuring that essential peripheral devices are attached and operational. This process consists of a test on the video card and video memory, a BIOS identification process (during which the BIOS version, manufacturer, and data are displayed on the monitor), and a memory test to ensure memory chips are working properly.

**preemptive multi-tasking** When the operating system processes the task assigned a higher priority before processing a task that has been assigned a lower priority.

**presentation software** An application program for creating dynamic slide shows, such as Microsoft PowerPoint or Apple Keynote.

**pretexting** The act of creating an invented scenario (the pretext) to convince someone to divulge information.

**printer** A common output device that creates tangible or hard copies of text and graphics.

**processing** Manipulating or organizing data into information.

**productivity software** Programs that enable a user to perform various tasks generally required in home, school, and business. Examples include word processing, spreadsheet, presentation, personal information management, and database programs.

**program** A series of instructions to be followed by a computer to accomplish a task.

**program file** Files that are used in the running of software programs and that do not store data.

**project management tools** Software designed to help assess the progress of a project as it moves toward completion.

**projector** A device that can project images from your computer onto a wall or viewing screen.

**proprietary (commercial) software** Custom software application that's owned and controlled by the company that created it.

**public domain** Copyrightable works whose copyright has expired, or that never had copyright protection.

**Q**

**quarantining** The placement (by antivirus software) of a computer virus in a secure area on the hard drive so that it won't spread infection to other files.

**QR (quick response) code** Technology that lets any piece of print in the real world host a live link to online information and video content.

**QWERTY keyboard** A keyboard that gets its name from the first six letters on the top-left row of alphabetic keys on the keyboard.

**R**

**RAID 0** The strategy of running two hard drives in one system, cutting in half the time it takes to write a file.

**RAID 1** The strategy of mirroring all the data written on one hard drive to a second hard drive, providing an instant backup of all data.

**random access memory (RAM)** The computer's temporary storage space or short-term memory. It's located in a set of chips on the system unit's motherboard, and its capacity is measured in megabytes or gigabytes.

**read-only memory (ROM)** A set of memory chips, located on the motherboard, that stores data and instructions that cannot be changed or erased; it holds all the instructions the computer needs to start up.

**read/write head** The mechanism that retrieves (reads) and records (writes) the magnetic data to and from a data disk.

**real property** Immoveable property such as land or a home (often called *real estate*).

**real-time operating system (RTOS)** A program with a specific purpose that must guarantee certain response times for particular computing tasks or else the machine's application is useless. Real-time operating systems are found in many types of robotic equipment.

**Really Simple Syndication (RSS)** An XML–based format that allows frequent updates of content on the Web.

**recommendation engines** AI systems that help people discover things they may like but are unlikely to discover on their own.

**recovery drive** A drive that contains all the information needed to reinstall your operating system if it should become corrupted. Often the manufacturer will have placed a utility on your system to create this.

**Recycle Bin** A folder on a Windows desktop in which deleted files from the hard drive are held until permanently purged from the system.

**redundant array of independent disks (RAID)** A set of strategies for using more than one hard drive in a computer system.

**registers** Special memory storage areas built into the CPU, which are the most expensive, fastest memory in your computer.

**registry** A portion of the hard drive containing all the different configurations (settings) used by the Windows operating system as well as by other applications.

**Reset this PC** A utility program in Windows 10 that attempts to diagnose and fix errors in Windows system files that are causing a computer to behave improperly.

**resolution** The clearness or sharpness of an image, which is controlled by the number of pixels displayed on the screen.

**restore point** A type of backup that doesn't affect your personal data files but saves all the apps, updates, drivers, and information needed to restore your computer system to the exact way it's configured at that time. That way, if something does go awry, you can return your system to the way it was before you started.

**root directory** The top level of the filing structure in a computer system. In Windows computers, the root directory of the hard drive is represented as C:\.

**rootkit** Programs that allow hackers to gain access to your computer and take almost complete control of it without your knowledge. These programs are designed to subvert normal login procedures to a computer and to hide their operations from normal detection methods.

**router** A device that routes packets of data between two or more networks.

**rules-based systems** Software that asks questions and responds based on preprogrammed algorithms. Early attempts at expert systems were rules based.

**S**

**sampling rate** The number of times per second a signal is measured and converted to a digital value. Sampling rates are measured in kilobits per second.

**satellite Internet** A way to connect to the Internet using a small satellite dish, which is placed outside the home and is connected to a computer with coaxial cable. The satellite company then sends the data to a satellite orbiting Earth. The satellite, in turn, sends the data back to the satellite dish and to the computer.

**scareware** A type of malware that's downloaded onto your computer and that tries to convince you that your computer is infected with a virus or other type of malware.

**script** A list of commands (mini-programs or macros) that can be executed on a computer without user interaction.

**search engine** A set of programs that searches the Web for specific words (or keywords) you wish to query (or look for) and that then returns a list of the websites on which those keywords are found.

**search engine optimization (SEO)** Designing a website to ensure ranking near the top of search engine results.

**sector** A section of a hard drive platter, wedge-shaped from the center of the platter to the edge.

**seek time** The time it takes for the hard drive's read/write heads to move over the surface of the disk to the correct track.

**semantic web (Web 3.0)** An evolving extension of the Web in which information is defined in such a way as to make it more easily readable by computers.

**semiconductor** Any material that can be controlled to either allow it to conduct electricity or act as an insulator.

**sensor** Any device that detects or measures something. Computing devices, especially smartphones, contain many sensors.

**server** A computer that provides resources to other computers on a network.

**service mark** Essentially the same as a trademark, but it applies to a service as opposed to a product.

**service set identifier (SSID)** A network name that wireless routers use to identify themselves.

**simulation programs** Software, often used for training purposes, that allows the user to experience or control an event as if it's reality.

**Sleep mode** A low-power mode for computing devices that saves electric power consumption and saves the last-used settings. When the device is "woken up," work is resumed more quickly than when cold-booting the device.

**smart home** A dwelling in which devices and appliances are automated or controlled by apps.

**smartphone** Phone with features of a computer including a wide assortment of apps, media players, high-quality cameras, and web connectivity.

**social commerce** A subset of e-commerce that uses social networks to assist in marketing and purchasing products.

**social engineering** Any technique that uses social skills to generate human interaction for the purpose of enticing individuals to reveal sensitive information.

**social media** Websites or apps that allow users to create and share content and/

or participate in social networking with others.

**social networking** A means by which people use the Internet to communicate and share information among their immediate friends and to meet and connect with others through common interests, experiences, and friends.

**software** The set of computer programs or instructions that tells the computer what to do and that enables it to perform different tasks.

**software license** An agreement between the user and the software developer that must be accepted before installing the software on a computer.

**software piracy** Violating a software license agreement by copying an application onto more computers than the license agreement permits.

**Software as a Service (SaaS)** Software that's delivered on demand over the Internet.

**solid-state drive (SSD)** A storage device that uses the same kind of memory that flash drives use but that can reach data in only a tenth of the time a flash drive requires.

**solid-state hybrid drive (SSHD)** A drive that is a combination of both a mechanical hard drive and an SSD in a single device.

**sound card** An expansion card that attaches to (or is integrated into) the motherboard inside the system unit and that enables the computer to produce sounds; also provides a connection for the speakers and microphone.

**spam** Unwanted or junk e-mail.

**spam filter** An option you can select in your e-mail account that places known or suspected spam messages into a folder other than your inbox.

**speakers** Output devices for sound.

**spear phishing** A targeted phishing attack that sends e-mails to people known to be customers of a company. Such attacks have a much greater chance of successfully getting individuals to reveal sensitive data.

**spooler** A program that helps coordinate all print jobs being sent to the printer at the same time.

**spreadsheet software** An application program such as Microsoft Excel or Lotus 1-2-3 that enables a user to do calculations and numerical analyses easily.

**spyware** An unwanted piggyback program that downloads with the software you want to install from the Internet and then runs in the background of your system.

**Start menu** A feature in Windows 10 that provides access to all applications in one convenient screen.

**stealth virus** A virus that temporarily erases its code from the files where it resides and hides in the active memory of the computer.

**stylus** A pen-shaped device used to tap or write on touch-sensitive screens.

**subscription software** A model whereby the user pays a fee to use the software. The software is downloaded and installed locally but is routinely updated by connection to the manufacturer's server.

**supercomputer** A specially designed computer that can perform complex calculations extremely rapidly; used in situations in which complex models requiring intensive mathematical calculations are needed (such as weather forecasting or atomic energy research).

**SuperFetch** A memory-management technique used by Windows. Monitors the applications you use the most and preloads them into your system memory so that they'll be ready to go.

**supervised learning** Training an AI system using a huge number of examples.

**surge protector** A device that protects computers and other electronic devices from power surges.

**surround sound** A type of audio processing that makes the listener experience sound as if it were coming from all directions.

**surround-sound system** A system of speakers set up in such a way that it surrounds an entire area (and the people in it) with sound.

**swap file (page file)** A temporary storage area on the hard drive where the operating system "swaps out" or moves the data or instructions from random access memory (RAM) that haven't recently been used. This process takes place when more RAM space is needed.

**switch** A device for transmitting data on a network that makes decisions, based on the media access control address of the data, as to where the data is to be sent.

**system clock** This internal clock is actually a special crystal that acts like a metronome, keeping a steady beat and controlling

when the CPU moves to the next stage of processing.

**system evaluation** The process of looking at a computer's subsystems, what they do, and how they perform to determine whether the computer system has the right hardware components to do what the user ultimately wants it to do.

**system files** The main files of an operating system.

**system requirements** The set of minimum storage, memory capacity, and processing standards recommended by the software manufacturer to ensure proper operation of a software application.

**System Restore** A utility in Windows that restores system settings to a specific previous date when everything was working properly.

**system restore point** In Windows, a snapshot of your entire system's settings used for restoring your system to a prior point in time.

**system software** The set of programs that enables a computer's hardware devices and application software to work together; it includes the operating system and utility programs.

**system unit** The metal or plastic case that holds all the physical parts of the computer together, including the computer's processor (its brains), its memory, and the many circuit boards that help the computer function.

# T

**tablet computer** A mobile computer, such as the Apple iPad, integrated into a flat multi-touch-sensitive screen. It uses an onscreen virtual keyboard.

**tag** Electronically identifying someone in a photo or post.

**tagging (social bookmarking)** Assigning a keyword or term to a web resource such as a web page, digital image, or video.

**tangible personal property** Property that has substance like your smartphone or car.

**Task Manager** A Windows utility that shows programs currently running and permits you to exit nonresponsive programs when you click End Task.

**taskbar** In later versions of Windows operating systems, a feature that displays open and favorite applications for easy access.

**tax preparation software** An application program, such as Intuit's TurboTax or

H&R Block's At Home, for preparing state and federal taxes. Each program offers a complete set of tax forms and instructions as well as expert advice on how to complete each form.

**template** A form included in many productivity applications that provides the basic structure for a particular kind of document, spreadsheet, or presentation.

**terabyte (TB)** 1,099,511,627,776 bytes or $2^{40}$ bytes.

**terms of use** Legal documents (or disclaimers) that delineate how copyrighted material can be used.

**texting** Using the Short Message Service (SMS) to send short messages between mobile devices.

**thrashing** A condition of excessive paging in which the operating system becomes sluggish.

**throughput** The actual speed of data transfer that's achieved. It's usually less than the data transfer rate.

**Thunderbolt port** A high-speed input/output port.

**time bomb** A virus that's triggered by the passage of time or on a certain date.

**top-level domain** The suffix, often of three letters (such as .com or .edu), in the domain name that indicates the kind of organization the host is.

**Tor (The Onion Router) browser** An app used to access the Dark Web, which allows you to locate hidden websites in the .onion domain.

**touch pad (trackpad)** A small, touch-sensitive surface at the base of a laptop keyboard that's used to direct the cursor.

**touch screen** A type of monitor (or display in a smartphone or tablet computer) that accepts input from a user touching the screen.

**track** A concentric circle that serves as a storage area on a hard drive platter.

**trademark** A word, phrase, symbol, or design—or a combination of these—that uniquely identifies and differentiates the goods (or services) of one party from those of another.

**transistor** Electrical switches built out of layers of a special type of material called a *semiconductor*.

**transmission media** The radio waves or the physical system (cable) that transports data on a network.

**Trojan horse** A computer program that appears to be something useful or desirable (such as a game or a screen saver), but at the same time does something malicious in the background without the user's knowledge.

**trolling** The act of posting inflammatory remarks online for the sheer pleasure of soliciting an angry or negative response.

**Turing test** A simple test to distinguish between a human and a computer system. Named after Alan Turing, a computing pioneer.

**twisted-pair cable** Cable made of copper wires that are twisted around each other and are surrounded by a plastic jacket (such as traditional home phone wire).

## U

**ultrabook** A full-featured but lightweight laptop computer that features a low-power processor and a solid-state drive; it tries to reduce its size and weight to extend battery life without sacrificing performance.

**unethical behavior** Not conforming to a set of approved standards of behavior—cheating on an exam, for example

**unicode** An encoding scheme that uses 16 bits instead of 8 bits. Unicode can represent nearly 1,115,000 code points and currently assigns more than 128,000 unique character symbols.

**Uniform Resource Locator (URL)** A website's unique address; an example is microsoft.com.

**universal serial bus (USB) port** A port that can connect a wide variety of peripheral devices to the computer, including keyboards, printers, mice, smartphones, external hard drives, flash drives, and digital cameras.

**UNIX** An operating system originally conceived in 1969 by Ken Thompson and Dennis Ritchie of AT&T's Bell Labs. In 1974, the UNIX code was rewritten in the standard programming language C. Today there are various commercial versions of UNIX.

**unshielded twisted-pair (UTP) cable** The most popular transmission media option for Ethernet networks. UTP cable is composed of four pairs of wires that are twisted around each other to reduce electrical interference.

**unsupervised learning** When an AI system can look at data on its own and build rules for deciding what it is seeing.

**urban legends** When hoaxes become so well known that they're incorporated into society as true events even though they're false.

**user interface** Part of the operating system that enables individuals to interact with the computer.

**utility program** A small program that performs many of the general housekeeping tasks for the computer, such as system maintenance and file compression.

## V

**vertical market software** Software that's developed for and customized to a specific industry's needs (such as a wood inventory system for a sawmill) as opposed to software that's useful across a range of industries (such as word processing software).

**video card (video adapter)** An expansion card that's installed inside a system unit to translate binary data (the 1s and 0s the computer uses) into the images viewed on the monitor.

**video log (vlog or video blog)** A personal online journal that uses video as the primary content in addition to text, images, and audio.

**video memory** Random access memory that's included as part of a video card.

**virtual desktops** A Windows 10 feature that allows you to organize groups of windows into different displays.

**virtual keyboard** A keyboard that displays on screen when text input is required.

**virtual memory** The space on the hard drive where the operating system stores data if there isn't enough random access memory to hold all of the programs you're currently trying to run.

**virtual private network (VPN)** A network that uses the public Internet communications infrastructure to build a secure, private network among various locations.

**virtual reality (VR)** An artificial environment that is immersive and interactive.

**virus** A computer program that attaches itself to another computer program (known as the host program) and attempts to spread itself to other computers when files are exchanged.

**virus signature** A portion of the virus code that's unique to a particular computer virus and that makes it identifiable by antivirus software.

**voice recognition software** Software that allows you to control your computing devices by speaking into the microphone instead of using a keyboard or mouse.

**VoIP (voice over Internet protocol)** A technology that facilitates making telephone calls across the Internet instead of using conventional telephone lines.

**volatile storage** Temporary storage, such as in random access memory. When the power is turned off, the data in volatile storage is cleared out.

## W

**warm boot** The process of restarting a computing device while it's powered on.

**Web 2.0** Tools and Web-based services that emphasize online collaboration and sharing among users.

**web authoring software** Programs you can use to design interactive web pages without knowing any HyperText Markup Language (HTML) code.

**Web-based e-mail** A type of e-mail system that's managed by a web browser and that allows access to e-mail from the Web.

**web browser (browser)** Software installed on a computer system that allows individuals to locate, view, and navigate the Web.

**web server** A computer running a specialized operating system that enables it to host web pages (and other information) and to provide requested web pages to clients.

**webcam** A small camera that sits on top of a computer monitor or that's built into a computing device and is usually used to transfer live video.

**webcast** The (usually live) broadcast of audio or video content over the Internet.

**white-hat hacker (ethical hacker)** A hacker who breaks into systems just for the challenge of it (and who doesn't wish to steal or wreak havoc on the systems). Such hackers tout themselves as experts who are performing a needed service for society by helping companies realize the vulnerabilities that exist in their systems.

**whole-house surge protector** A surge protector that's installed on (or near) the breaker panel of a home and that protects all electronic devices in the home from power surges.

**Wi-Fi** The 802.11 standard for wireless data transmissions established by the Institute of Electrical and Electronics Engineers (IEEE).

**wide area network (WAN)** A network made up of local area networks (LANs) connected over long distances.

**wiki** A type of website that allows anyone visiting the site to change its content by adding, removing, or editing the content.

**Windows** Microsoft's operating system that incorporates a user-friendly, visual interface.

**wireless Internet service provider (wireless ISP):** An ISP that provides service to wireless devices such as smartphones.

**wireless range extender** A device that amplifies your wireless signal to get it out to parts of your home that are experiencing poor connectivity.

**wizard** A step-by-step guide that walks a user through the necessary steps to complete a complicated task.

**word processing software** Programs used to create and edit written documents such as papers, letters, and résumés.

**World Wide Web (WWW or the Web)** The part of the Internet used the most. What distinguishes the web from the rest of the Internet are (1) its use of common communication protocols (such as Transmission Control Protocol/Internet protocol, or TCP/IP) and special languages (such as the HyperText Markup Language, or HTML) that enable different computers to talk to each other and display information in compatible formats and (2) its use of special links (called *hyperlinks*) that enable users to jump from one place to another on the Web.

**worm** A program that attempts to travel between systems through network connections to spread infections. Worms can run independently of host file execution and are active in spreading themselves.

**Z**

**zombie** A computer that is controlled by a hacker who uses it to launch attacks on other computer systems.

# Index